Machine Learning with PyTorch and Scikit-Learn

Develop machine learning and deep learning models with Python

Sebastian Raschka

Yuxi (Hayden) Liu

Vahid Mirjalili

BIRMINGHAM—MUMBAI

Machine Learning with PyTorch and Scikit-Learn

Producer: Tushar Gupta
Acquisition Editor – Peer Reviews: Saby Dsilva
Project Editor: Janice Gonsalves
Content Development Editor: Bhavesh Amin
Copy Editor: Safis Editing
Technical Editor: Aniket Shetty
Proofreader: Safis Editing
Indexer: Tejal Daruwale Soni
Presentation Designer: Pranit Padwal

First published: February 2022

Production reference: 5151122

Published by Packt Publishing Ltd.
Livery Place
35 Livery Street
Birmingham
B3 2PB, UK.

ISBN 978-1-80181-931-2

`www.packt.com`

Foreword

Over recent years, machine learning methods, with their ability to make sense of vast amounts of data and automate decisions, have found widespread applications in healthcare, robotics, biology, physics, consumer products, internet services, and various other industries.

Giant leaps in science usually come from a combination of powerful ideas and great tools. Machine learning is no exception. The success of data-driven learning methods is based on the ingenious ideas of thousands of talented researchers over the field's 60-year history. But their recent popularity is also fueled by the evolution of hardware and software solutions that make them scalable and accessible. The ecosystem of excellent libraries for numeric computing, data analysis, and machine learning built around Python like NumPy and scikit-learn gained wide adoption in research and industry. This has greatly helped propel Python to be the most popular programming language.

Massive improvements in computer vision, text, speech, and other tasks brought by the recent advent of deep learning techniques exemplify this theme. Approaches draw on neural network theory of the last four decades that started working remarkably well in combination with GPUs and highly optimized compute routines.

Our goal with building PyTorch over the past five years has been to give researchers the most flexible tool for expressing deep learning algorithms while taking care of the underlying engineering complexities. We benefited from the excellent Python ecosystem. In turn, we've been fortunate to see the community of very talented people build advanced deep learning models across various domains on top of PyTorch. The authors of this book were among them.

I've known Sebastian within this tight-knit community for a few years now. He has unmatched talent in easily explaining information and making the complex accessible. Sebastian contributed to many widely used machine learning software packages and authored dozens of excellent tutorials on deep learning and data visualization.

Mastery of both ideas and tools is also required to apply machine learning in practice. Getting started might feel intimidating, from making sense of theoretical concepts to figuring out which software packages to install.

Luckily, the book you're holding in your hands does a beautiful job of combining machine learning concepts and practical engineering steps to guide you in this journey. You're in for a delightful ride from the basics of data-driven techniques to the most novel deep learning architectures. Within every chapter, you will find concrete code examples applying the introduced methods to a practical task.

When the first edition came out in 2015, it set a very high bar for the *ML and Python* book category. But the excellence didn't stop there. With every edition, Sebastian and the team kept upgrading and refining the material as the deep learning revolution unfolded in new domains. In this new PyTorch edition, you'll find new chapters on transformer architectures and graph neural networks. These approaches are on the cutting edge of deep learning and have taken the fields of text understanding and molecular structure by storm in the last two years. You will get to practice them using new yet widely popular software packages in the ecosystem like Hugging Face, PyTorch Lightning, and PyTorch Geometric.

The excellent balance of theory and practice this book strikes is no surprise given the authors' combination of advanced research expertise and experience in solving problems hands-on. Sebastian Raschka and Vahid Mirjalili draw from their background in deep learning research for computer vision and computational biology. Hayden Liu brings the experience of applying machine learning methods to event prediction, recommendation systems, and other tasks in the industry. All of the authors share a deep passion for education, and it reflects in the approachable way the book goes from simple to advanced.

I'm confident that you will find this book invaluable both as a broad overview of the exciting field of machine learning and as a treasure of practical insights. I hope it inspires you to apply machine learning for the greater good in your problem area, whatever it might be.

Dmytro Dzhulgakov

PyTorch Core Maintainer

Contributors

About the authors

Dr. Sebastian Raschka is an Asst. Professor of Statistics at the University of Wisconsin-Madison focusing on machine learning and deep learning. His recent research focused on general challenges such as few-shot learning for working with limited data and developing deep neural networks for ordinal targets. Sebastian is also an avid open-source contributor, and in his new role as Lead AI Educator at Grid.ai, he plans to follow his passion for helping people to get into machine learning and AI.

Big thanks to Jitian Zhao and Ben Kaufman, with whom I had the pleasure to work on the new chapters on transformers and graph neural networks. I'm also very grateful for Hayden's and Vahid's help—this book wouldn't have been possible without you. Lastly, I want to thank Andrea Panizza, Tony Gitter, and Adam Bielski for helpful discussions on sections of the manuscript.

Yuxi (Hayden) Liu is a machine learning software engineer at Google and has worked as a machine learning scientist in a variety of data-driven domains. Hayden is the author of a series of ML books. His first book, *Python Machine Learning By Example*, was ranked the #1 bestseller in its category on Amazon in 2017 and 2018 and was translated into many languages. His other books include R Deep Learning Projects, *Hands-On Deep Learning Architectures with Python*, and *PyTorch 1.x Reinforcement Learning Cookbook*.

I would like to thank all the great people I worked with, especially my co-authors, my editors at Packt, and my reviewers. Without them, this book would be harder to read and to apply to real-world problems. Lastly, I'd like to thank all the readers for their support, which encouraged me to write the PyTorch edition of this bestselling ML book.

Dr. Vahid Mirjalili is a deep learning researcher focusing on computer vision applications. Vahid received a Ph.D. degree in both Mechanical Engineering and Computer Science from Michigan State University. During his Ph.D. journey, he developed novel computer vision algorithms to solve real-world problems and published several research articles that are highly cited in the computer vision community.

Other contributors

Benjamin Kaufman is a Ph.D. candidate at the University of Wisconsin-Madison in Biomedical Data Science. His research focuses on the development and application of machine learning methods for drug discovery. His work in this area has provided a deeper understanding of graph neural networks.

Jitian Zhao is a Ph.D. student at the University of Wisconsin-Madison, where she developed her interest in large-scale language models. She is passionate about deep learning in developing both real-world applications and theoretical support.

I would like to thank my parents for their support. They encouraged me to always pursue my dream and motivated me to be a good person.

About the reviewer

Roman Tezikov is an industrial research engineer and deep learning enthusiast with over four years of experience in advanced computer vision, NLP, and MLOps. As the co-creator of the ML-REPA community, he organized several workshops and meetups about ML reproducibility and pipeline automation. One of his current work challenges involves utilizing computer vision in the fashion industry. Roman was also a core developer of Catalyst – a PyTorch framework for accelerated deep learning.

Join our book's Discord space

Join our Discord community to meet like-minded people and learn alongside more than 2000 members at:

`https://packt.link/MLwPyTorch`

Table of Contents

Chapter 2: Training Simple Machine Learning Algorithms for Classification 19

Chapter 3: A Tour of Machine Learning Classifiers Using Scikit-Learn 53

Chapter 4: Building Good Training Datasets – Data Preprocessing 105

Chapter 5: Compressing Data via Dimensionality Reduction 139

Chapter 6: Learning Best Practices for Model Evaluation and Hyperparameter Tuning 171

Chapter 7: Combining Different Models for Ensemble Learning 205

Chapter 13: Going Deeper – The Mechanics of PyTorch 409

Chapter 14: Classifying Images with Deep Convolutional Neural Networks 451

Chapter 15: Modeling Sequential Data Using Recurrent Neural Networks 499

Chapter 16: Transformers – Improving Natural Language Processing with Attention Mechanisms 539

Chapter 17: Generative Adversarial Networks for Synthesizing New Data 589

Chapter 18: Graph Neural Networks for Capturing Dependencies in Graph Structured Data 637

Preface

Through exposure to the news and social media, you probably are familiar with the fact that machine learning has become one of the most exciting technologies of our time and age. Large companies, such as Microsoft, Google, Meta, Apple, Amazon, IBM, and many more, heavily invest in machine learning research and applications for good reasons. While it may seem that machine learning has become the buzzword of our time and age, it is certainly not hype. This exciting field opens the way to new possibilities and has become indispensable to our daily lives. Talking to the voice assistant on our smartphones, recommending the right product for our customers, preventing credit card fraud, filtering out spam from our e-mail inboxes, detecting and diagnosing medical diseases, the list goes on and on.

If you want to become a machine learning practitioner, a better problem solver, or even consider a career in machine learning research, then this book is for you! However, for a novice, the theoretical concepts behind machine learning can be quite overwhelming. Yet, many practical books that have been published in recent years will help you get started in machine learning by implementing powerful learning algorithms.

Getting exposed to practical code examples and working through example applications of machine learning is a great way to dive into this field. Concrete examples help to illustrate the broader concepts by putting the learned material directly into action. However, remember that with great power comes great responsibility! In addition to offering hands-on experience with machine learning using Python and Python-based machine learning libraries, this book also introduces the mathematical concepts behind machine learning algorithms, which is essential for using machine learning successfully. Thus, this book is different from a purely practical book; it is a book that discusses the necessary details regarding machine learning concepts, offers intuitive yet informative explanations on how machine learning algorithms work, how to use them, and most importantly, how to avoid the most common pitfalls.

In this book, we will embark on an exciting journey that covers all the essential topics and concepts to give you a head start in this field. If you find that your thirst for knowledge is not satisfied, this book references many useful resources that you can use to follow up on the essential breakthroughs in this field.

Who this book is for

This book is the ideal companion for learning how to apply machine learning and deep learning to a wide range of tasks and datasets. If you are a programmer who wants to keep up with the recent trends in technology, this book is definitely for you. Also, if you are a student or considering a career transition, this book will be both your introduction and a comprehensive guide to the world of machine learning.

What this book covers

Chapter 1, Giving Computers the Ability to Learn from Data, introduces you to the main subareas of machine learning to tackle various problem tasks. In addition, it discusses the essential steps for creating a typical machine learning model building pipeline that will guide us through the following chapters.

Chapter 2, Training Simple Machine Learning Algorithms for Classification, goes back to the origins of machine learning and introduces binary perceptron classifiers and adaptive linear neurons. This chapter is a gentle introduction to the fundamentals of pattern classification and focuses on the interplay of optimization algorithms and machine learning.

Chapter 3, A Tour of Machine Learning Classifiers Using Scikit-Learn, describes the essential machine learning algorithms for classification and provides practical examples using one of the most popular and comprehensive open-source machine learning libraries, scikit-learn.

Chapter 4, Building Good Training Datasets – Data Preprocessing, discusses how to deal with the most common problems in unprocessed datasets, such as missing data. It also discusses several approaches to identify the most informative features in datasets and teaches you how to prepare variables of different types as proper inputs for machine learning algorithms.

Chapter 5, Compressing Data via Dimensionality Reduction, describes the essential techniques to reduce the number of features in a dataset to smaller sets while retaining most of their useful and discriminatory information. It discusses the standard approach to dimensionality reduction via principal component analysis and compares it to supervised and nonlinear transformation techniques.

Chapter 6, Learning Best Practices for Model Evaluation and Hyperparameter Tuning, discusses the do's and don'ts for estimating the performances of predictive models. Moreover, it discusses different metrics for measuring the performance of our models and techniques to fine-tune machine learning algorithms.

Chapter 7, Combining Different Models for Ensemble Learning, introduces you to the different concepts of combining multiple learning algorithms effectively. It teaches you how to build ensembles of experts to overcome the weaknesses of individual learners, resulting in more accurate and reliable predictions.

Chapter 8, Applying Machine Learning to Sentiment Analysis, discusses the essential steps to transform textual data into meaningful representations for machine learning algorithms to predict the opinions of people based on their writing.

Chapter 9, Predicting Continuous Target Variables with Regression Analysis, discusses the essential techniques for modeling linear relationships between target and response variables to make predictions on a continuous scale. After introducing different linear models, it also talks about polynomial regression and tree-based approaches.

Chapter 10, Working with Unlabeled Data – Clustering Analysis, shifts the focus to a different subarea of machine learning, unsupervised learning. We apply algorithms from three fundamental families of clustering algorithms to find groups of objects that share a certain degree of similarity.

Chapter 11, Implementing a Multilayer Artificial Neural Network from Scratch, extends the concept of gradient-based optimization, which we first introduced in *Chapter 2, Training Simple Machine Learning Algorithms for Classification*, to build powerful, multilayer neural networks based on the popular backpropagation algorithm in Python.

Chapter 12, Parallelizing Neural Network Training with PyTorch, builds upon the knowledge from the previous chapter to provide you with a practical guide for training neural networks more efficiently. The focus of this chapter is on PyTorch, an open-source Python library that allows us to utilize multiple cores of modern GPUs and construct deep neural networks from common building blocks via a user-friendly and flexible API.

Chapter 13, Going Deeper – The Mechanics of PyTorch, picks up where the previous chapter left off and introduces more advanced concepts and functionality of PyTorch. PyTorch is an extraordinarily vast and sophisticated library, and this chapter walks you through concepts such as dynamic computation graphs and automatic differentiation. You will also learn how to use PyTorch's object-oriented API to implement complex neural networks and how PyTorch Lightning helps you with best practices and minimizing boilerplate code.

Chapter 14, Classifying Images with Deep Convolutional Neural Networks, introduces **convolutional neural networks (CNNs)**. A CNN represents a particular type of deep neural network architecture that is particularly well-suited for working with image datasets. Due to their superior performance compared to traditional approaches, CNNs are now widely used in computer vision to achieve state-of-the-art results for various image recognition tasks. Throughout this chapter, you will learn how convolutional layers can be used as powerful feature extractors for image classification.

Chapter 15, Modeling Sequential Data Using Recurrent Neural Networks, introduces another popular neural network architecture for deep learning that is especially well suited for working with text and other types of sequential data and time series data. As a warm-up exercise, this chapter introduces recurrent neural networks for predicting the sentiment of movie reviews. Then, we will teach recurrent networks to digest information from books in order to generate entirely new text.

Chapter 16, Transformers – Improving Natural Language Processing with Attention Mechanisms, focuses on the latest trends in natural language processing and explains how attention mechanisms help with modeling complex relationships in long sequences. In particular, this chapter describes the influential transformer architecture and state-of-the-art transformer models such as BERT and GPT.

Chapter 17, Generative Adversarial Networks for Synthesizing New Data, introduces a popular adversarial training regime for neural networks that can be used to generate new, realistic-looking images. The chapter starts with a brief introduction to autoencoders, which is a particular type of neural network architecture that can be used for data compression. The chapter then shows you how to combine the decoder part of an autoencoder with a second neural network that can distinguish between real and synthesized images. By letting two neural networks compete with each other in an adversarial training approach, you will implement a generative adversarial network that generates new handwritten digits.

Chapter 18, Graph Neural Networks for Capturing Dependencies in Graph Structured Data, goes beyond working with tabular datasets, images, and text. This chapter introduces graph neural networks that operate on graph-structured data, such as social media networks and molecules. After explaining the fundamentals of graph convolutions, this chapter includes a tutorial showing you how to implement predictive models for molecular data.

Chapter 19, Reinforcement Learning for Decision Making in Complex Environments, covers a subcategory of machine learning that is commonly used for training robots and other autonomous systems. This chapter starts by introducing the basics of **reinforcement learning** (**RL**) to become familiar with the agent/environment interactions, the reward process of RL systems, and the concept of learning from experience. After learning about the main categories of RL, you will implement and train an agent that can navigate in a grid world environment using the Q-learning algorithm. Finally, this chapter introduces the deep Q-learning algorithm, which is a variant of Q-learning that uses deep neural networks.

To get the most out of this book

Ideally, you are already comfortable with programming in Python to follow along with the code examples we provide to both illustrate and apply various algorithms and models. To get the most out of this book, a firm grasp of mathematical notation will be helpful as well.

A common laptop or desktop computer should be sufficient for running most of the code in this book, and we provide instructions for your Python environment in the first chapter. Later chapters will introduce additional libraries and installation recommendations when the need arises.

A recent **graphics processing unit** (**GPU**) can accelerate the code runtimes in the later deep learning chapters. However, a GPU is not required, and we also provide instructions for using free cloud resources.

Download the example code files

All code examples are available for download through GitHub at `https://github.com/rasbt/machine-learning-book`. We also have other code bundles from our rich catalog of books and videos available at `https://github.com/PacktPublishing/`. Check them out!

While we recommend using Jupyter Notebook for executing code interactively, all code examples are available in both a Python script (for example, `ch02/ch02.py`) and a Jupyter Notebook format (for example, `ch02/ch02.ipynb`). Furthermore, we recommend viewing the `README.md` file that accompanies each individual chapter for additional information and updates

Download the color images

We also provide a PDF file that has color images of the screenshots/diagrams used in this book. You can download it here: `https://static.packt-cdn.com/downloads/9781801819312_ColorImages.pdf`. In addition, lower resolution color images are embedded in the code notebooks of this book that come bundled with the example code files.

Conventions

There are a number of text conventions used throughout this book.

Here are some examples of these styles and an explanation of their meaning. Code words in text are shown as follows: "And already installed packages can be updated via the `--upgrade` flag."

A block of code is set as follows:

```
def __init__(self, eta=0.01, n_iter=50, random_state=1):
    self.eta = eta
    self.n_iter = n_iter
    self.random_state = random_state
```

Any input in the Python interpreter is written as follows (notice the >>> symbol). The expected output will be shown without the >>> symbol:

```
>>> v1 = np.array([1, 2, 3])
>>> v2 = 0.5 * v1
>>> np.arccos(v1.dot(v2) / (np.linalg.norm(v1) *
...           np.linalg.norm(v2)))
0.0
```

Any command-line input or output is written as follows:

```
pip install gym==0.20
```

New terms and **important words** are shown in bold. Words that you see on the screen, for example, in menus or dialog boxes, appear in the text like this: "Clicking the **Next** button moves you to the next screen."

Warnings or important notes appear in a box like this.

Tips and tricks appear like this.

Get in touch

Feedback from our readers is always welcome.

General feedback: Email `feedback@packtpub.com` and mention the book's title in the subject of your message. If you have questions about any aspect of this book, please email us at `questions@packtpub.com`.

Errata: Although we have taken every care to ensure the accuracy of our content, mistakes do happen. If you have found a mistake in this book we would be grateful if you would report this to us. Please visit, `http://www.packtpub.com/submit-errata`, selecting your book, clicking on the Errata Submission Form link, and entering the details.

Piracy: If you come across any illegal copies of our works in any form on the Internet, we would be grateful if you would provide us with the location address or website name. Please contact us at `copyright@packtpub.com` with a link to the material.

If you are interested in becoming an author: If there is a topic that you have expertise in and you are interested in either writing or contributing to a book, please visit `http://authors.packtpub.com`.

Share your thoughts

Once you've read *Machine Learning with PyTorch and Scikit-Learn*, we'd love to hear your thoughts! Scan the QR code below to go straight to the Amazon review page for this book and share your feedback.

https://packt.link/r/1801819319

Your review is important to us and the tech community and will help us make sure we're delivering excellent quality content.

Download a Free PDF copy of this book

Thanks for purchasing this book!

Do you like to read on the go but are unable to carry your print books everywhere?
Is your eBook purchase not compatible with the device of your choice?

Don't worry, now with every Packt book you get a DRM-free PDF version of that book at no cost.

Read anywhere, any place, on any device. Search, copy, and paste code from your favorite technical books directly into your application.

The perks don't stop there, you can get exclusive access to discounts, newsletters, and great free content in your inbox daily

Follow these simple steps to get the benefits:

1. Scan the QR code or visit the link below

`https://packt.link/free-ebook/9781801819312`

2. Submit your proof of purchase
3. That's it! We'll send your free PDF and other benefits to your email directly

1

Giving Computers the Ability to Learn from Data

In my opinion, **machine learning**, the application and science of algorithms that make sense of data, is the most exciting field of all the computer sciences! We are living in an age where data comes in abundance; using self-learning algorithms from the field of machine learning, we can turn this data into knowledge. Thanks to the many powerful open-source libraries that have been developed in recent years, there has probably never been a better time to break into the machine learning field and learn how to utilize powerful algorithms to spot patterns in data and make predictions about future events.

In this chapter, you will learn about the main concepts and different types of machine learning. Together with a basic introduction to the relevant terminology, we will lay the groundwork for successfully using machine learning techniques for practical problem solving.

In this chapter, we will cover the following topics:

- The general concepts of machine learning
- The three types of learning and basic terminology
- The building blocks for successfully designing machine learning systems
- Installing and setting up Python for data analysis and machine learning

Building intelligent machines to transform data into knowledge

In this age of modern technology, there is one resource that we have in abundance: a large amount of structured and unstructured data. In the second half of the 20th century, machine learning evolved as a subfield of **artificial intelligence** (**AI**) involving self-learning algorithms that derive knowledge from data to make predictions.

Instead of requiring humans to manually derive rules and build models from analyzing large amounts of data, machine learning offers a more efficient alternative for capturing the knowledge in data to gradually improve the performance of predictive models and make data-driven decisions.

Not only is machine learning becoming increasingly important in computer science research, but it is also playing an ever-greater role in our everyday lives. Thanks to machine learning, we enjoy robust email spam filters, convenient text and voice recognition software, reliable web search engines, recommendations on entertaining movies to watch, mobile check deposits, estimated meal delivery times, and much more. Hopefully, soon, we will add safe and efficient self-driving cars to this list. Also, notable progress has been made in medical applications; for example, researchers demonstrated that deep learning models can detect skin cancer with near-human accuracy (`https://www.nature.com/articles/nature21056`). Another milestone was recently achieved by researchers at DeepMind, who used deep learning to predict 3D protein structures, outperforming physics-based approaches by a substantial margin (`https://deepmind.com/blog/article/alphafold-a-solution-to-a-50-year-old-grand-challenge-in-biology`). While accurate 3D protein structure prediction plays an essential role in biological and pharmaceutical research, there have been many other important applications of machine learning in healthcare recently. For instance, researchers designed systems for predicting the oxygen needs of COVID-19 patients up to four days in advance to help hospitals allocate resources for those in need (`https://ai.facebook.com/blog/new-ai-research-to-help-predict-covid-19-resource-needs-from-a-series-of-x-rays/`). Another important topic of our day and age is climate change, which presents one of the biggest and most critical challenges. Today, many efforts are being directed toward developing intelligent systems to combat it (`https://www.forbes.com/sites/robtoews/2021/06/20/these-are-the-startups-applying-ai-to-tackle-climate-change`). One of the many approaches to tackling climate change is the emergent field of precision agriculture. Here, researchers aim to design computer vision-based machine learning systems to optimize resource deployment to minimize the use and waste of fertilizers.

The three different types of machine learning

In this section, we will take a look at the three types of machine learning: **supervised learning**, **unsupervised learning**, and **reinforcement learning**. We will learn about the fundamental differences between the three different learning types and, using conceptual examples, we will develop an understanding of the practical problem domains where they can be applied:

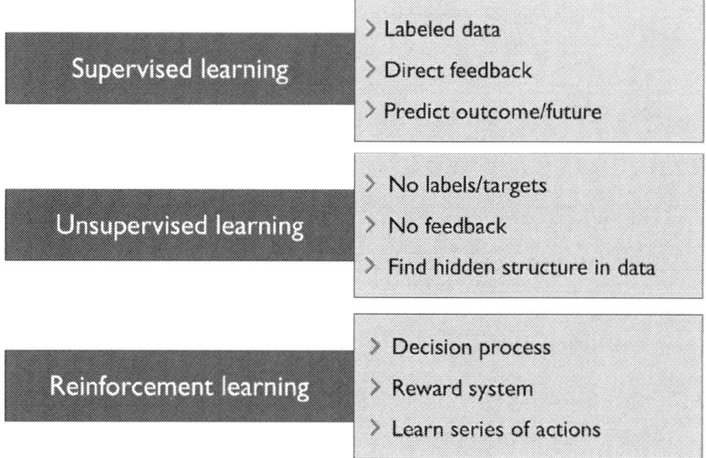

Figure 1.1: The three different types of machine learning

Making predictions about the future with supervised learning

The main goal in supervised learning is to learn a model from labeled training data that allows us to make predictions about unseen or future data. Here, the term "supervised" refers to a set of training examples (data inputs) where the desired output signals (labels) are already known. Supervised learning is then the process of modeling the relationship between the data inputs and the labels. Thus, we can also think of supervised learning as "label learning."

Figure 1.2 summarizes a typical supervised learning workflow, where the labeled training data is passed to a machine learning algorithm for fitting a predictive model that can make predictions on new, unlabeled data inputs:

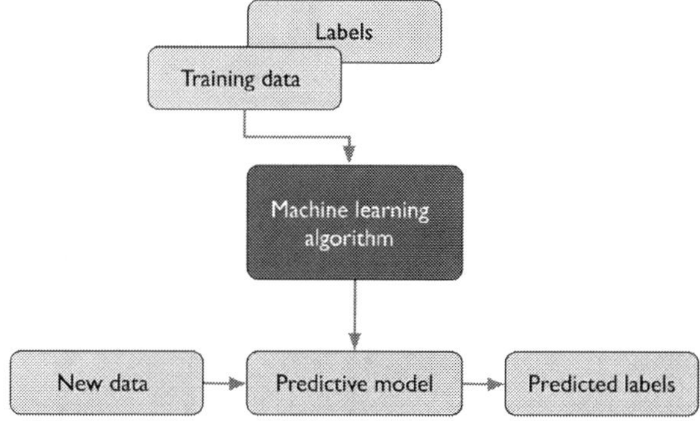

Figure 1.2: Supervised learning process

Considering the example of email spam filtering, we can train a model using a supervised machine learning algorithm on a corpus of labeled emails, which are correctly marked as spam or non-spam, to predict whether a new email belongs to either of the two categories. A supervised learning task with discrete class labels, such as in the previous email spam filtering example, is also called a **classification task**. Another subcategory of supervised learning is **regression**, where the outcome signal is a continuous value.

Classification for predicting class labels

Classification is a subcategory of supervised learning where the goal is to predict the categorical class labels of new instances or data points based on past observations. Those class labels are discrete, unordered values that can be understood as the group memberships of the data points. The previously mentioned example of email spam detection represents a typical example of a binary classification task, where the machine learning algorithm learns a set of rules to distinguish between two possible classes: spam and non-spam emails.

Figure 1.3 illustrates the concept of a binary classification task given 30 training examples; 15 training examples are labeled as class A and 15 training examples are labeled as class B. In this scenario, our dataset is two-dimensional, which means that each example has two values associated with it: x_1 and x_2. Now, we can use a supervised machine learning algorithm to learn a rule—the decision boundary represented as a dashed line—that can separate those two classes and classify new data into each of those two categories given its x_1 and x_2 values:

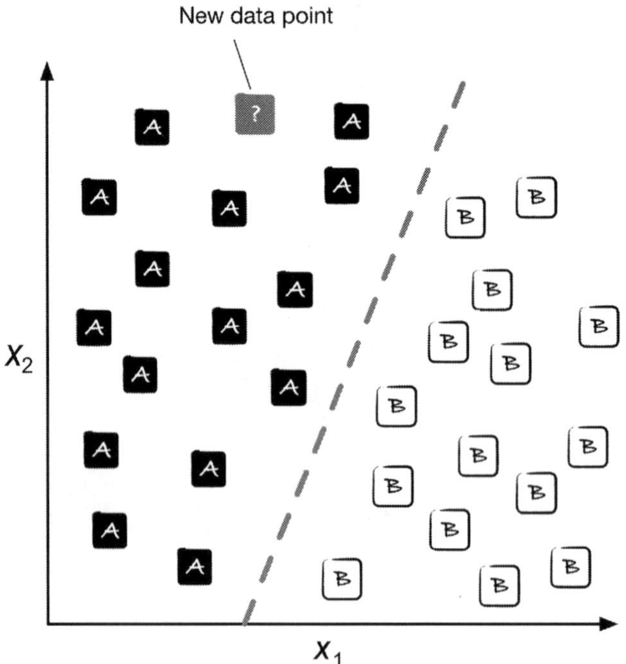

Figure 1.3: Classifying a new data point

However, the set of class labels does not have to be of a binary nature. The predictive model learned by a supervised learning algorithm can assign any class label that was presented in the training dataset to a new, unlabeled data point or instance.

A typical example of a **multiclass classification** task is handwritten character recognition. We can collect a training dataset that consists of multiple handwritten examples of each letter in the alphabet. The letters ("A," "B," "C," and so on) will represent the different unordered categories or class labels that we want to predict. Now, if a user provides a new handwritten character via an input device, our predictive model will be able to predict the correct letter in the alphabet with certain accuracy. However, our machine learning system will be unable to correctly recognize any of the digits between 0 and 9, for example, if they were not part of the training dataset.

Regression for predicting continuous outcomes

We learned in the previous section that the task of classification is to assign categorical, unordered labels to instances. A second type of supervised learning is the prediction of continuous outcomes, which is also called **regression analysis**. In regression analysis, we are given a number of predictor (**explanatory**) variables and a continuous response variable (**outcome**), and we try to find a relationship between those variables that allows us to predict an outcome.

Note that in the field of machine learning, the predictor variables are commonly called "features," and the response variables are usually referred to as "target variables." We will adopt these conventions throughout this book.

For example, let's assume that we are interested in predicting the math SAT scores of students. (The SAT is a standardized test frequently used for college admissions in the United States.) If there is a relationship between the time spent studying for the test and the final scores, we could use it as training data to learn a model that uses the study time to predict the test scores of future students who are planning to take this test.

Regression toward the mean

The term "regression" was devised by Francis Galton in his article *Regression towards Mediocrity in Hereditary Stature* in 1886. Galton described the biological phenomenon that the variance of height in a population does not increase over time.

He observed that the height of parents is not passed on to their children, but instead, their children's height regresses toward the population mean.

Figure 1.4 illustrates the concept of linear regression. Given a feature variable, x, and a target variable, y, we fit a straight line to this data that minimizes the distance—most commonly the average squared distance—between the data points and the fitted line.

We can now use the intercept and slope learned from this data to predict the target variable of new data:

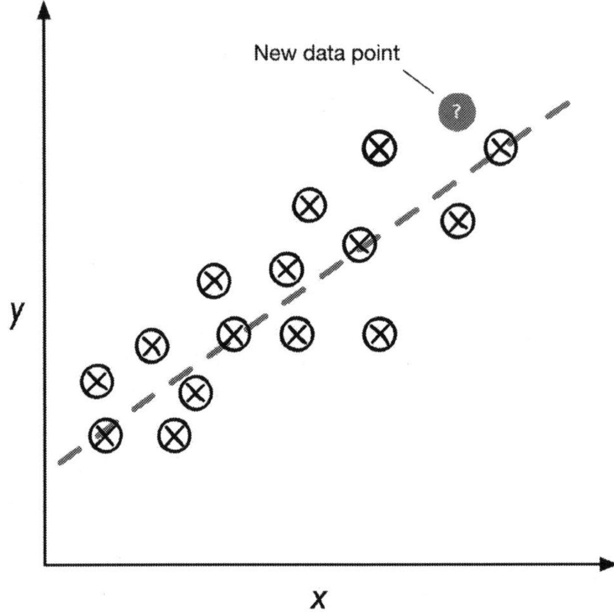

Figure 1.4: A linear regression example

Solving interactive problems with reinforcement learning

Another type of machine learning is **reinforcement learning**. In reinforcement learning, the goal is to develop a system (**agent**) that improves its performance based on interactions with the environment. Since the information about the current state of the environment typically also includes a so-called **reward signal**, we can think of reinforcement learning as a field related to supervised learning. However, in reinforcement learning, this feedback is not the correct ground truth label or value, but a measure of how well the action was measured by a reward function. Through its interaction with the environment, an agent can then use reinforcement learning to learn a series of actions that maximizes this reward via an exploratory trial-and-error approach or deliberative planning.

A popular example of reinforcement learning is a chess program. Here, the agent decides upon a series of moves depending on the state of the board (the environment), and the reward can be defined as **win** or **lose** at the end of the game:

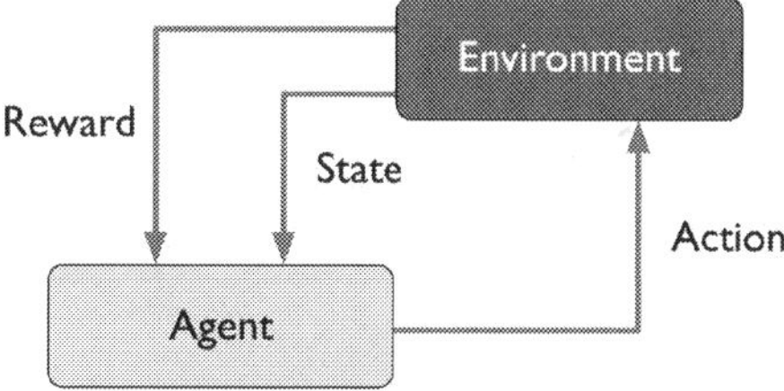

Figure 1.5: Reinforcement learning process

There are many different subtypes of reinforcement learning. However, a general scheme is that the agent in reinforcement learning tries to maximize the reward through a series of interactions with the environment. Each state can be associated with a positive or negative reward, and a reward can be defined as accomplishing an overall goal, such as winning or losing a game of chess. For instance, in chess, the outcome of each move can be thought of as a different state of the environment.

To explore the chess example further, let's think of visiting certain configurations on the chessboard as being associated with states that will more likely lead to winning—for instance, removing an opponent's chess piece from the board or threatening the queen. Other positions, however, are associated with states that will more likely result in losing the game, such as losing a chess piece to the opponent in the following turn. Now, in the game of chess, the reward (either positive for winning or negative for losing the game) will not be given until the end of the game. In addition, the final reward will also depend on how the opponent plays. For example, the opponent may sacrifice the queen but eventually win the game.

In sum, reinforcement learning is concerned with learning to choose a series of actions that maximizes the total reward, which could be earned either immediately after taking an action or via *delayed* feedback.

Discovering hidden structures with unsupervised learning

In supervised learning, we know the right answer (the label or target variable) beforehand when we train a model, and in reinforcement learning, we define a measure of reward for particular actions carried out by the agent. In unsupervised learning, however, we are dealing with unlabeled data or data of an unknown structure. Using unsupervised learning techniques, we are able to explore the structure of our data to extract meaningful information without the guidance of a known outcome variable or reward function.

Finding subgroups with clustering

Clustering is an exploratory data analysis or pattern discovery technique that allows us to organize a pile of information into meaningful subgroups (**clusters**) without having any prior knowledge of their group memberships. Each cluster that arises during the analysis defines a group of objects that share a certain degree of similarity but are more dissimilar to objects in other clusters, which is why clustering is also sometimes called **unsupervised classification.** Clustering is a great technique for structuring information and deriving meaningful relationships from data. For example, it allows marketers to discover customer groups based on their interests, in order to develop distinct marketing programs.

Figure 1.6 illustrates how clustering can be applied to organizing unlabeled data into three distinct groups or clusters (A, B, and C, in arbitrary order) based on the similarity of their features, x_1 and x_2:

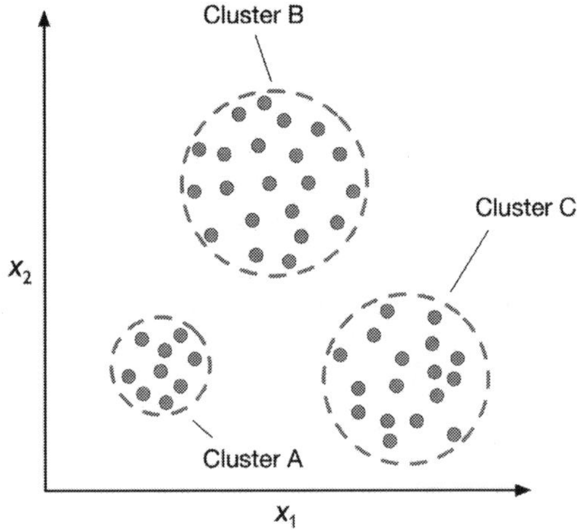

Figure 1.6: How clustering works

Dimensionality reduction for data compression

Another subfield of unsupervised learning is **dimensionality reduction.** Often, we are working with data of high dimensionality—each observation comes with a high number of measurements—that can present a challenge for limited storage space and the computational performance of machine learning algorithms. Unsupervised dimensionality reduction is a commonly used approach in feature preprocessing to remove noise from data, which can degrade the predictive performance of certain algorithms. Dimensionality reduction compresses the data onto a smaller dimensional subspace while retaining most of the relevant information.

Sometimes, dimensionality reduction can also be useful for visualizing data; for example, a high-dimensional feature set can be projected onto one-, two-, or three-dimensional feature spaces to visualize it via 2D or 3D scatterplots or histograms. *Figure 1.7* shows an example where nonlinear dimensionality reduction was applied to compress a 3D Swiss roll onto a new 2D feature subspace:

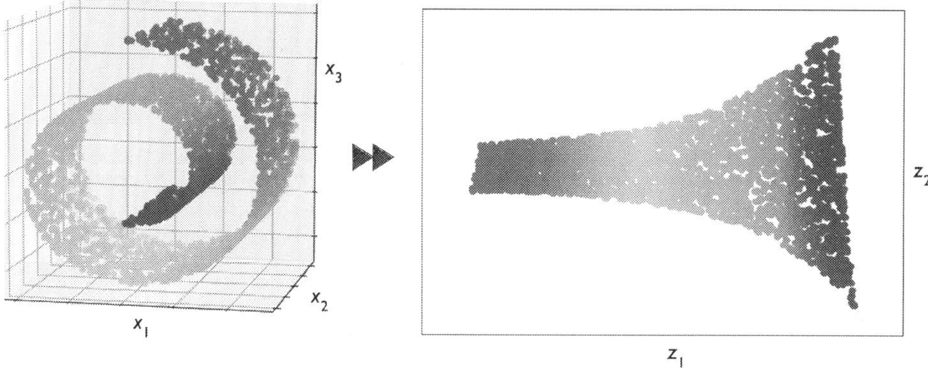

Figure 1.7: An example of dimensionality reduction from three to two dimensions

Introduction to the basic terminology and notations

Now that we have discussed the three broad categories of machine learning—supervised, unsupervised, and reinforcement learning—let's have a look at the basic terminology that we will be using throughout this book. The following subsection covers the common terms we will be using when referring to different aspects of a dataset, as well as the mathematical notation to communicate more precisely and efficiently.

As machine learning is a vast field and very interdisciplinary, you are guaranteed to encounter many different terms that refer to the same concepts sooner rather than later. The second subsection collects many of the most commonly used terms that are found in machine learning literature, which may be useful to you as a reference section when reading machine learning publications.

Notation and conventions used in this book

Figure 1.8 depicts an excerpt of the Iris dataset, which is a classic example in the field of machine learning (more information can be found at `https://archive.ics.uci.edu/ml/datasets/iris`). The Iris dataset contains the measurements of 150 Iris flowers from three different species—Setosa, Versicolor, and Virginica.

Here, each flower example represents one row in our dataset, and the flower measurements in centimeters are stored as columns, which we also call the **features** of the dataset:

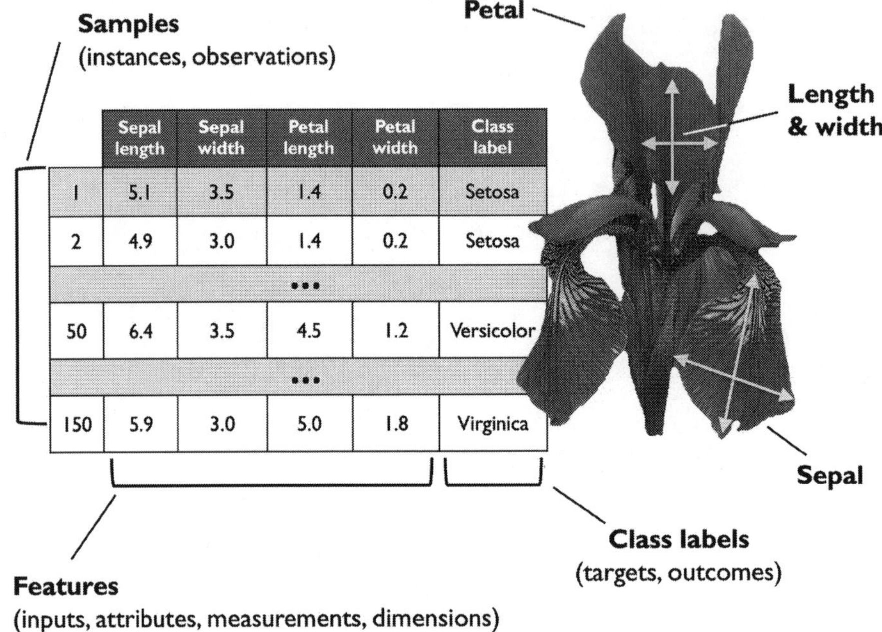

Figure 1.8: The Iris dataset

To keep the notation and implementation simple yet efficient, we will make use of some of the basics of linear algebra. In the following chapters, we will use a matrix notation to refer to our data. We will follow the common convention to represent each example as a separate row in a feature matrix, X, where each feature is stored as a separate column.

The Iris dataset, consisting of 150 examples and four features, can then be written as a 150×4 matrix, formally denoted as $\boldsymbol{X} \in \mathbb{R}^{150\times4}$:

$$\begin{bmatrix} x_1^{(1)} & x_2^{(1)} & x_3^{(1)} & x_4^{(1)} \\ x_1^{(2)} & x_2^{(2)} & x_3^{(2)} & x_4^{(2)} \\ \vdots & \vdots & \vdots & \vdots \\ x_1^{(150)} & x_2^{(150)} & x_3^{(150)} & x_4^{(150)} \end{bmatrix}$$

Notational conventions

For most parts of this book, unless noted otherwise, we will use the superscript *i* to refer to the *i*th training example, and the subscript *j* to refer to the *j*th dimension of the training dataset.

We will use lowercase, bold-face letters to refer to vectors ($\boldsymbol{x} \in \mathbb{R}^{n\times1}$) and uppercase, bold-face letters to refer to matrices ($\boldsymbol{X} \in \mathbb{R}^{n\times m}$). To refer to single elements in a vector or matrix, we will write the letters in italics ($x^{(n)}$ or $x_m^{(n)}$, respectively).

For example, $x_1^{(150)}$ refers to the first dimension of flower example 150, the sepal length. Each row in matrix $\boldsymbol{X}$ represents one flower instance and can be written as a four-dimensional row vector, $\boldsymbol{x}^{(i)} \in \mathbb{R}^{1\times4}$:

$$\boldsymbol{X}^{(i)} = \left[x_1^{(i)}\ x_2^{(i)}\ x_3^{(i)}\ x_4^{(i)}\right]$$

And each feature dimension is a 150-dimensional column vector, $\boldsymbol{X}^{(i)} \in \mathbb{R}^{150\times1}$. For example:

$$\boldsymbol{x}_j = \begin{bmatrix} x_j^{(1)} \\ x_j^{(2)} \\ \cdots \\ x_j^{(150)} \end{bmatrix}$$

Similarly, we can represent the target variables (here, class labels) as a 150-dimensional column vector:

$$\boldsymbol{y} = \begin{bmatrix} y^{(1)} \\ \cdots \\ y^{(150)} \end{bmatrix}, \text{where } y^{(i)} \in \{\text{Setosa, Versicolor, Virginica}\}$$

Machine learning terminology

Machine learning is a vast field and also very interdisciplinary as it brings together many scientists from other areas of research. As it happens, many terms and concepts have been rediscovered or redefined and may already be familiar to you but appear under different names. For your convenience, in the following list, you can find a selection of commonly used terms and their synonyms that you may find useful when reading this book and machine learning literature in general:

- **Training example:** A row in a table representing the dataset and synonymous with an observation, record, instance, or sample (in most contexts, sample refers to a collection of training examples).
- **Training:** Model fitting, for parametric models similar to parameter estimation.

- **Feature, abbrev.** x: A column in a data table or data (design) matrix. Synonymous with predictor, variable, input, attribute, or covariate.
- **Target, abbrev.** y: Synonymous with outcome, output, response variable, dependent variable, (class) label, and ground truth.
- **Loss function:** Often used synonymously with a *cost* function. Sometimes the loss function is also called an *error* function. In some literature, the term "loss" refers to the loss measured for a single data point, and the cost is a measurement that computes the loss (average or summed) over the entire dataset.

A roadmap for building machine learning systems

In previous sections, we discussed the basic concepts of machine learning and the three different types of learning. In this section, we will discuss the other important parts of a machine learning system accompanying the learning algorithm.

Figure 1.9 shows a typical workflow for using machine learning in predictive modeling, which we will discuss in the following subsections:

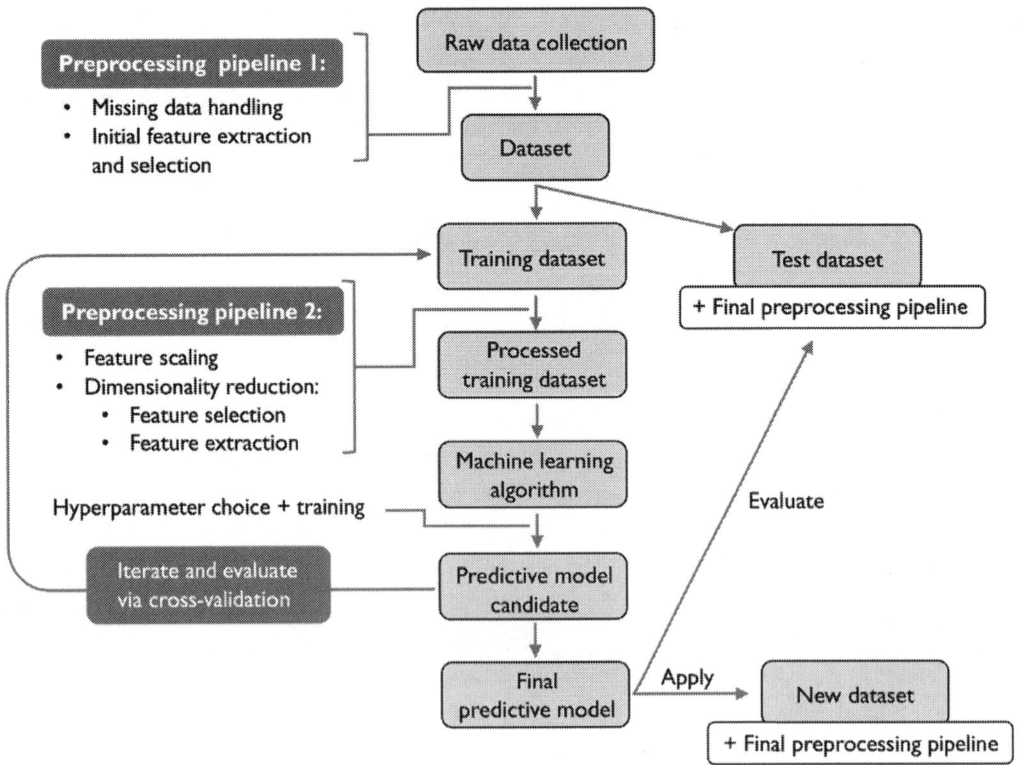

Figure 1.9: Predictive modeling workflow

Preprocessing – getting data into shape

Let's begin by discussing the roadmap for building machine learning systems. Raw data rarely comes in the form and shape that is necessary for the optimal performance of a learning algorithm. Thus, the preprocessing of the data is one of the most crucial steps in any machine learning application.

If we take the Iris flower dataset from the previous section as an example, we can think of the raw data as a series of flower images from which we want to extract meaningful features. Useful features could be centered around the color of the flowers or the height, length, and width of the flowers.

Many machine learning algorithms also require that the selected features are on the same scale for optimal performance, which is often achieved by transforming the features in the range [0, 1] or a standard normal distribution with zero mean and unit variance, as we will see in later chapters.

Some of the selected features may be highly correlated and therefore redundant to a certain degree. In those cases, dimensionality reduction techniques are useful for compressing the features onto a lower-dimensional subspace. Reducing the dimensionality of our feature space has the advantage that less storage space is required, and the learning algorithm can run much faster. In certain cases, dimensionality reduction can also improve the predictive performance of a model if the dataset contains a large number of irrelevant features (or noise); that is, if the dataset has a low signal-to-noise ratio.

To determine whether our machine learning algorithm not only performs well on the training dataset but also generalizes well to new data, we also want to randomly divide the dataset into separate training and test datasets. We use the training dataset to train and optimize our machine learning model, while we keep the test dataset until the very end to evaluate the final model.

Training and selecting a predictive model

As you will see in later chapters, many different machine learning algorithms have been developed to solve different problem tasks. An important point that can be summarized from David Wolpert's famous *No free lunch theorems* is that we can't get learning "for free" (*The Lack of A Priori Distinctions Between Learning Algorithms*, D.H. Wolpert, 1996; *No free lunch theorems for optimization*, D.H. Wolpert and W.G. Macready, 1997). We can relate this concept to the popular saying, *I suppose it is tempting, if the only tool you have is a hammer, to treat everything as if it were a nail* (Abraham Maslow, 1966). For example, each classification algorithm has its inherent biases, and no single classification model enjoys superiority if we don't make any assumptions about the task. In practice, it is therefore essential to compare at least a handful of different learning algorithms in order to train and select the best performing model. But before we can compare different models, we first have to decide upon a metric to measure performance. One commonly used metric is classification accuracy, which is defined as the proportion of correctly classified instances.

One legitimate question to ask is this: how do we know which model performs well on the final test dataset and real-world data if we don't use this test dataset for the model selection, but keep it for the final model evaluation? To address the issue embedded in this question, different techniques summarized as "cross-validation" can be used. In cross-validation, we further divide a dataset into training and validation subsets in order to estimate the generalization performance of the model.

Finally, we also cannot expect that the default parameters of the different learning algorithms provided by software libraries are optimal for our specific problem task. Therefore, we will make frequent use of hyperparameter optimization techniques that help us to fine-tune the performance of our model in later chapters.

We can think of those hyperparameters as parameters that are not learned from the data but represent the knobs of a model that we can turn to improve its performance. This will become much clearer in later chapters when we see actual examples.

Evaluating models and predicting unseen data instances

After we have selected a model that has been fitted on the training dataset, we can use the test dataset to estimate how well it performs on this unseen data to estimate the so-called *generalization error*. If we are satisfied with its performance, we can now use this model to predict new, future data. It is important to note that the parameters for the previously mentioned procedures, such as feature scaling and dimensionality reduction, are solely obtained from the training dataset, and the same parameters are later reapplied to transform the test dataset, as well as any new data instances—the performance measured on the test data may be overly optimistic otherwise.

Using Python for machine learning

Python is one of the most popular programming languages for data science, and thanks to its very active developer and open-source community, a large number of useful libraries for scientific computing and machine learning have been developed.

Although the performance of interpreted languages, such as Python, for computation-intensive tasks is inferior to lower-level programming languages, extension libraries such as NumPy and SciPy have been developed that build upon lower-layer Fortran and C implementations for fast vectorized operations on multidimensional arrays.

For machine learning programming tasks, we will mostly refer to the scikit-learn library, which is currently one of the most popular and accessible open-source machine learning libraries. In the later chapters, when we focus on a subfield of machine learning called *deep learning*, we will use the latest version of the PyTorch library, which specializes in training so-called *deep neural network* models very efficiently by utilizing graphics cards.

Installing Python and packages from the Python Package Index

Python is available for all three major operating systems—Microsoft Windows, macOS, and Linux—and the installer, as well as the documentation, can be downloaded from the official Python website: `https://www.python.org`.

The code examples provided in this book have been written for and tested in Python 3.9, and we generally recommend that you use the most recent version of Python 3 that is available. Some of the code may also be compatible with Python 2.7, but as the official support for Python 2.7 ended in 2019, and the majority of open-source libraries have already stopped supporting Python 2.7 (`https://python3statement.org`), we strongly advise that you use Python 3.9 or newer.

You can check your Python version by executing

```
python --version
```

or

```
python3 --version
```

in your terminal (or PowerShell if you are using Windows).

The additional packages that we will be using throughout this book can be installed via the `pip` installer program, which has been part of the Python Standard Library since Python 3.3. More information about `pip` can be found at `https://docs.python.org/3/installing/index.html`.

After we have successfully installed Python, we can execute `pip` from the terminal to install additional Python packages:

```
pip install SomePackage
```

Already installed packages can be updated via the `--upgrade` flag:

```
pip install SomePackage --upgrade
```

Using the Anaconda Python distribution and package manager

A highly recommended open-source package management system for installing Python for scientific computing contexts is conda by Continuum Analytics. Conda is free and licensed under a permissive open-source license. Its goal is to help with the installation and version management of Python packages for data science, math, and engineering across different operating systems. If you want to use conda, it comes in different flavors, namely Anaconda, Miniconda, and Miniforge:

- Anaconda comes with many scientific computing packages pre-installed. The Anaconda installer can be downloaded at `https://docs.anaconda.com/anaconda/install/`, and an Anaconda quick start guide is available at `https://docs.anaconda.com/anaconda/user-guide/getting-started/`.
- Miniconda is a leaner alternative to Anaconda (`https://docs.conda.io/en/latest/miniconda.html`). Essentially, it is similar to Anaconda but without any packages pre-installed, which many people (including the authors) prefer.
- Miniforge is similar to Miniconda but community-maintained and uses a different package repository (conda-forge) from Miniconda and Anaconda. We found that Miniforge is a great alternative to Miniconda. Download and installation instructions can be found in the GitHub repository at `https://github.com/conda-forge/miniforge`.

After successfully installing conda through either Anaconda, Miniconda, or Miniforge, we can install new Python packages using the following command:

```
conda install SomePackage
```

Existing packages can be updated using the following command:

```
conda update SomePackage
```

Packages that are not available through the official conda channel might be available via the community-supported conda-forge project (`https://conda-forge.org`), which can be specified via the `--channel conda-forge` flag. For example:

```
conda install SomePackage --channel conda-forge
```

Packages that are not available through the default conda channel or conda-forge can be installed via `pip` as explained earlier. For example:

```
pip install SomePackage
```

Packages for scientific computing, data science, and machine learning

Throughout the first half of this book, we will mainly use NumPy's multidimensional arrays to store and manipulate data. Occasionally, we will make use of pandas, which is a library built on top of NumPy that provides additional higher-level data manipulation tools that make working with tabular data even more convenient. To augment your learning experience and visualize quantitative data, which is often extremely useful to make sense of it, we will use the very customizable Matplotlib library.

The main machine learning library used in this book is scikit-learn (*Chapters 3* to *11*). *Chapter 12, Parallelizing Neural Network Training with PyTorch*, will then introduce the PyTorch library for deep learning.

The version numbers of the major Python packages that were used to write this book are mentioned in the following list. Please make sure that the version numbers of your installed packages are, ideally, equal to these version numbers to ensure that the code examples run correctly:

- NumPy 1.21.2
- SciPy 1.7.0
- Scikit-learn 1.0
- Matplotlib 3.4.3
- pandas 1.3.2

After installing these packages, you can double-check the installed version by importing the package in Python and accessing its `__version__` attribute, for example:

```
>>> import numpy
>>> numpy.__version__
'1.21.2'
```

For your convenience, we included a `python-environment-check.py` script in this book's complimentary code repository at `https://github.com/rasbt/machine-learning-book` so that you can check both your Python version and the package versions by executing this script.

Certain chapters will require additional packages and will provide information about the installations. For instance, do not worry about installing PyTorch at this point. *Chapter 12* will provide tips and instructions when you need them.

If you encounter errors even though your code matches the code in the chapter exactly, we recommend you first check the version numbers of the underlying packages before spending more time on debugging or reaching out to the publisher or authors. Sometimes, newer versions of libraries introduce backward-incompatible changes that could explain these errors.

If you do not want to change the package version in your main Python installation, we recommend using a virtual environment for installing the packages used in this book. If you use Python without the conda manager, you can use the `venv` library to create a new virtual environment. For example, you can create and activate the virtual environment via the following two commands:

```
python3 -m venv /Users/sebastian/Desktop/pyml-book
source /Users/sebastian/Desktop/pyml-book/bin/activate
```

Note that you need to activate the virtual environment every time you open a new terminal or PowerShell. You can find more information about `venv` at `https://docs.python.org/3/library/venv.html`.

If you are using Anaconda with the conda package manager, you can create and activate a virtual environment as follows:

```
conda create -n pyml python=3.9
conda activate pyml
```

Summary

In this chapter, we explored machine learning at a very high level and familiarized ourselves with the big picture and major concepts that we are going to explore in the following chapters in more detail. We learned that supervised learning is composed of two important subfields: classification and regression. While classification models allow us to categorize objects into known classes, we can use regression analysis to predict the continuous outcomes of target variables. Unsupervised learning not only offers useful techniques for discovering structures in unlabeled data, but it can also be useful for data compression in feature preprocessing steps.

We briefly went over the typical roadmap for applying machine learning to problem tasks, which we will use as a foundation for deeper discussions and hands-on examples in the following chapters. Finally, we set up our Python environment and installed and updated the required packages to get ready to see machine learning in action.

Later in this book, in addition to machine learning itself, we will introduce different techniques to preprocess a dataset, which will help you to get the best performance out of different machine learning algorithms. While we will cover classification algorithms quite extensively throughout the book, we will also explore different techniques for regression analysis and clustering.

We have an exciting journey ahead, covering many powerful techniques in the vast field of machine learning. However, we will approach machine learning one step at a time, building upon our knowledge gradually throughout the chapters of this book. In the following chapter, we will start this journey by implementing one of the earliest machine learning algorithms for classification, which will prepare us for *Chapter 3, A Tour of Machine Learning Classifiers Using Scikit-Learn,* where we will cover more advanced machine learning algorithms using the scikit-learn open-source machine learning library.

Join our book's Discord space

Join our Discord community to meet like-minded people and learn alongside more than 2000 members at:

`https://packt.link/MLwPyTorch`

2

Training Simple Machine Learning Algorithms for Classification

In this chapter, we will make use of two of the first algorithmically described machine learning algorithms for classification: the perceptron and adaptive linear neurons. We will start by implementing a perceptron step by step in Python and training it to classify different flower species in the Iris dataset. This will help us to understand the concept of machine learning algorithms for classification and how they can be efficiently implemented in Python.

Discussing the basics of optimization using adaptive linear neurons will then lay the groundwork for using more sophisticated classifiers via the scikit-learn machine learning library in *Chapter 3, A Tour of Machine Learning Classifiers Using Scikit-Learn*.

The topics that we will cover in this chapter are as follows:

- Building an understanding of machine learning algorithms
- Using pandas, NumPy, and Matplotlib to read in, process, and visualize data
- Implementing linear classifiers for 2-class problems in Python

Artificial neurons – a brief glimpse into the early history of machine learning

Before we discuss the perceptron and related algorithms in more detail, let's take a brief tour of the beginnings of machine learning. Trying to understand how the biological brain works in order to design an **artificial intelligence** (**AI**), Warren McCulloch and Walter Pitts published the first concept of a simplified brain cell, the so-called **McCulloch-Pitts** (**MCP**) neuron, in 1943 (*A Logical Calculus of the Ideas Immanent in Nervous Activity* by *W. S. McCulloch* and *W. Pitts*, *Bulletin of Mathematical Biophysics*, 5(4): 115-133, 1943).

Biological neurons are interconnected nerve cells in the brain that are involved in the processing and transmitting of chemical and electrical signals, which is illustrated in *Figure 2.1*:

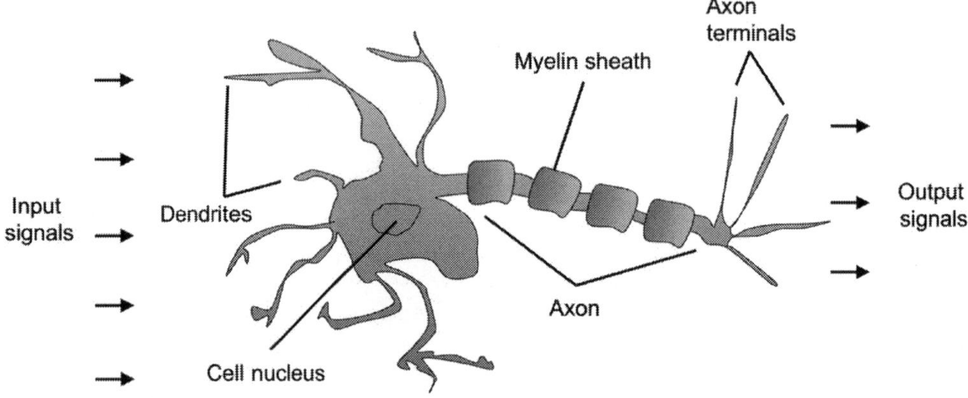

Figure 2.1: A neuron processing chemical and electrical signals

McCulloch and Pitts described such a nerve cell as a simple logic gate with binary outputs; multiple signals arrive at the dendrites, they are then integrated into the cell body, and, if the accumulated signal exceeds a certain threshold, an output signal is generated that will be passed on by the axon.

Only a few years later, Frank Rosenblatt published the first concept of the perceptron learning rule based on the MCP neuron model (*The Perceptron: A Perceiving and Recognizing Automaton* by *F. Rosenblatt, Cornell Aeronautical Laboratory*, 1957). With his perceptron rule, Rosenblatt proposed an algorithm that would automatically learn the optimal weight coefficients that would then be multiplied with the input features in order to make the decision of whether a neuron fires (transmits a signal) or not. In the context of supervised learning and classification, such an algorithm could then be used to predict whether a new data point belongs to one class or the other.

The formal definition of an artificial neuron

More formally, we can put the idea behind **artificial neurons** into the context of a binary classification task with two classes: 0 and 1. We can then define a decision function, $\sigma(z)$, that takes a linear combination of certain input values, x, and a corresponding weight vector, w, where z is the so-called net input $z = w_1x_1 + w_2x_2 + ... + w_mx_m$:

$$\boldsymbol{w} = \begin{bmatrix} w_1 \\ \vdots \\ w_m \end{bmatrix}, \quad \boldsymbol{x} = \begin{bmatrix} x_1 \\ \vdots \\ x_m \end{bmatrix}$$

Now, if the net input of a particular example, $x^{(i)}$, is greater than a defined threshold, θ, we predict class 1, and class 0 otherwise. In the perceptron algorithm, the decision function, $\sigma(\cdot)$, is a variant of a **unit step function**:

$$\sigma(z) = \begin{cases} 1 & \text{if } z \geq \theta \\ 0 & \text{otherwise} \end{cases}$$

To simplify the code implementation later, we can modify this setup via a couple of steps. First, we move the threshold, θ, to the left side of the equation:

$$z \geq \theta$$
$$z - \theta \geq 0$$

Second, we define a so-called *bias unit* as $b = -\theta$ and make it part of the net input:

$$z = w_1x_1 + \dots + w_mx_m + b = \boldsymbol{w}^T\boldsymbol{x} + b$$

Third, given the introduction of the bias unit and the redefinition of the net input z above, we can redefine the decision function as follows:

$$\sigma(z) = \begin{cases} 1 & \text{if } z \geq 0 \\ 0 & \text{otherwise} \end{cases}$$

Linear algebra basics: dot product and matrix transpose

In the following sections, we will often make use of basic notations from linear algebra. For example, we will abbreviate the sum of the products of the values in $\boldsymbol{x}$ and $\boldsymbol{w}$ using a vector dot product, whereas the superscript T stands for transpose, which is an operation that transforms a column vector into a row vector and vice versa. For example, assume we have the following two column vectors:

$$\boldsymbol{a} = \begin{bmatrix} a_1 \\ a_2 \\ a_3 \end{bmatrix}, \quad \boldsymbol{b} = \begin{bmatrix} b_1 \\ b_2 \\ b_3 \end{bmatrix}$$

Then, we can write the transpose of vector $\boldsymbol{a}$ as $\boldsymbol{a}^T = [a_1 \; a_2 \; a_3]$ and write the dot product as

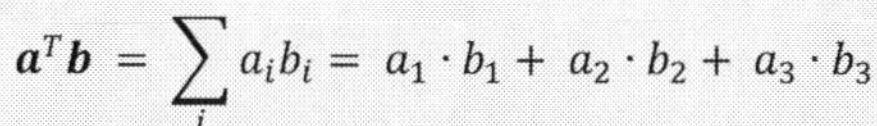

$$\boldsymbol{a}^T\boldsymbol{b} = \sum_i a_i b_i = a_1 \cdot b_1 + a_2 \cdot b_2 + a_3 \cdot b_3$$

Furthermore, the transpose operation can also be applied to matrices to reflect it over its diagonal, for example:

$$\begin{bmatrix} 1 & 2 \\ 3 & 4 \\ 5 & 6 \end{bmatrix}^T = \begin{bmatrix} 1 & 3 & 5 \\ 2 & 4 & 6 \end{bmatrix}$$

Please note that the transpose operation is strictly only defined for matrices; however, in the context of machine learning, we refer to $n \times 1$ or $1 \times m$ matrices when we use the term "vector."

In this book, we will only use very basic concepts from linear algebra; however, if you need a quick refresher, please take a look at Zico Kolter's excellent *Linear Algebra Review and Reference*, which is freely available at `http://www.cs.cmu.edu/~zkolter/course/linalg/linalg_notes.pdf`.

Figure 2.2 illustrates how the net input $z = \boldsymbol{w}^T\boldsymbol{x} + b$ is squashed into a binary output (0 or 1) by the decision function of the perceptron (left subfigure) and how it can be used to discriminate between two classes separable by a linear decision boundary (right subfigure):

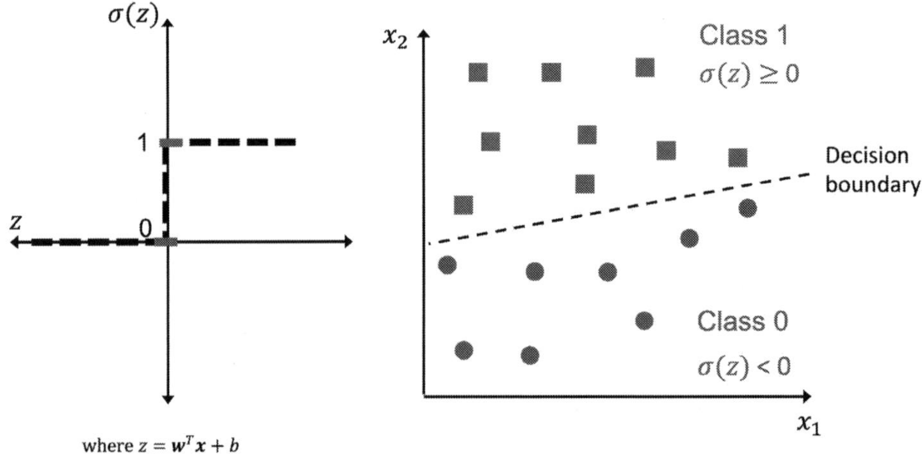

Figure 2.2: A threshold function producing a linear decision boundary for a binary classification problem

The perceptron learning rule

The whole idea behind the MCP neuron and Rosenblatt's *thresholded* perceptron model is to use a reductionist approach to mimic how a single neuron in the brain works: it either *fires* or it doesn't. Thus, Rosenblatt's classic perceptron rule is fairly simple, and the perceptron algorithm can be summarized by the following steps:

1. Initialize the weights and bias unit to 0 or small random numbers
2. For each training example, $\boldsymbol{x}^{(i)}$:
   a. Compute the output value, $\hat{y}^{(i)}$
   b. Update the weights and bias unit

Here, the output value is the class label predicted by the unit step function that we defined earlier, and the simultaneous update of the bias unit and each weight, w_j, in the weight vector, $\boldsymbol{w}$, can be more formally written as:

$$w_j := w_j + \Delta w_j$$
$$\text{and} \quad b := b + \Delta b$$

The update values ("deltas") are computed as follows:

$$\Delta w_j = \eta\left(y^{(i)} - \hat{y}^{(i)}\right)x_j^{(i)}$$
$$\text{and} \quad \Delta b = \eta\left(y^{(i)} - \hat{y}^{(i)}\right)$$

Note that unlike the bias unit, each weight, w_j, corresponds to a feature, x_j, in the dataset, which is involved in determining the update value, Δw_j, defined above. Furthermore, η is the **learning rate** (typically a constant between 0.0 and 1.0), $y^{(i)}$ is the **true class label** of the *i*th training example, and $\hat{y}^{(i)}$ is the **predicted class label.** It is important to note that the bias unit and all weights in the weight vector are being updated simultaneously, which means that we don't recompute the predicted label, $\hat{y}^{(i)}$, before the bias unit and all of the weights are updated via the respective update values, Δw_j and Δb. Concretely, for a two-dimensional dataset, we would write the update as:

$$\begin{aligned}\Delta w_1 &= \eta(y^{(i)} - \text{output}^{(i)})x_1^{(i)};\\ \Delta w_2 &= \eta(y^{(i)} - \text{output}^{(i)})x_2^{(i)};\\ \Delta b &= \eta(y^{(i)} - \text{output}^{(i)})\end{aligned}$$

Before we implement the perceptron rule in Python, let's go through a simple thought experiment to illustrate how beautifully simple this learning rule really is. In the two scenarios where the perceptron predicts the class label correctly, the bias unit and weights remain unchanged, since the update values are 0:

(1) $y^{(i)} = 0, \quad \hat{y}^{(i)} = 0, \quad \Delta w_j = \eta(0-0)x_j^{(i)} = 0, \quad \Delta b = \eta(0-0) = 0$

(2) $y^{(i)} = 1, \quad \hat{y}^{(i)} = 1, \quad \Delta w_j = \eta(1-1)x_j^{(i)} = 0, \quad \Delta b = \eta(1-1) = 0$

However, in the case of a wrong prediction, the weights are being pushed toward the direction of the positive or negative target class:

(3) $y^{(i)} = 1, \quad \hat{y}^{(i)} = 0, \quad \Delta w_j = \eta(1-0)x_j^{(i)} = \eta x_j^{(i)}, \quad \Delta b = \eta(1-0) = \eta$

(4) $y^{(i)} = 0, \quad \hat{y}^{(i)} = 1, \quad \Delta w_j = \eta(0-1)x_j^{(i)} = -\eta x_j^{(i)}, \quad \Delta b = \eta(0-1) = -\eta$

To get a better understanding of the feature value as a multiplicative factor, $x_j^{(i)}$, let's go through another simple example, where:

$$y^{(i)} = 1, \quad \hat{y}^{(i)} = 0, \quad \eta = 1$$

Let's assume that $x_j^{(i)} = 1.5$ and we misclassify this example as *class 0*. In this case, we would increase the corresponding weight by 2.5 in total so that the net input, $z = x_j^{(i)} \times w_j + b$, would be more positive the next time we encounter this example, and thus be more likely to be above the threshold of the unit step function to classify the example as *class 1*:

$\Delta w_j = (1-0)1.5 = 1.5, \quad \Delta b = (1-0) = 1$

The weight update, Δw_j, is proportional to the value of $x_j^{(i)}$. For instance, if we have another example, $x_j^{(i)} = 2$, that is incorrectly classified as *class 0*, we will push the decision boundary by an even larger extent to classify this example correctly the next time:

$\Delta w_j = (1-0)2 = 2, \quad \Delta b = (1-0) = 1$

It is important to note that the convergence of the perceptron is only guaranteed if the two classes are linearly separable, which means that the two classes can be perfectly separated by a linear decision boundary. (Interested readers can find the convergence proof in my lecture notes: `https://sebastianraschka.com/pdf/lecture-notes/stat453ss21/L03_perceptron_slides.pdf`). *Figure 2.3* shows visual examples of linearly separable and linearly inseparable scenarios:

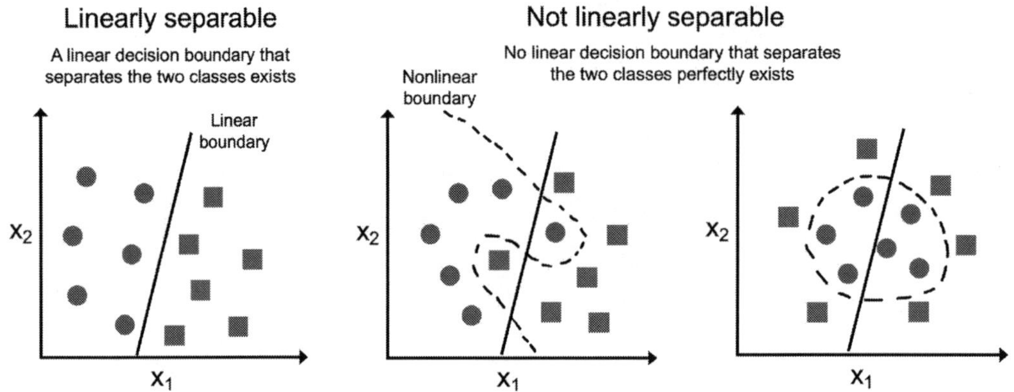

Figure 2.3: Examples of linearly and nonlinearly separable classes

If the two classes can't be separated by a linear decision boundary, we can set a maximum number of passes over the training dataset (**epochs**) and/or a threshold for the number of tolerated misclassifications—the perceptron would never stop updating the weights otherwise. Later in this chapter, we will cover the Adaline algorithm that produces linear decision boundaries and converges even if the classes are not perfectly linearly separable. In *Chapter 3*, we will learn about algorithms that can produce nonlinear decision boundaries.

Downloading the example code

If you bought this book directly from Packt, you can download the example code files from your account at `http://www.packtpub.com`. If you purchased this book elsewhere, you can download all code examples and datasets directly from `https://github.com/rasbt/machine-learning-book`.

Now, before we jump into the implementation in the next section, what you just learned can be summarized in a simple diagram that illustrates the general concept of the perceptron:

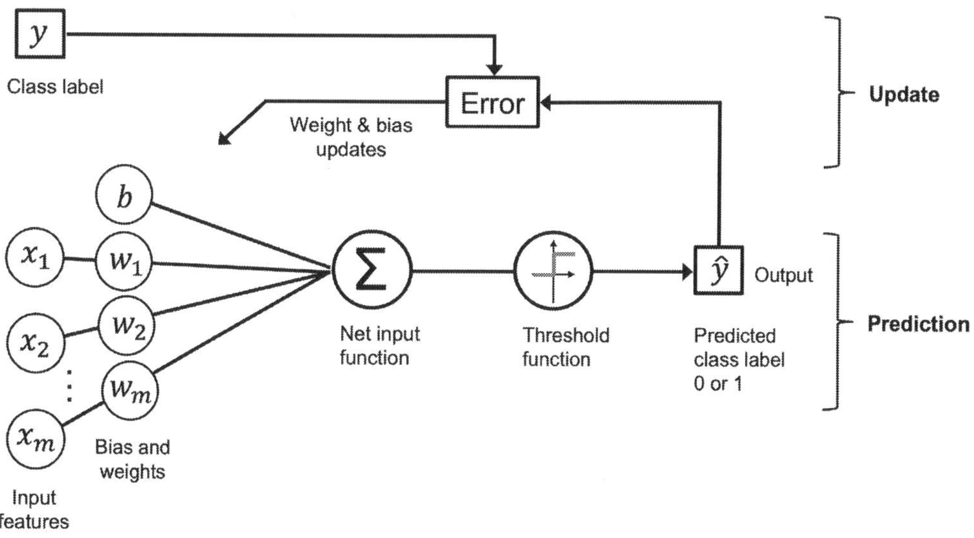

Figure 2.4: Weights and bias of the model are updated based on the error function

The preceding diagram illustrates how the perceptron receives the inputs of an example (*x*) and combines them with the bias unit (*b*) and weights (***w***) to compute the net input. The net input is then passed on to the threshold function, which generates a binary output of 0 or 1—the predicted class label of the example. During the learning phase, this output is used to calculate the error of the prediction and update the weights and bias unit.

Implementing a perceptron learning algorithm in Python

In the previous section, we learned how Rosenblatt's perceptron rule works; let's now implement it in Python and apply it to the Iris dataset that we introduced in *Chapter 1, Giving Computers the Ability to Learn from Data*.

An object-oriented perceptron API

We will take an object-oriented approach to defining the perceptron interface as a Python class, which will allow us to initialize new `Perceptron` objects that can learn from data via a `fit` method and make predictions via a separate `predict` method. As a convention, we append an underscore (_) to attributes that are not created upon the initialization of the object, but we do this by calling the object's other methods, for example, `self.w_`.

Additional resources for Python's scientific computing stack

If you are not yet familiar with Python's scientific libraries or need a refresher, please see the following resources:

- **NumPy:** https://sebastianraschka.com/blog/2020/numpy-intro.html
- **pandas:** https://pandas.pydata.org/pandas-docs/stable/user_guide/10min.html
- **Matplotlib:** https://matplotlib.org/stable/tutorials/introductory/usage.html

The following is the implementation of a perceptron in Python:

```
import numpy as np
class Perceptron:
    """Perceptron classifier.

    Parameters
    ------------
    eta : float
      Learning rate (between 0.0 and 1.0)
    n_iter : int
      Passes over the training dataset.
    random_state : int
      Random number generator seed for random weight
      initialization.

    Attributes
    -----------
    w_ : 1d-array
      Weights after fitting.
    b_ : Scalar
      Bias unit after fitting.

    errors_ : list
      Number of misclassifications (updates) in each epoch.

    """
    def __init__(self, eta=0.01, n_iter=50, random_state=1):
        self.eta = eta
        self.n_iter = n_iter
        self.random_state = random_state
```

```
    def fit(self, X, y):
        """Fit training data.

        Parameters
        ----------
        X : {array-like}, shape = [n_examples, n_features]
          Training vectors, where n_examples is the number of
          examples and n_features is the number of features.
        y : array-like, shape = [n_examples]
          Target values.

        Returns
        -------
        self : object

        """
        rgen = np.random.RandomState(self.random_state)
        self.w_ = rgen.normal(loc=0.0, scale=0.01,
                              size=X.shape[1])
        self.b_ = np.float_(0.)
        self.errors_ = []

        for _ in range(self.n_iter):
            errors = 0
            for xi, target in zip(X, y):
                update = self.eta * (target - self.predict(xi))
                self.w_ += update * xi
                self.b_ += update
                errors += int(update != 0.0)
            self.errors_.append(errors)
        return self

    def net_input(self, X):
        """Calculate net input"""
        return np.dot(X, self.w_) + self.b_

    def predict(self, X):
        """Return class label after unit step"""
        return np.where(self.net_input(X) >= 0.0, 1, 0)
```

Using this perceptron implementation, we can now initialize new `Perceptron` objects with a given learning rate, `eta` (η), and the number of epochs, `n_iter` (passes over the training dataset).

Via the `fit` method, we initialize the bias `self.b_` to an initial value 0 and the weights in `self.w_` to a vector, $\mathbb{R}^m$, where m stands for the number of dimensions (features) in the dataset.

Notice that the initial weight vector contains small random numbers drawn from a normal distribution with a standard deviation of 0.01 via `rgen.normal(loc=0.0, scale=0.01, size=1 + X.shape[1])`, where `rgen` is a NumPy random number generator that we seeded with a user-specified random seed so that we can reproduce previous results if desired.

Technically, we could initialize the weights to zero (in fact, this is done in the original perceptron algorithm). However, if we did that, then the learning rate η (`eta`) would have no effect on the decision boundary. If all the weights are initialized to zero, the learning rate parameter, `eta`, affects only the scale of the weight vector, not the direction. If you are familiar with trigonometry, consider a vector, $v1$ =[1 2 3], where the angle between $v1$ and a vector, $v2 = 0.5 \times v1$, would be exactly zero, as demonstrated by the following code snippet:

```
>>> v1 = np.array([1, 2, 3])
>>> v2 = 0.5 * v1
>>> np.arccos(v1.dot(v2) / (np.linalg.norm(v1) *
...           np.linalg.norm(v2)))
0.0
```

Here, `np.arccos` is the trigonometric inverse cosine, and `np.linalg.norm` is a function that computes the length of a vector. (Our decision to draw the random numbers from a random normal distribution—for example, instead of from a uniform distribution—and to use a standard deviation of `0.01` was arbitrary; remember, we are just interested in small random values to avoid the properties of all-zero vectors, as discussed earlier.)

As an optional exercise after reading this chapter, you can change `self.w_ = rgen.normal(loc=0.0, scale=0.01, size=X.shape[1])` to `self.w_ = np.zeros(X.shape[1])` and run the perceptron training code presented in the next section with different values for `eta`. You will observe that the decision boundary does not change.

NumPy array indexing

NumPy indexing for one-dimensional arrays works similarly to Python lists using the square-bracket (`[]`) notation. For two-dimensional arrays, the first indexer refers to the row number and the second indexer to the column number. For example, we would use `X[2, 3]` to select the third row and fourth column of a two-dimensional array, `X`.

After the weights have been initialized, the `fit` method loops over all individual examples in the training dataset and updates the weights according to the perceptron learning rule that we discussed in the previous section.

The class labels are predicted by the `predict` method, which is called in the `fit` method during training to get the class label for the weight update; but `predict` can also be used to predict the class labels of new data after we have fitted our model. Furthermore, we also collect the number of misclassifications during each epoch in the `self.errors_` list so that we can later analyze how well our perceptron performed during the training. The `np.dot` function that is used in the `net_input` method simply calculates the vector dot product, $\boldsymbol{w}^T\boldsymbol{x} + b$.

Vectorization: Replacing for loops with vectorized code

Instead of using NumPy to calculate the vector dot product between two arrays, `a` and `b`, via `a.dot(b)` or `np.dot(a, b)`, we could also perform the calculation in pure Python via `sum([i * j for i, j in zip(a, b)])`. However, the advantage of using NumPy over classic Python `for` loop structures is that its arithmetic operations are vectorized. Vectorization means that an elemental arithmetic operation is automatically applied to all elements in an array. By formulating our arithmetic operations as a sequence of instructions on an array, rather than performing a set of operations for each element at a time, we can make better use of our modern **central processing unit** (**CPU**) architectures with **single instruction, multiple data** (**SIMD**) support. Furthermore, NumPy uses highly optimized linear algebra libraries, such as **Basic Linear Algebra Subprograms** (**BLAS**) and **Linear Algebra Package** (**LAPACK**), that have been written in C or Fortran. Lastly, NumPy also allows us to write our code in a more compact and intuitive way using the basics of linear algebra, such as vector and matrix dot products.

Training a perceptron model on the Iris dataset

To test our perceptron implementation, we will restrict the following analyses and examples in the remainder of this chapter to two feature variables (dimensions). Although the perceptron rule is not restricted to two dimensions, considering only two features, sepal length and petal length, will allow us to visualize the decision regions of the trained model in a scatterplot for learning purposes.

Note that we will also only consider two flower classes, setosa and versicolor, from the Iris dataset for practical reasons—remember, the perceptron is a binary classifier. However, the perceptron algorithm can be extended to multi-class classification—for example, the **one-versus-all** (**OvA**) technique.

The OvA method for multi-class classification

OvA, which is sometimes also called **one-versus-rest (OvR)**, is a technique that allows us to extend any binary classifier to multi-class problems. Using OvA, we can train one classifier per class, where the particular class is treated as the positive class and the examples from all other classes are considered negative classes. If we were to classify a new, unlabeled data instance, we would use our *n* classifiers, where *n* is the number of class labels, and assign the class label with the highest confidence to the particular instance we want to classify. In the case of the perceptron, we would use OvA to choose the class label that is associated with the largest absolute net input value.

First, we will use the `pandas` library to load the Iris dataset directly from the *UCI Machine Learning Repository* into a `DataFrame` object and print the last five lines via the `tail` method to check that the data was loaded correctly:

```
>>> import os
>>> import pandas as pd
>>> s = 'https://archive.ics.uci.edu/ml/'\
...     'machine-learning-databases/iris/iris.data'
>>> print('From URL:', s)
From URL: https://archive.ics.uci.edu/ml/machine-learning-databases/iris/iris.
data
>>> df = pd.read_csv(s,
...                  header=None,
...                  encoding='utf-8')
>>> df.tail()
```

After executing the previous code, we should see the following output, which shows the last five lines of the Iris dataset:

	0	1	2	3	4
145	6.7	3.0	5.2	2.3	Iris-virginica
146	6.3	2.5	5.0	1.9	Iris-virginica
147	6.5	3.0	5.2	2.0	Iris-virginica
148	6.2	3.4	5.4	2.3	Iris-virginica
149	5.9	3.0	5.1	1.8	Iris-virginica

Figure 2.5: The last five lines of the Iris dataset

Loading the Iris dataset

You can find a copy of the Iris dataset (and all other datasets used in this book) in the code bundle of this book, which you can use if you are working offline or if the UCI server at `https://archive.ics.uci.edu/ml/machine-learning-databases/iris/iris.data` is temporarily unavailable. For instance, to load the Iris dataset from a local directory, you can replace this line,

```
df = pd.read_csv(
  'https://archive.ics.uci.edu/ml/'
  'machine-learning-databases/iris/iris.data',
  header=None, encoding='utf-8')
```

with the following one:

```
df = pd.read_csv(
  'your/local/path/to/iris.data',
  header=None, encoding='utf-8')
```

Next, we extract the first 100 class labels that correspond to the 50 Iris-setosa and 50 Iris-versicolor flowers and convert the class labels into the two integer class labels, `1` (versicolor) and `0` (setosa), that we assign to a vector, `y`, where the `values` method of a pandas `DataFrame` yields the corresponding NumPy representation.

Similarly, we extract the first feature column (sepal length) and the third feature column (petal length) of those 100 training examples and assign them to a feature matrix, `X`, which we can visualize via a two-dimensional scatterplot:

```
>>> import matplotlib.pyplot as plt
>>> import numpy as np
>>> # select setosa and versicolor
>>> y = df.iloc[0:100, 4].values
>>> y = np.where(y == 'Iris-setosa', 0, 1)
>>> # extract sepal length and petal length
>>> X = df.iloc[0:100, [0, 2]].values
>>> # plot data
>>> plt.scatter(X[:50, 0], X[:50, 1],
...             color='red', marker='o', label='Setosa')
>>> plt.scatter(X[50:100, 0], X[50:100, 1],
...             color='blue', marker='s', label='Versicolor')
>>> plt.xlabel('Sepal length [cm]')
>>> plt.ylabel('Petal length [cm]')
>>> plt.legend(loc='upper left')
>>> plt.show()
```

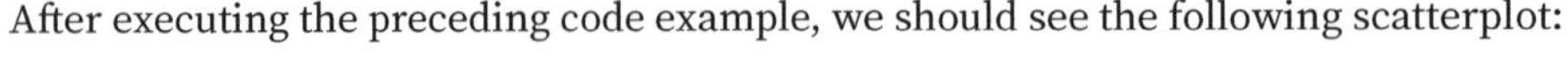

After executing the preceding code example, we should see the following scatterplot:

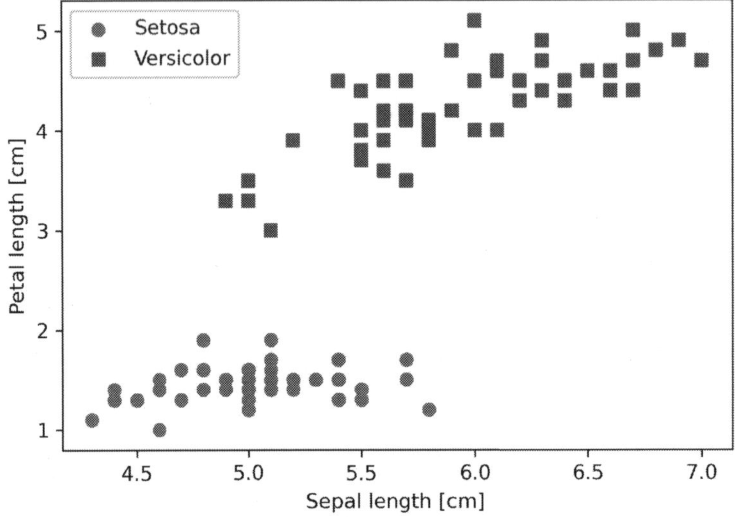

Figure 2.6: Scatterplot of setosa and versicolor flowers by sepal and petal length

Figure 2.6 shows the distribution of flower examples in the Iris dataset along the two feature axes: petal length and sepal length (measured in centimeters). In this two-dimensional feature subspace, we can see that a linear decision boundary should be sufficient to separate setosa from versicolor flowers. Thus, a linear classifier such as the perceptron should be able to classify the flowers in this dataset perfectly.

Now, it's time to train our perceptron algorithm on the Iris data subset that we just extracted. Also, we will plot the misclassification error for each epoch to check whether the algorithm converged and found a decision boundary that separates the two Iris flower classes:

```
>>> ppn = Perceptron(eta=0.1, n_iter=10)
>>> ppn.fit(X, y)
>>> plt.plot(range(1, len(ppn.errors_) + 1),
...          ppn.errors_, marker='o')
>>> plt.xlabel('Epochs')
>>> plt.ylabel('Number of updates')
>>> plt.show()
```

Note that the number of misclassification errors and the number of updates is the same, since the perceptron weights and bias are updated each time it misclassifies an example. After executing the preceding code, we should see the plot of the misclassification errors versus the number of epochs, as shown in *Figure 2.7*:

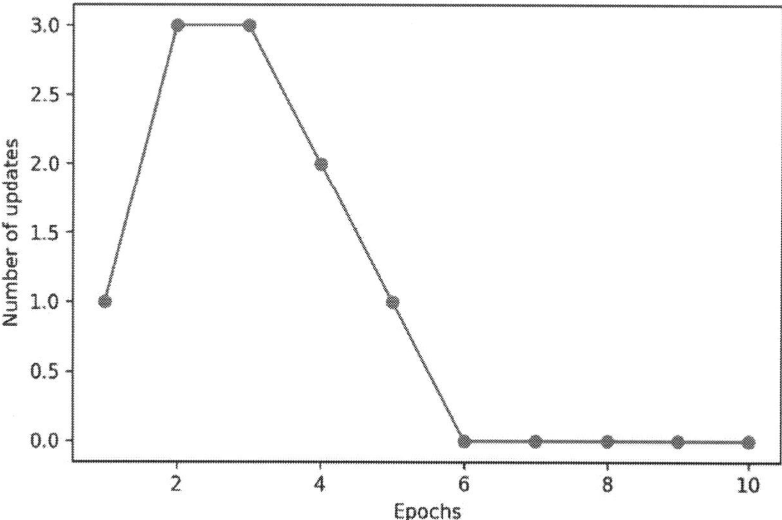

Figure 2.7: A plot of the misclassification errors against the number of epochs

As we can see in *Figure 2.7*, our perceptron converged after the sixth epoch and should now be able to classify the training examples perfectly. Let's implement a small convenience function to visualize the decision boundaries for two-dimensional datasets:

```
from matplotlib.colors import ListedColormap
def plot_decision_regions(X, y, classifier, resolution=0.02):
    # setup marker generator and color map
    markers = ('o', 's', '^', 'v', '<')
    colors = ('red', 'blue', 'lightgreen', 'gray', 'cyan')
    cmap = ListedColormap(colors[:len(np.unique(y))])

    # plot the decision surface
    x1_min, x1_max = X[:, 0].min() - 1, X[:, 0].max() + 1
    x2_min, x2_max = X[:, 1].min() - 1, X[:, 1].max() + 1
    xx1, xx2 = np.meshgrid(np.arange(x1_min, x1_max, resolution),
                           np.arange(x2_min, x2_max, resolution))
    lab = classifier.predict(np.array([xx1.ravel(), xx2.ravel()]).T)
    lab = lab.reshape(xx1.shape)
    plt.contourf(xx1, xx2, lab, alpha=0.3, cmap=cmap)
    plt.xlim(xx1.min(), xx1.max())
    plt.ylim(xx2.min(), xx2.max())
```

```
    # plot class examples
    for idx, cl in enumerate(np.unique(y)):
        plt.scatter(x=X[y == cl, 0],
                    y=X[y == cl, 1],
                    alpha=0.8,
                    c=colors[idx],
                    marker=markers[idx],
                    label=f'Class {cl}',
                    edgecolor='black')
```

First, we define a number of `colors` and `markers` and create a colormap from the list of colors via `ListedColormap`. Then, we determine the minimum and maximum values for the two features and use those feature vectors to create a pair of grid arrays, `xx1` and `xx2`, via the NumPy `meshgrid` function. Since we trained our perceptron classifier on two feature dimensions, we need to flatten the grid arrays and create a matrix that has the same number of columns as the Iris training subset so that we can use the `predict` method to predict the class labels, `lab`, of the corresponding grid points.

After reshaping the predicted class labels, `lab`, into a grid with the same dimensions as `xx1` and `xx2`, we can now draw a contour plot via Matplotlib's `contourf` function, which maps the different decision regions to different colors for each predicted class in the grid array:

```
>>> plot_decision_regions(X, y, classifier=ppn)
>>> plt.xlabel('Sepal length [cm]')
>>> plt.ylabel('Petal length [cm]')
>>> plt.legend(loc='upper left')
>>> plt.show()
```

After executing the preceding code example, we should now see a plot of the decision regions, as shown in *Figure 2.8*:

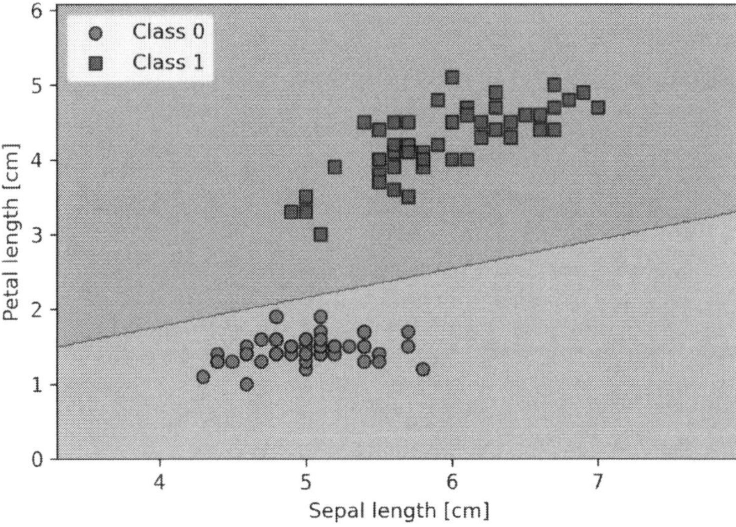

Figure 2.8: A plot of the perceptron's decision regions

As we can see in the plot, the perceptron learned a decision boundary that can classify all flower examples in the Iris training subset perfectly.

Perceptron convergence

Although the perceptron classified the two Iris flower classes perfectly, convergence is one of the biggest problems of the perceptron. Rosenblatt proved mathematically that the perceptron learning rule converges if the two classes can be separated by a linear hyperplane. However, if the classes cannot be separated perfectly by such a linear decision boundary, the weights will never stop updating unless we set a maximum number of epochs. Interested readers can find a summary of the proof in my lecture notes at `https://sebastianraschka.com/pdf/lecture-notes/stat453ss21/L03_perceptron_slides.pdf`.

Adaptive linear neurons and the convergence of learning

In this section, we will take a look at another type of single-layer **neural network** (**NN**): **ADAptive LInear NEuron** (**Adaline**). Adaline was published by Bernard Widrow and his doctoral student Tedd Hoff only a few years after Rosenblatt's perceptron algorithm, and it can be considered an improvement on the latter (*An Adaptive "Adaline" Neuron Using Chemical "Memistors"*, *Technical Report Number 1553-2* by *B. Widrow and colleagues*, *Stanford Electron Labs*, Stanford, CA, *October* 1960).

The Adaline algorithm is particularly interesting because it illustrates the key concepts of defining and minimizing continuous loss functions. This lays the groundwork for understanding other machine learning algorithms for classification, such as logistic regression, support vector machines, and multilayer neural networks, as well as linear regression models, which we will discuss in future chapters.

The key difference between the Adaline rule (also known as the **Widrow-Hoff rule**) and Rosenblatt's perceptron is that the weights are updated based on a linear activation function rather than a unit step function like in the perceptron. In Adaline, this linear activation function, $\sigma(z)$, is simply the identity function of the net input, so that $\sigma(z) = z$.

While the linear activation function is used for learning the weights, we still use a threshold function to make the final prediction, which is similar to the unit step function that we covered earlier.

The main differences between the perceptron and Adaline algorithm are highlighted in *Figure 2.9*:

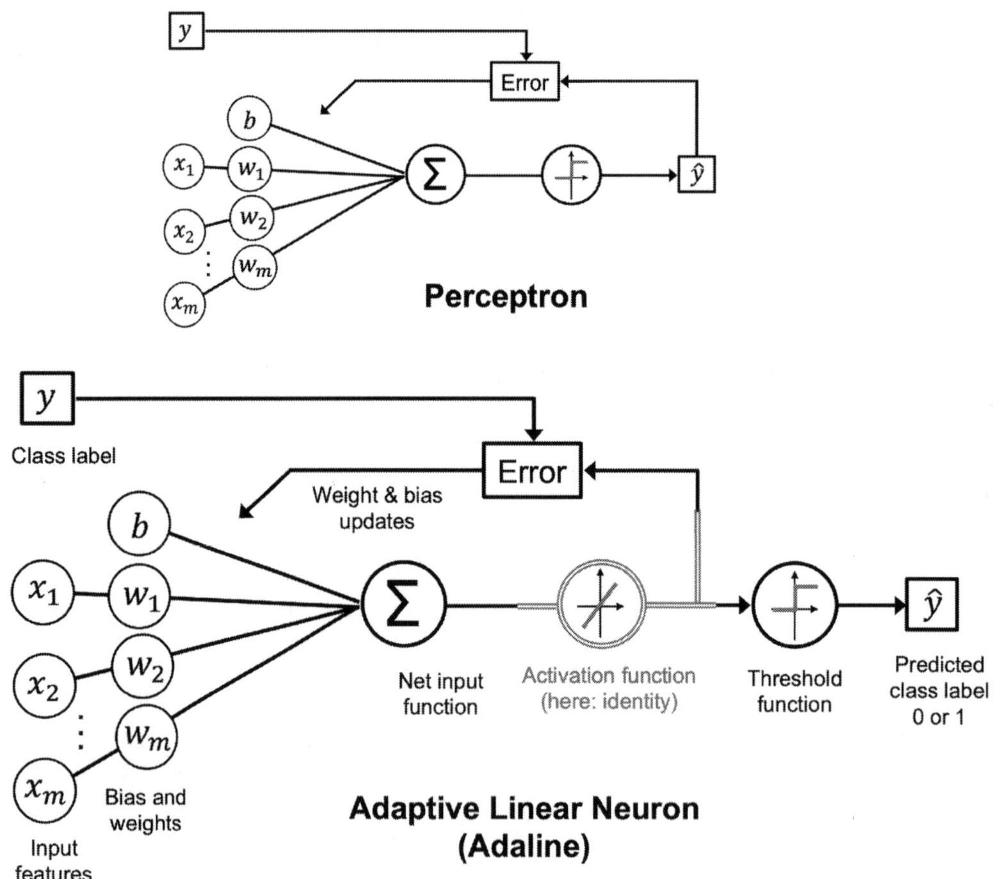

Figure 2.9: A comparison between a perceptron and the Adaline algorithm

As *Figure 2.9* indicates, the Adaline algorithm compares the true class labels with the linear activation function's continuous valued output to compute the model error and update the weights. In contrast, the perceptron compares the true class labels to the predicted class labels.

Minimizing loss functions with gradient descent

One of the key ingredients of supervised machine learning algorithms is a defined **objective function** that is to be optimized during the learning process. This objective function is often a loss or cost function that we want to minimize. In the case of Adaline, we can define the loss function, L, to learn the model parameters as the **mean squared error** (**MSE**) between the calculated outcome and the true class label:

$$L(\boldsymbol{w}, b) = \frac{1}{n}\sum_{i=1}^{n}\left(y^{(i)} - \sigma\left(z^{(i)}\right)\right)^2$$

The main advantage of this continuous linear activation function, in contrast to the unit step function, is that the loss function becomes differentiable. Another nice property of this loss function is that it is convex; thus, we can use a very simple yet powerful optimization algorithm called **gradient descent** to find the weights that minimize our loss function to classify the examples in the Iris dataset.

As illustrated in *Figure 2.10*, we can describe the main idea behind gradient descent as *climbing down a hill* until a local or global loss minimum is reached. In each iteration, we take a step in the opposite direction of the gradient, where the step size is determined by the value of the learning rate, as well as the slope of the gradient (for simplicity, the following figure visualizes this only for a single weight, w):

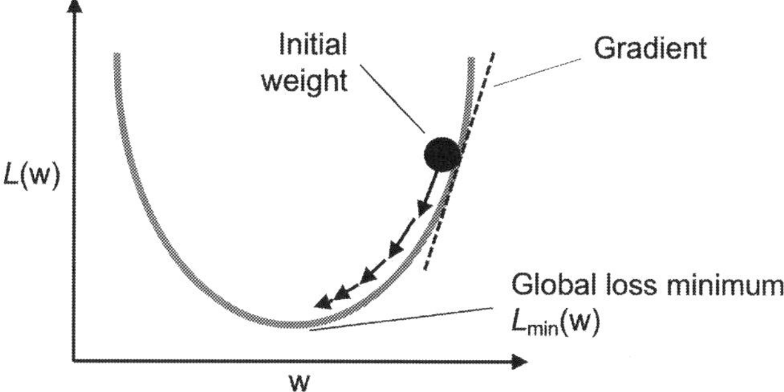

Figure 2.10: How gradient descent works

Using gradient descent, we can now update the model parameters by taking a step in the opposite direction of the gradient, $\nabla L(\boldsymbol{w}, b)$, of our loss function, $L(\boldsymbol{w}, b)$:

$$\boldsymbol{w} := \boldsymbol{w} + \Delta\boldsymbol{w}, \quad b := b + \Delta b$$

The parameter changes, $\Delta \boldsymbol{w}$ and Δb, are defined as the negative gradient multiplied by the learning rate, η:

$$\Delta \boldsymbol{w} = -\eta \nabla_w L(\boldsymbol{w}, b), \quad \Delta b = -\eta \nabla_b L(\boldsymbol{w}, b)$$

To compute the gradient of the loss function, we need to compute the partial derivative of the loss function with respect to each weight, w_j:

$$\frac{\partial L}{\partial w_j} = -\frac{2}{n} \sum_i \left(y^{(i)} - \sigma\left(z^{(i)}\right)\right) x_j^{(i)}$$

Similarly, we compute the partial derivative of the loss with respect to the bias as:

$$\frac{\partial L}{\partial b} = -\frac{2}{n} \sum_i \left(y^{(i)} - \sigma\left(z^{(i)}\right)\right)$$

Please note that the 2 in the numerator above is merely a constant scaling factor, and we could omit it without affecting the algorithm. Removing the scaling factor has the same effect as changing the learning rate by a factor of 2. The following information box explains where this scaling factor originates.

So we can write the weight update as:

$$\Delta w_j = -\eta \frac{\partial L}{\partial w_j} \text{ and } \Delta b = -\eta \frac{\partial L}{\partial b}$$

Since we update all parameters simultaneously, our Adaline learning rule becomes:

$$\boldsymbol{w} := \boldsymbol{w} + \Delta \boldsymbol{w}, \quad b := b + \Delta b$$

The mean squared error derivative

If you are familiar with calculus, the partial derivative of the MSE loss function with respect to the *j*th weight can be obtained as follows:

$$\frac{\partial L}{\partial w_j} = \frac{\partial}{\partial w_j} \frac{1}{n} \sum_i \left(y^{(i)} - \sigma\left(z^{(i)}\right)\right)^2 = \frac{1}{n} \frac{\partial}{\partial w_j} \sum_i \left(y^{(i)} - \sigma\left(z^{(i)}\right)\right)^2$$

$$= \frac{2}{n} \sum_i \left(y^{(i)} - \sigma\left(z^{(i)}\right)\right) \frac{\partial}{\partial w_j} \left(y^{(i)} - \sigma\left(z^{(i)}\right)\right)$$

$$= \frac{2}{n} \sum_i \left(y^{(i)} - \sigma\left(z^{(i)}\right)\right) \frac{\partial}{\partial w_j} \left(y^{(i)} - \sum_j \left(w_j x_j^{(i)} + b\right)\right)$$

$$= \frac{2}{n} \sum_i \left(y^{(i)} - \sigma\left(z^{(i)}\right)\right)\left(-x_j^{(i)}\right) = -\frac{2}{n} \sum_i \left(y^{(i)} - \sigma\left(z^{(i)}\right)\right) x_j^{(i)}$$

The same approach can be used to find partial derivative $\frac{\partial L}{\partial b}$ except that $\frac{\partial}{\partial b}\left(y^{(i)} - \sum_i \left(w_j^{(i)} x_j^{(i)} + b\right)\right)$ is equal to -1 and thus the last step simplifies to $-\frac{2}{n} \sum_i \left(y^{(i)} - \sigma\left(z^{(i)}\right)\right)$.

Although the Adaline learning rule looks identical to the perceptron rule, we should note that $\sigma(z^{(i)})$ with $z^{(i)} = \boldsymbol{w}^T\boldsymbol{x}^{(i)} + b$ is a real number and not an integer class label. Furthermore, the weight update is calculated based on all examples in the training dataset (instead of updating the parameters incrementally after each training example), which is why this approach is also referred to as **batch gradient descent**. To be more explicit and avoid confusion when talking about related concepts later in this chapter and this book, we will refer to this process as **full batch gradient descent**.

Implementing Adaline in Python

Since the perceptron rule and Adaline are very similar, we will take the perceptron implementation that we defined earlier and change the `fit` method so that the weight and bias parameters are now updated by minimizing the loss function via gradient descent:

```
class AdalineGD:
    """ADAptive LInear NEuron classifier.

    Parameters
    ------------
    eta : float
        Learning rate (between 0.0 and 1.0)
    n_iter : int
        Passes over the training dataset.
    random_state : int
        Random number generator seed for random weight initialization.

    Attributes
    -----------
    w_ : 1d-array
        Weights after fitting.
    b_ : Scalar
        Bias unit after fitting.
    losses_ : list
      Mean squared error loss function values in each epoch.

    """
    def __init__(self, eta=0.01, n_iter=50, random_state=1):
        self.eta = eta
        self.n_iter = n_iter
        self.random_state = random_state

    def fit(self, X, y):
        """ Fit training data.
```

```
        Parameters
        ----------
        X : {array-like}, shape = [n_examples, n_features]
            Training vectors, where n_examples
            is the number of examples and
            n_features is the number of features.
        y : array-like, shape = [n_examples]
            Target values.

        Returns
        -------
        self : object

        """
        rgen = np.random.RandomState(self.random_state)
        self.w_ = rgen.normal(loc=0.0, scale=0.01,
                              size=X.shape[1])
        self.b_ = np.float_(0.)
        self.losses_ = []

        for i in range(self.n_iter):
            net_input = self.net_input(X)
            output = self.activation(net_input)
            errors = (y - output)
            self.w_ += self.eta * 2.0 * X.T.dot(errors) / X.shape[0]
            self.b_ += self.eta * 2.0 * errors.mean()
            loss = (errors**2).mean()
            self.losses_.append(loss)
        return self

    def net_input(self, X):
        """Calculate net input"""
        return np.dot(X, self.w_) + self.b_

    def activation(self, X):
        """Compute linear activation"""
        return X

    def predict(self, X):
        """Return class label after unit step"""
```

```
        return np.where(self.activation(self.net_input(X))
                        >= 0.5, 1, 0)
```

Instead of updating the weights after evaluating each individual training example, as in the perceptron, we calculate the gradient based on the whole training dataset. For the bias unit, this is done via `self.eta * 2.0 * errors.mean()`, where `errors` is an array containing the partial derivative values $\frac{\partial}{\partial b}$. Similarly, we update the weights. However note that the weight updates via the partial derivatives $\frac{\partial L}{\partial w_j}$ involve the feature values x_j, which we can compute by multiplying `errors` with each feature value for each weight:

```
            for w_j in range(self.w_.shape[0]):
                self.w_[w_j] += self.eta *
                    (2.0 * (X[:, w_j]*errors)).mean()
```

To implement the weight update more efficiently without using a `for` loop, we can use a matrix-vector multiplication between our feature matrix and the error vector instead:

```
self.w_ += self.eta * 2.0 * X.T.dot(errors) / X.shape[0]
```

Please note that the `activation` method has no effect on the code since it is simply an identity function. Here, we added the activation function (computed via the `activation` method) to illustrate the general concept with regard to how information flows through a single-layer NN: features from the input data, net input, activation, and output.

In the next chapter, we will learn about a logistic regression classifier that uses a non-identity, nonlinear activation function. We will see that a logistic regression model is closely related to Adaline, with the only difference being its activation and loss function.

Now, similar to the previous perceptron implementation, we collect the loss values in a `self.losses_` list to check whether the algorithm converged after training.

Matrix multiplication

Performing a matrix multiplication is similar to calculating a vector dot-product where each row in the matrix is treated as a single row vector. This vectorized approach represents a more compact notation and results in a more efficient computation using NumPy. For example:

$$\begin{bmatrix} 1 & 2 & 3 \\ 4 & 5 & 6 \end{bmatrix} \times \begin{bmatrix} 7 \\ 8 \\ 9 \end{bmatrix} = \begin{bmatrix} 1 \times 7 + 2 \times 8 + 3 \times 9 \\ 4 \times 7 + 5 \times 8 + 6 \times 9 \end{bmatrix} = \begin{bmatrix} 50 \\ 122 \end{bmatrix}$$

Please note that in the preceding equation, we are multiplying a matrix with a vector, which is mathematically not defined. However, remember that we use the convention that this preceding vector is regarded as a 3×1 matrix.

In practice, it often requires some experimentation to find a good learning rate, η, for optimal convergence. So, let's choose two different learning rates, $\eta = 0.1$ and $\eta = 0.0001$, to start with and plot the loss functions versus the number of epochs to see how well the Adaline implementation learns from the training data.

Hyperparameters

The learning rate, η (eta), as well as the number of epochs (n_iter), are the so-called hyperparameters (or tuning parameters) of the perceptron and Adaline learning algorithms. In *Chapter 6, Learning Best Practices for Model Evaluation and Hyperparameter Tuning*, we will take a look at different techniques to automatically find the values of different hyperparameters that yield optimal performance of the classification model.

Let's now plot the loss against the number of epochs for the two different learning rates:

```
>>> fig, ax = plt.subplots(nrows=1, ncols=2, figsize=(10, 4))
>>> ada1 = AdalineGD(n_iter=15, eta=0.1).fit(X, y)
>>> ax[0].plot(range(1, len(ada1.losses_) + 1),
...            np.log10(ada1.losses_), marker='o')
>>> ax[0].set_xlabel('Epochs')
>>> ax[0].set_ylabel('log(Mean squared error)')
>>> ax[0].set_title('Adaline - Learning rate 0.1')
>>> ada2 = AdalineGD(n_iter=15, eta=0.0001).fit(X, y)
>>> ax[1].plot(range(1, len(ada2.losses_) + 1),
...            ada2.losses_, marker='o')
>>> ax[1].set_xlabel('Epochs')
>>> ax[1].set_ylabel('Mean squared error')
>>> ax[1].set_title('Adaline - Learning rate 0.0001')
>>> plt.show()
```

As we can see in the resulting loss function plots, we encountered two different types of problems. The left chart shows what could happen if we choose a learning rate that is too large. Instead of minimizing the loss function, the MSE becomes larger in every epoch, because we *overshoot* the global minimum. On the other hand, we can see that the loss decreases on the right plot, but the chosen learning rate, $\eta = 0.0001$, is so small that the algorithm would require a very large number of epochs to converge to the global loss minimum:

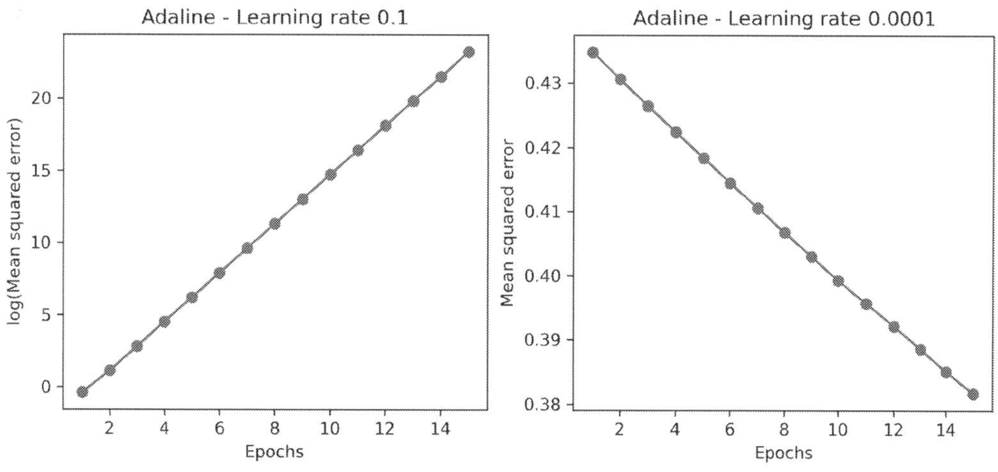

Figure 2.11: Error plots for suboptimal learning rates

Figure 2.12 illustrates what might happen if we change the value of a particular weight parameter to minimize the loss function, *L*. The left subfigure illustrates the case of a well-chosen learning rate, where the loss decreases gradually, moving in the direction of the global minimum.

The subfigure on the right, however, illustrates what happens if we choose a learning rate that is too large—we overshoot the global minimum:

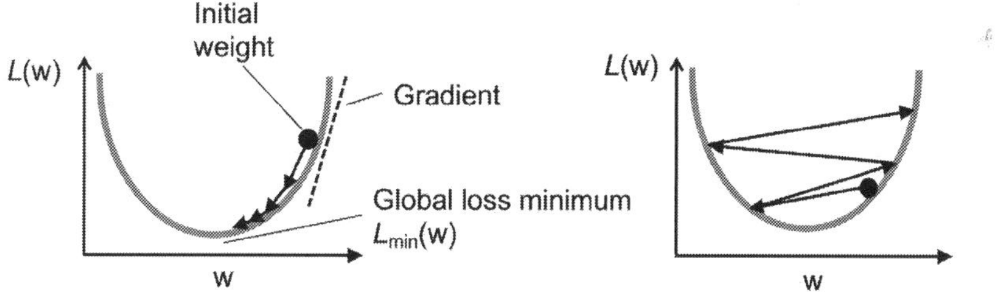

Figure 2.12: A comparison of a well-chosen learning rate and a learning rate that is too large

Improving gradient descent through feature scaling

Many machine learning algorithms that we will encounter throughout this book require some sort of feature scaling for optimal performance, which we will discuss in more detail in *Chapter 3, A Tour of Machine Learning Classifiers Using Scikit-Learn*, and *Chapter 4, Building Good Training Datasets – Data Preprocessing*.

Gradient descent is one of the many algorithms that benefit from feature scaling. In this section, we will use a feature scaling method called **standardization**. This normalization procedure helps gradient descent learning to converge more quickly; however, it does not make the original dataset normally distributed. Standardization shifts the mean of each feature so that it is centered at zero and each feature has a standard deviation of 1 (unit variance). For instance, to standardize the *j*th feature, we can simply subtract the sample mean, μ_j, from every training example and divide it by its standard deviation, σ_j:

$$x'_j = \frac{x_j - \mu_j}{\sigma_j}$$

Here, x_j is a vector consisting of the *j*th feature values of all training examples, *n*, and this standardization technique is applied to each feature, *j*, in our dataset.

One of the reasons why standardization helps with gradient descent learning is that it is easier to find a learning rate that works well for all weights (and the bias). If the features are on vastly different scales, a learning rate that works well for updating one weight might be too large or too small to update the other weight equally well. Overall, using standardized features can stabilize the training such that the optimizer has to go through fewer steps to find a good or optimal solution (the global loss minimum). *Figure 2.13* illustrates possible gradient updates with unscaled features (left) and standardized features (right), where the concentric circles represent the loss surface as a function of two model weights in a two-dimensional classification problem:

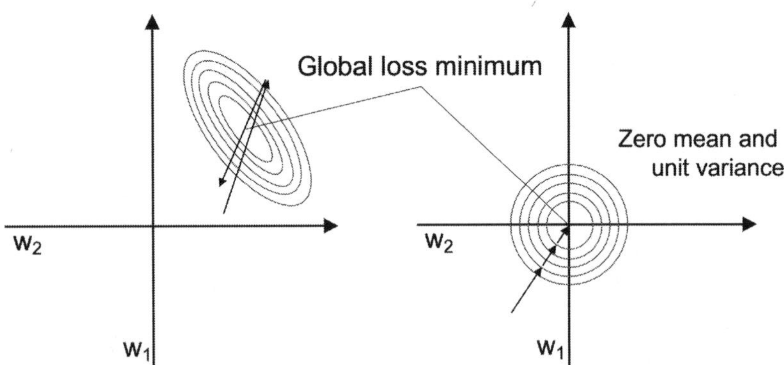

Figure 2.13: A comparison of unscaled and standardized features on gradient updates

Standardization can easily be achieved by using the built-in NumPy methods `mean` and `std`:

```
>>> X_std = np.copy(X)
>>> X_std[:,0] = (X[:,0] - X[:,0].mean()) / X[:,0].std()
>>> X_std[:,1] = (X[:,1] - X[:,1].mean()) / X[:,1].std()
```

After standardization, we will train Adaline again and see that it now converges after a small number of epochs using a learning rate of $\eta = 0.5$:

```
>>> ada_gd = AdalineGD(n_iter=20, eta=0.5)
>>> ada_gd.fit(X_std, y)
```

```
>>> plot_decision_regions(X_std, y, classifier=ada_gd)
>>> plt.title('Adaline - Gradient descent')
>>> plt.xlabel('Sepal length [standardized]')
>>> plt.ylabel('Petal length [standardized]')
>>> plt.legend(loc='upper left')
>>> plt.tight_layout()
>>> plt.show()
>>> plt.plot(range(1, len(ada_gd.losses_) + 1),
...          ada_gd.losses_, marker='o')
>>> plt.xlabel('Epochs')
>>> plt.ylabel('Mean squared error')
>>> plt.tight_layout()
>>> plt.show()
```

After executing this code, we should see a figure of the decision regions, as well as a plot of the declining loss, as shown in *Figure 2.14*:

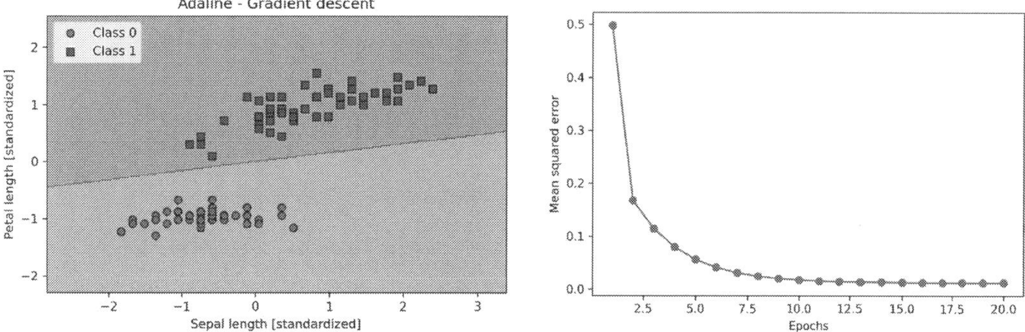

Figure 2.14: Plots of Adaline's decision regions and MSE by number of epochs

As we can see in the plots, Adaline has now converged after training on the standardized features. However, note that the MSE remains non-zero even though all flower examples were classified correctly.

Large-scale machine learning and stochastic gradient descent

In the previous section, we learned how to minimize a loss function by taking a step in the opposite direction of the loss gradient that is calculated from the whole training dataset; this is why this approach is sometimes also referred to as full batch gradient descent. Now imagine that we have a very large dataset with millions of data points, which is not uncommon in many machine learning applications. Running full batch gradient descent can be computationally quite costly in such scenarios, since we need to reevaluate the whole training dataset each time we take one step toward the global minimum.

A popular alternative to the batch gradient descent algorithm is **stochastic gradient descent (SGD)**, which is sometimes also called iterative or online gradient descent. Instead of updating the weights based on the sum of the accumulated errors over all training examples, $\boldsymbol{x}^{(i)}$:

$$\Delta w_j = \frac{2\eta}{n}\sum_i \left(y^{(i)} - \sigma\left(z^{(i)}\right)\right) x_j^{(i)}$$

we update the parameters incrementally for each training example, for instance:

$$\Delta w_j = \eta\left(y^{(i)} - \sigma\left(z^{(i)}\right)\right) x_j^{(i)}, \quad \Delta b = \eta\left(y^{(i)} - \sigma\left(z^{(i)}\right)\right)$$

Although SGD can be considered as an approximation of gradient descent, it typically reaches convergence much faster because of the more frequent weight updates. Since each gradient is calculated based on a single training example, the error surface is noisier than in gradient descent, which can also have the advantage that SGD can escape shallow local minima more readily if we are working with nonlinear loss functions, as we will see later in *Chapter 11, Implementing a Multilayer Artificial Neural Network from Scratch*. To obtain satisfying results via SGD, it is important to present training data in a random order; also, we want to shuffle the training dataset for every epoch to prevent cycles.

Adjusting the learning rate during training

In SGD implementations, the fixed learning rate, η, is often replaced by an adaptive learning rate that decreases over time, for example:

$$\frac{c_1}{[\text{number of iterations}] + c_2}$$

where c_1 and c_2 are constants. Note that SGD does not reach the global loss minimum but an area very close to it. And using an adaptive learning rate, we can achieve further annealing to the loss minimum.

Another advantage of SGD is that we can use it for **online learning**. In online learning, our model is trained on the fly as new training data arrives. This is especially useful if we are accumulating large amounts of data, for example, customer data in web applications. Using online learning, the system can immediately adapt to changes, and the training data can be discarded after updating the model if storage space is an issue.

Mini-batch gradient descent

A compromise between full batch gradient descent and SGD is so-called **mini-batch gradient descent**. Mini-batch gradient descent can be understood as applying full batch gradient descent to smaller subsets of the training data, for example, 32 training examples at a time. The advantage over full batch gradient descent is that convergence is reached faster via mini-batches because of the more frequent weight updates. Furthermore, mini-batch learning allows us to replace the `for` loop over the training examples in SGD with vectorized operations leveraging concepts from linear algebra (for example, implementing a weighted sum via a dot product), which can further improve the computational efficiency of our learning algorithm.

Since we already implemented the Adaline learning rule using gradient descent, we only need to make a few adjustments to modify the learning algorithm to update the weights via SGD. Inside the `fit` method, we will now update the weights after each training example. Furthermore, we will implement an additional `partial_fit` method, which does not reinitialize the weights, for online learning. In order to check whether our algorithm converged after training, we will calculate the loss as the average loss of the training examples in each epoch. Furthermore, we will add an option to shuffle the training data before each epoch to avoid repetitive cycles when we are optimizing the loss function; via the `random_state` parameter, we allow the specification of a random seed for reproducibility:

```
class AdalineSGD:
    """ADAptive LInear NEuron classifier.

    Parameters
    ------------
    eta : float
        Learning rate (between 0.0 and 1.0)
    n_iter : int
        Passes over the training dataset.
    shuffle : bool (default: True)
        Shuffles training data every epoch if True to prevent
        cycles.
    random_state : int
        Random number generator seed for random weight
        initialization.
```

```
    Attributes
    -----------
    w_ : 1d-array
        Weights after fitting.
    b_ : Scalar
        Bias unit after fitting.
    losses_ : list
        Mean squared error loss function value averaged over all
        training examples in each epoch.


    """
    def __init__(self, eta=0.01, n_iter=10,
                 shuffle=True, random_state=None):
        self.eta = eta
        self.n_iter = n_iter
        self.w_initialized = False
        self.shuffle = shuffle
        self.random_state = random_state

    def fit(self, X, y):
        """ Fit training data.

        Parameters
        ----------
        X : {array-like}, shape = [n_examples, n_features]
            Training vectors, where n_examples is the number of
            examples and n_features is the number of features.
        y : array-like, shape = [n_examples]
            Target values.

        Returns
        -------
        self : object

        """
        self._initialize_weights(X.shape[1])
        self.losses_ = []
        for i in range(self.n_iter):
            if self.shuffle:
```

```
            X, y = self._shuffle(X, y)
        losses = []
        for xi, target in zip(X, y):
            losses.append(self._update_weights(xi, target))
        avg_loss = np.mean(losses)
        self.losses_.append(avg_loss)
    return self

def partial_fit(self, X, y):
    """Fit training data without reinitializing the weights"""
    if not self.w_initialized:
        self._initialize_weights(X.shape[1])
    if y.ravel().shape[0] > 1:
        for xi, target in zip(X, y):
            self._update_weights(xi, target)
    else:
        self._update_weights(X, y)
    return self

def _shuffle(self, X, y):
    """Shuffle training data"""
    r = self.rgen.permutation(len(y))
    return X[r], y[r]

def _initialize_weights(self, m):
    """Initialize weights to small random numbers"""
    self.rgen = np.random.RandomState(self.random_state)
    self.w_ = self.rgen.normal(loc=0.0, scale=0.01,
                               size=m)
    self.b_ = np.float_(0.)
    self.w_initialized = True

def _update_weights(self, xi, target):
    """Apply Adaline learning rule to update the weights"""
    output = self.activation(self.net_input(xi))
    error = (target - output)
    self.w_ += self.eta * 2.0 * xi * (error)
    self.b_ += self.eta * 2.0 * error
    loss = error**2
    return loss
```

```
    def net_input(self, X):
        """Calculate net input"""
        return np.dot(X, self.w_) + self.b_

    def activation(self, X):
        """Compute linear activation"""
        return X

    def predict(self, X):
        """Return class label after unit step"""
        return np.where(self.activation(self.net_input(X))
                        >= 0.5, 1, 0)
```

The `_shuffle` method that we are now using in the `AdalineSGD` classifier works as follows: via the `permutation` function in `np.random`, we generate a random sequence of unique numbers in the range 0 to 100. Those numbers can then be used as indices to shuffle our feature matrix and class label vector.

We can then use the `fit` method to train the `AdalineSGD` classifier and use our `plot_decision_regions` to plot our training results:

```
>>> ada_sgd = AdalineSGD(n_iter=15, eta=0.01, random_state=1)
>>> ada_sgd.fit(X_std, y)
>>> plot_decision_regions(X_std, y, classifier=ada_sgd)
>>> plt.title('Adaline - Stochastic gradient descent')
>>> plt.xlabel('Sepal length [standardized]')
>>> plt.ylabel('Petal length [standardized]')
>>> plt.legend(loc='upper left')
>>> plt.tight_layout()
>>> plt.show()
>>> plt.plot(range(1, len(ada_sgd.losses_) + 1), ada_sgd.losses_,
...          marker='o')
>>> plt.xlabel('Epochs')
>>> plt.ylabel('Average loss')
>>> plt.tight_layout()
>>> plt.show()
```

The two plots that we obtain from executing the preceding code example are shown in *Figure 2.15*:

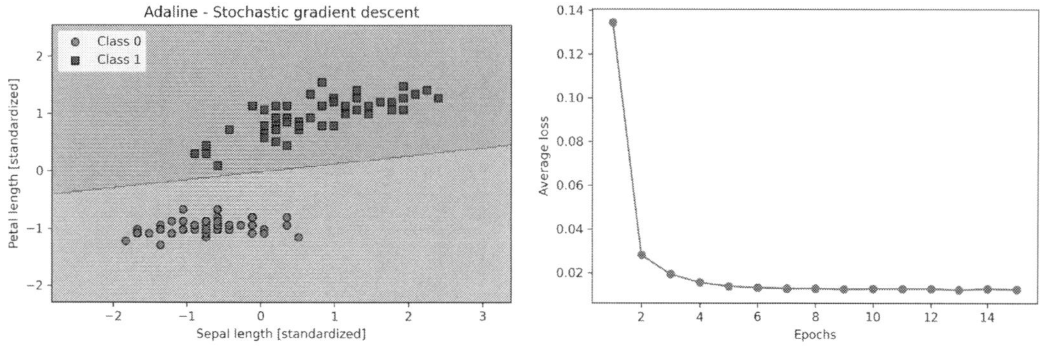

Figure 2.15: Decision regions and average loss plots after training an Adaline model using SGD

As you can see, the average loss goes down pretty quickly, and the final decision boundary after 15 epochs looks similar to the batch gradient descent Adaline. If we want to update our model, for example, in an online learning scenario with streaming data, we could simply call the `partial_fit` method on individual training examples—for instance, `ada_sgd.partial_fit(X_std[0, :], y[0])`.

Summary

In this chapter, we gained a good understanding of the basic concepts of linear classifiers for supervised learning. After we implemented a perceptron, we saw how we can train adaptive linear neurons efficiently via a vectorized implementation of gradient descent and online learning via SGD.

Now that we have seen how to implement simple classifiers in Python, we are ready to move on to the next chapter, where we will use the Python scikit-learn machine learning library to get access to more advanced and powerful machine learning classifiers, which are commonly used in academia as well as in industry.

The object-oriented approach that we used to implement the perceptron and Adaline algorithms will help with understanding the scikit-learn API, which is implemented based on the same core concepts that we used in this chapter: the `fit` and `predict` methods. Based on these core concepts, we will learn about logistic regression for modeling class probabilities and support vector machines for working with nonlinear decision boundaries. In addition, we will introduce a different class of supervised learning algorithms, tree-based algorithms, which are commonly combined into robust ensemble classifiers.

Join our book's Discord space

Join our Discord community to meet like-minded people and learn alongside more than 2000 members at:

`https://packt.link/MLwPyTorch`

3

A Tour of Machine Learning Classifiers Using Scikit-Learn

In this chapter, we will take a tour of a selection of popular and powerful machine learning algorithms that are commonly used in academia as well as in industry. While learning about the differences between several supervised learning algorithms for classification, we will also develop an appreciation of their individual strengths and weaknesses. In addition, we will take our first steps with the scikit-learn library, which offers a user-friendly and consistent interface for using those algorithms efficiently and productively.

The topics that will be covered throughout this chapter are as follows:

- An introduction to robust and popular algorithms for classification, such as logistic regression, support vector machines, decision trees, and *k*-nearest neighbors
- Examples and explanations using the scikit-learn machine learning library, which provides a wide variety of machine learning algorithms via a user-friendly Python API
- Discussions about the strengths and weaknesses of classifiers with linear and nonlinear decision boundaries

Choosing a classification algorithm

Choosing an appropriate classification algorithm for a particular problem task requires practice and experience; each algorithm has its own quirks and is based on certain assumptions. To paraphrase the **no free lunch theorem** by David H. Wolpert, no single classifier works best across all possible scenarios (*The Lack of A Priori Distinctions Between Learning Algorithms, Wolpert, David H, Neural Computation 8.7* (1996): 1341-1390). In practice, it is always recommended that you compare the performance of at least a handful of different learning algorithms to select the best model for the particular problem; these may differ in the number of features or examples, the amount of noise in a dataset, and whether the classes are linearly separable.

Eventually, the performance of a classifier—computational performance as well as predictive power—depends heavily on the underlying data that is available for learning. The five main steps that are involved in training a supervised machine learning algorithm can be summarized as follows:

1. Selecting features and collecting labeled training examples
2. Choosing a performance metric
3. Choosing a learning algorithm and training a model
4. Evaluating the performance of the model
5. Changing the settings of the algorithm and tuning the model.

Since the approach of this book is to build machine learning knowledge step by step, we will mainly focus on the main concepts of the different algorithms in this chapter and revisit topics such as feature selection and preprocessing, performance metrics, and hyperparameter tuning for more detailed discussions later in the book.

First steps with scikit-learn – training a perceptron

In *Chapter 2, Training Simple Machine Learning Algorithms for Classification*, you learned about two related learning algorithms for classification, the **perceptron** rule and **Adaline**, which we implemented in Python and NumPy by ourselves. Now we will take a look at the scikit-learn API, which, as mentioned, combines a user-friendly and consistent interface with a highly optimized implementation of several classification algorithms. The scikit-learn library offers not only a large variety of learning algorithms, but also many convenient functions to preprocess data and to fine-tune and evaluate our models. We will discuss this in more detail, together with the underlying concepts, in *Chapter 4, Building Good Training Datasets – Data Preprocessing*, and *Chapter 5, Compressing Data via Dimensionality Reduction*.

To get started with the scikit-learn library, we will train a perceptron model similar to the one that we implemented in *Chapter 2*. For simplicity, we will use the already familiar **Iris dataset** throughout the following sections. Conveniently, the Iris dataset is already available via scikit-learn, since it is a simple yet popular dataset that is frequently used for testing and experimenting with algorithms. Similar to the previous chapter, we will only use two features from the Iris dataset for visualization purposes.

We will assign the petal length and petal width of the 150 flower examples to the feature matrix, `X`, and the corresponding class labels of the flower species to the vector array, `y`:

```
>>> from sklearn import datasets
>>> import numpy as np
>>> iris = datasets.load_iris()
>>> X = iris.data[:, [2, 3]]
>>> y = iris.target
```

```
>>> print('Class labels:', np.unique(y))
Class labels: [0 1 2]
```

The np.unique(y) function returned the three unique class labels stored in iris.target, and as we can see, the Iris flower class names, Iris-setosa, Iris-versicolor, and Iris-virginica, are already stored as integers (here: 0, 1, 2). Although many scikit-learn functions and class methods also work with class labels in string format, using integer labels is a recommended approach to avoid technical glitches and improve computational performance due to a smaller memory footprint; furthermore, encoding class labels as integers is a common convention among most machine learning libraries.

To evaluate how well a trained model performs on unseen data, we will further split the dataset into separate training and test datasets. In *Chapter 6, Learning Best Practices for Model Evaluation and Hyperparameter Tuning*, we will discuss the best practices around model evaluation in more detail. Using the train_test_split function from scikit-learn's model_selection module, we randomly split the X and y arrays into 30 percent test data (45 examples) and 70 percent training data (105 examples):

```
>>> from sklearn.model_selection import train_test_split
>>> X_train, X_test, y_train, y_test = train_test_split(
...     X, y, test_size=0.3, random_state=1, stratify=y
... )
```

Note that the train_test_split function already shuffles the training datasets internally before splitting; otherwise, all examples from class 0 and class 1 would have ended up in the training datasets, and the test dataset would consist of 45 examples from class 2. Via the random_state parameter, we provided a fixed random seed (random_state=1) for the internal pseudo-random number generator that is used for shuffling the datasets prior to splitting. Using such a fixed random_state ensures that our results are reproducible.

Lastly, we took advantage of the built-in support for stratification via stratify=y. In this context, stratification means that the train_test_split method returns training and test subsets that have the same proportions of class labels as the input dataset. We can use NumPy's bincount function, which counts the number of occurrences of each value in an array, to verify that this is indeed the case:

```
>>> print('Labels counts in y:', np.bincount(y))
Labels counts in y: [50 50 50]
>>> print('Labels counts in y_train:', np.bincount(y_train))
Labels counts in y_train: [35 35 35]
>>> print('Labels counts in y_test:', np.bincount(y_test))
Labels counts in y_test: [15 15 15]
```

Many machine learning and optimization algorithms also require feature scaling for optimal performance, as we saw in the **gradient descent** example in *Chapter 2*. Here, we will standardize the features using the `StandardScaler` class from scikit-learn's `preprocessing` module:

```
>>> from sklearn.preprocessing import StandardScaler
>>> sc = StandardScaler()
>>> sc.fit(X_train)
>>> X_train_std = sc.transform(X_train)
>>> X_test_std = sc.transform(X_test)
```

Using the preceding code, we loaded the `StandardScaler` class from the `preprocessing` module and initialized a new `StandardScaler` object that we assigned to the `sc` variable. Using the `fit` method, `StandardScaler` estimated the parameters, μ (sample mean) and σ (standard deviation), for each feature dimension from the training data. By calling the `transform` method, we then standardized the training data using those estimated parameters, μ and σ. Note that we used the same scaling parameters to standardize the test dataset so that both the values in the training and test dataset are comparable with one another.

Having standardized the training data, we can now train a perceptron model. Most algorithms in scikit-learn already support multiclass classification by default via the **one-versus-rest** (**OvR**) method, which allows us to feed the three flower classes to the perceptron all at once. The code is as follows:

```
>>> from sklearn.linear_model import Perceptron
>>> ppn = Perceptron(eta0=0.1, random_state=1)
>>> ppn.fit(X_train_std, y_train)
```

The scikit-learn interface will remind you of our perceptron implementation in *Chapter 2*. After loading the `Perceptron` class from the `linear_model` module, we initialized a new `Perceptron` object and trained the model via the `fit` method. Here, the model parameter, `eta0`, is equivalent to the learning rate, `eta`, that we used in our own perceptron implementation.

As you will remember from *Chapter 2*, finding an appropriate learning rate requires some experimentation. If the learning rate is too large, the algorithm will overshoot the global loss minimum. If the learning rate is too small, the algorithm will require more epochs until convergence, which can make the learning slow—especially for large datasets. Also, we used the `random_state` parameter to ensure the reproducibility of the initial shuffling of the training dataset after each epoch.

Having trained a model in scikit-learn, we can make predictions via the `predict` method, just like in our own perceptron implementation in *Chapter 2*. The code is as follows:

```
>>> y_pred = ppn.predict(X_test_std)
>>> print('Misclassified examples: %d' % (y_test != y_pred).sum())
Misclassified examples: 1
```

Executing the code, we can see that the perceptron misclassifies 1 out of the 45 flower examples. Thus, the misclassification error on the test dataset is approximately 0.022, or 2.2 percent $\left(\frac{1}{45} \approx 0.022\right)$.

Classification error versus accuracy

Instead of the misclassification error, many machine learning practitioners report the classification accuracy of a model, which is simply calculated as follows:

1–*error* = 0.978, or 97.8 percent

Whether we use the classification error or accuracy is merely a matter of preference.

Note that scikit-learn also implements a large variety of different performance metrics that are available via the `metrics` module. For example, we can calculate the classification accuracy of the perceptron on the test dataset as follows:

```
>>> from sklearn.metrics import accuracy_score
>>> print('Accuracy: %.3f' % accuracy_score(y_test, y_pred))
Accuracy: 0.978
```

Here, `y_test` is the true class labels and `y_pred` is the class labels that we predicted previously. Alternatively, each classifier in scikit-learn has a `score` method, which computes a classifier's prediction accuracy by combining the `predict` call with `accuracy_score`, as shown here:

```
>>> print('Accuracy: %.3f' % ppn.score(X_test_std, y_test))
Accuracy: 0.978
```

Overfitting

Note that we will evaluate the performance of our models based on the test dataset in this chapter. In *Chapter 6*, you will learn about useful techniques, including graphical analysis, such as learning curves, to detect and prevent overfitting. Overfitting, which we will return to later in this chapter, means that the model captures the patterns in the training data well but fails to generalize well to unseen data.

Finally, we can use our `plot_decision_regions` function from *Chapter 2* to plot the **decision regions** of our newly trained perceptron model and visualize how well it separates the different flower examples. However, let's add a small modification to highlight the data instances from the test dataset via small circles:

```
from matplotlib.colors import ListedColormap
import matplotlib.pyplot as plt
def plot_decision_regions(X, y, classifier, test_idx=None,
                          resolution=0.02):
    # setup marker generator and color map
    markers = ('o', 's', '^', 'v', '<')
    colors = ('red', 'blue', 'lightgreen', 'gray', 'cyan')
    cmap = ListedColormap(colors[:len(np.unique(y))])
```

```
    # plot the decision surface
    x1_min, x1_max = X[:, 0].min() - 1, X[:, 0].max() + 1
    x2_min, x2_max = X[:, 1].min() - 1, X[:, 1].max() + 1
    xx1, xx2 = np.meshgrid(np.arange(x1_min, x1_max, resolution),
                           np.arange(x2_min, x2_max, resolution))
    lab = classifier.predict(np.array([xx1.ravel(), xx2.ravel()]).T)
    lab = lab.reshape(xx1.shape)
    plt.contourf(xx1, xx2, lab, alpha=0.3, cmap=cmap)
    plt.xlim(xx1.min(), xx1.max())
    plt.ylim(xx2.min(), xx2.max())

    # plot class examples
    for idx, cl in enumerate(np.unique(y)):
        plt.scatter(x=X[y == cl, 0],
                    y=X[y == cl, 1],
                    alpha=0.8,
                    c=colors[idx],
                    marker=markers[idx],
                    label=f'Class {cl}',
                    edgecolor='black')
    # highlight test examples
    if test_idx:
        # plot all examples
        X_test, y_test = X[test_idx, :], y[test_idx]

        plt.scatter(X_test[:, 0], X_test[:, 1],
                    c='none', edgecolor='black', alpha=1.0,
                    linewidth=1, marker='o',
                    s=100, label='Test set')
```

With the slight modification that we made to the `plot_decision_regions` function, we can now specify the indices of the examples that we want to mark on the resulting plots. The code is as follows:

```
>>> X_combined_std = np.vstack((X_train_std, X_test_std))
>>> y_combined = np.hstack((y_train, y_test))
>>> plot_decision_regions(X=X_combined_std,
...                       y=y_combined,
...                       classifier=ppn,
...                       test_idx=range(105, 150))
>>> plt.xlabel('Petal length [standardized]')
>>> plt.ylabel('Petal width [standardized]')
>>> plt.legend(loc='upper left')
>>> plt.tight_layout()
>>> plt.show()
```

As we can see in the resulting plot, the three flower classes can't be perfectly separated by a linear decision boundary:

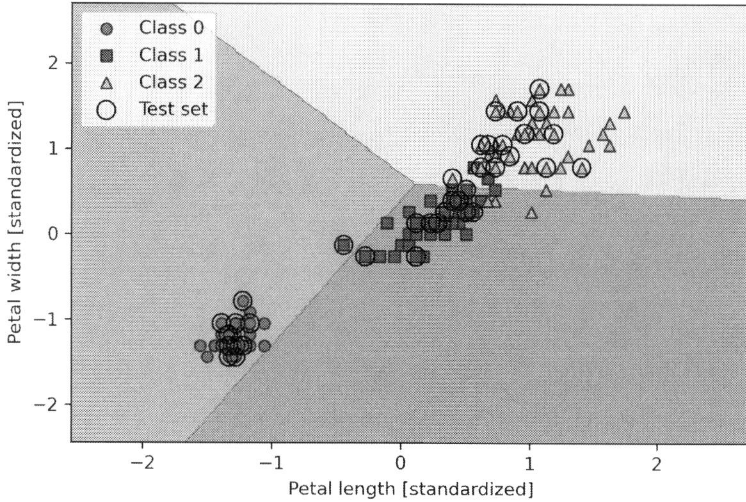

Figure 3.1: Decision boundaries of a multi-class perceptron model fitted to the Iris dataset

However, remember from our discussion in *Chapter 2* that the perceptron algorithm never converges on datasets that aren't perfectly linearly separable, which is why the use of the perceptron algorithm is typically not recommended in practice. In the following sections, we will look at more powerful linear classifiers that converge to a loss minimum even if the classes are not perfectly linearly separable.

Additional perceptron settings

The `Perceptron`, as well as other scikit-learn functions and classes, often has additional parameters that we omit for clarity. You can read more about those parameters using the `help` function in Python (for instance, `help(Perceptron)`) or by going through the excellent scikit-learn online documentation at `http://scikit-learn.org/stable/`.

Modeling class probabilities via logistic regression

Although the perceptron rule offers a nice and easy-going introduction to machine learning algorithms for classification, its biggest disadvantage is that it never converges if the classes are not perfectly linearly separable. The classification task in the previous section would be an example of such a scenario. The reason for this is that the weights are continuously being updated since there is always at least one misclassified training example present in each epoch. Of course, you can change the learning rate and increase the number of epochs, but be warned that the perceptron will never converge on this dataset.

To make better use of our time, we will now take a look at another simple, yet more powerful, algorithm for linear and binary classification problems: **logistic regression**. Note that, despite its name, logistic regression is a model for classification, not regression.

Logistic regression and conditional probabilities

Logistic regression is a classification model that is very easy to implement and performs very well on linearly separable classes. It is one of the most widely used algorithms for classification in industry. Similar to the perceptron and Adaline, the logistic regression model in this chapter is also a linear model for binary classification.

Logistic regression for multiple classes

Note that logistic regression can be readily generalized to multiclass settings, which is known as **multinomial logistic regression,** or **softmax regression.** More detailed coverage of multinomial logistic regression is outside the scope of this book, but the interested reader can find more information in my lecture notes at `https://sebastianraschka.com/pdf/lecture-notes/stat453ss21/L08_logistic__slides.pdf` or `https://www.youtube.com/watch?v=L0FU8NFpx4E`.

Another way to use logistic regression in multiclass settings is via the OvR technique, which we discussed previously.

To explain the main mechanics behind logistic regression as a probabilistic model for binary classification, let's first introduce the **odds**: the odds in favor of a particular event. The odds can be written as $\frac{p}{(1-p)}$, where p stands for the probability of the positive event. The term "positive event" does not necessarily mean "good," but refers to the event that we want to predict, for example, the probability that a patient has a certain disease given certain symptoms; we can think of the positive event as class label $y = 1$ and the symptoms as features $\boldsymbol{x}$. Hence, for brevity, we can define the probability p as $p := p(y = 1|\boldsymbol{x})$, the conditional probability that a particular example belongs to a certain class 1 given its features, $\boldsymbol{x}$.

We can then further define the **logit** function, which is simply the logarithm of the odds (log-odds):

$$\text{logit}(p) = \log\frac{p}{(1-p)}$$

Note that *log* refers to the natural logarithm, as it is the common convention in computer science. The *logit* function takes input values in the range 0 to 1 and transforms them into values over the entire real-number range.

Under the logistic model, we assume that there is a linear relationship between the weighted inputs (referred to as net inputs in *Chapter 2*) and the log-odds:

$$\text{logit}(p) = w_1x_1 + \cdots + w_mx_m + b = \sum_{i=j} w_jx_j + b = \boldsymbol{w}^T\boldsymbol{x} + b$$

While the preceding describes an assumption we make about the linear relationship between the log-odds and the net inputs, what we are actually interested in is the probability p, the class-membership probability of an example given its features. While the logit function maps the probability to a real-number range, we can consider the inverse of this function to map the real-number range back to a [0, 1] range for the probability p.

This inverse of the logit function is typically called the **logistic sigmoid function**, which is sometimes simply abbreviated to **sigmoid function** due to its characteristic S-shape:

$$\sigma(z) = \frac{1}{1 + e^{-z}}$$

Here, z is the net input, the linear combination of weights, and the inputs (that is, the features associated with the training examples):

$$z = \boldsymbol{w}^T\boldsymbol{x} + b$$

Now, let's simply plot the sigmoid function for some values in the range –7 to 7 to see how it looks:

```
>>> import matplotlib.pyplot as plt
>>> import numpy as np
>>> def sigmoid(z):
...     return 1.0 / (1.0 + np.exp(-z))
>>> z = np.arange(-7, 7, 0.1)
>>> sigma_z = sigmoid(z)
>>> plt.plot(z, sigma_z)
>>> plt.axvline(0.0, color='k')
>>> plt.ylim(-0.1, 1.1)
>>> plt.xlabel('z')
>>> plt.ylabel('$\sigma (z)$')
>>> # y axis ticks and gridline
>>> plt.yticks([0.0, 0.5, 1.0])
>>> ax = plt.gca()
>>> ax.yaxis.grid(True)
>>> plt.tight_layout()
>>> plt.show()
```

As a result of executing the previous code example, we should now see the S-shaped (sigmoidal) curve:

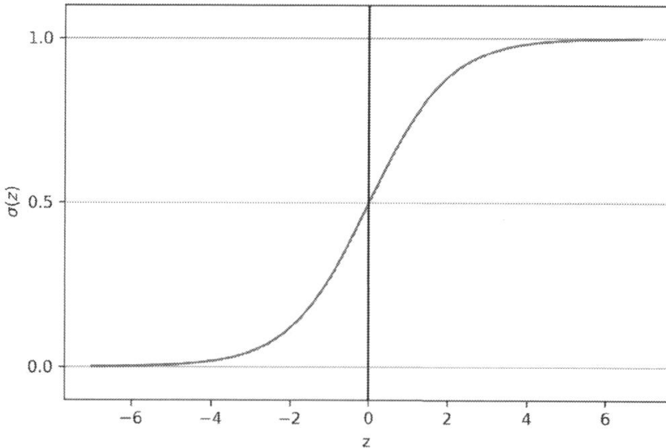

Figure 3.2: A plot of the logistic sigmoid function

We can see that $\sigma(z)$ approaches 1 if z goes toward infinity ($z \to \infty$) since e^{-z} becomes very small for large values of z. Similarly, $\sigma(z)$ goes toward 0 for $z \to -\infty$ as a result of an increasingly large denominator. Thus, we can conclude that this sigmoid function takes real-number values as input and transforms them into values in the range [0, 1] with an intercept at $\sigma(0) = 0.5$.

To build some understanding of the logistic regression model, we can relate it to *Chapter 2*. In Adaline, we used the identity function, $\sigma(z) = z$, as the activation function. In logistic regression, this activation function simply becomes the sigmoid function that we defined earlier.

The difference between Adaline and logistic regression is illustrated in the following figure, where the only difference is the activation function:

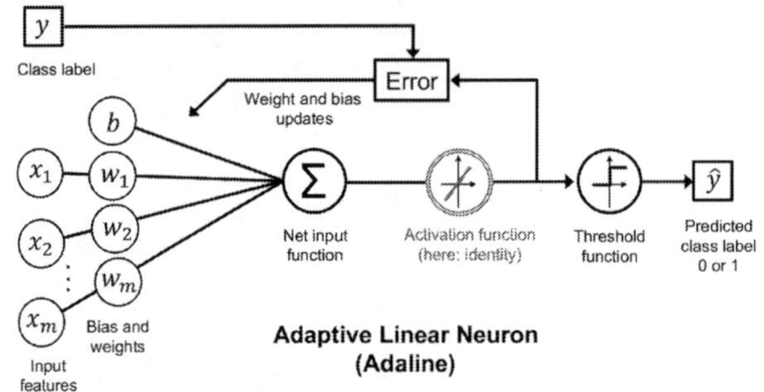

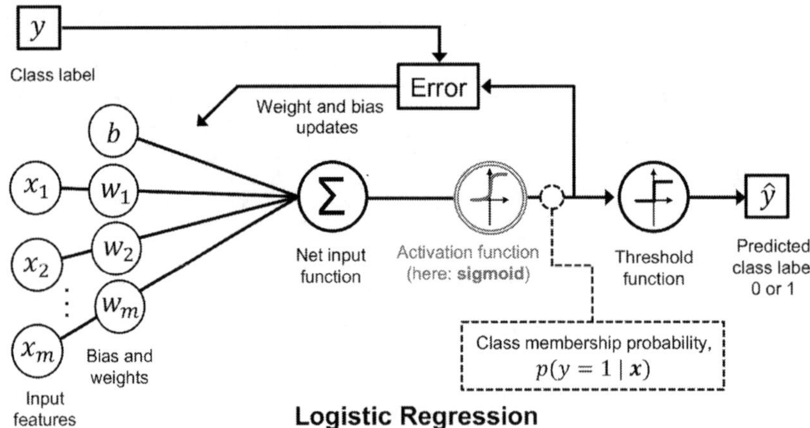

Figure 3.3: Logistic regression compared to Adaline

The output of the sigmoid function is then interpreted as the probability of a particular example belonging to class 1, $\sigma(z) = p(y = 1|\boldsymbol{x}; \boldsymbol{w}, b)$, given its features, x, and parameterized by the weights and bias, w and b. For example, if we compute $\sigma(z) = 0.8$ for a particular flower example, it means that the chance that this example is an `Iris-versicolor` flower is 80 percent. Therefore, the probability that this flower is an `Iris-setosa` flower can be calculated as $p(y = 0|\boldsymbol{x}; \boldsymbol{w}, b) = 1 - p(y = 1|\boldsymbol{x}; \boldsymbol{w}, b) = 0.2$, or 20 percent.

The predicted probability can then simply be converted into a binary outcome via a threshold function:

$$\hat{y} = \begin{cases} 1 & \text{if } \sigma(z) \geq 0.5 \\ 0 & \text{otherwise} \end{cases}$$

If we look at the preceding plot of the sigmoid function, this is equivalent to the following:

$$\hat{y} = \begin{cases} 1 & \text{if } z \geq 0.0 \\ 0 & \text{otherwise} \end{cases}$$

In fact, there are many applications where we are not only interested in the predicted class labels, but where the estimation of the class-membership probability is particularly useful (the output of the sigmoid function prior to applying the threshold function). Logistic regression is used in weather forecasting, for example, not only to predict whether it will rain on a particular day, but also to report the chance of rain. Similarly, logistic regression can be used to predict the chance that a patient has a particular disease given certain symptoms, which is why logistic regression enjoys great popularity in the field of medicine.

Learning the model weights via the logistic loss function

You have learned how we can use the logistic regression model to predict probabilities and class labels; now, let's briefly talk about how we fit the parameters of the model, for instance, the weights and bias unit, *w* and *b*. In the previous chapter, we defined the mean squared error loss function as follows:

$$L(\boldsymbol{w}, b|\boldsymbol{x}) = \sum_{i} \frac{1}{2}\left(\sigma\left(z^{(i)}\right) - y^{(i)}\right)^2$$

We minimized this function in order to learn the parameters for our Adaline classification model. To explain how we can derive the loss function for logistic regression, let's first define the likelihood, $\mathcal{L}$, that we want to maximize when we build a logistic regression model, assuming that the individual examples in our dataset are independent of one another. The formula is as follows:

$$\mathcal{L}(\boldsymbol{w}, b|\boldsymbol{x}) = p(y|\boldsymbol{x}; \boldsymbol{w}, b) = \prod_{i=1}^{n} p\left(y^{(i)}|\boldsymbol{x}^{(i)}; \boldsymbol{w}, b\right) = \prod_{i=1}^{n} \left(\sigma\left(z^{(i)}\right)\right)^{y^{(i)}} \left(1 - \sigma\left(z^{(i)}\right)\right)^{1-y^{(i)}}$$

In practice, it is easier to maximize the (natural) log of this equation, which is called the **log-likelihood** function:

$$l(\boldsymbol{w}, b|\boldsymbol{x}) = \log \mathcal{L}(\boldsymbol{w}, b|\boldsymbol{x}) = \sum_{i=1} \left[y^{(i)} \log\left(\sigma\left(z^{(i)}\right)\right) + \left(1 - y^{(i)}\right) \log\left(1 - \sigma\left(z^{(i)}\right)\right)\right]$$

Firstly, applying the log function reduces the potential for numerical underflow, which can occur if the likelihoods are very small. Secondly, we can convert the product of factors into a summation of factors, which makes it easier to obtain the derivative of this function via the addition trick, as you may remember from calculus.

Deriving the likelihood function

We can obtain the expression for the likelihood of the model given the data, $\mathcal{L}(\mathbf{w}, b \mid \mathbf{x})$, as follows. Given that we have a binary classification problem with class labels 0 and 1, we can think of the label 1 as a Bernoulli variable—it can take on two values, 0 and 1, with the probability p of being 1: $Y \sim Bern(p)$. For a single data point, we can write this probability as $P(Y = 1 \mid X = \mathrm{x}^{(i)}) = \sigma(z^{(i)})$ and $P(Y = 0 \mid X = \mathrm{x}^{(i)}) = 1 - \sigma(z^{(i)})$.

Putting these two expressions together, and using the shorthand $P(Y = y^{(i)} \mid X = \mathrm{x}^{(i)}) = p(y^{(i)} \mid \mathrm{x}^{(i)})$, we get the probability mass function of the Bernoulli variable:

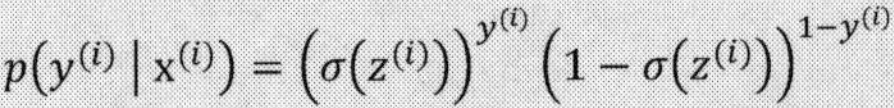

$$p(y^{(i)} \mid \mathrm{x}^{(i)}) = \left(\sigma(z^{(i)})\right)^{y^{(i)}} \left(1 - \sigma(z^{(i)})\right)^{1-y^{(i)}}$$

We can write the likelihood of the training labels given the assumption that all training examples are independent, using the multiplication rule to compute the probability that all events occur, as follows:

$$\mathcal{L}(\mathbf{w}, b \mid \mathbf{x}) = \prod_{i=1}^{n} p(y^{(i)} \mid \mathbf{x}^{(i)}; \mathbf{w}, b)$$

Now, substituting the probability mass function of the Bernoulli variable, we arrive at the expression of the likelihood, which we attempt to maximize by changing the model parameters:

$$\mathcal{L}(\mathbf{w}, b \mid \mathbf{x}) = \prod_{i=1}^{n} \left(\sigma(z^{(i)})\right)^{y^{(i)}} \left(1 - \sigma(z^{(i)})\right)^{1-y^{(i)}}$$

Now, we could use an optimization algorithm such as gradient ascent to maximize this log-likelihood function. (Gradient ascent works exactly the same way as gradient descent explained in *Chapter 2*, except that gradient ascent maximizes a function instead of minimizing it.) Alternatively, let's rewrite the log-likelihood as a loss function, L, that can be minimized using gradient descent as in *Chapter 2*:

$$L(\mathbf{w}, b) = \sum_{i=1}^{n} \left[-y^{(i)} \log\left(\sigma(z^{(i)})\right) - \left(1 - y^{(i)}\right) \log\left(1 - \sigma(z^{(i)})\right)\right]$$

To get a better grasp of this loss function, let's take a look at the loss that we calculate for one single training example:

$$L(\sigma(z), y; \mathbf{w}, b) = -y \log(\sigma(z)) - (1 - y) \log(1 - \sigma(z))$$

Looking at the equation, we can see that the first term becomes zero if $y = 0$, and the second term becomes zero if $y = 1$:

$$L(\sigma(z), y; \mathbf{w}, b) = \begin{cases} -\log(\sigma(z)) & \text{if } y = 1 \\ -\log(1 - \sigma(z)) & \text{if } y = 0 \end{cases}$$

Let's write a short code snippet to create a plot that illustrates the loss of classifying a single training example for different values of $\sigma(z)$:

```
>>> def loss_1(z):
...     return - np.log(sigmoid(z))
>>> def loss_0(z):
...     return - np.log(1 - sigmoid(z))
>>> z = np.arange(-10, 10, 0.1)
>>> sigma_z = sigmoid(z)
>>> c1 = [loss_1(x) for x in z]
>>> plt.plot(sigma_z, c1, label='L(w, b) if y=1')
>>> c0 = [loss_0(x) for x in z]
>>> plt.plot(sigma_z, c0, linestyle='--', label='L(w, b) if y=0')
>>> plt.ylim(0.0, 5.1)
>>> plt.xlim([0, 1])
>>> plt.xlabel('$\sigma(z)$')
>>> plt.ylabel('L(w, b)')
>>> plt.legend(loc='best')
>>> plt.tight_layout()
>>> plt.show()
```

The resulting plot shows the sigmoid activation on the x axis in the range 0 to 1 (the inputs to the sigmoid function were z values in the range –10 to 10) and the associated logistic loss on the y axis:

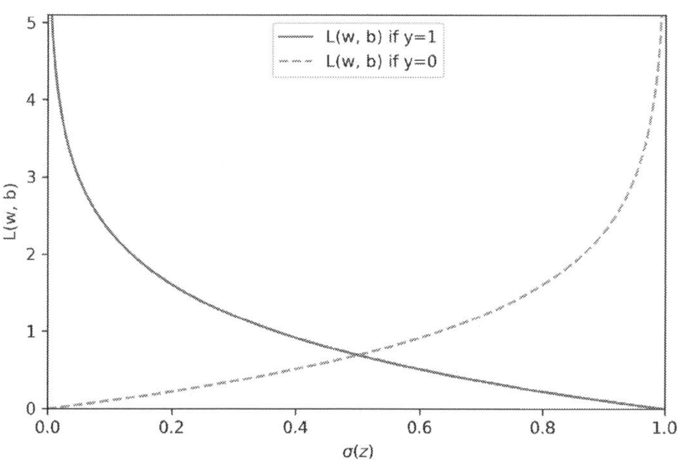

Figure 3.4: A plot of the loss function used in logistic regression

We can see that the loss approaches 0 (continuous line) if we correctly predict that an example belongs to class 1. Similarly, we can see on the y axis that the loss also approaches 0 if we correctly predict $y = 0$ (dashed line). However, if the prediction is wrong, the loss goes toward infinity. The main point is that we penalize wrong predictions with an increasingly larger loss.

Converting an Adaline implementation into an algorithm for logistic regression

If we were to implement logistic regression ourselves, we could simply substitute the loss function, *L*, in our Adaline implementation from *Chapter 2*, with the new loss function:

$$L(\boldsymbol{w}, b) = \frac{1}{n}\sum_{i=1}^{n}\left[-y^{(i)}\log\left(\sigma\left(z^{(i)}\right)\right) - \left(1 - y^{(i)}\right)\log\left(1 - \sigma\left(z^{(i)}\right)\right)\right]$$

We use this to compute the loss of classifying all training examples per epoch. Also, we need to swap the linear activation function with the sigmoid. If we make those changes to the Adaline code, we will end up with a working logistic regression implementation. The following is an implementation for full-batch gradient descent (but note that the same changes could be made to the stochastic gradient descent version as well):

```
class LogisticRegressionGD:
    """Gradient descent-based logistic regression classifier.

    Parameters
    ------------
    eta : float
      Learning rate (between 0.0 and 1.0)
    n_iter : int
      Passes over the training dataset.
    random_state : int
      Random number generator seed for random weight
      initialization.


    Attributes
    -----------
    w_ : 1d-array
      Weights after training.
    b_ : Scalar
      Bias unit after fitting.
    losses_ : list
      Mean squared error loss function values in each epoch.

    """
    def __init__(self, eta=0.01, n_iter=50, random_state=1):
        self.eta = eta
        self.n_iter = n_iter
        self.random_state = random_state
```

```
    def fit(self, X, y):
        """ Fit training data.

        Parameters
        ----------
        X : {array-like}, shape = [n_examples, n_features]
          Training vectors, where n_examples is the
          number of examples and n_features is the
          number of features.
        y : array-like, shape = [n_examples]
          Target values.

        Returns
        -------
        self : Instance of LogisticRegressionGD

        """
        rgen = np.random.RandomState(self.random_state)
        self.w_ = rgen.normal(loc=0.0, scale=0.01, size=X.shape[1])
        self.b_ = np.float_(0.)
        self.losses_ = []

        for i in range(self.n_iter):
            net_input = self.net_input(X)
            output = self.activation(net_input)
            errors = (y - output)
            self.w_ += self.eta * 2.0 * X.T.dot(errors) / X.shape[0]
            self.b_ += self.eta * 2.0 * errors.mean()
            loss = (-y.dot(np.log(output))
                   - ((1 - y).dot(np.log(1 - output)))
                    / X.shape[0])
            self.losses_.append(loss)
        return self

    def net_input(self, X):
        """Calculate net input"""
        return np.dot(X, self.w_) + self.b_

    def activation(self, z):
        """Compute logistic sigmoid activation"""
        return 1. / (1. + np.exp(-np.clip(z, -250, 250)))
```

```
    def predict(self, X):
        """Return class label after unit step"""
        return np.where(self.activation(self.net_input(X)) >= 0.5, 1, 0)
```

When we fit a logistic regression model, we have to keep in mind that it only works for binary classification tasks.

So, let's consider only setosa and versicolor flowers (classes `0` and `1`) and check that our implementation of logistic regression works:

```
>>> X_train_01_subset = X_train_std[(y_train == 0) | (y_train == 1)]
>>> y_train_01_subset = y_train[(y_train == 0) | (y_train == 1)]
>>> lrgd = LogisticRegressionGD(eta=0.3,
...                             n_iter=1000,
...                             random_state=1)
>>> lrgd.fit(X_train_01_subset,
...          y_train_01_subset)
>>> plot_decision_regions(X=X_train_01_subset,
...                       y=y_train_01_subset,
...                       classifier=lrgd)
>>> plt.xlabel('Petal length [standardized]')
>>> plt.ylabel('Petal width [standardized]')
>>> plt.legend(loc='upper left')
>>> plt.tight_layout()
>>> plt.show()
```

The resulting decision region plot looks as follows:

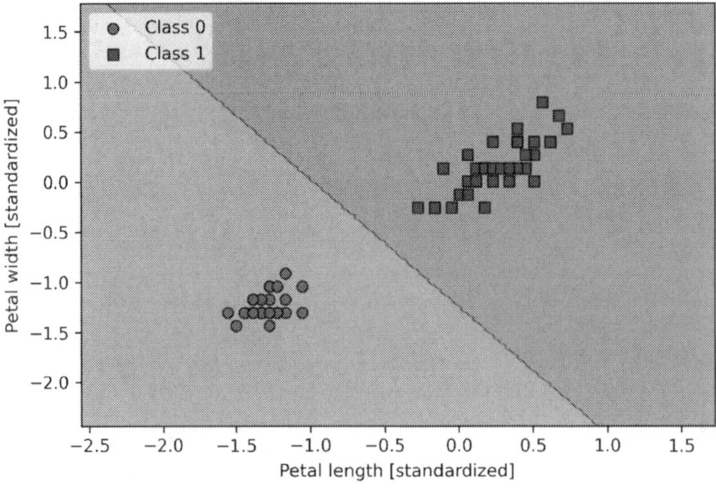

Figure 3.5: The decision region plot for the logistic regression model

The gradient descent learning algorithm for logistic regression

If you compared the `LogisticRegressionGD` in the previous code with the `AdalineGD` code from *Chapter 2*, you may have noticed that the weight and bias update rules remained unchanged (except for the scaling factor 2). Using calculus, we can show that the parameter updates via gradient descent are indeed similar for logistic regression and Adaline. However, please note that the following derivation of the gradient descent learning rule is intended for readers who are interested in the mathematical concepts behind the gradient descent learning rule for logistic regression. It is not essential for following the rest of this chapter.

Figure 3.6 summarizes how we can calculate the partial derivative of the log-likelihood function with respect to the *j*th weight:

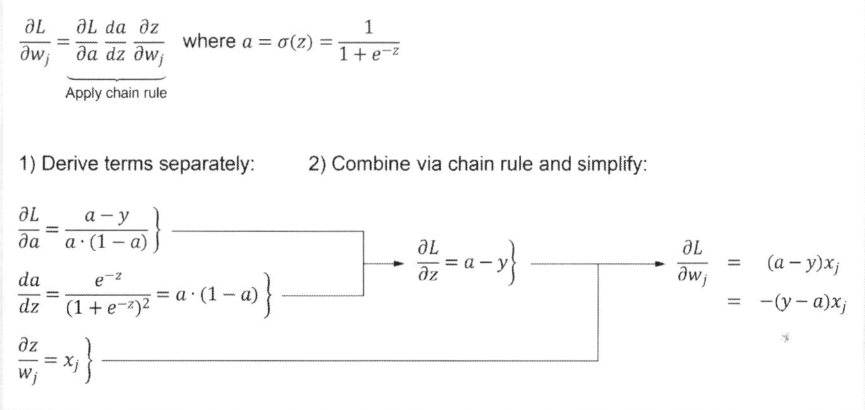

$$\frac{\partial L}{\partial w_j} = \underbrace{\frac{\partial L}{\partial a}\frac{da}{dz}\frac{\partial z}{\partial w_j}}_{\text{Apply chain rule}} \quad \text{where } a = \sigma(z) = \frac{1}{1+e^{-z}}$$

1) Derive terms separately:

$$\frac{\partial L}{\partial a} = \frac{a-y}{a\cdot(1-a)}$$

$$\frac{da}{dz} = \frac{e^{-z}}{(1+e^{-z})^2} = a\cdot(1-a)$$

$$\frac{\partial z}{w_j} = x_j$$

2) Combine via chain rule and simplify:

$$\frac{\partial L}{\partial z} = a - y$$

$$\frac{\partial L}{\partial w_j} = (a-y)x_j = -(y-a)x_j$$

Figure 3.6: Calculating the partial derivative of the log-likelihood function

Note that we omitted averaging over the training examples for brevity.

Remember from *Chapter 2* that we take steps in the opposite direction of the gradient. Hence, we flip $\frac{\partial L}{w_j} = -(y-a)x_j$ and update the *j*th weight as follows, including the learning rate η:

$$w_j := w_j + \eta(y-a)x_j$$

While the partial derivative of the loss function with respect to the bias unit is not shown, bias derivation follows the same overall concept using the chain rule, resulting in the following update rule:

$$b := b + \eta(y-a)$$

Both the weight and bias unit updates are equal to the ones for Adaline in *Chapter 2*.

Training a logistic regression model with scikit-learn

We just went through useful coding and math exercises in the previous subsection, which helped to illustrate the conceptual differences between Adaline and logistic regression. Now, let's learn how to use scikit-learn's more optimized implementation of logistic regression, which also supports multiclass settings off the shelf. Note that in recent versions of scikit-learn, the technique used for multiclass classification, multinomial, or OvR, is chosen automatically. In the following code example, we will use the `sklearn.linear_model.LogisticRegression` class as well as the familiar `fit` method to train the model on all three classes in the standardized flower training dataset. Also, we set `multi_class='ovr'` for illustration purposes. As an exercise for the reader, you may want to compare the results with `multi_class='multinomial'`. Note that the `multinomial` setting is now the default choice in scikit-learn's `LogisticRegression` class and recommended in practice for mutually exclusive classes, such as those found in the Iris dataset. Here, "mutually exclusive" means that each training example can only belong to a single class (in contrast to multilabel classification, where a training example can be a member of multiple classes).

Now, let's have a look at the code example:

```
>>> from sklearn.linear_model import LogisticRegression
>>> lr = LogisticRegression(C=100.0, solver='lbfgs',
...                         multi_class='ovr')
>>> lr.fit(X_train_std, y_train)
>>> plot_decision_regions(X_combined_std,
...                       y_combined,
...                       classifier=lr,
...                       test_idx=range(105, 150))
>>> plt.xlabel('Petal length [standardized]')
>>> plt.ylabel('Petal width [standardized]')
>>> plt.legend(loc='upper left')
>>> plt.tight_layout()
>>> plt.show()
```

After fitting the model on the training data, we plotted the decision regions, training examples, and test examples, as shown in *Figure 3.7*:

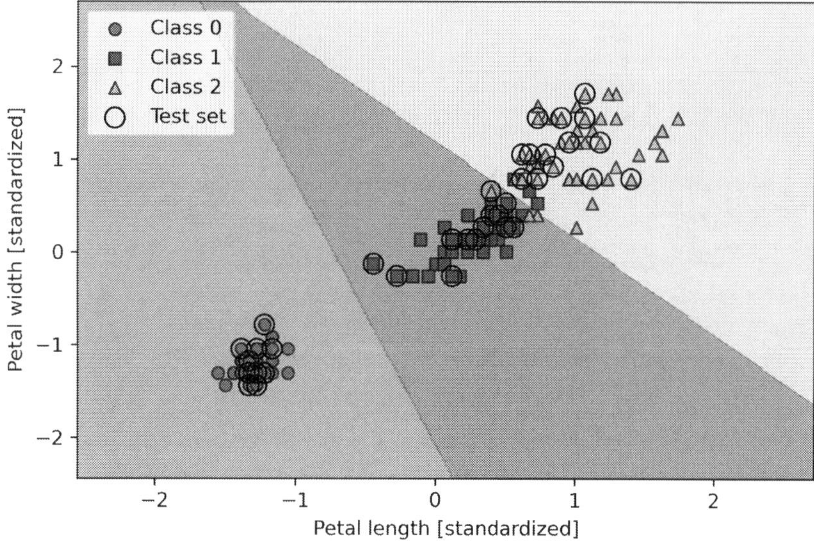

Figure 3.7: Decision regions for scikit-learn's multi-class logistic regression model

Algorithms for convex optimization

Note that there exist many different algorithms for solving optimization problems. For minimizing convex loss functions, such as the logistic regression loss, it is recommended to use more advanced approaches than regular **stochastic gradient descent** (**SGD**). In fact, scikit-learn implements a whole range of such optimization algorithms, which can be specified via the `solver` parameter, namely, `'newton-cg'`, `'lbfgs'`, `'liblinear'`, `'sag'`, and `'saga'`.

While the logistic regression loss is convex, most optimization algorithms should converge to the global loss minimum with ease. However, there are certain advantages of using one algorithm over the other. For example, in previous versions (for instance, v 0.21), scikit-learn used `'liblinear'` as a default, which cannot handle the multinomial loss and is limited to the OvR scheme for multiclass classification. However, in scikit-learn v 0.22, the default solver was changed to `'lbfgs'`, which stands for the limited-memory **Broyden–Fletcher–Goldfarb–Shanno** (**BFGS**) algorithm (`https://en.wikipedia.org/wiki/Limited-memory_BFGS`) and is more flexible in this regard.

Looking at the preceding code that we used to train the `LogisticRegression` model, you might now be wondering, "What is this mysterious parameter C?" We will discuss this parameter in the next subsection, where we will introduce the concepts of overfitting and regularization. However, before we move on to those topics, let's finish our discussion of class membership probabilities.

The probability that training examples belong to a certain class can be computed using the `predict_proba` method. For example, we can predict the probabilities of the first three examples in the test dataset as follows:

```
>>> lr.predict_proba(X_test_std[:3, :])
```

This code snippet returns the following array:

```
array([[3.81527885e-09, 1.44792866e-01, 8.55207131e-01],
       [8.34020679e-01, 1.65979321e-01, 3.25737138e-13],
       [8.48831425e-01, 1.51168575e-01, 2.62277619e-14]])
```

The first row corresponds to the class membership probabilities of the first flower, the second row corresponds to the class membership probabilities of the second flower, and so forth. Notice that the column-wise sum in each row is 1, as expected. (You can confirm this by executing `lr.predict_proba(X_test_std[:3, :]).sum(axis=1)`.)

The highest value in the first row is approximately 0.85, which means that the first example belongs to class 3 (`Iris-virginica`) with a predicted probability of 85 percent. So, as you may have already noticed, we can get the predicted class labels by identifying the largest column in each row, for example, using NumPy's `argmax` function:

```
>>> lr.predict_proba(X_test_std[:3, :]).argmax(axis=1)
```

The returned class indices are shown here (they correspond to `Iris-virginica`, `Iris-setosa`, and `Iris-setosa`):

```
array([2, 0, 0])
```

In the preceding code example, we computed the conditional probabilities and converted these into class labels manually by using NumPy's `argmax` function. In practice, the more convenient way of obtaining class labels when using scikit-learn is to call the `predict` method directly:

```
>>> lr.predict(X_test_std[:3, :])
array([2, 0, 0])
```

Lastly, a word of caution if you want to predict the class label of a single flower example: scikit-learn expects a two-dimensional array as data input; thus, we have to convert a single row slice into such a format first. One way to convert a single row entry into a two-dimensional data array is to use NumPy's `reshape` method to add a new dimension, as demonstrated here:

```
>>> lr.predict(X_test_std[0, :].reshape(1, -1))
array([2])
```

Tackling overfitting via regularization

Overfitting is a common problem in machine learning, where a model performs well on training data but does not generalize well to unseen data (test data). If a model suffers from overfitting, we also say that the model has a high variance, which can be caused by having too many parameters, leading to a model that is too complex given the underlying data. Similarly, our model can also suffer from **underfitting** (high bias), which means that our model is not complex enough to capture the pattern in the training data well and therefore also suffers from low performance on unseen data.

Although we have only encountered linear models for classification so far, the problems of overfitting and underfitting can be best illustrated by comparing a linear decision boundary to more complex, nonlinear decision boundaries, as shown in *Figure 3.8*:

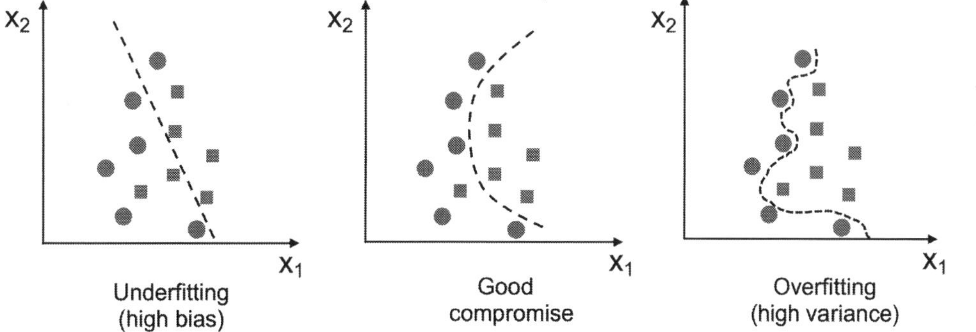

Figure 3.8: Examples of underfitted, well-fitted, and overfitted models

The bias-variance tradeoff

Often, researchers use the terms "bias" and "variance" or "bias-variance tradeoff" to describe the performance of a model—that is, you may stumble upon talks, books, or articles where people say that a model has a "high variance" or "high bias." So, what does that mean? In general, we might say that "high variance" is proportional to overfitting and "high bias" is proportional to underfitting.

In the context of machine learning models, variance measures the consistency (or variability) of the model prediction for classifying a particular example if we retrain the model multiple times, for example, on different subsets of the training dataset. We can say that the model is sensitive to the randomness in the training data. In contrast, bias measures how far off the predictions are from the correct values in general if we rebuild the model multiple times on different training datasets; bias is the measure of the systematic error that is not due to randomness.

If you are interested in the technical specification and derivation of the "bias" and "variance" terms, I've written about it in my lecture notes here: `https://sebastianraschka.com/pdf/lecture-notes/stat451fs20/08-model-eval-1-intro__notes.pdf`.

One way of finding a good bias-variance tradeoff is to tune the complexity of the model via regularization. Regularization is a very useful method for handling collinearity (high correlation among features), filtering out noise from data, and eventually preventing overfitting.

The concept behind regularization is to introduce additional information to penalize extreme parameter (weight) values. The most common form of regularization is so-called **L2 regularization** (sometimes also called L2 shrinkage or weight decay), which can be written as follows:

$$\frac{\lambda}{2n}\|\boldsymbol{w}\|^2 = \frac{\lambda}{2n}\sum_{j=1}^{m} w_j^2$$

Here, λ is the so-called **regularization parameter**. Note that the 2 in the denominator is merely a scaling factor, such that it cancels when computing the loss gradient. The sample size n is added to scale the regularization term similar to the loss.

Regularization and feature normalization

Regularization is another reason why feature scaling such as standardization is important. For regularization to work properly, we need to ensure that all our features are on comparable scales.

The loss function for logistic regression can be regularized by adding a simple regularization term, which will shrink the weights during model training:

$$L(\boldsymbol{w}, b) = \frac{1}{n}\sum_{i=1}^{n}\left[-y^{(i)}\log\left(\sigma\left(z^{(i)}\right)\right) - \left(1 - y^{(i)}\right)\log\left(1 - \sigma\left(z^{(i)}\right)\right)\right] + \frac{\lambda}{2n}\|\boldsymbol{w}\|^2$$

The partial derivative of the unregularized loss is defined as:

$$\frac{\partial L(\boldsymbol{w}, b)}{\partial w_j} = \left(\frac{1}{n}\sum_{i=1}^{n}\left(\sigma\left(\boldsymbol{w}^T\boldsymbol{x}^{(i)}\right) - y^{(i)}\right)x_j^{(i)}\right)$$

Adding the regularization term to the loss changes the partial derivative to the following form:

$$\frac{\partial L(\boldsymbol{w}, b)}{\partial w_j} = \left(\frac{1}{n}\sum_{i=1}^{n}\left(\sigma\left(\boldsymbol{w}^T\boldsymbol{x}^{(i)}\right) - y^{(i)}\right)x_j^{(i)}\right) + \frac{\lambda}{n}w_j$$

Via the regularization parameter, λ, we can then control how closely we fit the training data, while keeping the weights small. By increasing the value of λ, we increase the regularization strength. Please note that the bias unit, which is essentially an intercept term or negative threshold, as we learned in *Chapter 2*, is usually not regularized.

The parameter, `C`, that is implemented for the `LogisticRegression` class in scikit-learn comes from a convention in support vector machines, which will be the topic of the next section. The term `C` is inversely proportional to the regularization parameter, λ. Consequently, decreasing the value of the inverse regularization parameter, `C`, means that we are increasing the regularization strength, which we can visualize by plotting the L2 regularization path for the two weight coefficients:

```
>>> weights, params = [], []
>>> for c in np.arange(-5, 5):
...     lr = LogisticRegression(C=10.**c,
...                             multi_class='ovr')
...     lr.fit(X_train_std, y_train)
...     weights.append(lr.coef_[1])
...     params.append(10.**c)
>>> weights = np.array(weights)
>>> plt.plot(params, weights[:, 0],
...          label='Petal length')
>>> plt.plot(params, weights[:, 1], linestyle='--',
...          label='Petal width')
>>> plt.ylabel('Weight coefficient')
>>> plt.xlabel('C')
>>> plt.legend(loc='upper left')
>>> plt.xscale('log')
>>> plt.show()
```

By executing the preceding code, we fitted 10 logistic regression models with different values for the inverse-regularization parameter, `C`. For illustration purposes, we only collected the weight coefficients of class `1` (here, the second class in the dataset: `Iris-versicolor`) versus all classifiers—remember that we are using the OvR technique for multiclass classification.

As we can see in the resulting plot, the weight coefficients shrink if we decrease parameter C, that is, if we increase the regularization strength:

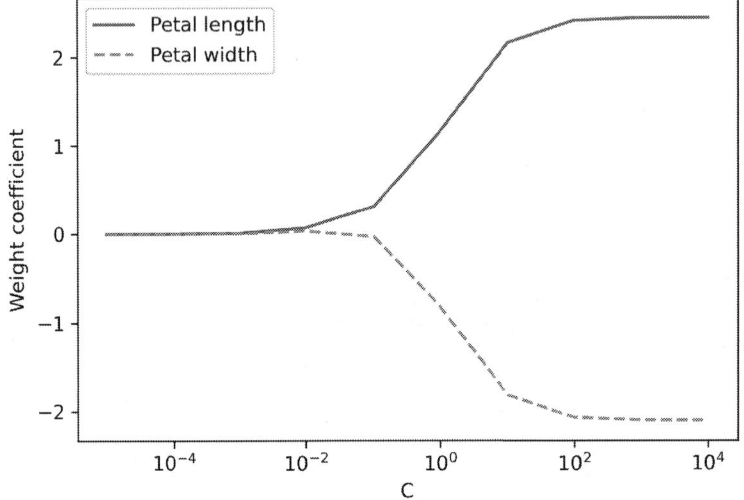

Figure 3.9: The impact of the inverse regularization strength parameter C on L2 regularized model results

Increasing the regularization strength can reduce overfitting, so we might ask why we don't strongly regularize all models by default. The reason is that we have to be careful when adjusting the regularization strength. For instance, if the regularization strength is too high and the weights coefficients approach zero, the model can perform very poorly due to underfitting, as illustrated in *Figure 3.8*.

An additional resource on logistic regression

Since in-depth coverage of the individual classification algorithms exceeds the scope of this book, *Logistic Regression: From Introductory to Advanced Concepts and Applications, Dr. Scott Menard, Sage Publications, 2009*, is recommended to readers who want to learn more about logistic regression.

Maximum margin classification with support vector machines

Another powerful and widely used learning algorithm is the **support vector machine** (**SVM**), which can be considered an extension of the perceptron. Using the perceptron algorithm, we minimized misclassification errors. However, in SVMs, our optimization objective is to maximize the margin. The margin is defined as the distance between the separating hyperplane (decision boundary) and the training examples that are closest to this hyperplane, which are the so-called **support vectors**.

This is illustrated in *Figure 3.10*:

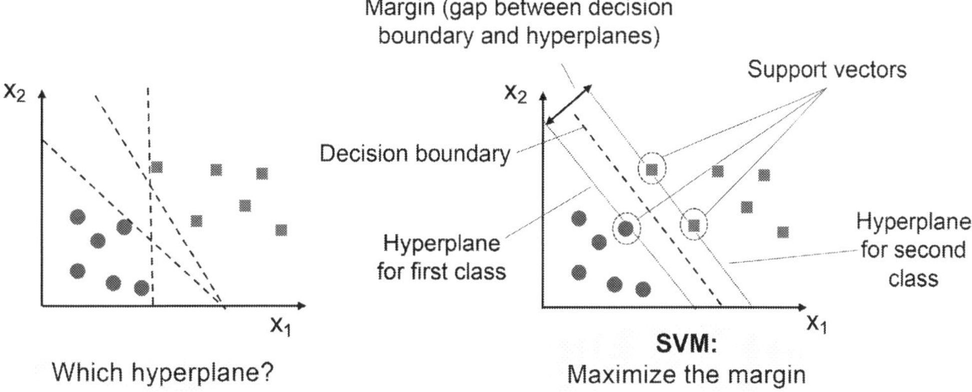

Figure 3.10: SVM maximizes the margin between the decision boundary and training data points

Maximum margin intuition

The rationale behind having decision boundaries with large margins is that they tend to have a lower generalization error, whereas models with small margins are more prone to overfitting.

Unfortunately, while the main intuition behind SVMs is relatively simple, the mathematics behind them is quite advanced and would require sound knowledge of constrained optimization.

Hence, the details behind maximum margin optimization in SVMs are beyond the scope of this book. However, we recommend the following resources if you are interested in learning more:

- Chris J.C. Burges' excellent explanation in *A Tutorial on Support Vector Machines for Pattern Recognition* (Data Mining and Knowledge Discovery, 2(2): 121-167, 1998)
- Vladimir Vapnik's book *The Nature of Statistical Learning Theory*, Springer Science+Business Media, Vladimir Vapnik, 2000
- Andrew Ng's very detailed lecture notes available at `https://see.stanford.edu/materials/aimlcs229/cs229-notes3.pdf`

Dealing with a nonlinearly separable case using slack variables

Although we don't want to dive much deeper into the more involved mathematical concepts behind the maximum-margin classification, let's briefly mention the so-called *slack variable*, which was introduced by Vladimir Vapnik in 1995 and led to the so-called **soft-margin classification.** The motivation for introducing the slack variable was that the linear constraints in the SVM optimization objective need to be relaxed for nonlinearly separable data to allow the convergence of the optimization in the presence of misclassifications, under appropriate loss penalization.

The use of the slack variable, in turn, introduces the variable, which is commonly referred to as *C* in SVM contexts. We can consider *C* as a hyperparameter for controlling the penalty for misclassification. Large values of *C* correspond to large error penalties, whereas we are less strict about misclassification errors if we choose smaller values for *C*. We can then use the *C* parameter to control the width of the margin and therefore tune the bias-variance tradeoff, as illustrated in *Figure 3.11*:

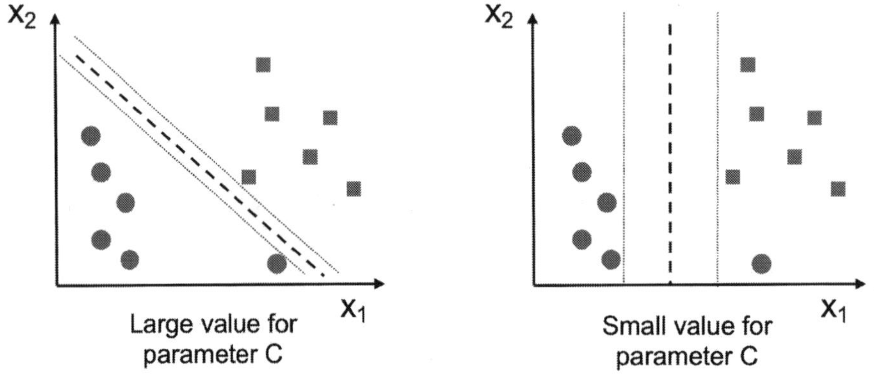

Figure 3.11: The impact of large and small values of the inverse regularization strength C on classification

This concept is related to regularization, which we discussed in the previous section in the context of regularized regression, where decreasing the value of `C` increases the bias (underfitting) and lowers the variance (overfitting) of the model.

Now that we have learned the basic concepts behind a linear SVM, let's train an SVM model to classify the different flowers in our Iris dataset:

```
>>> from sklearn.svm import SVC
>>> svm = SVC(kernel='linear', C=1.0, random_state=1)
>>> svm.fit(X_train_std, y_train)
>>> plot_decision_regions(X_combined_std,
...                       y_combined,
...                       classifier=svm,
...                       test_idx=range(105, 150))
>>> plt.xlabel('Petal length [standardized]')
>>> plt.ylabel('Petal width [standardized]')
>>> plt.legend(loc='upper left')
>>> plt.tight_layout()
>>> plt.show()
```

The three decision regions of the SVM, visualized after training the classifier on the Iris dataset by executing the preceding code example, are shown in *Figure 3.12*:

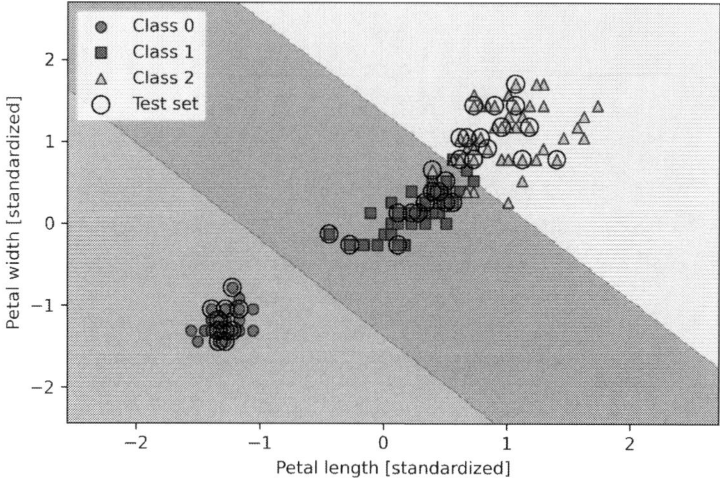

Figure 3.12: SVM's decision regions

Logistic regression versus SVMs

In practical classification tasks, linear logistic regression and linear SVMs often yield very similar results. Logistic regression tries to maximize the conditional likelihoods of the training data, which makes it more prone to outliers than SVMs, which mostly care about the points that are closest to the decision boundary (support vectors). On the other hand, logistic regression has the advantage of being a simpler model and can be implemented more easily, and is mathematically easier to explain. Furthermore, logistic regression models can be easily updated, which is attractive when working with streaming data.

Alternative implementations in scikit-learn

The scikit-learn library's `LogisticRegression` class, which we used in the previous sections, can make use of the LIBLINEAR library by setting `solver='liblinear'`. LIBLINEAR is a highly optimized C/C++ library developed at the National Taiwan University (`http://www.csie.ntu.edu.tw/~cjlin/liblinear/`).

Similarly, the `SVC` class that we used to train an SVM makes use of LIBSVM, which is an equivalent C/C++ library specialized for SVMs (`http://www.csie.ntu.edu.tw/~cjlin/libsvm/`).

The advantage of using LIBLINEAR and LIBSVM over, for example, native Python implementations is that they allow the extremely quick training of large amounts of linear classifiers. However, sometimes our datasets are too large to fit into computer memory. Thus, scikit-learn also offers alternative implementations via the `SGDClassifier` class, which also supports online learning via the `partial_fit` method. The concept behind the `SGDClassifier` class is similar to the stochastic gradient algorithm that we implemented in *Chapter 2* for Adaline.

We could initialize the SGD version of the perceptron (`loss='perceptron'`), logistic regression (`loss='log'`), and an SVM with default parameters (`loss='hinge'`), as follows:

```
>>> from sklearn.linear_model import SGDClassifier
>>> ppn = SGDClassifier(loss='perceptron')
>>> lr = SGDClassifier(loss='log')
>>> svm = SGDClassifier(loss='hinge')
```

Solving nonlinear problems using a kernel SVM

Another reason why SVMs enjoy high popularity among machine learning practitioners is that they can be easily **kernelized** to solve nonlinear classification problems. Before we discuss the main concept behind the so-called **kernel SVM**, the most common variant of SVMs, let's first create a synthetic dataset to see what such a nonlinear classification problem may look like.

Kernel methods for linearly inseparable data

Using the following code, we will create a simple dataset that has the form of an XOR gate using the `logical_xor` function from NumPy, where 100 examples will be assigned the class label `1`, and 100 examples will be assigned the class label `-1`:

```
>>> import matplotlib.pyplot as plt
>>> import numpy as np
>>> np.random.seed(1)
>>> X_xor = np.random.randn(200, 2)
>>> y_xor = np.logical_xor(X_xor[:, 0] > 0,
...                        X_xor[:, 1] > 0)
>>> y_xor = np.where(y_xor, 1, 0)
>>> plt.scatter(X_xor[y_xor == 1, 0],
...             X_xor[y_xor == 1, 1],
...             c='royalblue', marker='s',
...             label='Class 1')
```

```
>>> plt.scatter(X_xor[y_xor == 0, 0],
...             X_xor[y_xor == 0, 1],
...             c='tomato', marker='o',
...             label='Class 0')
>>> plt.xlim([-3, 3])
>>> plt.ylim([-3, 3])
>>> plt.xlabel('Feature 1')
>>> plt.ylabel('Feature 2')
>>> plt.legend(loc='best')
>>> plt.tight_layout()
>>> plt.show()
```

After executing the code, we will have an XOR dataset with random noise, as shown in *Figure 3.13*:

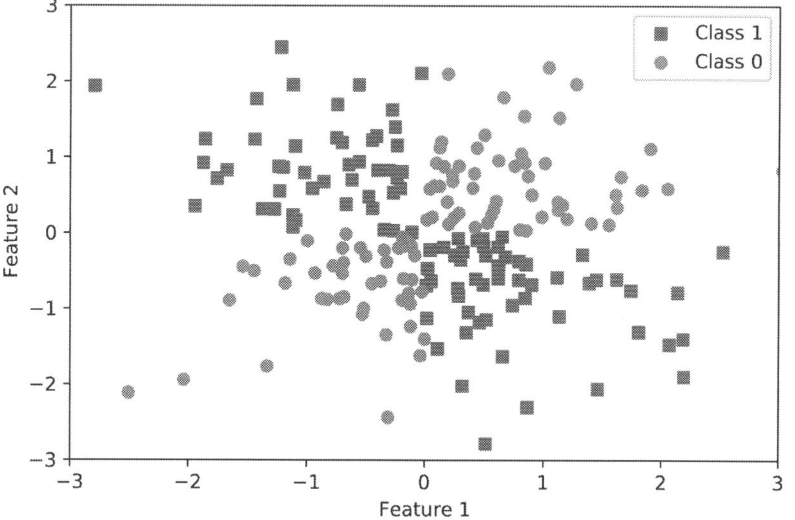

Figure 3.13: A plot of the XOR dataset

Obviously, we would not be able to separate the examples from the positive and negative class very well using a linear hyperplane as a decision boundary via the linear logistic regression or linear SVM model that we discussed in earlier sections.

The basic idea behind **kernel methods** for dealing with such linearly inseparable data is to create nonlinear combinations of the original features to project them onto a higher-dimensional space via a mapping function, ϕ, where the data becomes linearly separable. As shown in *Figure 3.14*, we can transform a two-dimensional dataset into a new three-dimensional feature space, where the classes become separable via the following projection:

$$\phi(x_1, x_2) = (z_1, z_2, z_3) = (x_1, x_2, x_1^2 + x_2^2)$$

This allows us to separate the two classes shown in the plot via a linear hyperplane that becomes a nonlinear decision boundary if we project it back onto the original feature space, as illustrated with the following concentric circle dataset:

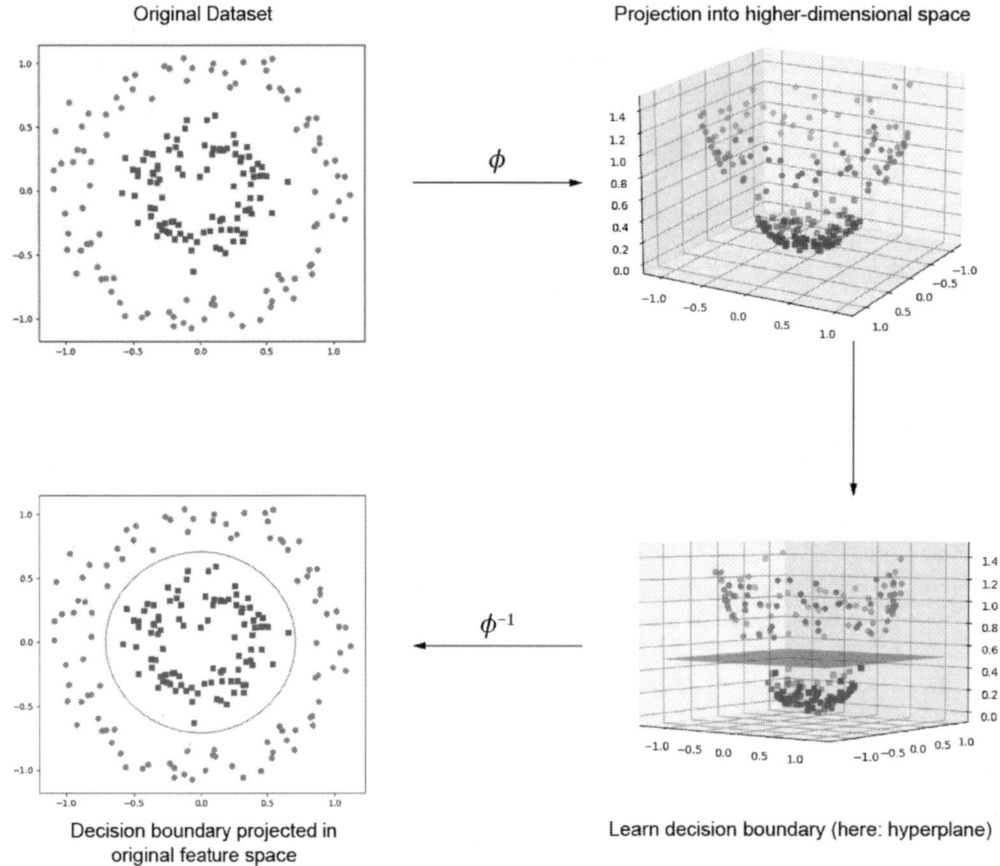

Figure 3.14: The process of classifying nonlinear data using kernel methods

Using the kernel trick to find separating hyperplanes in a high-dimensional space

To solve a nonlinear problem using an SVM, we would transform the training data into a higher-dimensional feature space via a mapping function, ϕ, and train a linear SVM model to classify the data in this new feature space. Then, we could use the same mapping function, ϕ, to transform new, unseen data to classify it using the linear SVM model.

However, one problem with this mapping approach is that the construction of the new features is computationally very expensive, especially if we are dealing with high-dimensional data. This is where the so-called **kernel trick** comes into play.

Although we did not go into much detail about how to solve the quadratic programming task to train an SVM, in practice, we just need to replace the dot product $\boldsymbol{x}^{(i)T}\boldsymbol{x}^{(j)}$ by $\phi\left(\boldsymbol{x}^{(i)}\right)^T \phi\left(\boldsymbol{x}^{(j)}\right)$. To save the expensive step of calculating this dot product between two points explicitly, we define a so-called **kernel function:**

$$\kappa\left(\boldsymbol{x}^{(i)}, \boldsymbol{x}^{(j)}\right) = \phi\left(\boldsymbol{x}^{(i)}\right)^T \phi\left(\boldsymbol{x}^{(j)}\right)$$

One of the most widely used kernels is the **radial basis function** (**RBF**) kernel, which can simply be called the **Gaussian kernel:**

$$\kappa\left(\boldsymbol{x}^{(i)}, \boldsymbol{x}^{(j)}\right) = \exp\left(-\frac{\left\|\boldsymbol{x}^{(i)} - \boldsymbol{x}^{(j)}\right\|^2}{2\sigma^2}\right)$$

This is often simplified to:

$$\kappa\left(\boldsymbol{x}^{(i)}, \boldsymbol{x}^{(j)}\right) = \exp\left(-\gamma\left\|\boldsymbol{x}^{(i)} - \boldsymbol{x}^{(j)}\right\|^2\right)$$

Here, $\gamma = \frac{1}{2\sigma^2}$ is a free parameter to be optimized.

Roughly speaking, the term "kernel" can be interpreted as a **similarity function** between a pair of examples. The minus sign inverts the distance measure into a similarity score, and, due to the exponential term, the resulting similarity score will fall into a range between 1 (for exactly similar examples) and 0 (for very dissimilar examples).

Now that we have covered the big picture behind the kernel trick, let's see if we can train a kernel SVM that is able to draw a nonlinear decision boundary that separates the XOR data well. Here, we simply use the `SVC` class from scikit-learn that we imported earlier and replace the `kernel='linear'` parameter with `kernel='rbf'`:

```
>>> svm = SVC(kernel='rbf', random_state=1, gamma=0.10, C=10.0)
>>> svm.fit(X_xor, y_xor)
>>> plot_decision_regions(X_xor, y_xor, classifier=svm)
>>> plt.legend(loc='upper left')
>>> plt.tight_layout()
>>> plt.show()
```

As we can see in the resulting plot, the kernel SVM separates the XOR data relatively well:

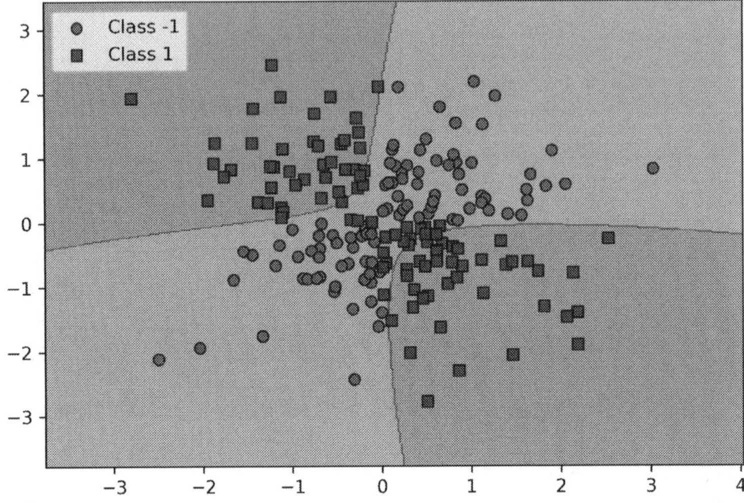

Figure 3.15: The decision boundary on the XOR data using a kernel method

The γ parameter, which we set to `gamma=0.1`, can be understood as a cut-off parameter for the Gaussian sphere. If we increase the value for γ, we increase the influence or reach of the training examples, which leads to a tighter and bumpier decision boundary. To get a better understanding of γ, let's apply an RBF kernel SVM to our Iris flower dataset:

```
>>> svm = SVC(kernel='rbf', random_state=1, gamma=0.2, C=1.0)
>>> svm.fit(X_train_std, y_train)
>>> plot_decision_regions(X_combined_std,
...                       y_combined, classifier=svm,
...                       test_idx=range(105, 150))
>>> plt.xlabel('Petal length [standardized]')
>>> plt.ylabel('Petal width [standardized]')
>>> plt.legend(loc='upper left')
>>> plt.tight_layout()
>>> plt.show()
```

Since we chose a relatively small value for γ, the resulting decision boundary of the RBF kernel SVM model will be relatively soft, as shown in *Figure 3.16*:

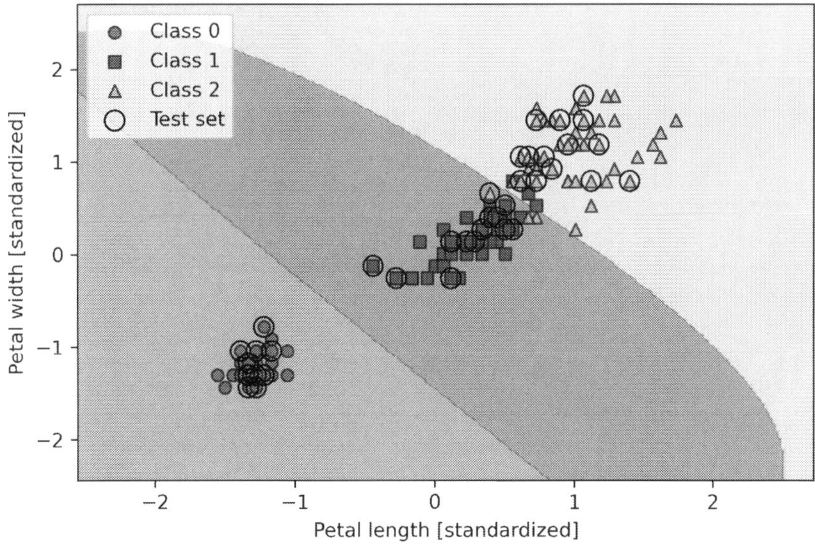

Figure 3.16: The decision boundaries on the Iris dataset using an RBF kernel SVM model with a small γ value

Now, let's increase the value of γ and observe the effect on the decision boundary:

```
>>> svm = SVC(kernel='rbf', random_state=1, gamma=100.0, C=1.0)
>>> svm.fit(X_train_std, y_train)
>>> plot_decision_regions(X_combined_std,
...                       y_combined, classifier=svm,
...                       test_idx=range(105,150))
>>> plt.xlabel('Petal length [standardized]')
>>> plt.ylabel('Petal width [standardized]')
>>> plt.legend(loc='upper left')
>>> plt.tight_layout()
>>> plt.show()
```

In *Figure 3.17*, we can now see that the decision boundary around the classes `0` and `1` is much tighter using a relatively large value of γ:

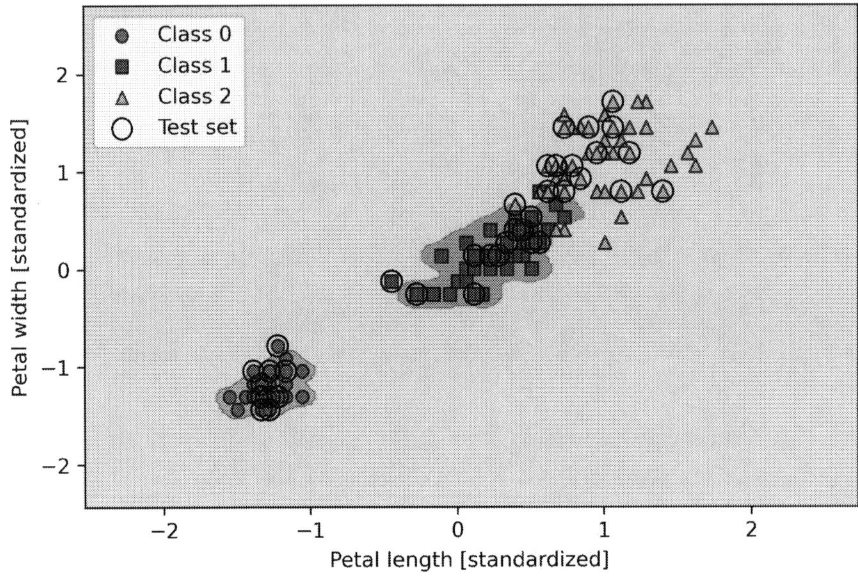

Figure 3.17: The decision boundaries on the Iris dataset using an RBF kernel SVM model with a large γ value

Although the model fits the training dataset very well, such a classifier will likely have a high generalization error on unseen data. This illustrates that the γ parameter also plays an important role in controlling overfitting or variance when the algorithm is too sensitive to fluctuations in the training dataset.

Decision tree learning

Decision tree classifiers are attractive models if we care about interpretability. As the name "decision tree" suggests, we can think of this model as breaking down our data by making a decision based on asking a series of questions.

Let's consider the following example in which we use a decision tree to decide upon an activity on a particular day:

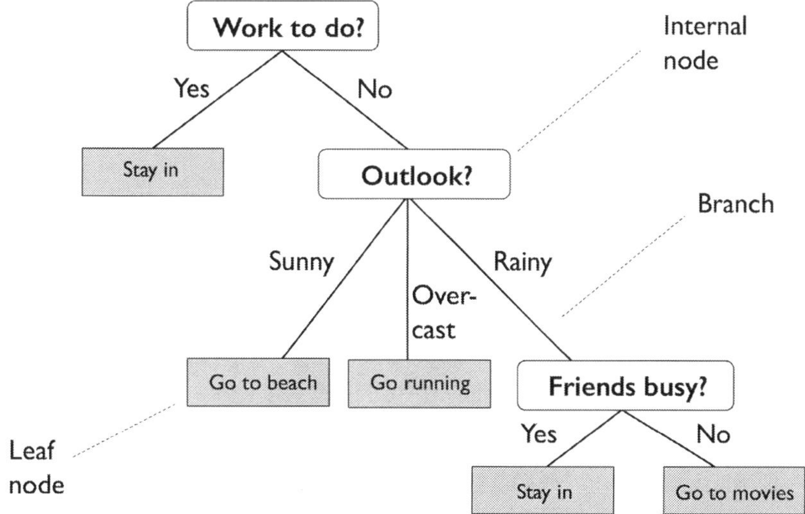

Figure 3.18: An example of a decision tree

Based on the features in our training dataset, the decision tree model learns a series of questions to infer the class labels of the examples. Although *Figure 3.18* illustrates the concept of a decision tree based on categorical variables, the same concept applies if our features are real numbers, like in the Iris dataset. For example, we could simply define a cut-off value along the **sepal width** feature axis and ask a binary question: "Is the sepal width ≥ 2.8 cm?"

Using the decision algorithm, we start at the tree root and split the data on the feature that results in the largest **information gain** (**IG**), which will be explained in more detail in the following section. In an iterative process, we can then repeat this splitting procedure at each child node until the leaves are pure. This means that the training examples at each node all belong to the same class. In practice, this can result in a very deep tree with many nodes, which can easily lead to overfitting. Thus, we typically want to **prune** the tree by setting a limit for the maximum depth of the tree.

Maximizing IG – getting the most bang for your buck

To split the nodes at the most informative features, we need to define an objective function to optimize via the tree learning algorithm. Here, our objective function is to maximize the IG at each split, which we define as follows:

$$IG(D_p, f) = I(D_p) - \sum_{j=1}^{m} \frac{N_j}{N_p} I(D_j)$$

Here, *f* is the feature to perform the split; D_p and D_j are the dataset of the parent and *j*th child node; *I* is our **impurity** measure; N_p is the total number of training examples at the parent node; and N_j is the number of examples in the *j*th child node. As we can see, the information gain is simply the difference between the impurity of the parent node and the sum of the child node impurities—the lower the impurities of the child nodes, the larger the information gain. However, for simplicity and to reduce the combinatorial search space, most libraries (including scikit-learn) implement binary decision trees. This means that each parent node is split into two child nodes, D_{left} and D_{right}:

$$IG(D_p, f) = I(D_p) - \frac{N_{left}}{N_p} I(D_{left}) - \frac{N_{right}}{N_p} I(D_{right})$$

The three impurity measures or splitting criteria that are commonly used in binary decision trees are **Gini impurity** (I_G), **entropy** (I_H), and the **classification error** (I_E). Let's start with the definition of entropy for all **non-empty** classes ($p(i|t) \neq 0$):

$$I_H(t) = -\sum_{i=1}^{c} p(i|t) \log_2 p(i|t)$$

Here, $p(i|t)$ is the proportion of the examples that belong to class *i* for a particular node, *t*. The entropy is therefore 0 if all examples at a node belong to the same class, and the entropy is maximal if we have a uniform class distribution. For example, in a binary class setting, the entropy is 0 if $p(i=1|t) = 1$ or $p(i=0|t) = 0$. If the classes are distributed uniformly with $p(i=1|t) = 0.5$ and $p(i=0|t) = 0.5$, the entropy is 1. Therefore, we can say that the entropy criterion attempts to maximize the mutual information in the tree.

To provide a visual intuition, let us visualize the entropy values for different class distributions via the following code:

```
>>> def entropy(p):
...     return - p * np.log2(p) - (1 - p) * np.log2((1 - p))
>>> x = np.arange(0.0, 1.0, 0.01)
>>> ent = [entropy(p) if p != 0 else None for p in x]
>>> plt.ylabel('Entropy')
>>> plt.xlabel('Class-membership probability p(i=1)')
>>> plt.plot(x, ent)
>>> plt.show()
```

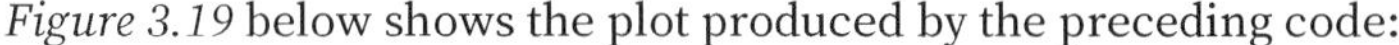

Figure 3.19 below shows the plot produced by the preceding code:

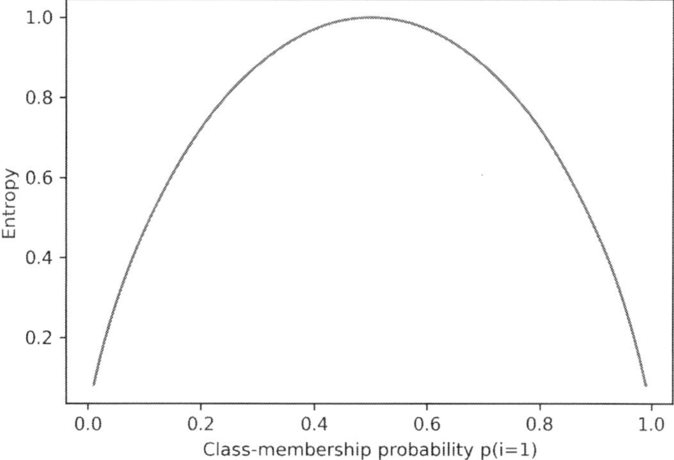

Figure 3.19: Entropy values for different class-membership probabilities

The Gini impurity can be understood as a criterion to minimize the probability of misclassification:

$$I_G(t) = \sum_{i=1}^{c} p(i|t)\,(1 - p(i|t)) = 1 - \sum_{i=1}^{c} p(i|t)^2$$

Similar to entropy, the Gini impurity is maximal if the classes are perfectly mixed, for example, in a binary class setting ($c = 2$):

$$I_G(t) = 1 - \sum_{i=1}^{c} 0.5^2 = 0.5$$

However, in practice, both the Gini impurity and entropy typically yield very similar results, and it is often not worth spending much time on evaluating trees using different impurity criteria rather than experimenting with different pruning cut-offs. In fact, as you will see later in *Figure 3.21*, both the Gini impurity and entropy have a similar shape.

Another impurity measure is the classification error:

$$I_E(t) = 1 - \max\{p(i|t)\}$$

This is a useful criterion for pruning, but not recommended for growing a decision tree, since it is less sensitive to changes in the class probabilities of the nodes. We can illustrate this by looking at the two possible splitting scenarios shown in *Figure 3.20*:

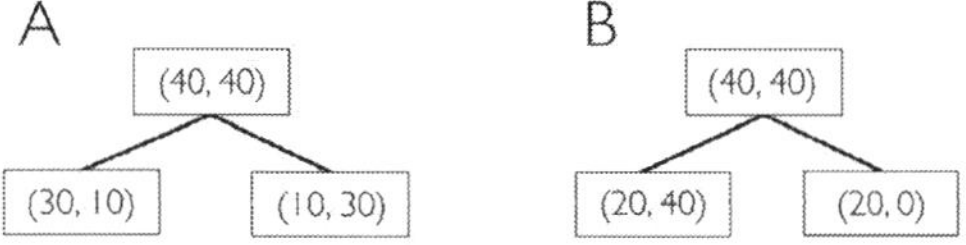

Figure 3.20: Decision tree data splits

We start with a dataset, D_p, at the parent node, which consists of 40 examples from class 1 and 40 examples from class 2 that we split into two datasets, D_{left} and D_{right}. The information gain using the classification error as a splitting criterion would be the same ($IG_E = 0.25$) in both scenarios, A and B:

$$I_E(D_p) = 1 - 0.5 = 0.5$$

$$A: \quad I_E(D_{left}) = 1 - \frac{3}{4} = 0.25$$

$$A: \quad I_E(D_{right}) = 1 - \frac{3}{4} = 0.25$$

$$A: \quad IG_E = 0.5 - \frac{4}{8}0.25 - \frac{4}{8}0.25 = 0.25$$

$$B: \quad I_E(D_{left}) = 1 - \frac{4}{6} = \frac{1}{3}$$

$$B: \quad I_E(D_{right}) = 1 - 1 = 0$$

$$B: \quad IG_E = 0.5 - \frac{6}{8} \times \frac{1}{3} - 0 = 0.25$$

However, the Gini impurity would favor the split in scenario B ($IG_G = 0.1\bar{6}$) over scenario A ($IG_G = 0.125$), which is indeed purer:

$$I_G(D_p) = 1 - (0.5^2 + 0.5^2) = 0.5$$

$$A: \quad I_G(D_{left}) = 1 - \left(\left(\frac{3}{4}\right)^2 + \left(\frac{1}{4}\right)^2\right) = \frac{3}{8} = 0.375$$

$$A: \quad I_G(D_{right}) = 1 - \left(\left(\frac{1}{4}\right)^2 + \left(\frac{3}{4}\right)^2\right) = \frac{3}{8} = 0.375$$

$$A: \quad IG_G = 0.5 - \frac{4}{8}0.375 - \frac{4}{8}0.375 = 0.125$$

$$B: \quad I_G(D_{left}) = 1 - \left(\left(\frac{2}{6}\right)^2 + \left(\frac{4}{6}\right)^2\right) = \frac{4}{9} = 0.\bar{4}$$

$$B: \quad I_G(D_{right}) = 1 - (1^2 + 0^2) = 0$$

$$B: \quad IG_G = 0.5 - \frac{6}{8}0.\bar{4} - 0 = 0.1\bar{6}$$

Similarly, the entropy criterion would also favor scenario B ($IG_H = 0.31$) over scenario A ($IG_H = 0.19$):

$$I_H(D_p) = -(0.5\log_2(0.5) + 0.5\log_2(0.5)) = 1$$

$$A: \quad I_H(D_{left}) = -\left(\frac{3}{4}\log_2\left(\frac{3}{4}\right) + \frac{1}{4}\log_2\left(\frac{1}{4}\right)\right) = 0.81$$

$$A: \quad I_H(D_{right}) = -\left(\frac{1}{4}\log_2\left(\frac{1}{4}\right) + \frac{3}{4}\log_2\left(\frac{3}{4}\right)\right) = 0.81$$

$$A: \quad IG_H = 1 - \frac{4}{8}0.81 - \frac{4}{8}0.81 = 0.19$$

$$B: \quad I_H(D_{left}) = -\left(\frac{2}{6}\log_2\left(\frac{2}{6}\right) + \frac{4}{6}\log_2\left(\frac{4}{6}\right)\right) = 0.92$$

$$B: \quad I_H(D_{right}) = 0$$

$$B: \quad IG_H = 1 - \frac{6}{8}0.92 - 0 = 0.31$$

For a more visual comparison of the three different impurity criteria that we discussed previously, let's plot the impurity indices for the probability range [0, 1] for class 1. Note that we will also add a scaled version of the entropy (entropy / 2) to observe that the Gini impurity is an intermediate measure between entropy and the classification error. The code is as follows:

```
>>> import matplotlib.pyplot as plt
>>> import numpy as np
>>> def gini(p):
...     return p*(1 - p) + (1 - p)*(1 - (1-p))
>>> def entropy(p):
...     return - p*np.log2(p) - (1 - p)*np.log2((1 - p))
>>> def error(p):
...     return 1 - np.max([p, 1 - p])
>>> x = np.arange(0.0, 1.0, 0.01)
>>> ent = [entropy(p) if p != 0 else None for p in x]
>>> sc_ent = [e*0.5 if e else None for e in ent]
>>> err = [error(i) for i in x]
>>> fig = plt.figure()
>>> ax = plt.subplot(111)
```

```
>>> for i, lab, ls, c, in zip([ent, sc_ent, gini(x), err],
...                           ['Entropy', 'Entropy (scaled)',
...                            'Gini impurity',
...                            'Misclassification error'],
...                           ['-', '-', '--', '-.'],
...                           ['black', 'lightgray',
...                            'red', 'green', 'cyan']):
...     line = ax.plot(x, i, label=lab,
...                    linestyle=ls, lw=2, color=c)
>>> ax.legend(loc='upper center', bbox_to_anchor=(0.5, 1.15),
...           ncol=5, fancybox=True, shadow=False)
>>> ax.axhline(y=0.5, linewidth=1, color='k', linestyle='--')
>>> ax.axhline(y=1.0, linewidth=1, color='k', linestyle='--')
>>> plt.ylim([0, 1.1])
>>> plt.xlabel('p(i=1)')
>>> plt.ylabel('impurity index')
>>> plt.show()
```

The plot produced by the preceding code example is as follows:

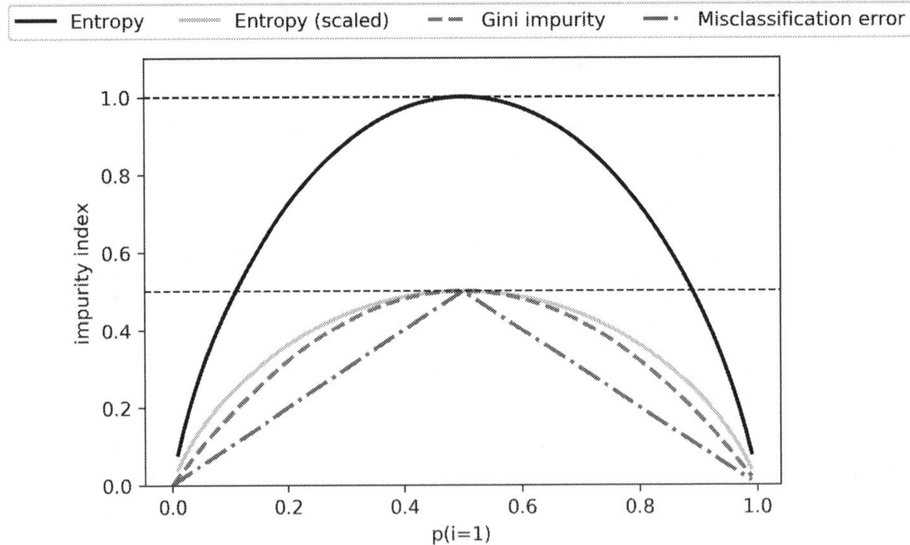

Figure 3.21: The different impurity indices for different class-membership probabilities between 0 and 1

Building a decision tree

Decision trees can build complex decision boundaries by dividing the feature space into rectangles. However, we have to be careful since the deeper the decision tree, the more complex the decision boundary becomes, which can easily result in overfitting. Using scikit-learn, we will now train a decision tree with a maximum depth of 4, using the Gini impurity as a criterion for impurity.

Although feature scaling may be desired for visualization purposes, note that feature scaling is not a requirement for decision tree algorithms. The code is as follows:

```
>>> from sklearn.tree import DecisionTreeClassifier
>>> tree_model = DecisionTreeClassifier(criterion='gini',
...                                     max_depth=4,
...                                     random_state=1)
>>> tree_model.fit(X_train, y_train)
>>> X_combined = np.vstack((X_train, X_test))
>>> y_combined = np.hstack((y_train, y_test))
>>> plot_decision_regions(X_combined,
...                       y_combined,
...                       classifier=tree_model,
...                       test_idx=range(105, 150))
>>> plt.xlabel('Petal length [cm]')
>>> plt.ylabel('Petal width [cm]')
>>> plt.legend(loc='upper left')
>>> plt.tight_layout()
>>> plt.show()
```

After executing the code example, we get the typical axis-parallel decision boundaries of the decision tree:

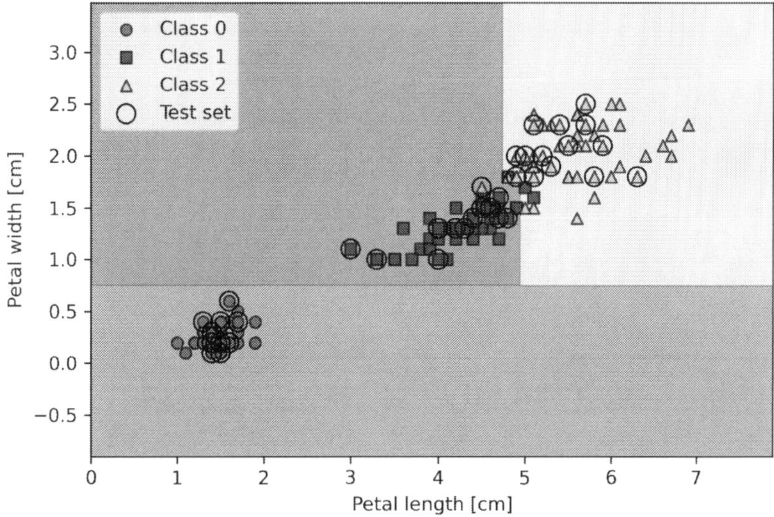

Figure 3.22: The decision boundaries of the Iris data using a decision tree

A nice feature in scikit-learn is that it allows us to readily visualize the decision tree model after training via the following code:

```
>>> from sklearn import tree
>>> feature_names = ['Sepal length', 'Sepal width',
...                  'Petal length', 'Petal width']
>>> tree.plot_tree(tree_model,
...                feature_names=feature_names,
...                filled=True)
>>> plt.show()
```

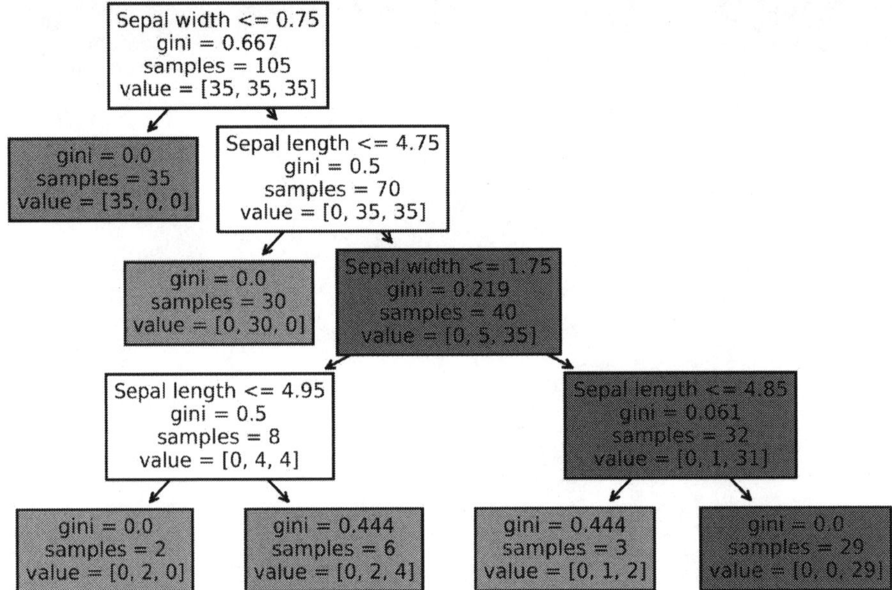

Figure 3.23: A decision tree model fit to the Iris dataset

Setting `filled=True` in the `plot_tree` function we called colors the nodes by the majority class label at that node. There are many additional options available, which you can find in the documentation at `https://scikit-learn.org/stable/modules/generated/sklearn.tree.plot_tree.html`.

Looking at the decision tree figure, we can now nicely trace back the splits that the decision tree determined from our training dataset. Regarding the feature splitting criterion at each node, note that the branches to the left correspond to "True" and branches to the right correspond to "False."

Looking at the root node, it starts with 105 examples at the top. The first split uses a sepal width cut-off ≤ 0.75 cm for splitting the root node into two child nodes with 35 examples (left child node) and 70 examples (right child node). After the first split, we can see that the left child node is already pure and only contains examples from the `Iris-setosa` class (Gini impurity = 0). The further splits on the right are then used to separate the examples from the `Iris-versicolor` and `Iris-virginica` class.

Looking at this tree, and the decision region plot of the tree, we can see that the decision tree does a very good job of separating the flower classes. Unfortunately, scikit-learn currently does not implement functionality to manually post-prune a decision tree. However, we could go back to our previous code example, change the `max_depth` of our decision tree to `3`, and compare it to our current model, but we leave this as an exercise for the interested reader.

Alternatively, scikit-learn provides an automatic cost complexity post-pruning procedure for decision trees. Interested readers can find more information about this more advanced topic in the following tutorial: `https://scikit-learn.org/stable/auto_examples/tree/plot_cost_complexity_pruning.html`.

Combining multiple decision trees via random forests

Ensemble methods have gained huge popularity in applications of machine learning during the last decade due to their good classification performance and robustness toward overfitting. While we are going to cover different ensemble methods, including **bagging** and **boosting**, later in *Chapter 7, Combining Different Models for Ensemble Learning*, let's discuss the decision tree-based **random forest** algorithm, which is known for its good scalability and ease of use. A random forest can be considered as an **ensemble** of decision trees. The idea behind a random forest is to average multiple (deep) decision trees that individually suffer from high variance to build a more robust model that has a better generalization performance and is less susceptible to overfitting. The random forest algorithm can be summarized in four simple steps:

1. Draw a random **bootstrap** sample of size n (randomly choose n examples from the training dataset with replacement).
2. Grow a decision tree from the bootstrap sample. At each node:
    a. Randomly select d features without replacement.
    b. Split the node using the feature that provides the best split according to the objective function, for instance, maximizing the information gain.
3. Repeat *steps 1-2* k times.
4. Aggregate the prediction by each tree to assign the class label by **majority vote**. Majority voting will be discussed in more detail in *Chapter 7*.

We should note one slight modification in *step 2* when we are training the individual decision trees: instead of evaluating all features to determine the best split at each node, we only consider a random subset of those.

Sampling with and without replacement

In case you are not familiar with the terms sampling "with" and "without" replacement, let's walk through a simple thought experiment. Let's assume that we are playing a lottery game where we randomly draw numbers from an urn. We start with an urn that holds five unique numbers, 0, 1, 2, 3, and 4, and we draw exactly one number on each turn. In the first round, the chance of drawing a particular number from the urn would be 1/5. Now, in sampling without replacement, we do not put the number back into the urn after each turn. Consequently, the probability of drawing a particular number from the set of remaining numbers in the next round depends on the previous round. For example, if we have a remaining set of numbers 0, 1, 2, and 4, the chance of drawing number 0 would become 1/4 in the next turn.

However, in random sampling with replacement, we always return the drawn number to the urn so that the probability of drawing a particular number at each turn does not change; we can draw the same number more than once. In other words, in sampling *with* replacement, the samples (numbers) are independent and have a covariance of zero. For example, the results from five rounds of drawing random numbers could look like this:

- Random sampling without replacement: 2, 1, 3, 4, 0
- Random sampling with replacement: 1, 3, 3, 4, 1

Although random forests don't offer the same level of interpretability as decision trees, a big advantage of random forests is that we don't have to worry so much about choosing good hyperparameter values. We typically don't need to prune the random forest since the ensemble model is quite robust to noise from averaging the predictions among the individual decision trees. The only parameter that we need to care about in practice is the number of trees, k, (*step 3*) that we choose for the random forest. Typically, the larger the number of trees, the better the performance of the random forest classifier at the expense of an increased computational cost.

Although it is less common in practice, other hyperparameters of the random forest classifier that can be optimized—using techniques that we will discuss in *Chapter 6, Learning Best Practices for Model Evaluation and Hyperparameter Tuning*—are the size, n, of the bootstrap sample (*step 1*) and the number of features, d, that are randomly chosen for each split (*step 2a*), respectively. Via the sample size, n, of the bootstrap sample, we control the bias-variance tradeoff of the random forest.

Decreasing the size of the bootstrap sample increases the diversity among the individual trees since the probability that a particular training example is included in the bootstrap sample is lower. Thus, shrinking the size of the bootstrap samples may increase the *randomness* of the random forest, and it can help to reduce the effect of overfitting. However, smaller bootstrap samples typically result in a lower overall performance of the random forest and a small gap between training and test performance, but a low test performance overall. Conversely, increasing the size of the bootstrap sample may increase the degree of overfitting. Because the bootstrap samples, and consequently the individual decision trees, become more similar to one another, they learn to fit the original training dataset more closely.

In most implementations, including the `RandomForestClassifier` implementation in scikit-learn, the size of the bootstrap sample is chosen to be equal to the number of training examples in the original training dataset, which usually provides a good bias-variance tradeoff. For the number of features, d, at each split, we want to choose a value that is smaller than the total number of features in the training dataset. A reasonable default that is used in scikit-learn and other implementations is $d = \sqrt{m}$, where m is the number of features in the training dataset.

Conveniently, we don't have to construct the random forest classifier from individual decision trees by ourselves because there is already an implementation in scikit-learn that we can use:

```
>>> from sklearn.ensemble import RandomForestClassifier
>>> forest = RandomForestClassifier(n_estimators=25,
...                                 random_state=1,
...                                 n_jobs=2)
>>> forest.fit(X_train, y_train)
>>> plot_decision_regions(X_combined, y_combined,
...                       classifier=forest, test_idx=range(105,150))
>>> plt.xlabel('Petal length [cm]')
>>> plt.ylabel('Petal width [cm]')
>>> plt.legend(loc='upper left')
>>> plt.tight_layout()
>>> plt.show()
```

After executing the preceding code, we should see the decision regions formed by the ensemble of trees in the random forest, as shown in *Figure 3.24*:

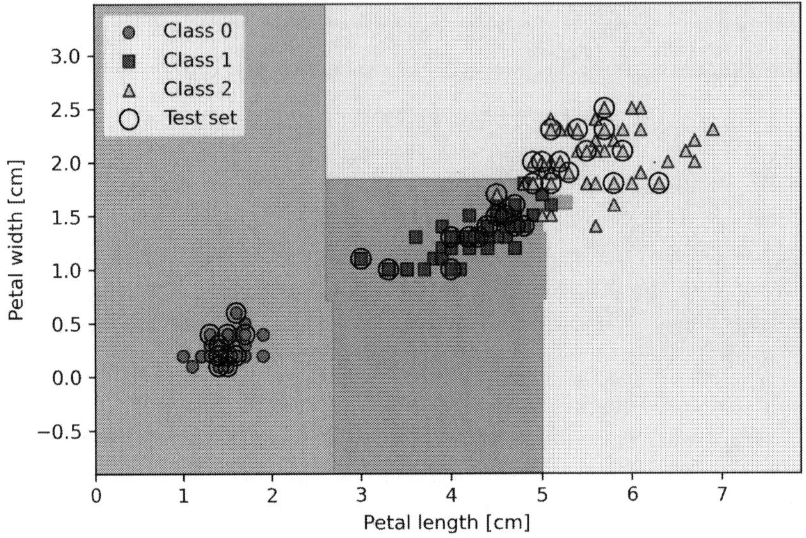

Figure 3.24: Decision boundaries on the Iris dataset using a random forest

Using the preceding code, we trained a random forest from 25 decision trees via the `n_estimators` parameter. By default, it uses the Gini impurity measure as a criterion to split the nodes. Although we are growing a very small random forest from a very small training dataset, we used the `n_jobs` parameter for demonstration purposes, which allows us to parallelize the model training using multiple cores of our computer (here, two cores). If you encounter errors with this code, your computer may not support multiprocessing. You can omit the `n_jobs` parameter or set it to `n_jobs=None`.

K-nearest neighbors – a lazy learning algorithm

The last supervised learning algorithm that we want to discuss in this chapter is the **k-nearest neighbor** (KNN) classifier, which is particularly interesting because it is fundamentally different from the learning algorithms that we have discussed so far.

KNN is a typical example of a **lazy learner**. It is called "lazy" not because of its apparent simplicity, but because it doesn't learn a discriminative function from the training data but memorizes the training dataset instead.

Parametric versus non-parametric models

Machine learning algorithms can be grouped into parametric and non-parametric models. Using parametric models, we estimate parameters from the training dataset to learn a function that can classify new data points without requiring the original training dataset anymore. Typical examples of parametric models are the perceptron, logistic regression, and the linear SVM. In contrast, non-parametric models can't be characterized by a fixed set of parameters, and the number of parameters changes with the amount of training data. Two examples of non-parametric models that we have seen so far are the decision tree classifier/random forest and the kernel (but not linear) SVM.

KNN belongs to a subcategory of non-parametric models described as instance-based learning. Models based on instance-based learning are characterized by memorizing the training dataset, and lazy learning is a special case of instance-based learning that is associated with no (zero) cost during the learning process.

The KNN algorithm itself is fairly straightforward and can be summarized by the following steps:

1. Choose the number of *k* and a distance metric
2. Find the *k*-nearest neighbors of the data record that we want to classify
3. Assign the class label by majority vote

Figure 3.25 illustrates how a new data point (?) is assigned the triangle class label based on majority voting among its five nearest neighbors:

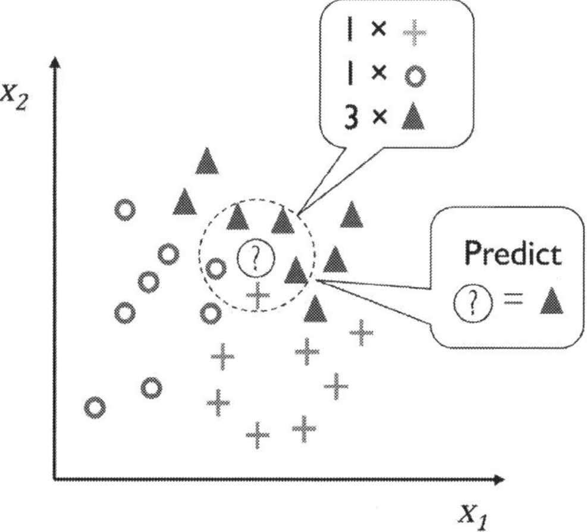

Figure 3.25: How k-nearest neighbors works

Based on the chosen distance metric, the KNN algorithm finds the *k* examples in the training dataset that are closest (most similar) to the point that we want to classify. The class label of the data point is then determined by a majority vote among its *k* nearest neighbors.

Advantages and disadvantages of memory-based approaches

The main advantage of such a memory-based approach is that the classifier immediately adapts as we collect new training data. However, the downside is that the computational complexity for classifying new examples grows linearly with the number of examples in the training dataset in the worst-case scenario—unless the dataset has very few dimensions (features) and the algorithm has been implemented using efficient data structures for querying the training data more effectively. Such data structures include k-d tree (`https://en.wikipedia.org/wiki/K-d_tree`) and ball tree (`https://en.wikipedia.org/wiki/Ball_tree`), which are both supported in scikit-learn. Furthermore, next to computational costs for querying data, large datasets can also be problematic in terms of limited storage capacities.

However, in many cases when we are working with relatively small to medium-sized datasets, memory-based methods can provide good predictive and computational performance and are thus a good choice for approaching many real-world problems. Recent examples of using nearest neighbor methods include predicting properties of pharmaceutical drug targets (*Machine Learning to Identify Flexibility Signatures of Class A GPCR Inhibition*, Biomolecules, 2020, Joe Bemister-Buffington, Alex J. Wolf, Sebastian Raschka, and Leslie A. Kuhn, `https://www.mdpi.com/2218-273X/10/3/454`) and state-of-the-art language models (*Efficient Nearest Neighbor Language Models*, 2021, Junxian He, Graham Neubig, and Taylor Berg-Kirkpatrick, `https://arxiv.org/abs/2109.04212`).

By executing the following code, we will now implement a KNN model in scikit-learn using a Euclidean distance metric:

```
>>> from sklearn.neighbors import KNeighborsClassifier
>>> knn = KNeighborsClassifier(n_neighbors=5, p=2,
...                            metric='minkowski')
>>> knn.fit(X_train_std, y_train)
>>> plot_decision_regions(X_combined_std, y_combined,
...                       classifier=knn, test_idx=range(105,150))
>>> plt.xlabel('Petal length [standardized]')
>>> plt.ylabel('Petal width [standardized]')
>>> plt.legend(loc='upper left')
>>> plt.tight_layout()
>>> plt.show()
```

By specifying five neighbors in the KNN model for this dataset, we obtain a relatively smooth decision boundary, as shown in *Figure 3.26*:

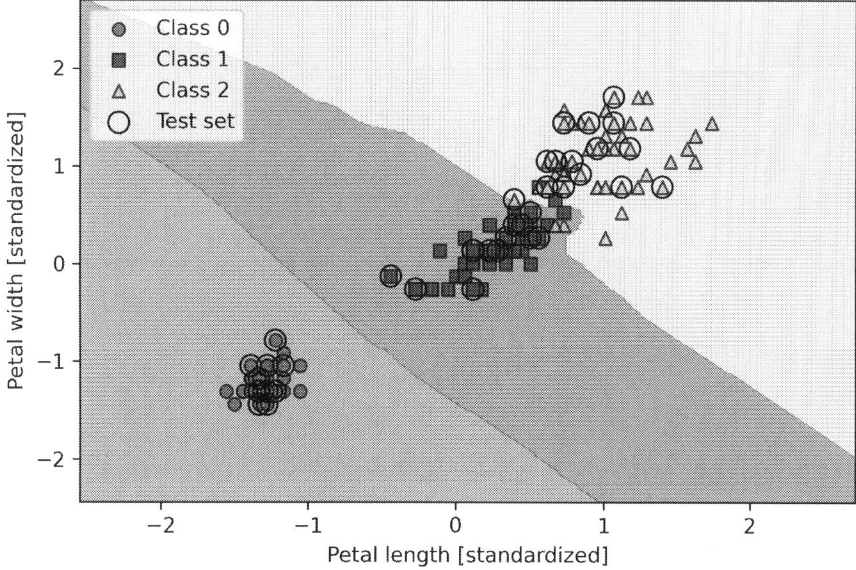

Figure 3.26: k-nearest neighbors' decision boundaries on the Iris dataset

Resolving ties

In the case of a tie, the scikit-learn implementation of the KNN algorithm will prefer the neighbors with a closer distance to the data record to be classified. If the neighbors have similar distances, the algorithm will choose the class label that comes first in the training dataset.

The *right* choice of *k* is crucial to finding a good balance between overfitting and underfitting. We also have to make sure that we choose a distance metric that is appropriate for the features in the dataset. Often, a simple Euclidean distance measure is used for real-value examples, for example, the flowers in our Iris dataset, which have features measured in centimeters. However, if we are using a Euclidean distance measure, it is also important to standardize the data so that each feature contributes equally to the distance. The `minkowski` distance that we used in the previous code is just a generalization of the Euclidean and Manhattan distance, which can be written as follows:

$$d\left(\boldsymbol{x}^{(i)}, \boldsymbol{x}^{(j)}\right) = \sqrt[p]{\sum_{k} \left|x_k^{(i)} - x_k^{(j)}\right|^p}$$

It becomes the Euclidean distance if we set the parameter `p=2` or the Manhattan distance at `p=1`. Many other distance metrics are available in scikit-learn and can be provided to the `metric` parameter. They are listed at `https://scikit-learn.org/stable/modules/generated/sklearn.metrics.DistanceMetric.html`.

Lastly, it is important to mention that KNN is very susceptible to overfitting due to the **curse of dimensionality**. The curse of dimensionality describes the phenomenon where the feature space becomes increasingly sparse for an increasing number of dimensions of a fixed-size training dataset. We can think of even the closest neighbors as being too far away in a high-dimensional space to give a good estimate.

We discussed the concept of regularization in the section about logistic regression as one way to avoid overfitting. However, in models where regularization is not applicable, such as decision trees and KNN, we can use feature selection and dimensionality reduction techniques to help us to avoid the curse of dimensionality. This will be discussed in more detail in the next two chapters.

Alternative machine learning implementations with GPU support

When working with large datasets, running k-nearest neighbors or fitting random forests with many estimators can require substantial computing resources and processing time. If you have a computer equipped with an NVIDIA GPU that is compatible with recent versions of NVIDIA's CUDA library, we recommend considering the RAPIDS ecosystem (`https://docs.rapids.ai/api`). For instance, RAPIDS' cuML (`https://docs.rapids.ai/api/cuml/stable/`) library implements many of scikit-learn's machine learning algorithms with GPU support to accelerate the processing speeds. You can find an introduction to cuML at `https://docs.rapids.ai/api/cuml/stable/estimator_intro.html`. If you are interested in learning more about the RAPIDS ecosystem, please also see the freely accessible journal article that we wrote in collaboration with the RAPIDS team: *Machine Learning in Python: Main Developments and Technology Trends in Data Science, Machine Learning, and Artificial Intelligence* (`https://www.mdpi.com/2078-2489/11/4/193`).

Summary

In this chapter, you learned about many different machine learning algorithms that are used to tackle linear and nonlinear problems. You have seen that decision trees are particularly attractive if we care about interpretability. Logistic regression is not only a useful model for online learning via SGD, but also allows us to predict the probability of a particular event.

Although SVMs are powerful linear models that can be extended to nonlinear problems via the kernel trick, they have many parameters that have to be tuned in order to make good predictions. In contrast, ensemble methods, such as random forests, don't require much parameter tuning and don't overfit as easily as decision trees, which makes them attractive models for many practical problem domains. The KNN classifier offers an alternative approach to classification via lazy learning that allows us to make predictions without any model training, but with a more computationally expensive prediction step.

However, even more important than the choice of an appropriate learning algorithm is the available data in our training dataset. No algorithm will be able to make good predictions without informative and discriminatory features.

In the next chapter, we will discuss important topics regarding the preprocessing of data, feature selection, and dimensionality reduction, which means that we will need to build powerful machine learning models. Later, in *Chapter 6, Learning Best Practices for Model Evaluation and Hyperparameter Tuning*, we will see how we can evaluate and compare the performance of our models and learn useful tricks to fine-tune the different algorithms.

Join our book's Discord space

Join our Discord community to meet like-minded people and learn alongside more than 2000 members at:

`https://packt.link/MLwPyTorch`

Building Good Training Datasets – Data Preprocessing

The quality of the data and the amount of useful information that it contains are key factors that determine how well a machine learning algorithm can learn. Therefore, it is absolutely critical to ensure that we examine and preprocess a dataset before we feed it to a machine learning algorithm. In this chapter, we will discuss the essential data preprocessing techniques that will help us to build good machine learning models.

The topics that we will cover in this chapter are as follows:

- Removing and imputing missing values from the dataset
- Getting categorical data into shape for machine learning algorithms
- Selecting relevant features for the model construction

Dealing with missing data

It is not uncommon in real-world applications for our training examples to be missing one or more values for various reasons. There could have been an error in the data collection process, certain measurements may not be applicable, or particular fields could have been simply left blank in a survey, for example. We typically see missing values as blank spaces in our data table or as placeholder strings such as `NaN`, which stands for "not a number," or `NULL` (a commonly used indicator of unknown values in relational databases). Unfortunately, most computational tools are unable to handle such missing values or will produce unpredictable results if we simply ignore them. Therefore, it is crucial that we take care of those missing values before we proceed with further analyses.

In this section, we will work through several practical techniques for dealing with missing values by removing entries from our dataset or imputing missing values from other training examples and features.

Identifying missing values in tabular data

Before we discuss several techniques for dealing with missing values, let's create a simple example `DataFrame` from a **comma-separated values (CSV)** file to get a better grasp of the problem:

```
>>> import pandas as pd
>>> from io import StringIO
>>> csv_data = \
... '''A,B,C,D
... 1.0,2.0,3.0,4.0
... 5.0,6.0,,8.0
... 10.0,11.0,12.0,'''
>>> # If you are using Python 2.7, you need
>>> # to convert the string to unicode:
>>> # csv_data = unicode(csv_data)
>>> df = pd.read_csv(StringIO(csv_data))
>>> df
        A       B       C       D
0     1.0     2.0     3.0     4.0
1     5.0     6.0     NaN     8.0
2    10.0    11.0    12.0     NaN
```

Using the preceding code, we read CSV-formatted data into a pandas `DataFrame` via the `read_csv` function and noticed that the two missing cells were replaced by `NaN`. The `StringIO` function in the preceding code example was simply used for the purposes of illustration. It allowed us to read the string assigned to `csv_data` into a pandas `DataFrame` as if it was a regular CSV file on our hard drive.

For a larger `DataFrame`, it can be tedious to look for missing values manually; in this case, we can use the `isnull` method to return a `DataFrame` with Boolean values that indicate whether a cell contains a numeric value (`False`) or if data is missing (`True`). Using the `sum` method, we can then return the number of missing values per column as follows:

```
>>> df.isnull().sum()
A      0
B      0
C      1
D      1
dtype: int64
```

This way, we can count the number of missing values per column; in the following subsections, we will take a look at different strategies for how to deal with this missing data.

Convenient data handling with pandas' DataFrame

Although scikit-learn was originally developed for working with NumPy arrays only, it can sometimes be more convenient to preprocess data using pandas' `DataFrame`. Nowadays, most scikit-learn functions support `DataFrame` objects as inputs, but since NumPy array handling is more mature in the scikit-learn API, it is recommended to use NumPy arrays when possible. Note that you can always access the underlying NumPy array of a `DataFrame` via the `values` attribute before you feed it into a scikit-learn estimator:

```
>>> df.values
array([[  1.,   2.,   3.,   4.],
       [  5.,   6.,  nan,   8.],
       [ 10.,  11.,  12.,  nan]])
```

Eliminating training examples or features with missing values

One of the easiest ways to deal with missing data is simply to remove the corresponding features (columns) or training examples (rows) from the dataset entirely; rows with missing values can easily be dropped via the `dropna` method:

```
>>> df.dropna(axis=0)
      A    B    C    D
0   1.0  2.0  3.0  4.0
```

Similarly, we can drop columns that have at least one `NaN` in any row by setting the `axis` argument to `1`:

```
>>> df.dropna(axis=1)
      A      B
0   1.0    2.0
1   5.0    6.0
2  10.0   11.0
```

The `dropna` method supports several additional parameters that can come in handy:

```
>>> # only drop rows where all columns are NaN
>>> # (returns the whole array here since we don't
>>> # have a row with all values NaN)
>>> df.dropna(how='all')
      A      B      C      D
0   1.0    2.0    3.0    4.0
1   5.0    6.0    NaN    8.0
2  10.0   11.0   12.0    NaN
```

```
>>> # drop rows that have fewer than 4 real values
>>> df.dropna(thresh=4)
     A     B     C     D
0   1.0   2.0   3.0   4.0
>>> # only drop rows where NaN appear in specific columns (here: 'C')
>>> df.dropna(subset=['C'])
     A     B     C     D
0   1.0   2.0   3.0   4.0
2  10.0  11.0  12.0   NaN
```

Although the removal of missing data seems to be a convenient approach, it also comes with certain disadvantages; for example, we may end up removing too many samples, which will make a reliable analysis impossible. Or, if we remove too many feature columns, we will run the risk of losing valuable information that our classifier needs to discriminate between classes. In the next section, we will look at one of the most commonly used alternatives for dealing with missing values: interpolation techniques.

Imputing missing values

Often, the removal of training examples or dropping of entire feature columns is simply not feasible, because we might lose too much valuable data. In this case, we can use different interpolation techniques to estimate the missing values from the other training examples in our dataset. One of the most common interpolation techniques is **mean imputation**, where we simply replace the missing value with the mean value of the entire feature column. A convenient way to achieve this is by using the `SimpleImputer` class from scikit-learn, as shown in the following code:

```
>>> from sklearn.impute import SimpleImputer
>>> import numpy as np
>>> imr = SimpleImputer(missing_values=np.nan, strategy='mean')
>>> imr = imr.fit(df.values)
>>> imputed_data = imr.transform(df.values)
>>> imputed_data
array([[  1.,   2.,   3.,   4.],
       [  5.,   6.,  7.5,   8.],
       [ 10.,  11.,  12.,   6.]])
```

Here, we replaced each `NaN` value with the corresponding mean, which is separately calculated for each feature column. Other options for the `strategy` parameter are `median` or `most_frequent`, where the latter replaces the missing values with the most frequent values. This is useful for imputing categorical feature values, for example, a feature column that stores an encoding of color names, such as red, green, and blue. We will encounter examples of such data later in this chapter.

Alternatively, an even more convenient way to impute missing values is by using pandas' `fillna` method and providing an imputation method as an argument. For example, using pandas, we could achieve the same mean imputation directly in the `DataFrame` object via the following command:

```
>>> df.fillna(df.mean())
```

	A	B	C	D
0	1.0	2.0	3.0	4.0
1	5.0	6.0	7.5	8.0
2	10.0	11.0	12.0	6.0

Figure 4.1: Replacing missing values in data with the mean

Additional imputation methods for missing data

For additional imputation techniques, including the `KNNImputer` based on a k-nearest neighbors approach to impute missing features by nearest neighbors, we recommend the scikit-learn imputation documentation at `https://scikit-learn.org/stable/modules/impute.html`.

Understanding the scikit-learn estimator API

In the previous section, we used the `SimpleImputer` class from scikit-learn to impute missing values in our dataset. The `SimpleImputer` class is part of the so-called **transformer** API in scikit-learn, which is used for implementing Python classes related to data transformation. (Please note that the scikit-learn transformer API is not to be confused with the transformer architecture that is used in natural language processing, which we will cover in more detail in *Chapter 16*, *Transformers – Improving Natural Language Processing with Attention Mechanisms*.) The two essential methods of those estimators are `fit` and `transform`. The `fit` method is used to learn the parameters from the training data, and the `transform` method uses those parameters to transform the data. Any data array that is to be transformed needs to have the same number of features as the data array that was used to fit the model.

Figure 4.2 illustrates how a scikit-learn transformer instance, fitted on the training data, is used to transform a training dataset as well as a new test dataset:

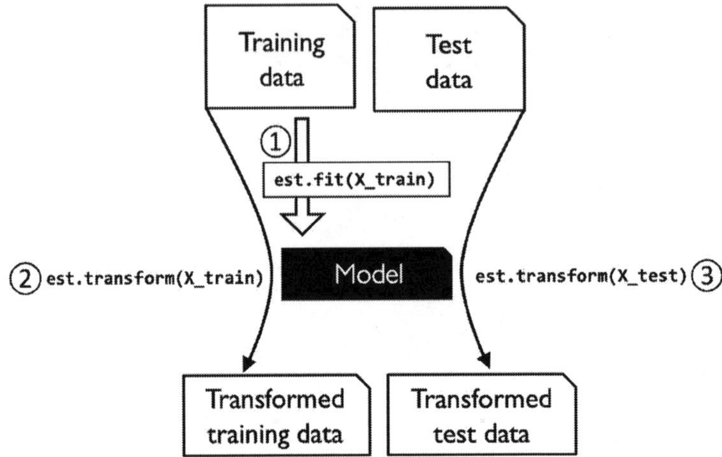

Figure 4.2: Using the scikit-learn API for data transformation

The classifiers that we used in *Chapter 3, A Tour of Machine Learning Classifiers Using Scikit-Learn*, belong to the so-called **estimators** in scikit-learn, with an API that is conceptually very similar to the scikit-learn transformer API. Estimators have a `predict` method but can also have a `transform` method, as you will see later in this chapter. As you may recall, we also used the `fit` method to learn the parameters of a model when we trained those estimators for classification. However, in supervised learning tasks, we additionally provide the class labels for fitting the model, which can then be used to make predictions about new, unlabeled data examples via the `predict` method, as illustrated in *Figure 4.3*:

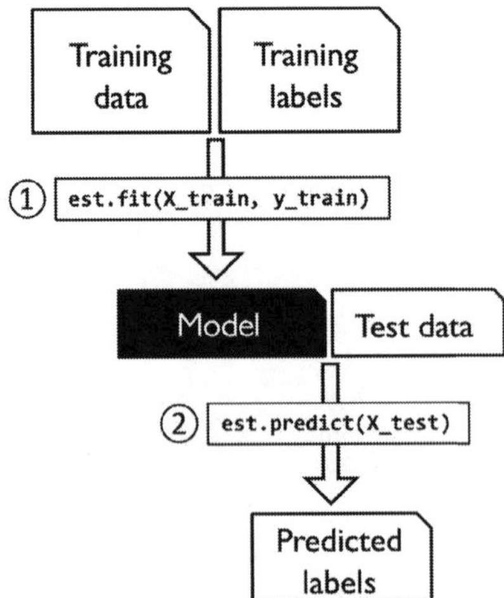

Figure 4.3: Using the scikit-learn API for predictive models such as classifiers

Handling categorical data

So far, we have only been working with numerical values. However, it is not uncommon for real-world datasets to contain one or more categorical feature columns. In this section, we will make use of simple yet effective examples to see how to deal with this type of data in numerical computing libraries.

When we are talking about categorical data, we have to further distinguish between **ordinal** and **nominal** features. Ordinal features can be understood as categorical values that can be sorted or ordered. For example, t-shirt size would be an ordinal feature, because we can define an order: $XL > L > M$. In contrast, nominal features don't imply any order; to continue with the previous example, we could think of t-shirt color as a nominal feature since it typically doesn't make sense to say that, for example, red is larger than blue.

Categorical data encoding with pandas

Before we explore different techniques for handling such categorical data, let's create a new `DataFrame` to illustrate the problem:

```
>>> import pandas as pd
>>> df = pd.DataFrame([
...             ['green', 'M', 10.1, 'class2'],
...             ['red', 'L', 13.5, 'class1'],
...             ['blue', 'XL', 15.3, 'class2']])
>>> df.columns = ['color', 'size', 'price', 'classlabel']
>>> df
    color  size  price  classlabel
0   green     M   10.1      class2
1     red     L   13.5      class1
2    blue    XL   15.3      class2
```

As we can see in the preceding output, the newly created `DataFrame` contains a nominal feature (`color`), an ordinal feature (`size`), and a numerical feature (`price`) column. The class labels (assuming that we created a dataset for a supervised learning task) are stored in the last column. The learning algorithms for classification that we discuss in this book do not use ordinal information in class labels.

Mapping ordinal features

To make sure that the learning algorithm interprets the ordinal features correctly, we need to convert the categorical string values into integers. Unfortunately, there is no convenient function that can automatically derive the correct order of the labels of our `size` feature, so we have to define the mapping manually. In the following simple example, let's assume that we know the numerical difference between features, for example, $XL = L + 1 = M + 2$:

```
>>> size_mapping = {'XL': 3,
...                 'L': 2,
...                 'M': 1}
```

```
>>> df['size'] = df['size'].map(size_mapping)
>>> df
   color  size  price  classlabel
0  green     1   10.1      class2
1    red     2   13.5      class1
2   blue     3   15.3      class2
```

If we want to transform the integer values back to the original string representation at a later stage, we can simply define a reverse-mapping dictionary, `inv_size_mapping = {v: k for k, v in size_mapping.items()}`, which can then be used via the pandas `map` method on the transformed feature column and is similar to the `size_mapping` dictionary that we used previously. We can use it as follows:

```
>>> inv_size_mapping = {v: k for k, v in size_mapping.items()}
>>> df['size'].map(inv_size_mapping)
0   M
1   L
2   XL
Name: size, dtype: object
```

Encoding class labels

Many machine learning libraries require that class labels are encoded as integer values. Although most estimators for classification in scikit-learn convert class labels to integers internally, it is considered good practice to provide class labels as integer arrays to avoid technical glitches. To encode the class labels, we can use an approach similar to the mapping of ordinal features discussed previously. We need to remember that class labels are *not* ordinal, and it doesn't matter which integer number we assign to a particular string label. Thus, we can simply enumerate the class labels, starting at `0`:

```
>>> import numpy as np
>>> class_mapping = {label: idx for idx, label in
...                  enumerate(np.unique(df['classlabel']))}
>>> class_mapping
{'class1': 0, 'class2': 1}
```

Next, we can use the mapping dictionary to transform the class labels into integers:

```
>>> df['classlabel'] = df['classlabel'].map(class_mapping)
>>> df
   color  size  price  classlabel
0  green     1   10.1           1
1    red     2   13.5           0
2   blue     3   15.3           1
```

We can reverse the key-value pairs in the mapping dictionary as follows to map the converted class labels back to the original string representation:

```
>>> inv_class_mapping = {v: k for k, v in class_mapping.items()}
>>> df['classlabel'] = df['classlabel'].map(inv_class_mapping)
>>> df
   color  size  price  classlabel
0  green     1   10.1      class2
1    red     2   13.5      class1
2   blue     3   15.3      class2
```

Alternatively, there is a convenient `LabelEncoder` class directly implemented in scikit-learn to achieve this:

```
>>> from sklearn.preprocessing import LabelEncoder
>>> class_le = LabelEncoder()
>>> y = class_le.fit_transform(df['classlabel'].values)
>>> y
array([1, 0, 1])
```

Note that the `fit_transform` method is just a shortcut for calling `fit` and `transform` separately, and we can use the `inverse_transform` method to transform the integer class labels back into their original string representation:

```
>>> class_le.inverse_transform(y)
array(['class2', 'class1', 'class2'], dtype=object)
```

Performing one-hot encoding on nominal features

In the previous *Mapping ordinal features* section, we used a simple dictionary mapping approach to convert the ordinal `size` feature into integers. Since scikit-learn's estimators for classification treat class labels as categorical data that does not imply any order (nominal), we used the convenient `LabelEncoder` to encode the string labels into integers. We could use a similar approach to transform the nominal `color` column of our dataset, as follows:

```
>>> X = df[['color', 'size', 'price']].values
>>> color_le = LabelEncoder()
>>> X[:, 0] = color_le.fit_transform(X[:, 0])
>>> X
array([[1, 1, 10.1],
       [2, 2, 13.5],
       [0, 3, 15.3]], dtype=object)
```

After executing the preceding code, the first column of the NumPy array, `X`, now holds the new `color` values, which are encoded as follows:

- `blue = 0`
- `green = 1`
- `red = 2`

If we stop at this point and feed the array to our classifier, we will make one of the most common mistakes in dealing with categorical data. Can you spot the problem? Although the color values don't come in any particular order, common classification models, such as the ones covered in the previous chapters, will now assume that `green` is larger than `blue`, and `red` is larger than `green`. Although this assumption is incorrect, a classifier could still produce useful results. However, those results would not be optimal.

A common workaround for this problem is to use a technique called **one-hot encoding**. The idea behind this approach is to create a new dummy feature for each unique value in the nominal feature column. Here, we would convert the `color` feature into three new features: `blue`, `green`, and `red`. Binary values can then be used to indicate the particular `color` of an example; for example, a `blue` example can be encoded as `blue=1`, `green=0`, `red=0`. To perform this transformation, we can use the `OneHotEncoder` that is implemented in scikit-learn's `preprocessing` module:

```
>>> from sklearn.preprocessing import OneHotEncoder
>>> X = df[['color', 'size', 'price']].values
>>> color_ohe = OneHotEncoder()
>>> color_ohe.fit_transform(X[:, 0].reshape(-1, 1)).toarray()
    array([[0., 1., 0.],
           [0., 0., 1.],
           [1., 0., 0.]])
```

Note that we applied the `OneHotEncoder` to only a single column, `(X[:, 0].reshape(-1, 1))`, to avoid modifying the other two columns in the array as well. If we want to selectively transform columns in a multi-feature array, we can use the `ColumnTransformer`, which accepts a list of `(name, transformer, column(s))` tuples as follows:

```
>>> from sklearn.compose import ColumnTransformer
>>> X = df[['color', 'size', 'price']].values
>>> c_transf = ColumnTransformer([
...     ('onehot', OneHotEncoder(), [0]),
...     ('nothing', 'passthrough', [1, 2])
... ])
>>> c_transf.fit_transform(X).astype(float)
    array([[0.0, 1.0, 0.0, 1, 10.1],
           [0.0, 0.0, 1.0, 2, 13.5],
           [1.0, 0.0, 0.0, 3, 15.3]])
```

In the preceding code example, we specified that we want to modify only the first column and leave the other two columns untouched via the `'passthrough'` argument.

An even more convenient way to create those dummy features via one-hot encoding is to use the `get_dummies` method implemented in pandas. Applied to a `DataFrame`, the `get_dummies` method will only convert string columns and leave all other columns unchanged:

```
>>> pd.get_dummies(df[['price', 'color', 'size']])
    price  size  color_blue  color_green  color_red
0    10.1     1           0            1          0
1    13.5     2           0            0          1
2    15.3     3           1            0          0
```

When we are using one-hot encoding datasets, we have to keep in mind that this introduces multicollinearity, which can be an issue for certain methods (for instance, methods that require matrix inversion). If features are highly correlated, matrices are computationally difficult to invert, which can lead to numerically unstable estimates. To reduce the correlation among variables, we can simply remove one feature column from the one-hot encoded array. Note that we do not lose any important information by removing a feature column, though; for example, if we remove the column `color_blue`, the feature information is still preserved since if we observe `color_green=0` and `color_red=0`, it implies that the observation must be `blue`.

If we use the `get_dummies` function, we can drop the first column by passing a `True` argument to the `drop_first` parameter, as shown in the following code example:

```
>>> pd.get_dummies(df[['price', 'color', 'size']],
...                drop_first=True)
    price  size  color_green  color_red
0    10.1     1            1          0
1    13.5     2            0          1
2    15.3     3            0          0
```

In order to drop a redundant column via the `OneHotEncoder`, we need to set `drop='first'` and set `categories='auto'` as follows:

```
>>> color_ohe = OneHotEncoder(categories='auto', drop='first')
>>> c_transf = ColumnTransformer([
...            ('onehot', color_ohe, [0]),
...            ('nothing', 'passthrough', [1, 2])
... ])
>>> c_transf.fit_transform(X).astype(float)
array([[  1. ,  0. ,  1. ,  10.1],
       [  0. ,  1. ,  2. ,  13.5],
       [  0. ,  0. ,  3. ,  15.3]])
```

Additional encoding schemes for nominal data

While one-hot encoding is the most common way to encode unordered categorical variables, several alternative methods exist. Some of these techniques can be useful when working with categorical features that have high cardinality (a large number of unique category labels). Examples include:

- Binary encoding, which produces multiple binary features similar to one-hot encoding but requires fewer feature columns, i.e., $\log_2(K)$ instead of $K - 1$, where K is the number of unique categories. In binary encoding, numbers are first converted into binary representations, and then each binary number position will form a new feature column.
- Count or frequency encoding, which replaces the label of each category by the number of times or frequency it occurs in the training set.

These methods, as well as additional categorical encoding schemes, are available via the scikit-learn-compatible `category_encoders` library: `https://contrib.scikit-learn.org/category_encoders/`.

While these methods are not guaranteed to perform better than one-hot encoding in terms of model performance, we can consider the choice of a categorical encoding scheme as an additional "hyperparameter" for improving model performance.

Optional: encoding ordinal features

If we are unsure about the numerical differences between the categories of ordinal features, or the difference between two ordinal values is not defined, we can also encode them using a threshold encoding with 0/1 values. For example, we can split the feature `size` with values `M`, `L`, and `XL` into two new features, `x > M` and `x > L`. Let's consider the original `DataFrame`:

```
>>> df = pd.DataFrame([['green', 'M', 10.1,
...                     'class2'],
...                    ['red', 'L', 13.5,
...                     'class1'],
...                    ['blue', 'XL', 15.3,
...                     'class2']])
>>> df.columns = ['color', 'size', 'price',
...               'classlabel']
>>> df
```

We can use the `apply` method of pandas' `DataFrame` to write custom lambda expressions in order to encode these variables using the value-threshold approach:

```
>>> df['x > M'] = df['size'].apply(
...     lambda x: 1 if x in {'L', 'XL'} else 0)
>>> df['x > L'] = df['size'].apply(
...     lambda x: 1 if x == 'XL' else 0)
```

```
>>> del df['size']
>>> df
```

Partitioning a dataset into separate training and test datasets

We briefly introduced the concept of partitioning a dataset into separate datasets for training and testing in *Chapter 1, Giving Computers the Ability to Learn from Data*, and *Chapter 3, A Tour of Machine Learning Classifiers Using Scikit-Learn*. Remember that comparing predictions to true labels in the test set can be understood as the unbiased performance evaluation of our model before we let it loose in the real world. In this section, we will prepare a new dataset, the **Wine** dataset. After we have preprocessed the dataset, we will explore different techniques for feature selection to reduce the dimensionality of a dataset.

The Wine dataset is another open-source dataset that is available from the UCI machine learning repository (`https://archive.ics.uci.edu/ml/datasets/Wine`); it consists of 178 wine examples with 13 features describing their different chemical properties.

Obtaining the Wine dataset

You can find a copy of the Wine dataset (and all other datasets used in this book) in the code bundle of this book, which you can use if you are working offline or the dataset at `https://archive.ics.uci.edu/ml/machine-learning-databases/wine/wine.data` is temporarily unavailable on the UCI server. For instance, to load the Wine dataset from a local directory, you can replace this line:

```
df = pd.read_csv(
    'https://archive.ics.uci.edu/ml/'
    'machine-learning-databases/wine/wine.data',
    header=None
)
```

with the following one:

```
df = pd.read_csv(
    'your/local/path/to/wine.data', header=None
)
```

Using the pandas library, we will directly read in the open-source Wine dataset from the UCI machine learning repository:

```
>>> df_wine = pd.read_csv('https://archive.ics.uci.edu/'
...                       'ml/machine-learning-databases/'
...                       'wine/wine.data', header=None)
```

```
>>> df_wine.columns = ['Class label', 'Alcohol',
...                    'Malic acid', 'Ash',
...                    'Alcalinity of ash', 'Magnesium',
...                    'Total phenols', 'Flavanoids',
...                    'Nonflavanoid phenols',
...                    'Proanthocyanins',
...                    'Color intensity', 'Hue',
...                    'OD280/OD315 of diluted wines',
...                    'Proline']
>>> print('Class labels', np.unique(df_wine['Class label']))
Class labels [1 2 3]
>>> df_wine.head()
```

The 13 different features in the Wine dataset, describing the chemical properties of the 178 wine examples, are listed in the following table:

	Class label	Alcohol	Malic acid	Ash	Alcalinity of ash	Magnesium	Total phenols	Flavanoids	Nonflavanoid phenols	Proanthocyanins	Color intensity	Hue	OD280/OD315 of diluted wines	Proline
0	1	14.23	1.71	2.43	15.6	127	2.80	3.06	0.28	2.29	5.64	1.04	3.92	1065
1	1	13.20	1.78	2.14	11.2	100	2.65	2.76	0.26	1.28	4.38	1.05	3.40	1050
2	1	13.16	2.36	2.67	18.6	101	2.80	3.24	0.30	2.81	5.68	1.03	3.17	1185
3	1	14.37	1.95	2.50	16.8	113	3.85	3.49	0.24	2.18	7.80	0.86	3.45	1480
4	1	13.24	2.59	2.87	21.0	118	2.80	2.69	0.39	1.82	4.32	1.04	2.93	735

Figure 4.4: A sample of the Wine dataset

The examples belong to one of three different classes, `1`, `2`, and `3`, which refer to the three different types of grape grown in the same region in Italy but derived from different wine cultivars, as described in the dataset summary (`https://archive.ics.uci.edu/ml/machine-learning-databases/wine/wine.names`).

A convenient way to randomly partition this dataset into separate test and training datasets is to use the `train_test_split` function from scikit-learn's `model_selection` submodule:

```
>>> from sklearn.model_selection import train_test_split
>>> X, y = df_wine.iloc[:, 1:].values, df_wine.iloc[:, 0].values
>>> X_train, X_test, y_train, y_test =\
...     train_test_split(X, y,
...                      test_size=0.3,
...                      random_state=0,
...                      stratify=y)
```

First, we assigned the NumPy array representation of the feature columns 1-13 to the variable `X` and we assigned the class labels from the first column to the variable `y`. Then, we used the `train_test_split` function to randomly split `X` and `y` into separate training and test datasets.

By setting `test_size=0.3`, we assigned 30 percent of the wine examples to `X_test` and `y_test`, and the remaining 70 percent of the examples were assigned to `X_train` and `y_train`, respectively. Providing the class label array `y` as an argument to `stratify` ensures that both training and test datasets have the same class proportions as the original dataset.

Choosing an appropriate ratio for partitioning a dataset into training and test datasets

If we are dividing a dataset into training and test datasets, we have to keep in mind that we are withholding valuable information that the learning algorithm could benefit from. Thus, we don't want to allocate too much information to the test set. However, the smaller the test set, the more inaccurate the estimation of the generalization error. Dividing a dataset into training and test datasets is all about balancing this tradeoff. In practice, the most commonly used splits are 60:40, 70:30, or 80:20, depending on the size of the initial dataset. However, for large datasets, 90:10 or 99:1 splits are also common and appropriate. For example, if the dataset contains more than 100,000 training examples, it might be fine to withhold only 10,000 examples for testing in order to get a good estimate of the generalization performance. More information and illustrations can be found in section one of my article *Model evaluation, model selection, and algorithm selection in machine learning*, which is freely available at `https://arxiv.org/pdf/1811.12808.pdf`. Also, we will revisit the topic of model evaluation and discuss it in more detail in *Chapter 6, Learning Best Practices for Model Evaluation and Hyperparameter Tuning*.

Moreover, instead of discarding the allocated test data after model training and evaluation, it is a common practice to retrain a classifier on the entire dataset, as it can improve the predictive performance of the model. While this approach is generally recommended, it could lead to worse generalization performance if the dataset is small and the test dataset contains outliers, for example. Also, after refitting the model on the whole dataset, we don't have any independent data left to evaluate its performance.

Bringing features onto the same scale

Feature scaling is a crucial step in our preprocessing pipeline that can easily be forgotten. **Decision trees** and **random forests** are two of the very few machine learning algorithms where we don't need to worry about feature scaling. Those algorithms are scale-invariant. However, the majority of machine learning and optimization algorithms behave much better if features are on the same scale, as we saw in *Chapter 2, Training Simple Machine Learning Algorithms for Classification*, when we implemented the **gradient descent optimization** algorithm.

The importance of feature scaling can be illustrated by a simple example. Let's assume that we have two features where one feature is measured on a scale from 1 to 10 and the second feature is measured on a scale from 1 to 100,000, respectively.

When we think of the squared error function in Adaline from *Chapter 2*, it makes sense to say that the algorithm will mostly be busy optimizing the weights according to the larger errors in the second feature. Another example is the **k-nearest neighbors** (**KNN**) algorithm with a Euclidean distance measure: the computed distances between examples will be dominated by the second feature axis.

Now, there are two common approaches to bringing different features onto the same scale: **normalization** and **standardization.** Those terms are often used quite loosely in different fields, and the meaning has to be derived from the context. Most often, normalization refers to the rescaling of the features to a range of [0, 1], which is a special case of **min-max scaling.** To normalize our data, we can simply apply the min-max scaling to each feature column, where the new value, $x_{norm}^{(i)}$, of an example, $x^{(i)}$, can be calculated as follows:

$$x_{norm}^{(i)} = \frac{x^{(i)} - x_{min}}{x_{max} - x_{min}}$$

Here, $x^{(i)}$ is a particular example, x_{min} is the smallest value in a feature column, and x_{max} is the largest value.

The min-max scaling procedure is implemented in scikit-learn and can be used as follows:

```
>>> from sklearn.preprocessing import MinMaxScaler
>>> mms = MinMaxScaler()
>>> X_train_norm = mms.fit_transform(X_train)
>>> X_test_norm = mms.transform(X_test)
```

Although normalization via min-max scaling is a commonly used technique that is useful when we need values in a bounded interval, standardization can be more practical for many machine learning algorithms, especially for optimization algorithms such as gradient descent. The reason is that many linear models, such as the logistic regression and SVM from *Chapter 3*, initialize the weights to 0 or small random values close to 0. Using standardization, we center the feature columns at mean 0 with standard deviation 1 so that the feature columns have the same parameters as a standard normal distribution (zero mean and unit variance), which makes it easier to learn the weights. However, we shall emphasize that standardization does not change the shape of the distribution, and it does not transform non-normally distributed data into normally distributed data. In addition to scaling data such that it has zero mean and unit variance, standardization maintains useful information about outliers and makes the algorithm less sensitive to them in contrast to min-max scaling, which scales the data to a limited range of values.

The procedure for standardization can be expressed by the following equation:

$$x_{std}^{(i)} = \frac{x^{(i)} - \mu_x}{\sigma_x}$$

Here, μ_x is the sample mean of a particular feature column, and σ_x is the corresponding standard deviation.

The following table illustrates the difference between the two commonly used feature scaling techniques, standardization and normalization, on a simple example dataset consisting of numbers 0 to 5:

Input	Standardized	Min-max normalized
0.0	-1.46385	0.0
1.0	-0.87831	0.2
2.0	-0.29277	0.4
3.0	0.29277	0.6
4.0	0.87831	0.8
5.0	1.46385	1.0

Table 4.1: A comparison between standardization and min-max normalization

You can perform the standardization and normalization shown in the table manually by executing the following code examples:

```
>>> ex = np.array([0, 1, 2, 3, 4, 5])
>>> print('standardized:', (ex - ex.mean()) / ex.std())
standardized: [-1.46385011  -0.87831007  -0.29277002  0.29277002
0.87831007  1.46385011]
>>> print('normalized:', (ex - ex.min()) / (ex.max() - ex.min()))
normalized: [ 0.  0.2  0.4  0.6  0.8  1. ]
```

Similar to the `MinMaxScaler` class, scikit-learn also implements a class for standardization:

```
>>> from sklearn.preprocessing import StandardScaler
>>> stdsc = StandardScaler()
>>> X_train_std = stdsc.fit_transform(X_train)
>>> X_test_std = stdsc.transform(X_test)
```

Again, it is also important to highlight that we fit the `StandardScaler` class only once—on the training data—and use those parameters to transform the test dataset or any new data point.

Other, more advanced methods for feature scaling are available from scikit-learn, such as `RobustScaler`. `RobustScaler` is especially helpful and recommended if we are working with small datasets that contain many outliers. Similarly, if the machine learning algorithm applied to this dataset is prone to **overfitting**, `RobustScaler` can be a good choice. Operating on each feature column independently, `RobustScaler` removes the median value and scales the dataset according to the 1st and 3rd quartile of the dataset (that is, the 25th and 75th quantile, respectively) such that more extreme values and outliers become less pronounced. The interested reader can find more information about `RobustScaler` in the official scikit-learn documentation at `https://scikit-learn.org/stable/modules/generated/sklearn.preprocessing.RobustScaler.html`.

Selecting meaningful features

If we notice that a model performs much better on a training dataset than on the test dataset, this observation is a strong indicator of overfitting. As we discussed in *Chapter 3, A Tour of Machine Learning Classifiers Using Scikit-Learn*, overfitting means the model fits the parameters too closely with regard to the particular observations in the training dataset but does not generalize well to new data; we say that the model has a **high variance**. The reason for the overfitting is that our model is too complex for the given training data. Common solutions to reduce the generalization error are as follows:

- Collect more training data
- Introduce a penalty for complexity via regularization
- Choose a simpler model with fewer parameters
- Reduce the dimensionality of the data

Collecting more training data is often not applicable. In *Chapter 6, Learning Best Practices for Model Evaluation and Hyperparameter Tuning*, we will learn about a useful technique to check whether more training data is helpful. In the following sections, we will look at common ways to reduce overfitting by regularization and dimensionality reduction via feature selection, which leads to simpler models by requiring fewer parameters to be fitted to the data. Then, in *Chapter 5, Compressing Data via Dimensionality Reduction*, we will take a look at additional feature extraction techniques.

L1 and L2 regularization as penalties against model complexity

You will recall from *Chapter 3* that **L2 regularization** is one approach to reduce the complexity of a model by penalizing large individual weights. We defined the squared L2 norm of our weight vector, $\boldsymbol{w}$, as follows:

$$L2: \quad \|\boldsymbol{w}\|_2^2 = \sum_{j=1}^{m} w_j^2$$

Another approach to reduce the model complexity is the related **L1 regularization**:

$$L1: \quad \|\boldsymbol{w}\|_1 = \sum_{j=1}^{m} |w_j|$$

Here, we simply replaced the square of the weights with the sum of the absolute values of the weights. In contrast to L2 regularization, L1 regularization usually yields sparse feature vectors, and most feature weights will be zero. Sparsity can be useful in practice if we have a high-dimensional dataset with many features that are irrelevant, especially in cases where we have more irrelevant dimensions than training examples. In this sense, L1 regularization can be understood as a technique for feature selection.

A geometric interpretation of L2 regularization

As mentioned in the previous section, L2 regularization adds a penalty term to the loss function that effectively results in less extreme weight values compared to a model trained with an unregularized loss function.

To better understand how L1 regularization encourages sparsity, let's take a step back and take a look at a geometric interpretation of regularization. Let's plot the contours of a convex loss function for two weight coefficients, w_1 and w_2.

Here, we will consider the **mean squared error** (**MSE**) loss function that we used for Adaline in *Chapter 2*, which computes the squared distances between the true and predicted class labels, y and $\hat{y}$, averaged over all N examples in the training set. Since the MSE is spherical, it is easier to draw than the loss function of logistic regression; however, the same concepts apply. Remember that our goal is to find the combination of weight coefficients that minimize the loss function for the training data, as shown in *Figure 4.5* (the point in the center of the ellipses):

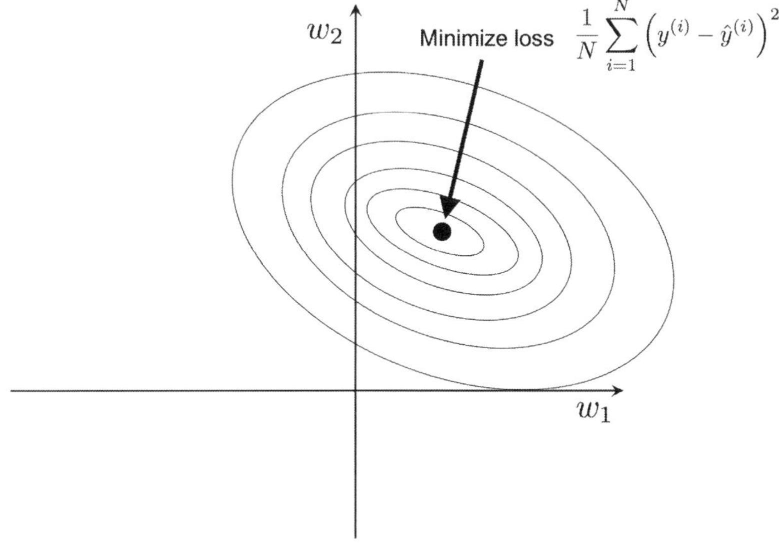

Figure 4.5: Minimizing the mean squared error loss function

We can think of regularization as adding a penalty term to the loss function to encourage smaller weights; in other words, we penalize large weights. Thus, by increasing the regularization strength via the regularization parameter, λ, we shrink the weights toward zero and decrease the dependence of our model on the training data. Let's illustrate this concept in the following figure for the L2 penalty term:

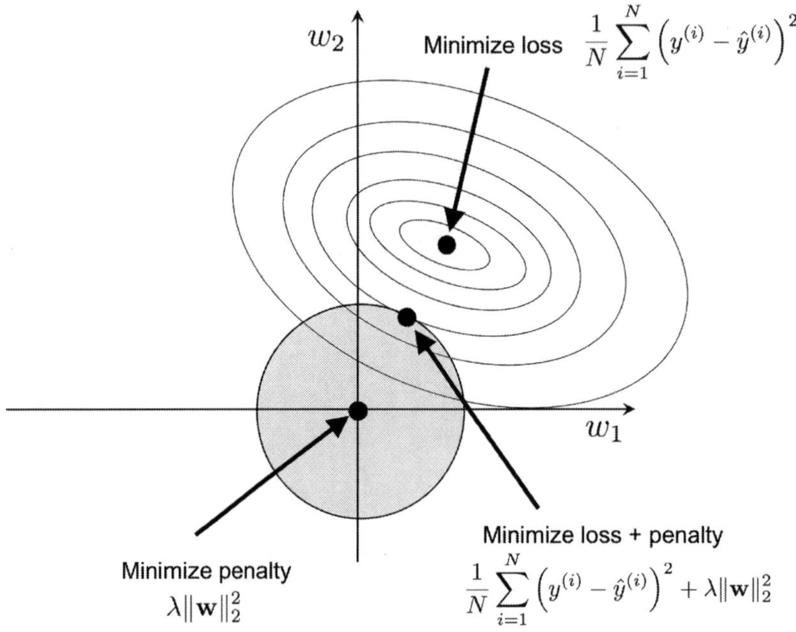

Figure 4.6: Applying L2 regularization to the loss function

The quadratic L2 regularization term is represented by the shaded ball. Here, our weight coefficients cannot exceed our regularization budget—the combination of the weight coefficients cannot fall outside the shaded area. On the other hand, we still want to minimize the loss function. Under the penalty constraint, our best effort is to choose the point where the L2 ball intersects with the contours of the unpenalized loss function. The larger the value of the regularization parameter, λ, gets, the faster the penalized loss grows, which leads to a narrower L2 ball. For example, if we increase the regularization parameter toward infinity, the weight coefficients will become effectively zero, denoted by the center of the L2 ball. To summarize the main message of the example, our goal is to minimize the sum of the unpenalized loss plus the penalty term, which can be understood as adding bias and preferring a simpler model to reduce the variance in the absence of sufficient training data to fit the model.

Sparse solutions with L1 regularization

Now, let's discuss L1 regularization and sparsity. The main concept behind L1 regularization is similar to what we discussed in the previous section. However, since the L1 penalty is the sum of the absolute weight coefficients (remember that the L2 term is quadratic), we can represent it as a diamond-shape budget, as shown in *Figure 4.7*:

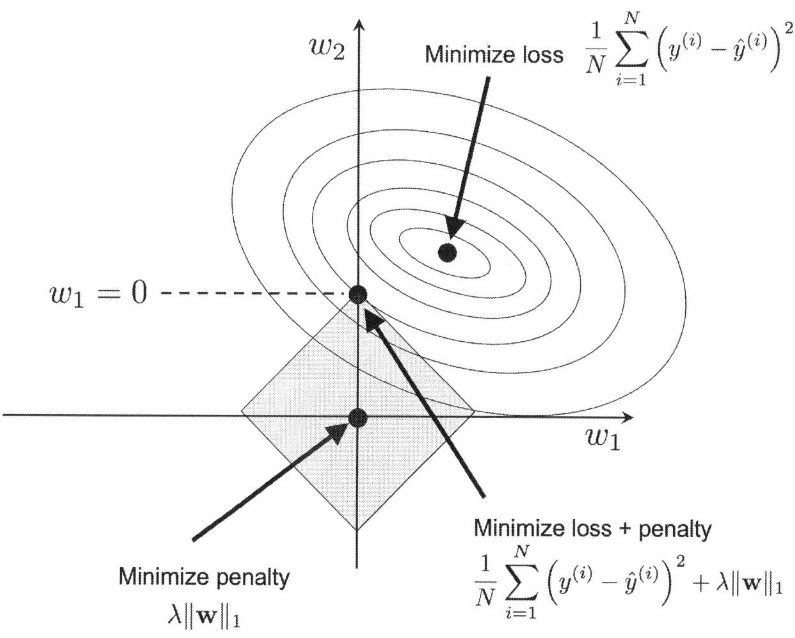

Figure 4.7: Applying L1 regularization to the loss function

In the preceding figure, we can see that the contour of the loss function touches the L1 diamond at $w_1 = 0$. Since the contours of an L1 regularized system are sharp, it is more likely that the optimum—that is, the intersection between the ellipses of the loss function and the boundary of the L1 diamond—is located on the axes, which encourages sparsity.

L1 regularization and sparsity

The mathematical details of why L1 regularization can lead to sparse solutions are beyond the scope of this book. If you are interested, an excellent explanation of L2 versus L1 regularization can be found in *Section 3.4*, *The Elements of Statistical Learning* by *Trevor Hastie, Robert Tibshirani*, and *Jerome Friedman, Springer Science+Business Media*, 2009.

For regularized models in scikit-learn that support L1 regularization, we can simply set the `penalty` parameter to `'l1'` to obtain a sparse solution:

```
>>> from sklearn.linear_model import LogisticRegression
>>> LogisticRegression(penalty='l1',
...                    solver='liblinear',
...                    multi_class='ovr')
```

Note that we also need to select a different optimization algorithm (for example, `solver='liblinear'`), since `'lbfgs'` currently does not support L1-regularized loss optimization. Applied to the standardized Wine data, the L1 regularized logistic regression would yield the following sparse solution:

```
>>> lr = LogisticRegression(penalty='l1',
...                         C=1.0,
...                         solver='liblinear',
...                         multi_class='ovr')
>>> # Note that C=1.0 is the default. You can increase
>>> # or decrease it to make the regularization effect
>>> # stronger or weaker, respectively.
>>> lr.fit(X_train_std, y_train)
>>> print('Training accuracy:', lr.score(X_train_std, y_train))
Training accuracy: 1.0
>>> print('Test accuracy:', lr.score(X_test_std, y_test))
Test accuracy: 1.0
```

Both training and test accuracies (both 100 percent) indicate that our model does a perfect job on both datasets. When we access the intercept terms via the `lr.intercept_` attribute, we can see that the array returns three values:

```
>>> lr.intercept_
    array([-1.26317363, -1.21537306, -2.37111954])
```

Since we fit the `LogisticRegression` object on a multiclass dataset via the **one-versus-rest (OvR)** approach, the first intercept belongs to the model that fits class 1 versus classes 2 and 3, the second value is the intercept of the model that fits class 2 versus classes 1 and 3, and the third value is the intercept of the model that fits class 3 versus classes 1 and 2:

```
>>> lr.coef_
array([[ 1.24647953,  0.18050894,  0.74540443, -1.16301108,
         0.        ,0.         ,  1.16243821,  0.        ,
         0.        ,  0.        ,  0.        ,  0.55620267,
         2.50890638],
       [-1.53919461, -0.38562247, -0.99565934,  0.36390047,
        -0.05892612, 0.         ,  0.66710883,  0.        ,
         0.        , -1.9318798 ,  1.23775092,  0.        ,
```

```
        -2.23280039],
      [ 0.13557571,  0.16848763,  0.35710712,  0.        ,
        0.        , 0.        , -2.43804744,  0.        ,
        0.        ,  1.56388787, -0.81881015, -0.49217022,
        0.        ]])
```

The weight array that we accessed via the `lr.coef_` attribute contains three rows of weight coefficients, one weight vector for each class. Each row consists of 13 weights, where each weight is multiplied by the respective feature in the 13-dimensional Wine dataset to calculate the net input:

$$z = w_1x_1 + \cdots + w_mx_m + b = \sum_{j=1}^{m} x_jw_j + b = \boldsymbol{w}^T\boldsymbol{x} + b$$

Accessing the bias unit and weight parameters of scikit-learn estimators

In scikit-learn, `intercept_` corresponds to the bias unit and `coef_` corresponds to the values w_j.

As a result of L1 regularization, which, as mentioned, serves as a method for feature selection, we just trained a model that is robust to the potentially irrelevant features in this dataset. Strictly speaking, though, the weight vectors from the previous example are not necessarily sparse because they contain more non-zero than zero entries. However, we could enforce sparsity (more zero entries) by further increasing the regularization strength—that is, choosing lower values for the `C` parameter.

In the last example on regularization in this chapter, we will vary the regularization strength and plot the regularization path—the weight coefficients of the different features for different regularization strengths:

```
>>> import matplotlib.pyplot as plt
>>> fig = plt.figure()
>>> ax = plt.subplot(111)
>>> colors = ['blue', 'green', 'red', 'cyan',
...           'magenta', 'yellow', 'black',
...           'pink', 'lightgreen', 'lightblue',
...           'gray', 'indigo', 'orange']
>>> weights, params = [], []
>>> for c in np.arange(-4., 6.):
...     lr = LogisticRegression(penalty='l1', C=10.**c,
...                             solver='liblinear',
...                             multi_class='ovr', random_state=0)
...     lr.fit(X_train_std, y_train)
...     weights.append(lr.coef_[1])
...     params.append(10**c)
```

```
>>> weights = np.array(weights)
>>> for column, color in zip(range(weights.shape[1]), colors):
...     plt.plot(params, weights[:, column],
...              label=df_wine.columns[column + 1],
...              color=color)
>>> plt.axhline(0, color='black', linestyle='--', linewidth=3)
>>> plt.xlim([10**(-5), 10**5])
>>> plt.ylabel('Weight coefficient')
>>> plt.xlabel('C (inverse regularization strength)')
>>> plt.xscale('log')
>>> plt.legend(loc='upper left')
>>> ax.legend(loc='upper center',
...           bbox_to_anchor=(1.38, 1.03),
...           ncol=1, fancybox=True)
>>> plt.show()
```

The resulting plot provides us with further insights into the behavior of L1 regularization. As we can see, all feature weights will be zero if we penalize the model with a strong regularization parameter ($C < 0.01$); C is the inverse of the regularization parameter, λ:

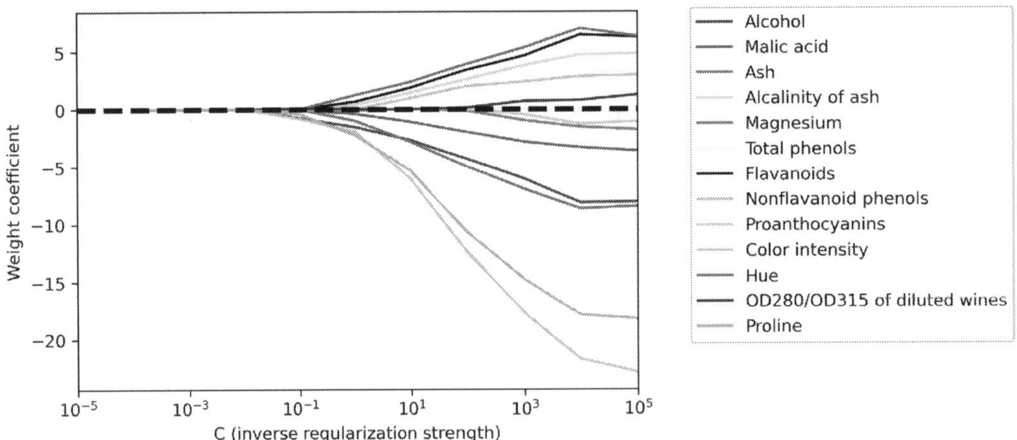

Figure 4.8: The impact of the value of the regularization strength hyperparameter C

Sequential feature selection algorithms

An alternative way to reduce the complexity of the model and avoid overfitting is **dimensionality reduction** via feature selection, which is especially useful for unregularized models. There are two main categories of dimensionality reduction techniques: **feature selection** and **feature extraction.** Via feature selection, we *select* a subset of the original features, whereas in feature extraction, we *derive* information from the feature set to construct a new feature subspace.

In this section, we will take a look at a classic family of feature selection algorithms. In the next chapter, *Chapter 5, Compressing Data via Dimensionality Reduction*, we will learn about different feature extraction techniques to compress a dataset onto a lower-dimensional feature subspace.

Sequential feature selection algorithms are a family of greedy search algorithms that are used to reduce an initial *d*-dimensional feature space to a *k*-dimensional feature subspace where $k<d$. The motivation behind feature selection algorithms is to automatically select a subset of features that are most relevant to the problem, to improve computational efficiency, or to reduce the generalization error of the model by removing irrelevant features or noise, which can be useful for algorithms that don't support regularization.

A classic sequential feature selection algorithm is **sequential backward selection** (**SBS**), which aims to reduce the dimensionality of the initial feature subspace with a minimum decay in the performance of the classifier to improve upon computational efficiency. In certain cases, SBS can even improve the predictive power of the model if a model suffers from overfitting.

Greedy search algorithms

Greedy algorithms make locally optimal choices at each stage of a combinatorial search problem and generally yield a suboptimal solution to the problem, in contrast to exhaustive search algorithms, which evaluate all possible combinations and are guaranteed to find the optimal solution. However, in practice, an exhaustive search is often computationally not feasible, whereas greedy algorithms allow for a less complex, computationally more efficient solution.

The idea behind the SBS algorithm is quite simple: SBS sequentially removes features from the full feature subset until the new feature subspace contains the desired number of features. To determine which feature is to be removed at each stage, we need to define the criterion function, *J*, that we want to minimize.

The criterion calculated by the criterion function can simply be the difference in the performance of the classifier before and after the removal of a particular feature. Then, the feature to be removed at each stage can simply be defined as the feature that maximizes this criterion; or in more simple terms, at each stage we eliminate the feature that causes the least performance loss after removal. Based on the preceding definition of SBS, we can outline the algorithm in four simple steps:

1. Initialize the algorithm with $k = d$, where d is the dimensionality of the full feature space, X_d.
2. Determine the feature, $\boldsymbol{x}^-$, that maximizes the criterion: $\boldsymbol{x}^- = \text{argmax}\, J(X_k - \boldsymbol{x})$, where $\boldsymbol{x} \in \boldsymbol{X}_k$.
3. Remove the feature, $\boldsymbol{x}^-$, from the feature set: $\boldsymbol{X}_{k-1} = X_k - \boldsymbol{x}^-$; $k = k - 1$.
4. Terminate if k equals the number of desired features; otherwise, go to *step 2*.

A resource on sequential feature algorithms

You can find a detailed evaluation of several sequential feature algorithms in *Comparative Study of Techniques for Large-Scale Feature Selection* by *F. Ferri, P. Pudil, M. Hatef,* and *J. Kittler*, pages 403-413, 1994.

To practice our coding skills and ability to implement our own algorithms, let's go ahead and implement it in Python from scratch:

```
from sklearn.base import clone
from itertools import combinations
import numpy as np
from sklearn.metrics import accuracy_score
from sklearn.model_selection import train_test_split

class SBS:
    def __init__(self, estimator, k_features,
                 scoring=accuracy_score,
                 test_size=0.25, random_state=1):
        self.scoring = scoring
        self.estimator = clone(estimator)
        self.k_features = k_features
        self.test_size = test_size
        self.random_state = random_state
    def fit(self, X, y):
        X_train, X_test, y_train, y_test = \
            train_test_split(X, y, test_size=self.test_size,
                             random_state=self.random_state)

        dim = X_train.shape[1]
        self.indices_ = tuple(range(dim))
        self.subsets_ = [self.indices_]
        score = self._calc_score(X_train, y_train,
                                 X_test, y_test, self.indices_)
        self.scores_ = [score]
        while dim > self.k_features:
            scores = []
            subsets = []

            for p in combinations(self.indices_, r=dim - 1):
                score = self._calc_score(X_train, y_train,
```

```
                                        X_test, y_test, p)
                scores.append(score)
                subsets.append(p)

            best = np.argmax(scores)
            self.indices_ = subsets[best]
            self.subsets_.append(self.indices_)
            dim -= 1

            self.scores_.append(scores[best])
        self.k_score_ = self.scores_[-1]

        return self

    def transform(self, X):
        return X[:, self.indices_]

    def _calc_score(self, X_train, y_train, X_test, y_test, indices):
        self.estimator.fit(X_train[:, indices], y_train)
        y_pred = self.estimator.predict(X_test[:, indices])
        score = self.scoring(y_test, y_pred)
        return score
```

In the preceding implementation, we defined the `k_features` parameter to specify the desired number of features we want to return. By default, we use `accuracy_score` from scikit-learn to evaluate the performance of a model (an estimator for classification) on the feature subsets.

Inside the `while` loop of the `fit` method, the feature subsets created by the `itertools.combination` function are evaluated and reduced until the feature subset has the desired dimensionality. In each iteration, the accuracy score of the best subset is collected in a list, `self.scores_`, based on the internally created test dataset, `X_test`. We will use those scores later to evaluate the results. The column indices of the final feature subset are assigned to `self.indices_`, which we can use via the `transform` method to return a new data array with the selected feature columns. Note that, instead of calculating the criterion explicitly inside the `fit` method, we simply removed the feature that is not contained in the best performing feature subset.

Now, let's see our SBS implementation in action using the KNN classifier from scikit-learn:

```
>>> import matplotlib.pyplot as plt
>>> from sklearn.neighbors import KNeighborsClassifier
>>> knn = KNeighborsClassifier(n_neighbors=5)
>>> sbs = SBS(knn, k_features=1)
>>> sbs.fit(X_train_std, y_train)
```

Although our SBS implementation already splits the dataset into a test and training dataset inside the `fit` function, we still fed the training dataset, `X_train`, to the algorithm. The SBS `fit` method will then create new training subsets for testing (validation) and training, which is why this test set is also called the **validation dataset**. This approach is necessary to prevent our *original* test set from becoming part of the training data.

Remember that our SBS algorithm collects the scores of the best feature subset at each stage, so let's move on to the more exciting part of our implementation and plot the classification accuracy of the KNN classifier that was calculated on the validation dataset. The code is as follows:

```
>>> k_feat = [len(k) for k in sbs.subsets_]
>>> plt.plot(k_feat, sbs.scores_, marker='o')
>>> plt.ylim([0.7, 1.02])
>>> plt.ylabel('Accuracy')
>>> plt.xlabel('Number of features')
>>> plt.grid()
>>> plt.tight_layout()
>>> plt.show()
```

As we can see in *Figure 4.9*, the accuracy of the KNN classifier improved on the validation dataset as we reduced the number of features, which is likely due to a decrease in the **curse of dimensionality** that we discussed in the context of the KNN algorithm in *Chapter 3*. Also, we can see in the following plot that the classifier achieved 100 percent accuracy for $k = \{3, 7, 8, 9, 10, 11, 12\}$:

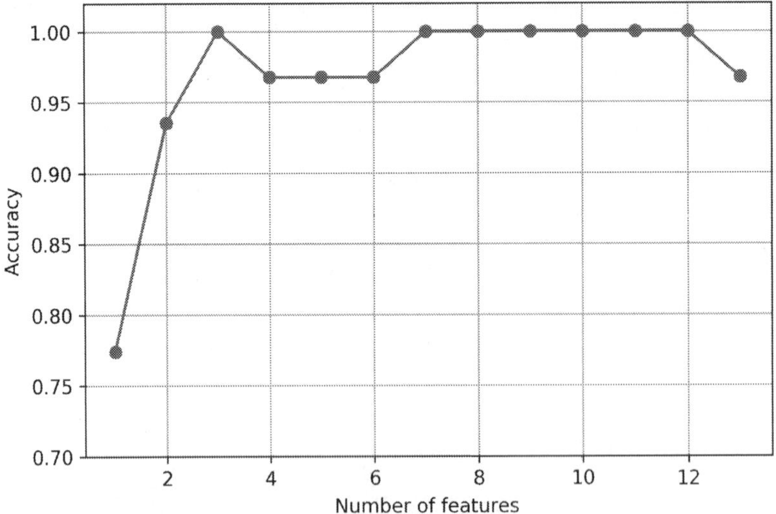

Figure 4.9: Impact of number of features on model accuracy

To satisfy our own curiosity, let's see what the smallest feature subset (k=3), which yielded such a good performance on the validation dataset, looks like:

```
>>> k3 = list(sbs.subsets_[10])
>>> print(df_wine.columns[1:][k3])
Index(['Alcohol', 'Malic acid', 'OD280/OD315 of diluted wines'],
dtype='object')
```

Using the preceding code, we obtained the column indices of the three-feature subset from the 11th position in the `sbs.subsets_` attribute and returned the corresponding feature names from the column index of the pandas Wine `DataFrame`.

Next, let's evaluate the performance of the KNN classifier on the original test dataset:

```
>>> knn.fit(X_train_std, y_train)
>>> print('Training accuracy:', knn.score(X_train_std, y_train))
Training accuracy: 0.967741935484
>>> print('Test accuracy:', knn.score(X_test_std, y_test))
Test accuracy: 0.962962962963
```

In the preceding code section, we used the complete feature set and obtained approximately 97 percent accuracy on the training dataset and approximately 96 percent accuracy on the test dataset, which indicates that our model already generalizes well to new data. Now, let's use the selected three-feature subset and see how well KNN performs:

```
>>> knn.fit(X_train_std[:, k3], y_train)
>>> print('Training accuracy:',
...       knn.score(X_train_std[:, k3], y_train))
Training accuracy: 0.951612903226
>>> print('Test accuracy:',
...       knn.score(X_test_std[:, k3], y_test))
Test accuracy: 0.925925925926
```

When using less than a quarter of the original features in the Wine dataset, the prediction accuracy on the test dataset declined slightly. This may indicate that those three features do not provide less discriminatory information than the original dataset. However, we also have to keep in mind that the Wine dataset is a small dataset and is very susceptible to randomness—that is, the way we split the dataset into training and test subsets, and how we split the training dataset further into a training and validation subset.

While we did not increase the performance of the KNN model by reducing the number of features, we shrank the size of the dataset, which can be useful in real-world applications that may involve expensive data collection steps. Also, by substantially reducing the number of features, we obtain simpler models, which are easier to interpret.

Feature selection algorithms in scikit-learn

You can find implementations of several different flavors of sequential feature selection related to the simple SBS that we implemented previously in the Python package `mlxtend` at `http://rasbt.github.io/mlxtend/user_guide/feature_selection/SequentialFeatureSelector/`. While our `mlxtend` implementation comes with many bells and whistles, we collaborated with the scikit-learn team to implement a simplified, user-friendly version, which has been part of the recent v0.24 release. The usage and behavior are very similar to the SBS code we implemented in this chapter. If you would like to learn more, please see the documentation at `https://scikit-learn.org/stable/modules/generated/sklearn.feature_selection.SequentialFeatureSelector.html`.

There are many more feature selection algorithms available via scikit-learn. These include recursive backward elimination based on feature weights, tree-based methods to select features by importance, and univariate statistical tests. A comprehensive discussion of the different feature selection methods is beyond the scope of this book, but a good summary with illustrative examples can be found at `http://scikit-learn.org/stable/modules/feature_selection.html`.

Assessing feature importance with random forests

In previous sections, you learned how to use L1 regularization to zero out irrelevant features via logistic regression and how to use the SBS algorithm for feature selection and apply it to a KNN algorithm. Another useful approach for selecting relevant features from a dataset is using a **random forest**, an ensemble technique that was introduced in *Chapter 3*. Using a random forest, we can measure the feature importance as the averaged impurity decrease computed from all decision trees in the forest, without making any assumptions about whether our data is linearly separable or not. Conveniently, the random forest implementation in scikit-learn already collects the feature importance values for us so that we can access them via the `feature_importances_` attribute after fitting a `RandomForestClassifier`. By executing the following code, we will now train a forest of 500 trees on the Wine dataset and rank the 13 features by their respective importance measures—remember from our discussion in *Chapter 3* that we don't need to use standardized or normalized features in tree-based models:

```
>>> from sklearn.ensemble import RandomForestClassifier
>>> feat_labels = df_wine.columns[1:]
>>> forest = RandomForestClassifier(n_estimators=500,
...                                 random_state=1)
>>> forest.fit(X_train, y_train)
>>> importances = forest.feature_importances_
>>> indices = np.argsort(importances)[::-1]
>>> for f in range(X_train.shape[1]):
...     print("%2d) %-*s %f" % (f + 1, 30,
...                             feat_labels[indices[f]],
```

```
...                             importances[indices[f]]))
>>> plt.title('Feature importance')
>>> plt.bar(range(X_train.shape[1]),
...         importances[indices],
...         align='center')
>>> plt.xticks(range(X_train.shape[1]),
...            feat_labels[indices], rotation=90)
>>> plt.xlim([-1, X_train.shape[1]])
>>> plt.tight_layout()
>>> plt.show()
 1) Proline                         0.185453
 2) Flavanoids                      0.174751
 3) Color intensity                 0.143920
 4) OD280/OD315 of diluted wines    0.136162
 5) Alcohol                         0.118529
 6) Hue                             0.058739
 7) Total phenols                   0.050872
 8) Magnesium                       0.031357
 9) Malic acid                      0.025648
 10) Proanthocyanins                0.025570
 11) Alcalinity of ash              0.022366
 12) Nonflavanoid phenols           0.013354
 13) Ash                            0.013279
```

After executing the code, we created a plot that ranks the different features in the Wine dataset by their relative importance; note that the feature importance values are normalized so that they sum up to 1.0:

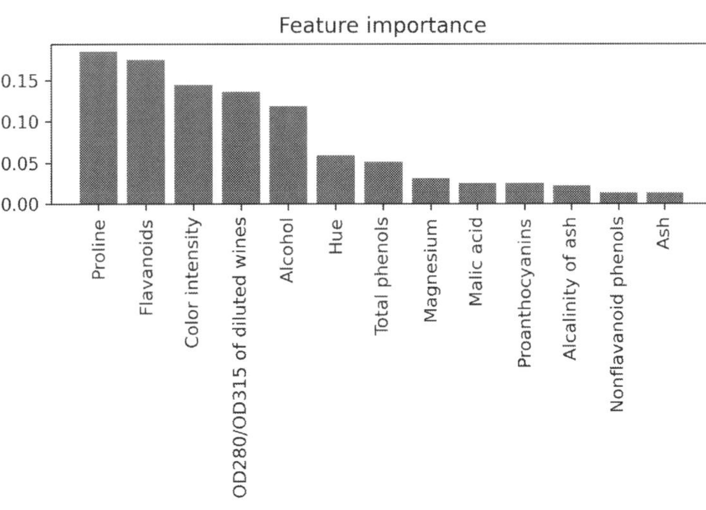

Figure 4.10: Random forest-based feature importance of the Wine dataset

We can conclude that the proline and flavonoid levels, the color intensity, the OD280/OD315 diffraction, and the alcohol concentration of wine are the most discriminative features in the dataset based on the average impurity decrease in the 500 decision trees. Interestingly, two of the top-ranked features in the plot are also in the three-feature subset selection from the SBS algorithm that we implemented in the previous section (alcohol concentration and OD280/OD315 of diluted wines).

However, as far as interpretability is concerned, the random forest technique comes with an important *gotcha* that is worth mentioning. If two or more features are highly correlated, one feature may be ranked very highly while the information on the other feature(s) may not be fully captured. On the other hand, we don't need to be concerned about this problem if we are merely interested in the predictive performance of a model rather than the interpretation of feature importance values.

To conclude this section about feature importance values and random forests, it is worth mentioning that scikit-learn also implements a `SelectFromModel` object that selects features based on a user-specified threshold after model fitting, which is useful if we want to use the `RandomForestClassifier` as a feature selector and intermediate step in a scikit-learn `Pipeline` object, which allows us to connect different preprocessing steps with an estimator, as you will see in *Chapter 6, Learning Best Practices for Model Evaluation and Hyperparameter Tuning*. For example, we could set the `threshold` to `0.1` to reduce the dataset to the five most important features using the following code:

```
>>> from sklearn.feature_selection import SelectFromModel
>>> sfm = SelectFromModel(forest, threshold=0.1, prefit=True)
>>> X_selected = sfm.transform(X_train)
>>> print('Number of features that meet this threshold',
...       'criterion:', X_selected.shape[1])
Number of features that meet this threshold criterion: 5
>>> for f in range(X_selected.shape[1]):
...     print("%2d) %-*s %f" % (f + 1, 30,
...                             feat_labels[indices[f]],
...                             importances[indices[f]]))
 1) Proline                        0.185453
 2) Flavanoids                     0.174751
 3) Color intensity                0.143920
 4) OD280/OD315 of diluted wines   0.136162
 5) Alcohol                        0.118529
```

Summary

We started this chapter by looking at useful techniques to make sure that we handle missing data correctly. Before we feed data to a machine learning algorithm, we also have to make sure that we encode categorical variables correctly, and in this chapter, we saw how we can map ordinal and nominal feature values to integer representations.

Moreover, we briefly discussed L1 regularization, which can help us to avoid overfitting by reducing the complexity of a model. As an alternative approach to removing irrelevant features, we used a sequential feature selection algorithm to select meaningful features from a dataset.

In the next chapter, you will learn about yet another useful approach to dimensionality reduction: feature extraction. It allows us to compress features onto a lower-dimensional subspace, rather than removing features entirely as in feature selection.

Join our book's Discord space

Join our Discord community to meet like-minded people and learn alongside more than 2000 members at:
`https://packt.link/MLwPyTorch`

5

Compressing Data via Dimensionality Reduction

In *Chapter 4, Building Good Training Datasets – Data Preprocessing*, you learned about the different approaches for reducing the dimensionality of a dataset using different feature selection techniques. An alternative approach to feature selection for dimensionality reduction is **feature extraction**. In this chapter, you will learn about two fundamental techniques that will help you to summarize the information content of a dataset by transforming it onto a new feature subspace of lower dimensionality than the original one. Data compression is an important topic in machine learning, and it helps us to store and analyze the increasing amounts of data that are produced and collected in the modern age of technology.

In this chapter, we will cover the following topics:

- Principal component analysis for unsupervised data compression
- Linear discriminant analysis as a supervised dimensionality reduction technique for maximizing class separability
- A brief overview of nonlinear dimensionality reduction techniques and t-distributed stochastic neighbor embedding for data visualization

Unsupervised dimensionality reduction via principal component analysis

Similar to feature selection, we can use different feature extraction techniques to reduce the number of features in a dataset. The difference between feature selection and feature extraction is that while we maintain the original features when we use feature selection algorithms, such as **sequential backward selection**, we use feature extraction to transform or project the data onto a new feature space.

In the context of dimensionality reduction, feature extraction can be understood as an approach to data compression with the goal of maintaining most of the relevant information. In practice, feature extraction is not only used to improve storage space or the computational efficiency of the learning algorithm but can also improve the predictive performance by reducing the **curse of dimensionality**—especially if we are working with non-regularized models.

The main steps in principal component analysis

In this section, we will discuss **principal component analysis** (**PCA**), an unsupervised linear transformation technique that is widely used across different fields, most prominently for feature extraction and dimensionality reduction. Other popular applications of PCA include exploratory data analysis and the denoising of signals in stock market trading, and the analysis of genome data and gene expression levels in the field of bioinformatics.

PCA helps us to identify patterns in data based on the correlation between features. In a nutshell, PCA aims to find the directions of maximum variance in high-dimensional data and projects the data onto a new subspace with equal or fewer dimensions than the original one. The orthogonal axes (principal components) of the new subspace can be interpreted as the directions of maximum variance given the constraint that the new feature axes are orthogonal to each other, as illustrated in *Figure 5.1*:

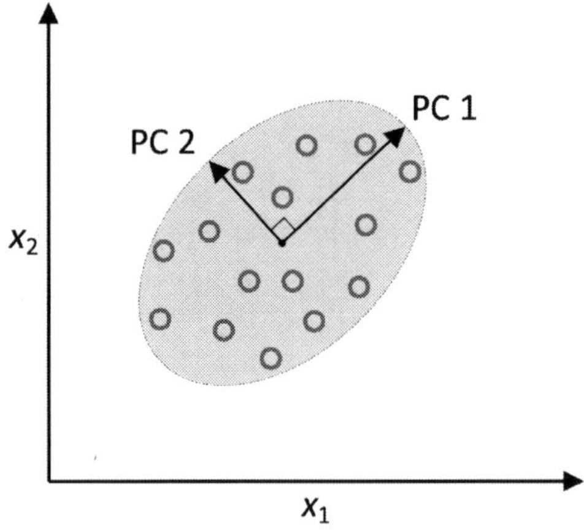

Figure 5.1: Using PCA to find the directions of maximum variance in a dataset

In *Figure 5.1*, x_1 and x_2 are the original feature axes, and **PC 1** and **PC 2** are the principal components.

If we use PCA for dimensionality reduction, we construct a $d \times k$-dimensional transformation matrix, $\boldsymbol{W}$, that allows us to map a vector of the features of the training example, $\boldsymbol{x}$, onto a new k-dimensional feature subspace that has fewer dimensions than the original d-dimensional feature space. For instance, the process is as follows. Suppose we have a feature vector, $\boldsymbol{x}$:

$$\boldsymbol{x} = [x_1, x_2, \dots, x_d], \quad \boldsymbol{x} \in \mathbb{R}^d$$

which is then transformed by a transformation matrix, $\boldsymbol{W} \in \mathbb{R}^{d \times k}$:

$$\boldsymbol{x}\boldsymbol{W} = \boldsymbol{z}$$

resulting in the output vector:

$$\boldsymbol{z} = [z_1, z_2, \dots, z_k], \quad \boldsymbol{z} \in \mathbb{R}^k$$

As a result of transforming the original d-dimensional data onto this new k-dimensional subspace (typically $k << d$), the first principal component will have the largest possible variance. All consequent principal components will have the largest variance given the constraint that these components are uncorrelated (orthogonal) to the other principal components—even if the input features are correlated, the resulting principal components will be mutually orthogonal (uncorrelated). Note that the PCA directions are highly sensitive to data scaling, and we need to standardize the features prior to PCA if the features were measured on different scales and we want to assign equal importance to all features.

Before looking at the PCA algorithm for dimensionality reduction in more detail, let's summarize the approach in a few simple steps:

1. Standardize the d-dimensional dataset.
2. Construct the covariance matrix.
3. Decompose the covariance matrix into its eigenvectors and eigenvalues.
4. Sort the eigenvalues by decreasing order to rank the corresponding eigenvectors.
5. Select k eigenvectors, which correspond to the k largest eigenvalues, where k is the dimensionality of the new feature subspace ($k \leq d$).
6. Construct a projection matrix, $\boldsymbol{W}$, from the "top" k eigenvectors.
7. Transform the d-dimensional input dataset, $\boldsymbol{X}$, using the projection matrix, $\boldsymbol{W}$, to obtain the new k-dimensional feature subspace.

In the following sections, we will perform a PCA step by step using Python as a learning exercise. Then, we will see how to perform a PCA more conveniently using scikit-learn.

Eigendecomposition: Decomposing a Matrix into Eigenvectors and Eigenvalues

Eigendecomposition, the factorization of a square matrix into so-called **eigenvalues** and **eigenvectors**, is at the core of the PCA procedure described in this section.

The covariance matrix is a special case of a square matrix: it's a symmetric matrix, which means that the matrix is equal to its transpose, $A = A^T$.

When we decompose such a symmetric matrix, the eigenvalues are real (rather than complex) numbers, and the eigenvectors are orthogonal (perpendicular) to each other. Furthermore, eigenvalues and eigenvectors come in pairs. If we decompose a covariance matrix into its eigenvectors and eigenvalues, the eigenvectors associated with the highest eigenvalue corresponds to the direction of maximum variance in the dataset. Here, this "direction" is a linear transformation of the dataset's feature columns.

While a more detailed discussion of eigenvalues and eigenvectors is beyond the scope of this book, a relatively thorough treatment with pointers to additional resources can be found on Wikipedia at `https://en.wikipedia.org/wiki/Eigenvalues_and_eigenvectors`.

Extracting the principal components step by step

In this subsection, we will tackle the first four steps of a PCA:

1. Standardizing the data
2. Constructing the covariance matrix
3. Obtaining the eigenvalues and eigenvectors of the covariance matrix
4. Sorting the eigenvalues by decreasing order to rank the eigenvectors

First, we will start by loading the Wine dataset that we worked with in *Chapter 4, Building Good Training Datasets – Data Preprocessing*:

```
>>> import pandas as pd
>>> df_wine = pd.read_csv(
...     'https://archive.ics.uci.edu/ml/'
...     'machine-learning-databases/wine/wine.data',
...     header=None
... )
```

Obtaining the Wine dataset

You can find a copy of the Wine dataset (and all other datasets used in this book) in the code bundle of this book, which you can use if you are working offline or the UCI server at `https://archive.ics.uci.edu/ml/machine-learning-databases/wine/wine.data` is temporarily unavailable. For instance, to load the Wine dataset from a local directory, you can replace the following lines:

```
df = pd.read_csv(
    'https://archive.ics.uci.edu/ml/'
    'machine-learning-databases/wine/wine.data',
    header=None
)
```

with these ones:

```
df = pd.read_csv(
    'your/local/path/to/wine.data',
    header=None
)
```

Next, we will process the Wine data into separate training and test datasets—using 70 percent and 30 percent of the data, respectively—and standardize it to unit variance:

```
>>> from sklearn.model_selection import train_test_split
>>> X, y = df_wine.iloc[:, 1:].values, df_wine.iloc[:, 0].values
>>> X_train, X_test, y_train, y_test = \
...     train_test_split(X, y, test_size=0.3,
...                      stratify=y,
...                      random_state=0)
>>> # standardize the features
>>> from sklearn.preprocessing import StandardScaler
>>> sc = StandardScaler()
>>> X_train_std = sc.fit_transform(X_train)
>>> X_test_std = sc.transform(X_test)
```

After completing the mandatory preprocessing by executing the preceding code, let's advance to the second step: constructing the covariance matrix. The symmetric $d \times d$-dimensional covariance matrix, where d is the number of dimensions in the dataset, stores the pairwise covariances between the different features. For example, the covariance between two features, x_j and x_k, on the population level can be calculated via the following equation:

$$\sigma_{jk} = \frac{1}{n-1} \sum_{i=1}^{n} \left(x_j^{(i)} - \mu_j\right)\left(x_k^{(i)} - \mu_k\right)$$

Here, μ_j and μ_k are the sample means of features j and k, respectively. Note that the sample means are zero if we standardized the dataset. A positive covariance between two features indicates that the features increase or decrease together, whereas a negative covariance indicates that the features vary in opposite directions. For example, the covariance matrix of three features can then be written as follows (note that Σ is the Greek uppercase letter sigma, which is not to be confused with the summation symbol):

$$\Sigma = \begin{bmatrix} \sigma_1^2 & \sigma_{12} & \sigma_{13} \\ \sigma_{21} & \sigma_2^2 & \sigma_{23} \\ \sigma_{31} & \sigma_{32} & \sigma_3^2 \end{bmatrix}$$

The eigenvectors of the covariance matrix represent the principal components (the directions of maximum variance), whereas the corresponding eigenvalues will define their magnitude. In the case of the Wine dataset, we would obtain 13 eigenvectors and eigenvalues from the 13×13-dimensional covariance matrix.

Now, for our third step, let's obtain the eigenpairs of the covariance matrix. If you have taken a linear algebra class, you may have learned that an eigenvector, v, satisfies the following condition:

$$\Sigma \boldsymbol{v} = \lambda \boldsymbol{v}$$

Here, λ is a scalar: the eigenvalue. Since the manual computation of eigenvectors and eigenvalues is a somewhat tedious and elaborate task, we will use the `linalg.eig` function from NumPy to obtain the eigenpairs of the Wine covariance matrix:

```
>>> import numpy as np
>>> cov_mat = np.cov(X_train_std.T)
>>> eigen_vals, eigen_vecs = np.linalg.eig(cov_mat)
>>> print('\nEigenvalues \n', eigen_vals)
Eigenvalues
[ 4.84274532  2.41602459  1.54845825  0.96120438  0.84166161
  0.6620634   0.51828472  0.34650377  0.3131368   0.10754642
  0.21357215  0.15362835  0.1808613 ]
```

Using the `numpy.cov` function, we computed the covariance matrix of the standardized training dataset. Using the `linalg.eig` function, we performed the eigendecomposition, which yielded a vector (`eigen_vals`) consisting of 13 eigenvalues and the corresponding eigenvectors stored as columns in a 13×13-dimensional matrix (`eigen_vecs`).

Eigendecomposition in NumPy

The `numpy.linalg.eig` function was designed to operate on both symmetric and non-symmetric square matrices. However, you may find that it returns complex eigenvalues in certain cases.

A related function, `numpy.linalg.eigh`, has been implemented to decompose Hermetian matrices, which is a numerically more stable approach to working with symmetric matrices such as the covariance matrix; `numpy.linalg.eigh` always returns real eigenvalues.

Total and explained variance

Since we want to reduce the dimensionality of our dataset by compressing it onto a new feature subspace, we only select the subset of the eigenvectors (principal components) that contains most of the information (variance). The eigenvalues define the magnitude of the eigenvectors, so we have to sort the eigenvalues by decreasing magnitude; we are interested in the top k eigenvectors based on the values of their corresponding eigenvalues. But before we collect those k most informative eigenvectors, let's plot the **variance explained ratios** of the eigenvalues. The variance explained ratio of an eigenvalue, λ_j, is simply the fraction of an eigenvalue, λ_j, and the total sum of the eigenvalues:

$$\text{Explained variance ratio} = \frac{\lambda_j}{\sum_{j=1}^{d} \lambda_j}$$

Using the NumPy `cumsum` function, we can then calculate the cumulative sum of explained variances, which we will then plot via Matplotlib's `step` function:

```
>>> tot = sum(eigen_vals)
>>> var_exp = [(i / tot) for i in
...            sorted(eigen_vals, reverse=True)]
>>> cum_var_exp = np.cumsum(var_exp)
>>> import matplotlib.pyplot as plt
>>> plt.bar(range(1,14), var_exp, align='center',
...         label='Individual explained variance')
>>> plt.step(range(1,14), cum_var_exp, where='mid',
...          label='Cumulative explained variance')
>>> plt.ylabel('Explained variance ratio')
>>> plt.xlabel('Principal component index')
>>> plt.legend(loc='best')
>>> plt.tight_layout()
>>> plt.show()
```

The resulting plot indicates that the first principal component alone accounts for approximately 40 percent of the variance.

Also, we can see that the first two principal components combined explain almost 60 percent of the variance in the dataset:

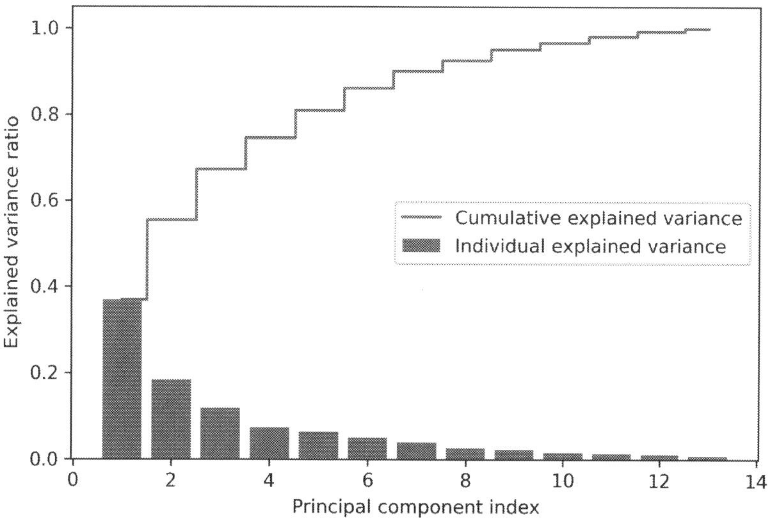

Figure 5.2: The proportion of the total variance captured by the principal components

Although the explained variance plot reminds us of the feature importance values that we computed in *Chapter 4, Building Good Training Datasets – Data Preprocessing*, via random forests, we should remind ourselves that PCA is an unsupervised method, which means that information about the class labels is ignored. Whereas a random forest uses the class membership information to compute the node impurities, variance measures the spread of values along a feature axis.

Feature transformation

Now that we have successfully decomposed the covariance matrix into eigenpairs, let's proceed with the last three steps to transform the Wine dataset onto the new principal component axes. The remaining steps we are going to tackle in this section are the following:

1. Select k eigenvectors, which correspond to the k largest eigenvalues, where k is the dimensionality of the new feature subspace ($k \leq d$).
2. Construct a projection matrix, $\boldsymbol{W}$, from the "top" k eigenvectors.
3. Transform the d-dimensional input dataset, $\boldsymbol{X}$, using the projection matrix, $\boldsymbol{W}$, to obtain the new k-dimensional feature subspace.

Or, in less technical terms, we will sort the eigenpairs by descending order of the eigenvalues, construct a projection matrix from the selected eigenvectors, and use the projection matrix to transform the data onto the lower-dimensional subspace.

We start by sorting the eigenpairs by decreasing order of the eigenvalues:

```
>>> # Make a list of (eigenvalue, eigenvector) tuples
>>> eigen_pairs = [(np.abs(eigen_vals[i]), eigen_vecs[:, i])
...                for i in range(len(eigen_vals))]
>>> # Sort the (eigenvalue, eigenvector) tuples from high to low
>>> eigen_pairs.sort(key=lambda k: k[0], reverse=True)
```

Next, we collect the two eigenvectors that correspond to the two largest eigenvalues, to capture about 60 percent of the variance in this dataset. Note that two eigenvectors have been chosen for the purpose of illustration, since we are going to plot the data via a two-dimensional scatterplot later in this subsection. In practice, the number of principal components has to be determined by a tradeoff between computational efficiency and the performance of the classifier:

```
>>> w = np.hstack((eigen_pairs[0][1][:, np.newaxis],
...                eigen_pairs[1][1][:, np.newaxis]))
>>> print('Matrix W:\n', w)
Matrix W:
[[-0.13724218  0.50303478]
 [ 0.24724326  0.16487119]
 [-0.02545159  0.24456476]
 [ 0.20694508 -0.11352904]
 [-0.15436582  0.28974518]
```

```
[-0.39376952  0.05080104]
[-0.41735106 -0.02287338]
[ 0.30572896  0.09048885]
[-0.30668347  0.00835233]
[ 0.07554066  0.54977581]
[-0.32613263 -0.20716433]
[-0.36861022 -0.24902536]
[-0.29669651  0.38022942]]
```

By executing the preceding code, we have created a 13×2-dimensional projection matrix, *W*, from the top two eigenvectors.

Mirrored projections

Depending on which versions of NumPy and LAPACK you are using, you may obtain the matrix, **W**, with its signs flipped. Please note that this is not an issue; if **v** is an eigenvector of a matrix, Σ, we have:

$$\Sigma \boldsymbol{v} = \lambda \boldsymbol{v}$$

Here, **v** is the eigenvector, and –**v** is also an eigenvector, which we can show as follows. Using basic algebra, we can multiply both sides of the equation by a scalar, α:

$$\alpha \Sigma \boldsymbol{v} = \alpha \lambda \boldsymbol{v}$$

Since matrix multiplication is associative for scalar multiplication, we can then rearrange this to the following:

$$\Sigma(\alpha \boldsymbol{v}) = \lambda(\alpha \boldsymbol{v})$$

Now, we can see that $\alpha \boldsymbol{v}$ is an eigenvector with the same eigenvalue, λ, for both $\alpha = 1$ and $\alpha = -1$. Hence, both **v** and –**v** are eigenvectors.

Using the projection matrix, we can now transform an example, *x* (represented as a 13-dimensional row vector), onto the PCA subspace (the principal components one and two) obtaining *x*′, now a two-dimensional example vector consisting of two new features:

$$x' = xW$$

```
>>> X_train_std[0].dot(w)
array([ 2.38299011,  0.45458499])
```

Similarly, we can transform the entire 124×13-dimensional training dataset onto the two principal components by calculating the matrix dot product:

$$X' = XW$$

```
>>> X_train_pca = X_train_std.dot(w)
```

Lastly, let's visualize the transformed Wine training dataset, now stored as an 124×2-dimensional matrix, in a two-dimensional scatterplot:

```
>>> colors = ['r', 'b', 'g']
>>> markers = ['o', 's', '^']
>>> for l, c, m in zip(np.unique(y_train), colors, markers):
...     plt.scatter(X_train_pca[y_train==l, 0],
...                 X_train_pca[y_train==l, 1],
...                 c=c, label=f'Class {l}', marker=m)
>>> plt.xlabel('PC 1')
>>> plt.ylabel('PC 2')
>>> plt.legend(loc='lower left')
>>> plt.tight_layout()
>>> plt.show()
```

As we can see in *Figure 5.3*, the data is more spread along the first principal component (*x* axis) than the second principal component (*y* axis), which is consistent with the explained variance ratio plot that we created in the previous subsection. However, we can tell that a linear classifier will likely be able to separate the classes well:

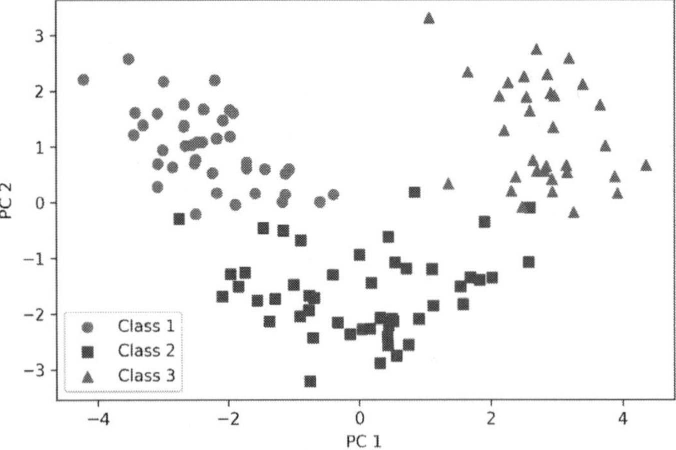

Figure 5.3: Data records from the Wine dataset projected onto a 2D feature space via PCA

Although we encoded the class label information for the purpose of illustration in the preceding scatterplot, we have to keep in mind that PCA is an unsupervised technique that doesn't use any class label information.

Principal component analysis in scikit-learn

Although the verbose approach in the previous subsection helped us to follow the inner workings of PCA, we will now discuss how to use the `PCA` class implemented in scikit-learn.

The `PCA` class is another one of scikit-learn's transformer classes, with which we first fit the model using the training data before we transform both the training data and the test dataset using the same model parameters. Now, let's use the `PCA` class from scikit-learn on the Wine training dataset, classify the transformed examples via logistic regression, and visualize the decision regions via the `plot_decision_regions` function that we defined in *Chapter 2*, *Training Simple Machine Learning Algorithms for Classification*:

```
from matplotlib.colors import ListedColormap
def plot_decision_regions(X, y, classifier, test_idx=None, resolution=0.02):

    # setup marker generator and color map
    markers = ('o', 's', '^', 'v', '<')
    colors = ('red', 'blue', 'lightgreen', 'gray', 'cyan')
    cmap = ListedColormap(colors[:len(np.unique(y))])

    # plot the decision surface
    x1_min, x1_max = X[:, 0].min() - 1, X[:, 0].max() + 1
    x2_min, x2_max = X[:, 1].min() - 1, X[:, 1].max() + 1
    xx1, xx2 = np.meshgrid(np.arange(x1_min, x1_max, resolution),
                           np.arange(x2_min, x2_max, resolution))
    lab = classifier.predict(np.array([xx1.ravel(), xx2.ravel()]).T)
    lab = lab.reshape(xx1.shape)
    plt.contourf(xx1, xx2, lab, alpha=0.3, cmap=cmap)
    plt.xlim(xx1.min(), xx1.max())
    plt.ylim(xx2.min(), xx2.max())

    # plot class examples
    for idx, cl in enumerate(np.unique(y)):
        plt.scatter(x=X[y == cl, 0],
                    y=X[y == cl, 1],
                    alpha=0.8,
                    c=colors[idx],
                    marker=markers[idx],
                    label=f'Class {cl}',
                    edgecolor='black')
```

For your convenience, you can place the preceding `plot_decision_regions` code into a separate code file in your current working directory, for example, `plot_decision_regions_script.py`, and import it into your current Python session:

```
>>> from sklearn.linear_model import LogisticRegression
>>> from sklearn.decomposition import PCA
>>> # initializing the PCA transformer and
>>> # logistic regression estimator:
>>> pca = PCA(n_components=2)
>>> lr = LogisticRegression(multi_class='ovr',
...                         random_state=1,
...                         solver='lbfgs')
>>> # dimensionality reduction:
>>> X_train_pca = pca.fit_transform(X_train_std)
>>> X_test_pca = pca.transform(X_test_std)
>>> # fitting the logistic regression model on the reduced dataset:
>>> lr.fit(X_train_pca, y_train)
>>> plot_decision_regions(X_train_pca, y_train, classifier=lr)
>>> plt.xlabel('PC 1')
>>> plt.ylabel('PC 2')
>>> plt.legend(loc='lower left')
>>> plt.tight_layout()
>>> plt.show()
```

By executing this code, we should now see the decision regions for the training data reduced to two principal component axes:

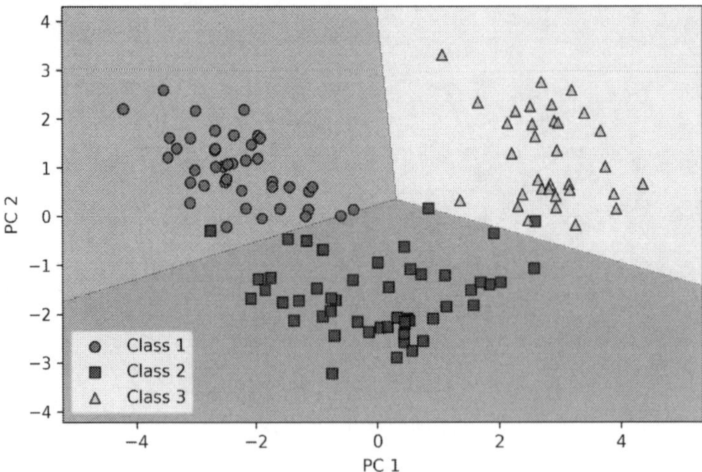

Figure 5.4: Training examples and logistic regression decision regions after using scikit-learn's PCA for dimensionality reduction

When we compare the PCA projections via scikit-learn with our own PCA implementation, we might see that the resulting plots are mirror images of each other. Note that this is not due to an error in either of those two implementations; the reason for this difference is that, depending on the eigen-solver, eigenvectors can have either negative or positive signs.

Not that it matters, but we could simply revert the mirror image by multiplying the data by -1 if we wanted to; note that eigenvectors are typically scaled to unit length 1. For the sake of completeness, let's plot the decision regions of the logistic regression on the transformed test dataset to see if it can separate the classes well:

```
>>> plot_decision_regions(X_test_pca, y_test, classifier=lr)
>>> plt.xlabel('PC 1')
>>> plt.ylabel('PC 2')
>>> plt.legend(loc='lower left')
>>> plt.tight_layout()
>>> plt.show()
```

After we plot the decision regions for the test dataset by executing the preceding code, we can see that logistic regression performs quite well on this small two-dimensional feature subspace and only misclassifies a few examples in the test dataset:

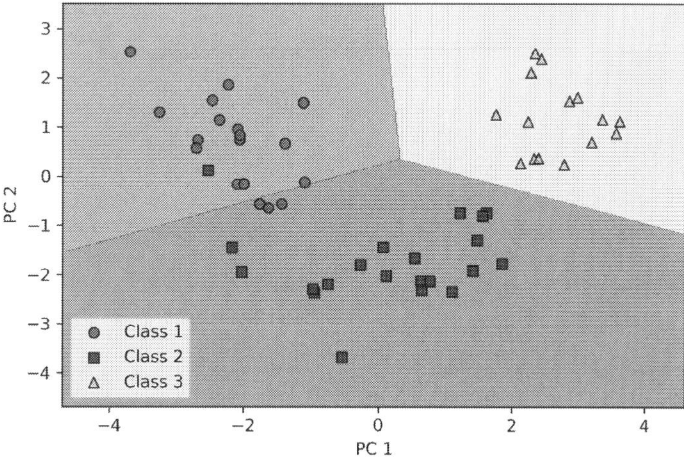

Figure 5.5: Test datapoints with logistic regression decision regions in the PCA-based feature space

If we are interested in the explained variance ratios of the different principal components, we can simply initialize the `PCA` class with the `n_components` parameter set to `None`, so all principal components are kept and the explained variance ratio can then be accessed via the `explained_variance_ratio_` attribute:

```
>>> pca = PCA(n_components=None)
>>> X_train_pca = pca.fit_transform(X_train_std)
>>> pca.explained_variance_ratio_
array([ 0.36951469, 0.18434927, 0.11815159, 0.07334252,
```

```
        0.06422108, 0.05051724, 0.03954654, 0.02643918,
        0.02389319, 0.01629614, 0.01380021, 0.01172226,
        0.00820609])
```

Note that we set `n_components=None` when we initialized the `PCA` class so that it will return all principal components in a sorted order, instead of performing a dimensionality reduction.

Assessing feature contributions

In this section, we will take a brief look at how we can assess the contributions of the original features to the principal components. As we learned, via PCA, we create principal components that represent linear combinations of the features. Sometimes, we are interested to know about how much each original feature contributes to a given principal component. These contributions are often called **loadings**.

The factor loadings can be computed by scaling the eigenvectors by the square root of the eigenvalues. The resulting values can then be interpreted as the correlation between the original features and the principal component. To illustrate this, let us plot the loadings for the first principal component.

First, we compute the 13×13-dimensional loadings matrix by multiplying the eigenvectors by the square root of the eigenvalues:

```
>>> loadings = eigen_vecs * np.sqrt(eigen_vals)
```

Then, we plot the loadings for the first principal component, `loadings[:, 0]`, which is the first column in this matrix:

```
>>> fig, ax = plt.subplots()
>>> ax.bar(range(13), loadings[:, 0], align='center')
>>> ax.set_ylabel('Loadings for PC 1')
>>> ax.set_xticks(range(13))
>>> ax.set_xticklabels(df_wine.columns[1:], rotation=90)
>>> plt.ylim([-1, 1])
>>> plt.tight_layout()
>>> plt.show()
```

In *Figure 5.6*, we can see that, for example, **Alcohol** has a negative correlation with the first principal component (approximately –0.3), whereas **Malic acid** has a positive correlation (approximately 0.54). Note that a value of 1 describes a perfect positive correlation whereas a value of –1 corresponds to a perfect negative correlation:

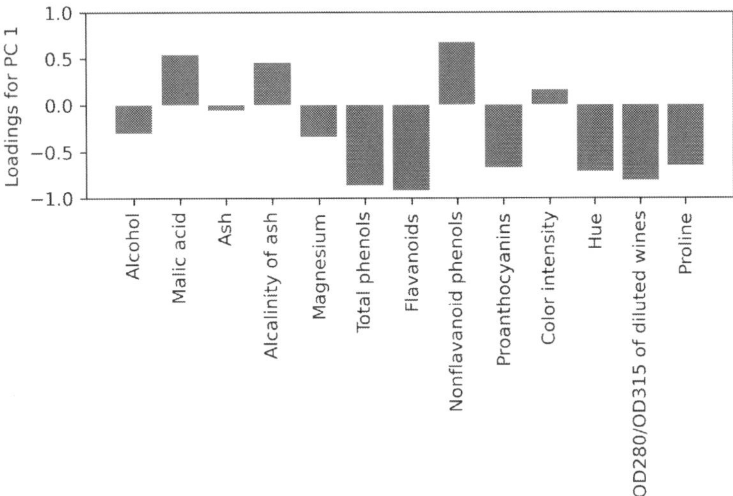

Figure 5.6: Feature correlations with the first principal component

In the preceding code example, we compute the factor loadings for our own PCA implementation. We can obtain the loadings from a fitted scikit-learn PCA object in a similar manner, where `pca.components_` represents the eigenvectors and `pca.explained_variance_` represents the eigenvalues:

```
>>> sklearn_loadings = pca.components_.T * np.sqrt(pca.explained_variance_)
```

To compare the scikit-learn PCA loadings with those we created previously, let us create a similar bar plot:

```
>>> fig, ax = plt.subplots()
>>> ax.bar(range(13), sklearn_loadings[:, 0], align='center')
>>> ax.set_ylabel('Loadings for PC 1')
>>> ax.set_xticks(range(13))
>>> ax.set_xticklabels(df_wine.columns[1:], rotation=90)
>>> plt.ylim([-1, 1])
>>> plt.tight_layout()
>>> plt.show()
```

As we can see, the bar plots look the same:

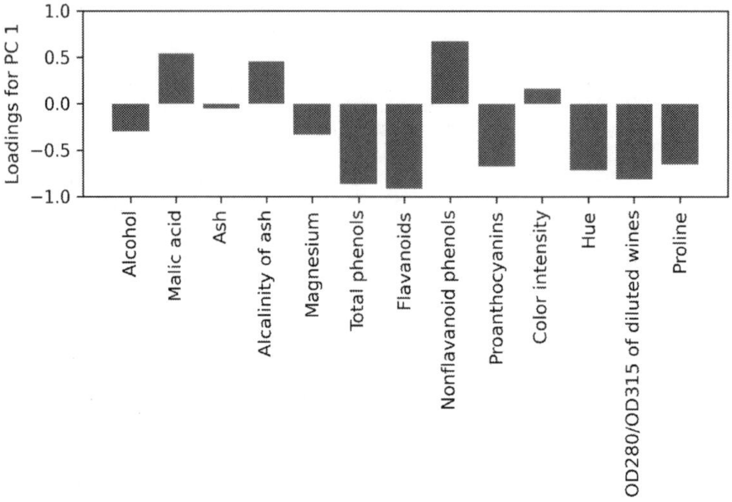

Figure 5.7: Feature correlations to the first principal component using scikit-learn

After exploring PCA as an unsupervised feature extraction technique, the next section will introduce **linear discriminant analysis (LDA)**, which is a linear transformation technique that takes class label information into account.

Supervised data compression via linear discriminant analysis

LDA can be used as a technique for feature extraction to increase computational efficiency and reduce the degree of overfitting due to the curse of dimensionality in non-regularized models. The general concept behind LDA is very similar to PCA, but whereas PCA attempts to find the orthogonal component axes of maximum variance in a dataset, the goal in LDA is to find the feature subspace that optimizes class separability. In the following sections, we will discuss the similarities between LDA and PCA in more detail and walk through the LDA approach step by step.

Principal component analysis versus linear discriminant analysis

Both PCA and LDA are *linear transformation techniques* that can be used to reduce the number of dimensions in a dataset; the former is an unsupervised algorithm, whereas the latter is supervised. Thus, we might think that LDA is a superior feature extraction technique for classification tasks compared to PCA. However, A.M. Martinez reported that preprocessing via PCA tends to result in better classification results in an image recognition task in certain cases, for instance, if each class consists of only a small number of examples (*PCA Versus LDA* by *A. M. Martinez* and *A. C. Kak, IEEE Transactions on Pattern Analysis and Machine Intelligence*, 23(2): 228-233, 2001).

Fisher LDA

LDA is sometimes also called **Fisher's LDA**. Ronald A. Fisher initially formulated *Fisher's Linear Discriminant* for two-class classification problems in 1936 (*The Use of Multiple Measurements in Taxonomic Problems, R. A. Fisher, Annals of Eugenics*, 7(2): 179-188, 1936). In 1948, Fisher's linear discriminant was generalized for multiclass problems by C. Radhakrishna Rao under the assumption of equal class covariances and normally distributed classes, which we now call LDA (*The Utilization of Multiple Measurements in Problems of Biological Classification* by *C. R. Rao, Journal of the Royal Statistical Society*. Series B (Methodological), 10(2): 159-203, 1948).

Figure 5.8 summarizes the concept of LDA for a two-class problem. Examples from class 1 are shown as circles, and examples from class 2 are shown as crosses:

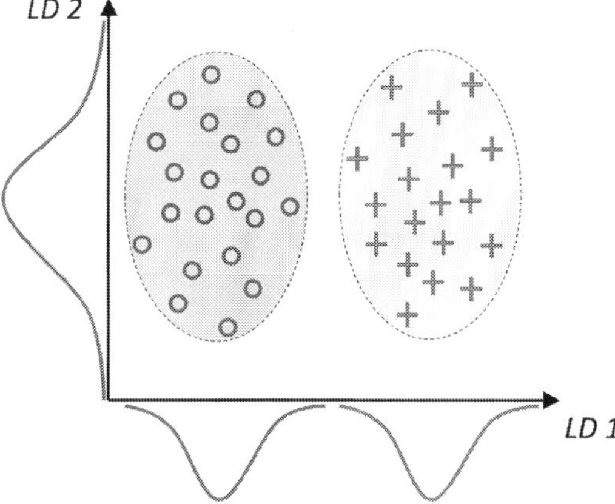

Figure 5.8: The concept of LDA for a two-class problem

A linear discriminant, as shown on the *x* axis (*LD 1*), would separate the two normal distributed classes well. Although the exemplary linear discriminant shown on the *y* axis (*LD 2*) captures a lot of the variance in the dataset, it would fail as a good linear discriminant since it does not capture any of the class-discriminatory information.

One assumption in LDA is that the data is normally distributed. Also, we assume that the classes have identical covariance matrices and that the training examples are statistically independent of each other. However, even if one, or more, of those assumptions is (slightly) violated, LDA for dimensionality reduction can still work reasonably well (*Pattern Classification 2nd Edition* by *R. O. Duda, P. E. Hart,* and *D. G. Stork, New York*, 2001).

The inner workings of linear discriminant analysis

Before we dive into the code implementation, let's briefly summarize the main steps that are required to perform LDA:

1. Standardize the *d*-dimensional dataset (*d* is the number of features).
2. For each class, compute the *d*-dimensional mean vector.
3. Construct the between-class scatter matrix, S_B, and the within-class scatter matrix, S_W.
4. Compute the eigenvectors and corresponding eigenvalues of the matrix, $\boldsymbol{S}_W^{-1}\boldsymbol{S}_B$.
5. Sort the eigenvalues by decreasing order to rank the corresponding eigenvectors.
6. Choose the *k* eigenvectors that correspond to the *k* largest eigenvalues to construct a *d*×*k*-dimensional transformation matrix, **W**; the eigenvectors are the columns of this matrix.
7. Project the examples onto the new feature subspace using the transformation matrix, **W**.

As we can see, LDA is quite similar to PCA in the sense that we are decomposing matrices into eigenvalues and eigenvectors, which will form the new lower-dimensional feature space. However, as mentioned before, LDA takes class label information into account, which is represented in the form of the mean vectors computed in *step 2*. In the following sections, we will discuss these seven steps in more detail, accompanied by illustrative code implementations.

Computing the scatter matrices

Since we already standardized the features of the Wine dataset in the PCA section at the beginning of this chapter, we can skip the first step and proceed with the calculation of the mean vectors, which we will use to construct the within-class scatter matrix and between-class scatter matrix, respectively. Each mean vector, $\boldsymbol{m}_i$, stores the mean feature value, μ_m, with respect to the examples of class *i*:

$$\boldsymbol{m}_i = \frac{1}{n_i}\sum_{\boldsymbol{x}\in D_i} \boldsymbol{x}_m$$

This results in three mean vectors:

$$\boldsymbol{m}_i = \begin{bmatrix} \mu_{i,alcohol} \\ \mu_{i,malic\ acid} \\ \vdots \\ \mu_{i,proline} \end{bmatrix}^T \quad i \in \{1,2,3\}$$

These mean vectors can be computed by the following code, where we compute one mean vector for each of the three labels:

```
>>> np.set_printoptions(precision=4)
>>> mean_vecs = []
>>> for label in range(1,4):
...     mean_vecs.append(np.mean(
...               X_train_std[y_train==label], axis=0))
...     print(f'MV {label}: {mean_vecs[label - 1]}\n')
```

```
MV 1: [ 0.9066  -0.3497  0.3201  -0.7189  0.5056  0.8807  0.9589  -0.5516
0.5416  0.2338  0.5897  0.6563  1.2075]
MV 2: [-0.8749  -0.2848  -0.3735  0.3157  -0.3848  -0.0433  0.0635  -0.0946
0.0703  -0.8286  0.3144  0.3608  -0.7253]
MV 3: [ 0.1992  0.866  0.1682  0.4148  -0.0451  -1.0286  -1.2876  0.8287
-0.7795  0.9649  -1.209  -1.3622  -0.4013]
```

Using the mean vectors, we can now compute the within-class scatter matrix, S_W:

$$\boldsymbol{S}_W = \sum_{i=1}^{c} \boldsymbol{S}_i$$

This is calculated by summing up the individual scatter matrices, S_i, of each individual class i:

$$\boldsymbol{S}_i = \sum_{x \in D_i} (\boldsymbol{x} - \boldsymbol{m}_i)(\boldsymbol{x} - \boldsymbol{m}_i)^T$$

```
>>> d = 13 # number of features
>>> S_W = np.zeros((d, d))
>>> for label, mv in zip(range(1, 4), mean_vecs):
...     class_scatter = np.zeros((d, d))
...     for row in X_train_std[y_train == label]:
...         row, mv = row.reshape(d, 1), mv.reshape(d, 1)
...         class_scatter += (row - mv).dot((row - mv).T)
...     S_W += class_scatter
>>> print('Within-class scatter matrix: '
...       f'{S_W.shape[0]}x{S_W.shape[1]}')
Within-class scatter matrix: 13x13
```

The assumption that we are making when we are computing the scatter matrices is that the class labels in the training dataset are uniformly distributed. However, if we print the number of class labels, we see that this assumption is violated:

```
>>> print('Class label distribution:',
...       np.bincount(y_train)[1:])
Class label distribution: [41 50 33]
```

Thus, we want to scale the individual scatter matrices, S_i, before we sum them up as the scatter matrix, S_W. When we divide the scatter matrices by the number of class-examples, n_i, we can see that computing the scatter matrix is in fact the same as computing the covariance matrix, Σ_i—the covariance matrix is a normalized version of the scatter matrix:

$$\Sigma_i = \frac{1}{n_i} \boldsymbol{S}_i = \frac{1}{n_i} \sum_{x \in D_i} (\boldsymbol{x} - \boldsymbol{m}_i)(\boldsymbol{x} - \boldsymbol{m}_i)^T$$

The code for computing the scaled within-class scatter matrix is as follows:

```
>>> d = 13 # number of features
>>> S_W = np.zeros((d, d))
>>> for label,mv in zip(range(1, 4), mean_vecs):
...     class_scatter = np.cov(X_train_std[y_train==label].T)
...     S_W += class_scatter
>>> print('Scaled within-class scatter matrix: '
...       f'{S_W.shape[0]}x{S_W.shape[1]}')
Scaled within-class scatter matrix: 13x13
```

After we compute the scaled within-class scatter matrix (or covariance matrix), we can move on to the next step and compute the between-class scatter matrix S_B:

$$\boldsymbol{S}_B = \sum_{i=1}^{c} n_i (\boldsymbol{m}_i - \boldsymbol{m})(\boldsymbol{m}_i - \boldsymbol{m})^T$$

Here, $\boldsymbol{m}$ is the overall mean that is computed, including examples from all *c* classes:

```
>>> mean_overall = np.mean(X_train_std, axis=0)
>>> mean_overall = mean_overall.reshape(d, 1)

>>> d = 13 # number of features
>>> S_B = np.zeros((d, d))
>>> for i, mean_vec in enumerate(mean_vecs):
...     n = X_train_std[y_train == i + 1, :].shape[0]
...     mean_vec = mean_vec.reshape(d, 1) # make column vector
...     S_B += n * (mean_vec - mean_overall).dot(
...     (mean_vec - mean_overall).T)
>>> print('Between-class scatter matrix: '
...       f'{S_B.shape[0]}x{S_B.shape[1]}')
Between-class scatter matrix: 13x13
```

Selecting linear discriminants for the new feature subspace

The remaining steps of the LDA are similar to the steps of the PCA. However, instead of performing the eigendecomposition on the covariance matrix, we solve the generalized eigenvalue problem of the matrix, $\boldsymbol{S}_W^{-1}\boldsymbol{S}_B$:

```
>>> eigen_vals, eigen_vecs =\
...     np.linalg.eig(np.linalg.inv(S_W).dot(S_B))
```

After we compute the eigenpairs, we can sort the eigenvalues in descending order:

```
>>> eigen_pairs = [(np.abs(eigen_vals[i]), eigen_vecs[:,i])
...                for i in range(len(eigen_vals))]
```

```
>>> eigen_pairs = sorted(eigen_pairs,
...               key=lambda k: k[0], reverse=True)
>>> print('Eigenvalues in descending order:\n')
>>> for eigen_val in eigen_pairs:
...     print(eigen_val[0])
Eigenvalues in descending order:
349.617808906
172.76152219
3.78531345125e-14
2.11739844822e-14
1.51646188942e-14
1.51646188942e-14
1.35795671405e-14
1.35795671405e-14
7.58776037165e-15
5.90603998447e-15
5.90603998447e-15
2.25644197857e-15
0.0
```

In LDA, the number of linear discriminants is at most $c - 1$, where c is the number of class labels, since the in-between scatter matrix, S_B, is the sum of c matrices with rank one or less. We can indeed see that we only have two nonzero eigenvalues (the eigenvalues 3-13 are not exactly zero, but this is due to the floating-point arithmetic in NumPy.)

Collinearity

Note that in the rare case of perfect collinearity (all aligned example points fall on a straight line), the covariance matrix would have rank one, which would result in only one eigenvector with a nonzero eigenvalue.

To measure how much of the class-discriminatory information is captured by the linear discriminants (eigenvectors), let's plot the linear discriminants by decreasing eigenvalues, similar to the explained variance plot that we created in the PCA section. For simplicity, we will call the content of class-discriminatory information **discriminability:**

```
>>> tot = sum(eigen_vals.real)
>>> discr = [(i / tot) for i in sorted(eigen_vals.real,
...                                    reverse=True)]
>>> cum_discr = np.cumsum(discr)
>>> plt.bar(range(1, 14), discr, align='center',
...         label='Individual discriminability')
```

```
>>> plt.step(range(1, 14), cum_discr, where='mid',
...          label='Cumulative discriminability')
>>> plt.ylabel('"Discriminability" ratio')
>>> plt.xlabel('Linear Discriminants')
>>> plt.ylim([-0.1, 1.1])
>>> plt.legend(loc='best')
>>> plt.tight_layout()
>>> plt.show()
```

As we can see in *Figure 5.9*, the first two linear discriminants alone capture 100 percent of the useful information in the Wine training dataset:

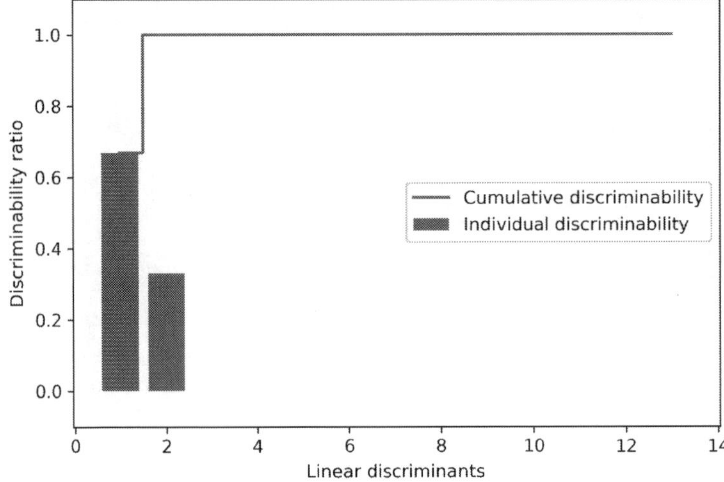

Figure 5.9: The top two discriminants capture 100 percent of the useful information

Let's now stack the two most discriminative eigenvector columns to create the transformation matrix, *W*:

```
>>> w = np.hstack((eigen_pairs[0][1][:, np.newaxis].real,
...                eigen_pairs[1][1][:, np.newaxis].real))
>>> print('Matrix W:\n', w)
Matrix W:
 [[-0.1481  -0.4092]
  [ 0.0908  -0.1577]
  [-0.0168  -0.3537]
  [ 0.1484   0.3223]
  [-0.0163  -0.0817]
  [ 0.1913   0.0842]
  [-0.7338   0.2823]
  [-0.075   -0.0102]
```

```
[ 0.0018   0.0907]
[ 0.294   -0.2152]
[-0.0328   0.2747]
[-0.3547  -0.0124]
[-0.3915  -0.5958]]
```

Projecting examples onto the new feature space

Using the transformation matrix W that we created in the previous subsection, we can now transform the training dataset by multiplying the matrices:

$$X' = XW$$

```
>>> X_train_lda = X_train_std.dot(w)
>>> colors = ['r', 'b', 'g']
>>> markers = ['o', 's', '^']
>>> for l, c, m in zip(np.unique(y_train), colors, markers):
...     plt.scatter(X_train_lda[y_train==l, 0],
...                 X_train_lda[y_train==l, 1] * (-1),
...                 c=c, label= f'Class {l}', marker=m)
>>> plt.xlabel('LD 1')
>>> plt.ylabel('LD 2')
>>> plt.legend(loc='lower right')
>>> plt.tight_layout()
>>> plt.show()
```

As we can see in *Figure 5.10*, the three Wine classes are now perfectly linearly separable in the new feature subspace:

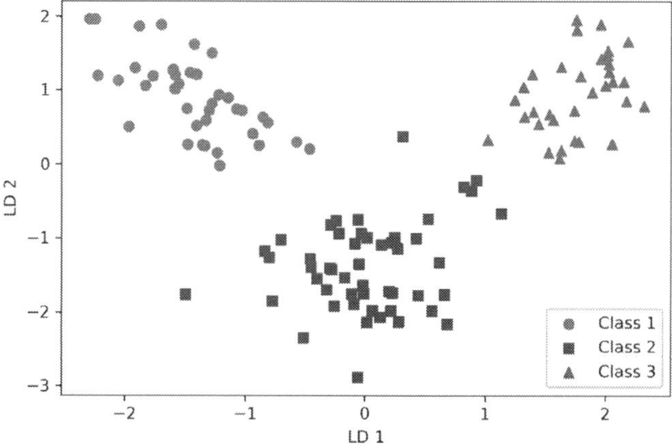

Figure 5.10: Wine classes perfectly separable after projecting the data onto the first two discriminants

LDA via scikit-learn

That step-by-step implementation was a good exercise to understand the inner workings of LDA and understand the differences between LDA and PCA. Now, let's look at the `LDA` class implemented in scikit-learn:

```
>>> # the following import statement is one line
>>> from sklearn.discriminant_analysis import LinearDiscriminantAnalysis as LDA
>>> lda = LDA(n_components=2)
>>> X_train_lda = lda.fit_transform(X_train_std, y_train)
```

Next, let's see how the logistic regression classifier handles the lower-dimensional training dataset after the LDA transformation:

```
>>> lr = LogisticRegression(multi_class='ovr', random_state=1,
...                         solver='lbfgs')
>>> lr = lr.fit(X_train_lda, y_train)
>>> plot_decision_regions(X_train_lda, y_train, classifier=lr)
>>> plt.xlabel('LD 1')
>>> plt.ylabel('LD 2')
>>> plt.legend(loc='lower left')
>>> plt.tight_layout()
>>> plt.show()
```

Looking at *Figure 5.11*, we can see that the logistic regression model misclassifies one of the examples from class 2:

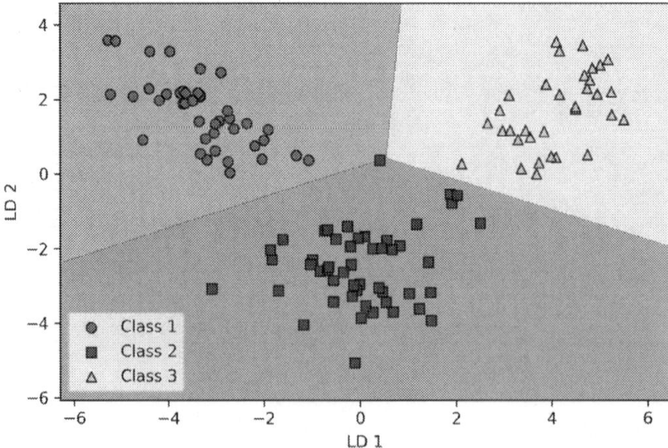

Figure 5.11: The logistic regression model misclassifies one of the classes

By lowering the regularization strength, we could probably shift the decision boundaries so that the logistic regression model classifies all examples in the training dataset correctly. However, and more importantly, let's take a look at the results on the test dataset:

```
>>> X_test_lda = lda.transform(X_test_std)
>>> plot_decision_regions(X_test_lda, y_test, classifier=lr)
>>> plt.xlabel('LD 1')
>>> plt.ylabel('LD 2')
>>> plt.legend(loc='lower left')
>>> plt.tight_layout()
>>> plt.show()
```

As we can see in *Figure 5.12*, the logistic regression classifier is able to get a perfect accuracy score for classifying the examples in the test dataset by only using a two-dimensional feature subspace, instead of the original 13 Wine features:

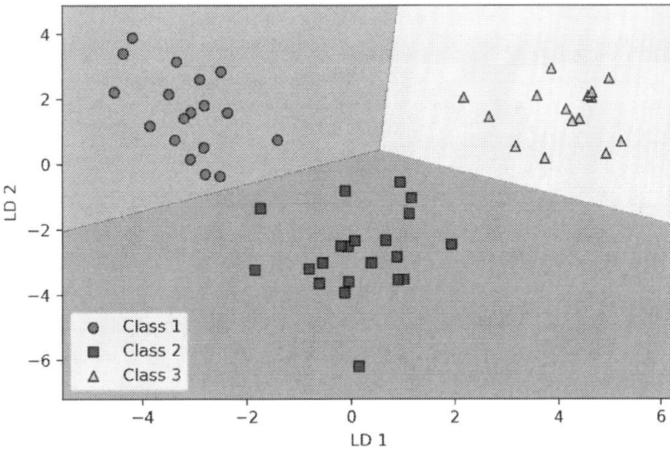

Figure 5.12: The logistic regression model works perfectly on the test data

Nonlinear dimensionality reduction and visualization

In the previous section, we covered linear transformation techniques, such as PCA and LDA, for feature extraction. In this section, we will discuss why considering nonlinear dimensionality reduction techniques might be worthwhile.

One nonlinear dimensionality reduction technique that is particularly worth highlighting is **t-distributed stochastic neighbor embedding** (t-SNE) since it is frequently used in literature to visualize high-dimensional datasets in two or three dimensions. We will see how we can apply t-SNE to plot images of handwritten images in a 2-dimensional feature space.

Why consider nonlinear dimensionality reduction?

Many machine learning algorithms make assumptions about the linear separability of the input data.

You have learned that the perceptron even requires perfectly linearly separable training data to converge. Other algorithms that we have covered so far assume that the lack of perfect linear separability is due to noise: Adaline, logistic regression, and the (standard) SVM to just name a few.

However, if we are dealing with nonlinear problems, which we may encounter rather frequently in real-world applications, linear transformation techniques for dimensionality reduction, such as PCA and LDA, may not be the best choice:

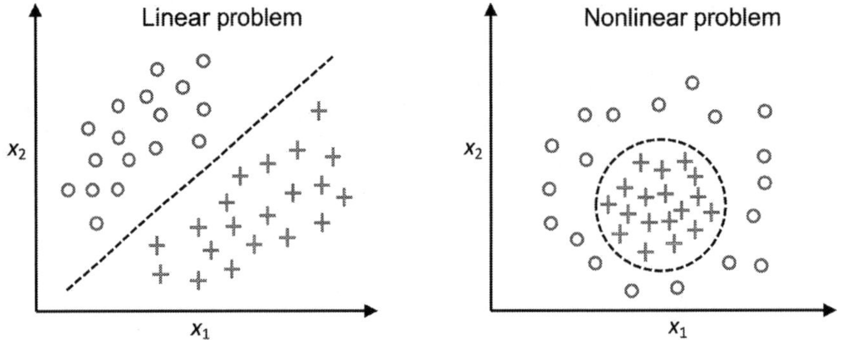

Figure 5.13: The difference between linear and nonlinear problems

The scikit-learn library implements a selection of advanced techniques for nonlinear dimensionality reduction that are beyond the scope of this book. The interested reader can find a nice overview of the current implementations in scikit-learn, complemented by illustrative examples, at `http://scikit-learn.org/stable/modules/manifold.html`.

The development and application of nonlinear dimensionality reduction techniques is also often referred to as manifold learning, where a manifold refers to a lower dimensional topological space embedded in a high-dimensional space. Algorithms for manifold learning have to capture the complicated structure of the data in order to project it onto a lower-dimensional space where the relationship between data points is preserved.

A classic example of manifold learning is the 3-dimensional Swiss roll illustrated in *Figure 5.14*:

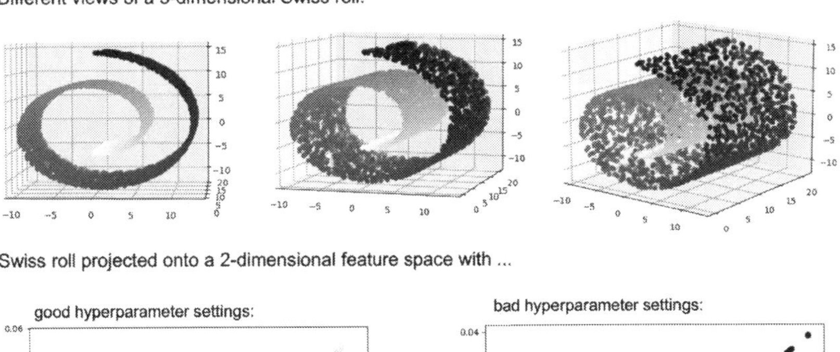

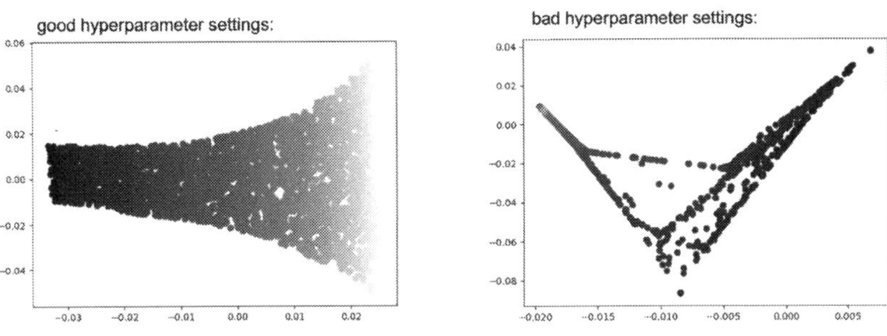

Figure 5.14: Three-dimensional Swiss roll projected into a lower, two-dimensional space

While nonlinear dimensionality reduction and manifold learning algorithms are very powerful, we should note that these techniques are notoriously hard to use, and with non-ideal hyperparameter choices, they may cause more harm than good. The reason behind this difficulty is that we are often working with high-dimensional datasets that we cannot readily visualize and where the structure is not obvious (unlike the Swiss roll example in *Figure 5.14*). Moreover, unless we project the dataset into two or three dimensions (which is often not sufficient for capturing more complicated relationships), it is hard or even impossible to assess the quality of the results. Hence, many people still rely on simpler techniques such as PCA and LDA for dimensionality reduction.

Visualizing data via t-distributed stochastic neighbor embedding

After introducing nonlinear dimensionality reduction and discussing some of its challenges, let's take a look at a hands-on example involving t-SNE, which is often used for visualizing complex datasets in two or three dimensions.

In a nutshell, t-SNE is modeling data points based on their pair-wise distances in the high-dimensional (original) feature space. Then, it finds a probability distribution of pair-wise distances in the new, lower-dimensional space that is close to the probability distribution of pair-wise distances in the original space. Or, in other words, t-SNE learns to embed data points into a lower-dimensional space such that the pairwise distances in the original space are preserved. You can find more details about this method in the original research paper *Visualizing data using t-SNE* by *Maaten and Hinton, Journal of Machine Learning Research*, 2018 (`https://www.jmlr.org/papers/volume9/vandermaaten08a/vandermaaten08a.pdf`). However, as the research paper title suggests, t-SNE is a technique intended for visualization purposes as it requires the whole dataset for the projection. Since it projects the points directly (unlike PCA, it does not involve a projection matrix), we cannot apply t-SNE to new data points.

The following code shows a quick demonstration of how t-SNE can be applied to a 64-dimensional dataset. First, we load the Digits dataset from scikit-learn, which consists of low-resolution handwritten digits (the numbers 0-9):

```
>>> from sklearn.datasets import load_digits
>>> digits = load_digits()
```

The digits are 8×8 grayscale images. The following code plots the first four images in the dataset, which consists of 1,797 images in total:

```
>>> fig, ax = plt.subplots(1, 4)
>>> for i in range(4):
>>>     ax[i].imshow(digits.images[i], cmap='Greys')
>>> plt.show()
```

As we can see in *Figure 5.15*, the images are relatively low resolution, 8×8 pixels (that is, 64 pixels per image):

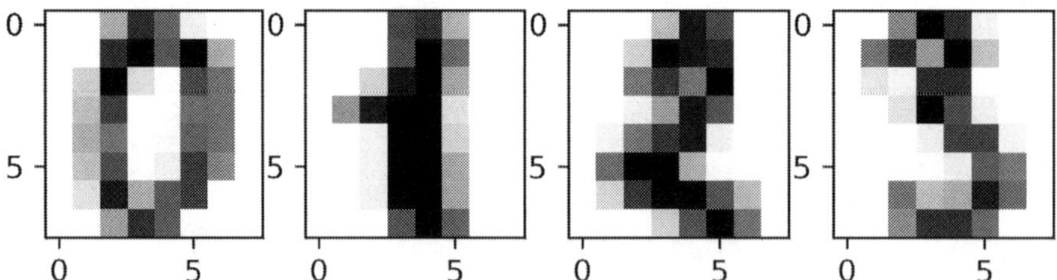

Figure 5.15: Low resolution images of handwritten digits

Note that the `digits.data` attribute lets us access a tabular version of this dataset where the examples are represented by the rows, and the columns correspond to the pixels:

```
>>> digits.data.shape
(1797, 64)
```

Next, let us assign the features (pixels) to a new variable `X_digits` and the labels to another new variable `y_digits`:

```
>>> y_digits = digits.target
>>> X_digits = digits.data
```

Then, we import the t-SNE class from scikit-learn and fit a new `tsne` object. Using `fit_transform`, we perform the t-SNE fitting and data transformation in one step:

```
>>> from sklearn.manifold import TSNE
>>> tsne = TSNE(n_components=2, init='pca',
...             random_state=123)
>>> X_digits_tsne = tsne.fit_transform(X_digits)
```

Using this code, we projected the 64-dimensional dataset onto a 2-dimensional space. We specified `init='pca'`, which initializes the t-SNE embedding using PCA as it is recommended in the research article *Initialization is critical for preserving global data structure in both t-SNE and UMAP* by *Kobak* and *Linderman*, *Nature Biotechnology Volume 39*, pages 156–157, 2021 (`https://www.nature.com/articles/s41587-020-00809-z`).

Note that t-SNE includes additional hyperparameters such as the perplexity and learning rate (often called **epsilon**), which we omitted in the example (we used the scikit-learn default values). In practice, we recommend you explore these parameters as well. More information about these parameters and their effects on the results can be found in the excellent article *How to Use t-SNE Effectively* by *Wattenberg*, *Viegas*, and *Johnson*, *Distill*, 2016 (`https://distill.pub/2016/misread-tsne/`).

Finally, let us visualize the 2D t-SNE embeddings using the following code:

```
>>> import matplotlib.patheffects as PathEffects
>>> def plot_projection(x, colors):

...     f = plt.figure(figsize=(8, 8))
...     ax = plt.subplot(aspect='equal')
...     for i in range(10):
...         plt.scatter(x[colors == i, 0],
...                     x[colors == i, 1])

...     for i in range(10):
...         xtext, ytext = np.median(x[colors == i, :], axis=0)
...         txt = ax.text(xtext, ytext, str(i), fontsize=24)
...         txt.set_path_effects([
...             PathEffects.Stroke(linewidth=5, foreground="w"),
...             PathEffects.Normal()])
```

```
>>> plot_projection(X_digits_tsne, y_digits)
>>> plt.show()
```

Like PCA, t-SNE is an unsupervised method, and in the preceding code, we use the class labels `y_digits` (0-9) only for visualization purposes via the functions color argument. Matplotlib's `PathEffects` are used for visual purposes, such that the class label is displayed in the center (via `np.median`) of data points belonging to each respective digit. The resulting plot is as follows:

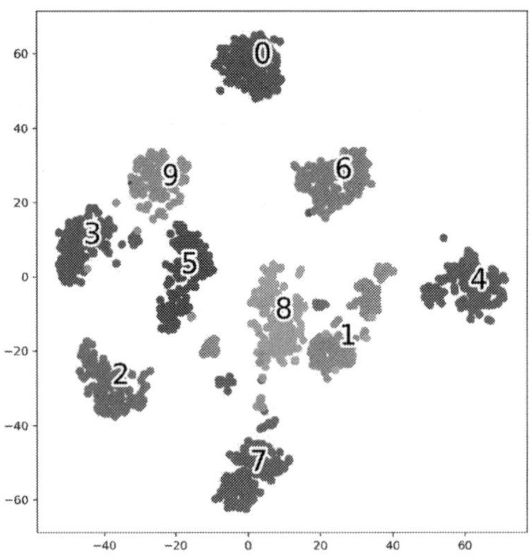

Figure 5.16: A visualization of how t-SNE embeds the handwritten digits in a 2D feature space

As we can see, t-SNE is able to separate the different digits (classes) nicely, although not perfectly. It might be possible to achieve better separation by tuning the hyperparameters. However, a certain degree of class mixing might be unavoidable due to illegible handwriting. For instance, by inspecting individual images, we might find that certain instances of the number 3 indeed look like the number 9, and so forth.

Uniform manifold approximation and projection

Another popular visualization technique is **uniform manifold approximation and projection (UMAP)**. While UMAP can produce similarly good results as t-SNE (for example, see the Kobak and Linderman paper referenced previously), it is typically faster, and it can also be used to project new data, which makes it more attractive as a dimensionality reduction technique in a machine learning context, similar to PCA. Interested readers can find more information about UMAP in the original paper: *UMAP: Uniform manifold approximation and projection for dimension reduction* by *McInnes, Healy*, and *Melville*, 2018 (`https://arxiv.org/abs/1802.03426`). A scikit-learn compatible implementation of UMAP can be found at `https://umap-learn.readthedocs.io`.

Summary

In this chapter, you learned about two fundamental dimensionality reduction techniques for feature extraction: PCA and LDA. Using PCA, we projected data onto a lower-dimensional subspace to maximize the variance along the orthogonal feature axes, while ignoring the class labels. LDA, in contrast to PCA, is a technique for supervised dimensionality reduction, which means that it considers class information in the training dataset to attempt to maximize the class separability in a linear feature space. Lastly, you also learned about t-SNE, which is a nonlinear feature extraction technique that can be used for visualizing data in two or three dimensions.

Equipped with PCA and LDA as fundamental data preprocessing techniques, you are now well prepared to learn about the best practices for efficiently incorporating different preprocessing techniques and evaluating the performance of different models in the next chapter.

Join our book's Discord space

Join our Discord community to meet like-minded people and learn alongside more than 2000 members at:
`https://packt.link/MLwPyTorch`

6

Learning Best Practices for Model Evaluation and Hyperparameter Tuning

In the previous chapters, we learned about the essential machine learning algorithms for classification and how to get our data into shape before we feed it into those algorithms. Now, it's time to learn about the best practices of building good machine learning models by fine-tuning the algorithms and evaluating the performance of the models. In this chapter, we will learn how to do the following:

- Assess the performance of machine learning models
- Diagnose the common problems of machine learning algorithms
- Fine-tune machine learning models
- Evaluate predictive models using different performance metrics

Streamlining workflows with pipelines

When we applied different preprocessing techniques in the previous chapters, such as standardization for feature scaling in *Chapter 4, Building Good Training Datasets – Data Preprocessing*, or principal component analysis for data compression in *Chapter 5, Compressing Data via Dimensionality Reduction*, you learned that we have to reuse the parameters that were obtained during the fitting of the training data to scale and compress any new data, such as the examples in the separate test dataset. In this section, you will learn about an extremely handy tool, the `Pipeline` class in scikit-learn. It allows us to fit a model including an arbitrary number of transformation steps and apply it to make predictions about new data.

Loading the Breast Cancer Wisconsin dataset

In this chapter, we will be working with the Breast Cancer Wisconsin dataset, which contains 569 examples of malignant and benign tumor cells. The first two columns in the dataset store the unique ID numbers of the examples and the corresponding diagnoses (`M` = malignant, `B` = benign), respectively. Columns 3-32 contain 30 real-valued features that have been computed from digitized images of the cell nuclei, which can be used to build a model to predict whether a tumor is benign or malignant. The Breast Cancer Wisconsin dataset has been deposited in the UCI Machine Learning Repository, and more detailed information about this dataset can be found at https://archive.ics.uci.edu/ml/datasets/Breast+Cancer+Wisconsin+(Diagnostic).

Obtaining the Breast Cancer Wisconsin dataset

You can find a copy of the dataset (and all other datasets used in this book) in the code bundle of this book, which you can use if you are working offline or the UCI server at https://archive.ics.uci.edu/ml/machine-learning-databases/breast-cancer-wisconsin/wdbc.data is temporarily unavailable. For instance, to load the dataset from a local directory, you can replace the following lines:

```
df = pd.read_csv(
    'https://archive.ics.uci.edu/ml/'
    'machine-learning-databases'
    '/breast-cancer-wisconsin/wdbc.data',
    header=None
)
```

with these:

```
df = pd.read_csv(
    'your/local/path/to/wdbc.data',
    header=None
)
```

In this section, we will read in the dataset and split it into training and test datasets in three simple steps:

1. We will start by reading in the dataset directly from the UCI website using pandas:

```
>>> import pandas as pd
>>> df = pd.read_csv('https://archive.ics.uci.edu/ml/'
...                  'machine-learning-databases'
...                  '/breast-cancer-wisconsin/wdbc.data',
...                  header=None)
```

2. Next, we will assign the 30 features to a NumPy array, `X`. Using a `LabelEncoder` object, we will transform the class labels from their original string representation (`'M'` and `'B'`) into integers:

```
>>> from sklearn.preprocessing import LabelEncoder
>>> X = df.loc[:, 2:].values
>>> y = df.loc[:, 1].values
>>> le = LabelEncoder()
>>> y = le.fit_transform(y)
>>> le.classes_
array(['B', 'M'], dtype=object)
```

3. After encoding the class labels (diagnosis) in an array, `y`, the malignant tumors are now represented as class `1`, and the benign tumors are represented as class `0`, respectively. We can double-check this mapping by calling the `transform` method of the fitted `LabelEncoder` on two dummy class labels:

```
>>> le.transform(['M', 'B'])
array([1, 0])
```

4. Before we construct our first model pipeline in the following subsection, let's divide the dataset into a separate training dataset (80 percent of the data) and a separate test dataset (20 percent of the data):

```
>>> from sklearn.model_selection import train_test_split
>>> X_train, X_test, y_train, y_test = \
...     train_test_split(X, y,
...                      test_size=0.20,
...                      stratify=y,
...                      random_state=1)
```

Combining transformers and estimators in a pipeline

In the previous chapter, you learned that many learning algorithms require input features on the same scale for optimal performance. Since the features in the Breast Cancer Wisconsin dataset are measured on various different scales, we will standardize the columns in the Breast Cancer Wisconsin dataset before we feed them to a linear classifier, such as logistic regression. Furthermore, let's assume that we want to compress our data from the initial 30 dimensions into a lower two-dimensional subspace via **principal component analysis** (**PCA**), a feature extraction technique for dimensionality reduction that was introduced in *Chapter 5*.

Instead of going through the model fitting and data transformation steps for the training and test datasets separately, we can chain the `StandardScaler`, `PCA`, and `LogisticRegression` objects in a pipeline:

```
>>> from sklearn.preprocessing import StandardScaler
>>> from sklearn.decomposition import PCA
>>> from sklearn.linear_model import LogisticRegression
>>> from sklearn.pipeline import make_pipeline
>>> pipe_lr = make_pipeline(StandardScaler(),
...                         PCA(n_components=2),
...                         LogisticRegression())
>>> pipe_lr.fit(X_train, y_train)
>>> y_pred = pipe_lr.predict(X_test)
>>> test_acc = pipe_lr.score(X_test, y_test)
>>> print(f'Test accuracy: {test_acc:.3f}')
Test accuracy: 0.956
```

The `make_pipeline` function takes an arbitrary number of scikit-learn transformers (objects that support the `fit` and `transform` methods as input), followed by a scikit-learn estimator that implements the `fit` and `predict` methods. In our preceding code example, we provided two scikit-learn transformers, `StandardScaler` and `PCA`, and a `LogisticRegression` estimator as inputs to the `make_pipeline` function, which constructs a scikit-learn `Pipeline` object from these objects.

We can think of a scikit-learn `Pipeline` as a meta-estimator or wrapper around those individual transformers and estimators. If we call the `fit` method of `Pipeline`, the data will be passed down a series of transformers via `fit` and `transform` calls on these intermediate steps until it arrives at the estimator object (the final element in a pipeline). The estimator will then be fitted to the transformed training data.

When we executed the `fit` method on the `pipe_lr` pipeline in the preceding code example, `StandardScaler` first performed `fit` and `transform` calls on the training data. Second, the transformed training data was passed on to the next object in the pipeline, `PCA`. Similar to the previous step, `PCA` also executed `fit` and `transform` on the scaled input data and passed it to the final element of the pipeline, the estimator.

Finally, the `LogisticRegression` estimator was fit to the training data after it underwent transformations via `StandardScaler` and `PCA`. Again, we should note that there is no limit to the number of intermediate steps in a pipeline; however, if we want to use the pipeline for prediction tasks, the last pipeline element has to be an estimator.

Similar to calling `fit` on a pipeline, pipelines also implement a `predict` method if the last step in the pipeline is an estimator. If we feed a dataset to the `predict` call of a `Pipeline` object instance, the data will pass through the intermediate steps via `transform` calls. In the final step, the estimator object will then return a prediction on the transformed data.

The pipelines of the scikit-learn library are immensely useful wrapper tools that we will use frequently throughout the rest of this book. To make sure that you've got a good grasp of how the `Pipeline` object works, please take a close look at *Figure 6.1*, which summarizes our discussion from the previous paragraphs:

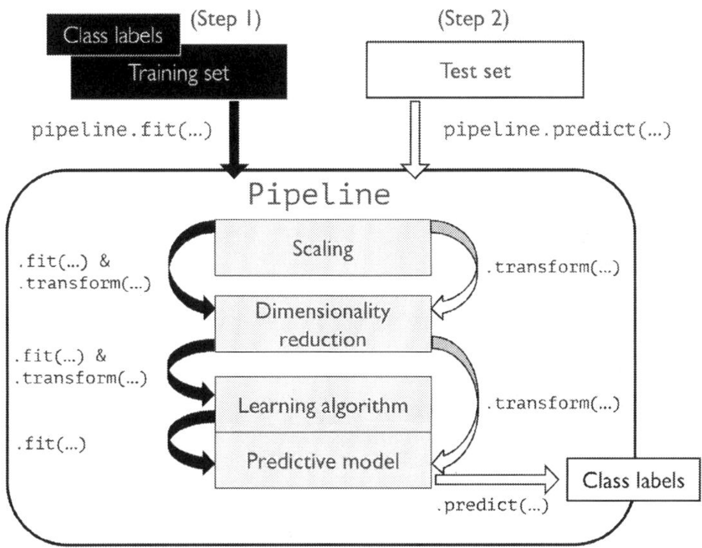

Figure 6.1: The inner workings of the Pipeline object

Using k-fold cross-validation to assess model performance

In this section, you will learn about the common cross-validation techniques **holdout cross-validation** and **k-fold cross-validation**, which can help us to obtain reliable estimates of the model's generalization performance, that is, how well the model performs on unseen data.

The holdout method

A classic and popular approach for estimating the generalization performance of machine learning models is the holdout method. Using the holdout method, we split our initial dataset into separate training and test datasets—the former is used for model training, and the latter is used to estimate its generalization performance. However, in typical machine learning applications, we are also interested in tuning and comparing different parameter settings to further improve the performance for making predictions on unseen data. This process is called **model selection**, with the name referring to a given classification problem for which we want to select the *optimal* values of *tuning parameters* (also called **hyperparameters**). However, if we reuse the same test dataset over and over again during model selection, it will become part of our training data and thus the model will be more likely to overfit. Despite this issue, many people still use the test dataset for model selection, which is not a good machine learning practice.

A better way of using the holdout method for model selection is to separate the data into three parts: a training dataset, a validation dataset, and a test dataset. The training dataset is used to fit the different models, and the performance on the validation dataset is then used for model selection. The advantage of having a test dataset that the model hasn't seen before during the training and model selection steps is that we can obtain a less biased estimate of its ability to generalize to new data. *Figure 6.2* illustrates the concept of holdout cross-validation, where we use a validation dataset to repeatedly evaluate the performance of the model after training using different hyperparameter values. Once we are satisfied with the tuning of hyperparameter values, we estimate the model's generalization performance on the test dataset:

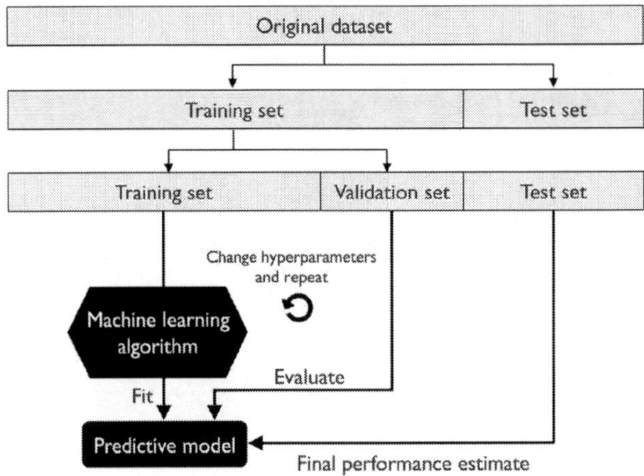

Figure 6.2: How to use training, validation, and test datasets

A disadvantage of the holdout method is that the performance estimate may be very sensitive to how we partition the training dataset into the training and validation subsets; the estimate will vary for different examples of the data. In the next subsection, we will take a look at a more robust technique for performance estimation, k-fold cross-validation, where we repeat the holdout method k times on k subsets of the training data.

K-fold cross-validation

In k-fold cross-validation, we randomly split the training dataset into k folds without replacement. Here, $k - 1$ folds, the so-called *training folds*, are used for the model training, and one fold, the so-called *test fold*, is used for performance evaluation. This procedure is repeated k times so that we obtain k models and performance estimates.

Sampling with and without replacement

We looked at an example to illustrate sampling with and without replacement in *Chapter 3*. If you haven't read that chapter, or want a refresher, refer to the information box titled *Sampling with and without replacement* in the *Combining multiple decision trees via random forests* section.

We then calculate the average performance of the models based on the different, independent test folds to obtain a performance estimate that is less sensitive to the sub-partitioning of the training data compared to the holdout method. Typically, we use k-fold cross-validation for model tuning, that is, finding the optimal hyperparameter values that yield a satisfying generalization performance, which is estimated from evaluating the model performance on the test folds.

Once we have found satisfactory hyperparameter values, we can retrain the model on the complete training dataset and obtain a final performance estimate using the independent test dataset. The rationale behind fitting a model to the whole training dataset after k-fold cross-validation is that first, we are typically interested in a single, final model (versus k individual models), and second, providing more training examples to a learning algorithm usually results in a more accurate and robust model.

Since k-fold cross-validation is a resampling technique without replacement, the advantage of this approach is that in each iteration, each example will be used exactly once, and the training and test folds are disjoint. Furthermore, all test folds are disjoint; that is, there is no overlap between the test folds. *Figure 6.3* summarizes the concept behind k-fold cross-validation with $k = 10$. The training dataset is divided into 10 folds, and during the 10 iterations, 9 folds are used for training, and 1 fold will be used as the test dataset for model evaluation.

Also, the estimated performances, E_i (for example, classification accuracy or error), for each fold are then used to calculate the estimated average performance, E, of the model:

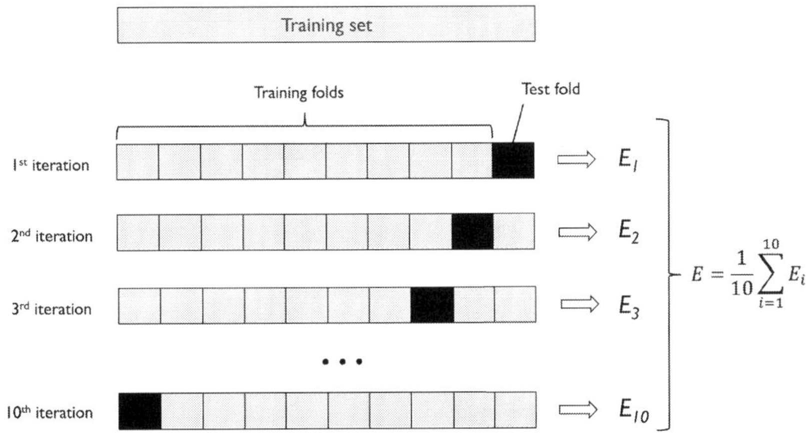

Figure 6.3: How k-fold cross-validation works

In summary, k-fold cross-validation makes better use of the dataset than the holdout method with a validation set, since in k-fold cross-validation all data points are being used for evaluation.

A good standard value for k in k-fold cross-validation is 10, as empirical evidence shows. For instance, experiments by Ron Kohavi on various real-world datasets suggest that 10-fold cross-validation offers the best tradeoff between bias and variance (*A Study of Cross-Validation and Bootstrap for Accuracy Estimation and Model Selection* by *Kohavi, Ron, International Joint Conference on Artificial Intelligence (IJCAI)*, 14 (12): 1137-43, 1995, `https://www.ijcai.org/Proceedings/95-2/Papers/016.pdf`).

However, if we are working with relatively small training sets, it can be useful to increase the number of folds. If we increase the value of k, more training data will be used in each iteration, which results in a lower pessimistic bias toward estimating the generalization performance by averaging the individual model estimates. However, large values of k will also increase the runtime of the cross-validation algorithm and yield estimates with higher variance, since the training folds will be more similar to each other. On the other hand, if we are working with large datasets, we can choose a smaller value for k, for example, $k = 5$, and still obtain an accurate estimate of the average performance of the model while reducing the computational cost of refitting and evaluating the model on the different folds.

Leave-one-out cross-validation

A special case of k-fold cross-validation is the **leave-one-out cross-validation (LOOCV)** method. In LOOCV, we set the number of folds equal to the number of training examples ($k = n$) so that only one training example is used for testing during each iteration, which is a recommended approach for working with very small datasets.

A slight improvement over the standard k-fold cross-validation approach is stratified k-fold cross-validation, which can yield better bias and variance estimates, especially in cases of unequal class proportions, which has also been shown in the same study by Ron Kohavi referenced previously in this section. In stratified cross-validation, the class label proportions are preserved in each fold to ensure that each fold is representative of the class proportions in the training dataset, which we will illustrate by using the `StratifiedKFold` iterator in scikit-learn:

```
>>> import numpy as np
>>> from sklearn.model_selection import StratifiedKFold
>>> kfold = StratifiedKFold(n_splits=10).split(X_train, y_train)
>>> scores = []
>>> for k, (train, test) in enumerate(kfold):
...     pipe_lr.fit(X_train[train], y_train[train])
...     score = pipe_lr.score(X_train[test], y_train[test])
...     scores.append(score)
...     print(f'Fold: {k+1:02d}, '
...           f'Class distr.: {np.bincount(y_train[train])}, '
...           f'Acc.: {score:.3f}')
Fold: 01, Class distr.: [256 153], Acc.: 0.935
Fold: 02, Class distr.: [256 153], Acc.: 0.935
Fold: 03, Class distr.: [256 153], Acc.: 0.957
Fold: 04, Class distr.: [256 153], Acc.: 0.957
```

```
Fold: 05, Class distr.: [256 153], Acc.: 0.935
Fold: 06, Class distr.: [257 153], Acc.: 0.956
Fold: 07, Class distr.: [257 153], Acc.: 0.978
Fold: 08, Class distr.: [257 153], Acc.: 0.933
Fold: 09, Class distr.: [257 153], Acc.: 0.956
Fold: 10, Class distr.: [257 153], Acc.: 0.956
>>> mean_acc = np.mean(scores)
>>> std_acc = np.std(scores)
>>> print(f'\nCV accuracy: {mean_acc:.3f} +/- {std_acc:.3f}')
CV accuracy: 0.950 +/- 0.014
```

First, we initialized the `StratifiedKFold` iterator from the `sklearn.model_selection` module with the `y_train` class labels in the training dataset, and we specified the number of folds via the `n_splits` parameter. When we used the `kfold` iterator to loop through the `k` folds, we used the returned indices in `train` to fit the logistic regression pipeline that we set up at the beginning of this chapter. Using the `pipe_lr` pipeline, we ensured that the examples were scaled properly (for instance, standardized) in each iteration. We then used the `test` indices to calculate the accuracy score of the model, which we collected in the `scores` list to calculate the average accuracy and the standard deviation of the estimate.

Although the previous code example was useful to illustrate how k-fold cross-validation works, scikit-learn also implements a k-fold cross-validation scorer, which allows us to evaluate our model using stratified k-fold cross-validation less verbosely:

```
>>> from sklearn.model_selection import cross_val_score
>>> scores = cross_val_score(estimator=pipe_lr,
...                          X=X_train,
...                          y=y_train,
...                          cv=10,
...                          n_jobs=1)
>>> print(f'CV accuracy scores: {scores}')
CV accuracy scores: [ 0.93478261  0.93478261  0.95652174
                      0.95652174  0.93478261  0.95555556
                      0.97777778  0.93333333  0.95555556
                      0.95555556]
>>> print(f'CV accuracy: {np.mean(scores):.3f} '
...       f'+/- {np.std(scores):.3f}')
CV accuracy: 0.950 +/- 0.014
```

An extremely useful feature of the `cross_val_score` approach is that we can distribute the evaluation of the different folds across multiple **central processing units** (**CPUs**) on our machine. If we set the `n_jobs` parameter to `1`, only one CPU will be used to evaluate the performances, just like in our `StratifiedKFold` example previously. However, by setting `n_jobs=2`, we could distribute the 10 rounds of cross-validation to two CPUs (if available on our machine), and by setting `n_jobs=-1`, we can use all available CPUs on our machine to do the computation in parallel.

Estimating generalization performance

Please note that a detailed discussion of how the variance of the generalization performance is estimated in cross-validation is beyond the scope of this book, but you can refer to a comprehensive article about model evaluation and cross-validation (*Model Evaluation, Model Selection, and Algorithm Selection in Machine Learning* by *S. Raschka*), which we share at `https://arxiv.org/abs/1811.12808`. This article also discusses alternative cross-validation techniques, such as the .632 and .632+ bootstrap cross-validation methods.

In addition, you can find a detailed discussion in an excellent article by M. Markatou and others (*Analysis of Variance of Cross-validation Estimators of the Generalization Error* by *M. Markatou, H. Tian, S. Biswas, and G. M. Hripcsak, Journal of Machine Learning Research*, 6: 1127-1168, 2005), which is available at `https://www.jmlr.org/papers/v6/markatou05a.html`.

Debugging algorithms with learning and validation curves

In this section, we will take a look at two very simple yet powerful diagnostic tools that can help us to improve the performance of a learning algorithm: **learning curves** and **validation curves**. In the next subsections, we will discuss how we can use learning curves to diagnose whether a learning algorithm has a problem with overfitting (high variance) or underfitting (high bias). Furthermore, we will take a look at validation curves, which can help us to address the common issues of learning algorithms.

Diagnosing bias and variance problems with learning curves

If a model is too complex for a given training dataset—for example, think of a very deep decision tree—the model tends to overfit the training data and does not generalize well to unseen data. Often, it can help to collect more training examples to reduce the degree of overfitting.

However, in practice, it can often be very expensive or simply not feasible to collect more data. By plotting the model training and validation accuracies as functions of the training dataset size, we can easily detect whether the model suffers from high variance or high bias, and whether the collection of more data could help to address this problem.

But before we discuss how to plot learning curves in scikit-learn, let's discuss those two common model issues by walking through the following illustration:

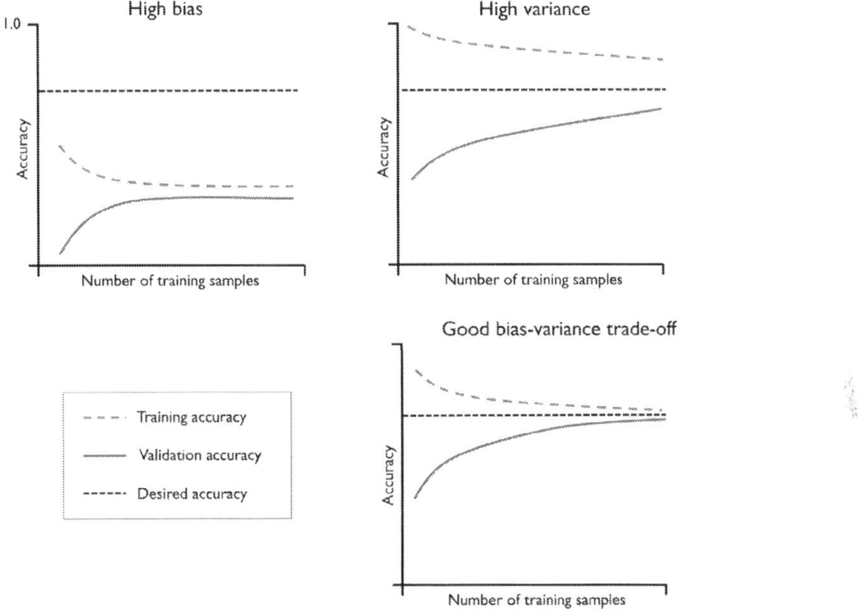

Figure 6.4: Common model issues

The graph in the upper left shows a model with a high bias. This model has both low training and cross-validation accuracy, which indicates that it underfits the training data. Common ways to address this issue are to increase the number of model parameters, for example, by collecting or constructing additional features, or by decreasing the degree of regularization, for example, in **support vector machine** (**SVM**) or logistic regression classifiers.

The graph in the upper-right shows a model that suffers from high variance, which is indicated by the large gap between the training and cross-validation accuracy. To address this problem of overfitting, we can collect more training data, reduce the complexity of the model, or increase the regularization parameter, for example.

For unregularized models, it can also help to decrease the number of features via feature selection (*Chapter 4*) or feature extraction (*Chapter 5*) to decrease the degree of overfitting. While collecting more training data usually tends to decrease the chance of overfitting, it may not always help, for example, if the training data is extremely noisy or the model is already very close to optimal.

In the next subsection, we will see how to address those model issues using validation curves, but let's first see how we can use the learning curve function from scikit-learn to evaluate the model:

```
>>> import matplotlib.pyplot as plt
>>> from sklearn.model_selection import learning_curve
>>> pipe_lr = make_pipeline(StandardScaler(),
...                         LogisticRegression(penalty='l2',
...                                            max_iter=10000))
>>> train_sizes, train_scores, test_scores =\
...                 learning_curve(estimator=pipe_lr,
...                                X=X_train,
...                                y=y_train,
...                                train_sizes=np.linspace(
...                                            0.1, 1.0, 10),
...                                cv=10,
...                                n_jobs=1)
>>> train_mean = np.mean(train_scores, axis=1)
>>> train_std = np.std(train_scores, axis=1)
>>> test_mean = np.mean(test_scores, axis=1)
>>> test_std = np.std(test_scores, axis=1)
>>> plt.plot(train_sizes, train_mean,
...          color='blue', marker='o',
...          markersize=5, label='Training accuracy')
>>> plt.fill_between(train_sizes,
...                  train_mean + train_std,
...                  train_mean - train_std,
...                  alpha=0.15, color='blue')
>>> plt.plot(train_sizes, test_mean,
...          color='green', linestyle='--',
...          marker='s', markersize=5,
...          label='Validation accuracy')
>>> plt.fill_between(train_sizes,
...                  test_mean + test_std,
...                  test_mean - test_std,
...                  alpha=0.15, color='green')
>>> plt.grid()
>>> plt.xlabel('Number of training examples')
>>> plt.ylabel('Accuracy')
>>> plt.legend(loc='lower right')
>>> plt.ylim([0.8, 1.03])
>>> plt.show()
```

Note that we passed `max_iter=10000` as an additional argument when instantiating the `LogisticRegression` object (which uses 1,000 iterations as a default) to avoid convergence issues for the smaller dataset sizes or extreme regularization parameter values (covered in the next section). After we have successfully executed the preceding code, we will obtain the following learning curve plot:

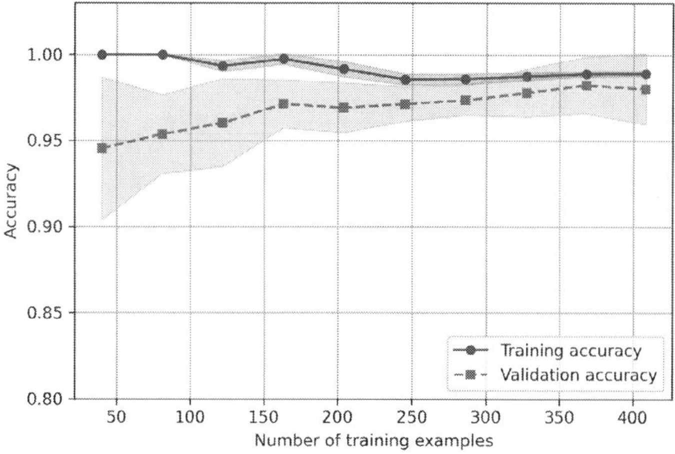

Figure 6.5: A learning curve showing training and validation dataset accuracy by the number of training examples

Via the `train_sizes` parameter in the `learning_curve` function, we can control the absolute or relative number of training examples that are used to generate the learning curves. Here, we set `train_sizes=np.linspace(0.1, 1.0, 10)` to use 10 evenly spaced, relative intervals for the training dataset sizes. By default, the `learning_curve` function uses stratified k-fold cross-validation to calculate the cross-validation accuracy of a classifier, and we set $k = 10$ via the `cv` parameter for 10-fold stratified cross-validation.

Then, we simply calculated the average accuracies from the returned cross-validated training and test scores for the different sizes of the training dataset, which we plotted using Matplotlib's `plot` function. Furthermore, we added the standard deviation of the average accuracy to the plot using the `fill_between` function to indicate the variance of the estimate.

As we can see in the preceding learning curve plot, our model performs quite well on both the training and validation datasets if it has seen more than 250 examples during training. We can also see that the training accuracy increases for training datasets with fewer than 250 examples, and the gap between validation and training accuracy widens—an indicator of an increasing degree of overfitting.

Addressing over- and underfitting with validation curves

Validation curves are a useful tool for improving the performance of a model by addressing issues such as overfitting or underfitting. Validation curves are related to learning curves, but instead of plotting the training and test accuracies as functions of the sample size, we vary the values of the model parameters, for example, the inverse regularization parameter, `C`, in logistic regression.

Let's go ahead and see how we create validation curves via scikit-learn:

```
>>> from sklearn.model_selection import validation_curve
>>> param_range = [0.001, 0.01, 0.1, 1.0, 10.0, 100.0]
>>> train_scores, test_scores = validation_curve(
...                             estimator=pipe_lr,
...                             X=X_train,
...                             y=y_train,
...                             param_name='logisticregression__C',
...                             param_range=param_range,
...                             cv=10)
>>> train_mean = np.mean(train_scores, axis=1)
>>> train_std = np.std(train_scores, axis=1)
>>> test_mean = np.mean(test_scores, axis=1)
>>> test_std = np.std(test_scores, axis=1)
>>> plt.plot(param_range, train_mean,
...          color='blue', marker='o',
...          markersize=5, label='Training accuracy')
>>> plt.fill_between(param_range, train_mean + train_std,
...                  train_mean - train_std, alpha=0.15,
...                  color='blue')
>>> plt.plot(param_range, test_mean,
...          color='green', linestyle='--',
...          marker='s', markersize=5,
...          label='Validation accuracy')
>>> plt.fill_between(param_range,
...                  test_mean + test_std,
...                  test_mean - test_std,
...                  alpha=0.15, color='green')
>>> plt.grid()
>>> plt.xscale('log')
>>> plt.legend(loc='lower right')
>>> plt.xlabel('Parameter C')
>>> plt.ylabel('Accuracy')
>>> plt.ylim([0.8, 1.0])
>>> plt.show()
```

Using the preceding code, we obtained the validation curve plot for the parameter C:

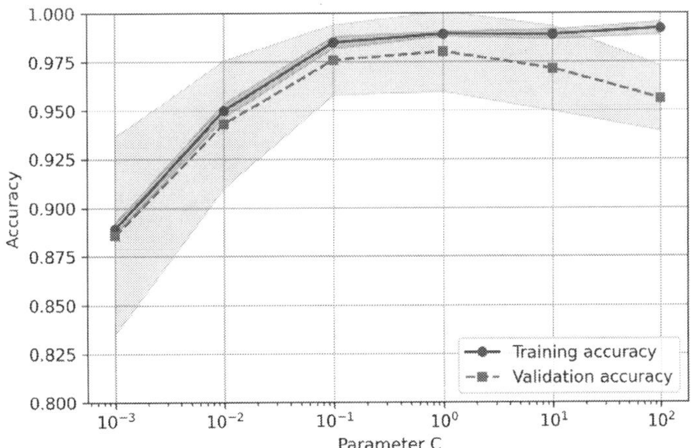

Figure 6.6: A validation curve plot for the SVM hyperparameter C

Similar to the `learning_curve` function, the `validation_curve` function uses stratified k-fold cross-validation by default to estimate the performance of the classifier. Inside the `validation_curve` function, we specified the parameter that we wanted to evaluate. In this case, it is `C`, the inverse regularization parameter of the `LogisticRegression` classifier, which we wrote as `'logisticregression__C'` to access the `LogisticRegression` object inside the scikit-learn pipeline for a specified value range that we set via the `param_range` parameter. Similar to the learning curve example in the previous section, we plotted the average training and cross-validation accuracies and the corresponding standard deviations.

Although the differences in the accuracy for varying values of `C` are subtle, we can see that the model slightly underfits the data when we increase the regularization strength (small values of `C`). However, for large values of `C`, it means lowering the strength of regularization, so the model tends to slightly overfit the data. In this case, the sweet spot appears to be between 0.1 and 1.0 of the `C` value.

Fine-tuning machine learning models via grid search

In machine learning, we have two types of parameters: those that are learned from the training data, for example, the weights in logistic regression, and the parameters of a learning algorithm that are optimized separately. The latter are the tuning parameters (or hyperparameters) of a model, for example, the regularization parameter in logistic regression or the maximum depth parameter of a decision tree.

In the previous section, we used validation curves to improve the performance of a model by tuning one of its hyperparameters. In this section, we will take a look at a popular hyperparameter optimization technique called **grid search**, which can further help to improve the performance of a model by finding the *optimal* combination of hyperparameter values.

Tuning hyperparameters via grid search

The grid search approach is quite simple: it's a brute-force exhaustive search paradigm where we specify a list of values for different hyperparameters, and the computer evaluates the model performance for each combination to obtain the optimal combination of values from this set:

```
>>> from sklearn.model_selection import GridSearchCV
>>> from sklearn.svm import SVC
>>> pipe_svc = make_pipeline(StandardScaler(),
...                          SVC(random_state=1))
>>> param_range = [0.0001, 0.001, 0.01, 0.1,
...                1.0, 10.0, 100.0, 1000.0]
>>> param_grid = [{'svc__C': param_range,
...                'svc__kernel': ['linear']},
...               {'svc__C': param_range,
...                'svc__gamma': param_range,
...                'svc__kernel': ['rbf']}]
>>> gs = GridSearchCV(estimator=pipe_svc,
...                   param_grid=param_grid,
...                   scoring='accuracy',
...                   cv=10,
...                   refit=True,
...                   n_jobs=-1)
>>> gs = gs.fit(X_train, y_train)
>>> print(gs.best_score_)
0.9846153846153847
>>> print(gs.best_params_)
{'svc__C': 100.0, 'svc__gamma': 0.001, 'svc__kernel': 'rbf'}
```

Using the preceding code, we initialized a `GridSearchCV` object from the `sklearn.model_selection` module to train and tune an SVM pipeline. We set the `param_grid` parameter of `GridSearchCV` to a list of dictionaries to specify the parameters that we'd want to tune. For the linear SVM, we only evaluated the inverse regularization parameter, `C`; for the **radial basis function** (**RBF**) kernel SVM, we tuned both the `svc__C` and `svc__gamma` parameters. Note that the `svc__gamma` parameter is specific to kernel SVMs.

`GridSearchCV` uses k-fold cross-validation for comparing models trained with different hyperparameter settings. Via the `cv=10` setting, it will carry out 10-fold cross-validation and compute the average accuracy (via `scoring='accuracy'`) across these 10-folds to assess the model performance. We set `n_jobs=-1` so that `GridSearchCV` can use all our processing cores to speed up the grid search by fitting models to the different folds in parallel, but if your machine has problems with this setting, you may change this setting to `n_jobs=None` for single processing.

After we used the training data to perform the grid search, we obtained the score of the best-performing model via the `best_score_` attribute and looked at its parameters, which can be accessed via the `best_params_` attribute. In this particular case, the RBF kernel SVM model with `svc__C = 100.0` yielded the best k-fold cross-validation accuracy: 98.5 percent.

Finally, we use the independent test dataset to estimate the performance of the best-selected model, which is available via the `best_estimator_` attribute of the `GridSearchCV` object:

```
>>> clf = gs.best_estimator_
>>> clf.fit(X_train, y_train)
>>> print(f'Test accuracy: {clf.score(X_test, y_test):.3f}')
Test accuracy: 0.974
```

Please note that fitting a model with the best settings (`gs.best_estimator_`) on the training set manually via `clf.fit(X_train, y_train)` after completing the grid search is not necessary. The `GridSearchCV` class has a `refit` parameter, which will refit the `gs.best_estimator_` to the whole training set automatically if we set `refit=True` (default).

Exploring hyperparameter configurations more widely with randomized search

Since grid search is an exhaustive search, it is guaranteed to find the optimal hyperparameter configuration if it is contained in the user-specified parameter grid. However, specifying large hyperparameter grids makes grid search very expensive in practice. An alternative approach for sampling different parameter combinations is randomized search. In randomized search, we draw hyperparameter configurations randomly from distributions (or discrete sets). In contrast to grid search, randomized search does not do an exhaustive search over the hyperparameter space. Still, it allows us to explore a wider range of hyperparameter value settings in a more cost- and time-effective manner. This concept is illustrated in *Figure 6.7*, which shows a fixed grid of nine hyperparameter settings being searched via grid search and randomized search:

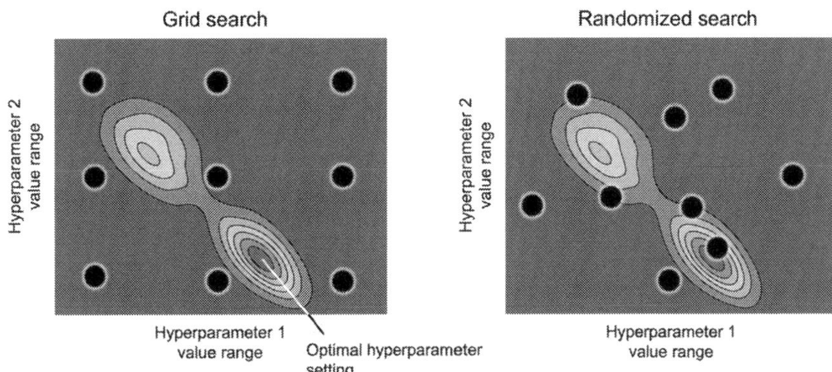

Figure 6.7: A comparison of grid search and randomized search for sampling nine different hyperparameter configurations each

The main takeaway is that while grid search only explores discrete, user-specified choices, it may miss good hyperparameter configurations if the search space is too scarce. Interested readers can find additional details about randomized search, along with empirical studies, in the following article: *Random Search for Hyper-Parameter Optimization* by *J. Bergstra, Y. Bengio, Journal of Machine Learning Research*, pp. 281-305, 2012, `https://www.jmlr.org/papers/volume13/bergstra12a/bergstra12a.`

Let's look at how we can use randomized search for tuning an SVM. Scikit-learn implements a `RandomizedSearchCV` class, which is analogous to the `GridSearchCV` we used in the previous subsection. The main difference is that we can specify distributions as part of our parameter grid and specify the total number of hyperparameter configurations to be evaluated. For example, let's consider the hyperparameter range we used for several hyperparameters when tuning the SVM in the grid search example in the previous section:

```
>>> import scipy.stats
>>> param_range = [0.0001, 0.001, 0.01, 0.1,
...                1.0, 10.0, 100.0, 1000.0]
```

Note that while `RandomizedSearchCV` can accept similar discrete lists of values as inputs for the parameter grid, which is useful when considering categorical hyperparameters, its main power lies in the fact that we can replace these lists with distributions to sample from. Thus, for example, we may substitute the preceding list with the following distribution from SciPy:

```
>>> param_range = scipy.stats.loguniform(0.0001, 1000.0)
```

For instance, using a loguniform distribution instead of a regular uniform distribution will ensure that in a sufficiently large number of trials, the same number of samples will be drawn from the [0.0001, 0.001] range as, for example, the [10.0, 100.0] range. To check its behavior, we can draw 10 random samples from this distribution via the `rvs(10)` method, as shown here:

```
>>> np.random.seed(1)
>>> param_range.rvs(10)
array([8.30145146e-02, 1.10222804e+01, 1.00184520e-04, 1.30715777e-02,
       1.06485687e-03, 4.42965766e-04, 2.01289666e-03, 2.62376594e-02,
       5.98924832e-02, 5.91176467e-01])
```

Specifying distributions

`RandomizedSearchCV` supports arbitrary distributions as long as we can sample from them by calling the `rvs()` method. A list of all distributions currently available via `scipy.stats` can be found here: `https://docs.scipy.org/doc/scipy/reference/stats.html#probability-distributions`.

Let's now see the `RandomizedSearchCV` in action and tune an SVM as we did with `GridSearchCV` in the previous section:

```
>>> from sklearn.model_selection import RandomizedSearchCV
>>> pipe_svc = make_pipeline(StandardScaler(),
...                          SVC(random_state=1))
```

```
>>> param_grid = [{'svc__C': param_range,
...                'svc__kernel': ['linear']},
...               {'svc__C': param_range,
...                'svc__gamma': param_range,
...                'svc__kernel': ['rbf']}]
>>> rs = RandomizedSearchCV(estimator=pipe_svc,
...                         param_distributions=param_grid,
...                         scoring='accuracy',
...                         refit=True,
...                         n_iter=20,
...                         cv=10,
...                         random_state=1,
...                         n_jobs=-1)

>>> rs = rs.fit(X_train, y_train)
>>> print(rs.best_score_)
0.9670531400966184

>>> print(rs.best_params_)
{'svc__C': 0.05971247755848464, 'svc__kernel': 'linear'}
```

Based on this code example, we can see that the usage is very similar to `GridSearchCV`, except that we could use distributions for specifying parameter ranges and specified the number of iterations—20 iterations—by setting `n_iter=20`.

More resource-efficient hyperparameter search with successive halving

Taking the idea of randomized search one step further, scikit-learn implements a successive halving variant, `HalvingRandomSearchCV`, that makes finding suitable hyperparameter configurations more efficient. Successive halving, given a large set of candidate configurations, successively throws out unpromising hyperparameter configurations until only one configuration remains. We can summarize the procedure via the following steps:

1. Draw a large set of candidate configurations via random sampling
2. Train the models with limited resources, for example, a small subset of the training data (as opposed to using the entire training set)
3. Discard the bottom 50 percent based on predictive performance
4. Go back to *step 2* with an increased amount of available resources

The steps are repeated until only one hyperparameter configuration remains. Note that there is also a successive halving implementation for the grid search variant called `HalvingGridSearchCV`, where all specified hyperparameter configurations are used in *step 1* instead of random samples.

In scikit-learn 1.0, `HalvingRandomSearchCV` is still experimental, which is why we have to enable it first:

```
>>> from sklearn.experimental import enable_halving_search_cv
```

(The above code may not work or be supported in future releases.)

After enabling the experimental support, we can use randomized search with successive halving as shown in the following:

```
>>> from sklearn.model_selection import HalvingRandomSearchCV

>>> hs = HalvingRandomSearchCV(pipe_svc,
...                            param_distributions=param_grid,
...                            n_candidates='exhaust',
...                            resource='n_samples',
...                            factor=1.5,
...                            random_state=1,
...                            n_jobs=-1)
```

The `resource='n_samples'` (default) setting specifies that we consider the training set size as the resource we vary between the rounds. Via the `factor` parameter, we can determine how many candidates are eliminated in each round. For example, setting `factor=2` eliminates half of the candidates, and setting `factor=1.5` means that only 100%/1.5 ≈ 66% of the candidates make it into the next round. Instead of choosing a fixed number of iterations as in `RandomizedSearchCV`, we set `n_candidates='exhaust'` (default), which will sample the number of hyperparameter configurations such that the maximum number of resources (here: training examples) are used in the last round.

We can then carry out the search similar to `RandomizedSearchCV`:

```
>>> hs = hs.fit(X_train, y_train)
>>> print(hs.best_score_)
0.9617647058823529

>>> print(hs.best_params_)
{'svc__C': 4.934834261073341, 'svc__kernel': 'linear'}
```

```
>>> clf = hs.best_estimator_
>>> print(f'Test accuracy: {hs.score(X_test, y_test):.3f}')
Test accuracy: 0.982
```

If we compare the results from `GridSearchCV` and `RandomizedSearchCV` from the previous two subsections with the model from `HalvingRandomSearchCV`, we can see that the latter yields a model that performs slightly better on the test set (98.2 percent accuracy as opposed to 97.4 percent).

Hyperparameter tuning with hyperopt

Another popular library for hyperparameter optimization is hyperopt (`https://github.com/hyperopt/hyperopt`), which implements several different methods for hyperparameter optimization, including randomized search and the **Tree-structured Parzen Estimators (TPE)** method. TPE is a Bayesian optimization method based on a probabilistic model that is continuously updated based on past hyperparameter evaluations and the associated performance scores instead of regarding these evaluations as independent events. You can find out more about TPE in *Algorithms for Hyper-Parameter Optimization. Bergstra J, Bardenet R, Bengio Y, Kegl B. NeurIPS 2011.* pp. 2546–2554, `https://dl.acm.org/doi/10.5555/2986459.2986743`.

While hyperopt provides a general-purpose interface for hyperparameter optimization, there is also a scikit-learn-specific package called hyperopt-sklearn for additional convenience: `https://github.com/hyperopt/hyperopt-sklearn`.

Algorithm selection with nested cross-validation

Using k-fold cross-validation in combination with grid search or randomized search is a useful approach for fine-tuning the performance of a machine learning model by varying its hyperparameter values, as we saw in the previous subsections. If we want to select among different machine learning algorithms, though, another recommended approach is **nested cross-validation**. In a nice study on the bias in error estimation, Sudhir Varma and Richard Simon concluded that the true error of the estimate is almost unbiased relative to the test dataset when nested cross-validation is used (*Bias in Error Estimation When Using Cross-Validation for Model Selection* by *S. Varma* and *R. Simon*, *BMC Bioinformatics*, 7(1): 91, 2006, `https://bmcbioinformatics.biomedcentral.com/articles/10.1186/1471-2105-7-91`).

In nested cross-validation, we have an outer k-fold cross-validation loop to split the data into training and test folds, and an inner loop is used to select the model using k-fold cross-validation on the training fold. After model selection, the test fold is then used to evaluate the model performance. *Figure 6.8* explains the concept of nested cross-validation with only five outer and two inner folds, which can be useful for large datasets where computational performance is important; this particular type of nested cross-validation is also known as **5×2 cross-validation:**

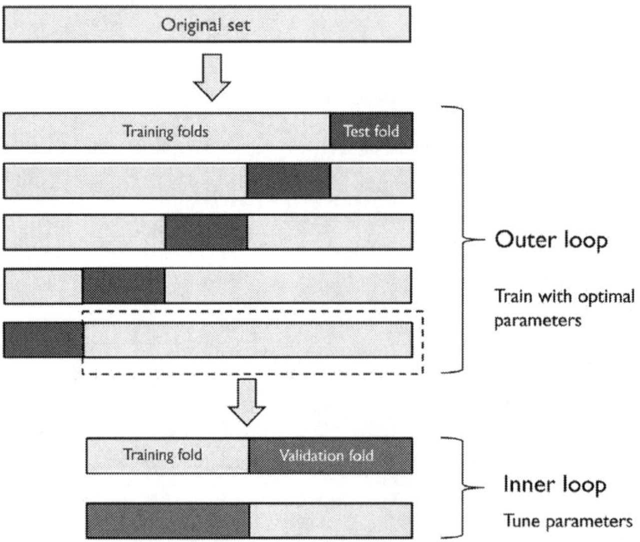

Figure 6.8: The concept of nested cross-validation

In scikit-learn, we can perform nested cross-validation with grid search as follows:

```
>>> param_range = [0.0001, 0.001, 0.01, 0.1,
...                1.0, 10.0, 100.0, 1000.0]
>>> param_grid = [{'svc__C': param_range,
...                'svc__kernel': ['linear']},
...               {'svc__C': param_range,
...                'svc__gamma': param_range,
...                'svc__kernel': ['rbf']}]
>>> gs = GridSearchCV(estimator=pipe_svc,
...                   param_grid=param_grid,
...                   scoring='accuracy',
...                   cv=2)
```

```
>>> scores = cross_val_score(gs, X_train, y_train,
...                          scoring='accuracy', cv=5)
>>> print(f'CV accuracy: {np.mean(scores):.3f} '
...       f'+/- {np.std(scores):.3f}')
CV accuracy: 0.974 +/- 0.015
```

The returned average cross-validation accuracy gives us a good estimate of what to expect if we tune the hyperparameters of a model and use it on unseen data.

For example, we can use the nested cross-validation approach to compare an SVM model to a simple decision tree classifier; for simplicity, we will only tune its depth parameter:

```
>>> from sklearn.tree import DecisionTreeClassifier
>>> gs = GridSearchCV(
...     estimator=DecisionTreeClassifier(random_state=0),
...     param_grid=[{'max_depth': [1, 2, 3, 4, 5, 6, 7, None]}],
...     scoring='accuracy',
...     cv=2
... )
>>> scores = cross_val_score(gs, X_train, y_train,
...                          scoring='accuracy', cv=5)
>>> print(f'CV accuracy: {np.mean(scores):.3f} '
...       f'+/- {np.std(scores):.3f}')
CV accuracy: 0.934 +/- 0.016
```

As we can see, the nested cross-validation performance of the SVM model (97.4 percent) is notably better than the performance of the decision tree (93.4 percent), and thus, we'd expect that it might be the better choice to classify new data that comes from the same population as this particular dataset.

Looking at different performance evaluation metrics

In the previous sections and chapters, we evaluated different machine learning models using prediction accuracy, which is a useful metric with which to quantify the performance of a model in general. However, there are several other performance metrics that can be used to measure a model's relevance, such as precision, recall, the **F1 score**, and **Matthews correlation coefficient** (MCC).

Reading a confusion matrix

Before we get into the details of different scoring metrics, let's take a look at a **confusion matrix**, a matrix that lays out the performance of a learning algorithm.

A confusion matrix is simply a square matrix that reports the counts of the **true positive** (**TP**), **true negative** (**TN**), **false positive** (**FP**), and **false negative** (**FN**) predictions of a classifier, as shown in *Figure 6.9*:

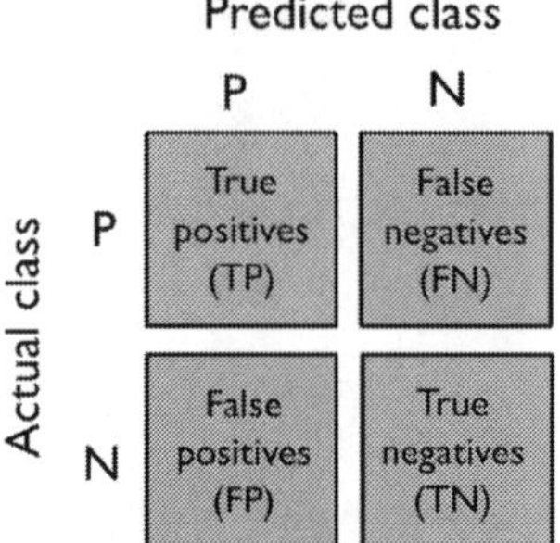

Figure 6.9: The confusion matrix

Although these metrics can be easily computed manually by comparing the actual and predicted class labels, scikit-learn provides a convenient `confusion_matrix` function that we can use, as follows:

```
>>> from sklearn.metrics import confusion_matrix
>>> pipe_svc.fit(X_train, y_train)
>>> y_pred = pipe_svc.predict(X_test)
>>> confmat = confusion_matrix(y_true=y_test, y_pred=y_pred)
>>> print(confmat)
[[71  1]
 [ 2 40]]
```

The array that was returned after executing the code provides us with information about the different types of error the classifier made on the test dataset. We can map this information onto the confusion matrix illustration in *Figure 6.9* using Matplotlib's `matshow` function:

```
>>> fig, ax = plt.subplots(figsize=(2.5, 2.5))
>>> ax.matshow(confmat, cmap=plt.cm.Blues, alpha=0.3)
>>> for i in range(confmat.shape[0]):
...     for j in range(confmat.shape[1]):
...         ax.text(x=j, y=i, s=confmat[i, j],
...                 va='center', ha='center')
>>> ax.xaxis.set_ticks_position('bottom')
>>> plt.xlabel('Predicted label')
>>> plt.ylabel('True label')
>>> plt.show()
```

Now, the following confusion matrix plot, with the added labels, should make the results a little bit easier to interpret:

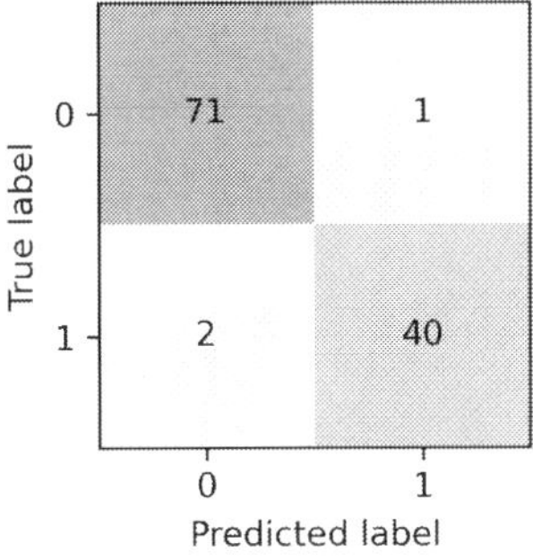

Figure 6.10: A confusion matrix for our data

Assuming that class `1` (malignant) is the positive class in this example, our model correctly classified 71 of the examples that belong to class `0` (TN) and 40 examples that belong to class `1` (TP), respectively. However, our model also incorrectly misclassified two examples from class `1` as class `0` (FN), and it predicted that one example is malignant although it is a benign tumor (FP). In the next subsection, we will learn how we can use this information to calculate various error metrics.

Optimizing the precision and recall of a classification model

Both the prediction **error** (**ERR**) and **accuracy** (**ACC**) provide general information about how many examples are misclassified. The error can be understood as the sum of all false predictions divided by the number of total predictions, and the accuracy is calculated as the sum of correct predictions divided by the total number of predictions, respectively:

$$ERR = \frac{FP + FN}{FP + FN + TP + TN}$$

The prediction accuracy can then be calculated directly from the error:

$$ACC = \frac{TP + TN}{FP + FN + TP + TN} = 1 - ERR$$

The **true positive rate** (**TPR**) and **false positive rate** (**FPR**) are performance metrics that are especially useful for imbalanced class problems:

$$FPR = \frac{FP}{N} = \frac{FP}{FP + TN}$$

$$TPR = \frac{TP}{P} = \frac{TP}{FN + TP}$$

In tumor diagnosis, for example, we are more concerned about the detection of malignant tumors in order to help a patient with the appropriate treatment. However, it is also important to decrease the number of benign tumors incorrectly classified as malignant (FP) to not unnecessarily concern patients. In contrast to the FPR, the TPR provides useful information about the fraction of positive (or relevant) examples that were correctly identified out of the total pool of positives (P).

The performance metrics **precision** (**PRE**) and **recall** (**REC**) are related to those TP and TN rates, and in fact, REC is synonymous with TPR:

$$REC = TPR = \frac{TP}{P} = \frac{TP}{FN + TP}$$

In other words, recall quantifies how many of the relevant records (the positives) are captured as such (the true positives). Precision quantifies how many of the records predicted as relevant (the sum of true and false positives) are actually relevant (true positives):

$$PRE = \frac{TP}{TP + FP}$$

Revisiting the malignant tumor detection example, optimizing for recall helps with minimizing the chance of not detecting a malignant tumor. However, this comes at the cost of predicting malignant tumors in patients although the patients are healthy (a high number of FPs). If we optimize for precision, on the other hand, we emphasize correctness if we predict that a patient has a malignant tumor. However, this comes at the cost of missing malignant tumors more frequently (a high number of FNs).

To balance the up- and downsides of optimizing PRE and REC, the harmonic mean of PRE and REC is used, the so-called F1 score:

$$F1 = 2\frac{PRE \times REC}{PRE + REC}$$

Further reading on precision and recall

If you are interested in a more thorough discussion of the different performance metrics, such as precision and recall, read David M. W. Powers' technical report *Evaluation: From Precision, Recall and F-Factor to ROC, Informedness, Markedness & Correlation*, which is freely available at `https://arxiv.org/abs/2010.16061`.

Lastly, a measure that summarizes a confusion matrix is the MCC, which is especially popular in biological research contexts. The MCC is calculated as follows:

$$MCC = \frac{TP \times TN - FP \times FN}{\sqrt{(TP + FP)(TP + FN)(TN + FP)(TN + FN)}}$$

In contrast to PRE, REC, and the F1 score, the MCC ranges between –1 and 1, and it takes all elements of a confusion matrix into account—for instance, the F1 score does not involve the TN. While the MCC values are harder to interpret than the F1 score, it is regarded as a superior metric, as described in the following article: *The advantages of the Matthews correlation coefficient (MCC) over F1 score and accuracy in binary classification evaluation* by *D. Chicco* and *G. Jurman*, *BMC Genomics*. pp. 281-305, 2012, `https://bmcgenomics.biomedcentral.com/articles/10.1186/s12864-019-6413-7`.

Those scoring metrics are all implemented in scikit-learn and can be imported from the `sklearn.metrics` module as shown in the following snippet:

```
>>> from sklearn.metrics import precision_score
>>> from sklearn.metrics import recall_score, f1_score
>>> from sklearn.metrics import matthews_corrcoef

>>> pre_val = precision_score(y_true=y_test, y_pred=y_pred)
>>> print(f'Precision: {pre_val:.3f}')
Precision: 0.976
>>> rec_val = recall_score(y_true=y_test, y_pred=y_pred)
>>> print(f'Recall: {rec_val:.3f}')
Recall: 0.952
>>> f1_val = f1_score(y_true=y_test, y_pred=y_pred)
>>> print(f'F1: {f1_val:.3f}')
F1: 0.964
>>> mcc_val = matthews_corrcoef(y_true=y_test, y_pred=y_pred)
>>> print(f'MCC: {mcc_val:.3f}')
MCC: 0.943
```

Furthermore, we can use a different scoring metric than accuracy in the `GridSearchCV` via the scoring parameter. A complete list of the different values that are accepted by the scoring parameter can be found at `http://scikit-learn.org/stable/modules/model_evaluation.html`.

Remember that the positive class in scikit-learn is the class that is labeled as class `1`. If we want to specify a different *positive label*, we can construct our own scorer via the `make_scorer` function, which we can then directly provide as an argument to the `scoring` parameter in `GridSearchCV` (in this example, using the `f1_score` as a metric):

```
>>> from sklearn.metrics import make_scorer
>>> c_gamma_range = [0.01, 0.1, 1.0, 10.0]
>>> param_grid = [{'svc__C': c_gamma_range,
...                'svc__kernel': ['linear']},
...               {'svc__C': c_gamma_range,
...                'svc__gamma': c_gamma_range,
...                'svc__kernel': ['rbf']}]
```

```
>>> scorer = make_scorer(f1_score, pos_label=0)
>>> gs = GridSearchCV(estimator=pipe_svc,
...                   param_grid=param_grid,
...                   scoring=scorer,
...                   cv=10)
>>> gs = gs.fit(X_train, y_train)
>>> print(gs.best_score_)
0.986202145696
>>> print(gs.best_params_)
{'svc__C': 10.0, 'svc__gamma': 0.01, 'svc__kernel': 'rbf'}
```

Plotting a receiver operating characteristic

Receiver operating characteristic (**ROC**) graphs are useful tools to select models for classification based on their performance with respect to the FPR and TPR, which are computed by shifting the decision threshold of the classifier. The diagonal of a ROC graph can be interpreted as *random guessing*, and classification models that fall below the diagonal are considered as worse than random guessing. A perfect classifier would fall into the top-left corner of the graph with a TPR of 1 and an FPR of 0. Based on the ROC curve, we can then compute the so-called **ROC area under the curve** (**ROC AUC**) to characterize the performance of a classification model.

Similar to ROC curves, we can compute **precision-recall curves** for different probability thresholds of a classifier. A function for plotting those precision-recall curves is also implemented in scikit-learn and is documented at `http://scikit-learn.org/stable/modules/generated/sklearn.metrics.precision_recall_curve.html`.

Executing the following code example, we will plot a ROC curve of a classifier that only uses two features from the Breast Cancer Wisconsin dataset to predict whether a tumor is benign or malignant. Although we are going to use the same logistic regression pipeline that we defined previously, we are only using two features this time. This is to make the classification task more challenging for the classifier, by withholding useful information contained in the other features, so that the resulting ROC curve becomes visually more interesting. For similar reasons, we are also reducing the number of folds in the `StratifiedKFold` validator to three. The code is as follows:

```
>>> from sklearn.metrics import roc_curve, auc
>>> from numpy import interp
>>> pipe_lr = make_pipeline(
...     StandardScaler(),
...     PCA(n_components=2),
...     LogisticRegression(penalty='l2', random_state=1,
...                        solver='lbfgs', C=100.0)
... )
>>> X_train2 = X_train[:, [4, 14]]
```

```
>>> cv = list(StratifiedKFold(n_splits=3).split(X_train, y_train))
>>> fig = plt.figure(figsize=(7, 5))
>>> mean_tpr = 0.0
>>> mean_fpr = np.linspace(0, 1, 100)
>>> all_tpr = []
>>> for i, (train, test) in enumerate(cv):
...     probas = pipe_lr.fit(
...         X_train2[train],
...         y_train[train]
...     ).predict_proba(X_train2[test])
...     fpr, tpr, thresholds = roc_curve(y_train[test],
...                                      probas[:, 1],
...                                      pos_label=1)
...     mean_tpr += interp(mean_fpr, fpr, tpr)
...     mean_tpr[0] = 0.0
...     roc_auc = auc(fpr, tpr)
...     plt.plot(fpr,
...              tpr,
...              label=f'ROC fold {i+1} (area = {roc_auc:.2f})')
>>> plt.plot([0, 1],
...          [0, 1],
...          linestyle='--',
...          color=(0.6, 0.6, 0.6),
...          label='Random guessing (area=0.5)')
>>> mean_tpr /= len(cv)
>>> mean_tpr[-1] = 1.0
>>> mean_auc = auc(mean_fpr, mean_tpr)
>>> plt.plot(mean_fpr, mean_tpr, 'k--',
...          label=f'Mean ROC (area = {mean_auc:.2f})', lw=2)
>>> plt.plot([0, 0, 1],
...          [0, 1, 1],
...          linestyle=':',
...          color='black',
...          label='Perfect performance (area=1.0)')
>>> plt.xlim([-0.05, 1.05])
>>> plt.ylim([-0.05, 1.05])
>>> plt.xlabel('False positive rate')
>>> plt.ylabel('True positive rate')
>>> plt.legend(loc='lower right')
>>> plt.show()
```

In the preceding code example, we used the already familiar `StratifiedKFold` class from scikit-learn and calculated the ROC performance of the `LogisticRegression` classifier in our `pipe_lr` pipeline using the `roc_curve` function from the `sklearn.metrics` module separately for each iteration. Furthermore, we interpolated the average ROC curve from the three folds via the `interp` function that we imported from NumPy and calculated the area under the curve via the `auc` function. The resulting ROC curve indicates that there is a certain degree of variance between the different folds, and the average ROC AUC (0.76) falls between a perfect score (1.0) and random guessing (0.5):

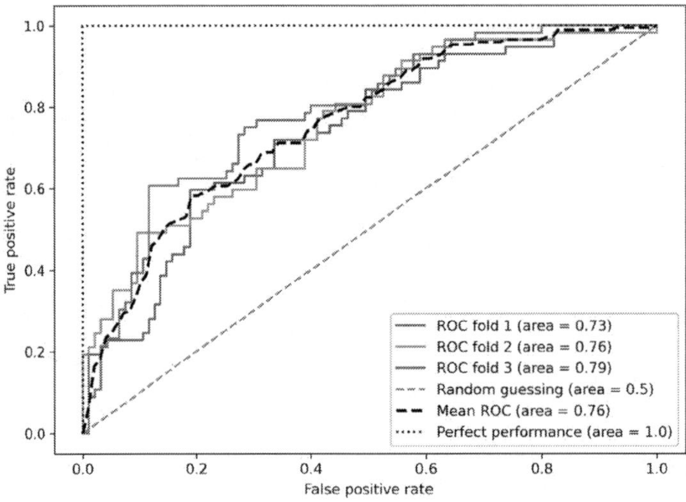

Figure 6.11: The ROC plot

Note that if we are just interested in the ROC AUC score, we could also directly import the `roc_auc_score` function from the `sklearn.metrics` submodule, which can be used similarly to the other scoring functions (for example, `precision_score`) that were introduced in the previous sections.

Reporting the performance of a classifier as the ROC AUC can yield further insights into a classifier's performance with respect to imbalanced samples. However, while the accuracy score can be interpreted as a single cutoff point on a ROC curve, A. P. Bradley showed that the ROC AUC and accuracy metrics mostly agree with each other: *The Use of the Area Under the ROC Curve in the Evaluation of Machine Learning Algorithms* by *A. P. Bradley*, *Pattern Recognition*, 30(7): 1145-1159, 1997, `https://reader.elsevier.com/reader/sd/pii/S0031320396001422`.

Scoring metrics for multiclass classification

The scoring metrics that we've discussed so far are specific to binary classification systems. However, scikit-learn also implements macro and micro averaging methods to extend those scoring metrics to multiclass problems via **one-vs.-all** (**OvA**) classification. The micro-average is calculated from the individual TPs, TNs, FPs, and FNs of the system. For example, the micro-average of the precision score in a *k*-class system can be calculated as follows:

$$PRE_{micro} = \frac{TP_1 + \cdots + TP_k}{TP_1 + \cdots + TP_k + FP_1 + \cdots + FP_k}$$

The macro-average is simply calculated as the average scores of the different systems:

$$PRE_{macro} = \frac{PRE_1 + \cdots + PRE_k}{k}$$

Micro-averaging is useful if we want to weight each instance or prediction equally, whereas macro-averaging weights all classes equally to evaluate the overall performance of a classifier with regard to the most frequent class labels.

If we are using binary performance metrics to evaluate multiclass classification models in scikit-learn, a normalized or weighted variant of the macro-average is used by default. The weighted macro-average is calculated by weighting the score of each class label by the number of true instances when calculating the average. The weighted macro-average is useful if we are dealing with class imbalances, that is, different numbers of instances for each label.

While the weighted macro-average is the default for multiclass problems in scikit-learn, we can specify the averaging method via the `average` parameter inside the different scoring functions that we import from the `sklearn.metrics` module, for example, the `precision_score` or `make_scorer` functions:

```
>>> pre_scorer = make_scorer(score_func=precision_score,
...                          pos_label=1,
...                          greater_is_better=True,
...                          average='micro')
```

Dealing with class imbalance

We've mentioned class imbalances several times throughout this chapter, and yet we haven't actually discussed how to deal with such scenarios appropriately if they occur. Class imbalance is a quite common problem when working with real-world data—examples from one class or multiple classes are over-represented in a dataset. We can think of several domains where this may occur, such as spam filtering, fraud detection, or screening for diseases.

Imagine that the Breast Cancer Wisconsin dataset that we've been working with in this chapter consisted of 90 percent healthy patients. In this case, we could achieve 90 percent accuracy on the test dataset by just predicting the majority class (benign tumor) for all examples, without the help of a supervised machine learning algorithm. Thus, training a model on such a dataset that achieves approximately 90 percent test accuracy would mean our model hasn't learned anything useful from the features provided in this dataset.

In this section, we will briefly go over some of the techniques that could help with imbalanced datasets. But before we discuss different methods to approach this problem, let's create an imbalanced dataset from our dataset, which originally consisted of 357 benign tumors (class `0`) and 212 malignant tumors (class `1`):

```
>>> X_imb = np.vstack((X[y == 0], X[y == 1][:40]))
>>> y_imb = np.hstack((y[y == 0], y[y == 1][:40]))
```

In this code snippet, we took all 357 benign tumor examples and stacked them with the first 40 malignant examples to create a stark class imbalance. If we were to compute the accuracy of a model that always predicts the majority class (benign, class `0`), we would achieve a prediction accuracy of approximately 90 percent:

```
>>> y_pred = np.zeros(y_imb.shape[0])
>>> np.mean(y_pred == y_imb) * 100
89.92443324937027
```

Thus, when we fit classifiers on such datasets, it would make sense to focus on other metrics than accuracy when comparing different models, such as precision, recall, the ROC curve—whatever we care most about in our application. For instance, our priority might be to identify the majority of patients with malignant cancer to recommend an additional screening, so recall should be our metric of choice. In spam filtering, where we don't want to label emails as spam if the system is not very certain, precision might be a more appropriate metric.

Aside from evaluating machine learning models, class imbalance influences a learning algorithm during model fitting itself. Since machine learning algorithms typically optimize a reward or loss function that is computed as a sum over the training examples that it sees during fitting, the decision rule is likely going to be biased toward the majority class.

In other words, the algorithm implicitly learns a model that optimizes the predictions based on the most abundant class in the dataset to minimize the loss or maximize the reward during training.

One way to deal with imbalanced class proportions during model fitting is to assign a larger penalty to wrong predictions on the minority class. Via scikit-learn, adjusting such a penalty is as convenient as setting the `class_weight` parameter to `class_weight='balanced'`, which is implemented for most classifiers.

Other popular strategies for dealing with class imbalance include upsampling the minority class, downsampling the majority class, and the generation of synthetic training examples. Unfortunately, there's no universally best solution or technique that works best across different problem domains. Thus, in practice, it is recommended to try out different strategies on a given problem, evaluate the results, and choose the technique that seems most appropriate.

The scikit-learn library implements a simple `resample` function that can help with the upsampling of the minority class by drawing new samples from the dataset with replacement. The following code will take the minority class from our imbalanced Breast Cancer Wisconsin dataset (here, class `1`) and repeatedly draw new samples from it until it contains the same number of examples as class label `0`:

```
>>> from sklearn.utils import resample
>>> print('Number of class 1 examples before:',
...       X_imb[y_imb == 1].shape[0])
Number of class 1 examples before: 40
>>> X_upsampled, y_upsampled = resample(
...         X_imb[y_imb == 1],
```

```
...          y_imb[y_imb == 1],
...          replace=True,
...          n_samples=X_imb[y_imb == 0].shape[0],
...          random_state=123)
>>> print('Number of class 1 examples after:',
...       X_upsampled.shape[0])
Number of class 1 examples after: 357
```

After resampling, we can then stack the original class `0` samples with the upsampled class `1` subset to obtain a balanced dataset as follows:

```
>>> X_bal = np.vstack((X[y == 0], X_upsampled))
>>> y_bal = np.hstack((y[y == 0], y_upsampled))
```

Consequently, a majority vote prediction rule would only achieve 50 percent accuracy:

```
>>> y_pred = np.zeros(y_bal.shape[0])
>>> np.mean(y_pred == y_bal) * 100
50
```

Similarly, we could downsample the majority class by removing training examples from the dataset. To perform downsampling using the `resample` function, we could simply swap the class `1` label with class `0` in the previous code example and vice versa.

Generating new training data to address class imbalance

Another technique for dealing with class imbalance is the generation of synthetic training examples, which is beyond the scope of this book. Probably the most widely used algorithm for synthetic training data generation is **Synthetic Minority Over-sampling Technique (SMOTE)**, and you can learn more about this technique in the original research article by *Nitesh Chawla* and others: *SMOTE: Synthetic Minority Over-sampling Technique, Journal of Artificial Intelligence Research*, 16: 321-357, 2002, which is available at `https://www.jair.org/index.php/jair/article/view/10302`. It is also highly recommended to check out imbalanced-learn, a Python library that is entirely focused on imbalanced datasets, including an implementation of SMOTE. You can learn more about imbalanced-learn at `https://github.com/scikit-learn-contrib/imbalanced-learn`.

Summary

At the beginning of this chapter, we discussed how to chain different transformation techniques and classifiers in convenient model pipelines that help us to train and evaluate machine learning models more efficiently. We then used those pipelines to perform k-fold cross-validation, one of the essential techniques for model selection and evaluation. Using k-fold cross-validation, we plotted learning and validation curves to diagnose common problems of learning algorithms, such as overfitting and underfitting.

Using grid search, randomized search, and successive halving, we further fine-tuned our model. We then used confusion matrices and various performance metrics to evaluate and optimize a model's performance for specific problem tasks. Finally, we concluded this chapter by discussing different methods for dealing with imbalanced data, which is a common problem in many real-world applications. Now, you should be well equipped with the essential techniques to build supervised machine learning models for classification successfully.

In the next chapter, we will look at ensemble methods: methods that allow us to combine multiple models and classification algorithms to boost the predictive performance of a machine learning system even further.

Join our book's Discord space

Join our Discord community to meet like-minded people and learn alongside more than 2000 members at:

`https://packt.link/MLwPyTorch`

7

Combining Different Models for Ensemble Learning

In the previous chapter, we focused on the best practices for tuning and evaluating different models for classification. In this chapter, we will build upon those techniques and explore different methods for constructing a set of classifiers that can often have a better predictive performance than any of its individual members. We will learn how to do the following:

- Make predictions based on majority voting
- Use bagging to reduce overfitting by drawing random combinations of the training dataset with repetition
- Apply boosting to build powerful models from weak learners that learn from their mistakes

Learning with ensembles

The goal of **ensemble methods** is to combine different classifiers into a meta-classifier that has better generalization performance than each individual classifier alone. For example, assuming that we collected predictions from 10 experts, ensemble methods would allow us to strategically combine those predictions by the 10 experts to come up with a prediction that was more accurate and robust than the predictions by each individual expert. As you will see later in this chapter, there are several different approaches for creating an ensemble of classifiers. This section will introduce a basic explanation of how ensembles work and why they are typically recognized for yielding a good generalization performance.

In this chapter, we will focus on the most popular ensemble methods that use the **majority voting** principle. Majority voting simply means that we select the class label that has been predicted by the majority of classifiers, that is, received more than 50 percent of the votes. Strictly speaking, the term "majority vote" refers to binary class settings only. However, it is easy to generalize the majority voting principle to multiclass settings, which is known as **plurality voting**. (In the UK, people distinguish between majority and plurality voting via the terms "absolute" and "relative" majority, respectively.)

Here, we select the class label that received the most votes (the mode). *Figure 7.1* illustrates the concept of majority and plurality voting for an ensemble of 10 classifiers, where each unique symbol (triangle, square, and circle) represents a unique class label:

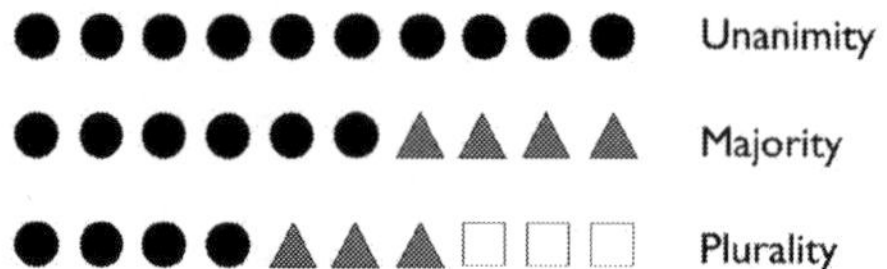

Figure 7.1: The different voting concepts

Using the training dataset, we start by training m different classifiers (C_1, ..., C_m). Depending on the technique, the ensemble can be built from different classification algorithms, for example, decision trees, support vector machines, logistic regression classifiers, and so on. Alternatively, we can also use the same base classification algorithm, fitting different subsets of the training dataset. One prominent example of this approach is the random forest algorithm combining different decision tree classifiers, which we covered in *Chapter 3, A Tour of Machine Learning Classifiers Using Scikit-Learn*. *Figure 7.2* illustrates the concept of a general ensemble approach using majority voting:

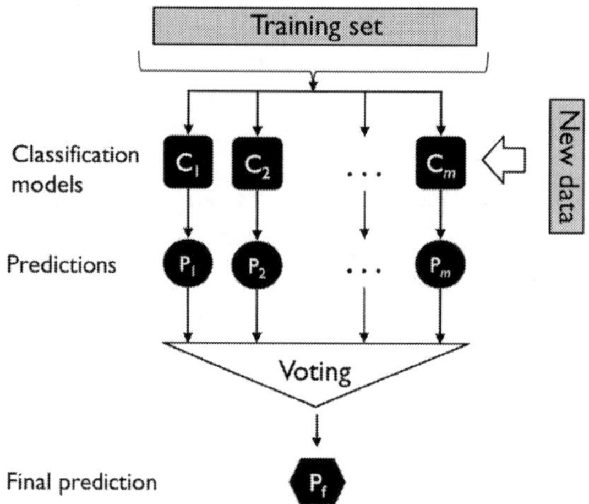

Figure 7.2: A general ensemble approach

To predict a class label via simple majority or plurality voting, we can combine the predicted class labels of each individual classifier, C_j, and select the class label, $\hat{y}$, that received the most votes:

$$\hat{y} = \text{mode}\{C_1(\boldsymbol{x}), C_2(\boldsymbol{x}), \dots, C_m(\boldsymbol{x})\}$$

(In statistics, the mode is the most frequent event or result in a set. For example, mode{1, 2, 1, 1, 2, 4, 5, 4} = 1.)

For example, in a binary classification task where class1 = –1 and class2 = +1, we can write the majority vote prediction as follows:

$$C(\boldsymbol{x}) = \text{sign}\left[\sum_{j}^{m} C_j(\boldsymbol{x})\right] = \begin{cases} 1 & \text{if } \sum_j C_j(\boldsymbol{x}) \geq 0 \\ -1 & \text{otherwise} \end{cases}$$

To illustrate why ensemble methods can work better than individual classifiers alone, let's apply some concepts of combinatorics. For the following example, we will make the assumption that all n-base classifiers for a binary classification task have an equal error rate, ε. Furthermore, we will assume that the classifiers are independent and the error rates are not correlated. Under those assumptions, we can simply express the error probability of an ensemble of base classifiers as a probability mass function of a binomial distribution:

$$P(y \geq k) = \sum_{k}^{n} \binom{n}{k} \varepsilon^k (1-\varepsilon)^{n-k} = \varepsilon_{\text{ensemble}}$$

Here, $\binom{n}{k}$ is the binomial coefficient *n choose* k. In other words, we compute the probability that the prediction of the ensemble is wrong. Now, let's take a look at a more concrete example of 11 base classifiers (n = 11), where each classifier has an error rate of 0.25 ($\varepsilon = 0.25$):

$$P(y \geq k) = \sum_{k=6}^{11} \binom{11}{k} 0.25^k (1-0.25)^{11-k} = 0.034$$

The binomial coefficient

The binomial coefficient refers to the number of ways we can choose subsets of k unordered elements from a set of size n; thus, it is often called "n choose k." Since the order does not matter here, the binomial coefficient is also sometimes referred to as *combination* or *combinatorial number*, and in its unabbreviated form, it is written as follows:

$$\frac{n!}{(n-k)!\,k!}$$

Here, the symbol (!) stands for factorial—for example, 3! = 3×2×1 = 6.

As you can see, the error rate of the ensemble (0.034) is much lower than the error rate of each individual classifier (0.25) if all the assumptions are met. Note that, in this simplified illustration, a 50-50 split by an even number of classifiers, n, is treated as an error, whereas this is only true half of the time. To compare such an idealistic ensemble classifier to a base classifier over a range of different base error rates, let's implement the probability mass function in Python:

```
>>> from scipy.special import comb
>>> import math
>>> def ensemble_error(n_classifier, error):
```

```
...     k_start = int(math.ceil(n_classifier / 2.))
...     probs = [comb(n_classifier, k) *
...              error**k *
...              (1-error)**(n_classifier - k)
...              for k in range(k_start, n_classifier + 1)]
...     return sum(probs)
>>> ensemble_error(n_classifier=11, error=0.25)
0.03432750701904297
```

After we have implemented the `ensemble_error` function, we can compute the ensemble error rates for a range of different base errors from 0.0 to 1.0 to visualize the relationship between ensemble and base errors in a line graph:

```
>>> import numpy as np
>>> import matplotlib.pyplot as plt
>>> error_range = np.arange(0.0, 1.01, 0.01)
>>> ens_errors = [ensemble_error(n_classifier=11, error=error)
...               for error in error_range]
>>> plt.plot(error_range, ens_errors,
...          label='Ensemble error',
...          linewidth=2)
>>> plt.plot(error_range, error_range,
...          linestyle='--', label='Base error',
...          linewidth=2)
>>> plt.xlabel('Base error')
>>> plt.ylabel('Base/Ensemble error')
>>> plt.legend(loc='upper left')
>>> plt.grid(alpha=0.5)
>>> plt.show()
```

As you can see in the resulting plot, the error probability of an ensemble is always better than the error of an individual base classifier, as long as the base classifiers perform better than random guessing ($\varepsilon < 0.5$).

Note that the y axis depicts the base error (dotted line) as well as the ensemble error (continuous line):

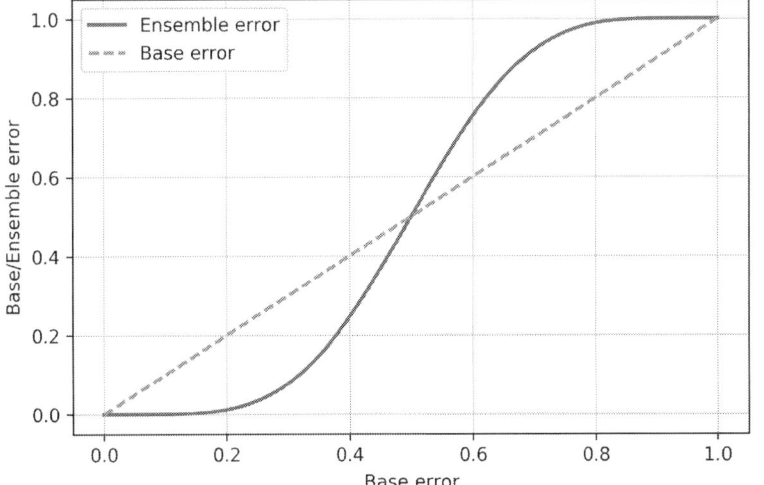

Figure 7.3: A plot of the ensemble error versus the base error

Combining classifiers via majority vote

After the short introduction to ensemble learning in the previous section, let's start with a warm-up exercise and implement a simple ensemble classifier for majority voting in Python.

Plurality voting

Although the majority voting algorithm that we will discuss in this section also generalizes to multiclass settings via plurality voting, the term "majority voting" will be used for simplicity, as is often the case in the literature.

Implementing a simple majority vote classifier

The algorithm that we are going to implement in this section will allow us to combine different classification algorithms associated with individual weights for confidence. Our goal is to build a stronger meta-classifier that balances out the individual classifiers' weaknesses on a particular dataset. In more precise mathematical terms, we can write the weighted majority vote as follows:

$$\hat{y} = \arg\max_{i} \sum_{j=1}^{m} w_j \chi_A \big(C_j(\boldsymbol{x}) = i\big)$$

Here, w_j is a weight associated with a base classifier, C_j; $\hat{y}$ is the predicted class label of the ensemble; A is the set of unique class labels; χ_A (Greek chi) is the characteristic function or indicator function, which returns 1 if the predicted class of the jth classifier matches i ($C_j(x) = i$). For equal weights, we can simplify this equation and write it as follows:

$$\hat{y} = \text{mode}\{C_1(\boldsymbol{x}), C_2(\boldsymbol{x}), \ldots, C_m(\boldsymbol{x})\}$$

To better understand the concept of *weighting*, we will now take a look at a more concrete example. Let's assume that we have an ensemble of three base classifiers, $C_j(j \in \{1, 2, 3\})$, and we want to predict the class label, $C_j(\boldsymbol{x}) \in \{0, 1\}$, of a given example, $\boldsymbol{x}$. Two out of three base classifiers predict the class label 0, and one, C_3, predicts that the example belongs to class 1. If we weight the predictions of each base classifier equally, the majority vote predicts that the example belongs to class 0:

$$C_1(\boldsymbol{x}) \rightarrow 0, \quad C_2(\boldsymbol{x}) \rightarrow 0, \quad C_3(\boldsymbol{x}) \rightarrow 1$$

$$\hat{y} = \text{mode}\{0, 0, 1\} = 0$$

Now, let's assign a weight of 0.6 to C_3, and let's weight C_1 and C_2 by a coefficient of 0.2:

$$\hat{y} = \arg\max_i \sum_{j=1}^{m} w_j \chi_A\big(C_j(\boldsymbol{x}) = i\big)$$

$$= \arg\max_i [0.2 \times i_0 + 0.2 \times i_0, 0.6 \times i_1] = 1$$

More simply, since 3×0.2 = 0.6, we can say that the prediction made by C_3 has three times more weight than the predictions by C_1 or C_2, which we can write as follows:

$$\hat{y} = \text{mode}\{0, 0, 1, 1, 1\} = 1$$

To translate the concept of the weighted majority vote into Python code, we can use NumPy's convenient `argmax` and `bincount` functions, where `bincount` counts the number of occurrences of each class label. The `argmax` function then returns the index position of the highest count, corresponding to the majority class label (this assumes that class labels start at 0):

```
>>> import numpy as np
>>> np.argmax(np.bincount([0, 0, 1],
...                      weights=[0.2, 0.2, 0.6]))
1
```

As you will remember from the discussion on logistic regression in *Chapter 3*, certain classifiers in scikit-learn can also return the probability of a predicted class label via the `predict_proba` method. Using the predicted class probabilities instead of the class labels for majority voting can be useful if the classifiers in our ensemble are well calibrated. The modified version of the majority vote for predicting class labels from probabilities can be written as follows:

$$\hat{y} = \arg\max_i \sum_{j=1}^{m} w_j p_{ij}$$

Here, p_{ij} is the predicted probability of the jth classifier for class label i.

To continue with our previous example, let's assume that we have a binary classification problem with class labels $i \in \{0, 1\}$ and an ensemble of three classifiers, $C_j (j \in \{1, 2, 3\})$. Let's assume that the classifiers C_j return the following class membership probabilities for a particular example, $\boldsymbol{x}$:

$$C_1(\boldsymbol{x}) \to [0.9, 0.1], \quad C_2(\boldsymbol{x}) \to [0.8, 0.2], \quad C_3(\boldsymbol{x}) \to [0.4, 0.6]$$

Using the same weights as previously (0.2, 0.2, and 0.6), we can then calculate the individual class probabilities as follows:

$$\begin{aligned} p(i_0|\boldsymbol{x}) &= 0.2 \times 0.9 + 0.2 \times 0.8 + 0.6 \times 0.4 = 0.58 \\ p(i_1|\boldsymbol{x}) &= 0.2 \times 0.1 + 0.2 \times 0.2 + 0.6 \times 0.6 = 0.42 \\ \hat{y} &= \arg\max_i [p(i_0|\boldsymbol{x}), p(i_1|\boldsymbol{x})] = 0 \end{aligned}$$

To implement the weighted majority vote based on class probabilities, we can again make use of NumPy, using `np.average` and `np.argmax`:

```
>>> ex = np.array([[0.9, 0.1],
...                [0.8, 0.2],
...                [0.4, 0.6]])
>>> p = np.average(ex, axis=0, weights=[0.2, 0.2, 0.6])
>>> p
array([0.58, 0.42])
>>> np.argmax(p)
0
```

Putting everything together, let's now implement `MajorityVoteClassifier` in Python:

```
from sklearn.base import BaseEstimator
from sklearn.base import ClassifierMixin
from sklearn.preprocessing import LabelEncoder
from sklearn.base import clone
from sklearn.pipeline import _name_estimators
import numpy as np
import operator
class MajorityVoteClassifier(BaseEstimator, ClassifierMixin):
    def __init__(self, classifiers, vote='classlabel', weights=None):

        self.classifiers = classifiers
        self.named_classifiers = {
            key: value for key,
            value in _name_estimators(classifiers)
        }
        self.vote = vote
```

```
        self.weights = weights

    def fit(self, X, y):
        if self.vote not in ('probability', 'classlabel'):
            raise ValueError(f"vote must be 'probability' "
                             f"or 'classlabel'"
                             f"; got (vote={self.vote})")
        if self.weights and
        len(self.weights) != len(self.classifiers):
            raise ValueError(f'Number of classifiers and'
                             f' weights must be equal'
                             f'; got {len(self.weights)} weights,'
                             f' {len(self.classifiers)} classifiers')
        # Use LabelEncoder to ensure class labels start
        # with 0, which is important for np.argmax
        # call in self.predict
        self.lablenc_ = LabelEncoder()
        self.lablenc_.fit(y)
        self.classes_ = self.lablenc_.classes_
        self.classifiers_ = []
        for clf in self.classifiers:
            fitted_clf = clone(clf).fit(X,
                               self.lablenc_.transform(y))
            self.classifiers_.append(fitted_clf)
        return self
```

We've added a lot of comments to the code to explain the individual parts. However, before we implement the remaining methods, let's take a quick break and discuss some of the code that may look confusing at first. We used the `BaseEstimator` and `ClassifierMixin` parent classes to get some base functionality *for free*, including the `get_params` and `set_params` methods to set and return the classifier's parameters, as well as the `score` method to calculate the prediction accuracy.

Next, we will add the `predict` method to predict the class label via a majority vote based on the class labels if we initialize a new `MajorityVoteClassifier` object with `vote='classlabel'`. Alternatively, we will be able to initialize the ensemble classifier with `vote='probability'` to predict the class label based on the class membership probabilities. Furthermore, we will also add a `predict_proba` method to return the averaged probabilities, which is useful when computing the **receiver operating characteristic area under the curve** (**ROC AUC**):

```
    def predict(self, X):
        if self.vote == 'probability':
            maj_vote = np.argmax(self.predict_proba(X), axis=1)
        else: # 'classlabel' vote
```

```
        # Collect results from clf.predict calls
        predictions = np.asarray([
            clf.predict(X) for clf in self.classifiers_
        ]).T

        maj_vote = np.apply_along_axis(
            lambda x: np.argmax(
                np.bincount(x, weights=self.weights)
            ),
            axis=1, arr=predictions
        )
    maj_vote = self.lablenc_.inverse_transform(maj_vote)
    return maj_vote

def predict_proba(self, X):
    probas = np.asarray([clf.predict_proba(X)
                         for clf in self.classifiers_])
    avg_proba = np.average(probas, axis=0,
                           weights=self.weights)
    return avg_proba

def get_params(self, deep=True):
    if not deep:
        return super().get_params(deep=False)
    else:
        out = self.named_classifiers.copy()
        for name, step in self.named_classifiers.items():
            for key, value in step.get_params(
                    deep=True).items():
                out[f'{name}__{key}'] = value
        return out
```

Also, note that we defined our own modified version of the `get_params` method to use the `_name_estimators` function to access the parameters of individual classifiers in the ensemble; this may look a little bit complicated at first, but it will make perfect sense when we use grid search for hyperparameter tuning in later sections.

VotingClassifier in scikit-learn

Although the `MajorityVoteClassifier` implementation is very useful for demonstration purposes, we implemented a more sophisticated version of this majority vote classifier in scikit-learn based on the implementation in the first edition of this book. The ensemble classifier is available as `sklearn.ensemble.VotingClassifier` in scikit-learn version 0.17 and newer. You can find out more about `VotingClassifier` at `https://scikit-learn.org/stable/modules/generated/sklearn.ensemble.VotingClassifier.html`

Using the majority voting principle to make predictions

Now it is time to put the `MajorityVoteClassifier` that we implemented in the previous section into action. But first, let's prepare a dataset that we can test it on. Since we are already familiar with techniques to load datasets from CSV files, we will take a shortcut and load the Iris dataset from scikit-learn's `datasets` module. Furthermore, we will only select two features, *sepal width* and *petal length*, to make the classification task more challenging for illustration purposes. Although our `MajorityVoteClassifier` generalizes to multiclass problems, we will only classify flower examples from the `Iris-versicolor` and `Iris-virginica` classes, with which we will compute the ROC AUC later. The code is as follows:

```
>>> from sklearn import datasets
>>> from sklearn.model_selection import train_test_split
>>> from sklearn.preprocessing import StandardScaler
>>> from sklearn.preprocessing import LabelEncoder
>>> iris = datasets.load_iris()
>>> X, y = iris.data[50:, [1, 2]], iris.target[50:]
>>> le = LabelEncoder()
>>> y = le.fit_transform(y)
```

Class membership probabilities from decision trees

Note that scikit-learn uses the `predict_proba` method (if applicable) to compute the ROC AUC score. In *Chapter 3*, we saw how the class probabilities are computed in logistic regression models. In decision trees, the probabilities are calculated from a frequency vector that is created for each node at training time. The vector collects the frequency values of each class label computed from the class label distribution at that node. Then, the frequencies are normalized so that they sum up to 1. Similarly, the class labels of the k-nearest neighbors are aggregated to return the normalized class label frequencies in the k-nearest neighbors algorithm. Although the normalized probabilities returned by both the decision tree and k-nearest neighbors classifier may look similar to the probabilities obtained from a logistic regression model, we have to be aware that they are actually not derived from probability mass functions.

Next, we will split the Iris examples into 50 percent training and 50 percent test data:

```
>>> X_train, X_test, y_train, y_test =\
...     train_test_split(X, y,
...                      test_size=0.5,
...                      random_state=1,
...                      stratify=y)
```

Using the training dataset, we now will train three different classifiers:

- Logistic regression classifier
- Decision tree classifier
- k-nearest neighbors classifier

We will then evaluate the model performance of each classifier via 10-fold cross-validation on the training dataset before we combine them into an ensemble classifier:

```
>>> from sklearn.model_selection import cross_val_score
>>> from sklearn.linear_model import LogisticRegression
>>> from sklearn.tree import DecisionTreeClassifier
>>> from sklearn.neighbors import KNeighborsClassifier
>>> from sklearn.pipeline import Pipeline
>>> import numpy as np
>>> clf1 = LogisticRegression(penalty='l2',
...                           C=0.001,
...                           solver='lbfgs',
...                           random_state=1)
>>> clf2 = DecisionTreeClassifier(max_depth=1,
...                               criterion='entropy',
...                               random_state=0)
>>> clf3 = KNeighborsClassifier(n_neighbors=1,
...                             p=2,
...                             metric='minkowski')
>>> pipe1 = Pipeline([['sc', StandardScaler()],
...                   ['clf', clf1]])
>>> pipe3 = Pipeline([['sc', StandardScaler()],
...                   ['clf', clf3]])
>>> clf_labels = ['Logistic regression', 'Decision tree', 'KNN']
>>> print('10-fold cross validation:\n')
>>> for clf, label in zip([pipe1, clf2, pipe3], clf_labels):
...     scores = cross_val_score(estimator=clf,
...                              X=X_train,
...                              y=y_train,
```

```
...                              cv=10,
...                              scoring='roc_auc')
...     print(f'ROC AUC: {scores.mean():.2f} '
...           f'(+/- {scores.std():.2f}) [{label}]')
```

The output that we receive, as shown in the following snippet, shows that the predictive performances of the individual classifiers are almost equal:

```
10-fold cross validation:
ROC AUC: 0.92 (+/- 0.15) [Logistic regression]
ROC AUC: 0.87 (+/- 0.18) [Decision tree]
ROC AUC: 0.85 (+/- 0.13) [KNN]
```

You may be wondering why we trained the logistic regression and k-nearest neighbors classifier as part of a pipeline. The reason behind it is that, as discussed in *Chapter 3*, both the logistic regression and k-nearest neighbors algorithms (using the Euclidean distance metric) are not scale-invariant, in contrast to decision trees. Although the Iris features are all measured on the same scale (cm), it is a good habit to work with standardized features.

Now, let's move on to the more exciting part and combine the individual classifiers for majority rule voting in our `MajorityVoteClassifier`:

```
>>> mv_clf = MajorityVoteClassifier(
...     classifiers=[pipe1, clf2, pipe3]
... )
>>> clf_labels += ['Majority voting']
>>> all_clf = [pipe1, clf2, pipe3, mv_clf]
>>> for clf, label in zip(all_clf, clf_labels):
...     scores = cross_val_score(estimator=clf,
...                              X=X_train,
...                              y=y_train,
...                              cv=10,
...                              scoring='roc_auc')
...     print(f'ROC AUC: {scores.mean():.2f} '
...           f'(+/- {scores.std():.2f}) [{label}]')
ROC AUC: 0.92 (+/- 0.15) [Logistic regression]
ROC AUC: 0.87 (+/- 0.18) [Decision tree]
ROC AUC: 0.85 (+/- 0.13) [KNN]
ROC AUC: 0.98 (+/- 0.05) [Majority voting]
```

As you can see, the performance of `MajorityVotingClassifier` has improved over the individual classifiers in the 10-fold cross-validation evaluation.

Evaluating and tuning the ensemble classifier

In this section, we are going to compute the ROC curves from the test dataset to check that `MajorityVoteClassifier` generalizes well with unseen data. We must remember that the test dataset is not to be used for model selection; its purpose is merely to report an unbiased estimate of the generalization performance of a classifier system:

```
>>> from sklearn.metrics import roc_curve
>>> from sklearn.metrics import auc
>>> colors = ['black', 'orange', 'blue', 'green']
>>> linestyles = [':', '--', '-.', '-']
>>> for clf, label, clr, ls \
...     in zip(all_clf, clf_labels, colors, linestyles):
...     # assuming the label of the positive class is 1
...     y_pred = clf.fit(X_train,
...                      y_train).predict_proba(X_test)[:, 1]
...     fpr, tpr, thresholds = roc_curve(y_true=y_test,
...                                      y_score=y_pred)
...     roc_auc = auc(x=fpr, y=tpr)
...     plt.plot(fpr, tpr,
...              color=clr,
...              linestyle=ls,
...              label=f'{label} (auc = {roc_auc:.2f})')
>>> plt.legend(loc='lower right')
>>> plt.plot([0, 1], [0, 1],
...          linestyle='--',
...          color='gray',
...          linewidth=2)
>>> plt.xlim([-0.1, 1.1])
>>> plt.ylim([-0.1, 1.1])
>>> plt.grid(alpha=0.5)
>>> plt.xlabel('False positive rate (FPR)')
>>> plt.ylabel('True positive rate (TPR)')
>>> plt.show()
```

As you can see in the resulting ROC, the ensemble classifier also performs well on the test dataset (ROC AUC = 0.95). However, you can see that the logistic regression classifier performs similarly well on the same dataset, which is probably due to the high variance (in this case, the sensitivity of how we split the dataset) given the small size of the dataset:

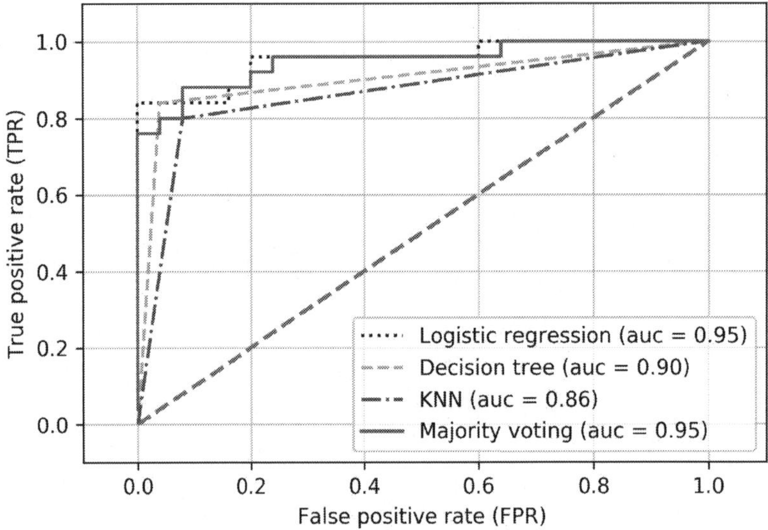

Figure 7.4: The ROC curve for the different classifiers

Since we only selected two features for the classification examples, it would be interesting to see what the decision region of the ensemble classifier actually looks like.

Although it is not necessary to standardize the training features prior to model fitting, because our logistic regression and k-nearest neighbors pipelines will automatically take care of it, we will standardize the training dataset so that the decision regions of the decision tree will be on the same scale for visual purposes. The code is as follows:

```
>>> sc = StandardScaler()
>>> X_train_std = sc.fit_transform(X_train)
>>> from itertools import product
>>> x_min = X_train_std[:, 0].min() - 1
>>> x_max = X_train_std[:, 0].max() + 1
>>> y_min = X_train_std[:, 1].min() - 1
>>>
>>> y_max = X_train_std[:, 1].max() + 1
```

```
>>> xx, yy = np.meshgrid(np.arange(x_min, x_max, 0.1),
...                      np.arange(y_min, y_max, 0.1))
>>> f, axarr = plt.subplots(nrows=2, ncols=2,
...                         sharex='col',
...                         sharey='row',
...                         figsize=(7, 5))
>>> for idx, clf, tt in zip(product([0, 1], [0, 1]),
...                         all_clf, clf_labels):
...     clf.fit(X_train_std, y_train)
...     Z = clf.predict(np.c_[xx.ravel(), yy.ravel()])
...     Z = Z.reshape(xx.shape)
...     axarr[idx[0], idx[1]].contourf(xx, yy, Z, alpha=0.3)
...     axarr[idx[0], idx[1]].scatter(X_train_std[y_train==0, 0],
...                                   X_train_std[y_train==0, 1],
...                                   c='blue',
...                                   marker='^',
...                                   s=50)
...     axarr[idx[0], idx[1]].scatter(X_train_std[y_train==1, 0],
...                                   X_train_std[y_train==1, 1],
...                                   c='green',
...                                   marker='o',
...                                   s=50)
...     axarr[idx[0], idx[1]].set_title(tt)
>>> plt.text(-3.5, -5.,
...          s='Sepal width [standardized]',
...          ha='center', va='center', fontsize=12)
>>> plt.text(-12.5, 4.5,
...          s='Petal length [standardized]',
...          ha='center', va='center',
...          fontsize=12, rotation=90)
>>> plt.show()
```

Interestingly, but also as expected, the decision regions of the ensemble classifier seem to be a hybrid of the decision regions from the individual classifiers. At first glance, the majority vote decision boundary looks a lot like the decision of the decision tree stump, which is orthogonal to the *y* axis for *sepal width* ≥ 1.

However, you can also notice the nonlinearity from the k-nearest neighbor classifier mixed in:

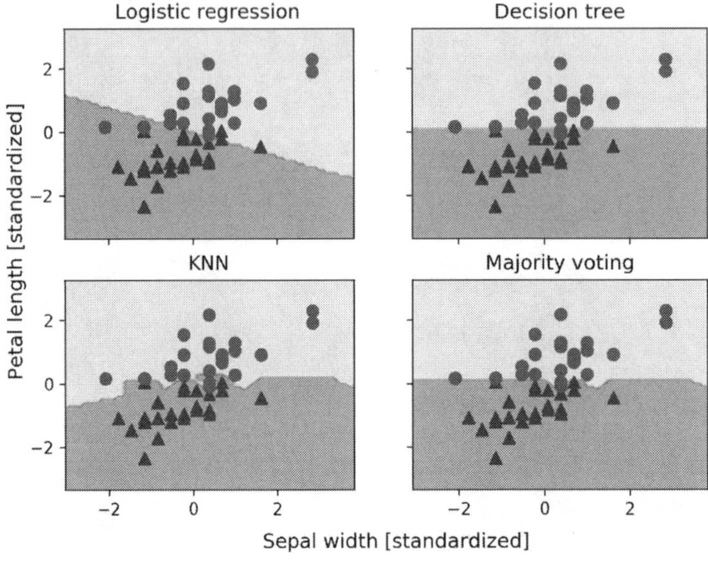

Figure 7.5: The decision boundaries for the different classifiers

Before we tune the individual classifier's parameters for ensemble classification, let's call the `get_params` method to get a basic idea of how we can access the individual parameters inside a `GridSearchCV` object:

```
>>> mv_clf.get_params()
{'decisiontreeclassifier':
 DecisionTreeClassifier(class_weight=None, criterion='entropy',
                        max_depth=1, max_features=None,
                        max_leaf_nodes=None, min_samples_leaf=1,
                        min_samples_split=2,
                        min_weight_fraction_leaf=0.0,
                        random_state=0, splitter='best'),
 'decisiontreeclassifier__class_weight': None,
 'decisiontreeclassifier__criterion': 'entropy',
 [...]
 'decisiontreeclassifier__random_state': 0,
 'decisiontreeclassifier__splitter': 'best',
 'pipeline-1':
 Pipeline(steps=[('sc', StandardScaler(copy=True, with_mean=True,
                                       with_std=True)),
                 ('clf', LogisticRegression(C=0.001,
```

```
                                           class_weight=None,
                                           dual=False,
                                           fit_intercept=True,
                                           intercept_scaling=1,
                                           max_iter=100,
                                           multi_class='ovr',
                                           penalty='l2',
                                           random_state=0,
                                           solver='liblinear',
                                           tol=0.0001,
                                           verbose=0))]),
'pipeline-1__clf':
LogisticRegression(C=0.001, class_weight=None, dual=False,
                   fit_intercept=True, intercept_scaling=1,
                   max_iter=100, multi_class='ovr',
                   penalty='l2', random_state=0,
                   solver='liblinear', tol=0.0001, verbose=0),
'pipeline-1__clf__C': 0.001,
'pipeline-1__clf__class_weight': None,
'pipeline-1__clf__dual': False,
[...]
'pipeline-1__sc__with_std': True,
'pipeline-2':
Pipeline(steps=[('sc', StandardScaler(copy=True, with_mean=True,
                                      with_std=True)),
                ('clf', KNeighborsClassifier(algorithm='auto',
                                             leaf_size=30,
                                             metric='minkowski',
                                             metric_params=None,
                                             n_neighbors=1,
                                             p=2,
                                             weights='uniform'))]),
'pipeline-2__clf':
KNeighborsClassifier(algorithm='auto', leaf_size=30,
                     metric='minkowski', metric_params=None,
                     n_neighbors=1, p=2, weights='uniform'),
'pipeline-2__clf__algorithm': 'auto',
[...]
'pipeline-2__sc__with_std': True}
```

Based on the values returned by the get_params method, we now know how to access the individual classifier's attributes. Let's now tune the inverse regularization parameter, C, of the logistic regression classifier and the decision tree depth via a grid search for demonstration purposes:

```
>>> from sklearn.model_selection import GridSearchCV
>>> params = {'decisiontreeclassifier__max_depth': [1, 2],
...           'pipeline-1__clf__C': [0.001, 0.1, 100.0]}
>>> grid = GridSearchCV(estimator=mv_clf,
...                     param_grid=params,
...                     cv=10,
...                     scoring='roc_auc')
>>> grid.fit(X_train, y_train)
```

After the grid search has completed, we can print the different hyperparameter value combinations and the average ROC AUC scores computed via 10-fold cross-validation as follows:

```
>>> for r, _ in enumerate(grid.cv_results_['mean_test_score']):
...     mean_score = grid.cv_results_['mean_test_score'][r]
...     std_dev = grid.cv_results_['std_test_score'][r]
...     params = grid.cv_results_['params'][r]
...     print(f'{mean_score:.3f} +/- {std_dev:.2f} {params}')
0.983 +/- 0.05 {'decisiontreeclassifier__max_depth': 1,
                'pipeline-1__clf__C': 0.001}
0.983 +/- 0.05 {'decisiontreeclassifier__max_depth': 1,
                'pipeline-1__clf__C': 0.1}
0.967 +/- 0.10 {'decisiontreeclassifier__max_depth': 1,
                'pipeline-1__clf__C': 100.0}
0.983 +/- 0.05 {'decisiontreeclassifier__max_depth': 2,
                'pipeline-1__clf__C': 0.001}
0.983 +/- 0.05 {'decisiontreeclassifier__max_depth': 2,
                'pipeline-1__clf__C': 0.1}
0.967 +/- 0.10 {'decisiontreeclassifier__max_depth': 2,
                'pipeline-1__clf__C': 100.0}
>>> print(f'Best parameters: {grid.best_params_}')
Best parameters: {'decisiontreeclassifier__max_depth': 1,
                  'pipeline-1__clf__C': 0.001}
>>> print(f'ROC AUC : {grid.best_score_:.2f}')
ROC AUC: 0.98
```

As you can see, we get the best cross-validation results when we choose a lower regularization strength (`C=0.001`), whereas the tree depth does not seem to affect the performance at all, suggesting that a decision stump is sufficient to separate the data. To remind ourselves that it is a bad practice to use the test dataset more than once for model evaluation, we are not going to estimate the generalization performance of the tuned hyperparameters in this section. We will move on swiftly to an alternative approach for ensemble learning: **bagging**.

Building ensembles using stacking

The majority vote approach we implemented in this section is not to be confused with stacking. The stacking algorithm can be understood as a two-level ensemble, where the first level consists of individual classifiers that feed their predictions to the second level, where another classifier (typically logistic regression) is fit to the level-one classifier predictions to make the final predictions. For more information on stacking, see the following resources:

- The stacking algorithm has been described in more detail by David H. Wolpert in *Stacked generalization*, *Neural Networks*, 5(2):241-259, 1992 (`https://www.sciencedirect.com/science/article/pii/S0893608005800231`).
- Interested readers can find our video tutorial about stacking on YouTube at `https://www.youtube.com/watch?v=8T2emza6g80`.
- A scikit-learn compatible version of a stacking classifier is available from mlxtend: `http://rasbt.github.io/mlxtend/user_guide/classifier/StackingCVClassifier/`.
- Also, a `StackingClassifier` has recently been added to scikit-learn (available in version 0.22 and newer); for more information, please see the documentation at `https://scikit-learn.org/stable/modules/generated/sklearn.ensemble.StackingClassifier.html`.

Bagging – building an ensemble of classifiers from bootstrap samples

Bagging is an ensemble learning technique that is closely related to the `MajorityVoteClassifier` that we implemented in the previous section. However, instead of using the same training dataset to fit the individual classifiers in the ensemble, we draw bootstrap samples (random samples with replacement) from the initial training dataset, which is why bagging is also known as *bootstrap aggregating*.

The concept of bagging is summarized in *Figure 7.6*:

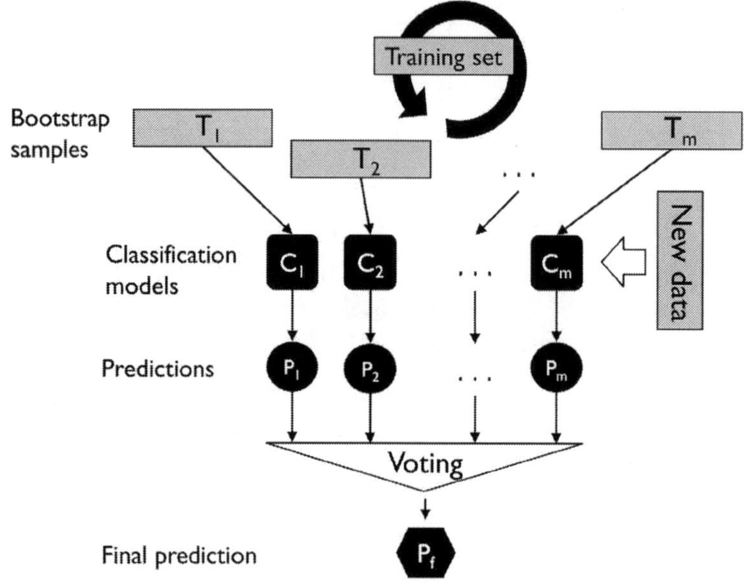

Figure 7.6: The concept of bagging

In the following subsections, we will work through a simple example of bagging by hand and use scikit-learn for classifying wine examples.

Bagging in a nutshell

To provide a more concrete example of how the bootstrap aggregating of a bagging classifier works, let's consider the example shown in *Figure 7.7*. Here, we have seven different training instances (denoted as indices 1-7) that are sampled randomly with replacement in each round of bagging. Each bootstrap sample is then used to fit a classifier, C_j, which is most typically an unpruned decision tree:

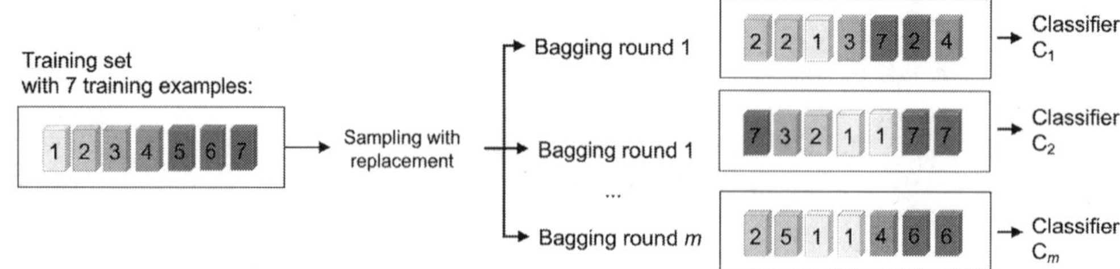

Figure 7.7: An example of bagging

As you can see from *Figure 7.7*, each classifier receives a random subset of examples from the training dataset. We denote these random samples obtained via bagging as *Bagging round 1*, *Bagging round 2*, and so on. Each subset contains a certain portion of duplicates and some of the original examples don't appear in a resampled dataset at all due to sampling with replacement. Once the individual classifiers are fit to the bootstrap samples, the predictions are combined using majority voting.

Note that bagging is also related to the random forest classifier that we introduced in *Chapter 3*. In fact, random forests are a special case of bagging where we also use random feature subsets when fitting the individual decision trees.

Model ensembles using bagging

Bagging was first proposed by Leo Breiman in a technical report in 1994; he also showed that bagging can improve the accuracy of unstable models and decrease the degree of overfitting. We highly recommend that you read about his research in *Bagging predictors* by *L. Breiman, Machine Learning*, 24(2):123-140, 1996, which is freely available online, to learn more details about bagging.

Applying bagging to classify examples in the Wine dataset

To see bagging in action, let's create a more complex classification problem using the Wine dataset that was introduced in *Chapter 4, Building Good Training Datasets – Data Preprocessing*. Here, we will only consider the Wine classes 2 and 3, and we will select two features – `Alcohol` and `OD280/OD315 of diluted wines`:

```
>>> import pandas as pd
>>> df_wine = pd.read_csv('https://archive.ics.uci.edu/ml/'
...                       'machine-learning-databases/'
...                       'wine/wine.data',
...                       header=None)
>>> df_wine.columns = ['Class label', 'Alcohol',
...                    'Malic acid', 'Ash',
...                    'Alcalinity of ash',
...                    'Magnesium', 'Total phenols',
...                    'Flavanoids', 'Nonflavanoid phenols',
...                    'Proanthocyanins',
...                    'Color intensity', 'Hue',
...                    'OD280/OD315 of diluted wines',
...                    'Proline']
>>> # drop 1 class
>>> df_wine = df_wine[df_wine['Class label'] != 1]
>>> y = df_wine['Class label'].values
>>> X = df_wine[['Alcohol',
...              'OD280/OD315 of diluted wines']].values
```

Next, we will encode the class labels into binary format and split the dataset into 80 percent training and 20 percent test datasets:

```
>>> from sklearn.preprocessing import LabelEncoder
>>> from sklearn.model_selection import train_test_split
>>> le = LabelEncoder()
>>> y = le.fit_transform(y)
>>> X_train, X_test, y_train, y_test =\
...             train_test_split(X, y,
...                              test_size=0.2,
...                              random_state=1,
...                              stratify=y)
```

Obtaining the Wine dataset

You can find a copy of the Wine dataset (and all other datasets used in this book) in the code bundle of this book, which you can use if you are working offline or the UCI server at `https://archive.ics.uci.edu/ml/machine-learning-databases/wine/wine.data` is temporarily unavailable. For instance, to load the Wine dataset from a local directory, take the following lines:

```
df = pd.read_csv('https://archive.ics.uci.edu/ml/'
                 'machine-learning-databases'
                 '/wine/wine.data',
                 header=None)
```

and replace them with these:

```
df = pd.read_csv('your/local/path/to/wine.data',
                 header=None)
```

A `BaggingClassifier` algorithm is already implemented in scikit-learn, which we can import from the `ensemble` submodule. Here, we will use an unpruned decision tree as the base classifier and create an ensemble of 500 decision trees fit on different bootstrap samples of the training dataset:

```
>>> from sklearn.ensemble import BaggingClassifier
>>> tree = DecisionTreeClassifier(criterion='entropy',
...                               random_state=1,
...                               max_depth=None)
>>> bag = BaggingClassifier(base_estimator=tree,
...                         n_estimators=500,
...                         max_samples=1.0,
...                         max_features=1.0,
...                         bootstrap=True,
```

```
...                           bootstrap_features=False,
...                           n_jobs=1,
...                           random_state=1)
```

Next, we will calculate the accuracy score of the prediction on the training and test datasets to compare the performance of the bagging classifier to the performance of a single unpruned decision tree:

```
>>> from sklearn.metrics import accuracy_score
>>> tree = tree.fit(X_train, y_train)
>>> y_train_pred = tree.predict(X_train)
>>> y_test_pred = tree.predict(X_test)
>>> tree_train = accuracy_score(y_train, y_train_pred)
>>> tree_test = accuracy_score(y_test, y_test_pred)
>>> print(f'Decision tree train/test accuracies '
...       f'{tree_train:.3f}/{tree_test:.3f}')
Decision tree train/test accuracies 1.000/0.833
```

Based on the accuracy values that we printed here, the unpruned decision tree predicts all the class labels of the training examples correctly; however, the substantially lower test accuracy indicates high variance (overfitting) of the model:

```
>>> bag = bag.fit(X_train, y_train)
>>> y_train_pred = bag.predict(X_train)
>>> y_test_pred = bag.predict(X_test)
>>> bag_train = accuracy_score(y_train, y_train_pred)
>>> bag_test = accuracy_score(y_test, y_test_pred)
>>> print(f'Bagging train/test accuracies '
...       f'{bag_train:.3f}/{bag_test:.3f}')
Bagging train/test accuracies 1.000/0.917
```

Although the training accuracies of the decision tree and bagging classifier are similar on the training dataset (both 100 percent), we can see that the bagging classifier has a slightly better generalization performance, as estimated on the test dataset. Next, let's compare the decision regions between the decision tree and the bagging classifier:

```
>>> x_min = X_train[:, 0].min() - 1
>>> x_max = X_train[:, 0].max() + 1
>>> y_min = X_train[:, 1].min() - 1
>>> y_max = X_train[:, 1].max() + 1
>>> xx, yy = np.meshgrid(np.arange(x_min, x_max, 0.1),
...                      np.arange(y_min, y_max, 0.1))
>>> f, axarr = plt.subplots(nrows=1, ncols=2,
...                         sharex='col',
...                         sharey='row',
```

```
...                             figsize=(8, 3))
>>> for idx, clf, tt in zip([0, 1],
...                             [tree, bag],
...                             ['Decision tree', 'Bagging']):
...     clf.fit(X_train, y_train)
...
...     Z = clf.predict(np.c_[xx.ravel(), yy.ravel()])
...     Z = Z.reshape(xx.shape)
...     axarr[idx].contourf(xx, yy, Z, alpha=0.3)
...     axarr[idx].scatter(X_train[y_train==0, 0],
...                        X_train[y_train==0, 1],
...                        c='blue', marker='^')
...     axarr[idx].scatter(X_train[y_train==1, 0],
...                        X_train[y_train==1, 1],
...                        c='green', marker='o')
...     axarr[idx].set_title(tt)
>>> axarr[0].set_ylabel('OD280/OD315 of diluted wines', fontsize=12)
>>> plt.tight_layout()
>>> plt.text(0, -0.2,
...          s='Alcohol',
...          ha='center',
...          va='center',
...          fontsize=12,
...          transform=axarr[1].transAxes)
>>> plt.show()
```

As we can see in the resulting plot, the piece-wise linear decision boundary of the three-node deep decision tree looks smoother in the bagging ensemble:

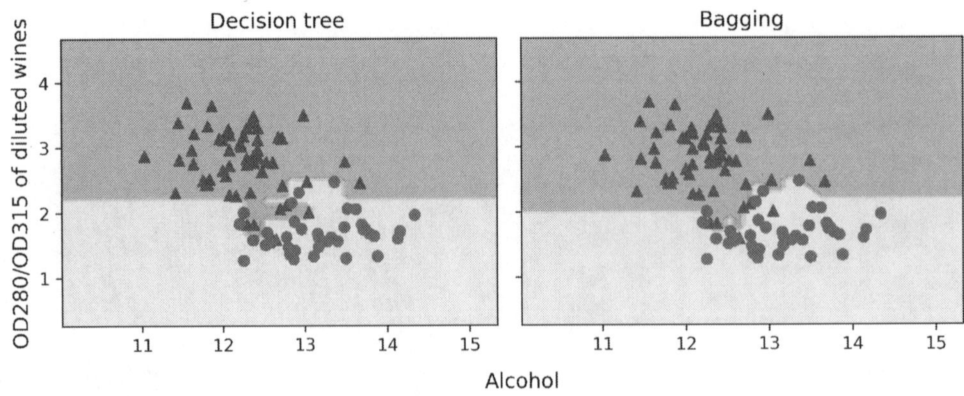

Figure 7.8: The piece-wise linear decision boundary of a decision tree versus bagging

We only looked at a very simple bagging example in this section. In practice, more complex classification tasks and a dataset's high dimensionality can easily lead to overfitting in single decision trees, and this is where the bagging algorithm can really play to its strengths. Finally, we must note that the bagging algorithm can be an effective approach to reducing the variance of a model. However, bagging is ineffective in reducing model bias, that is, models that are too simple to capture the trends in the data well. This is why we want to perform bagging on an ensemble of classifiers with low bias, for example, unpruned decision trees.

Leveraging weak learners via adaptive boosting

In this last section about ensemble methods, we will discuss **boosting**, with a special focus on its most common implementation: **Adaptive Boosting** (**AdaBoost**).

AdaBoost recognition

The original idea behind AdaBoost was formulated by Robert E. Schapire in 1990 in *The Strength of Weak Learnability, Machine Learning*, 5(2): 197-227, 1990, URL: `http://rob.schapire.net/papers/strengthofweak.pdf`. After Robert Schapire and Yoav Freund presented the AdaBoost algorithm in the *Proceedings of the Thirteenth International Conference* (ICML 1996), AdaBoost became one of the most widely used ensemble methods in the years that followed (*Experiments with a New Boosting Algorithm* by *Y. Freund, R. E. Schapire*, and others, *ICML*, volume 96, 148-156, 1996). In 2003, Freund and Schapire received the Gödel Prize for their groundbreaking work, which is a prestigious prize for the most outstanding publications in the field of computer science.

In boosting, the ensemble consists of very simple base classifiers, also often referred to as **weak learners**, which often only have a slight performance advantage over random guessing—a typical example of a weak learner is a decision tree stump. The key concept behind boosting is to focus on training examples that are hard to classify, that is, to let the weak learners subsequently learn from misclassified training examples to improve the performance of the ensemble.

The following subsections will introduce the algorithmic procedure behind the general concept of boosting and AdaBoost. Lastly, we will use scikit-learn for a practical classification example.

How adaptive boosting works

In contrast to bagging, the initial formulation of the boosting algorithm uses random subsets of training examples drawn from the training dataset without replacement; the original boosting procedure can be summarized in the following four key steps:

1. Draw a random subset (sample) of training examples, d_1, without replacement from the training dataset, D, to train a weak learner, C_1.
2. Draw a second random training subset, d_2, without replacement from the training dataset and add 50 percent of the examples that were previously misclassified to train a weak learner, C_2.

3. Find the training examples, d_3, in the training dataset, D, which C_1 and C_2 disagree upon, to train a third weak learner, C_3.
4. Combine the weak learners C_1, C_2, and C_3 via majority voting.

As discussed by Leo Breiman (*Bias, variance, and arcing classifiers*, 1996), boosting can lead to a decrease in bias as well as variance compared to bagging models. In practice, however, boosting algorithms such as AdaBoost are also known for their high variance, that is, the tendency to overfit the training data (*An improvement of AdaBoost to avoid overfitting* by *G. Raetsch, T. Onoda,* and *K. R. Mueller*. *Proceedings of the International Conference on Neural Information Processing, CiteSeer*, 1998).

In contrast to the original boosting procedure described here, AdaBoost uses the complete training dataset to train the weak learners, where the training examples are reweighted in each iteration to build a strong classifier that learns from the mistakes of the previous weak learners in the ensemble.

Before we dive deeper into the specific details of the AdaBoost algorithm, let's take a look at *Figure 7.9* to get a better grasp of the basic concept behind AdaBoost:

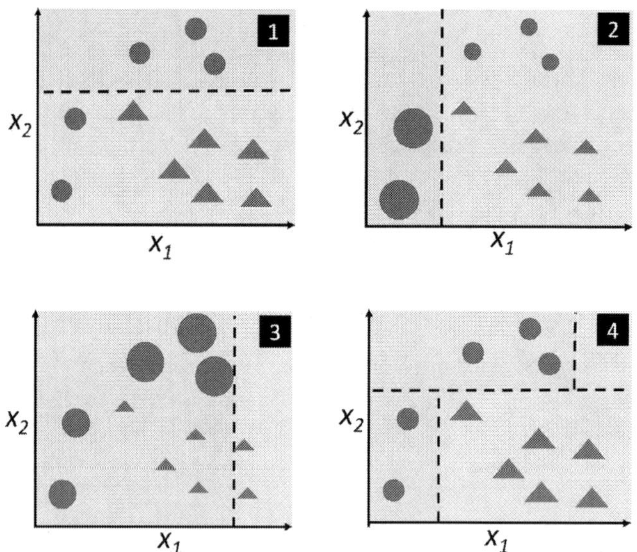

Figure 7.9: The concept of AdaBoost to improve weak learners

To walk through the AdaBoost illustration step by step, we will start with subfigure **1**, which represents a training dataset for binary classification where all training examples are assigned equal weights. Based on this training dataset, we train a decision stump (shown as a dashed line) that tries to classify the examples of the two classes (triangles and circles), as well as possibly minimizing the loss function (or the impurity score in the special case of decision tree ensembles).

For the next round (subfigure **2**), we assign a larger weight to the two previously misclassified examples (circles). Furthermore, we lower the weight of the correctly classified examples. The next decision stump will now be more focused on the training examples that have the largest weights—the training examples that are supposedly hard to classify.

The weak learner shown in subfigure 2 misclassifies three different examples from the circle class, which are then assigned a larger weight, as shown in subfigure 3.

Assuming that our AdaBoost ensemble only consists of three rounds of boosting, we then combine the three weak learners trained on different reweighted training subsets by a weighted majority vote, as shown in subfigure 4.

Now that we have a better understanding of the basic concept of AdaBoost, let's take a more detailed look at the algorithm using pseudo code. For clarity, we will denote element-wise multiplication by the cross symbol (×) and the dot-product between two vectors by a dot symbol (·):

1. Set the weight vector, w, to uniform weights, where $\sum_i w_i = 1$.
2. For j in m boosting rounds, do the following:
    a. Train a weighted weak learner: $C_j = \text{train}(X, y, w)$.
    b. Predict class labels: $\hat{\boldsymbol{y}} = \text{predict}(C_j, \boldsymbol{X})$.
    c. Compute the weighted error rate: $\varepsilon = \boldsymbol{w} \cdot (\hat{\boldsymbol{y}} \neq \boldsymbol{y})$.
    d. Compute the coefficient: $\alpha_j = 0.5 \log \frac{1-\varepsilon}{\varepsilon}$.
    e. Update the weights: $\boldsymbol{w} := \boldsymbol{w} \times \exp(-\alpha_j \times \hat{\boldsymbol{y}} \times \boldsymbol{y})$.
    f. Normalize the weights to sum to 1: $\boldsymbol{w} := \boldsymbol{w} / \sum_i w_i$.
3. Compute the final prediction: $\hat{\boldsymbol{y}} = \left(\sum_{j=1}^{m} \left(\alpha_j \times \text{predict}(C_j, \boldsymbol{X})\right) > 0\right)$.

Note that the expression $(\hat{\boldsymbol{y}} \neq \boldsymbol{y})$ in *step 2c* refers to a binary vector consisting of 1s and 0s, where a 1 is assigned if the prediction is incorrect and 0 is assigned otherwise.

Although the AdaBoost algorithm seems to be pretty straightforward, let's walk through a more concrete example using a training dataset consisting of 10 training examples, as illustrated in *Figure 7.10*:

Index	x	y	Weights	$\hat{y}$(x <= 3.0)?	Correct?	Updated weights
1	1.0	1	0.1	1	Yes	0.072
2	2.0	1	0.1	1	Yes	0.072
3	3.0	1	0.1	1	Yes	0.072
4	4.0	-1	0.1	-1	Yes	0.072
5	5.0	-1	0.1	-1	Yes	0.072
6	6.0	-1	0.1	-1	Yes	0.072
7	7.0	1	0.1	-1	No	0.167
8	8.0	1	0.1	-1	No	0.167
9	9.0	1	0.1	-1	No	0.167
10	10.0	-1	0.1	-1	Yes	0.072

Figure 7.10: Running 10 training examples through the AdaBoost algorithm

The first column of the table depicts the indices of training examples 1 to 10. In the second column, you can see the feature values of the individual samples, assuming this is a one-dimensional dataset. The third column shows the true class label, y_i, for each training sample, x_i, where $y_i \in \{1, -1\}$. The initial weights are shown in the fourth column; we initialize the weights uniformly (assigning the same constant value) and normalize them to sum to 1. In the case of the 10-sample training dataset, we therefore assign 0.1 to each weight, w_i, in the weight vector, $\boldsymbol{w}$. The predicted class labels, $\hat{\boldsymbol{y}}$, are shown in the fifth column, assuming that our splitting criterion is $x \leq 3.0$. The last column of the table then shows the updated weights based on the update rules that we defined in the pseudo code.

Since the computation of the weight updates may look a little bit complicated at first, we will now follow the calculation step by step. We will start by computing the weighted error rate, ε (`epsilon`), as described in *step 2c*:

```
>>> y = np.array([1, 1, 1, -1, -1, -1,  1,  1,  1, -1])
>>> yhat = np.array([1, 1, 1, -1, -1, -1, -1, -1, -1, -1])
>>> correct = (y == yhat)
>>> weights = np.full(10, 0.1)
>>> print(weights)
[0.1 0.1 0.1 0.1 0.1 0.1 0.1 0.1 0.1 0.1]
>>> epsilon = np.mean(~correct)
>>> print(epsilon)
0.3
```

Note that `correct` is a Boolean array consisting of `True` and `False` values where `True` indicates that a prediction is correct. Via `~correct`, we invert the array such that `np.mean(~correct)` computes the proportion of incorrect predictions (`True` counts as the value 1 and `False` as 0), that is, the classification error.

Next, we will compute the coefficient, α_j—shown in *step 2d*—which will later be used in *step 2e* to update the weights, as well as for the weights in the majority vote prediction (*step 3*):

```
>>> alpha_j = 0.5 * np.log((1-epsilon) / epsilon)
>>> print(alpha_j)
0.42364893019360184
```

After we have computed the coefficient, α_j (`alpha_j`), we can now update the weight vector using the following equation:

$$\boldsymbol{w} := \boldsymbol{w} \times \exp(-\alpha_j \times \hat{\boldsymbol{y}} \times \boldsymbol{y})$$

Here, $\hat{\boldsymbol{y}} \times \boldsymbol{y}$ is an element-wise multiplication between the vectors of the predicted and true class labels, respectively. Thus, if a prediction, $\hat{y}_i$, is correct, $\hat{y}_i \times y_i$ will have a positive sign so that we decrease the ith weight, since α_j is a positive number as well:

```
>>> update_if_correct = 0.1 * np.exp(-alpha_j * 1 * 1)
>>> print(update_if_correct)
0.06546536707079771
```

Similarly, we will increase the ith weight if $\hat{y}_i$ predicted the label incorrectly, like this:

```
>>> update_if_wrong_1 = 0.1 * np.exp(-alpha_j * 1 * -1)
>>> print(update_if_wrong_1)
0.1527525231651947
```

Alternatively, it's like this:

```
>>> update_if_wrong_2 = 0.1 * np.exp(-alpha_j * -1 * 1)
>>> print(update_if_wrong_2)
0.1527525231651947
```

We can use these values to update the weights as follows:

```
>>> weights = np.where(correct == 1,
...                    update_if_correct,
...                    update_if_wrong_1)
>>> print(weights)
array([0.06546537, 0.06546537, 0.06546537, 0.06546537, 0.06546537,
       0.06546537, 0.15275252, 0.15275252, 0.15275252, 0.06546537])
```

The code above assigned the `update_if_correct` value to all correct predictions and the `update_if_wrong_1` value to all wrong predictions. We omitted using `update_if_wrong_2` for simplicity, since it is similar to `update_if_wrong_1` anyway.

After we have updated each weight in the weight vector, we normalize the weights so that they sum up to 1 (*step 2f*):

$$\boldsymbol{w} := \frac{\boldsymbol{w}}{\sum_i w_i}$$

In code, we can accomplish that as follows:

```
>>> normalized_weights = weights / np.sum(weights)
>>> print(normalized_weights)
[0.07142857 0.07142857 0.07142857 0.07142857 0.07142857 0.07142857
 0.16666667 0.16666667 0.16666667 0.07142857]
```

Thus, each weight that corresponds to a correctly classified example will be reduced from the initial value of 0.1 to 0.0714 for the next round of boosting. Similarly, the weights of the incorrectly classified examples will increase from 0.1 to 0.1667.

Applying AdaBoost using scikit-learn

The previous subsection introduced AdaBoost in a nutshell. Skipping to the more practical part, let's now train an AdaBoost ensemble classifier via scikit-learn. We will use the same Wine subset that we used in the previous section to train the bagging meta-classifier.

Via the `base_estimator` attribute, we will train the `AdaBoostClassifier` on 500 decision tree stumps:

```
>>> from sklearn.ensemble import AdaBoostClassifier
>>> tree = DecisionTreeClassifier(criterion='entropy',
...                               random_state=1,
...                               max_depth=1)
>>> ada = AdaBoostClassifier(base_estimator=tree,
...                          n_estimators=500,
...                          learning_rate=0.1,
...                          random_state=1)
>>> tree = tree.fit(X_train, y_train)
>>> y_train_pred = tree.predict(X_train)
>>> y_test_pred = tree.predict(X_test)
>>> tree_train = accuracy_score(y_train, y_train_pred)
>>> tree_test = accuracy_score(y_test, y_test_pred)
>>> print(f'Decision tree train/test accuracies '
...       f'{tree_train:.3f}/{tree_test:.3f}')
Decision tree train/test accuracies 0.916/0.875
```

As you can see, the decision tree stump seems to underfit the training data in contrast to the unpruned decision tree that we saw in the previous section:

```
>>> ada = ada.fit(X_train, y_train)
>>> y_train_pred = ada.predict(X_train)
>>> y_test_pred = ada.predict(X_test)
>>> ada_train = accuracy_score(y_train, y_train_pred)
>>> ada_test = accuracy_score(y_test, y_test_pred)
>>> print(f'AdaBoost train/test accuracies '
...       f'{ada_train:.3f}/{ada_test:.3f}')
AdaBoost train/test accuracies 1.000/0.917
```

Here, you can see that the AdaBoost model predicts all class labels of the training dataset correctly and also shows a slightly improved test dataset performance compared to the decision tree stump. However, you can also see that we introduced additional variance with our attempt to reduce the model bias—a greater gap between training and test performance.

Although we used another simple example for demonstration purposes, we can see that the performance of the AdaBoost classifier is slightly improved compared to the decision stump and achieved very similar accuracy scores as the bagging classifier that we trained in the previous section. However, we must note that it is considered bad practice to select a model based on the repeated usage of the test dataset. The estimate of the generalization performance may be overoptimistic, which we discussed in more detail in *Chapter 6, Learning Best Practices for Model Evaluation and Hyperparameter Tuning*.

Lastly, let's check what the decision regions look like:

```
>>> x_min = X_train[:, 0].min() - 1
>>> x_max = X_train[:, 0].max() + 1
>>> y_min = X_train[:, 1].min() - 1
>>> y_max = X_train[:, 1].max() + 1
>>> xx, yy = np.meshgrid(np.arange(x_min, x_max, 0.1),
...                      np.arange(y_min, y_max, 0.1))
>>> f, axarr = plt.subplots(1, 2,
...                         sharex='col',
...                         sharey='row',
...                         figsize=(8, 3))
>>> for idx, clf, tt in zip([0, 1],
...                         [tree, ada],
...                         ['Decision tree', 'AdaBoost']):
...     clf.fit(X_train, y_train)
...     Z = clf.predict(np.c_[xx.ravel(), yy.ravel()])
...     Z = Z.reshape(xx.shape)
...     axarr[idx].contourf(xx, yy, Z, alpha=0.3)
...     axarr[idx].scatter(X_train[y_train==0, 0],
...                        X_train[y_train==0, 1],
...                        c='blue',
...                        marker='^')
...     axarr[idx].scatter(X_train[y_train==1, 0],
...                        X_train[y_train==1, 1],
...                        c='green',
...                        marker='o')
...     axarr[idx].set_title(tt)
...     axarr[0].set_ylabel('OD280/OD315 of diluted wines', fontsize=12)
>>> plt.tight_layout()
>>> plt.text(0, -0.2,
...          s='Alcohol',
...          ha='center',
...          va='center',
...          fontsize=12,
...          transform=axarr[1].transAxes)
>>> plt.show()
```

By looking at the decision regions, you can see that the decision boundary of the AdaBoost model is substantially more complex than the decision boundary of the decision stump. In addition, note that the AdaBoost model separates the feature space very similarly to the bagging classifier that we trained in the previous section:

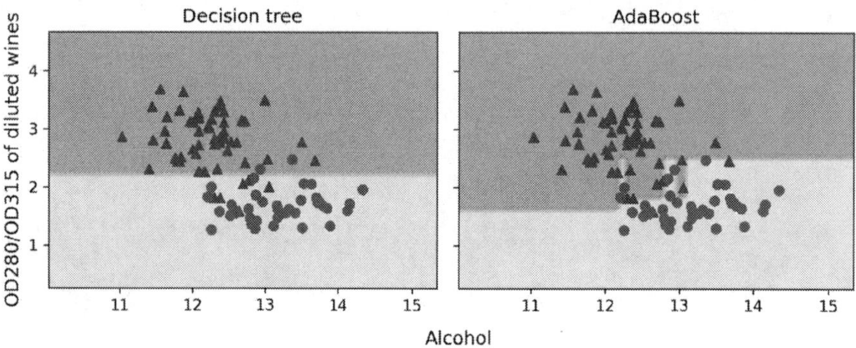

Figure 7.11: The decision boundaries of the decision tree versus AdaBoost

As concluding remarks about ensemble techniques, it is worth noting that ensemble learning increases the computational complexity compared to individual classifiers. In practice, we need to think carefully about whether we want to pay the price of increased computational costs for an often relatively modest improvement in predictive performance.

An often-cited example of this tradeoff is the famous $1 million *Netflix Prize*, which was won using ensemble techniques. The details about the algorithm were published in *The BigChaos Solution to the Netflix Grand Prize* by *A. Toescher, M. Jahrer*, and *R. M. Bell, Netflix Prize documentation*, 2009, which is available at `http://www.stat.osu.edu/~dmsl/GrandPrize2009_BPC_BigChaos.pdf`. The winning team received the $1 million grand prize money; however, Netflix never implemented their model due to its complexity, which made it infeasible for a real-world application:

> *"We evaluated some of the new methods offline but the additional accuracy gains that we measured did not seem to justify the engineering effort needed to bring them into a production environment."*
>
> `http://techblog.netflix.com/2012/04/netflix-recommendations-beyond-5-stars.html`

Gradient boosting – training an ensemble based on loss gradients

Gradient boosting is another variant of the boosting concept introduced in the previous section, that is, successively training weak learners to create a strong ensemble. Gradient boosting is an extremely important topic because it forms the basis of popular machine learning algorithms such as XGBoost, which is well-known for winning Kaggle competitions.

The gradient boosting algorithm may appear a bit daunting at first. So, in the following subsections, we will cover it step by step, starting with a general overview. Then, we will see how gradient boosting is used for classification and walk through an example. Finally, after we've introduced the fundamental concepts of gradient boosting, we will take a brief look at popular implementations, such as XGBoost, and we will see how we can use gradient boosting in practice.

Comparing AdaBoost with gradient boosting

Fundamentally, gradient boosting is very similar to AdaBoost, which we discussed previously in this chapter. AdaBoost trains decision tree stumps based on errors of the previous decision tree stump. In particular, the errors are used to compute sample weights in each round as well as for computing a classifier weight for each decision tree stump when combining the individual stumps into an ensemble. We stop training once a maximum number of iterations (decision tree stumps) is reached. Like AdaBoost, gradient boosting fits decision trees in an iterative fashion using prediction errors. However, gradient boosting trees are usually deeper than decision tree stumps and have typically a maximum depth of 3 to 6 (or a maximum number of 8 to 64 leaf nodes). Also, in contrast to AdaBoost, gradient boosting does not use the prediction errors for assigning sample weights; they are used directly to form the target variable for fitting the next tree. Moreover, instead of having an individual weighting term for each tree, like in AdaBoost, gradient boosting uses a global learning rate that is the same for each tree.

As you can see, AdaBoost and gradient boosting share several similarities but differ in certain key aspects. In the following subsection, we will sketch the general outline of the gradient boosting algorithm.

Outlining the general gradient boosting algorithm

In this section, we will look at gradient boosting for classification. For simplicity, we will look at a binary classification example. Interested readers can find the generalization to the multi-class setting with logistic loss in *Section 4.6. Multiclass logistic regression and classification* of the original gradient boosting paper written by Friedman in 2001, *Greedy function approximation: A gradient boosting machine*, `https://projecteuclid.org/journals/annals-of-statistics/volume-29/issue-5/Greedy-function-approximation-A-gradient-boostingmachine/10.1214/aos/1013203451.full`.

Gradient boosting for regression

Note that the procedure behind gradient boosting is a bit more complicated than AdaBoost. We omit a simpler regression example, which was given in Friedman's paper, for brevity, but interested readers are encouraged to also consider my complementary video tutorial on gradient boosting for regression, which is available at: `https://www.youtube.com/watch?v=zblsrxc7XpM`.

In essence, gradient boosting builds a series of trees, where each tree is fit on the error—the difference between the label and the predicted value—of the previous tree. In each round, the tree ensemble improves as we are nudging each tree more in the right direction via small updates. These updates are based on a loss gradient, which is how gradient boosting got its name.

The following steps will introduce the general algorithm behind gradient boosting. After illustrating the main steps, we will dive into some of its parts in more detail and walk through a hands-on example in the next subsections.

1. Initialize a model to return a constant prediction value. For this, we use a decision tree root node; that is, a decision tree with a single leaf node. We denote the value returned by the tree as $\hat{y}$, and we find this value by minimizing a differentiable loss function L that we will define later:

   $$F_0(x) = \arg\min_{\hat{y}} \sum_{i=1}^{n} L(y_i, \hat{y})$$

   Here, n refers to the n training examples in our dataset.

2. For each tree $m = 1, ..., M$, where M is a user-specified total number of trees, we carry out the following computations outlined in *steps 2a* to *2d* below:

   a. Compute the difference between a predicted value $F(x_i) = \hat{y}_i$ and the class label y_i. This value is sometimes called the *pseudo-response* or *pseudo-residual*. More formally, we can write this pseudo-residual as the negative gradient of the loss function with respect to the predicted values:

   $$r_{im} = -\left[\frac{\partial L(y_i, F(x_i))}{\partial F(x_i)}\right]_{F(x)=F_{m-1}(x)} \quad \text{for } i = 1, \dots, n$$

   Note that in the notation above $F(x)$ is the prediction of the previous tree, $F_{m-1}(x)$. So, in the first round, this refers to the constant value from the tree (single leaf node) from step 1.

   b. Fit a tree to the pseudo-residuals r_{im}. We use the notation R_{jm} to denote the $j = 1 \dots J_m$ leaf nodes of the resulting tree in iteration m.

c. For each leaf node R_{jm}, we compute the following output value:

$$\gamma_{jm} = \arg\min_{\gamma} \sum_{x_i \in R_{jm}} L(y_i, F_{m-1}(x_i) + \gamma)$$

In the next subsection, we will dive deeper into how this γ_{jm} is computed by minimizing the loss function. At this point, we can already note that leaf nodes R_{jm} may contain more than one training example, hence the summation.

d. Update the model by adding the output values γ_m to the previous tree:

$$F_m(x) = F_{m-1}(x) + \eta\gamma_m$$

However, instead of adding the full predicted values of the current tree γ_m to the previous tree F_{m-1}, we scale γ_m by a learning rate η, which is typically a small value between 0.01 and 1. In other words, we update the model incrementally by taking small steps, which helps avoid overfitting.

Now, after looking at the general structure of gradient boosting, we will adopt these mechanics to look at gradient boosting for classification.

Explaining the gradient boosting algorithm for classification

In this subsection, we will go over the details for implementing the gradient boosting algorithm for binary classification. In this context, we will be using the logistic loss function that we introduced for logistic regression in *Chapter 3, A Tour of Machine Learning Classifiers Using Scikit-Learn*. For a single training example, we can specify the logistic loss as follows:

$$L_i = -y_i \log p_i + (1 - y_i) \log(1 - p_i)$$

In *Chapter 3*, we also introduced the log(odds):

$$\hat{y} = \log(\text{odds}) = \log\left(\frac{p}{1-p}\right)$$

For reasons that will make sense later, we will use these log(odds) to rewrite the logistic function as follows (omitting intermediate steps here):

$$L_i = \log\left(1 + e^{\hat{y}_i}\right) - y_i\hat{y}_i$$

Now, we can define the partial derivative of the loss function with respect to these log(odds), $\hat{y}$. The derivative of this loss function with respect to the log(odds) is:

$$\frac{\partial L_i}{\partial \hat{y}_i} - \frac{e^{\hat{y}_i}}{1 + e^{\hat{y}_i}} - y_i = p_\iota - y_\iota$$

After specifying these mathematical definitions, let us now revisit the general gradient boosting *steps 1* to *2d* from the previous section and reformulate them for this binary classification scenario.

1. Create a root node that minimizes the logistic loss. It turns out that the loss is minimized if the root node returns the log(odds), $\hat{y}$.
2. For each tree $m = 1, ..., M$, where M is a user-specified number of total trees, we carry out the following computations outlined in *steps 2a* to *2d*:

    a. We convert the log(odds) into a probability using the familiar logistic function that we used in logistic regression (in *Chapter 3*):

    $$p = \frac{1}{1 + e^{-\hat{y}}}$$

    Then, we compute the pseudo-residual, which is the negative partial derivative of the loss with respect to the log(odds), which turns out to be the difference between the class label and the predicted probability:

    $$-\frac{\partial L_i}{\partial \hat{y}_i} = y_i - p_i$$

    b. Fit a new tree to the pseudo-residuals.

    c. For each leaf node R_{jm}, compute a value γ_{jm} that minimizes the logistic loss function. This includes a summarization step for dealing with leaf nodes that contain multiple training examples:

    $$\begin{aligned}\gamma_{jm} &= \underset{\gamma}{\arg\min} \sum_{x_i \in R_{jm}} L(y_i, F_{m-1}(x_i) + \gamma) \\ &= \log\left(1 + e^{\hat{y}_i + \gamma}\right) - y_i(\hat{y}_i + \gamma)\end{aligned}$$

    Skipping over intermediate mathematical details, this results in the following:

    $$\gamma_{jm} = \frac{\sum_i y_i - p_i}{\sum_i p_i(i - p_i)}$$

    Note that the summation here is only over the examples at the node corresponding to the leaf node R_{jm} and not the complete training set.

    d. Update the model by adding the gamma value from *step 2c* with learning rate η:

    $$F_m(x) = F_{m-1}(x) + \eta\gamma_m$$

Outputting log(odds) vs probabilities

Why do the trees return log(odds) values and not probabilities? This is because we cannot just add up probability values and arrive at a meaningful result. (So, technically speaking, gradient boosting for classification uses regression trees.)

In this section, we adopted the general gradient boosting algorithm and specified it for binary classification, for instance, by replacing the generic loss function with the logistic loss and the predicted values with the log(odds). However, many of the individual steps may still seem very abstract, and in the next section, we will apply these steps to a concrete example.

Illustrating gradient boosting for classification

The previous two subsections went over the condensed mathematical details of the gradient boosting algorithm for binary classification. To make these concepts clearer, let's apply it to a small toy example, that is, a training dataset of the following three examples shown in *Figure 7.12*:

	Feature x_1	Feature x_2	Class label y
1	1.12	1.4	1
2	2.45	2.1	0
3	3.54	1.2	1

Figure 7.12: Toy dataset for explaining gradient boosting

Let's start with *step 1*, constructing the root node and computing the log(odds), and *step 2a*, converting the log(odds) into class-membership probabilities and computing the pseudo-residuals. Note that based on what we have learned in *Chapter 3*, the odds can be computed as the number of successes divided by the number of failures. Here, we regard label 1 as success and label 0 as failure, so the odds are computed as: odds = 2/1. Carrying out steps *1* and *2a*, we get the following results shown in *Figure 7.13*:

	Feature x_1	Feature x_2	Class label y	Step 1: $\hat{y}$ = log(odds)	Step 2a: $p = \frac{1}{1+e^{-\hat{y}}}$	Step 2a: $r = y - p$
1	1.12	1.4	1	0.69	0.67	0.33
2	2.45	2.1	0	0.69	0.67	-0.67
3	3.54	1.2	1	0.69	0.67	0.33

Figure 7.13: Results from the first round of applying step 1 and step 2a

Next, in *step 2b*, we fit a new tree on the pseudo-residuals r. Then, in *step 2c*, we compute the output values, γ, for this tree as shown in *Figure 7.14*:

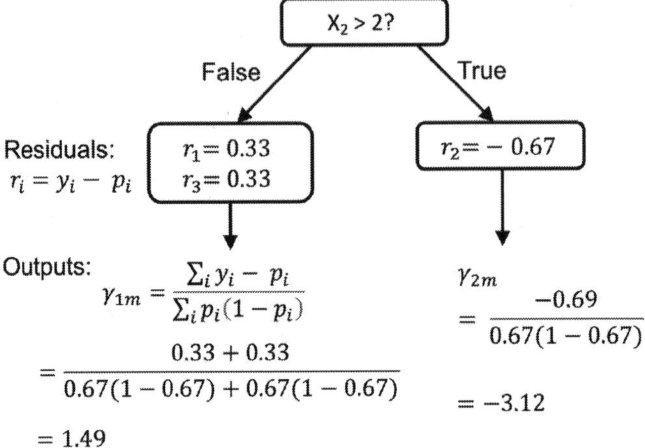

Figure 7.14: An illustration of steps 2b and 2c, which fits a tree to the residuals and computes the output values for each leaf node

(Note that we artificially limit the tree to have only two leaf nodes, which helps illustrate what happens if a leaf node contains more than one example.)

Then, in the final *step 2d*, we update the previous model and the current model. Assuming a learning rate of $\eta = 0.1$, the resulting prediction for the first training example is shown in *Figure 7.15*:

	Feature x_1	Feature x_2	Class label y
1	1.12	1.4	1
2	2.45	2.1	0
3	3.54	1.2	1

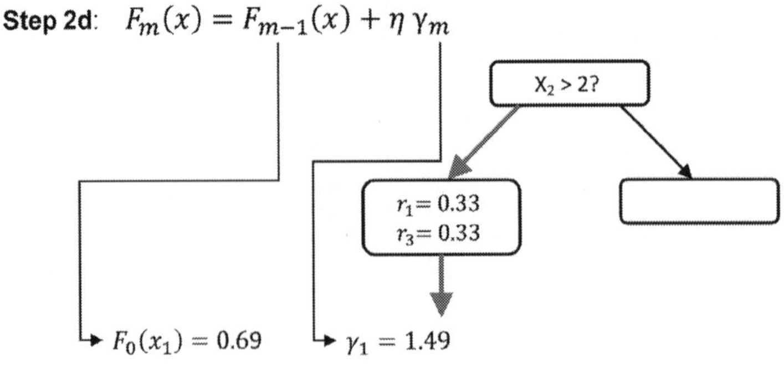

$F_1(x_1) = 0.69 + 0.1 \times 1.49 = 0.839$

Figure 7.15: The update of the previous model shown in the context of the first training example

Now that we have completed *steps 2a* to *2d* of the first round, $m = 1$, we can proceed to execute *steps 2a* to *2d* for the second round, $m = 2$. In the second round, we use the log(odds) returned by the updated model, for example, $F_1(x_1) = 0.839$, as input to *step 2A*. The new values we obtain in the second round are shown in *Figure 7.16*:

	x_1	x_2	y	Step 1: $F_0(x) = \hat{y}$ = log(odds)	Step 2a: $p = \frac{1}{1+e^{-\hat{y}}}$	Step 2a: $r = y - p$	New log(odds) $\hat{y} = F_1(x)$	Step 2a: p	Step 2a: r
1	1.12	1.4	1	0.69	0.67	0.33	0.839	0.698	0.302
2	2.45	2.1	0	0.69	0.67	-0.67	0.378	0.593	-0.593
3	3.54	1.2	1	0.69	0.67	0.33	0.839	0.698	0.302

Round $m = 1$ Round $m = 2$

Figure 7.16: Values from the second round next to the values from the first round

We can already see that the predicted probabilities are higher for the positive class and lower for the negative class. Consequently, the residuals are getting smaller, too. Note that the process of *steps 2a* to *2d* is repeated until we have fit *M* trees or the residuals are smaller than a user-specified threshold value. Then, once the gradient boosting algorithm has completed, we can use it to predict the class labels by thresholding the probability values of the final model, $F_M(x)$ at 0.5, like logistic regression in *Chapter 3*. However, in contrast to logistic regression, gradient boosting consists of multiple trees and produces nonlinear decision boundaries. In the next section, we will look at how gradient boosting looks in action.

Using XGBoost

After covering the nitty-gritty details behind gradient boosting, let's finally look at how we can use gradient boosting code implementations.

In scikit-learn, gradient boosting is implemented as `sklearn.ensemble.GradientBoostingClassifier` (see `https://scikit-learn.org/stable/modules/generated/sklearn.ensemble.GradientBoostingClassifier.html` for more details). It is important to note that gradient boosting is a sequential process that can be slow to train. However, in recent years a more popular implementation of gradient boosting has emerged, namely, XGBoost.

XGBoost proposed several tricks and approximations that speed up the training process substantially. Hence, the name XGBoost, which stands for extreme gradient boosting. Moreover, these approximations and tricks result in very good predictive performances. In fact, XGBoost gained popularity as it has been the winning solution for many Kaggle competitions.

Next to XGBoost, there are also other popular implementations of gradient boosting, for example, LightGBM and CatBoost. Inspired by LightGBM, scikit-learn now also implements a `HistGradientBoostingClassifier`, which is more performant than the original gradient boosting classifier (`GradientBoostingClassifier`).

You can find more details about these methods via the resources below:

- **XGBoost**: https://xgboost.readthedocs.io/en/stable/
- **LightGBM**: https://lightgbm.readthedocs.io/en/latest/
- **CatBoost**: https://catboost.ai
- **HistGradientBoostingClassifier**: https://scikit-learn.org/stable/modules/generated/sklearn.ensemble.HistGradientBoostingClassifier.html

However, since XGBoost is still among the most popular gradient boosting implementations, we will see how we can use it in practice. First, we need to install it, for example via `pip`:

```
pip install xgboost
```

Installing XGBoost

For this chapter, we used XGBoost version 1.5.0, which can be installed via:

```
pip install XGBoost==1.5.0
```

You can find more information about the installation details at https://xgboost.readthedocs.io/en/stable/install.html

Fortunately, XGBoost's `XGBClassifier` follows the scikit-learn API. So, using it is relatively straightforward:

```
>>> import xgboost as xgb
>>> model = xgb.XGBClassifier(n_estimators=1000, learning_rate=0.01,
...                           max_depth=4, random_state=1,
...                           use_label_encoder=False)

>>> gbm = model.fit(X_train, y_train)
>>> y_train_pred = gbm.predict(X_train)
>>> y_test_pred = gbm.predict(X_test)

>>> gbm_train = accuracy_score(y_train, y_train_pred)
>>> gbm_test = accuracy_score(y_test, y_test_pred)
>>> print(f'XGboost train/test accuracies '
...       f'{gbm_train:.3f}/{gbm_test:.3f}')
XGboost train/test accuracies 0.968/0.917
```

Here, we fit the gradient boosting classifier with 1,000 trees (rounds) and a learning rate of 0.01. Typically, a learning rate between 0.01 and 0.1 is recommended. However, remember that the learning rate is used for scaling the predictions from the individual rounds. So, intuitively, the lower the learning rate, the more estimators are required to achieve accurate predictions.

Next, we have the `max_depth` for the individual decision trees, which we set to 4. Since we are still boosting weak learners, a value between 2 and 6 is reasonable, but larger values may also work well depending on the dataset.

Finally, `use_label_encoder=False` disables a warning message which informs users that XGBoost is not converting labels by default anymore, and it expects users to provide labels in an integer format starting with label 0. (There is nothing to worry about here, since we have been following this format throughout this book.)

There are many more settings available, and a detailed discussion is out of the scope of this book. However, interested readers can find more details in the original documentation at `https://xgboost.readthedocs.io/en/latest/python/python_api.html#xgboost.XGBClassifier`.

Summary

In this chapter, we looked at some of the most popular and widely used techniques for ensemble learning. Ensemble methods combine different classification models to cancel out their individual weaknesses, which often results in stable and well-performing models that are very attractive for industrial applications as well as machine learning competitions.

At the beginning of this chapter, we implemented `MajorityVoteClassifier` in Python, which allows us to combine different algorithms for classification. We then looked at bagging, a useful technique for reducing the variance of a model by drawing random bootstrap samples from the training dataset and combining the individually trained classifiers via majority vote. Lastly, we learned about boosting in the form of AdaBoost and gradient boosting, which are algorithms based on training weak learners that subsequently learn from mistakes.

Throughout the previous chapters, we learned a lot about different learning algorithms, tuning, and evaluation techniques. In the next chapter, we will look at a particular application of machine learning, sentiment analysis, which has become an interesting topic in the internet and social media era.

Join our book's Discord space

Join our Discord community to meet like-minded people and learn alongside more than 2000 members at:

`https://packt.link/MLwPyTorch`

8

Applying Machine Learning to Sentiment Analysis

In the modern internet and social media age, people's opinions, reviews, and recommendations have become a valuable resource for political science and businesses. Thanks to modern technologies, we are now able to collect and analyze such data most efficiently. In this chapter, we will delve into a subfield of **natural language processing** (NLP) called **sentiment analysis** and learn how to use machine learning algorithms to classify documents based on their sentiment: the attitude of the writer. In particular, we are going to work with a dataset of 50,000 movie reviews from the **Internet Movie Database** (**IMDb**) and build a predictor that can distinguish between positive and negative reviews.

The topics that we will cover in this chapter include the following:

- Cleaning and preparing text data
- Building feature vectors from text documents
- Training a machine learning model to classify positive and negative movie reviews
- Working with large text datasets using out-of-core learning
- Inferring topics from document collections for categorization

Preparing the IMDb movie review data for text processing

As mentioned, sentiment analysis, sometimes also called **opinion mining**, is a popular subdiscipline of the broader field of NLP; it is concerned with analyzing the sentiment of documents. A popular task in sentiment analysis is the classification of documents based on the expressed opinions or emotions of the authors with regard to a particular topic.

In this chapter, we will be working with a large dataset of movie reviews from IMDb that has been collected by Andrew Maas and others (*Learning Word Vectors for Sentiment Analysis* by *A. L. Maas, R. E. Daly, P. T. Pham, D. Huang, A. Y. Ng*, and *C. Potts, Proceedings of the 49th Annual Meeting of the Association for Computational Linguistics: Human Language Technologies*, pages 142–150, Portland, Oregon, USA, Association for Computational Linguistics, June 2011). The movie review dataset consists of 50,000 polar movie reviews that are labeled as either positive or negative; here, positive means that a movie was rated with more than six stars on IMDb, and negative means that a movie was rated with fewer than five stars on IMDb. In the following sections, we will download the dataset, preprocess it into a useable format for machine learning tools, and extract meaningful information from a subset of these movie reviews to build a machine learning model that can predict whether a certain reviewer liked or disliked a movie.

Obtaining the movie review dataset

A compressed archive of the movie review dataset (84.1 MB) can be downloaded from `http://ai.stanford.edu/~amaas/data/sentiment/` as a gzip-compressed tarball archive:

- If you are working with Linux or macOS, you can open a new terminal window, `cd` into the download directory, and execute `tar -zxf aclImdb_v1.tar.gz` to decompress the dataset.
- If you are working with Windows, you can download a free archiver, such as 7-Zip (`http://www.7-zip.org`), to extract the files from the download archive.
- Alternatively, you can unpack the gzip-compressed tarball archive directly in Python as follows:

```
>>> import tarfile
>>> with tarfile.open('aclImdb_v1.tar.gz', 'r:gz') as tar:
...     tar.extractall()
```

Preprocessing the movie dataset into a more convenient format

Having successfully extracted the dataset, we will now assemble the individual text documents from the decompressed download archive into a single CSV file. In the following code section, we will be reading the movie reviews into a pandas `DataFrame` object, which can take up to 10 minutes on a standard desktop computer.

To visualize the progress and estimated time until completion, we will use the **Python Progress Indicator** (**PyPrind**, `https://pypi.python.org/pypi/PyPrind/`) package, which was developed several years ago for such purposes. PyPrind can be installed by executing the `pip install pyprind` command:

```
>>> import pyprind
>>> import pandas as pd
>>> import os
>>> import sys
>>> # change the 'basepath' to the directory of the
>>> # unzipped movie dataset
>>> basepath = 'aclImdb'
```

```
>>>
>>> labels = {'pos': 1, 'neg': 0}
>>> pbar = pyprind.ProgBar(50000, stream=sys.stdout)
>>> df = pd.DataFrame()
>>> for s in ('test', 'train'):
...     for l in ('pos', 'neg'):
...         path = os.path.join(basepath, s, l)
...         for file in sorted(os.listdir(path)):
...             with open(os.path.join(path, file),
...                       'r', encoding='utf-8') as infile:
...                 txt = infile.read()
...             df = df.append([[txt, labels[l]]],
...                            ignore_index=True)
...             pbar.update()
>>> df.columns = ['review', 'sentiment']
0%                          100%
[##############################] | ETA: 00:00:00
Total time elapsed: 00:00:25
```

In the preceding code, we first initialized a new progress bar object, `pbar`, with 50,000 iterations, which was the number of documents we were going to read in. Using the nested `for` loops, we iterated over the `train` and `test` subdirectories in the main `aclImdb` directory and read the individual text files from the `pos` and `neg` subdirectories that we eventually appended to the `df` pandas `DataFrame`, together with an integer class label (1 = positive and 0 = negative).

Since the class labels in the assembled dataset are sorted, we will now shuffle the `DataFrame` using the `permutation` function from the `np.random` submodule—this will be useful for splitting the dataset into training and test datasets in later sections, when we will stream the data from our local drive directly.

For our own convenience, we will also store the assembled and shuffled movie review dataset as a CSV file:

```
>>> import numpy as np
>>> np.random.seed(0)
>>> df = df.reindex(np.random.permutation(df.index))
>>> df.to_csv('movie_data.csv', index=False, encoding='utf-8')
```

Since we are going to use this dataset later in this chapter, let's quickly confirm that we have successfully saved the data in the right format by reading in the CSV and printing an excerpt of the first three examples:

```
>>> df = pd.read_csv('movie_data.csv', encoding='utf-8')
>>> # the following column renaming is necessary on some computers:
>>> df = df.rename(columns={"0": "review", "1": "sentiment"})
>>> df.head(3)
```

If you are running the code examples in a Jupyter notebook, you should now see the first three examples of the dataset, as shown in *Figure 8.1*:

	review	sentiment
0	In 1974, the teenager Martha Moxley (Maggie Gr...	1
1	OK... so... I really like Kris Kristofferson a...	0
2	***SPOILER*** Do not read this, if you think a...	0

Figure 8.1: The first three rows of the movie review dataset

As a sanity check, before we proceed to the next section, let's make sure that the `DataFrame` contains all 50,000 rows:

```
>>> df.shape
(50000, 2)
```

Introducing the bag-of-words model

You may remember from *Chapter 4, Building Good Training Datasets – Data Preprocessing*, that we have to convert categorical data, such as text or words, into a numerical form before we can pass it on to a machine learning algorithm. In this section, we will introduce the **bag-of-words** model, which allows us to represent text as numerical feature vectors. The idea behind bag-of-words is quite simple and can be summarized as follows:

1. We create a vocabulary of unique tokens—for example, words—from the entire set of documents.
2. We construct a feature vector from each document that contains the counts of how often each word occurs in the particular document.

Since the unique words in each document represent only a small subset of all the words in the bag-of-words vocabulary, the feature vectors will mostly consist of zeros, which is why we call them **sparse**. Do not worry if this sounds too abstract; in the following subsections, we will walk through the process of creating a simple bag-of-words model step by step.

Transforming words into feature vectors

To construct a bag-of-words model based on the word counts in the respective documents, we can use the `CountVectorizer` class implemented in scikit-learn. As you will see in the following code section, `CountVectorizer` takes an array of text data, which can be documents or sentences, and constructs the bag-of-words model for us:

```
>>> import numpy as np
>>> from sklearn.feature_extraction.text import CountVectorizer
>>> count = CountVectorizer()
>>> docs = np.array(['The sun is shining',
```

```
...                     'The weather is sweet',
...                     'The sun is shining, the weather is sweet,'
...                     'and one and one is two'])
>>> bag = count.fit_transform(docs)
```

By calling the `fit_transform` method on `CountVectorizer`, we constructed the vocabulary of the bag-of-words model and transformed the following three sentences into sparse feature vectors:

- `'The sun is shining'`
- `'The weather is sweet'`
- `'The sun is shining, the weather is sweet, and one and one is two'`

Now, let's print the contents of the vocabulary to get a better understanding of the underlying concepts:

```
>>> print(count.vocabulary_)
{'and': 0,
'two': 7,
'shining': 3,
'one': 2,
'sun': 4,
'weather': 8,
'the': 6,
'sweet': 5,
'is': 1}
```

As you can see from executing the preceding command, the vocabulary is stored in a Python dictionary that maps the unique words to integer indices. Next, let's print the feature vectors that we just created:

```
>>> print(bag.toarray())
[[0 1 0 1 1 0 1 0 0]
 [0 1 0 0 0 1 1 0 1]
 [2 3 2 1 1 1 2 1 1]]
```

Each index position in the feature vectors shown here corresponds to the integer values that are stored as dictionary items in the `CountVectorizer` vocabulary. For example, the first feature at index position `0` resembles the count of the word `'and'`, which only occurs in the last document, and the word `'is'`, at index position `1` (the second feature in the document vectors), occurs in all three sentences. These values in the feature vectors are also called the **raw term frequencies**: *tf*(*t*, *d*)—the number of times a term, *t*, occurs in a document, *d*. It should be noted that, in the bag-of-words model, the word or term order in a sentence or document does not matter. The order in which the term frequencies appear in the feature vector is derived from the vocabulary indices, which are usually assigned alphabetically.

N-gram models

The sequence of items in the bag-of-words model that we just created is also called the 1-gram or unigram model—each item or token in the vocabulary represents a single word. More generally, the contiguous sequences of items in NLP—words, letters, or symbols—are also called *n-grams*. The choice of the number, *n*, in the n-gram model depends on the particular application; for example, a study by Ioannis Kanaris and others revealed that n-grams of size 3 and 4 yield good performances in the anti-spam filtering of email messages (*Words versus character n-grams for anti-spam filtering* by *Ioannis Kanaris, Konstantinos Kanaris, Ioannis Houvardas,* and *Efstathios Stamatatos, International Journal on Artificial Intelligence Tools, World Scientific Publishing Company,* 16(06): 1047-1067, 2007).

To summarize the concept of the n-gram representation, the 1-gram and 2-gram representations of our first document, "the sun is shining", would be constructed as follows:

- 1-gram: "the", "sun", "is", "shining"
- 2-gram: "the sun", "sun is", "is shining"

The `CountVectorizer` class in scikit-learn allows us to use different n-gram models via its `ngram_range` parameter. While a 1-gram representation is used by default, we could switch to a 2-gram representation by initializing a new `CountVectorizer` instance with `ngram_range=(2,2)`.

Assessing word relevancy via term frequency-inverse document frequency

When we are analyzing text data, we often encounter words that occur across multiple documents from both classes. These frequently occurring words typically don't contain useful or discriminatory information. In this subsection, you will learn about a useful technique called the **term frequency-inverse document frequency (tf-idf)**, which can be used to downweight these frequently occurring words in the feature vectors. The tf-idf can be defined as the product of the term frequency and the inverse document frequency:

$$tf\text{-}idf(t, d) = tf(t, d) \times idf(t, d)$$

Here, $tf(t, d)$ is the term frequency that we introduced in the previous section, and $idf(t, d)$ is the inverse document frequency, which can be calculated as follows:

$$idf(t,d) = \log\frac{n_d}{1 + df(d,t)}$$

Here, n_d is the total number of documents, and $df(d, t)$ is the number of documents, *d*, that contain the term *t*. Note that adding the constant 1 to the denominator is optional and serves the purpose of assigning a non-zero value to terms that occur in none of the training examples; the *log* is used to ensure that low document frequencies are not given too much weight.

The scikit-learn library implements yet another transformer, the `TfidfTransformer` class, which takes the raw term frequencies from the `CountVectorizer` class as input and transforms them into tf-idfs:

```
>>> from sklearn.feature_extraction.text import TfidfTransformer
>>> tfidf = TfidfTransformer(use_idf=True,
...                          norm='l2',
...                          smooth_idf=True)
>>> np.set_printoptions(precision=2)
>>> print(tfidf.fit_transform(count.fit_transform(docs))
...       .toarray())
[[ 0.    0.43  0.    0.56  0.56  0.    0.43  0.    0.  ]
 [ 0.    0.43  0.    0.    0.    0.56  0.43  0.    0.56]
 [ 0.5   0.45  0.5   0.19  0.19  0.19  0.3   0.25  0.19]]
```

As you saw in the previous subsection, the word `'is'` had the largest term frequency in the third document, being the most frequently occurring word. However, after transforming the same feature vector into tf-idfs, the word `'is'` is now associated with a relatively small tf-idf (0.45) in the third document, since it is also present in the first and second document and thus is unlikely to contain any useful discriminatory information.

However, if we'd manually calculated the tf-idfs of the individual terms in our feature vectors, we would have noticed that `TfidfTransformer` calculates the tf-idfs slightly differently compared to the standard textbook equations that we defined previously. The equation for the inverse document frequency implemented in scikit-learn is computed as follows:

$$idf(t,d) = \log\frac{1+n_d}{1+df(d,t)}$$

Similarly, the tf-idf computed in scikit-learn deviates slightly from the default equation we defined earlier:

$$\textit{tf-idf}(t, d) = tf(t, d) \times (idf(t, d) + 1)$$

Note that the "+1" in the previous idf equation is due to setting `smooth_idf=True` in the previous code example, which is helpful for assigning zero weight (that is, $idf(t, d) = \log(1) = 0$) to terms that occur in all documents.

While it is also more typical to normalize the raw term frequencies before calculating the tf-idfs, the `TfidfTransformer` class normalizes the tf-idfs directly. By default (`norm='l2'`), scikit-learn's `TfidfTransformer` applies the L2-normalization, which returns a vector of length 1 by dividing an unnormalized feature vector, v, by its L2-norm:

$$v_{norm} = \frac{v}{\|v\|_2} = \frac{v}{\sqrt{v_1^2 + v_2^2 + \cdots + v_n^2}} = \frac{v}{\left(\sum_{i=1}^{n} v_i^2\right)^{1/2}}$$

To make sure that we understand how `TfidfTransformer` works, let's walk through an example and calculate the tf-idf of the word `'is'` in the third document. The word `'is'` has a term frequency of 3 (*tf* = 3) in the third document, and the document frequency of this term is 3 since the term `'is'` occurs in all three documents (*df* = 3). Thus, we can calculate the inverse document frequency as follows:

$$idf(\text{"is"}, d_3) = \log\frac{1+3}{1+3} = 0$$

Now, in order to calculate the tf-idf, we simply need to add 1 to the inverse document frequency and multiply it by the term frequency:

$$tf\text{-}idf(\text{"is"}, d_3) = 3 \times (0+1) = 3$$

If we repeated this calculation for all terms in the third document, we'd obtain the following tf-idf vectors: `[3.39, 3.0, 3.39, 1.29, 1.29, 1.29, 2.0, 1.69, 1.29]`. However, notice that the values in this feature vector are different from the values that we obtained from `TfidfTransformer` that we used previously. The final step that we are missing in this tf-idf calculation is the L2-normalization, which can be applied as follows:

$$\begin{aligned} tf\text{-}idf(d_3)_{norm} &= \frac{[3.39, 3.0, 3.39, 1.29, 1.29, 1.29, 2.0, 1.69, 1.29]}{\sqrt{3.39^2 + 3.0^2 + 3.39^2 + 1.29^2 + 1.29^2 + 1.29^2 + 2.0^2 + 1.69^2 + 1.29^2}} \\ &= [0.5, 0.45, 0.5, 0.19, 0.19, 0.19, 0.3, 0.25, 0.19] \end{aligned}$$

$$tf\text{-}idf(\text{"is"}, d_3) = 0.45$$

As you can see, the results now match the results returned by scikit-learn's `TfidfTransformer`, and since you now understand how tf-idfs are calculated, let's proceed to the next section and apply those concepts to the movie review dataset.

Cleaning text data

In the previous subsections, we learned about the bag-of-words model, term frequencies, and tf-idfs. However, the first important step—before we build our bag-of-words model—is to clean the text data by stripping it of all unwanted characters.

To illustrate why this is important, let's display the last 50 characters from the first document in the reshuffled movie review dataset:

```
>>> df.loc[0, 'review'][-50:]
'is seven.<br /><br />Title (Brazil): Not Available'
```

As you can see here, the text contains HTML markup as well as punctuation and other non-letter characters. While HTML markup does not contain many useful semantics, punctuation marks can represent useful, additional information in certain NLP contexts. However, for simplicity, we will now remove all punctuation marks except for emoticon characters, such as :), since those are certainly useful for sentiment analysis.

To accomplish this task, we will use Python's **regular expression** (**regex**) library, `re`, as shown here:

```
>>> import re
>>> def preprocessor(text):
...     text = re.sub('<[^>]*>', '', text)
...     emoticons = re.findall('(?::|;|=)(?:-)?(?:\)|\(|D|P)',
...                            text)
...     text = (re.sub('[\W]+', ' ', text.lower()) +
...             ' '.join(emoticons).replace('-', ''))
...     return text
```

Via the first regex, `<[^>]*>`, in the preceding code section, we tried to remove all of the HTML markup from the movie reviews. Although many programmers generally advise against the use of regex to parse HTML, this regex should be sufficient to *clean* this particular dataset. Since we are only interested in removing HTML markup and do not plan to use the HTML markup further, using regex to do the job should be acceptable. However, if you prefer to use sophisticated tools for removing HTML markup from text, you can take a look at Python's HTML parser module, which is described at `https://docs.python.org/3/library/html.parser.html`. After we removed the HTML markup, we used a slightly more complex regex to find emoticons, which we temporarily stored as emoticons. Next, we removed all non-word characters from the text via the regex `[\W]+` and converted the text into lowercase characters.

Dealing with word capitalization

In the context of this analysis, we assume that the capitalization of a word—for example, whether it appears at the beginning of a sentence—does not contain semantically relevant information. However, note that there are exceptions; for instance, we remove the notation of proper names. But again, in the context of this analysis, it is a simplifying assumption that the letter case does not contain information that is relevant for sentiment analysis.

Eventually, we added the temporarily stored emoticons to the end of the processed document string. Additionally, we removed the *nose* character (- in :-)) from the emoticons for consistency.

Regular expressions

Although regular expressions offer an efficient and convenient approach to searching for characters in a string, they also come with a steep learning curve. Unfortunately, an in-depth discussion of regular expressions is beyond the scope of this book. However, you can find a great tutorial on the Google Developers portal at `https://developers.google.com/edu/python/regular-expressions` or you can check out the official documentation of Python's `re` module at `https://docs.python.org/3.9/library/re.html`.

Although the addition of the emoticon characters to the end of the cleaned document strings may not look like the most elegant approach, we must note that the order of the words doesn't matter in our bag-of-words model if our vocabulary consists of only one-word tokens. But before we talk more about the splitting of documents into individual terms, words, or tokens, let's confirm that our `preprocessor` function works correctly:

```
>>> preprocessor(df.loc[0, 'review'][-50:])
'is seven title brazil not available'
>>> preprocessor("</a>This :) is :( a test :-)!")
'this is a test :) :( :)'
```

Lastly, since we will make use of the *cleaned* text data over and over again during the next sections, let's now apply our `preprocessor` function to all the movie reviews in our `DataFrame`:

```
>>> df['review'] = df['review'].apply(preprocessor)
```

Processing documents into tokens

After successfully preparing the movie review dataset, we now need to think about how to split the text corpora into individual elements. One way to *tokenize* documents is to split them into individual words by splitting the cleaned documents at their whitespace characters:

```
>>> def tokenizer(text):
...     return text.split()
>>> tokenizer('runners like running and thus they run')
['runners', 'like', 'running', 'and', 'thus', 'they', 'run']
```

In the context of tokenization, another useful technique is **word stemming**, which is the process of transforming a word into its root form. It allows us to map related words to the same stem. The original stemming algorithm was developed by Martin F. Porter in 1979 and is hence known as the **Porter stemmer** algorithm (*An algorithm for suffix stripping* by *Martin F. Porter, Program: Electronic Library and Information Systems,* 14(3): 130–137, 1980). The **Natural Language Toolkit** (**NLTK**, `http://www.nltk.org`) for Python implements the Porter stemming algorithm, which we will use in the following code section. To install the NLTK, you can simply execute `conda install nltk` or `pip install nltk`.

NLTK online book

Although the NLTK is not the focus of this chapter, I highly recommend that you visit the NLTK website as well as read the official NLTK book, which is freely available at `http://www.nltk.org/book/`, if you are interested in more advanced applications in NLP.

The following code shows how to use the Porter stemming algorithm:

```
>>> from nltk.stem.porter import PorterStemmer
>>> porter = PorterStemmer()
```

```
>>> def tokenizer_porter(text):
...     return [porter.stem(word) for word in text.split()]
>>> tokenizer_porter('runners like running and thus they run')
['runner', 'like', 'run', 'and', 'thu', 'they', 'run']
```

Using the `PorterStemmer` from the `nltk` package, we modified our `tokenizer` function to reduce words to their root form, which was illustrated by the simple preceding example where the word `'running'` was *stemmed* to its root form `'run'`.

Stemming algorithms

The Porter stemming algorithm is probably the oldest and simplest stemming algorithm. Other popular stemming algorithms include the newer Snowball stemmer (Porter2 or English stemmer) and the Lancaster stemmer (Paice/Husk stemmer). While both the Snowball and Lancaster stemmers are faster than the original Porter stemmer, the Lancaster stemmer is also notorious for being more aggressive than the Porter stemmer, which means that it will produce shorter and more obscure words. These alternative stemming algorithms are also available through the NLTK package (`http://www.nltk.org/api/nltk.stem.html`).

While stemming can create non-real words, such as `'thu'` (from `'thus'`), as shown in the previous example, a technique called *lemmatization* aims to obtain the canonical (grammatically correct) forms of individual words—the so-called *lemmas*. However, lemmatization is computationally more difficult and expensive compared to stemming and, in practice, it has been observed that stemming and lemmatization have little impact on the performance of text classification (*Influence of Word Normalization on Text Classification*, by *Michal Toman, Roman Tesar*, and *Karel Jezek*, *Proceedings of InSciT*, pages 354–358, 2006).

Before we jump into the next section, where we will train a machine learning model using the bag-of-words model, let's briefly talk about another useful topic called **stop word removal**. Stop words are simply those words that are extremely common in all sorts of texts and probably bear no (or only a little) useful information that can be used to distinguish between different classes of documents. Examples of stop words are *is*, *and*, *has*, and *like*. Removing stop words can be useful if we are working with raw or normalized term frequencies rather than tf-idfs, which already downweight the frequently occurring words.

To remove stop words from the movie reviews, we will use the set of 127 English stop words that is available from the NLTK library, which can be obtained by calling the `nltk.download` function:

```
>>> import nltk
>>> nltk.download('stopwords')
```

After we download the stop words set, we can load and apply the English stop word set as follows:

```
>>> from nltk.corpus import stopwords
>>> stop = stopwords.words('english')
>>> [w for w in tokenizer_porter('a runner likes'
...  ' running and runs a lot')
...  if w not in stop]
['runner', 'like', 'run', 'run', 'lot']
```

Training a logistic regression model for document classification

In this section, we will train a logistic regression model to classify the movie reviews into *positive* and *negative* reviews based on the bag-of-words model. First, we will divide the `DataFrame` of cleaned text documents into 25,000 documents for training and 25,000 documents for testing:

```
>>> X_train = df.loc[:25000, 'review'].values
>>> y_train = df.loc[:25000, 'sentiment'].values
>>> X_test = df.loc[25000:, 'review'].values
>>> y_test = df.loc[25000:, 'sentiment'].values
```

Next, we will use a `GridSearchCV` object to find the optimal set of parameters for our logistic regression model using 5-fold stratified cross-validation:

```
>>> from sklearn.model_selection import GridSearchCV
>>> from sklearn.pipeline import Pipeline
>>> from sklearn.linear_model import LogisticRegression
>>> from sklearn.feature_extraction.text import TfidfVectorizer
>>> tfidf = TfidfVectorizer(strip_accents=None,
...                         lowercase=False,
...                         preprocessor=None)
>>> small_param_grid = [
...     {
...         'vect__ngram_range': [(1, 1)],
...         'vect__stop_words': [None],
...         'vect__tokenizer': [tokenizer, tokenizer_porter],
...         'clf__penalty': ['l2'],
...         'clf__C': [1.0, 10.0]
...     },
...     {
...         'vect__ngram_range': [(1, 1)],
...         'vect__stop_words': [stop, None],
...         'vect__tokenizer': [tokenizer],
```

```
...         'vect__use_idf':[False],
...         'vect__norm':[None],
...         'clf__penalty': ['l2'],
...         'clf__C': [1.0, 10.0]
...     },
... ]
>>> lr_tfidf = Pipeline([
...     ('vect', tfidf),
...     ('clf', LogisticRegression(solver='liblinear'))
... ])
>>> gs_lr_tfidf = GridSearchCV(lr_tfidf, small_param_grid,
...                            scoring='accuracy', cv=5,
...                            verbose=2, n_jobs=1)
>>> gs_lr_tfidf.fit(X_train, y_train)
```

Note that for the logistic regression classifier, we are using the LIBLINEAR solver as it can perform better than the default choice (`'lbfgs'`) for relatively large datasets.

Multiprocessing via the n_jobs parameter

Please note that we highly recommend setting `n_jobs=-1` (instead of `n_jobs=1`, as in the previous code example) to utilize all available cores on your machine and speed up the grid search. However, some Windows users reported issues when running the previous code with the `n_jobs=-1` setting related to pickling the `tokenizer` and `tokenizer_porter` functions for multiprocessing on Windows. Another workaround would be to replace those two functions, `[tokenizer, tokenizer_porter]`, with `[str.split]`. However, note that replacement by the simple `str.split` would not support stemming.

When we initialized the `GridSearchCV` object and its parameter grid using the preceding code, we restricted ourselves to a limited number of parameter combinations, since the number of feature vectors, as well as the large vocabulary, can make the grid search computationally quite expensive. Using a standard desktop computer, our grid search may take 5-10 minutes to complete.

In the previous code example, we replaced `CountVectorizer` and `TfidfTransformer` from the previous subsection with `TfidfVectorizer`, which combines `CountVectorizer` with the `TfidfTransformer`. Our `param_grid` consisted of two parameter dictionaries. In the first dictionary, we used `TfidfVectorizer` with its default settings (`use_idf=True`, `smooth_idf=True`, and `norm='l2'`) to calculate the tf-idfs; in the second dictionary, we set those parameters to `use_idf=False`, `smooth_idf=False`, and `norm=None` in order to train a model based on raw term frequencies. Furthermore, for the logistic regression classifier itself, we trained models using L2 regularization via the penalty parameter and compared different regularization strengths by defining a range of values for the inverse-regularization parameter `C`. As an optional exercise, you are also encouraged to add L1 regularization to the parameter grid by changing `'clf__penalty': ['l2']` to `'clf__penalty': ['l2', 'l1']`.

After the grid search has finished, we can print the best parameter set:

```
>>> print(f'Best parameter set: {gs_lr_tfidf.best_params_}')
Best parameter set: {'clf__C': 10.0, 'clf__penalty': 'l2', 'vect__ngram_range':
(1, 1), 'vect__stop_words': None, 'vect__tokenizer': <function tokenizer at
0x169932dc0>}
```

As you can see in the preceding output, we obtained the best grid search results using the regular `tokenizer` without Porter stemming, no stop word library, and tf-idfs in combination with a logistic regression classifier that uses L2-regularization with the regularization strength `C` of `10.0`.

Using the best model from this grid search, let's print the average 5-fold cross-validation accuracy scores on the training dataset and the classification accuracy on the test dataset:

```
>>> print(f'CV Accuracy: {gs_lr_tfidf.best_score_:.3f}')
CV Accuracy: 0.897
>>> clf = gs_lr_tfidf.best_estimator_
>>> print(f'Test Accuracy: {clf.score(X_test, y_test):.3f}')
Test Accuracy: 0.899
```

The results reveal that our machine learning model can predict whether a movie review is positive or negative with 90 percent accuracy.

The naïve Bayes classifier

A still very popular classifier for text classification is the naïve Bayes classifier, which gained popularity in applications of email spam filtering. Naïve Bayes classifiers are easy to implement, computationally efficient, and tend to perform particularly well on relatively small datasets compared to other algorithms. Although we don't discuss naïve Bayes classifiers in this book, the interested reader can find an article about naïve Bayes text classification that is freely available on arXiv (*Naive Bayes and Text Classification I – Introduction and Theory* by *S. Raschka, Computing Research Repository* (*CoRR*), abs/1410.5329, 2014, `http://arxiv.org/pdf/1410.5329v3.pdf`). Different versions of naïve Bayes classifiers referenced in this article are implemented in scikit-learn. You can find an overview page with links to the respective code classes here: `https://scikit-learn.org/stable/modules/naive_bayes.html`.

Working with bigger data – online algorithms and out-of-core learning

If you executed the code examples in the previous section, you may have noticed that it could be computationally quite expensive to construct the feature vectors for the 50,000-movie review dataset during a grid search. In many real-world applications, it is not uncommon to work with even larger datasets that can exceed our computer's memory.

Since not everyone has access to supercomputer facilities, we will now apply a technique called **out-of-core learning**, which allows us to work with such large datasets by fitting the classifier incrementally on smaller batches of a dataset.

Text classification with recurrent neural networks

In *Chapter 15, Modeling Sequential Data Using Recurrent Neural Networks,* we will revisit this dataset and train a deep learning-based classifier (a recurrent neural network) to classify the reviews in the IMDb movie review dataset. This neural network-based classifier follows the same out-of-core principle using the stochastic gradient descent optimization algorithm, but does not require the construction of a bag-of-words model.

Back in *Chapter 2, Training Simple Machine Learning Algorithms for Classification,* the concept of **stochastic gradient descent** was introduced; it is an optimization algorithm that updates the model's weights using one example at a time. In this section, we will make use of the `partial_fit` function of `SGDClassifier` in scikit-learn to stream the documents directly from our local drive and train a logistic regression model using small mini-batches of documents.

First, we will define a `tokenizer` function that cleans the unprocessed text data from the `movie_data.csv` file that we constructed at the beginning of this chapter and separates it into word tokens while removing stop words:

```
>>> import numpy as np
>>> import re
>>> from nltk.corpus import stopwords
>>> stop = stopwords.words('english')
>>> def tokenizer(text):
...     text = re.sub('<[^>]*>', '', text)
...     emoticons = re.findall('(?::|;|=)(?:-)?(?:\)|\(|D|P)',
...                            text)
...     text = re.sub('[\W]+', ' ', text.lower()) \
...                   + ' '.join(emoticons).replace('-', '')
...     tokenized = [w for w in text.split() if w not in stop]
...     return tokenized
```

Next, we will define a generator function, `stream_docs`, that reads in and returns one document at a time:

```
>>> def stream_docs(path):
...     with open(path, 'r', encoding='utf-8') as csv:
...         next(csv) # skip header
...         for line in csv:
...             text, label = line[:-3], int(line[-2])
...             yield text, label
```

To verify that our stream_docs function works correctly, let's read in the first document from the movie_data.csv file, which should return a tuple consisting of the review text as well as the corresponding class label:

```
>>> next(stream_docs(path='movie_data.csv'))
('"In 1974, the teenager Martha Moxley ... ',1)
```

We will now define a function, get_minibatch, that will take a document stream from the stream_docs function and return a particular number of documents specified by the size parameter:

```
>>> def get_minibatch(doc_stream, size):
...     docs, y = [], []
...     try:
...         for _ in range(size):
...             text, label = next(doc_stream)
...             docs.append(text)
...             y.append(label)
...     except StopIteration:
...         return None, None
...     return docs, y
```

Unfortunately, we can't use CountVectorizer for out-of-core learning since it requires holding the complete vocabulary in memory. Also, TfidfVectorizer needs to keep all the feature vectors of the training dataset in memory to calculate the inverse document frequencies. However, another useful vectorizer for text processing implemented in scikit-learn is HashingVectorizer. HashingVectorizer is data-independent and makes use of the hashing trick via the 32-bit MurmurHash3 function by Austin Appleby (you can find more information about MurmurHash at https://en.wikipedia.org/wiki/MurmurHash):

```
>>> from sklearn.feature_extraction.text import HashingVectorizer
>>> from sklearn.linear_model import SGDClassifier
>>> vect = HashingVectorizer(decode_error='ignore',
...                          n_features=2**21,
...                          preprocessor=None,
...                          tokenizer=tokenizer)
>>> clf = SGDClassifier(loss='log', random_state=1)
>>> doc_stream = stream_docs(path='movie_data.csv')
```

Using the preceding code, we initialized HashingVectorizer with our tokenizer function and set the number of features to 2**21. Furthermore, we reinitialized a logistic regression classifier by setting the loss parameter of SGDClassifier to 'log'. Note that by choosing a large number of features in HashingVectorizer, we reduce the chance of causing hash collisions, but we also increase the number of coefficients in our logistic regression model.

Now comes the really interesting part—having set up all the complementary functions, we can start the out-of-core learning using the following code:

```
>>> import pyprind
>>> pbar = pyprind.ProgBar(45)
>>> classes = np.array([0, 1])
>>> for _ in range(45):
...     X_train, y_train = get_minibatch(doc_stream, size=1000)
...     if not X_train:
...         break
...     X_train = vect.transform(X_train)
...     clf.partial_fit(X_train, y_train, classes=classes)
...     pbar.update()
0%                          100%
[##############################] | ETA: 00:00:00
Total time elapsed: 00:00:21
```

Again, we made use of the PyPrind package to estimate the progress of our learning algorithm. We initialized the progress bar object with 45 iterations and, in the following `for` loop, we iterated over 45 mini-batches of documents where each mini-batch consists of 1,000 documents. Having completed the incremental learning process, we will use the last 5,000 documents to evaluate the performance of our model:

```
>>> X_test, y_test = get_minibatch(doc_stream, size=5000)
>>> X_test = vect.transform(X_test)
>>> print(f'Accuracy: {clf.score(X_test, y_test):.3f}')
Accuracy: 0.868
```

NoneType error

Please note that if you encounter a `NoneType` error, you may have executed the `X_test, y_test = get_minibatch(...)` code twice. Via the previous loop, we have 45 iterations where we fetch 1,000 documents each. Hence, there are exactly 5,000 documents left for testing, which we assign via:

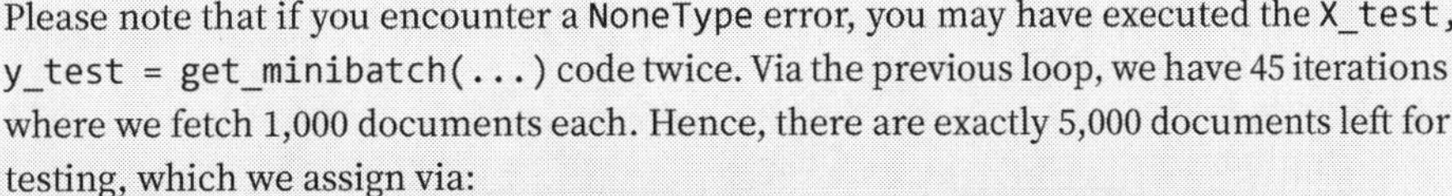

```
>>> X_test, y_test = get_minibatch(doc_stream, size=5000)
```

If we execute this code twice, then there are not enough documents left in the generator, and `X_test` returns `None`. Hence, if you encounter the `NoneType` error, you have to start at the previous `stream_docs(...)` code again.

As you can see, the accuracy of the model is approximately 87 percent, slightly below the accuracy that we achieved in the previous section using the grid search for hyperparameter tuning. However, out-of-core learning is very memory efficient, and it took less than a minute to complete.

Finally, we can use the last 5,000 documents to update our model:

```
>>> clf = clf.partial_fit(X_test, y_test)
```

The word2vec model

A more modern alternative to the bag-of-words model is word2vec, an algorithm that Google released in 2013 (*Efficient Estimation of Word Representations in Vector Space* by *T. Mikolov, K. Chen, G. Corrado,* and *J. Dean*, `https://arxiv.org/abs/1301.3781`).

The word2vec algorithm is an unsupervised learning algorithm based on neural networks that attempts to automatically learn the relationship between words. The idea behind word2vec is to put words that have similar meanings into similar clusters, and via clever vector spacing, the model can reproduce certain words using simple vector math, for example, *king* – *man* + *woman* = *queen*.

The original C-implementation with useful links to the relevant papers and alternative implementations can be found at `https://code.google.com/p/word2vec/`.

Topic modeling with latent Dirichlet allocation

Topic modeling describes the broad task of assigning topics to unlabeled text documents. For example, a typical application is the categorization of documents in a large text corpus of newspaper articles. In applications of topic modeling, we then aim to assign category labels to those articles, for example, sports, finance, world news, politics, and local news. Thus, in the context of the broad categories of machine learning that we discussed in *Chapter 1, Giving Computers the Ability to Learn from Data*, we can consider topic modeling as a clustering task, a subcategory of unsupervised learning.

In this section, we will discuss a popular technique for topic modeling called **latent Dirichlet allocation** (**LDA**). However, note that while latent Dirichlet allocation is often abbreviated as LDA, it is not to be confused with *linear discriminant analysis*, a supervised dimensionality reduction technique that was introduced in *Chapter 5, Compressing Data via Dimensionality Reduction*.

Decomposing text documents with LDA

Since the mathematics behind LDA is quite involved and requires knowledge of Bayesian inference, we will approach this topic from a practitioner's perspective and interpret LDA using layman's terms. However, the interested reader can read more about LDA in the following research paper: *Latent Dirichlet Allocation*, by *David M. Blei, Andrew Y. Ng*, and *Michael I. Jordan, Journal of Machine Learning Research 3*, pages: 993-1022, Jan 2003, `https://www.jmlr.org/papers/volume3/blei03a/blei03a.pdf`.

LDA is a generative probabilistic model that tries to find groups of words that appear frequently together across different documents. These frequently appearing words represent our topics, assuming that each document is a mixture of different words. The input to an LDA is the bag-of-words model that we discussed earlier in this chapter.

Given a bag-of-words matrix as input, LDA decomposes it into two new matrices:

- A document-to-topic matrix
- A word-to-topic matrix

LDA decomposes the bag-of-words matrix in such a way that if we multiply those two matrices together, we will be able to reproduce the input, the bag-of-words matrix, with the lowest possible error. In practice, we are interested in those topics that LDA found in the bag-of-words matrix. The only downside may be that we must define the number of topics beforehand—the number of topics is a hyperparameter of LDA that has to be specified manually.

LDA with scikit-learn

In this subsection, we will use the `LatentDirichletAllocation` class implemented in scikit-learn to decompose the movie review dataset and categorize it into different topics. In the following example, we will restrict the analysis to 10 different topics, but readers are encouraged to experiment with the hyperparameters of the algorithm to further explore the topics that can be found in this dataset.

First, we are going to load the dataset into a pandas `DataFrame` using the local `movie_data.csv` file of the movie reviews that we created at the beginning of this chapter:

```
>>> import pandas as pd
>>> df = pd.read_csv('movie_data.csv', encoding='utf-8')
>>> # the following is necessary on some computers:
>>> df = df.rename(columns={"0": "review", "1": "sentiment"})
```

Next, we are going to use the already familiar `CountVectorizer` to create the bag-of-words matrix as input to the LDA.

For convenience, we will use scikit-learn's built-in English stop word library via `stop_words='english'`:

```
>>> from sklearn.feature_extraction.text import CountVectorizer
>>> count = CountVectorizer(stop_words='english',
...                         max_df=.1,
...                         max_features=5000)
>>> X = count.fit_transform(df['review'].values)
```

Notice that we set the maximum document frequency of words to be considered to 10 percent (`max_df=.1`) to exclude words that occur too frequently across documents. The rationale behind the removal of frequently occurring words is that these might be common words appearing across all documents that are, therefore, less likely to be associated with a specific topic category of a given document. Also, we limited the number of words to be considered to the most frequently occurring 5,000 words (`max_features=5000`), to limit the dimensionality of this dataset to improve the inference performed by LDA. However, both `max_df=.1` and `max_features=5000` are hyperparameter values chosen arbitrarily, and readers are encouraged to tune them while comparing the results.

The following code example demonstrates how to fit a `LatentDirichletAllocation` estimator to the bag-of-words matrix and infer the 10 different topics from the documents (note that the model fitting can take up to 5 minutes or more on a laptop or standard desktop computer):

```
>>> from sklearn.decomposition import LatentDirichletAllocation
>>> lda = LatentDirichletAllocation(n_components=10,
...                                 random_state=123,
...                                 learning_method='batch')
>>> X_topics = lda.fit_transform(X)
```

By setting `learning_method='batch'`, we let the `lda` estimator do its estimation based on all available training data (the bag-of-words matrix) in one iteration, which is slower than the alternative `'online'` learning method, but can lead to more accurate results (setting `learning_method='online'` is analogous to online or mini-batch learning, which we discussed in *Chapter 2, Training Simple Machine Learning Algorithms for Classification*, and previously in this chapter).

Expectation-maximization

The scikit-learn library's implementation of LDA uses the **expectation-maximization (EM)** algorithm to update its parameter estimates iteratively. We haven't discussed the EM algorithm in this chapter, but if you are curious to learn more, please see the excellent overview on Wikipedia (`https://en.wikipedia.org/wiki/Expectation-maximization_algorithm`) and the detailed tutorial on how it is used in LDA in Colorado Reed's tutorial, *Latent Dirichlet Allocation: Towards a Deeper Understanding*, which is freely available at `http://obphio.us/pdfs/lda_tutorial.pdf`.

After fitting the LDA, we now have access to the `components_` attribute of the `lda` instance, which stores a matrix containing the word importance (here, `5000`) for each of the 10 topics in increasing order:

```
>>> lda.components_.shape
(10, 5000)
```

To analyze the results, let's print the five most important words for each of the 10 topics. Note that the word importance values are ranked in increasing order. Thus, to print the top five words, we need to sort the topic array in reverse order:

```
>>> n_top_words = 5
>>> feature_names = count.get_feature_names_out()
>>> for topic_idx, topic in enumerate(lda.components_):
...     print(f'Topic {(topic_idx + 1)}:')
...     print(' '.join([feature_names[i]
...                     for i in topic.argsort()\
...                     [:-n_top_words - 1:-1]]))
Topic 1:
```

```
worst minutes awful script stupid
Topic 2:
family mother father children girl
Topic 3:
american war dvd music tv
Topic 4:
human audience cinema art sense
Topic 5:
police guy car dead murder
Topic 6:
horror house sex girl woman
Topic 7:
role performance comedy actor performances
Topic 8:
series episode war episodes tv
Topic 9:
book version original read novel
Topic 10:
action fight guy guys cool
```

Based on reading the five most important words for each topic, you may guess that the LDA identified the following topics:

1. Generally bad movies (not really a topic category)
2. Movies about families
3. War movies
4. Art movies
5. Crime movies
6. Horror movies
7. Comedy movie reviews
8. Movies somehow related to TV shows
9. Movies based on books
10. Action movies

To confirm that the categories make sense based on the reviews, let's plot three movies from the horror movie category (horror movies belong to category 6 at index position 5):

```
>>> horror = X_topics[:, 5].argsort()[::-1]
>>> for iter_idx, movie_idx in enumerate(horror[:3]):
...     print(f'\nHorror movie #{(iter_idx + 1)}:')
...     print(df['review'][movie_idx][:300], '...')
Horror movie #1:
House of Dracula works from the same basic premise as House of Frankenstein
from the year before; namely that Universal's three most famous monsters;
Dracula, Frankenstein's Monster and The Wolf Man are appearing in the movie
together. Naturally, the film is rather messy therefore, but the fact that ...
```

```
Horror movie #2:
Okay, what the hell kind of TRASH have I been watching now? "The Witches'
Mountain" has got to be one of the most incoherent and insane Spanish
exploitation flicks ever and yet, at the same time, it's also strangely
compelling. There's absolutely nothing that makes sense here and I even doubt
there ...
Horror movie #3:
<br /><br />Horror movie time, Japanese style. Uzumaki/Spiral was a total
freakfest from start to finish. A fun freakfest at that, but at times it was
a tad too reliant on kitsch rather than the horror. The story is difficult to
summarize succinctly: a carefree, normal teenage girl starts coming fac ...
```

Using the preceding code example, we printed the first 300 characters from the top three horror movies. The reviews—even though we don't know which exact movie they belong to—sound like reviews of horror movies (however, one might argue that `Horror movie #2` could also be a good fit for topic category 1: *Generally bad movies*).

Summary

In this chapter, you learned how to use machine learning algorithms to classify text documents based on their polarity, which is a basic task in sentiment analysis in the field of NLP. Not only did you learn how to encode a document as a feature vector using the bag-of-words model, but you also learned how to weight the term frequency by relevance using tf-idf.

Working with text data can be computationally quite expensive due to the large feature vectors that are created during this process; in the last section, we covered how to utilize out-of-core or incremental learning to train a machine learning algorithm without loading the whole dataset into a computer's memory.

Lastly, you were introduced to the concept of topic modeling using LDA to categorize the movie reviews into different categories in an unsupervised fashion.

So far, in this book, we have covered many machine learning concepts, best practices, and supervised models for classification. In the next chapter, we will look at another subcategory of supervised learning, *regression analysis*, which lets us predict outcome variables on a continuous scale, in contrast to the categorical class labels of the classification models that we have been working with so far.

Join our book's Discord space

Predicting Continuous Target Variables with Regression Analysis

Throughout the previous chapters, you learned a lot about the main concepts behind **supervised learning** and trained many different models for classification tasks to predict group memberships or categorical variables. In this chapter, we will dive into another subcategory of supervised learning: **regression analysis**.

Regression models are used to predict target variables on a continuous scale, which makes them attractive for addressing many questions in science. They also have applications in industry, such as understanding relationships between variables, evaluating trends, or making forecasts. One example is predicting the sales of a company in future months.

In this chapter, we will discuss the main concepts of regression models and cover the following topics:

- Exploring and visualizing datasets
- Looking at different approaches to implementing linear regression models
- Training regression models that are robust to outliers
- Evaluating regression models and diagnosing common problems
- Fitting regression models to nonlinear data

Introducing linear regression

The goal of linear regression is to model the relationship between one or multiple features and a continuous target variable. In contrast to classification—a different subcategory of supervised learning—regression analysis aims to predict outputs on a continuous scale rather than categorical class labels.

In the following subsections, you will be introduced to the most basic type of linear regression, **simple linear regression**, and understand how to relate it to the more general, multivariate case (linear regression with multiple features).

Simple linear regression

The goal of simple (**univariate**) linear regression is to model the relationship between a single feature (**explanatory variable**, x) and a continuous-valued **target** (**response variable**, y). The equation of a linear model with one explanatory variable is defined as follows:

$$y = w_1 x + b$$

Here, the parameter (bias unit), b, represents the y axis intercept and w_1 is the weight coefficient of the explanatory variable. Our goal is to learn the weights of the linear equation to describe the relationship between the explanatory variable and the target variable, which can then be used to predict the responses of new explanatory variables that were not part of the training dataset.

Based on the linear equation that we defined previously, linear regression can be understood as finding the best-fitting straight line through the training examples, as shown in *Figure 9.1*:

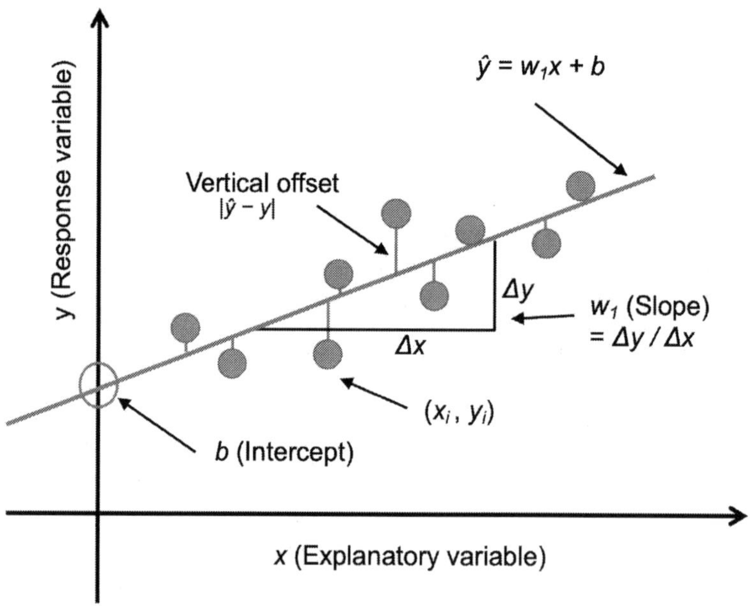

Figure 9.1: A simple one-feature linear regression example

This best-fitting line is also called the **regression line**, and the vertical lines from the regression line to the training examples are the so-called **offsets** or **residuals**—the errors of our prediction.

Multiple linear regression

The previous section introduced simple linear regression, a special case of linear regression with one explanatory variable. Of course, we can also generalize the linear regression model to multiple explanatory variables; this process is called **multiple linear regression**:

$$y = w_1x_1 + \ldots + w_mx_m + b = \sum_{i=1}^{m} w_ix_i + b = w^T\boldsymbol{x} + b$$

Figure 9.2 shows how the two-dimensional, fitted hyperplane of a multiple linear regression model with two features could look:

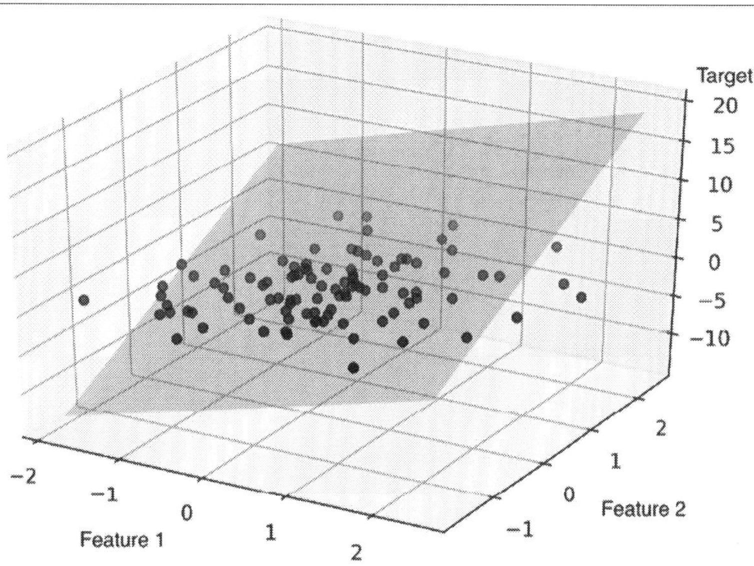

Figure 9.2: A two-feature linear regression model

As you can see, visualizations of multiple linear regression hyperplanes in a three-dimensional scatterplot are already challenging to interpret when looking at static figures. Since we have no good means of visualizing hyperplanes with two dimensions in a scatterplot (multiple linear regression models fit to datasets with three or more features), the examples and visualizations in this chapter will mainly focus on the univariate case, using simple linear regression. However, simple and multiple linear regression are based on the same concepts and the same evaluation techniques; the code implementations that we will discuss in this chapter are also compatible with both types of regression model.

Exploring the Ames Housing dataset

Before we implement the first linear regression model, we will discuss a new dataset, the Ames Housing dataset, which contains information about individual residential property in Ames, Iowa, from 2006 to 2010. The dataset was collected by Dean De Cock in 2011, and additional information is available via the following links:

- A report describing the dataset: `http://jse.amstat.org/v19n3/decock.pdf`
- Detailed documentation regarding the dataset's features: `http://jse.amstat.org/v19n3/decock/DataDocumentation.txt`
- The dataset in a tab-separated format: `http://jse.amstat.org/v19n3/decock/AmesHousing.txt`

As with each new dataset, it is always helpful to explore the data through a simple visualization, to get a better feeling of what we are working with, which is what we will do in the following subsections.

Loading the Ames Housing dataset into a DataFrame

In this section, we will load the Ames Housing dataset using the pandas `read_csv` function, which is fast and versatile and a recommended tool for working with tabular data stored in a plaintext format.

The Ames Housing dataset consists of 2,930 examples and 80 features. For simplicity, we will only work with a subset of the features, shown in the following list. However, if you are curious, follow the link to the full dataset description provided at the beginning of this section, and you are encouraged to explore other variables in this dataset after reading this chapter.

The features we will be working with, including the target variable, are as follows:

- `Overall Qual`: Rating for the overall material and finish of the house on a scale from 1 (very poor) to 10 (excellent)
- `Overall Cond`: Rating for the overall condition of the house on a scale from 1 (very poor) to 10 (excellent)
- `Gr Liv Area`: Above grade (ground) living area in square feet
- `Central Air`: Central air conditioning (N=no, Y=yes)
- `Total Bsmt SF`: Total square feet of the basement area
- `SalePrice`: Sale price in U.S. dollars ($)

For the rest of this chapter, we will regard the sale price (`SalePrice`) as our target variable—the variable that we want to predict using one or more of the five explanatory variables. Before we explore this dataset further, let's load it into a pandas `DataFrame`:

```
import pandas as pd

columns = ['Overall Qual', 'Overall Cond', 'Gr Liv Area',
           'Central Air', 'Total Bsmt SF', 'SalePrice']
```

```
df = pd.read_csv('http://jse.amstat.org/v19n3/decock/AmesHousing.txt',
                 sep='\t',
                 usecols=columns)

df.head()
```

To confirm that the dataset was loaded successfully, we can display the first five lines of the dataset, as shown in *Figure 9.3*:

	Overall Qual	Overall Cond	Total Bsmt SF	Central Air	Gr Liv Area	SalePrice
0	6	5	1080.0	Y	1656	215000
1	5	6	882.0	Y	896	105000
2	6	6	1329.0	Y	1329	172000
3	7	5	2110.0	Y	2110	244000
4	5	5	928.0	Y	1629	189900

Figure 9.3: The first five rows of the housing dataset

After loading the dataset, let's also check the dimensions of the `DataFrame` to make sure that it contains the expected number of rows:

```
>>> df.shape
(2930, 6)
```

As we can see, the `DataFrame` contains 2,930 rows, as expected.

Another aspect we have to take care of is the `'Central Air'` variable, which is encoded as type `string`, as we can see in *Figure 9.3*. As we learned in *Chapter 4, Building Good Training Datasets – Data Preprocessing*, we can use the `.map` method to convert `DataFrame` columns. The following code will convert the string `'Y'` to the integer 1, and the string `'N'` to the integer 0:

```
>>> df['Central Air'] = df['Central Air'].map({'N': 0, 'Y': 1})
```

Lastly, let's check whether any of the data frame columns contain missing values:

```
>>> df.isnull().sum()
Overall Qual     0
Overall Cond     0
Total Bsmt SF    1
Central Air      0
Gr Liv Area      0
SalePrice        0
dtype: int64
```

As we can see, the `Total Bsmt SF` feature variable contains one missing value. Since we have a relatively large dataset, the easiest way to deal with this missing feature value is to remove the corresponding example from the dataset (for alternative methods, please see *Chapter 4*):

```
>>> df = df.dropna(axis=0)
>>> df.isnull().sum()

Overall Qual     0
Overall Cond     0
Total Bsmt SF    0
Central Air      0
Gr Liv Area      0
SalePrice        0
dtype: int64
```

Visualizing the important characteristics of a dataset

Exploratory data analysis (EDA) is an important and recommended first step prior to the training of a machine learning model. In the rest of this section, we will use some simple yet useful techniques from the graphical EDA toolbox that may help us to visually detect the presence of outliers, the distribution of the data, and the relationships between features.

First, we will create a **scatterplot matrix** that allows us to visualize the pair-wise correlations between the different features in this dataset in one place. To plot the scatterplot matrix, we will use the `scatterplotmatrix` function from the mlxtend library (`http://rasbt.github.io/mlxtend/`), which is a Python library that contains various convenience functions for machine learning and data science applications in Python.

You can install the `mlxtend` package via `conda install mlxtend` or `pip install mlxtend`. For this chapter, we used mlxtend version 0.19.0.

Once the installation is complete, you can import the package and create the scatterplot matrix as follows:

```
>>> import matplotlib.pyplot as plt
>>> from mlxtend.plotting import scatterplotmatrix
>>> scatterplotmatrix(df.values, figsize=(12, 10),
...                   names=df.columns, alpha=0.5)
>>> plt.tight_layout()
plt.show()
```

As you can see in *Figure 9.4*, the scatterplot matrix provides us with a useful graphical summary of the relationships in a dataset:

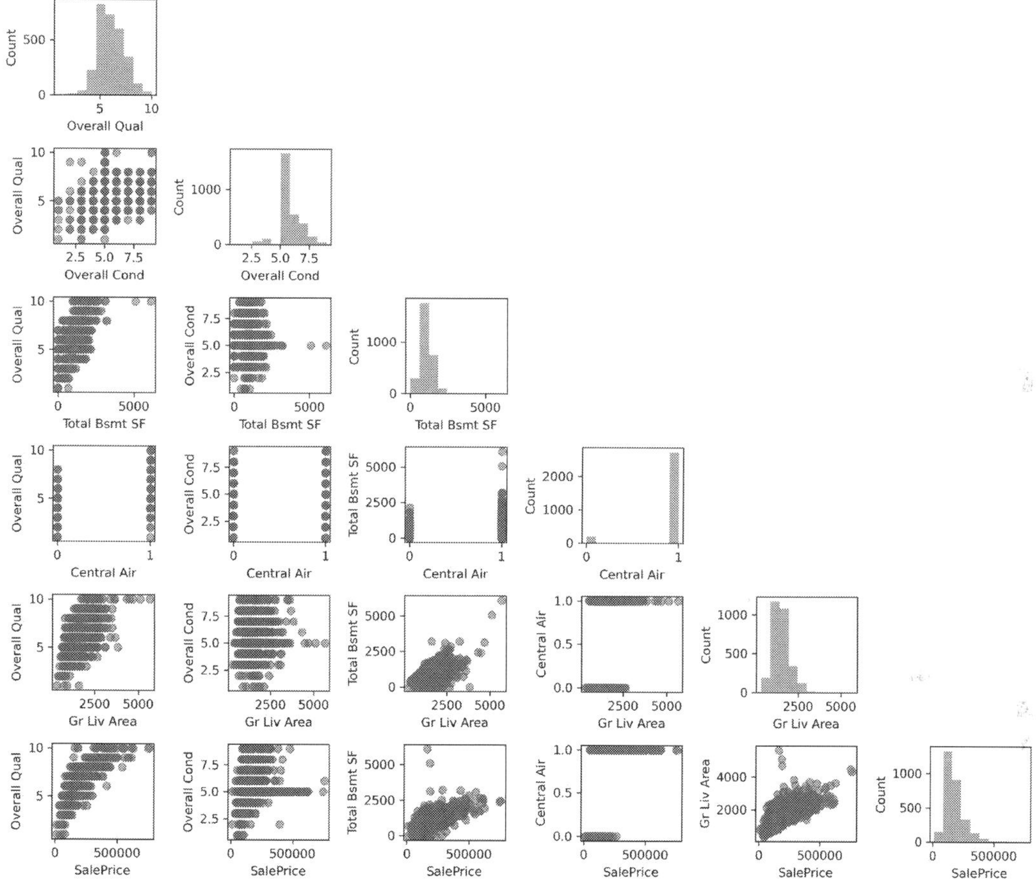

Figure 9.4: A scatterplot matrix of our data

Using this scatterplot matrix, we can now quickly see how the data is distributed and whether it contains outliers. For example, we can see (fifth column from the left of the bottom row) that there is a somewhat linear relationship between the size of the living area above ground (`Gr Liv Area`) and the sale price (`SalePrice`).

Furthermore, we can see in the histogram—the lower-right subplot in the scatterplot matrix—that the `SalePrice` variable seems to be skewed by several outliers.

The normality assumption of linear regression

Note that in contrast to common belief, training a linear regression model does not require that the explanatory or target variables are normally distributed. The normality assumption is only a requirement for certain statistics and hypothesis tests that are beyond the scope of this book (for more information on this topic, please refer to *Introduction to Linear Regression Analysis* by *Douglas C. Montgomery, Elizabeth A. Peck,* and *G. Geoffrey Vining, Wiley,* pages: 318-319, 2012).

Looking at relationships using a correlation matrix

In the previous section, we visualized the data distributions of the Ames Housing dataset variables in the form of histograms and scatterplots. Next, we will create a correlation matrix to quantify and summarize linear relationships between variables. A correlation matrix is closely related to the covariance matrix that we covered in the section *Unsupervised dimensionality reduction via principal component analysis* in *Chapter 5, Compressing Data via Dimensionality Reduction.* We can interpret the correlation matrix as being a rescaled version of the covariance matrix. In fact, the correlation matrix is identical to a covariance matrix computed from standardized features.

The correlation matrix is a square matrix that contains the **Pearson product-moment correlation coefficient** (often abbreviated as **Pearson's r**), which measures the linear dependence between pairs of features. The correlation coefficients are in the range –1 to 1. Two features have a perfect positive correlation if $r = 1$, no correlation if $r = 0$, and a perfect negative correlation if $r = -1$. As mentioned previously, Pearson's correlation coefficient can simply be calculated as the covariance between two features, x and y (numerator), divided by the product of their standard deviations (denominator):

$$r = \frac{\sum_{i=1}^{n}\left[\left(x^{(i)} - \mu_x\right)\left(y^{(i)} - \mu_y\right)\right]}{\sqrt{\sum_{i=1}^{n}\left(x^{(i)} - \mu_x\right)^2}\sqrt{\sum_{i=1}^{n}\left(y^{(i)} - \mu_y\right)^2}} = \frac{\sigma_{xy}}{\sigma_x \sigma_y}$$

Here, μ denotes the mean of the corresponding feature, σ_{xy} is the covariance between the features x and y, and σ_x and σ_y are the features' standard deviations.

Covariance versus correlation for standardized features

We can show that the covariance between a pair of standardized features is, in fact, equal to their linear correlation coefficient. To show this, let's first standardize the features *x* and *y* to obtain their z-scores, which we will denote as *x'* and *y'*, respectively:

$$x' = \frac{x - \mu_x}{\sigma_x},\ y' = \frac{y - \mu_y}{\sigma_y}$$

Remember that we compute the (population) covariance between two features as follows:

$$\sigma_{xy} = \frac{1}{n}\sum_{i}^{n}\left(x^{(i)} - \mu_x\right)\left(y^{(i)} - \mu_y\right)$$

Since standardization centers a feature variable at mean zero, we can now calculate the covariance between the scaled features as follows:

$$\sigma'_{xy} = \frac{1}{n}\sum_{i}^{n}\left(x'^{(i)} - 0\right)\left(y'^{(i)} - 0\right)$$

Through resubstitution, we then get the following result:

$$\sigma'_{xy} = \frac{1}{n}\sum_{i}^{n}\left(\frac{x - \mu_x}{\sigma_x}\right)\left(\frac{y - \mu_y}{\sigma_y}\right)$$

$$\sigma'_{xy} = \frac{1}{n \cdot \sigma_x\sigma_y}\sum_{i}^{n}\left(x^{(i)} - \mu_x\right)\left(y^{(i)} - \mu_y\right)$$

Finally, we can simplify this equation as follows:

$$\sigma'_{xy} = \frac{\sigma_{xy}}{\sigma_x\sigma_y}$$

In the following code example, we will use NumPy's `corrcoef` function on the five feature columns that we previously visualized in the scatterplot matrix, and we will use mlxtend's `heatmap` function to plot the correlation matrix array as a heat map:

```
>>> import numpy as np
>>> from mlxtend.plotting import heatmap


>>> cm = np.corrcoef(df.values.T)
>>> hm = heatmap(cm, row_names=df.columns, column_names=df.columns)
>>> plt.tight_layout()
>>> plt.show()
```

As you can see in *Figure 9.5*, the correlation matrix provides us with another useful summary graphic that can help us to select features based on their respective linear correlations:

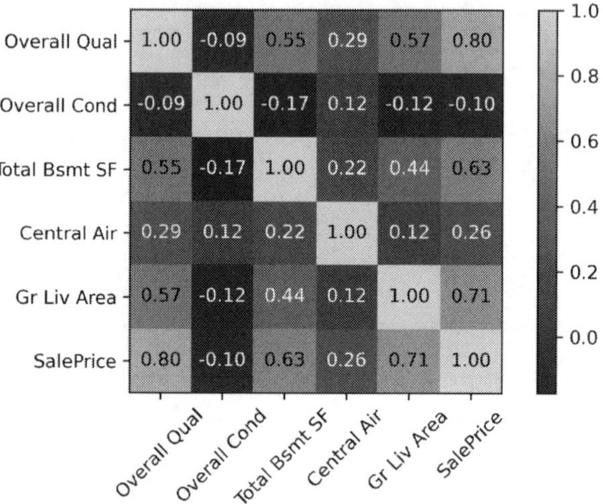

Figure 9.5: A correlation matrix of the selected variables

To fit a linear regression model, we are interested in those features that have a high correlation with our target variable, `SalePrice`. Looking at the previous correlation matrix, we can see that `SalePrice` shows the largest correlation with the `Gr Liv Area` variable (`0.71`), which seems to be a good choice for an exploratory variable to introduce the concepts of a simple linear regression model in the following section.

Implementing an ordinary least squares linear regression model

At the beginning of this chapter, we mentioned that linear regression can be understood as obtaining the best-fitting straight line through the examples of our training data. However, we have neither defined the term *best-fitting* nor have we discussed the different techniques of fitting such a model. In the following subsections, we will fill in the missing pieces of this puzzle using the **ordinary least squares** (**OLS**) method (sometimes also called **linear least squares**) to estimate the parameters of the linear regression line that minimizes the sum of the squared vertical distances (residuals or errors) to the training examples.

Solving regression for regression parameters with gradient descent

Consider our implementation of the **Adaptive Linear Neuron** (**Adaline**) from *Chapter 2, Training Simple Machine Learning Algorithms for Classification*. You will remember that the artificial neuron uses a linear activation function. Also, we defined a loss function, $L(\boldsymbol{w})$, which we minimized to learn the weights via optimization algorithms, such as **gradient descent** (**GD**) and **stochastic gradient descent** (**SGD**).

This loss function in Adaline is the **mean squared error** (**MSE**), which is identical to the loss function that we use for OLS:

$$L(\boldsymbol{w}, b) = \frac{1}{2n}\sum_{i=1}^{n}\left(y^{(i)} - \hat{y}^{(i)}\right)^2$$

Here, $\hat{y}$ is the predicted value $\hat{y} = \boldsymbol{w}^T\boldsymbol{x} + b$ (note that the term $\frac{1}{2}$ is just used for convenience to derive the update rule of GD). Essentially, OLS regression can be understood as Adaline without the threshold function so that we obtain continuous target values instead of the class labels `0` and `1`. To demonstrate this, let's take the GD implementation of Adaline from *Chapter 2* and remove the threshold function to implement our first linear regression model:

```
class LinearRegressionGD:
    def __init__(self, eta=0.01, n_iter=50, random_state=1):
        self.eta = eta
        self.n_iter = n_iter
        self.random_state = random_state

    def fit(self, X, y):
        rgen = np.random.RandomState(self.random_state)
        self.w_ = rgen.normal(loc=0.0, scale=0.01, size=X.shape[1])
        self.b_ = np.array([0.])
        self.losses_ = []

        for i in range(self.n_iter):
            output = self.net_input(X)
            errors = (y - output)
            self.w_ += self.eta * 2.0 * X.T.dot(errors) / X.shape[0]
            self.b_ += self.eta * 2.0 * errors.mean()
            loss = (errors**2).mean()
            self.losses_.append(loss)
        return self

    def net_input(self, X):
        return np.dot(X, self.w_) + self.b_

    def predict(self, X):
        return self.net_input(X)
```

Weight updates with gradient descent

If you need a refresher about how the weights are updated—taking a step in the opposite direction of the gradient—please revisit the *Adaptive linear neurons and the convergence of learning* section in *Chapter 2*.

To see our `LinearRegressionGD` regressor in action, let's use the `Gr Living Area` (size of the living area above ground in square feet) feature from the Ames Housing dataset as the explanatory variable and train a model that can predict `SalePrice`. Furthermore, we will standardize the variables for better convergence of the GD algorithm. The code is as follows:

```
>>> X = df[['Gr Liv Area']].values
>>> y = df['SalePrice'].values
>>> from sklearn.preprocessing import StandardScaler
>>> sc_x = StandardScaler()
>>> sc_y = StandardScaler()
>>> X_std = sc_x.fit_transform(X)
>>> y_std = sc_y.fit_transform(y[:, np.newaxis]).flatten()
>>> lr = LinearRegressionGD(eta=0.1)
>>> lr.fit(X_std, y_std)
```

Notice the workaround regarding `y_std`, using `np.newaxis` and `flatten`. Most data preprocessing classes in scikit-learn expect data to be stored in two-dimensional arrays. In the previous code example, the use of `np.newaxis` in `y[:, np.newaxis]` added a new dimension to the array. Then, after `StandardScaler` returned the scaled variable, we converted it back to the original one-dimensional array representation using the `flatten()` method for our convenience.

We discussed in *Chapter 2* that it is always a good idea to plot the loss as a function of the number of epochs (complete iterations) over the training dataset when we are using optimization algorithms, such as GD, to check that the algorithm converged to a loss minimum (here, a *global* loss minimum):

```
>>> plt.plot(range(1, lr.n_iter+1), lr.losses_)
>>> plt.ylabel('MSE')
>>> plt.xlabel('Epoch')
>>> plt.show()
```

As you can see in *Figure 9.6*, the GD algorithm converged approximately after the tenth epoch:

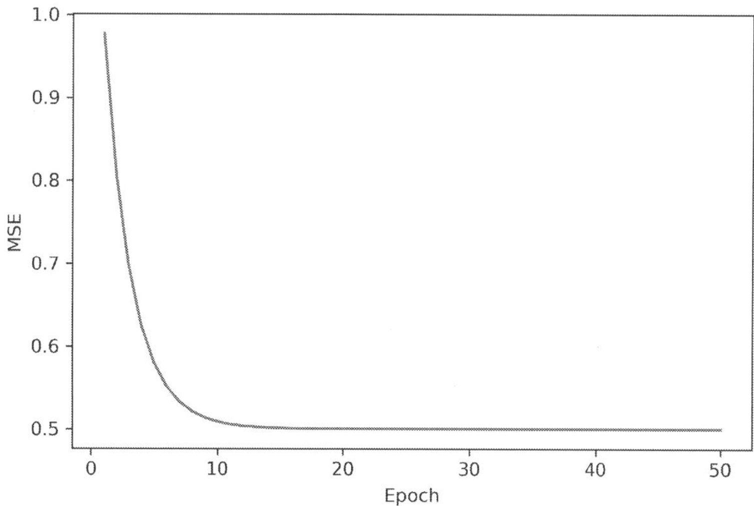

Figure 9.6: The loss function versus the number of epochs

Next, let's visualize how well the linear regression line fits the training data. To do so, we will define a simple helper function that will plot a scatterplot of the training examples and add the regression line:

```
>>> def lin_regplot(X, y, model):
...     plt.scatter(X, y, c='steelblue', edgecolor='white', s=70)
...     plt.plot(X, model.predict(X), color='black', lw=2)
```

Now, we will use this `lin_regplot` function to plot the living area against the sale price:

```
>>> lin_regplot(X_std, y_std, lr)
>>> plt.xlabel(' Living area above ground (standardized)')
>>> plt.ylabel('Sale price (standardized)')
>>> plt.show()
```

As you can see in *Figure 9.7*, the linear regression line reflects the general trend that house prices tend to increase with the size of the living area:

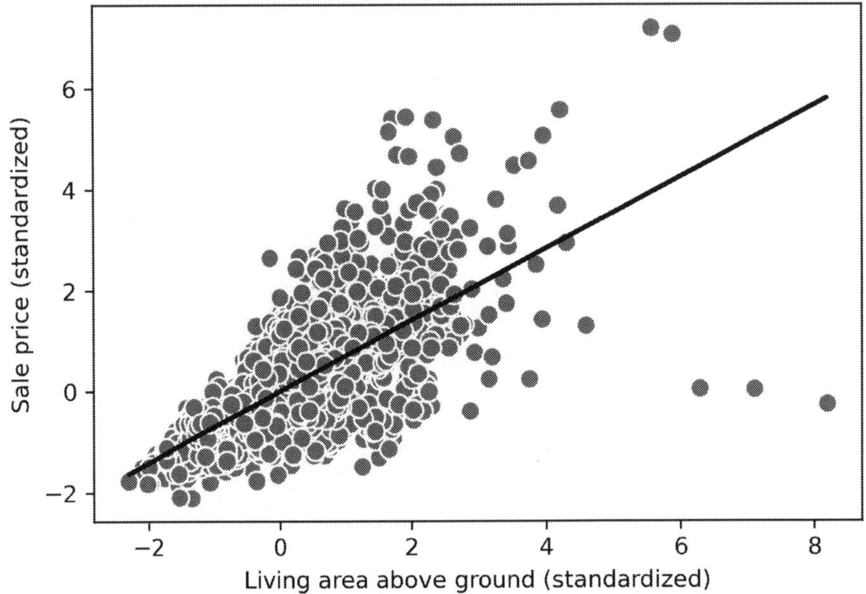

Figure 9.7: A linear regression plot of sale prices versus living area size

Although this observation makes sense, the data also tells us that the living area size does not explain house prices very well in many cases. Later in this chapter, we will discuss how to quantify the performance of a regression model. Interestingly, we can also observe several outliers, for example, the three data points corresponding to a standardized living area greater than 6. We will discuss how we can deal with outliers later in this chapter.

In certain applications, it may also be important to report the predicted outcome variables on their original scale. To scale the predicted price back onto the original *price in U.S. dollars* scale, we can simply apply the `inverse_transform` method of `StandardScaler`:

```
>>> feature_std = sc_x.transform(np.array([[2500]]))
>>> target_std = lr.predict(feature_std)
>>> target_reverted = sc_y.inverse_transform(target_std.reshape(-1, 1))
>>> print(f'Sales price: ${target_reverted.flatten()[0]:.2f}')
Sales price: $292507.07
```

In this code example, we used the previously trained linear regression model to predict the price of a house with an aboveground living area of 2,500 square feet. According to our model, such a house will be worth $292,507.07.

As a side note, it is also worth mentioning that we technically don't have to update the intercept parameter (for instance, the bias unit, *b*) if we are working with standardized variables, since the *y* axis intercept is always 0 in those cases. We can quickly confirm this by printing the model parameters:

```
>>> print(f'Slope: {lr.w_[0]:.3f}')
Slope: 0.707
>>> print(f'Intercept: {lr.b_[0]:.3f}')
Intercept: -0.000
```

Estimating the coefficient of a regression model via scikit-learn

In the previous section, we implemented a working model for regression analysis; however, in a real-world application, we may be interested in more efficient implementations. For example, many of scikit-learn's estimators for regression make use of the least squares implementation in SciPy (`scipy.linalg.lstsq`), which, in turn, uses highly optimized code optimizations based on the **Linear Algebra Package** (**LAPACK**). The linear regression implementation in scikit-learn also works (better) with unstandardized variables, since it does not use (S)GD-based optimization, so we can skip the standardization step:

```
>>> from sklearn.linear_model import LinearRegression
>>> slr = LinearRegression()
>>> slr.fit(X, y)
>>> y_pred = slr.predict(X)
>>> print(f'Slope: {slr.coef_[0]:.3f}')
Slope: 111.666
>>> print(f'Intercept: {slr.intercept_:.3f}')
Intercept: 13342.979
```

As you can see from executing this code, scikit-learn's `LinearRegression` model, fitted with the unstandardized `Gr Liv Area` and `SalePrice` variables, yielded different model coefficients, since the features have not been standardized. However, when we compare it to our GD implementation by plotting `SalePrice` against `Gr Liv Area`, we can qualitatively see that it fits the data similarly well:

```
>>> lin_regplot(X, y, slr)
>>> plt.xlabel('Living area above ground in square feet')
>>> plt.ylabel('Sale price in U.S. dollars')
>>> plt.tight_layout()
>>> plt.show()
```

For instance, we can see that the overall result looks identical to our GD implementation:

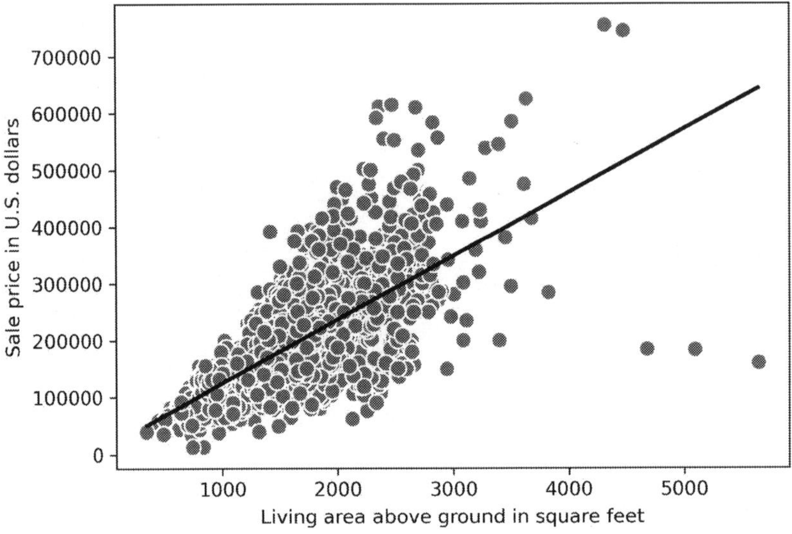

Figure 9.8: A linear regression plot using scikit-learn

Analytical solutions of linear regression

As an alternative to using machine learning libraries, there is also a closed-form solution for solving OLS involving a system of linear equations that can be found in most introductory statistics textbooks:

$$w = (X^T X)^{-1} X^T y$$

We can implement it in Python as follows:

```
# adding a column vector of "ones"
>>> Xb = np.hstack((np.ones((X.shape[0], 1)), X))
>>> w = np.zeros(X.shape[1])
>>> z = np.linalg.inv(np.dot(Xb.T, Xb))
>>> w = np.dot(z, np.dot(Xb.T, y))
>>> print(f'Slope: {w[1]:.3f}')
Slope: 111.666
>>> print(f'Intercept: {w[0]:.3f}')
Intercept: 13342.979
```

The advantage of this method is that it is guaranteed to find the optimal solution analytically. However, if we are working with very large datasets, it can be computationally too expensive to invert the matrix in this formula (sometimes also called the normal equation), or the matrix containing the training examples may be singular (non-invertible), which is why we may prefer iterative methods in certain cases.

If you are interested in more information on how to obtain normal equations, take a look at Dr. Stephen Pollock's chapter *The Classical Linear Regression Model*, from his lectures at the University of Leicester, which is available for free at `http://www.le.ac.uk/users/dsgp1/COURSES/MESOMET/ECMETXT/06mesmet.pdf`.

Also, if you want to compare linear regression solutions obtained via GD, SGD, the closed-form solution, QR factorization, and singular vector decomposition, you can use the `LinearRegression` class implemented in mlxtend (`http://rasbt.github.io/mlxtend/user_guide/regressor/LinearRegression/`), which lets users toggle between these options. Another great library to recommend for regression modeling in Python is statsmodels, which implements more advanced linear regression models, as illustrated at `https://www.statsmodels.org/stable/examples/index.html#regression`.

Fitting a robust regression model using RANSAC

Linear regression models can be heavily impacted by the presence of outliers. In certain situations, a very small subset of our data can have a big effect on the estimated model coefficients. Many statistical tests can be used to detect outliers, but these are beyond the scope of the book. However, removing outliers always requires our own judgment as data scientists as well as our domain knowledge.

As an alternative to throwing out outliers, we will look at a robust method of regression using the **RANdom SAmple Consensus** (**RANSAC**) algorithm, which fits a regression model to a subset of the data, the so-called **inliers**.

We can summarize the iterative RANSAC algorithm as follows:

1. Select a random number of examples to be inliers and fit the model.
2. Test all other data points against the fitted model and add those points that fall within a user-given tolerance to the inliers.
3. Refit the model using all inliers.
4. Estimate the error of the fitted model versus the inliers.
5. Terminate the algorithm if the performance meets a certain user-defined threshold or if a fixed number of iterations was reached; go back to *step 1* otherwise.

Let's now use a linear model in combination with the RANSAC algorithm as implemented in scikit-learn's `RANSACRegressor` class:

```
>>> from sklearn.linear_model import RANSACRegressor
>>> ransac = RANSACRegressor(
...     LinearRegression(),
...     max_trials=100, # default value
...     min_samples=0.95,
...     residual_threshold=None, # default value
...     random_state=123)
>>> ransac.fit(X, y)
```

We set the maximum number of iterations of the `RANSACRegressor` to 100, and using `min_samples=0.95`, we set the minimum number of the randomly chosen training examples to be at least 95 percent of the dataset.

By default (via `residual_threshold=None`), scikit-learn uses the **MAD** estimate to select the inlier threshold, where MAD stands for the **median absolute deviation** of the target values, `y`. However, the choice of an appropriate value for the inlier threshold is problem-specific, which is one disadvantage of RANSAC.

Many different approaches have been developed in recent years to select a good inlier threshold automatically. You can find a detailed discussion in *Automatic Estimation of the Inlier Threshold in Robust Multiple Structures Fitting* by *R. Toldo* and *A. Fusiello, Springer*, 2009 (in *Image Analysis and Processing–ICIAP 2009*, pages: 123-131).

Once we have fitted the RANSAC model, let's obtain the inliers and outliers from the fitted RANSAC linear regression model and plot them together with the linear fit:

```
>>> inlier_mask = ransac.inlier_mask_
>>> outlier_mask = np.logical_not(inlier_mask)
>>> line_X = np.arange(3, 10, 1)
>>> line_y_ransac = ransac.predict(line_X[:, np.newaxis])
>>> plt.scatter(X[inlier_mask], y[inlier_mask],
...             c='steelblue', edgecolor='white',
...             marker='o', label='Inliers')
>>> plt.scatter(X[outlier_mask], y[outlier_mask],
...             c='limegreen', edgecolor='white',
...             marker='s', label='Outliers')
>>> plt.plot(line_X, line_y_ransac, color='black', lw=2)
>>> plt.xlabel('Living area above ground in square feet')
>>> plt.ylabel('Sale price in U.S. dollars')
>>> plt.legend(loc='upper left')
>>> plt.tight_layout()
>>> plt.show()
```

As you can see in *Figure 9.9*, the linear regression model was fitted on the detected set of inliers, which are shown as circles:

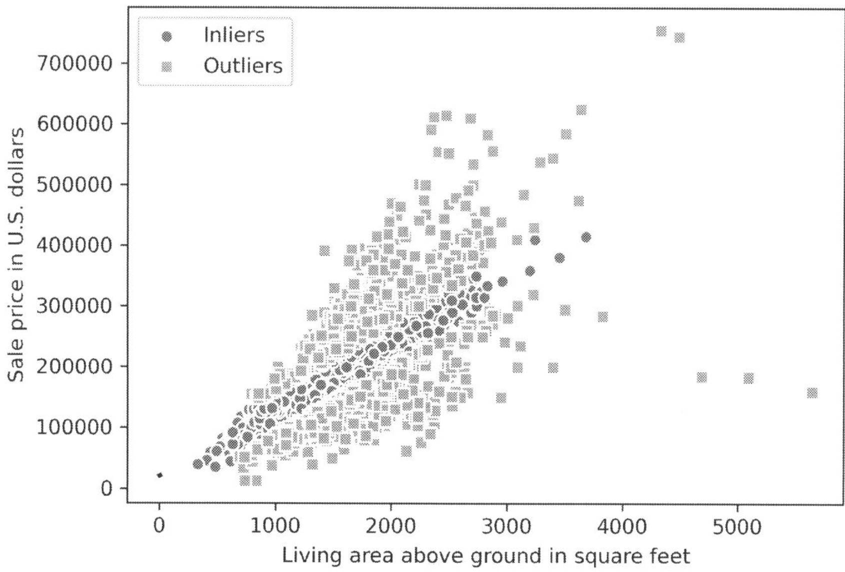

Figure 9.9: Inliers and outliers identified via a RANSAC linear regression model

When we print the slope and intercept of the model by executing the following code, the linear regression line will be slightly different from the fit that we obtained in the previous section without using RANSAC:

```
>>> print(f'Slope: {ransac.estimator_.coef_[0]:.3f}')
Slope: 106.348
>>> print(f'Intercept: {ransac.estimator_.intercept_:.3f}')
Intercept: 20190.093
```

Remember that we set the `residual_threshold` parameter to `None`, so RANSAC was using the MAD to compute the threshold for flagging inliers and outliers. The MAD, for this dataset, can be computed as follows:

```
>>> def median_absolute_deviation(data):
...     return np.median(np.abs(data - np.median(data)))
>>> median_absolute_deviation(y)
37000.00
```

So, if we want to identify fewer data points as outliers, we can choose a `residual_threshold` value greater than the preceding MAD. For example, *Figure 9.10* shows the inliers and outliers of a RANSAC linear regression model with a residual threshold of 65,000:

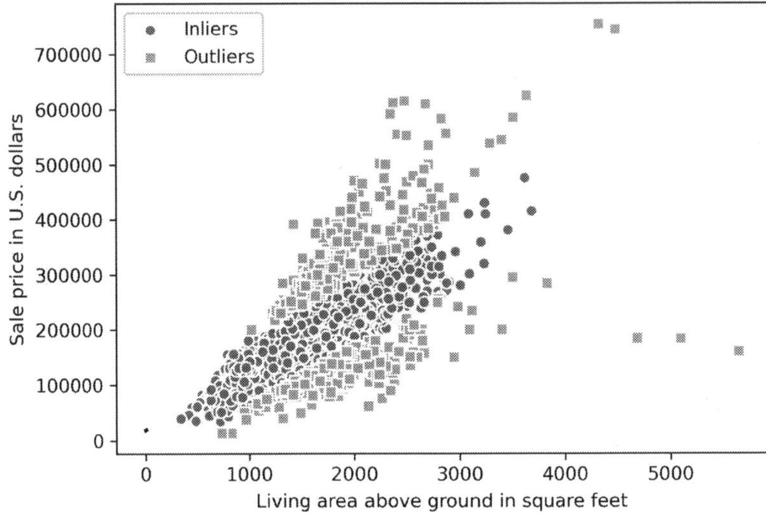

Figure 9.10: Inliers and outliers determined by a RANSAC linear regression model with a larger residual threshold

Using RANSAC, we reduced the potential effect of the outliers in this dataset, but we don't know whether this approach will have a positive effect on the predictive performance for unseen data or not. Thus, in the next section, we will look at different approaches for evaluating a regression model, which is a crucial part of building systems for predictive modeling.

Evaluating the performance of linear regression models

In the previous section, you learned how to fit a regression model on training data. However, you discovered in previous chapters that it is crucial to test the model on data that it hasn't seen during training to obtain a more unbiased estimate of its generalization performance.

As you may remember from *Chapter 6, Learning Best Practices for Model Evaluation and Hyperparameter Tuning*, we want to split our dataset into separate training and test datasets, where we will use the former to fit the model and the latter to evaluate its performance on unseen data to estimate the generalization performance. Instead of proceeding with the simple regression model, we will now use all five features in the dataset and train a multiple regression model:

```
>>> from sklearn.model_selection import train_test_split
>>> target = 'SalePrice'
>>> features = df.columns[df.columns != target]
>>> X = df[features].values
>>> y = df[target].values
```

```
>>> X_train, X_test, y_train, y_test = train_test_split(
...     X, y, test_size=0.3, random_state=123)
>>> slr = LinearRegression()
>>> slr.fit(X_train, y_train)
>>> y_train_pred = slr.predict(X_train)
>>> y_test_pred = slr.predict(X_test)
```

Since our model uses multiple explanatory variables, we can't visualize the linear regression line (or hyperplane, to be precise) in a two-dimensional plot, but we can plot the residuals (the differences or vertical distances between the actual and predicted values) versus the predicted values to diagnose our regression model. **Residual plots** are a commonly used graphical tool for diagnosing regression models. They can help to detect nonlinearity and outliers and check whether the errors are randomly distributed.

Using the following code, we will now plot a residual plot where we simply subtract the true target variables from our predicted responses:

```
>>> x_max = np.max(
...     [np.max(y_train_pred), np.max(y_test_pred)])
>>> x_min = np.min(
...     [np.min(y_train_pred), np.min(y_test_pred)])

>>> fig, (ax1, ax2) = plt.subplots(
...     1, 2, figsize=(7, 3), sharey=True)

>>> ax1.scatter(
...     y_test_pred, y_test_pred - y_test,
...     c='limegreen', marker='s',
...     edgecolor='white',
...     label='Test data')
>>> ax2.scatter(
...     y_train_pred, y_train_pred - y_train,
...     c='steelblue', marker='o', edgecolor='white',
...     label='Training data')
>>> ax1.set_ylabel('Residuals')

>>> for ax in (ax1, ax2):
...     ax.set_xlabel('Predicted values')
...     ax.legend(loc='upper left')
...     ax.hlines(y=0, xmin=x_min-100, xmax=x_max+100,\
...         color='black', lw=2)
>>> plt.tight_layout()
>>> plt.show()
```

After executing the code, we should see residual plots for the test and training datasets with a line passing through the x axis origin, as shown in *Figure 9.11*:

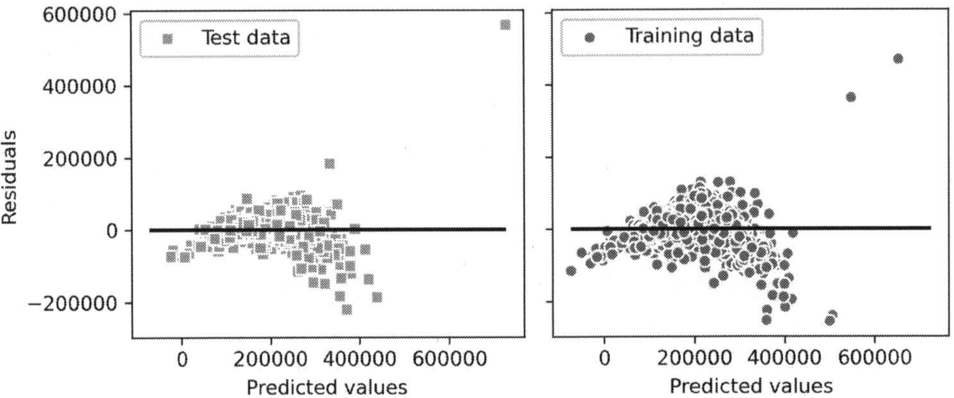

Figure 9.11: Residual plots of our data

In the case of a perfect prediction, the residuals would be exactly zero, which we will probably never encounter in realistic and practical applications. However, for a good regression model, we would expect the errors to be randomly distributed and the residuals to be randomly scattered around the centerline. If we see patterns in a residual plot, it means that our model is unable to capture some explanatory information, which has leaked into the residuals, as you can see to a degree in our previous residual plot. Furthermore, we can also use residual plots to detect outliers, which are represented by the points with a large deviation from the centerline.

Another useful quantitative measure of a model's performance is the **mean squared error** (**MSE**) that we discussed earlier as our loss function that we minimized to fit the linear regression model. The following is a version of the MSE without the $\frac{1}{2}$ scaling factor that is often used to simplify the loss derivative in gradient descent:

$$MSE = \frac{1}{n}\sum_{i=1}^{n}\left(y^{(i)} - \hat{y}^{(i)}\right)^2$$

Similar to prediction accuracy in classification contexts, we can use the MSE for cross-validation and model selection as discussed in *Chapter 6*.

Like classification accuracy, MSE also normalizes according to the sample size, n. This makes it possible to compare across different sample sizes (for example, in the context of learning curves) as well.

Let's now compute the MSE of our training and test predictions:

```
>>> from sklearn.metrics import mean_squared_error
>>> mse_train = mean_squared_error(y_train, y_train_pred)
>>> mse_test = mean_squared_error(y_test, y_test_pred)
```

```
>>> print(f'MSE train: {mse_train:.2f}')
MSE train: 1497216245.85
>>> print(f'MSE test: {mse_test:.2f}')
MSE test: 1516565821.00
```

We can see that the MSE on the training dataset is less than on the test set, which is an indicator that our model is slightly overfitting the training data in this case. Note that it can be more intuitive to show the error on the original unit scale (here, dollar instead of dollar-squared), which is why we may choose to compute the square root of the MSE, called *root mean squared error*, or the **mean absolute error** (**MAE**), which emphasizes incorrect prediction slightly less:

$$MAE = \frac{1}{n}\sum_{i=1}^{n} |y^{(i)} - \hat{y}^{(i)}|$$

We can compute the MAE similar to the MSE:

```
>>> from sklearn.metrics import mean_absolute_error
>>> mae_train = mean_absolute_error(y_train, y_train_pred)
>>> mae_test = mean_absolute_error(y_test, y_test_pred)
>>> print(f'MAE train: {mae_train:.2f}')
MAE train: 25983.03
>>> print(f'MAE test: {mae_test:.2f}')
MAE test: 24921.29
```

Based on the test set MAE, we can say that the model makes an error of approximately $25,000 on average.

When we use the MAE or MSE for comparing models, we need to be aware that these are unbounded in contrast to the classification accuracy, for example. In other words, the interpretations of the MAE and MSE depend on the dataset and feature scaling. For example, if the sale prices were presented as multiples of 1,000 (with the K suffix), the same model would yield a lower MAE compared to a model that worked with unscaled features. To further illustrate this point,

$$|\$500K - 550K| < |\$500{,}000 - 550{,}000|$$

Thus, it may sometimes be more useful to report the **coefficient of determination** (R^2), which can be understood as a standardized version of the MSE, for better interpretability of the model's performance. Or, in other words, R^2 is the fraction of response variance that is captured by the model. The R^2 value is defined as:

$$R^2 = 1 - \frac{SSE}{SST}$$

Here, SSE is the sum of squared errors, which is similar to the MSE but does not include the normalization by sample size n:

$$SSE = \sum_{i=1}^{n} (y^{(i)} - \hat{y}^{(i)})^2$$

And SST is the total sum of squares:

$$SST = \sum_{i=1}^{n} (y^{(i)} - \mu_y)^2$$

In other words, SST is simply the variance of the response.

Now, let's briefly show that R^2 is indeed just a rescaled version of the MSE:

$$\begin{aligned} R^2 &= 1 - \frac{\frac{1}{n}SSE}{\frac{1}{n}SST} \\ &= \frac{\frac{1}{n}\sum_{i=1}^{n}(y^{(i)} - \hat{y}^{(i)})^2}{\frac{1}{n}\sum_{i=1}^{n}(y^{(i)} - \mu_y)^2} \\ &= 1 - \frac{MSE}{Var(y)} \end{aligned}$$

For the training dataset, R^2 is bounded between 0 and 1, but it can become negative for the test dataset. A negative R^2 means that the regression model fits the data worse than a horizontal line representing the sample mean. (In practice, this often happens in the case of extreme overfitting, or if we forget to scale the test set in the same manner we scaled the training set.) If $R^2 = 1$, the model fits the data perfectly with a corresponding $MSE = 0$.

Evaluated on the training data, the R^2 of our model is 0.77, which isn't great but also not too bad given that we only work with a small set of features. However, the R^2 on the test dataset is only slightly smaller, at 0.75, which indicates that the model is only overfitting slightly:

```
>>> from sklearn.metrics import r2_score
>>> train_r2 = r2_score(y_train, y_train_pred)
>>> test_r2 = r2_score(y_test, y_test_pred)
>>> print(f'R^2 train: {train_r2:.3f}, {test_r2:.3f}')
R^2 train: 0.77, test: 0.75
```

Using regularized methods for regression

As we discussed in *Chapter 3, A Tour of Machine Learning Classifiers Using Scikit-Learn*, regularization is one approach to tackling the problem of overfitting by adding additional information and thereby shrinking the parameter values of the model to induce a penalty against complexity. The most popular approaches to regularized linear regression are the so-called **ridge regression**, **least absolute shrinkage and selection operator** (LASSO), and **elastic net**.

Ridge regression is an L2 penalized model where we simply add the squared sum of the weights to the MSE loss function:

$$L(\boldsymbol{w})_{Ridge} = \sum_{i=1}^{n}\left(y^{(i)} - \hat{y}^{(i)}\right)^2 + \lambda||\boldsymbol{w}||_2^2$$

Here, the L2 term is defined as follows:

$$\lambda||\boldsymbol{w}||_2^2 = \lambda\sum_{j=1}^{m} w_j^2$$

By increasing the value of hyperparameter λ, we increase the regularization strength and thereby shrink the weights of our model. Please note that, as mentioned in *Chapter 3*, the bias unit b is not regularized.

An alternative approach that can lead to sparse models is LASSO. Depending on the regularization strength, certain weights can become zero, which also makes LASSO useful as a supervised feature selection technique:

$$L(\boldsymbol{w})_{Lasso} = \sum_{i=1}^{n}\left(y^{(i)} - \hat{y}^{(i)}\right)^2 + \lambda||\boldsymbol{w}||_1$$

Here, the L1 penalty for LASSO is defined as the sum of the absolute magnitudes of the model weights, as follows:

$$\lambda||\boldsymbol{w}||_1 = \lambda\sum_{j=1}^{m} |w_j|$$

However, a limitation of LASSO is that it selects at most n features if $m > n$, where n is the number of training examples. This may be undesirable in certain applications of feature selection. In practice, however, this property of LASSO is often an advantage because it avoids saturated models. The saturation of a model occurs if the number of training examples is equal to the number of features, which is a form of overparameterization. As a consequence, a saturated model can always fit the training data perfectly but is merely a form of interpolation and thus is not expected to generalize well.

A compromise between ridge regression and LASSO is elastic net, which has an L1 penalty to generate sparsity and an L2 penalty such that it can be used for selecting more than n features if $m > n$:

$$L(\boldsymbol{w})_{Elastic\ Net} = \sum_{i=1}^{n}\left(y^{(i)} - \hat{y}^{(i)}\right)^2 + \lambda_2||\boldsymbol{w}||_2^2 + \lambda_1||\boldsymbol{w}||_1$$

Those regularized regression models are all available via scikit-learn, and their usage is similar to the regular regression model except that we have to specify the regularization strength via the parameter λ, for example, optimized via k-fold cross-validation.

A ridge regression model can be initialized via:

```
>>> from sklearn.linear_model import Ridge
>>> ridge = Ridge(alpha=1.0)
```

Note that the regularization strength is regulated by the parameter `alpha`, which is similar to the parameter λ. Likewise, we can initialize a LASSO regressor from the `linear_model` submodule:

```
>>> from sklearn.linear_model import Lasso
>>> lasso = Lasso(alpha=1.0)
```

Lastly, the `ElasticNet` implementation allows us to vary the L1 to L2 ratio:

```
>>> from sklearn.linear_model import ElasticNet
>>> elanet = ElasticNet(alpha=1.0, l1_ratio=0.5)
```

For example, if we set `l1_ratio` to 1.0, the `ElasticNet` regressor would be equal to LASSO regression. For more detailed information about the different implementations of linear regression, please refer to the documentation at `http://scikit-learn.org/stable/modules/linear_model.html`.

Turning a linear regression model into a curve – polynomial regression

In the previous sections, we assumed a linear relationship between explanatory and response variables. One way to account for the violation of linearity assumption is to use a polynomial regression model by adding polynomial terms:

$$y = w_1x + w_2x^2 + \ldots + w_dx^d + b$$

Here, d denotes the degree of the polynomial. Although we can use polynomial regression to model a nonlinear relationship, it is still considered a multiple linear regression model because of the linear regression coefficients, $\boldsymbol{w}$. In the following subsections, we will see how we can add such polynomial terms to an existing dataset conveniently and fit a polynomial regression model.

Adding polynomial terms using scikit-learn

We will now learn how to use the `PolynomialFeatures` transformer class from scikit-learn to add a quadratic term ($d = 2$) to a simple regression problem with one explanatory variable. Then, we will compare the polynomial to the linear fit by following these steps:

1. Add a second-degree polynomial term:

```
>>> from sklearn.preprocessing import PolynomialFeatures
>>> X = np.array([ 258.0, 270.0, 294.0, 320.0, 342.0,
...                368.0, 396.0, 446.0, 480.0, 586.0])\
...               [:, np.newaxis]
>>> y = np.array([ 236.4, 234.4, 252.8, 298.6, 314.2,
...                342.2, 360.8, 368.0, 391.2, 390.8])
>>> lr = LinearRegression()
>>> pr = LinearRegression()
>>> quadratic = PolynomialFeatures(degree=2)
>>> X_quad = quadratic.fit_transform(X)
```

2. Fit a simple linear regression model for comparison:

```
>>> lr.fit(X, y)
>>> X_fit = np.arange(250, 600, 10)[:, np.newaxis]
>>> y_lin_fit = lr.predict(X_fit)
```

3. Fit a multiple regression model on the transformed features for polynomial regression:

```
>>> pr.fit(X_quad, y)
>>> y_quad_fit = pr.predict(quadratic.fit_transform(X_fit))
```

4. Plot the results:

```
>>> plt.scatter(X, y, label='Training points')
>>> plt.plot(X_fit, y_lin_fit,
...          label='Linear fit', linestyle='--')
>>> plt.plot(X_fit, y_quad_fit,
...          label='Quadratic fit')
>>> plt.xlabel('Explanatory variable')
>>> plt.ylabel('Predicted or known target values')
>>> plt.legend(loc='upper left')
>>> plt.tight_layout()
>>> plt.show()
```

In the resulting plot, you can see that the polynomial fit captures the relationship between the response and explanatory variables much better than the linear fit:

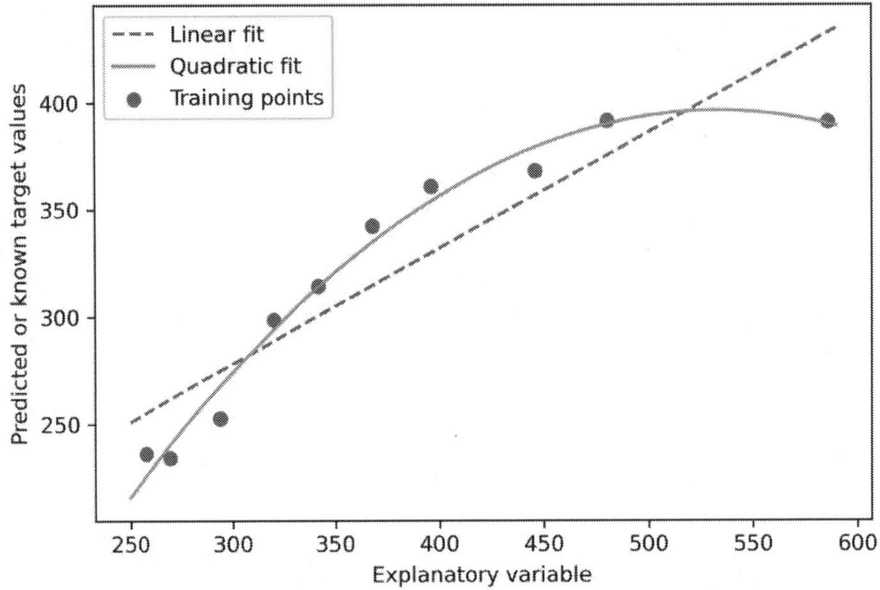

Figure 9.12: A comparison of a linear and quadratic model

Next, we will compute the MSE and R^2 evaluation metrics:

```
>>> y_lin_pred = lr.predict(X)
>>> y_quad_pred = pr.predict(X_quad)
>>> mse_lin = mean_squared_error(y, y_lin_pred)
>>> mse_quad = mean_squared_error(y, y_quad_pred)
>>> print(f'Training MSE linear: {mse_lin:.3f}'
          f', quadratic: {mse_quad:.3f}')
Training MSE linear: 569.780, quadratic: 61.330
>>> r2_lin = r2_score(y, y_lin_pred)
>>> r2_quad = r2_score(y, y_quad_pred)
>>> print(f'Training R^2 linear: {r2_lin:.3f}'
          f', quadratic: {r2_quad:.3f}')
Training R^2 linear: 0.832, quadratic: 0.982
```

As you can see after executing the code, the MSE decreased from 570 (linear fit) to 61 (quadratic fit); also, the coefficient of determination reflects a closer fit of the quadratic model ($R^2 = 0.982$) as opposed to the linear fit ($R^2 = 0.832$) in this particular toy problem.

Modeling nonlinear relationships in the Ames Housing dataset

In the preceding subsection, you learned how to construct polynomial features to fit nonlinear relationships in a toy problem; let's now take a look at a more concrete example and apply those concepts to the data in the Ames Housing dataset. By executing the following code, we will model the relationship between sale prices and the living area above ground using second-degree (quadratic) and third-degree (cubic) polynomials and compare that to a linear fit.

We start by removing the three outliers with a living area greater than 4,000 square feet, which we can see in previous figures, such as in *Figure 9.8*, so that these outliers don't skew our regression fits:

```
>>> X = df[['Gr Liv Area']].values
>>> y = df['SalePrice'].values
>>> X = X[(df['Gr Liv Area'] < 4000)]
>>> y = y[(df['Gr Liv Area'] < 4000)]
```

Next, we fit the regression models:

```
>>> regr = LinearRegression()

>>> # create quadratic and cubic features
>>> quadratic = PolynomialFeatures(degree=2)
>>> cubic = PolynomialFeatures(degree=3)
>>> X_quad = quadratic.fit_transform(X)
>>> X_cubic = cubic.fit_transform(X)

>>> # fit to features
>>> X_fit = np.arange(X.min()-1, X.max()+2, 1)[:, np.newaxis]
>>> regr = regr.fit(X, y)
>>> y_lin_fit = regr.predict(X_fit)
>>> linear_r2 = r2_score(y, regr.predict(X))
>>> regr = regr.fit(X_quad, y)
>>> y_quad_fit = regr.predict(quadratic.fit_transform(X_fit))
>>> quadratic_r2 = r2_score(y, regr.predict(X_quad))
>>> regr = regr.fit(X_cubic, y)
>>> y_cubic_fit = regr.predict(cubic.fit_transform(X_fit))
>>> cubic_r2 = r2_score(y, regr.predict(X_cubic))

>>> # plot results
>>> plt.scatter(X, y, label='Training points', color='lightgray')
>>> plt.plot(X_fit, y_lin_fit,
...          label=f'Linear (d=1), $R^2$={linear_r2:.2f}',
```

```
...           color='blue',
...           lw=2,
...           linestyle=':')
>>> plt.plot(X_fit, y_quad_fit,
...           label=f'Quadratic (d=2), $R^2$={quadratic_r2:.2f}',
...           color='red',
...           lw=2,
...           linestyle='-')
>>> plt.plot(X_fit, y_cubic_fit,
...           label=f'Cubic (d=3), $R^2$={cubic_r2:.2f}',
...           color='green',
...           lw=2,
...           linestyle='--')
>>> plt.xlabel('Living area above ground in square feet')
>>> plt.ylabel('Sale price in U.S. dollars')
>>> plt.legend(loc='upper left')
>>> plt.show()
```

The resulting plot is shown in *Figure 9.13*:

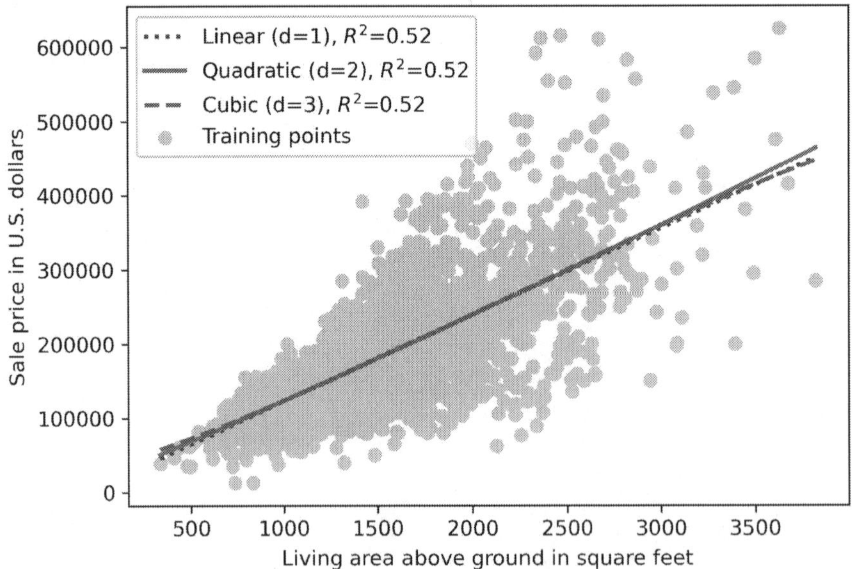

Figure 9.13: A comparison of different curves fitted to the sale price and living area data

As we can see, using quadratic or cubic features does not really have an effect. That's because the relationship between the two variables appears to be linear. So, let's take a look at another feature, namely, `Overall Qual`. The `Overall Qual` variable rates the overall quality of the material and finish of the houses and is given on a scale from 1 to 10, where 10 is best:

```
>>> X = df[['Overall Qual']].values
>>> y = df['SalePrice'].values
```

After specifying the `X` and `y` variables, we can reuse the previous code and obtain the plot in *Figure 9.14*:

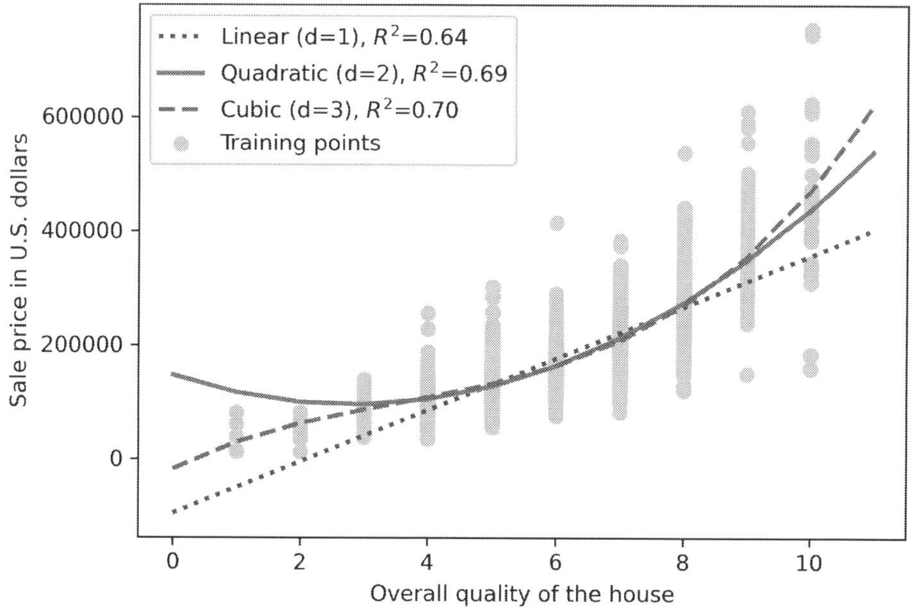

Figure 9.14: A linear, quadratic, and cubic fit on the sale price and house quality data

As you can see, the quadratic and cubic fits capture the relationship between sale prices and the overall quality of the house better than the linear fit. However, you should be aware that adding more and more polynomial features increases the complexity of a model and therefore increases the chance of overfitting. Thus, in practice, it is always recommended to evaluate the performance of the model on a separate test dataset to estimate the generalization performance.

Dealing with nonlinear relationships using random forests

In this section, we are going to look at **random forest** regression, which is conceptually different from the previous regression models in this chapter. A random forest, which is an ensemble of multiple **decision trees**, can be understood as the sum of piecewise linear functions, in contrast to the global linear and polynomial regression models that we discussed previously. In other words, via the decision tree algorithm, we subdivide the input space into smaller regions that become more manageable.

Decision tree regression

An advantage of the decision tree algorithm is that it works with arbitrary features and does not require any transformation of the features if we are dealing with nonlinear data because decision trees analyze one feature at a time, rather than taking weighted combinations into account. (Likewise, normalizing or standardizing features is not required for decision trees.) As mentioned in *Chapter 3, A Tour of Machine Learning Classifiers Using Scikit-Learn*, we grow a decision tree by iteratively splitting its nodes until the leaves are pure or a stopping criterion is satisfied. When we used decision trees for classification, we defined entropy as a measure of impurity to determine which feature split maximizes the **information gain** (**IG**), which can be defined as follows for a binary split:

$$IG(D_p, x_i) = I(D_p) - \frac{N_{left}}{N_p} I(D_{left}) - \frac{N_{right}}{N_p} I(D_{right})$$

Here, x_i is the feature to perform the split, N_p is the number of training examples in the parent node, I is the impurity function, D_p is the subset of training examples at the parent node, and D_{left} and D_{right} are the subsets of training examples at the left and right child nodes after the split. Remember that our goal is to find the feature split that maximizes the information gain; in other words, we want to find the feature split that reduces the impurities in the child nodes most. In *Chapter 3*, we discussed Gini impurity and entropy as measures of impurity, which are both useful criteria for classification. To use a decision tree for regression, however, we need an impurity metric that is suitable for continuous variables, so we define the impurity measure of a node, t, as the MSE instead:

$$I(t) = MSE(t) = \frac{1}{N_t} \sum_{i \in D_t} (y^{(i)} - \hat{y}_t)^2$$

Here, N_t is the number of training examples at node t, D_t is the training subset at node t, $y^{(i)}$ is the true target value, and $\hat{y}_t$ is the predicted target value (sample mean):

$$\hat{y}_t = \frac{1}{N_t} \sum_{i \in D_t} y^{(i)}$$

In the context of decision tree regression, the MSE is often referred to as **within-node variance**, which is why the splitting criterion is also better known as **variance reduction**.

To see what the line fit of a decision tree looks like, let's use the `DecisionTreeRegressor` implemented in scikit-learn to model the relationship between the `SalePrice` and `Gr Living Area` variables. Note that `SalePrice` and `Gr Living Area` do not necessarily represent a nonlinear relationship, but this feature combination still demonstrates the general aspects of a regression tree quite nicely:

```
>>> from sklearn.tree import DecisionTreeRegressor
>>> X = df[['Gr Liv Area']].values
>>> y = df['SalePrice'].values
>>> tree = DecisionTreeRegressor(max_depth=3)
>>> tree.fit(X, y)
```

```
>>> sort_idx = X.flatten().argsort()
>>> lin_regplot(X[sort_idx], y[sort_idx], tree)
>>> plt.xlabel('Living area above ground in square feet')
>>> plt.ylabel('Sale price in U.S. dollars')>>> plt.show()
```

As you can see in the resulting plot, the decision tree captures the general trend in the data. And we can imagine that a regression tree could also capture trends in nonlinear data relatively well. However, a limitation of this model is that it does not capture the continuity and differentiability of the desired prediction. In addition, we need to be careful about choosing an appropriate value for the depth of the tree so as to not overfit or underfit the data; here, a depth of three seemed to be a good choice.

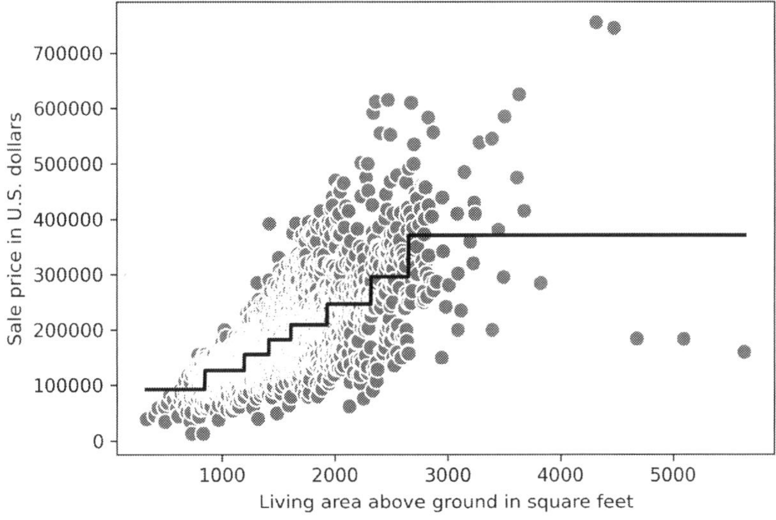

Figure 9.15: A decision tree regression plot

You are encouraged to experiment with deeper decision trees. Note that the relationship between `Gr Living Area` and `SalePrice` is rather linear, so you are also encouraged to apply the decision tree to the `Overall Qual` variable instead.

In the next section, we will look at a more robust way of fitting regression trees: random forests.

Random forest regression

As you learned in *Chapter 3*, the random forest algorithm is an ensemble technique that combines multiple decision trees. A random forest usually has a better generalization performance than an individual decision tree due to randomness, which helps to decrease the model's variance. Other advantages of random forests are that they are less sensitive to outliers in the dataset and don't require much parameter tuning. The only parameter in random forests that we typically need to experiment with is the number of trees in the ensemble. The basic random forest algorithm for regression is almost identical to the random forest algorithm for classification that we discussed in *Chapter 3*. The only difference is that we use the MSE criterion to grow the individual decision trees, and the predicted target variable is calculated as the average prediction across all decision trees.

Now, let's use all the features in the Ames Housing dataset to fit a random forest regression model on 70 percent of the examples and evaluate its performance on the remaining 30 percent, as we have done previously in the *Evaluating the performance of linear regression models* section. The code is as follows:

```
>>> target = 'SalePrice'
>>> features = df.columns[df.columns != target]
>>> X = df[features].values
>>> y = df[target].values
>>> X_train, X_test, y_train, y_test = train_test_split(
...     X, y, test_size=0.3, random_state=123)

>>> from sklearn.ensemble import RandomForestRegressor
>>> forest = RandomForestRegressor(
...     n_estimators=1000,
...     criterion='squared_error',
...     random_state=1,
...     n_jobs=-1)
>>> forest.fit(X_train, y_train)
>>> y_train_pred = forest.predict(X_train)
>>> y_test_pred = forest.predict(X_test)
>>> mae_train = mean_absolute_error(y_train, y_train_pred)
>>> mae_test = mean_absolute_error(y_test, y_test_pred)
>>> print(f'MAE train: {mae_train:.2f}')
MAE train: 8305.18
>>> print(f'MAE test: {mae_test:.2f}')
MAE test: 20821.77
>>> r2_train = r2_score(y_train, y_train_pred)
>>> r2_test =r2_score(y_test, y_test_pred)
>>> print(f'R^2 train: {r2_train:.2f}')
R^2 train: 0.98
>>> print(f'R^2 test: {r2_test:.2f}')
R^2 test: 0.85
```

Unfortunately, you can see that the random forest tends to overfit the training data. However, it's still able to explain the relationship between the target and explanatory variables relatively well ($R^2 = 0.85$ on the test dataset). For comparison, the linear model from the previous section, *Evaluating the performance of linear regression models*, which was fit to the same dataset, was overfitting less but performed worse on the test set ($R^2 = 0.75$).

Lastly, let's also take a look at the residuals of the prediction:

```
>>> x_max = np.max([np.max(y_train_pred), np.max(y_test_pred)])
>>> x_min = np.min([np.min(y_train_pred), np.min(y_test_pred)])

>>> fig, (ax1, ax2) = plt.subplots(1, 2, figsize=(7, 3), sharey=True)
```

```
>>> ax1.scatter(y_test_pred, y_test_pred - y_test,
...             c='limegreen', marker='s', edgecolor='white',
...             label='Test data')
>>> ax2.scatter(y_train_pred, y_train_pred - y_train,
...             c='steelblue', marker='o', edgecolor='white',
...             label='Training data')
>>> ax1.set_ylabel('Residuals')

>>> for ax in (ax1, ax2):
...     ax.set_xlabel('Predicted values')
...     ax.legend(loc='upper left')
...     ax.hlines(y=0, xmin=x_min-100, xmax=x_max+100,
...               color='black', lw=2)

>>> plt.tight_layout()
>>> plt.show()
```

As it was already summarized by the R^2 coefficient, you can see that the model fits the training data better than the test data, as indicated by the outliers in the *y* axis direction. Also, the distribution of the residuals does not seem to be completely random around the zero center point, indicating that the model is not able to capture all the exploratory information. However, the residual plot indicates a large improvement over the residual plot of the linear model that we plotted earlier in this chapter.

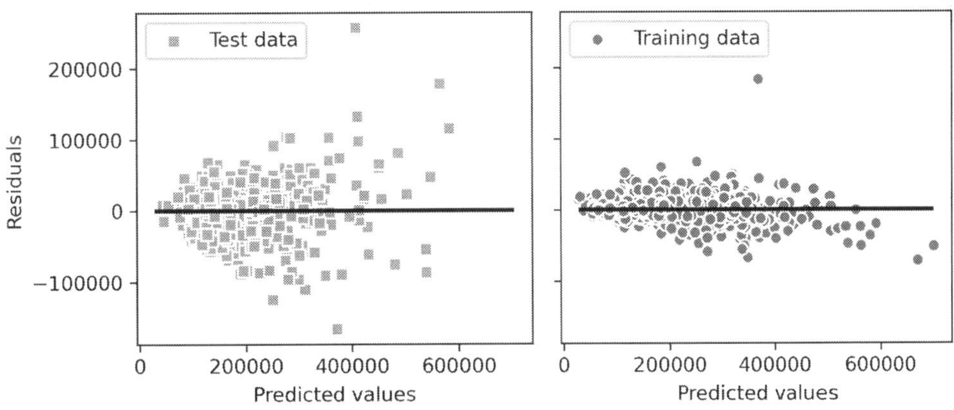

Figure 9.16: The residuals of the random forest regression

Ideally, our model error should be random or unpredictable. In other words, the error of the predictions should not be related to any of the information contained in the explanatory variables; rather, it should reflect the randomness of the real-world distributions or patterns. If we find patterns in the prediction errors, for example, by inspecting the residual plot, it means that the residual plots contain predictive information. A common reason for this could be that explanatory information is leaking into those residuals.

Unfortunately, there is not a universal approach for dealing with non-randomness in residual plots, and it requires experimentation. Depending on the data that is available to us, we may be able to improve the model by transforming variables, tuning the hyperparameters of the learning algorithm, choosing simpler or more complex models, removing outliers, or including additional variables.

Summary

At the beginning of this chapter, you learned about simple linear regression analysis to model the relationship between a single explanatory variable and a continuous response variable. We then discussed a useful explanatory data analysis technique to look at patterns and anomalies in data, which is an important first step in predictive modeling tasks.

We built our first model by implementing linear regression using a gradient-based optimization approach. You then saw how to utilize scikit-learn's linear models for regression and also implement a robust regression technique (RANSAC) as an approach for dealing with outliers. To assess the predictive performance of regression models, we computed the mean sum of squared errors and the related R^2 metric. Furthermore, we also discussed a useful graphical approach for diagnosing the problems of regression models: the residual plot.

After we explored how regularization can be applied to regression models to reduce the model complexity and avoid overfitting, we also covered several approaches for modeling nonlinear relationships, including polynomial feature transformation and random forest regressors.

We discussed supervised learning, classification, and regression analysis in detail in the previous chapters. In the next chapter, we are going to learn about another interesting subfield of machine learning, unsupervised learning, and also how to use cluster analysis to find hidden structures in data in the absence of target variables.

Join our book's Discord space

Join our Discord community to meet like-minded people and learn alongside more than 2000 members at:

`https://packt.link/MLwPyTorch`

10

Working with Unlabeled Data – Clustering Analysis

In the previous chapters, we used supervised learning techniques to build machine learning models, using data where the answer was already known—the class labels were already available in our training data. In this chapter, we will switch gears and explore cluster analysis, a category of **unsupervised learning** techniques that allows us to discover hidden structures in data where we do not know the right answer upfront. The goal of **clustering** is to find a natural grouping in data so that items in the same cluster are more similar to each other than to those from different clusters.

Given its exploratory nature, clustering is an exciting topic, and in this chapter, you will learn about the following concepts, which can help us to organize data into meaningful structures:

- Finding centers of similarity using the popular **k-means** algorithm
- Taking a bottom-up approach to building hierarchical clustering trees
- Identifying arbitrary shapes of objects using a density-based clustering approach

Grouping objects by similarity using k-means

In this section, we will learn about one of the most popular clustering algorithms, k-means, which is widely used in academia as well as in industry. Clustering (or cluster analysis) is a technique that allows us to find groups of similar objects that are more related to each other than to objects in other groups. Examples of business-oriented applications of clustering include the grouping of documents, music, and movies by different topics, or finding customers that share similar interests based on common purchase behaviors as a basis for recommendation engines.

k-means clustering using scikit-learn

As you will see in a moment, the k-means algorithm is extremely easy to implement, but it is also computationally very efficient compared to other clustering algorithms, which might explain its popularity. The k-means algorithm belongs to the category of **prototype-based clustering.**

We will discuss two other categories of clustering, **hierarchical** and **density-based clustering**, later in this chapter.

Prototype-based clustering means that each cluster is represented by a prototype, which is usually either the **centroid** (*average*) of similar points with continuous features, or the **medoid** (the most *representative* or the point that minimizes the distance to all other points that belong to a particular cluster) in the case of categorical features. While k-means is very good at identifying clusters with a spherical shape, one of the drawbacks of this clustering algorithm is that we have to specify the number of clusters, *k*, *a priori*. An inappropriate choice for *k* can result in poor clustering performance. Later in this chapter, we will discuss the **elbow** method and **silhouette plots**, which are useful techniques to evaluate the quality of a clustering to help us determine the optimal number of clusters, *k*.

Although k-means clustering can be applied to data in higher dimensions, we will walk through the following examples using a simple two-dimensional dataset for the purpose of visualization:

```
>>> from sklearn.datasets import make_blobs
>>> X, y = make_blobs(n_samples=150,
...                   n_features=2,
...                   centers=3,
...                   cluster_std=0.5,
...                   shuffle=True,
...                   random_state=0)
>>> import matplotlib.pyplot as plt
>>> plt.scatter(X[:, 0],
...             X[:, 1],
...             c='white',
...             marker='o',
...             edgecolor='black',
...             s=50)
>>> plt.xlabel('Feature 1')
>>> plt.ylabel('Feature 2')
>>> plt.grid()
>>> plt.tight_layout()
>>> plt.show()
```

The dataset that we just created consists of 150 randomly generated points that are roughly grouped into three regions with higher density, which is visualized via a two-dimensional scatterplot:

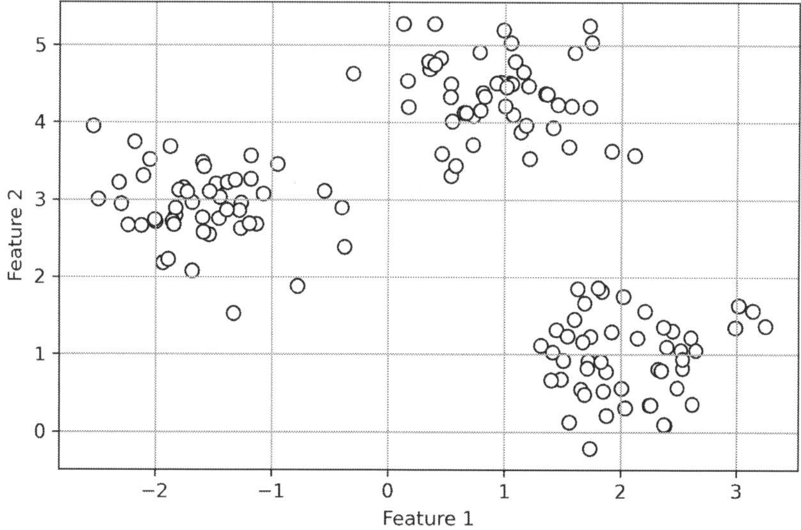

Figure 10.1: A scatterplot of our unlabeled dataset

In real-world applications of clustering, we do not have any ground-truth category information (information provided as empirical evidence as opposed to inference) about those examples; if we were given class labels, this task would fall into the category of supervised learning. Thus, our goal is to group the examples based on their feature similarities, which can be achieved using the k-means algorithm, as summarized by the following four steps:

1. Randomly pick k centroids from the examples as initial cluster centers
2. Assign each example to the nearest centroid, $\mu^{(j)}, j \in \{1, \dots, k\}$
3. Move the centroids to the center of the examples that were assigned to it
4. Repeat *steps 2* and *3* until the cluster assignments do not change or a user-defined tolerance or maximum number of iterations is reached

Now, the next question is, *how do we measure similarity between objects*? We can define similarity as the opposite of distance, and a commonly used distance for clustering examples with continuous features is the **squared Euclidean distance** between two points, $\boldsymbol{x}$ and $\boldsymbol{y}$, in m-dimensional space:

$$d(\boldsymbol{x}, \boldsymbol{y})^2 = \sum_{j=1}^{m} \left(x_j - y_j\right)^2 = \|\boldsymbol{x} - \boldsymbol{y}\|_2^2$$

Note that, in the preceding equation, the index j refers to the jth dimension (feature column) of the example inputs, x and y. In the rest of this section, we will use the superscripts i and j to refer to the index of the example (data record) and cluster index, respectively.

Based on this Euclidean distance metric, we can describe the k-means algorithm as a simple optimization problem, an iterative approach for minimizing the within-cluster **sum of squared errors** (**SSE**), which is sometimes also called **cluster inertia**:

$$SSE = \sum_{i=1}^{n} \sum_{j=1}^{k} w^{(i,j)} \left\| \boldsymbol{x}^{(i)} - \boldsymbol{\mu}^{(j)} \right\|_2^2$$

Here, $\boldsymbol{\mu}^{(j)}$ is the representative point (centroid) for cluster j. $w^{(i,j)} = 1$ if the example, $x^{(i)}$, is in cluster j, or 0 otherwise.

$$w^{(i,j)} = \begin{cases} 1, & \text{if } \boldsymbol{x}^{(i)} \in j \\ 0, & \text{otherwise} \end{cases}$$

Now that you have learned how the simple k-means algorithm works, let's apply it to our example dataset using the `KMeans` class from scikit-learn's `cluster` module:

```
>>> from sklearn.cluster import KMeans
>>> km = KMeans(n_clusters=3,
...             init='random',
...             n_init=10,
...             max_iter=300,
...             tol=1e-04,
...             random_state=0)
>>> y_km = km.fit_predict(X)
```

Using the preceding code, we set the number of desired clusters to 3; having to specify the number of clusters *a priori* is one of the limitations of k-means. We set `n_init=10` to run the k-means clustering algorithms 10 times independently, with different random centroids to choose the final model as the one with the lowest SSE. Via the `max_iter` parameter, we specify the maximum number of iterations for each single run (here, `300`). Note that the k-means implementation in scikit-learn stops early if it converges before the maximum number of iterations is reached. However, it is possible that k-means does not reach convergence for a particular run, which can be problematic (computationally expensive) if we choose relatively large values for `max_iter`. One way to deal with convergence problems is to choose larger values for `tol`, which is a parameter that controls the tolerance with regard to the changes in the within-cluster SSE to declare convergence. In the preceding code, we chose a tolerance of `1e-04` (=0.0001).

A problem with k-means is that one or more clusters can be empty. Note that this problem does not exist for k-medoids or fuzzy C-means, an algorithm that we will discuss later in this section. However, this problem is accounted for in the current k-means implementation in scikit-learn. If a cluster is empty, the algorithm will search for the example that is farthest away from the centroid of the empty cluster. Then, it will reassign the centroid to be this farthest point.

Feature scaling

When we are applying k-means to real-world data using a Euclidean distance metric, we want to make sure that the features are measured on the same scale and apply z-score standardization or min-max scaling if necessary.

Having predicted the cluster labels, `y_km`, and discussed some of the challenges of the k-means algorithm, let's now visualize the clusters that k-means identified in the dataset together with the cluster centroids. These are stored under the `cluster_centers_` attribute of the fitted `KMeans` object:

```
>>> plt.scatter(X[y_km == 0, 0],
...             X[y_km == 0, 1],
...             s=50, c='lightgreen',
...             marker='s', edgecolor='black',
...             label='Cluster 1')
>>> plt.scatter(X[y_km == 1, 0],
...             X[y_km == 1, 1],
...             s=50, c='orange',
...             marker='o', edgecolor='black',
...             label='Cluster 2')
>>> plt.scatter(X[y_km == 2, 0],
...             X[y_km == 2, 1],
...             s=50, c='lightblue',
...             marker='v', edgecolor='black',
...             label='Cluster 3')
>>> plt.scatter(km.cluster_centers_[:, 0],
...             km.cluster_centers_[:, 1],
...             s=250, marker='*',
...             c='red', edgecolor='black',
...             label='Centroids')
>>> plt.xlabel('Feature 1')
>>> plt.ylabel('Feature 2')
>>> plt.legend(scatterpoints=1)
>>> plt.grid()
>>> plt.tight_layout()
>>> plt.show()
```

In *Figure 10.2*, you can see that k-means placed the three centroids at the center of each sphere, which looks like a reasonable grouping given this dataset:

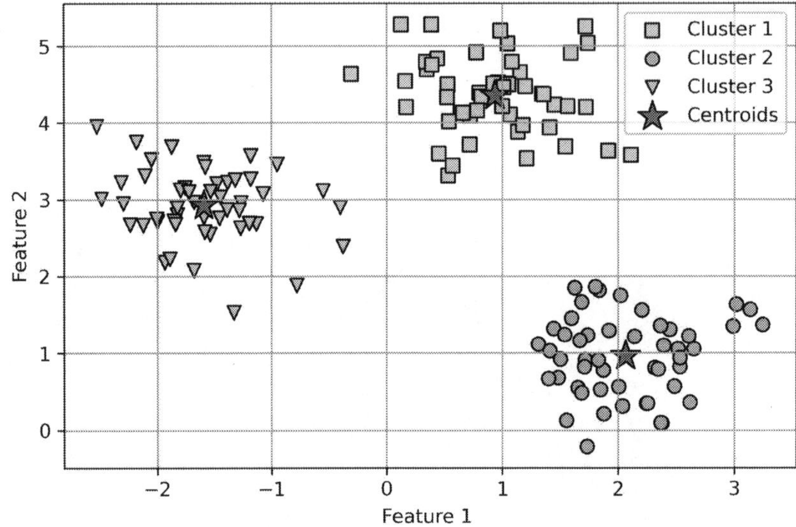

Figure 10.2: The k-means clusters and their centroids

Although k-means worked well on this toy dataset, we still have the drawback of having to specify the number of clusters, *k*, *a priori*. The number of clusters to choose may not always be so obvious in real-world applications, especially if we are working with a higher-dimensional dataset that cannot be visualized. The other properties of k-means are that clusters do not overlap and are not hierarchical, and we also assume that there is at least one item in each cluster. Later in this chapter, we will encounter different types of clustering algorithms, hierarchical and density-based clustering. Neither type of algorithm requires us to specify the number of clusters upfront or assume spherical structures in our dataset.

In the next subsection, we will cover a popular variant of the classic k-means algorithm called **k-means++**. While it doesn't address those assumptions and drawbacks of k-means that were discussed in the previous paragraph, it can greatly improve the clustering results through more clever seeding of the initial cluster centers.

A smarter way of placing the initial cluster centroids using k-means++

So far, we have discussed the classic k-means algorithm, which uses a random seed to place the initial centroids, which can sometimes result in bad clusterings or slow convergence if the initial centroids are chosen poorly. One way to address this issue is to run the k-means algorithm multiple times on a dataset and choose the best-performing model in terms of the SSE.

Another strategy is to place the initial centroids far away from each other via the k-means++ algorithm, which leads to better and more consistent results than the classic k-means (*k-means++: The Advantages of Careful Seeding* by *D. Arthur* and *S. Vassilvitskii* in *Proceedings of the eighteenth annual ACM-SIAM symposium on Discrete algorithms*, pages 1027-1035. *Society for Industrial and Applied Mathematics*, 2007).

The initialization in k-means++ can be summarized as follows:

1. Initialize an empty set, **M**, to store the k centroids being selected.
2. Randomly choose the first centroid, $\boldsymbol{\mu}^{(j)}$, from the input examples and assign it to **M**.
3. For each example, $\boldsymbol{x}^{(i)}$, that is not in **M**, find the minimum squared distance, $d(\boldsymbol{x}^{(i)}, \mathbf{M})^2$, to any of the centroids in **M**.
4. To randomly select the next centroid, $\boldsymbol{\mu}^{(p)}$, use a weighted probability distribution equal to $\frac{d(\boldsymbol{\mu}^{(p)},\mathbf{M})^2}{\sum_i d(\boldsymbol{x}^{(i)},\mathbf{M})^2}$. For instance, we collect all points in an array and choose a weighted random sampling, such that the larger the squared distance, the more likely a point gets chosen as the centroid.
5. Repeat *steps 3* and *4* until k centroids are chosen.
6. Proceed with the classic k-means algorithm.

To use k-means++ with scikit-learn's `KMeans` object, we just need to set the `init` parameter to `'k-means++'`. In fact, `'k-means++'` is the default argument to the `init` parameter, which is strongly recommended in practice. The only reason we didn't use it in the previous example was to not introduce too many concepts all at once. The rest of this section on k-means will use k-means++, but you are encouraged to experiment more with the two different approaches (classic k-means via `init='random'` versus k-means++ via `init='k-means++'`) for placing the initial cluster centroids.

Hard versus soft clustering

Hard clustering describes a family of algorithms where each example in a dataset is assigned to exactly one cluster, as in the k-means and k-means++ algorithms that we discussed earlier in this chapter. In contrast, algorithms for **soft clustering** (sometimes also called **fuzzy clustering**) assign an example to one or more clusters. A popular example of soft clustering is the **fuzzy C-means** (**FCM**) algorithm (also called **soft k-means** or **fuzzy k-means**). The original idea goes back to the 1970s, when Joseph C. Dunn first proposed an early version of fuzzy clustering to improve k-means (*A Fuzzy Relative of the ISODATA Process and Its Use in Detecting Compact Well-Separated Clusters*, 1973). Almost a decade later, James C. Bedzek published his work on the improvement of the fuzzy clustering algorithm, which is now known as the FCM algorithm (*Pattern Recognition with Fuzzy Objective Function Algorithms, Springer Science+Business Media*, 2013).

The FCM procedure is very similar to k-means. However, we replace the hard cluster assignment with probabilities for each point belonging to each cluster. In k-means, we could express the cluster membership of an example, x, with a sparse vector of binary values:

$$\begin{bmatrix} x \in \mu^{(1)} & \rightarrow & w^{(i,j)} = 0 \\ x \in \mu^{(2)} & \rightarrow & w^{(i,j)} = 1 \\ x \in \mu^{(3)} & \rightarrow & w^{(i,j)} = 0 \end{bmatrix}$$

Here, the index position with value 1 indicates the cluster centroid, $\boldsymbol{\mu}^{(j)}$, that the example is assigned to (assuming $k = 3, j \in \{1, 2, 3\}$). In contrast, a membership vector in FCM could be represented as follows:

$$\begin{bmatrix} x \in \mu^{(1)} & \rightarrow & w^{(i,j)} = 0.1 \\ x \in \mu^{(2)} & \rightarrow & w^{(i,j)} = 0.85 \\ x \in \mu^{(3)} & \rightarrow & w^{(i,j)} = 0.05 \end{bmatrix}$$

Here, each value falls in the range [0, 1] and represents a probability of membership of the respective cluster centroid. The sum of the memberships for a given example is equal to 1. As with the k-means algorithm, we can summarize the FCM algorithm in four key steps:

1. Specify the number of k centroids and randomly assign the cluster memberships for each point
2. Compute the cluster centroids, $\boldsymbol{\mu}^{(j)}, j \in \{1, \ldots, k\}$
3. Update the cluster memberships for each point
4. Repeat *steps 2* and *3* until the membership coefficients do not change or a user-defined tolerance or maximum number of iterations is reached

The objective function of FCM—we abbreviate it as J_m—looks very similar to the within-cluster SSE that we minimize in k-means:

$$J_m = \sum_{i=1}^{n} \sum_{j=1}^{k} w^{(i,j)^m} \left\| \boldsymbol{x}^{(i)} - \boldsymbol{\mu}^{(j)} \right\|_2^2$$

However, note that the membership indicator, $w^{(i,j)}$, is not a binary value as in k-means ($w^{(i,j)} \in \{0, 1\}$), but a real value that denotes the cluster membership probability ($w^{(i,j)} \in [0, 1]$). You also may have noticed that we added an additional exponent to $w^{(i,j)}$; the exponent m, any number greater than or equal to one (typically $m = 2$), is the so-called **fuzziness coefficient** (or simply **fuzzifier**), which controls the degree of *fuzziness*.

The larger the value of m, the smaller the cluster membership, $w^{(i,j)}$, becomes, which leads to fuzzier clusters. The cluster membership probability itself is calculated as follows:

$$w^{(i,j)} = \left[\sum_{c=1}^{k} \left(\frac{\left\| \boldsymbol{x}^{(i)} - \boldsymbol{\mu}^{(j)} \right\|_2}{\left\| \boldsymbol{x}^{(i)} - \boldsymbol{\mu}^{(c)} \right\|_2} \right)^{\frac{2}{m-1}} \right]^{-1}$$

For example, if we chose three cluster centers, as in the previous k-means example, we could calculate the membership of $\boldsymbol{x}^{(i)}$ belonging to the $\boldsymbol{\mu}^{(j)}$ cluster as follows:

$$w^{(i,j)} = \left[\left(\frac{\left\| \boldsymbol{x}^{(i)} - \boldsymbol{\mu}^{(j)} \right\|_2}{\left\| \boldsymbol{x}^{(i)} - \boldsymbol{\mu}^{(1)} \right\|_2} \right)^{\frac{2}{m-1}} + \left(\frac{\left\| \boldsymbol{x}^{(i)} - \boldsymbol{\mu}^{(j)} \right\|_2}{\left\| \boldsymbol{x}^{(i)} - \boldsymbol{\mu}^{(2)} \right\|_2} \right)^{\frac{2}{m-1}} + \left(\frac{\left\| \boldsymbol{x}^{(i)} - \boldsymbol{\mu}^{(j)} \right\|_2}{\left\| \boldsymbol{x}^{(i)} - \boldsymbol{\mu}^{(3)} \right\|_2} \right)^{\frac{2}{m-1}} \right]^{-1}$$

The center, $\boldsymbol{\mu}^{(j)}$, of a cluster itself is calculated as the mean of all examples weighted by the degree to which each example belongs to that cluster ($w^{(i,j)^m}$):

$$\boldsymbol{\mu}^{(j)} = \frac{\sum_{i=1}^{n} w^{(i,j)^m} \boldsymbol{x}^{(i)}}{\sum_{i=1}^{n} w^{(i,j)^m}}$$

Just by looking at the equation to calculate the cluster memberships, we can say that each iteration in FCM is more expensive than an iteration in k-means. On the other hand, FCM typically requires fewer iterations overall to reach convergence. However, it has been found, in practice, that both k-means and FCM produce very similar clustering outputs, as described in a study (*Comparative Analysis of k-means and Fuzzy C-Means Algorithms* by *S. Ghosh* and *S. K. Dubey*, *IJACSA*, 4: 35–38, 2013). Unfortunately, the FCM algorithm is not implemented in scikit-learn currently, but interested readers can try out the FCM implementation from the scikit-fuzzy package, which is available at `https://github.com/scikit-fuzzy/scikit-fuzzy`.

Using the elbow method to find the optimal number of clusters

One of the main challenges in unsupervised learning is that we do not know the definitive answer. We don't have the ground-truth class labels in our dataset that allow us to apply the techniques that we used in *Chapter 6*, *Learning Best Practices for Model Evaluation and Hyperparameter Tuning*, to evaluate the performance of a supervised model. Thus, to quantify the quality of clustering, we need to use intrinsic metrics—such as the within-cluster SSE (distortion)—to compare the performance of different k-means clustering models.

Conveniently, we don't need to compute the within-cluster SSE explicitly when we are using scikit-learn, as it is already accessible via the `inertia_` attribute after fitting a `KMeans` model:

```
>>> print(f'Distortion: {km.inertia_:.2f}')
Distortion: 72.48
```

Based on the within-cluster SSE, we can use a graphical tool, the so-called **elbow method**, to estimate the optimal number of clusters, *k*, for a given task. We can say that if *k* increases, the distortion will decrease. This is because the examples will be closer to the centroids they are assigned to. The idea behind the elbow method is to identify the value of *k* where the distortion begins to increase most rapidly, which will become clearer if we plot the distortion for different values of *k*:

```
>>> distortions = []
>>> for i in range(1, 11):
...     km = KMeans(n_clusters=i,
...                 init='k-means++',
...                 n_init=10,
...                 max_iter=300,
...                 random_state=0)
...     km.fit(X)
...     distortions.append(km.inertia_)
```

```
>>> plt.plot(range(1,11), distortions, marker='o')
>>> plt.xlabel('Number of clusters')
>>> plt.ylabel('Distortion')
>>> plt.tight_layout()
>>> plt.show()
```

As you can see in *Figure 10.3*, the *elbow* is located at $k = 3$, so this is supporting evidence that $k = 3$ is indeed a good choice for this dataset:

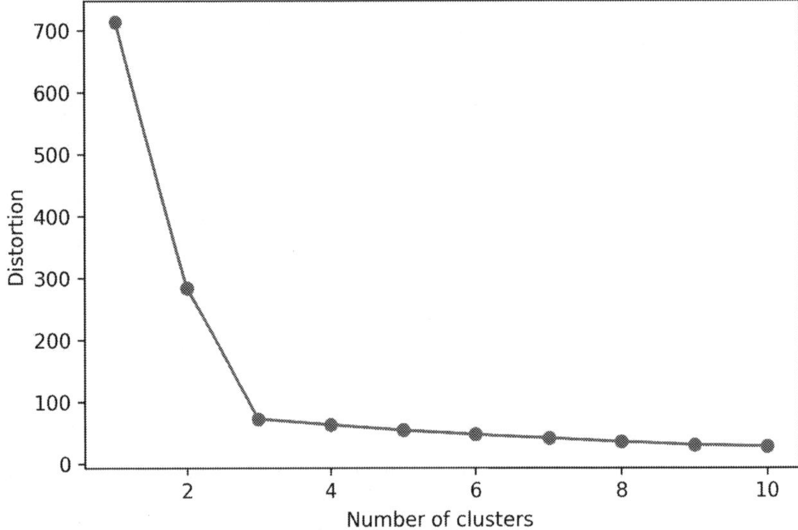

Figure 10.3: Finding the optimal number of clusters using the elbow method

Quantifying the quality of clustering via silhouette plots

Another intrinsic metric to evaluate the quality of a clustering is **silhouette analysis**, which can also be applied to clustering algorithms other than k-means that we will discuss later in this chapter. Silhouette analysis can be used as a graphical tool to plot a measure of how tightly grouped the examples in the clusters are. To calculate the **silhouette coefficient** of a single example in our dataset, we can apply the following three steps:

1. Calculate the **cluster cohesion**, $a^{(i)}$, as the average distance between an example, $x^{(i)}$, and all other points in the same cluster.
2. Calculate the **cluster separation**, $b^{(i)}$, from the next closest cluster as the average distance between the example, $x^{(i)}$, and all examples in the nearest cluster.
3. Calculate the silhouette, $s^{(i)}$, as the difference between cluster cohesion and separation divided by the greater of the two, as shown here:

$$s^{(i)} = \frac{b^{(i)} - a^{(i)}}{max\{b^{(i)}, a^{(i)}\}}$$

The silhouette coefficient is bounded in the range –1 to 1. Based on the preceding equation, we can see that the silhouette coefficient is 0 if the cluster separation and cohesion are equal ($b^{(i)} = a^{(i)}$). Furthermore, we get close to an ideal silhouette coefficient of 1 if $b^{(i)} >> a^{(i)}$, since $b^{(i)}$ quantifies how dissimilar an example is from other clusters, and $a^{(i)}$ tells us how similar it is to the other examples in its own cluster.

The silhouette coefficient is available as `silhouette_samples` from scikit-learn's `metric` module, and optionally, the `silhouette_scores` function can be imported for convenience. The `silhouette_scores` function calculates the average silhouette coefficient across all examples, which is equivalent to `numpy.mean(silhouette_samples(...))`. By executing the following code, we will now create a plot of the silhouette coefficients for a k-means clustering with $k = 3$:

```
>>> km = KMeans(n_clusters=3,
...             init='k-means++',
...             n_init=10,
...             max_iter=300,
...             tol=1e-04,
...             random_state=0)
>>> y_km = km.fit_predict(X)

>>> import numpy as np
>>> from matplotlib import cm
>>> from sklearn.metrics import silhouette_samples
>>> cluster_labels = np.unique(y_km)
>>> n_clusters = cluster_labels.shape[0]
>>> silhouette_vals = silhouette_samples(
...     X, y_km, metric='euclidean'
... )
>>> y_ax_lower, y_ax_upper = 0, 0
>>> yticks = []
>>> for i, c in enumerate(cluster_labels):
...     c_silhouette_vals = silhouette_vals[y_km == c]
...     c_silhouette_vals.sort()
...     y_ax_upper += len(c_silhouette_vals)
...     color = cm.jet(float(i) / n_clusters)
...     plt.barh(range(y_ax_lower, y_ax_upper),
...              c_silhouette_vals,
...              height=1.0,
...              edgecolor='none',
...              color=color)
...     yticks.append((y_ax_lower + y_ax_upper) / 2.)
...     y_ax_lower += len(c_silhouette_vals)
```

```
>>> silhouette_avg = np.mean(silhouette_vals)
>>> plt.axvline(silhouette_avg,
...             color="red",
...             linestyle="--")
>>> plt.yticks(yticks, cluster_labels + 1)
>>> plt.ylabel('Cluster')
>>> plt.xlabel('Silhouette coefficient')
>>> plt.tight_layout()
>>> plt.show()
```

Through a visual inspection of the silhouette plot, we can quickly scrutinize the sizes of the different clusters and identify clusters that contain *outliers*:

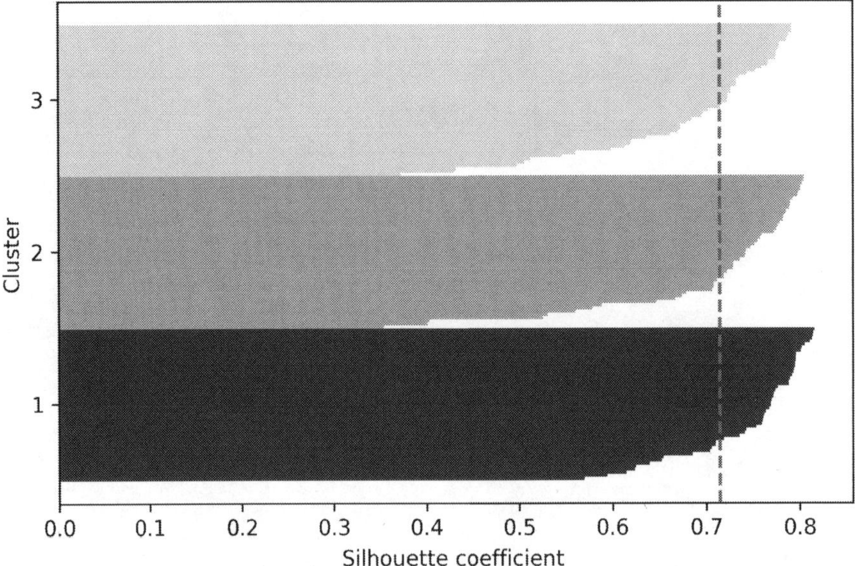

Figure 10.4: A silhouette plot for a good example of clustering

However, as you can see in the preceding silhouette plot, the silhouette coefficients are not close to 0 and are approximately equally far away from the average silhouette score, which is, in this case, an indicator of *good* clustering. Furthermore, to summarize the goodness of our clustering, we added the average silhouette coefficient to the plot (dotted line).

To see what a silhouette plot looks like for a relatively *bad* clustering, let's seed the k-means algorithm with only two centroids:

```
>>> km = KMeans(n_clusters=2,
...             init='k-means++',
...             n_init=10,
...             max_iter=300,
...             tol=1e-04,
...             random_state=0)
>>> y_km = km.fit_predict(X)
>>> plt.scatter(X[y_km == 0, 0],
...             X[y_km == 0, 1],
...             s=50, c='lightgreen',
...             edgecolor='black',
...             marker='s',
...             label='Cluster 1')
>>> plt.scatter(X[y_km == 1, 0],
...             X[y_km == 1, 1],
...             s=50,
...             c='orange',
...             edgecolor='black',
...             marker='o',
...             label='Cluster 2')
>>> plt.scatter(km.cluster_centers_[:, 0],
...             km.cluster_centers_[:, 1],
...             s=250,
...             marker='*',
...             c='red',
...             label='Centroids')
>>> plt.xlabel('Feature 1')
>>> plt.ylabel('Feature 2')
>>> plt.legend()
>>> plt.grid()
>>> plt.tight_layout()
>>> plt.show()
```

As you can see in *Figure 10.5*, one of the centroids falls between two of the three spherical groupings of the input data.

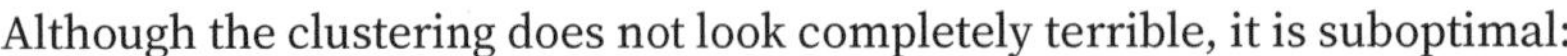

Although the clustering does not look completely terrible, it is suboptimal:

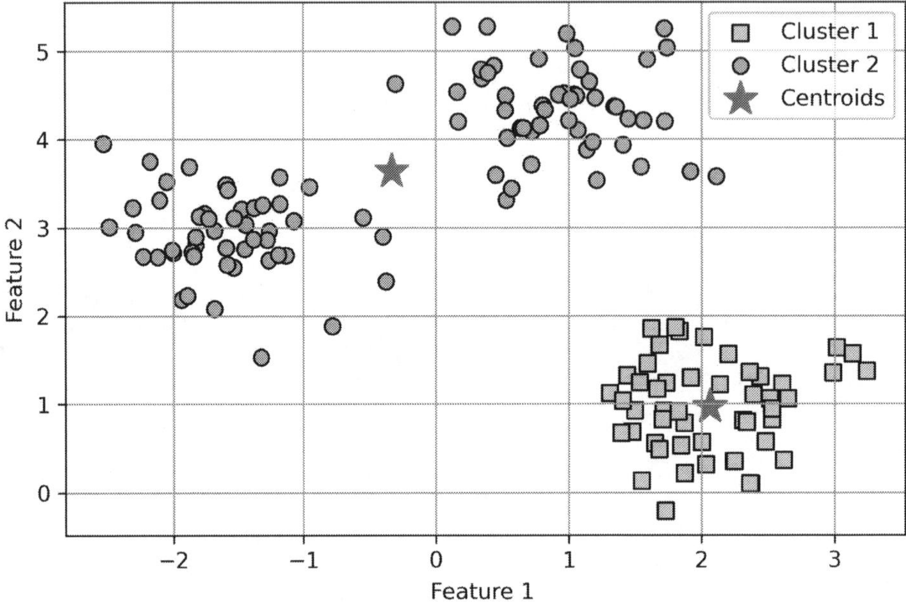

Figure 10.5: A suboptimal example of clustering

Please keep in mind that we typically do not have the luxury of visualizing datasets in two-dimensional scatterplots in real-world problems, since we typically work with data in higher dimensions. So, next, we will create the silhouette plot to evaluate the results:

```
>>> cluster_labels = np.unique(y_km)
>>> n_clusters = cluster_labels.shape[0]
>>> silhouette_vals = silhouette_samples(
...     X, y_km, metric='euclidean'
... )
>>> y_ax_lower, y_ax_upper = 0, 0
>>> yticks = []
>>> for i, c in enumerate(cluster_labels):
...     c_silhouette_vals = silhouette_vals[y_km == c]
...     c_silhouette_vals.sort()
...     y_ax_upper += len(c_silhouette_vals)
...     color = cm.jet(float(i) / n_clusters)
...     plt.barh(range(y_ax_lower, y_ax_upper),
...              c_silhouette_vals,
...              height=1.0,
...              edgecolor='none',
...              color=color)
```

```
...     yticks.append((y_ax_lower + y_ax_upper) / 2.)
...     y_ax_lower += len(c_silhouette_vals)
>>> silhouette_avg = np.mean(silhouette_vals)
>>> plt.axvline(silhouette_avg, color="red", linestyle="--")
>>> plt.yticks(yticks, cluster_labels + 1)
>>> plt.ylabel('Cluster')
>>> plt.xlabel('Silhouette coefficient')
>>> plt.tight_layout()
>>> plt.show()
```

As you can see in *Figure 10.6*, the silhouettes now have visibly different lengths and widths, which is evidence of a relatively *bad* or at least *suboptimal* clustering:

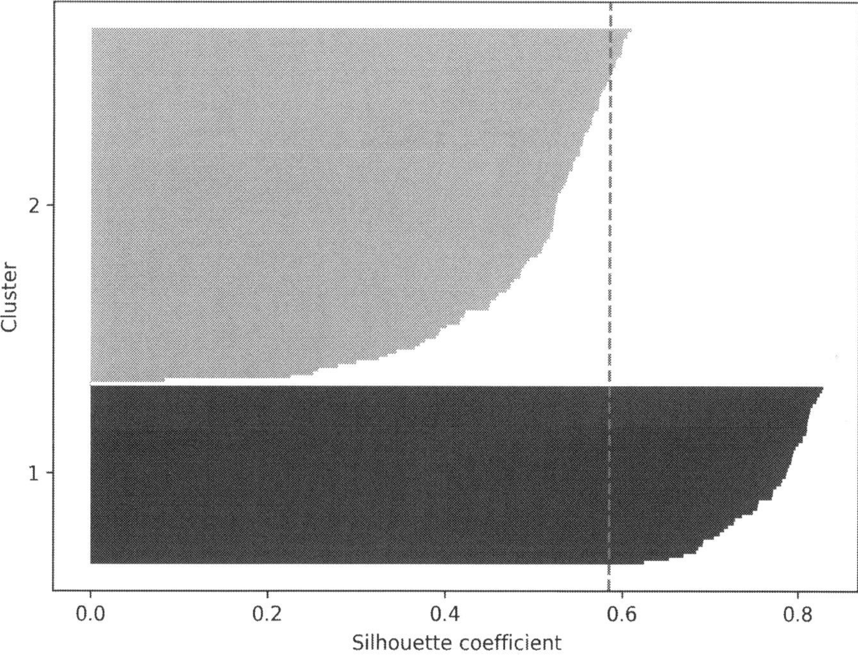

Figure 10.6: A silhouette plot for a suboptimal example of clustering

Now, after we have gained a good understanding of how clustering works, the next section will introduce hierarchical clustering as an alternative approach to k-means.

Organizing clusters as a hierarchical tree

In this section, we will look at an alternative approach to prototype-based clustering: **hierarchical clustering.** One advantage of the hierarchical clustering algorithm is that it allows us to plot **dendrograms** (visualizations of a binary hierarchical clustering), which can help with the interpretation of the results by creating meaningful taxonomies. Another advantage of this hierarchical approach is that we do not need to specify the number of clusters upfront.

The two main approaches to hierarchical clustering are **agglomerative** and **divisive** hierarchical clustering. In divisive hierarchical clustering, we start with one cluster that encompasses the complete dataset, and we iteratively split the cluster into smaller clusters until each cluster only contains one example. In this section, we will focus on agglomerative clustering, which takes the opposite approach. We start with each example as an individual cluster and merge the closest pairs of clusters until only one cluster remains.

Grouping clusters in a bottom-up fashion

The two standard algorithms for agglomerative hierarchical clustering are **single linkage** and **complete linkage.** Using single linkage, we compute the distances between the most similar members for each pair of clusters and merge the two clusters for which the distance between the most similar members is the smallest. The complete linkage approach is similar to single linkage but, instead of comparing the most similar members in each pair of clusters, we compare the most dissimilar members to perform the merge. This is shown in *Figure 10.7*:

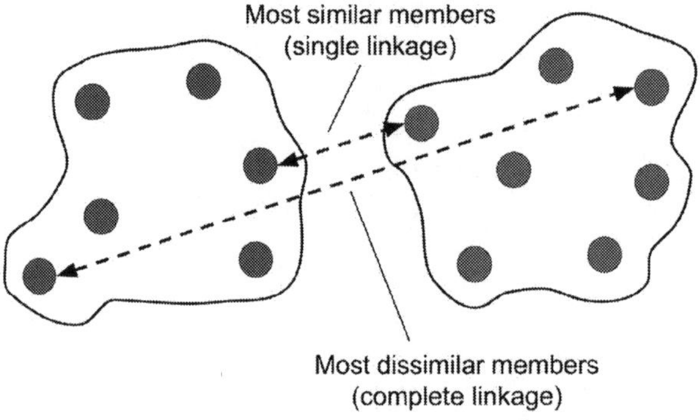

Figure 10.7: The complete linkage approach

Alternative types of linkages

Other commonly used algorithms for agglomerative hierarchical clustering include average linkage and Ward's linkage. In average linkage, we merge the cluster pairs based on the minimum average distances between all group members in the two clusters. In Ward's linkage, the two clusters that lead to the minimum increase of the total within-cluster SSE are merged.

In this section, we will focus on agglomerative clustering using the complete linkage approach. Hierarchical complete linkage clustering is an iterative procedure that can be summarized by the following steps:

1. Compute a pair-wise distance matrix of all examples.
2. Represent each data point as a singleton cluster.

3. Merge the two closest clusters based on the distance between the most dissimilar (distant) members.
4. Update the cluster linkage matrix.
5. Repeat *steps 2-4* until one single cluster remains.

Next, we will discuss how to compute the distance matrix (*step 1*). But first, let's generate a random data sample to work with. The rows represent different observations (IDs 0-4), and the columns are the different features (`X`, `Y`, `Z`) of those examples:

```
>>> import pandas as pd
>>> import numpy as np
>>> np.random.seed(123)
>>> variables = ['X', 'Y', 'Z']
>>> labels = ['ID_0', 'ID_1', 'ID_2', 'ID_3', 'ID_4']
>>> X = np.random.random_sample([5, 3])*10
>>> df = pd.DataFrame(X, columns=variables, index=labels)
>>> df
```

After executing the preceding code, we should now see the following `DataFrame` containing the randomly generated examples:

	X	Y	Z
ID_0	6.964692	2.861393	2.268515
ID_1	5.513148	7.194690	4.231065
ID_2	9.807642	6.848297	4.809319
ID_3	3.921175	3.431780	7.290497
ID_4	4.385722	0.596779	3.980443

Figure 10.8: A randomly generated data sample

Performing hierarchical clustering on a distance matrix

To calculate the distance matrix as input for the hierarchical clustering algorithm, we will use the `pdist` function from SciPy's `spatial.distance` submodule:

```
>>> from scipy.spatial.distance import pdist, squareform
>>> row_dist = pd.DataFrame(squareform(
...                         pdist(df, metric='euclidean')),
...                         columns=labels, index=labels)
>>> row_dist
```

Using the preceding code, we calculated the Euclidean distance between each pair of input examples in our dataset based on the features X, Y, and Z.

We provided the condensed distance matrix—returned by pdist—as input to the squareform function to create a symmetrical matrix of the pair-wise distances, as shown here:

	ID_0	ID_1	ID_2	ID_3	ID_4
ID_0	0.000000	4.973534	5.516653	5.899885	3.835396
ID_1	4.973534	0.000000	4.347073	5.104311	6.698233
ID_2	5.516653	4.347073	0.000000	7.244262	8.316594
ID_3	5.899885	5.104311	7.244262	0.000000	4.382864
ID_4	3.835396	6.698233	8.316594	4.382864	0.000000

Figure 10.9: The calculated pair-wise distances of our data

Next, we will apply the complete linkage agglomeration to our clusters using the linkage function from SciPy's cluster.hierarchy submodule, which returns a so-called **linkage matrix**.

However, before we call the linkage function, let's take a careful look at the function documentation:

```
>>> from scipy.cluster.hierarchy import linkage
>>> help(linkage)
[...]
Parameters:
  y : ndarray
    A condensed or redundant distance matrix. A condensed
    distance matrix is a flat array containing the upper
    triangular of the distance matrix. This is the form
    that pdist returns. Alternatively, a collection of m
    observation vectors in n dimensions may be passed as
    an m by n array.

  method : str, optional
    The linkage algorithm to use. See the Linkage Methods
    section below for full descriptions.

  metric : str, optional
    The distance metric to use. See the distance.pdist
    function for a list of valid distance metrics.

  Returns:
  Z : ndarray
```

```
    The hierarchical clustering encoded as a linkage matrix.
[...]
```

Based on the function description, we understand that we can use a condensed distance matrix (upper triangular) from the `pdist` function as an input attribute. Alternatively, we could also provide the initial data array and use the `'euclidean'` metric as a function argument in `linkage`. However, we should not use the `squareform` distance matrix that we defined earlier, since it would yield different distance values than expected. To sum it up, the three possible scenarios are listed here:

- **Incorrect approach:** Using the `squareform` distance matrix as shown in the following code snippet leads to incorrect results:

```
>>> row_clusters = linkage(row_dist,
...                        method='complete',
...                        metric='euclidean')
```

- **Correct approach:** Using the condensed distance matrix as shown in the following code example yields the correct linkage matrix:

```
>>> row_clusters = linkage(pdist(df, metric='euclidean'),
...                        method='complete')
```

- **Correct approach:** Using the complete input example matrix (the so-called design matrix) as shown in the following code snippet also leads to a correct linkage matrix similar to the preceding approach:

```
>>> row_clusters = linkage(df.values,
...                        method='complete',
...                        metric='euclidean')
```

To take a closer look at the clustering results, we can turn those results into a pandas `DataFrame` (best viewed in a Jupyter notebook) as follows:

```
>>> pd.DataFrame(row_clusters,
...              columns=['row label 1',
...                       'row label 2',
...                       'distance',
...                       'no. of items in clust.'],
...              index=[f'cluster {(i + 1)}' for i in
...                     range(row_clusters.shape[0])])
```

As shown in *Figure 10.10*, the linkage matrix consists of several rows where each row represents one merge. The first and second columns denote the most dissimilar members in each cluster, and the third column reports the distance between those members.

The last column returns the count of the members in each cluster:

	row label 1	row label 2	distance	no. of items in clust.
cluster 1	0.0	4.0	3.835396	2.0
cluster 2	1.0	2.0	4.347073	2.0
cluster 3	3.0	5.0	5.899885	3.0
cluster 4	6.0	7.0	8.316594	5.0

Figure 10.10: The linkage matrix

Now that we have computed the linkage matrix, we can visualize the results in the form of a dendrogram:

```
>>> from scipy.cluster.hierarchy import dendrogram
>>> # make dendrogram black (part 1/2)
>>> # from scipy.cluster.hierarchy import set_link_color_palette
>>> # set_link_color_palette(['black'])
>>> row_dendr = dendrogram(
...     row_clusters,
...     labels=labels,
...     # make dendrogram black (part 2/2)
...     # color_threshold=np.inf
... )
>>> plt.tight_layout()
>>> plt.ylabel('Euclidean distance')
>>> plt.show()
```

If you are executing the preceding code or reading an e-book version of this book, you will notice that the branches in the resulting dendrogram are shown in different colors. The color scheme is derived from a list of Matplotlib colors that are cycled for the distance thresholds in the dendrogram. For example, to display the dendrograms in black, you can uncomment the respective sections that were inserted in the preceding code:

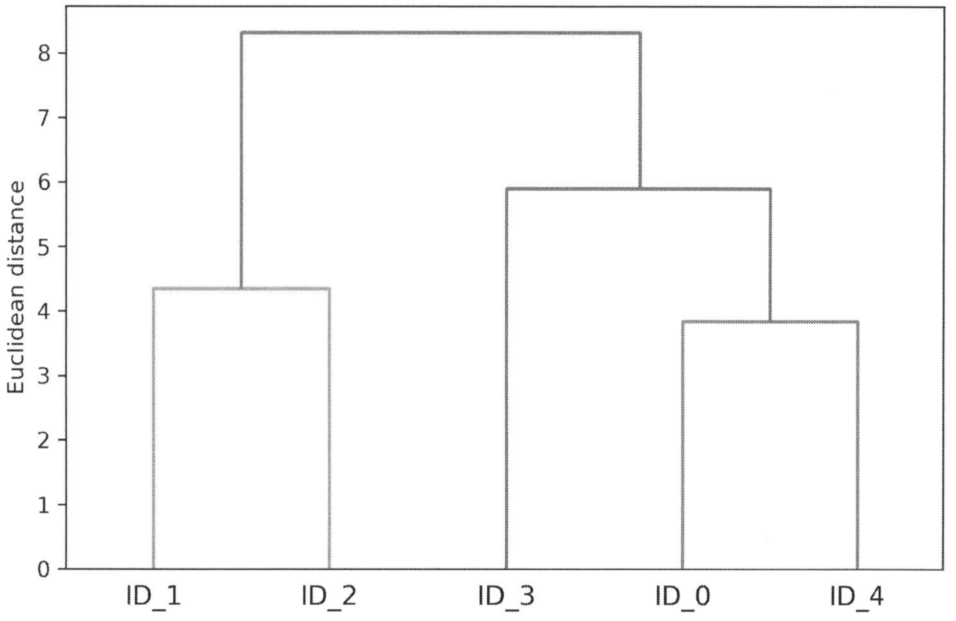

Figure 10.11: A dendrogram of our data

Such a dendrogram summarizes the different clusters that were formed during the agglomerative hierarchical clustering; for example, you can see that the examples `ID_0` and `ID_4`, followed by `ID_1` and `ID_2`, are the most similar ones based on the Euclidean distance metric.

Attaching dendrograms to a heat map

In practical applications, hierarchical clustering dendrograms are often used in combination with a **heat map**, which allows us to represent the individual values in the data array or matrix containing our training examples with a color code. In this section, we will discuss how to attach a dendrogram to a heat map plot and order the rows in the heat map correspondingly.

However, attaching a dendrogram to a heat map can be a little bit tricky, so let's go through this procedure step by step:

1. We create a new `figure` object and define the x axis position, y axis position, width, and height of the dendrogram via the `add_axes` attribute. Furthermore, we rotate the dendrogram 90 degrees counterclockwise. The code is as follows:

```
>>> fig = plt.figure(figsize=(8, 8), facecolor='white')
>>> axd = fig.add_axes([0.09, 0.1, 0.2, 0.6])
>>> row_dendr = dendrogram(row_clusters,
...                        orientation='left')
>>> # note: for matplotlib < v1.5.1, please use
>>> # orientation='right'
```

2. Next, we reorder the data in our initial `DataFrame` according to the clustering labels that can be accessed from the `dendrogram` object, which is essentially a Python dictionary, via the `leaves` key. The code is as follows:

```
>>> df_rowclust = df.iloc[row_dendr['leaves'][::-1]]
```

3. Now, we construct the heat map from the reordered `DataFrame` and position it next to the dendrogram:

```
>>> axm = fig.add_axes([0.23, 0.1, 0.6, 0.6])
>>> cax = axm.matshow(df_rowclust,
...                   interpolation='nearest',
...                   cmap='hot_r')
```

4. Finally, we modify the aesthetics of the dendrogram by removing the axis ticks and hiding the axis spines. Also, we add a color bar and assign the feature and data record names to the x and y axis tick labels, respectively:

```
>>> axd.set_xticks([])
>>> axd.set_yticks([])
>>> for i in axd.spines.values():
...     i.set_visible(False)
>>> fig.colorbar(cax)
>>> axm.set_xticklabels([''] + list(df_rowclust.columns))
>>> axm.set_yticklabels([''] + list(df_rowclust.index))
>>> plt.show()
```

After following the previous steps, the heat map should be displayed with the dendrogram attached:

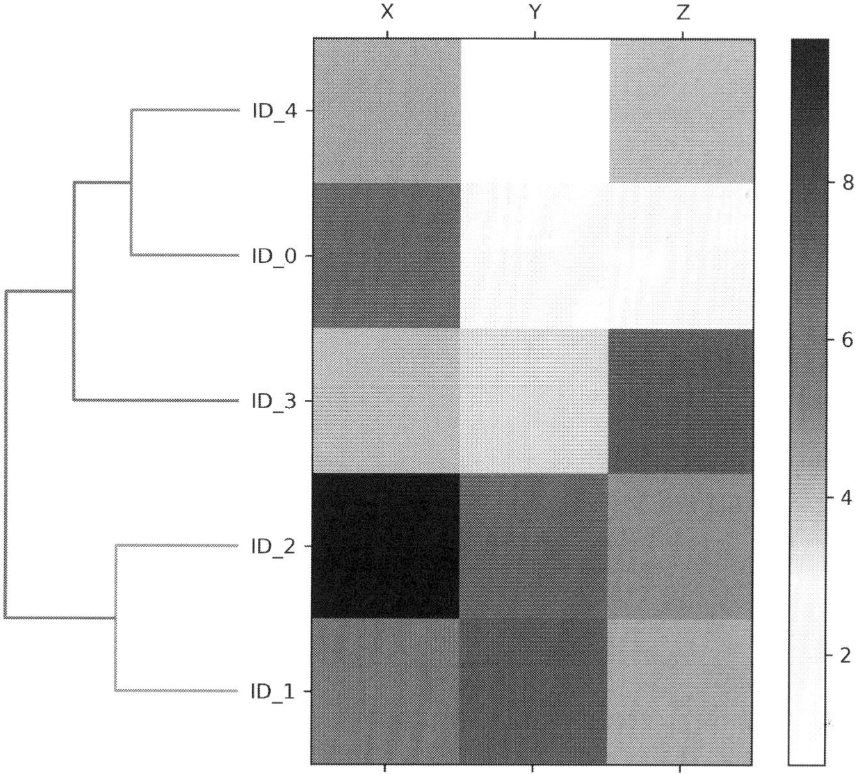

Figure 10.12: A heat map and dendrogram of our data

As you can see, the order of rows in the heat map reflects the clustering of the examples in the dendrogram. In addition to a simple dendrogram, the color-coded values of each example and feature in the heat map provide us with a nice summary of the dataset.

Applying agglomerative clustering via scikit-learn

In the previous subsection, you saw how to perform agglomerative hierarchical clustering using SciPy. However, there is also an `AgglomerativeClustering` implementation in scikit-learn, which allows us to choose the number of clusters that we want to return. This is useful if we want to prune the hierarchical cluster tree.

By setting the `n_cluster` parameter to `3`, we will now cluster the input examples into three groups using the same complete linkage approach based on the Euclidean distance metric as before:

```
>>> from sklearn.cluster import AgglomerativeClustering
>>> ac = AgglomerativeClustering(n_clusters=3,
...                              affinity='euclidean',
...                              linkage='complete')
>>> labels = ac.fit_predict(X)
>>> print(f'Cluster labels: {labels}')
Cluster labels: [1 0 0 2 1]
```

Looking at the predicted cluster labels, we can see that the first and the fifth examples (`ID_0` and `ID_4`) were assigned to one cluster (label `1`), and the examples `ID_1` and `ID_2` were assigned to a second cluster (label `0`). The example `ID_3` was put into its own cluster (label `2`). Overall, the results are consistent with the results that we observed in the dendrogram. We should note, though, that `ID_3` is more similar to `ID_4` and `ID_0` than to `ID_1` and `ID_2`, as shown in the preceding dendrogram figure; this is not clear from scikit-learn's clustering results. Let's now rerun the `AgglomerativeClustering` using `n_cluster=2` in the following code snippet:

```
>>> ac = AgglomerativeClustering(n_clusters=2,
...                              affinity='euclidean',
...                              linkage='complete')
>>> labels = ac.fit_predict(X)
>>> print(f'Cluster labels: {labels}')
Cluster labels: [0 1 1 0 0]
```

As you can see, in this *pruned* clustering hierarchy, label `ID_3` was assigned to the same cluster as `ID_0` and `ID_4`, as expected.

Locating regions of high density via DBSCAN

Although we can't cover the vast number of different clustering algorithms in this chapter, let's at least include one more approach to clustering: **density-based spatial clustering of applications with noise** (**DBSCAN**), which does not make assumptions about spherical clusters like k-means, nor does it partition the dataset into hierarchies that require a manual cut-off point. As its name implies, density-based clustering assigns cluster labels based on dense regions of points. In DBSCAN, the notion of density is defined as the number of points within a specified radius, ε.

According to the DBSCAN algorithm, a special label is assigned to each example (data point) using the following criteria:

- A point is considered a **core point** if at least a specified number (MinPts) of neighboring points fall within the specified radius, ε
- A **border point** is a point that has fewer neighbors than MinPts within ε, but lies within the ε radius of a core point
- All other points that are neither core nor border points are considered **noise points**

After labeling the points as core, border, or noise, the DBSCAN algorithm can be summarized in two simple steps:

1. Form a separate cluster for each core point or connected group of core points. (Core points are connected if they are no farther away than ε.)
2. Assign each border point to the cluster of its corresponding core point.

To get a better understanding of what the result of DBSCAN can look like, before jumping to the implementation, let's summarize what we have just learned about core points, border points, and noise points in *Figure 10.13*:

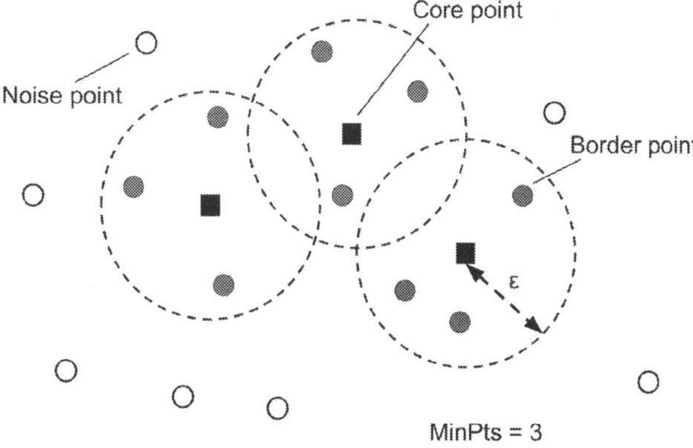

Figure 10.13: Core, noise, and border points for DBSCAN

One of the main advantages of using DBSCAN is that it does not assume that the clusters have a spherical shape as in k-means. Furthermore, DBSCAN is different from k-means and hierarchical clustering in that it doesn't necessarily assign each point to a cluster but is capable of removing noise points.

For a more illustrative example, let's create a new dataset of half-moon-shaped structures to compare k-means clustering, hierarchical clustering, and DBSCAN:

```
>>> from sklearn.datasets import make_moons
>>> X, y = make_moons(n_samples=200,
...                   noise=0.05,
...                   random_state=0)
>>> plt.scatter(X[:, 0], X[:, 1])
>>> plt.xlabel('Feature 1')
>>> plt.ylabel('Feature 2')
>>> plt.tight_layout()
>>> plt.show()
```

As you can see in the resulting plot, there are two visible, half-moon-shaped groups consisting of 100 examples (data points) each:

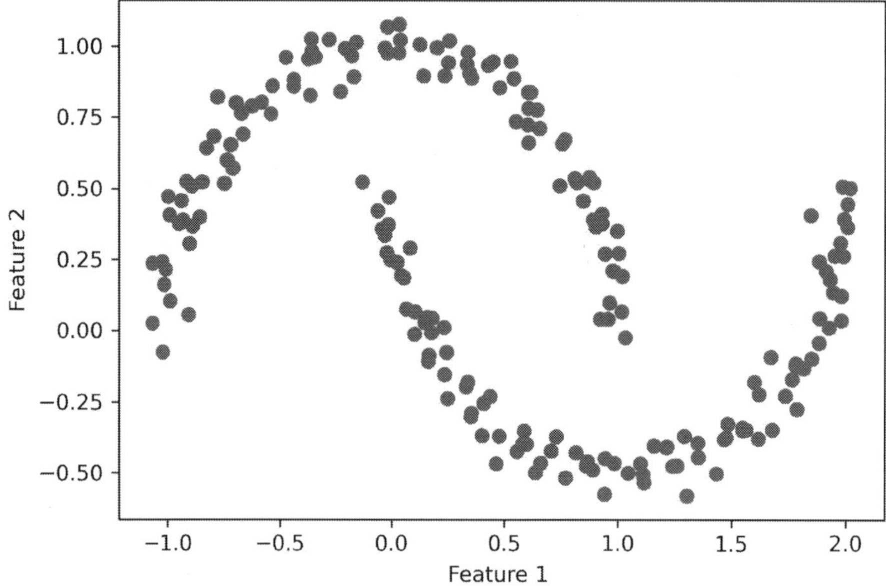

Figure 10.14: A two-feature half-moon-shaped dataset

We will start by using the k-means algorithm and complete linkage clustering to see if one of those previously discussed clustering algorithms can successfully identify the half-moon shapes as separate clusters. The code is as follows:

```
>>> f, (ax1, ax2) = plt.subplots(1, 2, figsize=(8, 3))
>>> km = KMeans(n_clusters=2,
...             random_state=0)
>>> y_km = km.fit_predict(X)
>>> ax1.scatter(X[y_km == 0, 0],
...             X[y_km == 0, 1],
...             c='lightblue',
...             edgecolor='black',
...             marker='o',
...             s=40,
...             label='cluster 1')
```

```
>>> ax1.scatter(X[y_km == 1, 0],
...             X[y_km == 1, 1],
...             c='red',
...             edgecolor='black',
...             marker='s',
...             s=40,
...             label='cluster 2')
>>> ax1.set_title('K-means clustering')
>>> ax1.set_xlabel('Feature 1')
>>> ax1.set_ylabel('Feature 2')

>>> ac = AgglomerativeClustering(n_clusters=2,
...                              affinity='euclidean',
...                              linkage='complete')
>>> y_ac = ac.fit_predict(X)
>>> ax2.scatter(X[y_ac == 0, 0],
...             X[y_ac == 0, 1],
...             c='lightblue',
...             edgecolor='black',
...             marker='o',
...             s=40,
...             label='Cluster 1')
>>> ax2.scatter(X[y_ac == 1, 0],
...             X[y_ac == 1, 1],
...             c='red',
...             edgecolor='black',
...             marker='s',
...             s=40,
...             label='Cluster 2')
>>> ax2.set_title('Agglomerative clustering')
>>> ax2.set_xlabel('Feature 1')
>>> ax2.set_ylabel('Feature 2')
>>> plt.legend()
>>> plt.tight_layout()
>>> plt.show()
```

Based on the visualized clustering results, we can see that the k-means algorithm was unable to separate the two clusters, and also, the hierarchical clustering algorithm was challenged by those complex shapes:

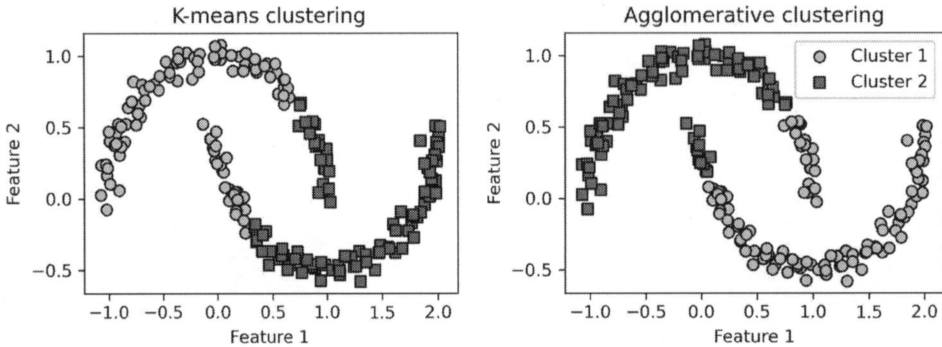

Figure 10.15: k-means and agglomerative clustering on the half-moon-shaped dataset

Finally, let's try the DBSCAN algorithm on this dataset to see if it can find the two half-moon-shaped clusters using a density-based approach:

```
>>> from sklearn.cluster import DBSCAN
>>> db = DBSCAN(eps=0.2,
...             min_samples=5,
...             metric='euclidean')
>>> y_db = db.fit_predict(X)
>>> plt.scatter(X[y_db == 0, 0],
...             X[y_db == 0, 1],
...             c='lightblue',
...             edgecolor='black',
...             marker='o',
...             s=40,
...             label='Cluster 1')
>>> plt.scatter(X[y_db == 1, 0],
...             X[y_db == 1, 1],
...             c='red',
...             edgecolor='black',
...             marker='s',
...             s=40,
...             label='Cluster 2')
>>> plt.xlabel('Feature 1')
>>> plt.ylabel('Feature 2')
>>> plt.legend()
>>> plt.tight_layout()
>>> plt.show()
```

The DBSCAN algorithm can successfully detect the half-moon shapes, which highlights one of the strengths of DBSCAN—clustering data of arbitrary shapes:

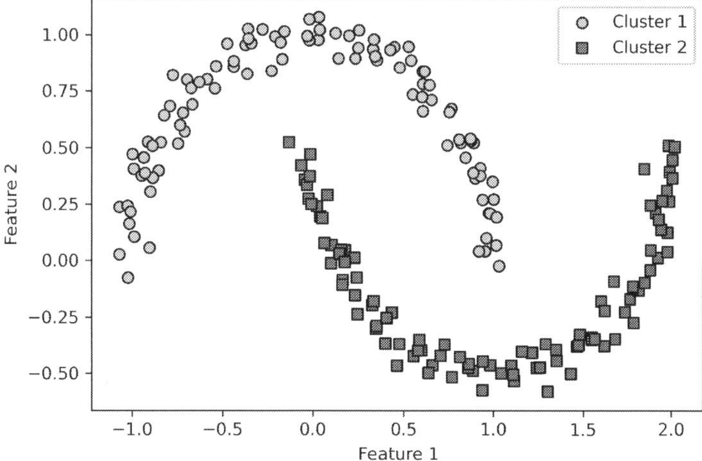

Figure 10.16: DBSCAN clustering on the half-moon-shaped dataset

However, we should also note some of the disadvantages of DBSCAN. With an increasing number of features in our dataset—assuming a fixed number of training examples—the negative effect of the **curse of dimensionality** increases. This is especially a problem if we are using the Euclidean distance metric. However, the problem of the curse of dimensionality is not unique to DBSCAN: it also affects other clustering algorithms that use the Euclidean distance metric, for example, k-means and hierarchical clustering algorithms. In addition, we have two hyperparameters in DBSCAN (MinPts and ε) that need to be optimized to yield good clustering results. Finding a good combination of MinPts and ε can be problematic if the density differences in the dataset are relatively large.

Graph-based clustering

So far, we have seen three of the most fundamental categories of clustering algorithms: prototype-based clustering with k-means, agglomerative hierarchical clustering, and density-based clustering via DBSCAN. However, there is also a fourth class of more advanced clustering algorithms that we have not covered in this chapter: graph-based clustering. Probably the most prominent members of the graph-based clustering family are the spectral clustering algorithms.

Although there are many different implementations of spectral clustering, what they all have in common is that they use the eigenvectors of a similarity or distance matrix to derive the cluster relationships. Since spectral clustering is beyond the scope of this book, you can read the excellent tutorial by Ulrike von Luxburg to learn more about this topic (*A tutorial on spectral clustering*, *Statistics and Computing*, 17(4): 395-416, 2007). It is freely available from arXiv at `http://arxiv.org/pdf/0711.0189v1.pdf`.

Note that, in practice, it is not always obvious which clustering algorithm will perform best on a given dataset, especially if the data comes in multiple dimensions that make it hard or impossible to visualize. Furthermore, it is important to emphasize that a successful clustering does not only depend on the algorithm and its hyperparameters; rather, the choice of an appropriate distance metric and the use of domain knowledge that can help to guide the experimental setup can be even more important.

In the context of the curse of dimensionality, it is thus common practice to apply dimensionality reduction techniques prior to performing clustering. Such dimensionality reduction techniques for unsupervised datasets include principal component analysis and t-SNE, which we covered in *Chapter 5, Compressing Data via Dimensionality Reduction*. Also, it is particularly common to compress datasets down to two-dimensional subspaces, which allows us to visualize the clusters and assigned labels using two-dimensional scatterplots, which are particularly helpful for evaluating the results.

Summary

In this chapter, you learned about three different clustering algorithms that can help us with the discovery of hidden structures or information in data. We started with a prototype-based approach, k-means, which clusters examples into spherical shapes based on a specified number of cluster centroids. Since clustering is an unsupervised method, we do not enjoy the luxury of ground-truth labels to evaluate the performance of a model. Thus, we used intrinsic performance metrics, such as the elbow method or silhouette analysis, as an attempt to quantify the quality of clustering.

We then looked at a different approach to clustering: agglomerative hierarchical clustering. Hierarchical clustering does not require specifying the number of clusters upfront, and the result can be visualized in a dendrogram representation, which can help with the interpretation of the results. The last clustering algorithm that we covered in this chapter was DBSCAN, an algorithm that groups points based on local densities and is capable of handling outliers and identifying non-globular shapes.

After this excursion into the field of unsupervised learning, it is now time to introduce some of the most exciting machine learning algorithms for supervised learning: multilayer artificial neural networks. After their recent resurgence, neural networks are once again the hottest topic in machine learning research. Thanks to recently developed deep learning algorithms, neural networks are considered state of the art for many complex tasks such as image classification, natural language processing, and speech recognition. In *Chapter 11, Implementing a Multilayer Artificial Neural Network from Scratch*, we will construct our own multilayer neural network. In *Chapter 12, Parallelizing Neural Network Training with PyTorch*, we will work with the PyTorch library, which specializes in training neural network models with multiple layers very efficiently by utilizing graphics processing units.

Join our book's Discord space

Join our Discord community to meet like-minded people and learn alongside more than 2000 members at:

`https://packt.link/MLwPyTorch`

11

Implementing a Multilayer Artificial Neural Network from Scratch

As you may know, deep learning is getting a lot of attention from the press and is, without doubt, the hottest topic in the machine learning field. Deep learning can be understood as a subfield of machine learning that is concerned with training artificial **neural networks** (**NNs**) with many layers efficiently. In this chapter, you will learn the basic concepts of artificial NNs so that you are well equipped for the following chapters, which will introduce advanced Python-based deep learning libraries and **deep neural network** (**DNN**) architectures that are particularly well suited for image and text analyses.

The topics that we will cover in this chapter are as follows:

- Gaining a conceptual understanding of multilayer NNs
- Implementing the fundamental backpropagation algorithm for NN training from scratch
- Training a basic multilayer NN for image classification

Modeling complex functions with artificial neural networks

At the beginning of this book, we started our journey through machine learning algorithms with artificial neurons in *Chapter 2, Training Simple Machine Learning Algorithms for Classification*. Artificial neurons represent the building blocks of the multilayer artificial NNs that we will discuss in this chapter.

The basic concept behind artificial NNs was built upon hypotheses and models of how the human brain works to solve complex problem tasks. Although artificial NNs have gained a lot of popularity in recent years, early studies of NNs go back to the 1940s, when Warren McCulloch and Walter Pitts first described how neurons could work. (*A logical calculus of the ideas immanent in nervous activity*, by *W. S. McCulloch* and *W. Pitts*, *The Bulletin of Mathematical Biophysics*, 5(4):115–133, 1943.)

However, in the decades that followed the first implementation of the **McCulloch-Pitts neuron** model—Rosenblatt's perceptron in the 1950s—many researchers and machine learning practitioners slowly began to lose interest in NNs since no one had a good solution for training an NN with multiple layers. Eventually, interest in NNs was rekindled in 1986 when D.E. Rumelhart, G.E. Hinton, and R.J. Williams were involved in the (re)discovery and popularization of the backpropagation algorithm to train NNs more efficiently, which we will discuss in more detail later in this chapter (*Learning representations by backpropagating errors*, by *D.E. Rumelhart, G.E. Hinton,* and *R.J. Williams, Nature,* 323 (6088): 533–536, 1986). Readers who are interested in the history of **artificial intelligence** (**AI**), machine learning, and NNs are also encouraged to read the Wikipedia article on the so-called *AI winters*, which are the periods of time where a large portion of the research community lost interest in the study of NNs (`https://en.wikipedia.org/wiki/AI_winter`).

However, NNs are more popular today than ever thanks to the many breakthroughs that have been made in the previous decade, which resulted in what we now call deep learning algorithms and architectures—NNs that are composed of many layers. NNs are a hot topic not only in academic research but also in big technology companies, such as Facebook, Microsoft, Amazon, Uber, Google, and many more that invest heavily in artificial NNs and deep learning research.

As of today, complex NNs powered by deep learning algorithms are considered state-of-the-art solutions for complex problem solving such as image and voice recognition. Some of the recent applications include:

- Predicting COVID-19 resource needs from a series of X-rays (`https://arxiv.org/abs/2101.04909`)
- Modeling virus mutations (`https://science.sciencemag.org/content/371/6526/284`)
- Leveraging data from social media platforms to manage extreme weather events (`https://onlinelibrary.wiley.com/doi/abs/10.1111/1468-5973.12311`)
- Improving photo descriptions for people who are blind or visually impaired (`https://tech.fb.com/how-facebook-is-using-ai-to-improve-photo-descriptions-for-people-who-are-blind-or-visually-impaired/`)

Single-layer neural network recap

This chapter is all about multilayer NNs, how they work, and how to train them to solve complex problems. However, before we dig deeper into a particular multilayer NN architecture, let's briefly reiterate some of the concepts of single-layer NNs that we introduced in *Chapter 2*, namely, the **ADAp-tive LInear NEuron** (**Adaline**) algorithm, which is shown in *Figure 11.1*:

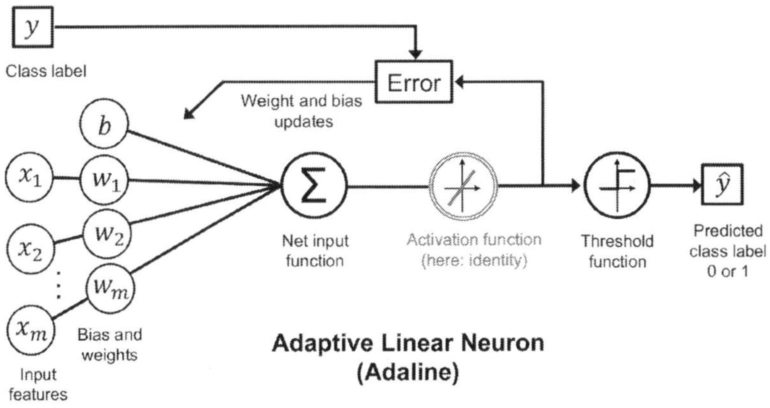

Figure 11.1: The Adaline algorithm

In *Chapter 2*, we implemented the Adaline algorithm to perform binary classification, and we used the gradient descent optimization algorithm to learn the weight coefficients of the model. In every epoch (pass over the training dataset), we updated the weight vector $\boldsymbol{w}$ and bias unit b using the following update rule:

$$\boldsymbol{w} := \boldsymbol{w} + \Delta\boldsymbol{w}, \quad b := b + \Delta b$$

where $\Delta w_j = -\eta \frac{\partial L}{\partial w_j}$ and $\Delta b = -\eta \frac{\partial L}{\partial b}$ for the bias unit and each weight w_j in the weight vector $\boldsymbol{w}$.

In other words, we computed the gradient based on the whole training dataset and updated the weights of the model by taking a step in the opposite direction of the loss gradient $\nabla L(\boldsymbol{w})$. (For simplicity, we will focus on the weights and omit the bias unit in the following paragraphs; however, as you remember from *Chapter 2*, the same concepts apply.) In order to find the optimal weights of the model, we optimized an objective function that we defined as the **mean of squared errors** (**MSE**) loss function $L(\boldsymbol{w})$. Furthermore, we multiplied the gradient by a factor, the **learning rate** η, which we had to choose carefully to balance the speed of learning against the risk of overshooting the global minimum of the loss function.

In gradient descent optimization, we updated all weights simultaneously after each epoch, and we defined the partial derivative for each weight w_j in the weight vector, $\boldsymbol{w}$, as follows:

$$\frac{\partial L}{\partial w_j} = \frac{\partial}{\partial w_j}\frac{1}{n}\sum_i \left(y^{(i)} - a^{(i)}\right)^2 = -\frac{2}{n}\sum_i \left(y^{(i)} - a^{(i)}\right)x_j^{(i)}$$

Here, $y^{(i)}$ is the target class label of a particular sample $x^{(i)}$, and $a^{(i)}$ is the activation of the neuron, which is a linear function in the special case of Adaline.

Furthermore, we defined the activation function $\sigma(\cdot)$ as follows:

$$\sigma(\cdot) = z = a$$

Here, the net input, z, is a linear combination of the weights that are connecting the input layer to the output layer:

$$z = \sum_j w_j x_j + b = \boldsymbol{w}^T \boldsymbol{x} + b$$

While we used the activation $\sigma(\cdot)$ to compute the gradient update, we implemented a threshold function to squash the continuous-valued output into binary class labels for prediction:

$$\hat{y} = \begin{cases} 1 & \text{if } z \geq 0; \\ 0 & \text{otherwise} \end{cases}$$

Single-layer naming convention

Note that although Adaline consists of two layers, one input layer and one output layer, it is called a single-layer network because of its single link between the input and output layers.

Also, we learned about a certain *trick* to accelerate the model learning, the so-called **stochastic gradient descent** (**SGD**) optimization. SGD approximates the loss from a single training sample (online learning) or a small subset of training examples (mini-batch learning). We will make use of this concept later in this chapter when we implement and train a **multilayer perceptron** (**MLP**). Apart from faster learning—due to the more frequent weight updates compared to gradient descent—its noisy nature is also regarded as beneficial when training multilayer NNs with nonlinear activation functions, which do not have a convex loss function. Here, the added noise can help to escape local loss minima, but we will discuss this topic in more detail later in this chapter.

Introducing the multilayer neural network architecture

In this section, you will learn how to connect multiple single neurons to a multilayer feedforward NN; this special type of *fully connected* network is also called **MLP**.

Figure 11.2 illustrates the concept of an MLP consisting of two layers:

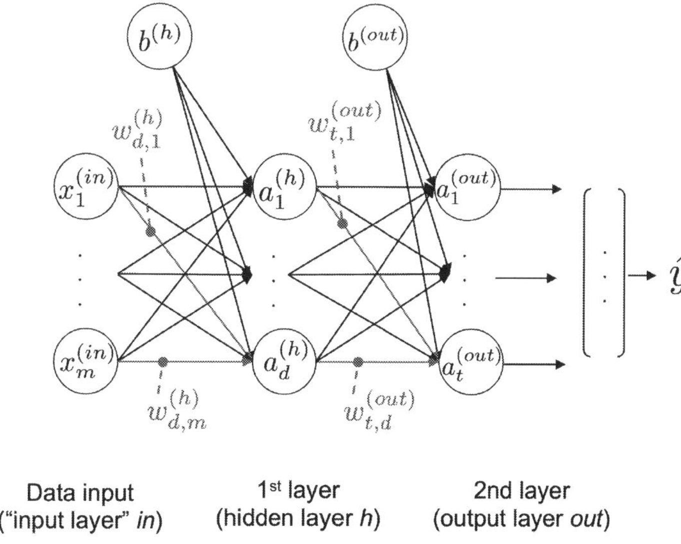

Figure 11.2: A two-layer MLP

Next to the data input, the MLP depicted in *Figure 11.2* has one hidden layer and one output layer. The units in the hidden layer are fully connected to the input features, and the output layer is fully connected to the hidden layer. If such a network has more than one hidden layer, we also call it a **deep NN**. (Note that in some contexts, the inputs are also regarded as a layer. However, in this case, it would make the Adaline model, which is a single-layer neural network, a two-layer neural network, which may be counterintuitive.)

Adding additional hidden layers

We can add any number of hidden layers to the MLP to create deeper network architectures. Practically, we can think of the number of layers and units in an NN as additional hyperparameters that we want to optimize for a given problem task using the cross-validation technique, which we discussed in *Chapter 6, Learning Best Practices for Model Evaluation and Hyperparameter Tuning*.

However, the loss gradients for updating the network's parameters, which we will calculate later via backpropagation, will become increasingly small as more layers are added to a network. This vanishing gradient problem makes model learning more challenging. Therefore, special algorithms have been developed to help train such DNN structures; this is known as **deep learning**, which we will discuss in more detail in the following chapters.

As shown in *Figure 11.2*, we denote the ith activation unit in the lth layer as $a_i^{(l)}$. To make the math and code implementations a bit more intuitive, we will not use numerical indices to refer to layers, but we will use the *in* superscript for the input features, the h superscript for the hidden layer, and the *out* superscript for the output layer. For instance, $x_i^{(in)}$ refers to the ith input feature value, $a_i^{(h)}$ refers to the ith unit in the hidden layer, and $a_i^{(out)}$ refers to the ith unit in the output layer. Note that the *b*'s in *Figure 11.2* denote the bias units. In fact, $\boldsymbol{b}^{(h)}$ and $\boldsymbol{b}^{(out)}$ are vectors with the number of elements being equal to the number of nodes in the layer they correspond to. For example, $\boldsymbol{b}^{(h)}$ stores d bias units, where d is the number of nodes in the hidden layer. If this sounds confusing, don't worry. Looking at the code implementation later, where we initialize weight matrices and bias unit vectors, will help clarify these concepts.

Each node in layer l is connected to all nodes in layer $l + 1$ via a weight coefficient. For example, the connection between the kth unit in layer l to the jth unit in layer $l + 1$ will be written as $w_{j,k}^{(l+1)}$. Referring back to *Figure 11.2*, we denote the weight matrix that connects the input to the hidden layer as $\boldsymbol{W}^{(h)}$, and we write the matrix that connects the hidden layer to the output layer as $\boldsymbol{W}^{(out)}$.

While one unit in the output layer would suffice for a binary classification task, we saw a more general form of an NN in the preceding figure, which allows us to perform multiclass classification via a generalization of the **one-versus-all (OvA)** technique. To better understand how this works, remember the **one-hot** representation of categorical variables that we introduced in *Chapter 4, Building Good Training Datasets – Data Preprocessing*.

For example, we can encode the three class labels in the familiar Iris dataset (0=*Setosa*, 1=*Versicolor*, 2=*Virginica*) as follows:

$$0 = \begin{bmatrix} 1 \\ 0 \\ 0 \end{bmatrix}, 1 = \begin{bmatrix} 0 \\ 1 \\ 0 \end{bmatrix}, 2 = \begin{bmatrix} 0 \\ 0 \\ 1 \end{bmatrix}$$

This one-hot vector representation allows us to tackle classification tasks with an arbitrary number of unique class labels present in the training dataset.

If you are new to NN representations, the indexing notation (subscripts and superscripts) may look a little bit confusing at first. What may seem overly complicated at first will make much more sense in later sections when we vectorize the NN representation. As introduced earlier, we summarize the weights that connect the input and hidden layers by a $d \times m$ dimensional matrix $\boldsymbol{W}^{(h)}$, where d is the number of hidden units and m is the number of input units.

Activating a neural network via forward propagation

In this section, we will describe the process of **forward propagation** to calculate the output of an MLP model. To understand how it fits into the context of learning an MLP model, let's summarize the MLP learning procedure in three simple steps:

1. Starting at the input layer, we forward propagate the patterns of the training data through the network to generate an output.
2. Based on the network's output, we calculate the loss that we want to minimize using a loss function that we will describe later.

3. We backpropagate the loss, find its derivative with respect to each weight and bias unit in the network, and update the model.

Finally, after we repeat these three steps for multiple epochs and learn the weight and bias parameters of the MLP, we use forward propagation to calculate the network output and apply a threshold function to obtain the predicted class labels in the one-hot representation, which we described in the previous section.

Now, let's walk through the individual steps of forward propagation to generate an output from the patterns in the training data. Since each unit in the hidden layer is connected to all units in the input layers, we first calculate the activation unit of the hidden layer $a_1^{(h)}$ as follows:

$$z_1^{(h)} = x_1^{(in)} w_{1,1}^{(h)} + x_2^{(in)} w_{1,2}^{(h)} + \cdots + x_m^{(in)} w_{1,m}^{(h)}$$

$$a_1^{(h)} = \sigma\left(z_1^{(h)}\right)$$

Here, $z_1^{(h)}$ is the net input and $\sigma(\cdot)$ is the activation function, which has to be differentiable to learn the weights that connect the neurons using a gradient-based approach. To be able to solve complex problems such as image classification, we need nonlinear activation functions in our MLP model, for example, the sigmoid (logistic) activation function that we remember from the section about logistic regression in *Chapter 3, A Tour of Machine Learning Classifiers Using Scikit-Learn*:

$$\sigma(z) = \frac{1}{1 + e^{-z}}$$

As you may recall, the sigmoid function is an *S*-shaped curve that maps the net input *z* onto a logistic distribution in the range 0 to 1, which cuts the *y* axis at *z* = 0, as shown in *Figure 11.3*:

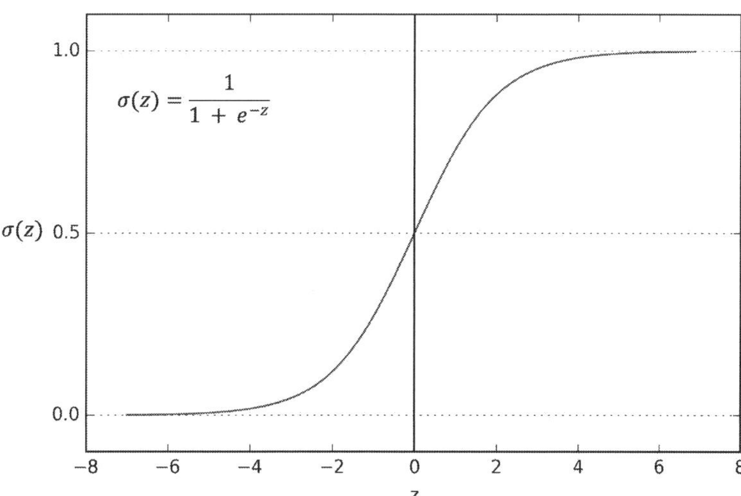

Figure 11.3: The sigmoid activation function

MLP is a typical example of a feedforward artificial NN. The term **feedforward** refers to the fact that each layer serves as the input to the next layer without loops, in contrast to recurrent NNs—an architecture that we will discuss later in this chapter and discuss in more detail in *Chapter 15, Modeling Sequential Data Using Recurrent Neural Networks*. The term *multilayer perceptron* may sound a little bit confusing since the artificial neurons in this network architecture are typically sigmoid units, not perceptrons. We can think of the neurons in the MLP as logistic regression units that return values in the continuous range between 0 and 1.

For purposes of code efficiency and readability, we will now write the activation in a more compact form using the concepts of basic linear algebra, which will allow us to vectorize our code implementation via NumPy rather than writing multiple nested and computationally expensive Python `for` loops:

$$z^{(h)} = \boldsymbol{x}^{(in)}\boldsymbol{W}^{(h)T} + \boldsymbol{b}^{(h)}$$

$$a^{(h)} = \sigma\left(\boldsymbol{z}^{(h)}\right)$$

Here, $\boldsymbol{x}^{(in)}$ is our $1\times m$ dimensional feature vector. $\boldsymbol{W}^{(h)}$ is a $d\times m$ dimensional weight matrix where d is the number of units in the hidden layer; consequently, the transposed matrix $\boldsymbol{W}^{(h)T}$ is $m\times d$ dimensional. The bias vector $\boldsymbol{b}^{(h)}$ consists of d bias units (one bias unit per hidden node).

After matrix-vector multiplication, we obtain the $1\times d$ dimensional net input vector $\boldsymbol{z}^{(h)}$ to calculate the activation $\boldsymbol{a}^{(h)}$ (where $\boldsymbol{a}^{(h)} \in \mathbb{R}^{1\times d}$).

Furthermore, we can generalize this computation to all n examples in the training dataset:

$$\boldsymbol{Z}^{(h)} = \boldsymbol{X}^{(in)}\boldsymbol{W}^{(h)T} + \boldsymbol{b}^{(h)}$$

Here, $\boldsymbol{X}^{(in)}$ is now an $n\times m$ matrix, and the matrix multiplication will result in an $n\times d$ dimensional net input matrix, $\boldsymbol{Z}^{(h)}$. Finally, we apply the activation function $\sigma(\cdot)$ to each value in the net input matrix to get the $n\times d$ activation matrix in the next layer (here, the output layer):

$$\boldsymbol{A}^{(h)} = \sigma\left(\boldsymbol{Z}^{(h)}\right)$$

Similarly, we can write the activation of the output layer in vectorized form for multiple examples:

$$\boldsymbol{Z}^{(out)} = \boldsymbol{A}^{(h)}\boldsymbol{W}^{(out)T} + \boldsymbol{b}^{(out)}$$

Here, we multiply the transpose of the $t\times d$ matrix $\boldsymbol{W}^{(out)}$ (t is the number of output units) by the $n\times d$ dimensional matrix, $\boldsymbol{A}^{(h)}$, and add the t dimensional bias vector $\boldsymbol{b}^{(out)}$ to obtain the $n\times t$ dimensional matrix, $\boldsymbol{Z}^{(out)}$. (The rows in this matrix represent the outputs for each example.)

Lastly, we apply the sigmoid activation function to obtain the continuous-valued output of our network:

$$\boldsymbol{A}^{(out)} = \sigma\left(\boldsymbol{Z}^{(out)}\right)$$

Similar to $\boldsymbol{Z}^{(out)}$, $\boldsymbol{A}^{(out)}$ is an $n\times t$ dimensional matrix.

Classifying handwritten digits

In the previous section, we covered a lot of the theory around NNs, which can be a little bit overwhelming if you are new to this topic. Before we continue with the discussion of the algorithm for learning the weights of the MLP model, backpropagation, let's take a short break from the theory and see an NN in action.

Additional resources on backpropagation

The NN theory can be quite complex; thus, we want to provide readers with additional resources that cover some of the topics we discuss in this chapter in more detail or from a different perspective:

- *Chapter 6, Deep Feedforward Networks, Deep Learning*, by *I. Goodfellow, Y. Bengio*, and *A. Courville*, MIT Press, 2016 (manuscripts freely accessible at `http://www.deeplearningbook.org`).
- *Pattern Recognition and Machine Learning*, by *C. M. Bishop*, Springer New York, 2006.
- Lecture video slides from Sebastian Raschka's deep learning course:

  `https://sebastianraschka.com/blog/2021/dl-course.html#l08-multinomial-logistic-regression--softmax-regression`

  `https://sebastianraschka.com/blog/2021/dl-course.html#l09-multilayer-perceptrons-and-backpropration`

In this section, we will implement and train our first multilayer NN to classify handwritten digits from the popular **Mixed National Institute of Standards and Technology** (**MNIST**) dataset that has been constructed by Yann LeCun and others and serves as a popular benchmark dataset for machine learning algorithms (*Gradient-Based Learning Applied to Document Recognition* by *Y. LeCun, L. Bottou, Y. Bengio*, and *P. Haffner*, *Proceedings of the IEEE*, 86(11): 2278-2324, 1998).

Obtaining and preparing the MNIST dataset

The MNIST dataset is publicly available at `http://yann.lecun.com/exdb/mnist/` and consists of the following four parts:

1. **Training dataset images:** `train-images-idx3-ubyte.gz` (9.9 MB, 47 MB unzipped, and 60,000 examples)
2. **Training dataset labels:** `train-labels-idx1-ubyte.gz` (29 KB, 60 KB unzipped, and 60,000 labels)
3. **Test dataset images:** `t10k-images-idx3-ubyte.gz` (1.6 MB, 7.8 MB unzipped, and 10,000 examples)
4. **Test dataset labels:** `t10k-labels-idx1-ubyte.gz` (5 KB, 10 KB unzipped, and 10,000 labels)

The MNIST dataset was constructed from two datasets of the US **National Institute of Standards and Technology** (**NIST**). The training dataset consists of handwritten digits from 250 different people, 50 percent high school students, and 50 percent employees from the Census Bureau. Note that the test dataset contains handwritten digits from different people following the same split.

Instead of downloading the abovementioned dataset files and preprocessing them into NumPy arrays ourselves, we will use scikit-learn's new `fetch_openml` function, which allows us to load the MNIST dataset more conveniently:

```
>>> from sklearn.datasets import fetch_openml
>>> X, y = fetch_openml('mnist_784', version=1,
...                     return_X_y=True)
>>> X = X.values
>>> y = y.astype(int).values
```

In scikit-learn, the `fetch_openml` function downloads the MNIST dataset from OpenML (`https://www.openml.org/d/554`) as pandas `DataFrame` and Series objects, which is why we use the `.values` attribute to obtain the underlying NumPy arrays. (If you are using a scikit-learn version older than 1.0, `fetch_openml` downloads NumPy arrays directly so you can omit using the `.values` attribute.) The $n \times m$ dimensional `X` array consists of 70,000 images with 784 pixels each, and the `y` array stores the corresponding 70,000 class labels, which we can confirm by checking the dimensions of the arrays as follows:

```
>>> print(X.shape)
(70000, 784)
>>> print(y.shape)
(70000,)
```

The images in the MNIST dataset consist of 28×28 pixels, and each pixel is represented by a grayscale intensity value. Here, `fetch_openml` already unrolled the 28×28 pixels into one-dimensional row vectors, which represent the rows in our `X` array (784 per row or image) above. The second array (y) returned by the `fetch_openml` function contains the corresponding target variable, the class labels (integers 0-9) of the handwritten digits.

Next, let's normalize the pixels values in MNIST to the range –1 to 1 (originally 0 to 255) via the following code line:

```
>>> X = ((X / 255.) - .5) * 2
```

The reason behind this is that gradient-based optimization is much more stable under these conditions, as discussed in *Chapter 2*. Note that we scaled the images on a pixel-by-pixel basis, which is different from the feature-scaling approach that we took in previous chapters.

Previously, we derived scaling parameters from the training dataset and used these to scale each column in the training dataset and test dataset. However, when working with image pixels, centering them at zero and rescaling them to a [–1, 1] range is also common and usually works well in practice.

To get an idea of how those images in MNIST look, let's visualize examples of the digits 0-9 after reshaping the 784-pixel vectors from our feature matrix into the original 28×28 image that we can plot via Matplotlib's `imshow` function:

```
>>> import matplotlib.pyplot as plt
>>> fig, ax = plt.subplots(nrows=2, ncols=5,
...                        sharex=True, sharey=True)
>>> ax = ax.flatten()
>>> for i in range(10):
...     img = X[y == i][0].reshape(28, 28)
...     ax[i].imshow(img, cmap='Greys')
>>> ax[0].set_xticks([])
>>> ax[0].set_yticks([])
>>> plt.tight_layout()
>>> plt.show()
```

We should now see a plot of the 2×5 subfigures showing a representative image of each unique digit:

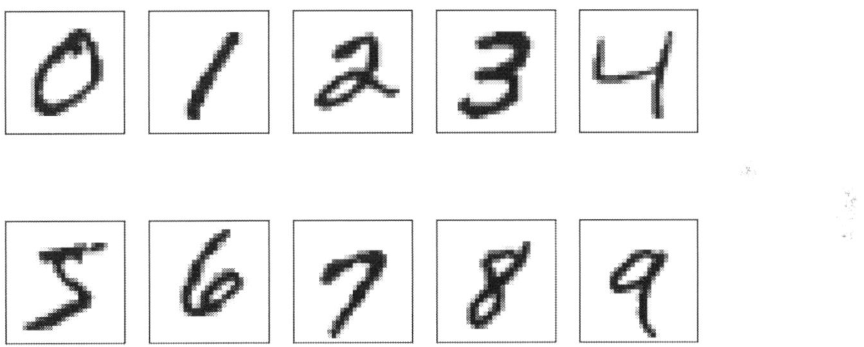

Figure 11.4: A plot showing one randomly chosen handwritten digit from each class

In addition, let's also plot multiple examples of the same digit to see how different the handwriting for each really is:

```
>>> fig, ax = plt.subplots(nrows=5,
...                        ncols=5,
...                        sharex=True,
...                        sharey=True)
>>> ax = ax.flatten()
```

```
>>> for i in range(25):
...     img = X[y == 7][i].reshape(28, 28)
...     ax[i].imshow(img, cmap='Greys')
>>> ax[0].set_xticks([])
>>> ax[0].set_yticks([])
>>> plt.tight_layout()
>>> plt.show()
```

After executing the code, we should now see the first 25 variants of the digit 7:

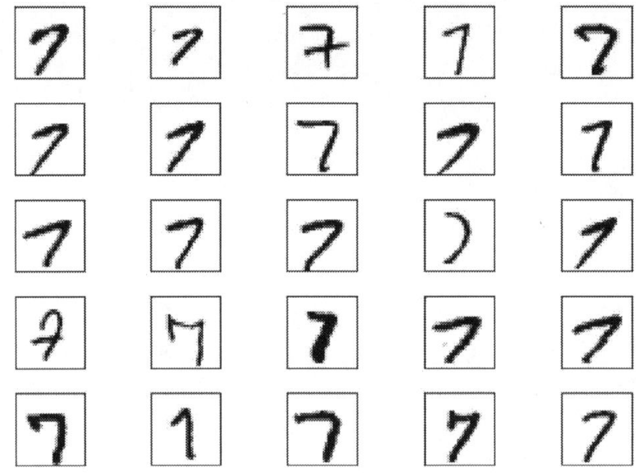

Figure 11.5: Different variants of the handwritten digit 7

Finally, let's divide the dataset into training, validation, and test subsets. The following code will split the dataset such that 55,000 images are used for training, 5,000 images for validation, and 10,000 images for testing:

```
>>> from sklearn.model_selection import train_test_split
>>> X_temp, X_test, y_temp, y_test = train_test_split(
...     X, y, test_size=10000, random_state=123, stratify=y
... )
>>> X_train, X_valid, y_train, y_valid = train_test_split(
...     X_temp, y_temp, test_size=5000,
...     random_state=123, stratify=y_temp
... )
```

Implementing a multilayer perceptron

In this subsection, we will now implement an MLP from scratch to classify the images in the MNIST dataset. To keep things simple, we will implement an MLP with only one hidden layer. Since the approach may seem a little bit complicated at first, you are encouraged to download the sample code for this chapter from the Packt Publishing website or from GitHub (`https://github.com/rasbt/machine-learning-book`) so that you can view this MLP implementation annotated with comments and syntax highlighting for better readability.

If you are not running the code from the accompanying Jupyter Notebook file or don't have access to the internet, copy the `NeuralNetMLP` code from this chapter into a Python script file in your current working directory (for example, `neuralnet.py`), which you can then import into your current Python session via the following command:

```
from neuralnet import NeuralNetMLP
```

The code will contain parts that we have not talked about yet, such as the backpropagation algorithm. Do not worry if not all the code makes immediate sense to you; we will follow up on certain parts later in this chapter. However, going over the code at this stage can make it easier to follow the theory later.

So, let's look at the following implementation of an MLP, starting with the two helper functions to compute the logistic sigmoid activation and to convert integer class label arrays to one-hot encoded labels:

```
import numpy as np

def sigmoid(z):
    return 1. / (1. + np.exp(-z))


def int_to_onehot(y, num_labels):

    ary = np.zeros((y.shape[0], num_labels))
    for i, val in enumerate(y):
        ary[i, val] = 1

    return ary
```

Below, we implement the main class for our MLP, which we call `NeuralNetMLP`. There are three class methods, `.__init__()`, `.forward()`, and `.backward()`, that we will discuss one by one, starting with the `__init__` constructor:

```
class NeuralNetMLP:

    def __init__(self, num_features, num_hidden,
                 num_classes, random_seed=123):
        super().__init__()

        self.num_classes = num_classes

        # hidden
        rng = np.random.RandomState(random_seed)

        self.weight_h = rng.normal(
            loc=0.0, scale=0.1, size=(num_hidden, num_features))
        self.bias_h = np.zeros(num_hidden)

        # output
        self.weight_out = rng.normal(
            loc=0.0, scale=0.1, size=(num_classes, num_hidden))
        self.bias_out = np.zeros(num_classes)
```

The `__init__` constructor instantiates the weight matrices and bias vectors for the hidden and the output layer. Next, let's see how these are used in the `forward` method to make predictions:

```
    def forward(self, x):
        # Hidden layer

        # input dim: [n_examples, n_features]
        #        dot [n_hidden, n_features].T
        # output dim: [n_examples, n_hidden]
        z_h = np.dot(x, self.weight_h.T) + self.bias_h
        a_h = sigmoid(z_h)

        # Output layer
        # input dim: [n_examples, n_hidden]
        #        dot [n_classes, n_hidden].T
        # output dim: [n_examples, n_classes]
        z_out = np.dot(a_h, self.weight_out.T) + self.bias_out
        a_out = sigmoid(z_out)
        return a_h, a_out
```

The `forward` method takes in one or more training examples and returns the predictions. In fact, it returns both the activation values from the hidden layer and the output layer, `a_h` and `a_out`. While `a_out` represents the class-membership probabilities that we can convert to class labels, which we care about, we also need the activation values from the hidden layer, `a_h`, to optimize the model parameters; that is, the weight and bias units of the hidden and output layers.

Finally, let's talk about the `backward` method, which updates the weight and bias parameters of the neural network:

```
    def backward(self, x, a_h, a_out, y):

        #########################
        ### Output layer weights
        #########################

        # one-hot encoding
        y_onehot = int_to_onehot(y, self.num_classes)

        # Part 1: dLoss/dOutWeights
        ## = dLoss/dOutAct * dOutAct/dOutNet * dOutNet/dOutWeight
        ## where DeltaOut = dLoss/dOutAct * dOutAct/dOutNet
        ## for convenient re-use

        # input/output dim: [n_examples, n_classes]
        d_loss__d_a_out = 2.*(a_out - y_onehot) / y.shape[0]

        # input/output dim: [n_examples, n_classes]
        d_a_out__d_z_out = a_out * (1. - a_out) # sigmoid derivative

        # output dim: [n_examples, n_classes]
        delta_out = d_loss__d_a_out * d_a_out__d_z_out

        # gradient for output weights

        # [n_examples, n_hidden]
        d_z_out__dw_out = a_h

        # input dim: [n_classes, n_examples]
        #           dot [n_examples, n_hidden]
        # output dim: [n_classes, n_hidden]
        d_loss__dw_out = np.dot(delta_out.T, d_z_out__dw_out)
        d_loss__db_out = np.sum(delta_out, axis=0)
```

```
        ##################################
        # Part 2: dLoss/dHiddenWeights
        ## = DeltaOut * dOutNet/dHiddenAct * dHiddenAct/dHiddenNet
        #    * dHiddenNet/dWeight

        # [n_classes, n_hidden]
        d_z_out__a_h = self.weight_out

        # output dim: [n_examples, n_hidden]
        d_loss__a_h = np.dot(delta_out, d_z_out__a_h)

        # [n_examples, n_hidden]
        d_a_h__d_z_h = a_h * (1. - a_h) # sigmoid derivative

        # [n_examples, n_features]
        d_z_h__d_w_h = x

        # output dim: [n_hidden, n_features]
        d_loss__d_w_h = np.dot((d_loss__a_h * d_a_h__d_z_h).T,
                                d_z_h__d_w_h)
        d_loss__d_b_h = np.sum((d_loss__a_h * d_a_h__d_z_h), axis=0)

        return (d_loss__dw_out, d_loss__db_out,
                d_loss__d_w_h, d_loss__d_b_h)
```

The `backward` method implements the so-called *backpropagation* algorithm, which calculates the gradients of the loss with respect to the weight and bias parameters. Similar to Adaline, these gradients are then used to update these parameters via gradient descent. Note that multilayer NNs are more complex than their single-layer siblings, and we will go over the mathematical concepts of how to compute the gradients in a later section after discussing the code. For now, just consider the `backward` method as a way for computing gradients that are used for the gradient descent updates. For simplicity, the loss function this derivation is based on is the same MSE loss that we used in Adaline. In later chapters, we will look at alternative loss functions, such as multi-category cross-entropy loss, which is a generalization of the binary logistic regression loss to multiple classes.

Looking at this code implementation of the `NeuralNetMLP` class, you may have noticed that this object-oriented implementation differs from the familiar scikit-learn API that is centered around the `.fit()` and `.predict()` methods. Instead, the main methods of the `NeuralNetMLP` class are the `.forward()` and `.backward()` methods. One of the reasons behind this is that it makes a complex neural network a bit easier to understand in terms of how the information flows through the networks.

Another reason is that this implementation is relatively similar to how more advanced deep learning libraries such as PyTorch operate, which we will introduce and use in the upcoming chapters to implement more complex neural networks.

After we have implemented the `NeuralNetMLP` class, we use the following code to instantiate a new `NeuralNetMLP` object:

```
>>> model = NeuralNetMLP(num_features=28*28,
...                      num_hidden=50,
...                      num_classes=10)
```

The `model` accepts MNIST images reshaped into 784-dimensional vectors (in the format of `X_train`, `X_valid`, or `X_test`, which we defined previously) for the 10 integer classes (digits 0-9). The hidden layer consists of 50 nodes. Also, as you may be able to tell from looking at the previously defined `.forward()` method, we use a sigmoid activation function after the first hidden layer and output layer to keep things simple. In later chapters, we will learn about alternative activation functions for both the hidden and output layers.

Figure 11.6 summarizes the neural network architecture that we instantiated above:

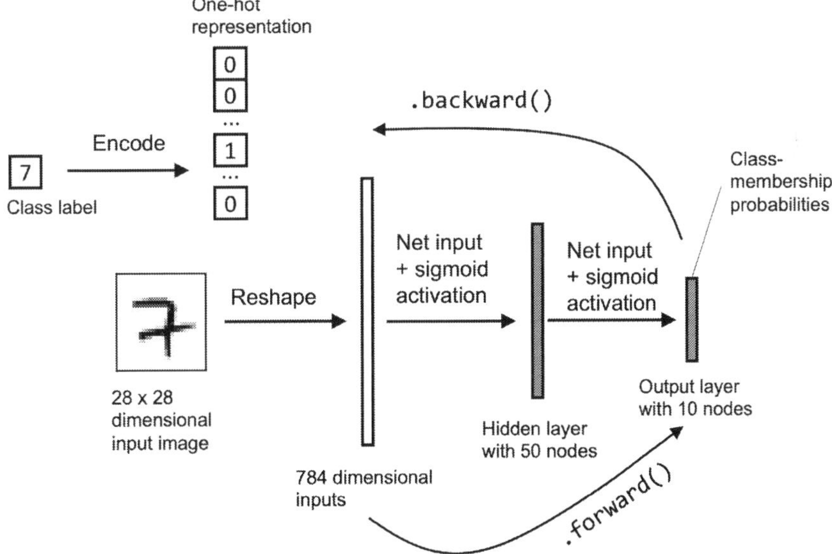

Figure 11.6: The NN architecture for labeling handwritten digits

In the next subsection, we are going to implement the training function that we can use to train the network on mini-batches of the data via backpropagation.

Coding the neural network training loop

Now that we have implemented the `NeuralNetMLP` class in the previous subsection and initiated a model, the next step is to train the model. We will tackle this in multiple steps. First, we will define some helper functions for data loading. Second, we will embed these functions into the training loop that iterates over the dataset in multiple epochs.

The first function we are going to define is a mini-batch generator, which takes in our dataset and divides it into mini-batches of a desired size for stochastic gradient descent training. The code is as follows:

```
>>> import numpy as np
>>> num_epochs = 50
>>> minibatch_size = 100

>>> def minibatch_generator(X, y, minibatch_size):
...     indices = np.arange(X.shape[0])
...     np.random.shuffle(indices)
...     for start_idx in range(0, indices.shape[0] - minibatch_size
...                            + 1, minibatch_size):
...         batch_idx = indices[start_idx:start_idx + minibatch_size]
...         yield X[batch_idx], y[batch_idx]
```

Before we move on to the next functions, let's confirm that the mini-batch generator works as intended and produces mini-batches of the desired size. The following code will attempt to iterate through the dataset, and then we will print the dimension of the mini-batches. Note that in the following code examples, we will remove the `break` statements. The code is as follows:

```
>>> # iterate over training epochs
>>> for i in range(num_epochs):
...     # iterate over minibatches
...     minibatch_gen = minibatch_generator(
...         X_train, y_train, minibatch_size)
...     for X_train_mini, y_train_mini in minibatch_gen:
...         break
...     break
>>> print(X_train_mini.shape)
(100, 784)
>>> print(y_train_mini.shape)
(100,)
```

As we can see, the network returns mini-batches of size 100 as intended.

Next, we have to define our loss function and performance metric that we can use to monitor the training process and evaluate the model. The MSE loss and accuracy function can be implemented as follows:

```
>>> def mse_loss(targets, probas, num_labels=10):
...     onehot_targets = int_to_onehot(
...         targets, num_labels=num_labels
...     )
...     return np.mean((onehot_targets - probas)**2)

>>> def accuracy(targets, predicted_labels):
...     return np.mean(predicted_labels == targets)
```

Let's test the preceding function and compute the initial validation set MSE and accuracy of the model we instantiated in the previous section:

```
>>> _, probas = model.forward(X_valid)
>>> mse = mse_loss(y_valid, probas)
>>> print(f'Initial validation MSE: {mse:.1f}')
Initial validation MSE: 0.3

>>> predicted_labels = np.argmax(probas, axis=1)
>>> acc = accuracy(y_valid, predicted_labels)
>>> print(f'Initial validation accuracy: {acc*100:.1f}%')
Initial validation accuracy: 9.4%
```

In this code example, note that `model.forward()` returns the hidden and output layer activations. Remember that we have 10 output nodes (one corresponding to each unique class label). Hence, when computing the MSE, we first converted the class labels into one-hot encoded class labels in the `mse_loss()` function. In practice, it does not make a difference whether we average over the row or the columns of the squared-difference matrix first, so we simply call `np.mean()` without any axis specification so that it returns a scalar.

The output layer activations, since we used the logistic sigmoid function, are values in the range [0, 1]. For each input, the output layer produces 10 values in the range [0, 1], so we used the `np.argmax()` function to select the index position of the largest value, which yields the predicted class label. We then compared the true labels with the predicted class labels to compute the accuracy via the `accuracy()` function we defined. As we can see from the preceding output, the accuracy is not very high. However, given that we have a balanced dataset with 10 classes, a prediction accuracy of approximately 10 percent is what we would expect for an untrained model producing random predictions.

Using the previous code, we can compute the performance on, for example, the whole training set if we provide `y_train` as input to targets and the predicted labels from feeding the model with `X_train`. However, in practice, our computer memory is usually a limiting factor for how much data the model can ingest in one forward pass (due to the large matrix multiplications). Hence, we are defining our MSE and accuracy computation based on our previous mini-batch generator. The following function will compute the MSE and accuracy incrementally by iterating over the dataset one mini-batch at a time to be more memory-efficient:

```
>>> def compute_mse_and_acc(nnet, X, y, num_labels=10,
...                         minibatch_size=100):
...     mse, correct_pred, num_examples = 0., 0, 0
...     minibatch_gen = minibatch_generator(X, y, minibatch_size)
...     for i, (features, targets) in enumerate(minibatch_gen):
...         _, probas = nnet.forward(features)
...         predicted_labels = np.argmax(probas, axis=1)
...         onehot_targets = int_to_onehot(
...             targets, num_labels=num_labels
...         )
...         loss = np.mean((onehot_targets - probas)**2)
...         correct_pred += (predicted_labels == targets).sum()
...         num_examples += targets.shape[0]
...         mse += loss
...     mse = mse/i
...     acc = correct_pred/num_examples
...     return mse, acc
```

Before we implement the training loop, let's test the function and compute the initial training set MSE and accuracy of the model we instantiated in the previous section and make sure it works as intended:

```
>>> mse, acc = compute_mse_and_acc(model, X_valid, y_valid)
>>> print(f'Initial valid MSE: {mse:.1f}')
Initial valid MSE: 0.3
>>> print(f'Initial valid accuracy: {acc*100:.1f}%')
Initial valid accuracy: 9.4%
```

As we can see from the results, our generator approach produces the same results as the previously defined MSE and accuracy functions, except for a small rounding error in the MSE (0.27 versus 0.28), which is negligible for our purposes.

Let's now get to the main part and implement the code to train our model:

```
>>> def train(model, X_train, y_train, X_valid, y_valid, num_epochs,
...           learning_rate=0.1):
...     epoch_loss = []
```

```
...     epoch_train_acc = []
...     epoch_valid_acc = []
...
...     for e in range(num_epochs):
...         # iterate over minibatches
...         minibatch_gen = minibatch_generator(
...             X_train, y_train, minibatch_size)
...         for X_train_mini, y_train_mini in minibatch_gen:
...             #### Compute outputs ####
...             a_h, a_out = model.forward(X_train_mini)

...             #### Compute gradients ####
...             d_loss__d_w_out, d_loss__d_b_out, \
...             d_loss__d_w_h, d_loss__d_b_h = \
...                 model.backward(X_train_mini, a_h, a_out,
...                                y_train_mini)
...
...             #### Update weights ####
...             model.weight_h -= learning_rate * d_loss__d_w_h
...             model.bias_h -= learning_rate * d_loss__d_b_h
...             model.weight_out -= learning_rate * d_loss__d_w_out
...             model.bias_out -= learning_rate * d_loss__d_b_out
...
...         #### Epoch Logging ####
...         train_mse, train_acc = compute_mse_and_acc(
...             model, X_train, y_train
...         )
...         valid_mse, valid_acc = compute_mse_and_acc(
...             model, X_valid, y_valid
...         )
...         train_acc, valid_acc = train_acc*100, valid_acc*100
...         epoch_train_acc.append(train_acc)
...         epoch_valid_acc.append(valid_acc)
...         epoch_loss.append(train_mse)
...         print(f'Epoch: {e+1:03d}/{num_epochs:03d} '
...               f'| Train MSE: {train_mse:.2f} '
...               f'| Train Acc: {train_acc:.2f}% '
...               f'| Valid Acc: {valid_acc:.2f}%')
...
...     return epoch_loss, epoch_train_acc, epoch_valid_acc
```

On a high level, the `train()` function iterates over multiple epochs, and in each epoch, it used the previously defined `minibatch_generator()` function to iterate over the whole training set in mini-batches for stochastic gradient descent training. Inside the mini-batch generator `for` loop, we obtain the outputs from the model, `a_h` and `a_out`, via its `.forward()` method. Then, we compute the loss gradients via the model's `.backward()` method—the theory will be explained in a later section. Using the loss gradients, we update the weights by adding the negative gradient multiplied by the learning rate. This is the same concept that we discussed earlier for Adaline. For example, to update the model weights of the hidden layer, we defined the following line:

```
model.weight_h -= learning_rate * d_loss__d_w_h
```

For a single weight, w_j, this corresponds to the following partial derivative-based update:

$$w_j := w_j - \eta \frac{\partial L}{\partial w_j}$$

Finally, the last portion of the previous code computes the losses and prediction accuracies on the training and test sets to track the training progress.

Let's now execute this function to train our model for 50 epochs, which may take a few minutes to finish:

```
>>> np.random.seed(123) # for the training set shuffling
>>> epoch_loss, epoch_train_acc, epoch_valid_acc = train(
...     model, X_train, y_train, X_valid, y_valid,
...     num_epochs=50, learning_rate=0.1)
```

During training, we should see the following output:

```
Epoch: 001/050 | Train MSE: 0.05 | Train Acc: 76.17% | Valid Acc: 76.02%
Epoch: 002/050 | Train MSE: 0.03 | Train Acc: 85.46% | Valid Acc: 84.94%
Epoch: 003/050 | Train MSE: 0.02 | Train Acc: 87.89% | Valid Acc: 87.64%
Epoch: 004/050 | Train MSE: 0.02 | Train Acc: 89.36% | Valid Acc: 89.38%
Epoch: 005/050 | Train MSE: 0.02 | Train Acc: 90.21% | Valid Acc: 90.16%
...
Epoch: 048/050 | Train MSE: 0.01 | Train Acc: 95.57% | Valid Acc: 94.58%
Epoch: 049/050 | Train MSE: 0.01 | Train Acc: 95.55% | Valid Acc: 94.54%
Epoch: 050/050 | Train MSE: 0.01 | Train Acc: 95.59% | Valid Acc: 94.74%
```

The reason why we print all this output is that, in NN training, it is really useful to compare training and validation accuracy. This helps us judge whether the network model performs well, given the architecture and hyperparameters. For example, if we observe a low training and validation accuracy, there is likely an issue with the training dataset, or the hyperparameters' settings are not ideal.

In general, training (deep) NNs is relatively expensive compared with the other models we've discussed so far. Thus, we want to stop it early in certain circumstances and start over with different hyperparameter settings. On the other hand, if we find that it increasingly tends to overfit the training data (noticeable by an increasing gap between training and validation dataset performance), we may want to stop the training early, as well.

In the next subsection, we will discuss the performance of our NN model in more detail.

Evaluating the neural network performance

Before we discuss backpropagation, the training procedure of NNs, in more detail in the next section, let's look at the performance of the model that we trained in the previous subsection.

In `train()`, we collected the training loss and the training and validation accuracy for each epoch so that we can visualize the results using Matplotlib. Let's look at the training MSE loss first:

```
>>> plt.plot(range(len(epoch_loss)), epoch_loss)
>>> plt.ylabel('Mean squared error')
>>> plt.xlabel('Epoch')
>>> plt.show()
```

The preceding code plots the loss over the 50 epochs, as shown in *Figure 11.7*:

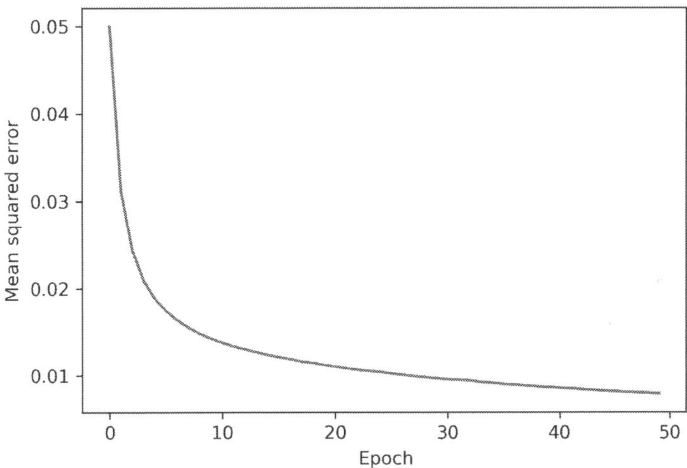

Figure 11.7: A plot of the MSE by the number of training epochs

As we can see, the loss decreased substantially during the first 10 epochs and seems to slowly converge in the last 10 epochs. However, the small slope between epoch 40 and epoch 50 indicates that the loss would further decrease with training over additional epochs.

Next, let's take a look at the training and validation accuracy:

```
>>> plt.plot(range(len(epoch_train_acc)), epoch_train_acc,
...          label='Training')
>>> plt.plot(range(len(epoch_valid_acc)), epoch_valid_acc,
...          label='Validation')
>>> plt.ylabel('Accuracy')
>>> plt.xlabel('Epochs')
>>> plt.legend(loc='lower right')
>>> plt.show()
```

The preceding code examples plot those accuracy values over the 50 training epochs, as shown in *Figure 11.8*:

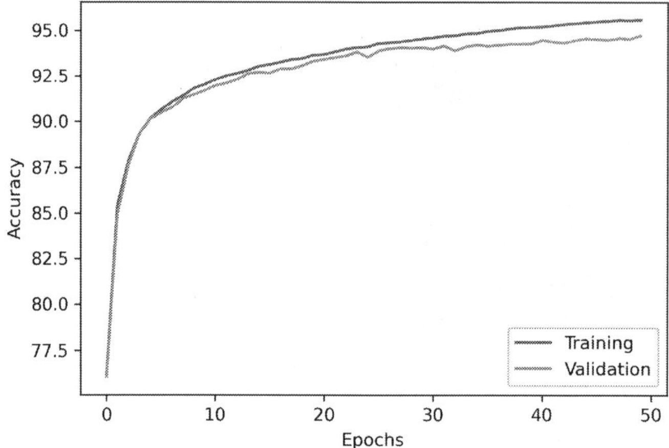

Figure 11.8: Classification accuracy by the number of training epochs

The plot reveals that the gap between training and validation accuracy increases as we train for more epochs. At approximately the 25th epoch, the training and validation accuracy values are almost equal, and then, the network starts to slightly overfit the training data.

Reducing overfitting

One way to decrease the effect of overfitting is to increase the regularization strength via L2 regularization, which we introduced in *Chapter 3, A Tour of Machine Learning Classifiers Using Scikit-Learn*. Another useful technique for tackling overfitting in NNs is dropout, which will be covered in *Chapter 14, Classifying Images with Deep Convolutional Neural Networks*.

Finally, let's evaluate the generalization performance of the model by calculating the prediction accuracy on the test dataset:

```
>>> test_mse, test_acc = compute_mse_and_acc(model, X_test, y_test)
>>> print(f'Test accuracy: {test_acc*100:.2f}%')
Test accuracy: 94.51%
```

We can see that the test accuracy is very close to the validation set accuracy corresponding to the last epoch (94.74%), which we reported during the training in the last subsection. Moreover, the respective training accuracy is only minimally higher at 95.59%, reaffirming that our model only slightly overfits the training data.

To further fine-tune the model, we could change the number of hidden units, the learning rate, or use various other tricks that have been developed over the years but are beyond the scope of this book. In *Chapter 14, Classifying Images with Deep Convolutional Neural Networks*, you will learn about a different NN architecture that is known for its good performance on image datasets.

Also, the chapter will introduce additional performance-enhancing tricks such as adaptive learning rates, more sophisticated SGD-based optimization algorithms, batch normalization, and dropout.

Other common tricks that are beyond the scope of the following chapters include:

- Adding skip-connections, which are the main contribution of residual NNs (*Deep residual learning for image recognition* by *K. He, X. Zhang, S. Ren,* and *J. Sun, Proceedings of the IEEE Conference on Computer Vision and Pattern Recognition*, pp. 770-778, 2016)
- Using learning rate schedulers that change the learning rate during training (*Cyclical learning rates for training neural networks* by *L.N. Smith, 2017 IEEE Winter Conference on Applications of Computer Vision (WACV)*, pp. 464-472, 2017)
- Attaching loss functions to earlier layers in the networks as it's being done in the popular Inception v3 architecture (*Rethinking the Inception architecture for computer vision by C. Szegedy, V. Vanhoucke, S. Ioffe, J. Shlens,* and *Z. Wojna, Proceedings of the IEEE Conference on Computer Vision and Pattern Recognition*, pp. 2818-2826, 2016)

Lastly, let's take a look at some of the images that our MLP struggles with by extracting and plotting the first 25 misclassified samples from the test set:

```
>>> X_test_subset = X_test[:1000, :]
>>> y_test_subset = y_test[:1000]
>>> _, probas = model.forward(X_test_subset)
>>> test_pred = np.argmax(probas, axis=1)
>>> misclassified_images = \
...      X_test_subset[y_test_subset != test_pred][:25]
>>> misclassified_labels = test_pred[y_test_subset != test_pred][:25]
>>> correct_labels = y_test_subset[y_test_subset != test_pred][:25]

>>> fig, ax = plt.subplots(nrows=5, ncols=5,
...                        sharex=True, sharey=True,
...                        figsize=(8, 8))
>>> ax = ax.flatten()
>>> for i in range(25):
...     img = misclassified_images[i].reshape(28, 28)
...     ax[i].imshow(img, cmap='Greys', interpolation='nearest')
...     ax[i].set_title(f'{i+1}) '
...                     f'True: {correct_labels[i]}\n'
...                     f' Predicted: {misclassified_labels[i]}')

>>> ax[0].set_xticks([])
>>> ax[0].set_yticks([])
>>> plt.tight_layout()
>>> plt.show()
```

We should now see a 5×5 subplot matrix where the first number in the subtitles indicates the plot index, the second number represents the true class label (`True`), and the third number stands for the predicted class label (`Predicted`):

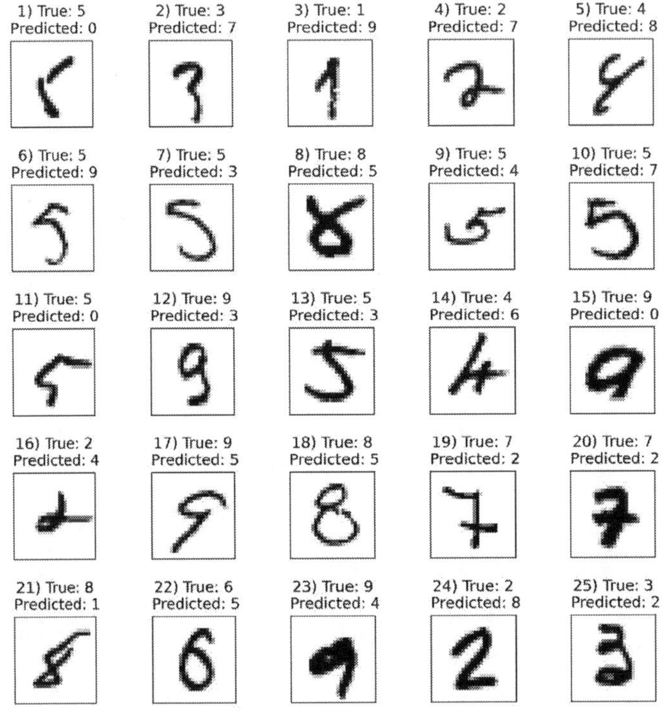

Figure 11.9: Handwritten digits that the model fails to classify correctly

As we can see in *Figure 11.9*, among others, the network finds 7s challenging when they include a horizontal line as in examples 19 and 20. Looking back at an earlier figure in this chapter where we plotted different training examples of the number 7, we can hypothesize that the handwritten digit 7 with a horizontal line is underrepresented in our dataset and is often misclassified.

Training an artificial neural network

Now that we have seen an NN in action and have gained a basic understanding of how it works by looking over the code, let's dig a little bit deeper into some of the concepts, such as the loss computation and the backpropagation algorithm that we implemented to learn the model parameters.

Computing the loss function

As mentioned previously, we used an MSE loss (as in Adaline) to train the multilayer NN as it makes the derivation of the gradients a bit easier to follow. In later chapters, we will discuss other loss functions, such as the multi-category cross-entropy loss (a generalization of the binary logistic regression loss), which is a more common choice for training NN classifiers.

In the previous section, we implemented an MLP for multiclass classification that returns an output vector of t elements that we need to compare to the t×1 dimensional target vector in the one-hot encoding representation. If we predict the class label of an input image with class label 2, using this MLP, the activation of the third layer and the target may look like this:

$$a^{(out)} = \begin{bmatrix} 0.1 \\ 0.9 \\ \vdots \\ 0.3 \end{bmatrix}, \quad y = \begin{bmatrix} 0 \\ 1 \\ \vdots \\ 0 \end{bmatrix}$$

Thus, our MSE loss either has to sum or average over the t activation units in our network in addition to averaging over the n examples in the dataset or mini-batch:

$$L(\boldsymbol{W}, \boldsymbol{b}) = \frac{1}{n} \sum_{i=1}^{n} \frac{1}{t} \sum_{j=1}^{t} \left(y_j^{[i]} - a_j^{(out)[i]} \right)^2$$

Here, again, the superscript $[i]$ is the index of a particular example in our training dataset.

Remember that our goal is to minimize the loss function $L(\boldsymbol{W})$; thus, we need to calculate the partial derivative of the parameters $\boldsymbol{W}$ with respect to each weight for every layer in the network:

$$\frac{\partial}{\partial w_{j,l}^{(l)}} = L(\boldsymbol{W}, \boldsymbol{b})$$

In the next section, we will talk about the backpropagation algorithm, which allows us to calculate those partial derivatives to minimize the loss function.

Note that $\boldsymbol{W}$ consists of multiple matrices. In an MLP with one hidden layer, we have the weight matrix, $\boldsymbol{W}^{(h)}$, which connects the input to the hidden layer, and $\boldsymbol{W}^{(out)}$, which connects the hidden layer to the output layer. A visualization of the three-dimensional tensor $\boldsymbol{W}$ is provided in *Figure 11.10*:

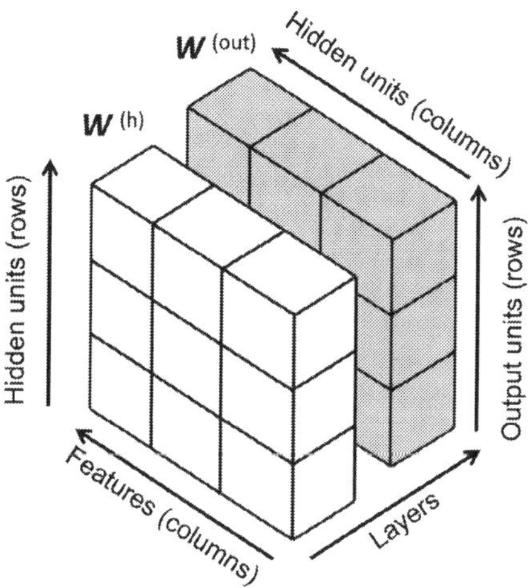

Figure 11.10: A visualization of a three-dimensional tensor

In this simplified figure, it may seem that both $W^{(h)}$ and $W^{(out)}$ have the same number of rows and columns, which is typically not the case unless we initialize an MLP with the same number of hidden units, output units, and input features.

If this sounds confusing, stay tuned for the next section, where we will discuss the dimensionality of $W^{(h)}$ and $W^{(out)}$ in more detail in the context of the backpropagation algorithm. Also, you are encouraged to read through the code of `NeuralNetMLP` again, which is annotated with helpful comments about the dimensionality of the different matrices and vector transformations.

Developing your understanding of backpropagation

Although backpropagation was introduced to the neural network community more than 30 years ago (*Learning representations by backpropagating errors*, by *D.E. Rumelhart*, *G.E. Hinton*, and *R.J. Williams*, *Nature*, 323: 6088, pages 533–536, 1986), it remains one of the most widely used algorithms for training artificial NNs very efficiently. If you are interested in additional references regarding the history of backpropagation, Juergen Schmidhuber wrote a nice survey article, *Who Invented Backpropagation?*, which you can find online at `http://people.idsia.ch/~juergen/who-invented-backpropagation.html`.

This section will provide both a short, clear summary and the bigger picture of how this fascinating algorithm works before we dive into more mathematical details. In essence, we can think of backpropagation as a very computationally efficient approach to compute the partial derivatives of a complex, non-convex loss function in multilayer NNs. Here, our goal is to use those derivatives to learn the weight coefficients for parameterizing such a multilayer artificial NN. The challenge in the parameterization of NNs is that we are typically dealing with a very large number of model parameters in a high-dimensional feature space. In contrast to loss functions of single-layer NNs such as Adaline or logistic regression, which we have seen in previous chapters, the error surface of an NN loss function is not convex or smooth with respect to the parameters. There are many bumps in this high-dimensional loss surface (local minima) that we have to overcome in order to find the global minimum of the loss function.

You may recall the concept of the chain rule from your introductory calculus classes. The chain rule is an approach to compute the derivative of a complex, nested function, such as $f(g(x))$, as follows:

$$\frac{d}{dx}[f(g(x))] = \frac{df}{dg} \cdot \frac{dg}{dx}$$

Similarly, we can use the chain rule for an arbitrarily long function composition. For example, let's assume that we have five different functions, $f(x)$, $g(x)$, $h(x)$, $u(x)$, and $v(x)$, and let F be the function composition: $F(x) = f(g(h(u(v(x)))))$. Applying the chain rule, we can compute the derivative of this function as follows:

$$\frac{dF}{dx} = \frac{d}{dx}F(x) = \frac{d}{dx}f(g(h(u(v(x))))) = \frac{df}{dg} \cdot \frac{dg}{dh} \cdot \frac{dh}{du} \cdot \frac{du}{dv} \cdot \frac{dv}{dx}$$

In the context of computer algebra, a set of techniques, known as **automatic differentiation**, has been developed to solve such problems very efficiently. If you are interested in learning more about automatic differentiation in machine learning applications, read A.G. Baydin and B.A. Pearlmutter's article, *Automatic Differentiation of Algorithms for Machine Learning*, arXiv preprint arXiv:1404.7456, 2014, which is freely available on arXiv at `http://arxiv.org/pdf/1404.7456.pdf`.

Automatic differentiation comes with two modes, the forward and reverse modes; backpropagation is simply a special case of reverse-mode automatic differentiation. The key point is that applying the chain rule in forward mode could be quite expensive since we would have to multiply large matrices for each layer (Jacobians) that we would eventually multiply by a vector to obtain the output.

The trick of reverse mode is that we traverse the chain rule from right to left. We multiply a matrix by a vector, which yields another vector that is multiplied by the next matrix, and so on. Matrix-vector multiplication is computationally much cheaper than matrix-matrix multiplication, which is why backpropagation is one of the most popular algorithms used in NN training.

A basic calculus refresher

To fully understand backpropagation, we need to borrow certain concepts from differential calculus, which is outside the scope of this book. However, you can refer to a review chapter of the most fundamental concepts, which you might find useful in this context. It discusses function derivatives, partial derivatives, gradients, and the Jacobian. This text is freely accessible at `https://sebastianraschka.com/pdf/books/dlb/appendix_d_calculus.pdf`. If you are unfamiliar with calculus or need a brief refresher, consider reading this text as an additional supporting resource before reading the next section.

Training neural networks via backpropagation

In this section, we will go through the math of backpropagation to understand how you can learn the weights in an NN very efficiently. Depending on how comfortable you are with mathematical representations, the following equations may seem relatively complicated at first.

In a previous section, we saw how to calculate the loss as the difference between the activation of the last layer and the target class label. Now, we will see how the backpropagation algorithm works to update the weights in our MLP model from a mathematical perspective, which we implemented in the `.backward()` method of the `NeuralNetMLP()` class. As we recall from the beginning of this chapter, we first need to apply forward propagation to obtain the activation of the output layer, which we formulated as follows:

$$\boldsymbol{Z}^{(h)} = \boldsymbol{X}^{(in)}\boldsymbol{W}^{(h)T} + \boldsymbol{b}^{(h)} \quad \text{(net input of the hidden layer)}$$

$$\boldsymbol{A}^{(h)} = \sigma\left(\boldsymbol{Z}^{(h)}\right) \quad \text{(activation of the hidden layer)}$$

$$\boldsymbol{Z}^{(out)} = \boldsymbol{A}^{(h)}\boldsymbol{W}^{(out)T} + \boldsymbol{b}^{(out)} \quad \text{(net input of the output layer)}$$

$$\boldsymbol{A}^{(out)} = \sigma\left(\boldsymbol{Z}^{(out)}\right) \quad \text{(activation of the output layer)}$$

Concisely, we just forward-propagate the input features through the connections in the network, as shown by the arrows in *Figure 11.11* for a network with two input features, three hidden nodes, and two output nodes:

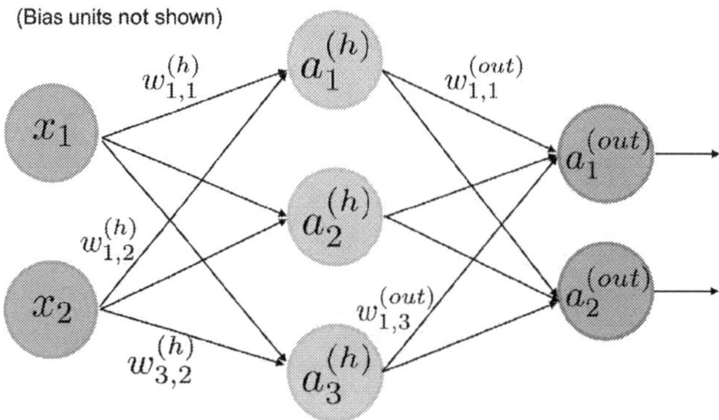

Figure 11.11: Forward-propagating the input features of an NN

In backpropagation, we propagate the error from right to left. We can think of this as an application of the chain rule to the computation of the forward pass to compute the gradient of the loss with respect to the model weights (and bias units). For simplicity, we will illustrate this process for the partial derivative used to update the first weight in the weight matrix of the output layer. The paths of the computation we backpropagate are highlighted via the bold arrows below:

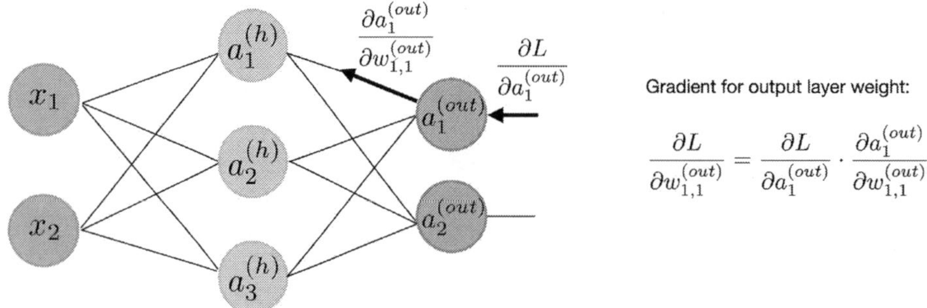

Figure 11.12: Backpropagating the error of an NN

If we include the net inputs z explicitly, the partial derivative computation shown in the previous figure expands as follows:

$$\frac{\partial L}{\partial w_{1,1}^{(out)}} = \frac{\partial L}{\partial a_1^{(out)}} \cdot \frac{\partial a_1^{(out)}}{\partial z_1^{(out)}} \cdot \frac{\partial z_1^{(out)}}{\partial w_{1,1}^{(out)}}$$

To compute this partial derivative, which is used to update $w_{1,1}^{(out)}$, we can compute the three individual partial derivative terms and multiply the results. For simplicity, we will omit averaging over the individual examples in the mini-batch, so we drop the $\frac{1}{n}\sum_{i=1}^{n}$ averaging term from the following equations.

Let's start with $\frac{\partial L}{\partial a_1^{(out)}}$, which is the partial derivative of the MSE loss (which simplifies to the squared error if we omit the mini-batch dimension) with respect to the predicted output score of the first output node:

$$\frac{\partial L}{\partial a_1^{(out)}} = \frac{\partial}{\partial a_1^{(out)}} \left(y_1 - a_1^{(out)}\right)^2 = 2\left(a_1^{(out)} - y\right)$$

The next term is the derivative of the logistic sigmoid activation function that we used in the output layer:

$$\frac{\partial a_1^{(out)}}{\partial z_1^{(out)}} = \frac{\partial}{\partial z_1^{(out)}} \frac{1}{1 + e^{z_1^{(out)}}} = \quad \dots \quad = \left(\frac{1}{1 + e^{z_1^{(out)}}}\right)\left(1 - \frac{1}{1 + e^{z_1^{(out)}}}\right)$$

$$= a_1^{(out)}\left(1 - a_1^{(out)}\right)$$

Lastly, we compute the derivative of the net input with respect to the weight:

$$\frac{\partial z_1^{(out)}}{\partial w_{1,1}^{(out)}} = \frac{\partial}{\partial w_{1,1}^{(out)}} a_1^{(h)} w_{1,1}^{(out)} + b_1^{(out)} = a_1^{(h)}$$

Putting all of it together, we get the following:

$$\frac{\partial L}{\partial w_{1,1}^{(out)}} = \frac{\partial L}{\partial a_1^{(out)}} \cdot \frac{\partial a_1^{(out)}}{\partial z_1^{(out)}} \cdot \frac{\partial z_1^{(out)}}{\partial w_{1,1}^{(out)}} = 2\left(a_1^{(out)} - y\right) \cdot a_1^{(out)}\left(1 - a_1^{(out)}\right) \cdot a_1^{(h)}$$

We then use this value to update the weight via the familiar stochastic gradient descent update with a learning rate of η:

$$w_{1,1}^{(out)} := w_{1,1}^{(out)} - \eta \frac{\partial L}{\partial w_{1,1}^{(out)}}$$

In our code implementation of `NeuralNetMLP()`, we implemented the computation $\frac{\partial L}{\partial w_{1,1}^{(out)}}$ in vectorized form in the `.backward()` method as follows:

```
        # Part 1: dLoss/dOutWeights
        ## = dLoss/dOutAct * dOutAct/dOutNet * dOutNet/dOutWeight
        ## where DeltaOut = dLoss/dOutAct * dOutAct/dOutNet for convenient re-use

        # input/output dim: [n_examples, n_classes]
        d_loss__d_a_out = 2.*(a_out - y_onehot) / y.shape[0]

        # input/output dim: [n_examples, n_classes]
        d_a_out__d_z_out = a_out * (1. - a_out) # sigmoid derivative

        # output dim: [n_examples, n_classes]
        delta_out = d_loss__d_a_out * d_a_out__d_z_out # "delta (rule)
                                                       # placeholder"

        # gradient for output weights

        # [n_examples, n_hidden]
```

```
d_z_out__dw_out = a_h

# input dim: [n_classes, n_examples] dot [n_examples, n_hidden]
# output dim: [n_classes, n_hidden]
d_loss__dw_out = np.dot(delta_out.T, d_z_out__dw_out)
d_loss__db_out = np.sum(delta_out, axis=0)
```

As annotated in the code snippet above, we created the following "delta" placeholder variable:

$$\delta_1^{(out)} = \frac{\partial L}{\partial a_1^{(out)}} \cdot \frac{\partial a_1^{(out)}}{\partial z_1^{(out)}}$$

This is because $\delta^{(out)}$ terms are involved in computing the partial derivatives (or gradients) of the hidden layer weights as well; hence, we can reuse $\delta^{(out)}$.

Speaking of hidden layer weights, *Figure 11.13* illustrates how to compute the partial derivative of the loss with respect to the first weight of the hidden layer:

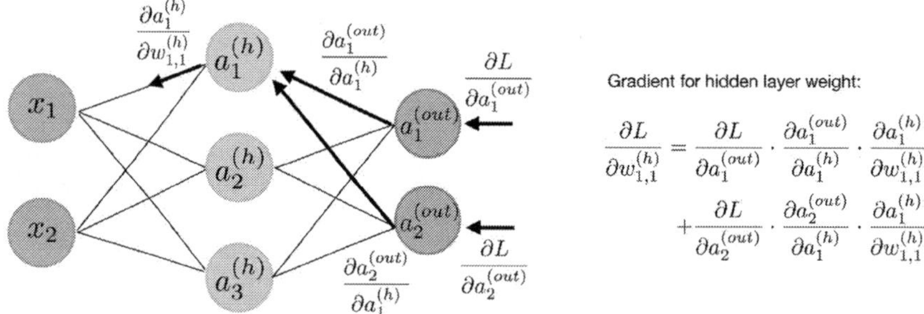

Figure 11.13: Computing the partial derivatives of the loss with respect to the first hidden layer weight

It is important to highlight that since the weight $w_{1,1}^{(h)}$ is connected to both output nodes, we have to use the *multi-variable* chain rule to sum the two paths highlighted with bold arrows. As before, we can expand it to include the net inputs z and then solve the individual terms:

$$\frac{\partial L}{\partial w_{1,1}^{(out)}} = \frac{\partial L}{\partial a_1^{(out)}} \cdot \frac{\partial a_1^{(out)}}{\partial z_1^{(out)}} \cdot \frac{\partial z_1^{(out)}}{\partial a_1^{(h)}} \cdot \frac{\partial a_1^{(h)}}{\partial z_1^{(h)}} \cdot \frac{\partial z_1^{(h)}}{\partial w_{1,1}^{(h)}}$$

$$+ \frac{\partial L}{\partial a_2^{(out)}} \cdot \frac{\partial a_2^{(out)}}{\partial z_2^{(out)}} \cdot \frac{\partial z_2^{(out)}}{\partial a_1^{(h)}} \cdot \frac{\partial a_1^{(h)}}{\partial z_1^{(h)}} \cdot \frac{\partial z_1^{(h)}}{\partial w_{1,1}^{(h)}}$$

Notice that if we reuse $\delta^{(out)}$ computed previously, this equation can be simplified as follows:

$$\frac{\partial L}{\partial w_{1,1}^{(h)}} = \delta_1^{(out)} \cdot \frac{\partial z_1^{(out)}}{\partial a_1^{(h)}} \cdot \frac{\partial a_1^{(h)}}{\partial z_1^{(h)}} \cdot \frac{\partial z_1^{(h)}}{\partial w_{1,1}^{(h)}}$$

$$+ \delta_2^{(out)} \cdot \frac{\partial z_2^{(out)}}{\partial a_1^{(h)}} \cdot \frac{\partial a_1^{(h)}}{\partial z_1^{(h)}} \cdot \frac{\partial z_1^{(h)}}{\partial w_{1,1}^{(h)}}$$

The preceding terms can be individually solved relatively easily, as we have done previously, because there are no new derivatives involved. For example, $\frac{\partial a_1^{(h)}}{\partial z_1^{(h)}}$ is the derivative of the sigmoid activation, that is, $a_1^{(h)}(1 - a_1^{(h)})$, and so forth. We'll leave solving the individual parts as an optional exercise for you.

About convergence in neural networks

You might be wondering why we did not use regular gradient descent but instead used mini-batch learning to train our NN for the handwritten digit classification earlier. You may recall our discussion on SGD that we used to implement online learning. In online learning, we compute the gradient based on a single training example ($k = 1$) at a time to perform the weight update. Although this is a stochastic approach, it often leads to very accurate solutions with a much faster convergence than regular gradient descent. Mini-batch learning is a special form of SGD where we compute the gradient based on a subset k of the n training examples with $1 < k < n$. Mini-batch learning has an advantage over online learning in that we can make use of our vectorized implementations to improve computational efficiency. However, we can update the weights much faster than in regular gradient descent. Intuitively, you can think of mini-batch learning as predicting the voter turnout of a presidential election from a poll by asking only a representative subset of the population rather than asking the entire population (which would be equal to running the actual election).

Multilayer NNs are much harder to train than simpler algorithms such as Adaline, logistic regression, or support vector machines. In multilayer NNs, we typically have hundreds, thousands, or even billions of weights that we need to optimize. Unfortunately, the output function has a rough surface, and the optimization algorithm can easily become trapped in local minima, as shown in *Figure 11.14*:

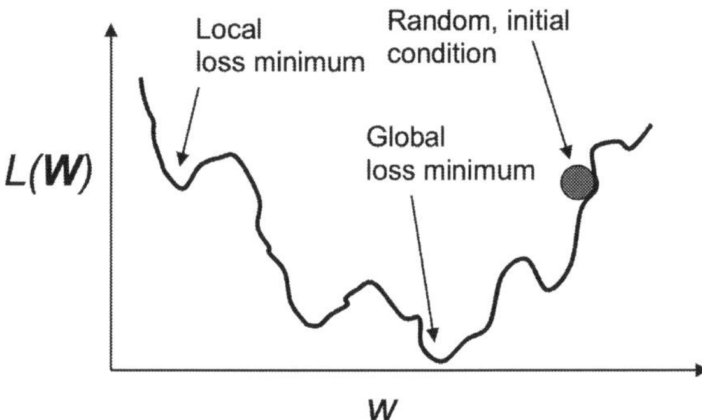

Figure 11.14: Optimization algorithms can become trapped in local minima

Note that this representation is extremely simplified since our NN has many dimensions; it makes it impossible to visualize the actual loss surface for the human eye. Here, we only show the loss surface for a single weight on the x axis. However, the main message is that we do not want our algorithm to get trapped in local minima. By increasing the learning rate, we can more readily escape such local minima. On the other hand, we also increase the chance of overshooting the global optimum if the learning rate is too large. Since we initialize the weights randomly, we start with a solution to the optimization problem that is typically hopelessly wrong.

A few last words about the neural network implementation

You may be wondering why we went through all of this theory just to implement a simple multilayer artificial network that can classify handwritten digits instead of using an open source Python machine learning library. In fact, we will introduce more complex NN models in the next chapters, which we will train using the open source PyTorch library (`https://pytorch.org`).

Although the from-scratch implementation in this chapter seems a bit tedious at first, it was a good exercise for understanding the basics behind backpropagation and NN training. A basic understanding of algorithms is crucial for applying machine learning techniques appropriately and successfully.

Now that you have learned how feedforward NNs work, we are ready to explore more sophisticated DNNs using PyTorch, which allows us to construct NNs more efficiently, as we will see in *Chapter 12, Parallelizing Neural Network Training with PyTorch*.

PyTorch, which was originally released in September 2016, has gained a lot of popularity among machine learning researchers, who use it to construct DNNs because of its ability to optimize mathematical expressions for computations on multidimensional arrays utilizing **graphics processing units** (**GPUs**).

Lastly, we should note that scikit-learn also includes a basic MLP implementation, `MLPClassifier`, which you can find at `https://scikit-learn.org/stable/modules/generated/sklearn.neural_network.MLPClassifier.html`. While this implementation is great and very convenient for training basic MLPs, we strongly recommend specialized deep learning libraries, such as PyTorch, for implementing and training multilayer NNs.

Summary

In this chapter, you have learned the basic concepts behind multilayer artificial NNs, which are currently the hottest topic in machine learning research. In *Chapter 2, Training Simple Machine Learning Algorithms for Classification*, we started our journey with simple single-layer NN structures and now we have connected multiple neurons to a powerful NN architecture to solve complex problems such as handwritten digit recognition. We demystified the popular backpropagation algorithm, which is one of the building blocks of many NN models that are used in deep learning. After learning about the backpropagation algorithm in this chapter, we are well equipped for exploring more complex DNN architectures. In the remaining chapters, we will cover more advanced deep learning concepts and PyTorch, an open source library that allows us to implement and train multilayer NNs more efficiently.

Join our book's Discord space

Join our Discord community to meet like-minded people and learn alongside more than 2000 members at:

`https://packt.link/MLwPyTorch`

12

Parallelizing Neural Network Training with PyTorch

In this chapter, we will move on from the mathematical foundations of machine learning and deep learning to focus on PyTorch. PyTorch is one of the most popular deep learning libraries currently available, and it lets us implement **neural networks** (**NNs**) much more efficiently than any of our previous NumPy implementations. In this chapter, we will start using PyTorch and see how it brings significant benefits to training performance.

This chapter will begin the next stage of our journey into machine learning and deep learning, and we will explore the following topics:

- How PyTorch improves training performance
- Working with PyTorch's `Dataset` and `DataLoader` to build input pipelines and enable efficient model training
- Working with PyTorch to write optimized machine learning code
- Using the `torch.nn` module to implement common deep learning architectures conveniently
- Choosing activation functions for artificial NNs

PyTorch and training performance

PyTorch can speed up our machine learning tasks significantly. To understand how it can do this, let's begin by discussing some of the performance challenges we typically run into when we execute expensive calculations on our hardware. Then, we will take a high-level look at what PyTorch is and what our learning approach will be in this chapter.

Performance challenges

The performance of computer processors has, of course, been continuously improving in recent years. That allows us to train more powerful and complex learning systems, which means that we can improve the predictive performance of our machine learning models. Even the cheapest desktop computer hardware that's available right now comes with processing units that have multiple cores.

In the previous chapters, we saw that many functions in scikit-learn allow us to spread those computations over multiple processing units. However, by default, Python is limited to execution on one core due to the **global interpreter lock** (**GIL**). So, although we indeed take advantage of Python's multiprocessing library to distribute our computations over multiple cores, we still have to consider that the most advanced desktop hardware rarely comes with more than 8 or 16 such cores.

You will recall from *Chapter 11, Implementing a Multilayer Artificial Neural Network from Scratch,* that we implemented a very simple **multilayer perceptron** (**MLP**) with only one hidden layer consisting of 100 units. We had to optimize approximately 80,000 weight parameters ([784*100 + 100] + [100 * 10] + 10 = 79,510) for a very simple image classification task. The images in MNIST are rather small (28×28), and we can only imagine the explosion in the number of parameters if we wanted to add additional hidden layers or work with images that have higher pixel densities. Such a task would quickly become unfeasible for a single processing unit. The question then becomes, how can we tackle such problems more effectively?

The obvious solution to this problem is to use **graphics processing units** (**GPUs**), which are real workhorses. You can think of a graphics card as a small computer cluster inside your machine. Another advantage is that modern GPUs are great value compared to the state-of-the-art **central processing units** (**CPUs**), as you can see in the following overview:

Specifications	Intel® Core™ i9-11900KB Processor	NVIDIA GeForce® RTX™ 3080 Ti
Base Clock Frequency	3.3 GHz	1.37 GHz
Cores	16 (32 threads)	10240
Memory Bandwidth	45.8 GB/s	912.1 GB/s
Floating-Point Calculations	742 GFLOPS	34.10 TFLOPS
Cost	~ $540.00	~ $1200.00

Figure 12.1: Comparison of a state-of-the-art CPU and GPU

The sources for the information in *Figure 12.1* are the following websites (date accessed: July 2021):

- `https://ark.intel.com/content/www/us/en/ark/products/215570/intel-core-i9-11900kb-processor-24m-cache-up-to-4-90-ghz.html`
- `https://www.nvidia.com/en-us/geforce/graphics-cards/30-series/rtx-3080-3080ti/`

At 2.2 times the price of a modern CPU, we can get a GPU that has 640 times more cores and is capable of around 46 times more floating-point calculations per second. So, what is holding us back from utilizing GPUs for our machine learning tasks? The challenge is that writing code to target GPUs is not as simple as executing Python code in our interpreter. There are special packages, such as CUDA and OpenCL, that allow us to target the GPU. However, writing code in CUDA or OpenCL is probably not the most convenient way to implement and run machine learning algorithms. The good news is that this is what PyTorch was developed for!

What is PyTorch?

PyTorch is a scalable and multiplatform programming interface for implementing and running machine learning algorithms, including convenience wrappers for deep learning. PyTorch was primarily developed by the researchers and engineers from the **Facebook AI Research** (**FAIR**) lab. Its development also involves many contributions from the community. PyTorch was initially released in September 2016 and is free and open source under the modified BSD license. Many machine learning researchers and practitioners from academia and industry have adapted PyTorch to develop deep learning solutions, such as Tesla Autopilot, Uber's Pyro, and Hugging Face's Transformers (`https://pytorch.org/ecosystem/`).

To improve the performance of training machine learning models, PyTorch allows execution on CPUs, GPUs, and XLA devices such as TPUs. However, its greatest performance capabilities can be discovered when using GPUs and XLA devices. PyTorch supports CUDA-enabled and ROCm GPUs officially. PyTorch's development is based on the Torch library (`www.torch.ch`). As its name implies, the Python interface is the primary development focus of PyTorch.

PyTorch is built around a computation graph composed of a set of nodes. Each node represents an operation that may have zero or more inputs or outputs. PyTorch provides an imperative programming environment that evaluates operations, executes computation, and returns concrete values immediately. Hence, the computation graph in PyTorch is defined implicitly, rather than constructed in advance and executed after.

Mathematically, tensors can be understood as a generalization of scalars, vectors, matrices, and so on. More concretely, a scalar can be defined as a rank-0 tensor, a vector can be defined as a rank-1 tensor, a matrix can be defined as a rank-2 tensor, and matrices stacked in a third dimension can be defined as rank-3 tensors. Tensors in PyTorch are similar to NumPy's arrays, except that tensors are optimized for automatic differentiation and can run on GPUs.

To make the concept of a tensor clearer, consider *Figure 12.2*, which represents tensors of ranks 0 and 1 in the first row, and tensors of ranks 2 and 3 in the second row:

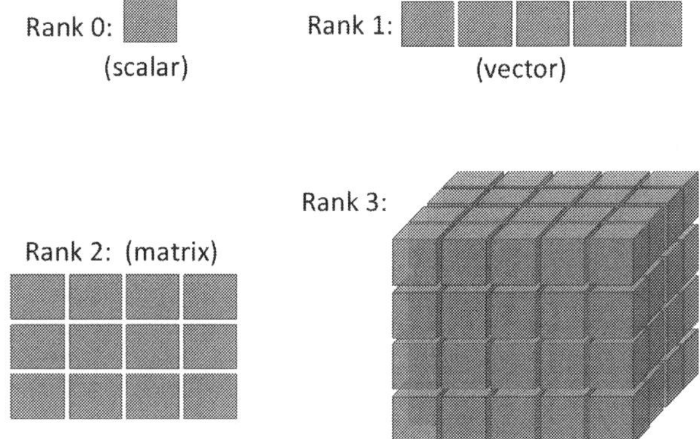

Figure 12.2: Different types of tensor in PyTorch

Now that we know what PyTorch is, let's see how to use it.

How we will learn PyTorch

First, we are going to cover PyTorch's programming model, in particular, creating and manipulating tensors. Then, we will see how to load data and utilize the `torch.utils.data` module, which will allow us to iterate through a dataset efficiently. In addition, we will discuss the existing, ready-to-use datasets in the `torch.utils.data.Dataset` submodule and learn how to use them.

After learning about these basics, the PyTorch neural network `torch.nn` module will be introduced. Then, we will move forward to building machine learning models, learn how to compose and train the models, and learn how to save the trained models on disk for future evaluation.

First steps with PyTorch

In this section, we will take our first steps in using the low-level PyTorch API. After installing PyTorch, we will cover how to create tensors in PyTorch and different ways of manipulating them, such as changing their shape, data type, and so on.

Installing PyTorch

To install PyTorch, we recommend consulting the latest instructions on the official `https://pytorch.org` website. Below, we will outline the basic steps that will work on most systems.

Depending on how your system is set up, you can typically just use Python's `pip` installer and install PyTorch from PyPI by executing the following from your terminal:

```
pip install torch torchvision
```

This will install the latest *stable* version, which is 1.9.0 at the time of writing. To install the 1.9.0 version, which is guaranteed to be compatible with the following code examples, you can modify the preceding command as follows:

```
pip install torch==1.9.0 torchvision==0.10.0
```

If you want to use GPUs (recommended), you need a compatible NVIDIA graphics card that supports CUDA and cuDNN. If your machine satisfies these requirements, you can install PyTorch with GPU support, as follows:

```
pip install torch==1.9.0+cu111 torchvision==0.10.0+cu111 -f https://download.
pytorch.org/whl/torch_stable.html
```

for CUDA 11.1 or:

```
pip install torch==1.9.0 torchvision==0.10.0\  -f https://download.pytorch.org/
whl/torch_stable.html
```

for CUDA 10.2 as of the time of writing.

As macOS binaries don't support CUDA, you can install from source: `https://pytorch.org/get-started/locally/#mac-from-source`.

For more information about the installation and setup process, please see the official recommendations at `https://pytorch.org/get-started/locally/`.

Note that PyTorch is under active development; therefore, every couple of months, new versions are released with significant changes. You can verify your PyTorch version from your terminal, as follows:

```
python -c 'import torch; print(torch.__version__)'
```

Troubleshooting your installation of PyTorch

If you experience problems with the installation procedure, read more about system- and platform-specific recommendations that are provided at `https://pytorch.org/get-started/locally/`. Note that all the code in this chapter can be run on your CPU; using a GPU is entirely optional but recommended if you want to fully enjoy the benefits of PyTorch. For example, while training some NN models on a CPU could take a week, the same models could be trained in just a few hours on a modern GPU. If you have a graphics card, refer to the installation page to set it up appropriately. In addition, you may find this setup guide helpful, which explains how to install the NVIDIA graphics card drivers, CUDA, and cuDNN on Ubuntu (not required but recommended requirements for running PyTorch on a GPU): `https://sebastianraschka.com/pdf/books/dlb/appendix_h_cloud-computing.pdf`. Furthermore, as you will see in *Chapter 17, Generative Adversarial Networks for Synthesizing New Data*, you can also train your models using a GPU for free via Google Colab.

Creating tensors in PyTorch

Now, let's consider a few different ways of creating tensors, and then see some of their properties and how to manipulate them. Firstly, we can simply create a tensor from a list or a NumPy array using the `torch.tensor` or the `torch.from_numpy` function as follows:

```
>>> import torch
>>> import numpy as np
>>> np.set_printoptions(precision=3)
>>> a = [1, 2, 3]
>>> b = np.array([4, 5, 6], dtype=np.int32)
>>> t_a = torch.tensor(a)
>>> t_b = torch.from_numpy(b)
>>> print(t_a)
>>> print(t_b)
tensor([1, 2, 3])
tensor([4, 5, 6], dtype=torch.int32)
```

This resulted in tensors `t_a` and `t_b`, with their properties, `shape=(3,)` and `dtype=int32`, adopted from their source. Similar to NumPy arrays, we can also see these properties:

```
>>> t_ones = torch.ones(2, 3)
>>> t_ones.shape
torch.Size([2, 3])
>>> print(t_ones)
```

```
tensor([[1., 1., 1.],
        [1., 1., 1.]])
```

Finally, creating a tensor of random values can be done as follows:

```
>>> rand_tensor = torch.rand(2,3)
>>> print(rand_tensor)
tensor([[0.1409, 0.2848, 0.8914],
        [0.9223, 0.2924, 0.7889]])
```

Manipulating the data type and shape of a tensor

Learning ways to manipulate tensors is necessary to make them compatible for input to a model or an operation. In this section, you will learn how to manipulate tensor data types and shapes via several PyTorch functions that cast, reshape, transpose, and squeeze (remove dimensions).

The `torch.to()` function can be used to change the data type of a tensor to a desired type:

```
>>> t_a_new = t_a.to(torch.int64)
>>> print(t_a_new.dtype)
torch.int64
```

See `https://pytorch.org/docs/stable/tensor_attributes.html` for all other data types.

As you will see in upcoming chapters, certain operations require that the input tensors have a certain number of dimensions (that is, rank) associated with a certain number of elements (shape). Thus, we might need to change the shape of a tensor, add a new dimension, or squeeze an unnecessary dimension. PyTorch provides useful functions (or operations) to achieve this, such as `torch.transpose()`, `torch.reshape()`, and `torch.squeeze()`. Let's take a look at some examples:

- Transposing a tensor:

  ```
  >>> t = torch.rand(3, 5)
  >>> t_tr = torch.transpose(t, 0, 1)
  >>> print(t.shape, ' --> ', t_tr.shape)
  torch.Size([3, 5])  -->  torch.Size([5, 3])
  ```

- Reshaping a tensor (for example, from a 1D vector to a 2D array):

  ```
  >>> t = torch.zeros(30)
  >>> t_reshape = t.reshape(5, 6)
  >>> print(t_reshape.shape)
  torch.Size([5, 6])
  ```

- Removing the unnecessary dimensions (dimensions that have size 1, which are not needed):

  ```
  >>> t = torch.zeros(1, 2, 1, 4, 1)
  >>> t_sqz = torch.squeeze(t, 2)
  >>> print(t.shape, ' --> ', t_sqz.shape)
  torch.Size([1, 2, 1, 4, 1])  -->  torch.Size([1, 2, 4, 1])
  ```

Applying mathematical operations to tensors

Applying mathematical operations, in particular linear algebra operations, is necessary for building most machine learning models. In this subsection, we will cover some widely used linear algebra operations, such as element-wise product, matrix multiplication, and computing the norm of a tensor.

First, let's instantiate two random tensors, one with uniform distribution in the range [-1, 1) and the other with a standard normal distribution:

```
>>> torch.manual_seed(1)
>>> t1 = 2 * torch.rand(5, 2) - 1
>>> t2 = torch.normal(mean=0, std=1, size=(5, 2))
```

Note that `torch.rand` returns a tensor filled with random numbers from a uniform distribution in the range of [0, 1).

Notice that `t1` and `t2` have the same shape. Now, to compute the element-wise product of `t1` and `t2`, we can use the following:

```
>>> t3 = torch.multiply(t1, t2)
>>> print(t3)
tensor([[ 0.4426, -0.3114],
        [ 0.0660, -0.5970],
        [ 1.1249,  0.0150],
        [ 0.1569,  0.7107],
        [-0.0451, -0.0352]])
```

To compute the mean, sum, and standard deviation along a certain axis (or axes), we can use `torch.mean()`, `torch.sum()`, and `torch.std()`. For example, the mean of each column in `t1` can be computed as follows:

```
>>> t4 = torch.mean(t1, axis=0)
>>> print(t4)
tensor([-0.1373,  0.2028])
```

The matrix-matrix product between `t1` and `t2` (that is, $t_1 \times t_2^T$, where the superscript T is for transpose) can be computed by using the `torch.matmul()` function as follows:

```
>>> t5 = torch.matmul(t1, torch.transpose(t2, 0, 1))
>>> print(t5)
tensor([[ 0.1312,  0.3860, -0.6267, -1.0096, -0.2943],
        [ 0.1647, -0.5310,  0.2434,  0.8035,  0.1980],
        [-0.3855, -0.4422,  1.1399,  1.5558,  0.4781],
        [ 0.1822, -0.5771,  0.2585,  0.8676,  0.2132],
        [ 0.0330,  0.1084, -0.1692, -0.2771, -0.0804]])
```

On the other hand, computing $t_1^T \times t_2$ is performed by transposing `t1`, resulting in an array of size 2×2:

```
>>> t6 = torch.matmul(torch.transpose(t1, 0, 1), t2)
>>> print(t6)
tensor([[ 1.7453,  0.3392],
        [-1.6038, -0.2180]])
```

Finally, the `torch.linalg.norm()` function is useful for computing the L^p norm of a tensor. For example, we can calculate the L^2 norm of `t1` as follows:

```
>>> norm_t1 = torch.linalg.norm(t1, ord=2, dim=1)
>>> print(norm_t1)
tensor([0.6785, 0.5078, 1.1162, 0.5488, 0.1853])
```

To verify that this code snippet computes the L^2 norm of `t1` correctly, you can compare the results with the following NumPy function: `np.sqrt(np.sum(np.square(t1.numpy()), axis=1))`.

Split, stack, and concatenate tensors

In this subsection, we will cover PyTorch operations for splitting a tensor into multiple tensors, or the reverse: stacking and concatenating multiple tensors into a single one.

Assume that we have a single tensor, and we want to split it into two or more tensors. For this, PyTorch provides a convenient `torch.chunk()` function, which divides an input tensor into a list of equally sized tensors. We can determine the desired number of splits as an integer using the `chunks` argument to split a tensor along the desired dimension specified by the `dim` argument. In this case, the total size of the input tensor along the specified dimension must be divisible by the desired number of splits. Alternatively, we can provide the desired sizes in a list using the `torch.split()` function. Let's have a look at an example of both these options:

- Providing the number of splits:

  ```
  >>> torch.manual_seed(1)
  >>> t = torch.rand(6)
  >>> print(t)
  tensor([0.7576, 0.2793, 0.4031, 0.7347, 0.0293, 0.7999])
  >>> t_splits = torch.chunk(t, 3)
  >>> [item.numpy() for item in t_splits]
  [array([0.758, 0.279], dtype=float32),
   array([0.403, 0.735], dtype=float32),
   array([0.029, 0.8  ], dtype=float32)]
  ```

  In this example, a tensor of size 6 was divided into a list of three tensors each with size 2. If the tensor size is not divisible by the `chunks` value, the last chunk will be smaller.

- Providing the sizes of different splits:

  Alternatively, instead of defining the number of splits, we can also specify the sizes of the output tensors directly. Here, we are splitting a tensor of size 5 into tensors of sizes 3 and 2:

```
>>> torch.manual_seed(1)
>>> t = torch.rand(5)
>>> print(t)
tensor([0.7576, 0.2793, 0.4031, 0.7347, 0.0293])
>>> t_splits = torch.split(t, split_size_or_sections=[3, 2])
>>> [item.numpy() for item in t_splits]
[array([0.758, 0.279, 0.403], dtype=float32),
 array([0.735, 0.029], dtype=float32)]
```

Sometimes, we are working with multiple tensors and need to concatenate or stack them to create a single tensor. In this case, PyTorch functions such as `torch.stack()` and `torch.cat()` come in handy. For example, let's create a 1D tensor, `A`, containing 1s with size `3`, and a 1D tensor, `B`, containing 0s with size `2`, and concatenate them into a 1D tensor, `C`, of size `5`:

```
>>> A = torch.ones(3)
>>> B = torch.zeros(2)
>>> C = torch.cat([A, B], axis=0)
>>> print(C)
tensor([1., 1., 1., 0., 0.])
```

If we create 1D tensors `A` and `B`, both with size `3`, then we can stack them together to form a 2D tensor, `S`:

```
>>> A = torch.ones(3)
>>> B = torch.zeros(3)
>>> S = torch.stack([A, B], axis=1)
>>> print(S)
tensor([[1., 0.],
        [1., 0.],
        [1., 0.]])
```

The PyTorch API has many operations that you can use for building a model, processing your data, and more. However, covering every function is outside the scope of this book, where we will focus on the most essential ones. For the full list of operations and functions, you can refer to the documentation page of PyTorch at `https://pytorch.org/docs/stable/index.html`.

Building input pipelines in PyTorch

When we are training a deep NN model, we usually train the model incrementally using an iterative optimization algorithm such as stochastic gradient descent, as we have seen in previous chapters.

As mentioned at the beginning of this chapter, `torch.nn` is a module for building NN models. In cases where the training dataset is rather small and can be loaded as a tensor into the memory, we can directly use this tensor for training. In typical use cases, however, when the dataset is too large to fit into the computer memory, we will need to load the data from the main storage device (for example, the hard drive or solid-state drive) in chunks, that is, batch by batch. (Note the use of the term "batch" instead of "mini-batch" in this chapter to stay close to the PyTorch terminology.) In addition, we may need to construct a data-processing pipeline to apply certain transformations and preprocessing steps to our data, such as mean centering, scaling, or adding noise to augment the training procedure and to prevent overfitting.

Applying preprocessing functions manually every time can be quite cumbersome. Luckily, PyTorch provides a special class for constructing efficient and convenient preprocessing pipelines. In this section, we will see an overview of different methods for constructing a PyTorch `Dataset` and `DataLoader`, and implementing data loading, shuffling, and batching.

Creating a PyTorch DataLoader from existing tensors

If the data already exists in the form of a tensor object, a Python list, or a NumPy array, we can easily create a dataset loader using the `torch.utils.data.DataLoader()` class. It returns an object of the `DataLoader` class, which we can use to iterate through the individual elements in the input dataset. As a simple example, consider the following code, which creates a dataset from a list of values from 0 to 5:

```
>>> from torch.utils.data import DataLoader
>>> t = torch.arange(6, dtype=torch.float32)
>>> data_loader = DataLoader(t)
```

We can easily iterate through a dataset entry by entry as follows:

```
>>> for item in data_loader:
...     print(item)
tensor([0.])
tensor([1.])
tensor([2.])
tensor([3.])
tensor([4.])
tensor([5.])
```

If we want to create batches from this dataset, with a desired batch size of 3, we can do this with the `batch_size` argument as follows:

```
>>> data_loader = DataLoader(t, batch_size=3, drop_last=False)
>>> for i, batch in enumerate(data_loader, 1):
...     print(f'batch {i}:', batch)
batch 1: tensor([0., 1., 2.])
batch 2: tensor([3., 4., 5.])
```

This will create two batches from this dataset, where the first three elements go into batch #1, and the remaining elements go into batch #2. The optional `drop_last` argument is useful for cases when the number of elements in the tensor is not divisible by the desired batch size. We can drop the last non-full batch by setting `drop_last` to `True`. The default value for `drop_last` is `False`.

We can always iterate through a dataset directly, but as you just saw, `DataLoader` provides an automatic and customizable batching to a dataset.

Combining two tensors into a joint dataset

Often, we may have the data in two (or possibly more) tensors. For example, we could have a tensor for features and a tensor for labels. In such cases, we need to build a dataset that combines these tensors, which will allow us to retrieve the elements of these tensors in tuples.

Assume that we have two tensors, `t_x` and `t_y`. Tensor `t_x` holds our feature values, each of size 3, and `t_y` stores the class labels. For this example, we first create these two tensors as follows:

```
>>> torch.manual_seed(1)
>>> t_x = torch.rand([4, 3], dtype=torch.float32)
>>> t_y = torch.arange(4)
```

Now, we want to create a joint dataset from these two tensors. We first need to create a `Dataset` class as follows:

```
>>> from torch.utils.data import Dataset
>>> class JointDataset(Dataset):
...     def __init__(self, x, y):
...         self.x = x
...         self.y = y
...
...     def __len__(self):
...         return len(self.x)
...
```

```
...     def __getitem__(self, idx):
...         return self.x[idx], self.y[idx]
```

A custom Dataset class must contain the following methods to be used by the data loader later on:

- `__init__()`: This is where the initial logic happens, such as reading existing arrays, loading a file, filtering data, and so forth.
- `__getitem__()`: This returns the corresponding sample to the given index.

Then we create a joint dataset of t_x and t_y with the custom Dataset class as follows:

```
>>> from torch.utils.data import TensorDataset
>>> joint_dataset = TensorDataset(t_x, t_y)
```

Finally, we can print each example of the joint dataset as follows:

```
>>> for example in joint_dataset:
...     print('  x: ', example[0], '  y: ', example[1])
  x:  tensor([0.7576, 0.2793, 0.4031])  y:  tensor(0)
  x:  tensor([0.7347, 0.0293, 0.7999])  y:  tensor(1)
  x:  tensor([0.3971, 0.7544, 0.5695])  y:  tensor(2)
  x:  tensor([0.4388, 0.6387, 0.5247])  y:  tensor(3)
```

We can also simply utilize the `torch.utils.data.TensorDataset` class, if the second dataset is a labeled dataset in the form of tensors. So, instead of using our self-defined Dataset class, JointDataset, we can create a joint dataset as follows:

```
>>> joint_dataset = TensorDataset(t_x, t_y)
```

Note that a common source of error could be that the element-wise correspondence between the original features (x) and labels (y) might be lost (for example, if the two datasets are shuffled separately). However, once they are merged into one dataset, it is safe to apply these operations.

If we have a dataset created from the list of image filenames on disk, we can define a function to load the images from these filenames. You will see an example of applying multiple transformations to a dataset later in this chapter.

Shuffle, batch, and repeat

As was mentioned in *Chapter 2, Training Simple Machine Learning Algorithms for Classification*, when training an NN model using stochastic gradient descent optimization, it is important to feed training data as randomly shuffled batches. You have already seen how to specify the batch size using the `batch_size` argument of a data loader object. Now, in addition to creating batches, you will see how to shuffle and reiterate over the datasets. We will continue working with the previous joint dataset.

First, let's create a shuffled version data loader from the `joint_dataset` dataset:

```
>>> torch.manual_seed(1)
>>> data_loader = DataLoader(dataset=joint_dataset, batch_size=2, shuffle=True)
```

Here, each batch contains two data records (*x*) and the corresponding labels (*y*). Now we iterate through the data loader entry by entry as follows:

```
>>> for i, batch in enumerate(data_loader, 1):
...     print(f'batch {i}:', 'x:', batch[0],
              '\n       y:', batch[1])
batch 1: x: tensor([[0.4388, 0.6387, 0.5247],
        [0.3971, 0.7544, 0.5695]])
         y: tensor([3, 2])
batch 2: x: tensor([[0.7576, 0.2793, 0.4031],
        [0.7347, 0.0293, 0.7999]])
         y: tensor([0, 1])
```

The rows are shuffled without losing the one-to-one correspondence between the entries in `x` and `y`.

In addition, when training a model for multiple epochs, we need to shuffle and iterate over the dataset by the desired number of epochs. So, let's iterate over the batched dataset twice:

```
>>> for epoch in range(2):
>>>     print(f'epoch {epoch+1}')
>>>     for i, batch in enumerate(data_loader, 1):
...         print(f'batch {i}:', 'x:', batch[0],
                  '\n       y:', batch[1])
epoch 1
batch 1: x: tensor([[0.7347, 0.0293, 0.7999],
        [0.3971, 0.7544, 0.5695]])
         y: tensor([1, 2])
batch 2: x: tensor([[0.4388, 0.6387, 0.5247],
        [0.7576, 0.2793, 0.4031]])
         y: tensor([3, 0])
epoch 2
batch 1: x: tensor([[0.3971, 0.7544, 0.5695],
        [0.7576, 0.2793, 0.4031]])
         y: tensor([2, 0])
batch 2: x: tensor([[0.7347, 0.0293, 0.7999],
        [0.4388, 0.6387, 0.5247]])
         y: tensor([1, 3])
```

This results in two different sets of batches. In the first epoch, the first batch contains a pair of values [y=1, y=2], and the second batch contains a pair of values [y=3, y=0]. In the second epoch, two batches contain a pair of values, [y=2, y=0] and [y=1, y=3] respectively. For each iteration, the elements within a batch are also shuffled.

Creating a dataset from files on your local storage disk

In this section, we will build a dataset from image files stored on disk. There is an image folder associated with the online content of this chapter. After downloading the folder, you should be able to see six images of cats and dogs in JPEG format.

This small dataset will show how building a dataset from stored files generally works. To accomplish this, we are going to use two additional modules: `Image` in `PIL` to read the image file contents and `transforms` in `torchvision` to decode the raw contents and resize the images.

> The `PIL.Image` and `torchvision.transforms` modules provide a lot of additional and useful functions, which are beyond the scope of the book. You are encouraged to browse through the official documentation to learn more about these functions:
>
> `https://pillow.readthedocs.io/en/stable/reference/Image.html` for `PIL.Image`
>
> `https://pytorch.org/vision/stable/transforms.html` for `torchvision.transforms`

Before we start, let's take a look at the content of these files. We will use the `pathlib` library to generate a list of image files:

```
>>> import pathlib
>>> imgdir_path = pathlib.Path('cat_dog_images')
>>> file_list = sorted([str(path) for path in
... imgdir_path.glob('*.jpg')])
>>> print(file_list)
['cat_dog_images/dog-03.jpg', 'cat_dog_images/cat-01.jpg', 'cat_dog_images/cat-02.jpg', 'cat_dog_images/cat-03.jpg', 'cat_dog_images/dog-01.jpg', 'cat_dog_images/dog-02.jpg']
```

Next, we will visualize these image examples using Matplotlib:

```
>>> import matplotlib.pyplot as plt
>>> import os
>>> from PIL import Image
>>> fig = plt.figure(figsize=(10, 5))
>>> for i, file in enumerate(file_list):
...     img = Image.open(file)
...     print('Image shape:', np.array(img).shape)
...     ax = fig.add_subplot(2, 3, i+1)
...     ax.set_xticks([]); ax.set_yticks([])
```

```
...     ax.imshow(img)
...     ax.set_title(os.path.basename(file), size=15)
>>> plt.tight_layout()
>>> plt.show()
Image shape: (900, 1200, 3)
Image shape: (900, 1200, 3)
Image shape: (900, 1200, 3)
Image shape: (900, 742, 3)
Image shape: (800, 1200, 3)
Image shape: (800, 1200, 3)
```

Figure 12.3 shows the example images:

Figure 12.3: Images of cats and dogs

Just from this visualization and the printed image shapes, we can already see that the images have different aspect ratios. If you print the aspect ratios (or data array shapes) of these images, you will see that some images are 900 pixels high and 1200 pixels wide (900×1200), some are 800×1200, and one is 900×742. Later, we will preprocess these images to a consistent size. Another point to consider is that the labels for these images are provided within their filenames. So, we extract these labels from the list of filenames, assigning label `1` to dogs and label `0` to cats:

```
>>> labels = [1 if 'dog' in
...           os.path.basename(file) else 0
...                   for file in file_list]
>>> print(labels)
[0, 0, 0, 1, 1, 1]
```

Now, we have two lists: a list of filenames (or paths of each image) and a list of their labels. In the previous section, you learned how to create a joint dataset from two arrays. Here, we will do the following:

```
>>> class ImageDataset(Dataset):
...     def __init__(self, file_list, labels):
...         self.file_list = file_list
```

```
...         self.labels = labels
...
...     def __getitem__(self, index):
...         file = self.file_list[index]
...         label = self.labels[index]
...         return file, label
...
...     def __len__(self):
...         return len(self.labels)

>>> image_dataset = ImageDataset(file_list, labels)
>>> for file, label in image_dataset:
...     print(file, label)


cat_dog_images/cat-01.jpg 0
cat_dog_images/cat-02.jpg 0
cat_dog_images/cat-03.jpg 0
cat_dog_images/dog-01.jpg 1
cat_dog_images/dog-02.jpg 1
cat_dog_images/dog-03.jpg 1
```

The joint dataset has filenames and labels.

Next, we need to apply transformations to this dataset: load the image content from its file path, decode the raw content, and resize it to a desired size, for example, 80×120. As mentioned before, we use the `torchvision.transforms` module to resize the images and convert the loaded pixels into tensors as follows:

```
>>> import torchvision.transforms as transforms
>>> img_height, img_width = 80, 120
>>> transform = transforms.Compose([
...     transforms.ToTensor(),
...     transforms.Resize((img_height, img_width)),
... ])
```

Now we update the `ImageDataset` class with the `transform` we just defined:

```
>>> class ImageDataset(Dataset):
...     def __init__(self, file_list, labels, transform=None):
...         self.file_list = file_list
...         self.labels = labels
...         self.transform = transform
...
```

```
...     def __getitem__(self, index):
...         img = Image.open(self.file_list[index])
...         if self.transform is not None:
...             img = self.transform(img)
...         label = self.labels[index]
...         return img, label
...
...     def __len__(self):
...         return len(self.labels)
>>>
>>> image_dataset = ImageDataset(file_list, labels, transform)
```

Finally, we visualize these transformed image examples using Matplotlib:

```
>>> fig = plt.figure(figsize=(10, 6))
>>> for i, example in enumerate(image_dataset):
...     ax = fig.add_subplot(2, 3, i+1)
...     ax.set_xticks([]); ax.set_yticks([])
...     ax.imshow(example[0].numpy().transpose((1, 2, 0)))
...     ax.set_title(f'{example[1]}', size=15)
...
>>> plt.tight_layout()
>>> plt.show()
```

This results in the following visualization of the retrieved example images, along with their labels:

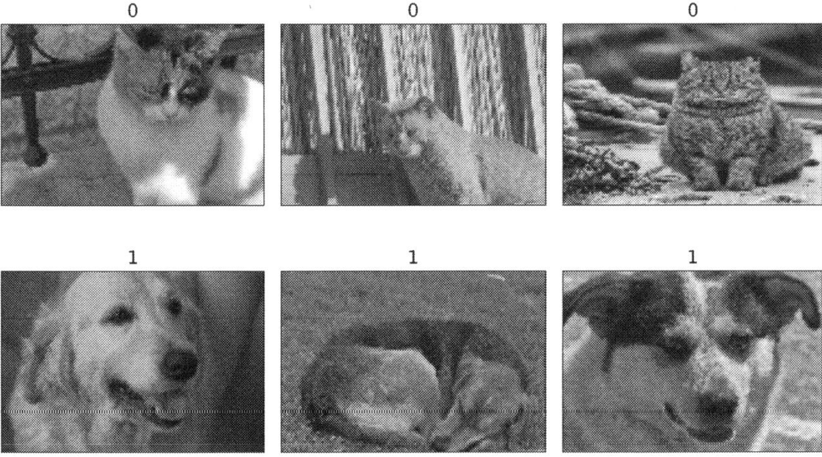

Figure 12.4: Images are labeled

The `__getitem__` method in the `ImageDataset` class wraps all four steps into a single function, including the loading of the raw content (images and labels), decoding the images into tensors, and resizing the images. The function then returns a dataset that we can iterate over and apply other operations that we learned about in the previous sections via a data loader, such as shuffling and batching.

Fetching available datasets from the torchvision.datasets library

The `torchvision.datasets` library provides a nice collection of freely available image datasets for training or evaluating deep learning models. Similarly, the `torchtext.datasets` library provides datasets for natural language. Here, we use `torchvision.datasets` as an example.

The `torchvision` datasets (`https://pytorch.org/vision/stable/datasets.html`) are nicely formatted and come with informative descriptions, including the format of features and labels and their type and dimensionality, as well as the link to the original source of the dataset. Another advantage is that these datasets are all subclasses of `torch.utils.data.Dataset`, so all the functions we covered in the previous sections can be used directly. So, let's see how to use these datasets in action.

First, if you haven't already installed `torchvision` together with PyTorch earlier, you need to install the `torchvision` library via `pip` from the command line:

```
pip install torchvision
```

You can take a look at the list of available datasets at `https://pytorch.org/vision/stable/datasets.html`.

In the following paragraphs, we will cover fetching two different datasets: CelebA (`celeb_a`) and the MNIST digit dataset.

Let's first work with the CelebA dataset (`http://mmlab.ie.cuhk.edu.hk/projects/CelebA.html`) with `torchvision.datasets.CelebA` (`https://pytorch.org/vision/stable/datasets.html#celeba`). The description of `torchvision.datasets.CelebA` provides some useful information to help us understand the structure of this dataset:

- The database has three subsets, `'train'`, `'valid'`, and `'test'`. We can select a specific subset or load all of them with the `split` parameter.
- The images are stored in `PIL.Image` format. And we can obtain a transformed version using a custom `transform` function, such as `transforms.ToTensor` and `transforms.Resize`.
- There are different types of targets we can use, including `'attributes'`, `'identity'`, and `'landmarks'`. `'attributes'` is 40 facial attributes for the person in the image, such as facial expression, makeup, hair properties, and so on; `'identity'` is the person ID for an image; and `'landmarks'` refers to the dictionary of extracted facial points, such as the position of the eyes, nose, and so on.

Next, we will call the `torchvision.datasets.CelebA` class to download the data, store it on disk in a designated folder, and load it into a `torch.utils.data.Dataset` object:

```
>>> import torchvision
>>> image_path = './'
>>> celeba_dataset = torchvision.datasets.CelebA(
...     image_path, split='train', target_type='attr', download=True
... )
1443490838/? [01:28<00:00, 6730259.81it/s]
26721026/? [00:03<00:00, 8225581.57it/s]
3424458/? [00:00<00:00, 14141274.46it/s]
6082035/? [00:00<00:00, 21695906.49it/s]
12156055/? [00:00<00:00, 12002767.35it/s]
2836386/? [00:00<00:00, 3858079.93it/s]
```

You may run into a `BadZipFile: File is not a zip file` error, or `RuntimeError: The daily quota of the file img_align_celeba.zip is exceeded and it can't be downloaded. This is a limitation of Google Drive and can only be overcome by trying again later`; it just means that Google Drive has a daily maximum quota that is exceeded by the CelebA files. To work around it, you can manually download the files from the source: `http://mmlab.ie.cuhk.edu.hk/projects/CelebA.html`. In the downloaded folder, `celeba/`, you can unzip the `img_align_celeba.zip` file. The `image_path` is the root of the downloaded folder, `celeba/`. If you have already downloaded the files once, you can simply set `download=False`. For additional information and guidance, we highly recommend to see accompanying code notebook at `https://github.com/rasbt/machine-learning-book/blob/main/ch12/ch12_part1.ipynb`.

Now that we have instantiated the datasets, let's check if the object is of the `torch.utils.data.Dataset` class:

```
>>> assert isinstance(celeba_dataset, torch.utils.data.Dataset)
```

As mentioned, the dataset is already split into train, test, and validation datasets, and we only load the train set. And we only use the `'attributes'` target. In order to see what the data examples look like, we can execute the following code:

```
>>> example = next(iter(celeba_dataset))
>>> print(example)
(<PIL.JpegImagePlugin.JpegImageFile image mode=RGB size=178x218 at
0x120C6C668>, tensor([0, 1, 1, 0, 0, 0, 0, 0, 0, 0, 0, 1, 0, 0, 0, 0, 0, 0, 1,
1, 0, 1, 0, 0, 1, 0, 0, 1, 0, 0, 0, 1, 1, 0, 1, 0, 1, 0, 0, 1]))
```

Note that the sample in this dataset comes in a tuple of `(PIL.Image, attributes)`. If we want to pass this dataset to a supervised deep learning model during training, we have to reformat it as a tuple of `(features tensor, label)`. For the label, we will use the `'Smiling'` category from the attributes as an example, which is the 31st element.

Finally, let's take the first 18 examples from it to visualize them with their `'Smiling'` labels:

```
>>> from itertools import islice
>>> fig = plt.figure(figsize=(12, 8))
>>> for i, (image, attributes) in islice(enumerate(celeba_dataset), 18):
...     ax = fig.add_subplot(3, 6, i+1)
...     ax.set_xticks([]); ax.set_yticks([])
...     ax.imshow(image)
...     ax.set_title(f'{attributes[31]}', size=15)
>>> plt.show()
```

The examples and their labels that are retrieved from `celeba_dataset` are shown in *Figure 12.5*:

Figure 12.5: Model predicts smiling celebrities

This was all we needed to do to fetch and use the CelebA image dataset.

Next, we will proceed with the second dataset from `torchvision.datasets.MNIST` (`https://pytorch.org/vision/stable/datasets.html#mnist`). Let's see how it can be used to fetch the MNIST digit dataset:

- The database has two partitions, `'train'` and `'test'`. We need to select a specific subset to load.
- The images are stored in `PIL.Image` format. And we can obtain a transformed version using a custom `transform` function, such as `transforms.ToTensor` and `transforms.Resize`.
- There are 10 classes for the target, from `0` to `9`.

Now, we can download the `'train'` partition, convert the elements to tuples, and visualize 10 examples:

```
>>> mnist_dataset = torchvision.datasets.MNIST(image_path, 'train',
download=True)
>>> assert isinstance(mnist_dataset, torch.utils.data.Dataset)
>>> example = next(iter(mnist_dataset))
>>> print(example)
(<PIL.Image.Image image mode=L size=28x28 at 0x126895B00>, 5)
>>> fig = plt.figure(figsize=(15, 6))
>>> for i, (image, label) in  islice(enumerate(mnist_dataset), 10):
...     ax = fig.add_subplot(2, 5, i+1)
...     ax.set_xticks([]); ax.set_yticks([])
...     ax.imshow(image, cmap='gray_r')
...     ax.set_title(f'{label}', size=15)
>>> plt.show()
```

The retrieved example handwritten digits from this dataset are shown as follows:

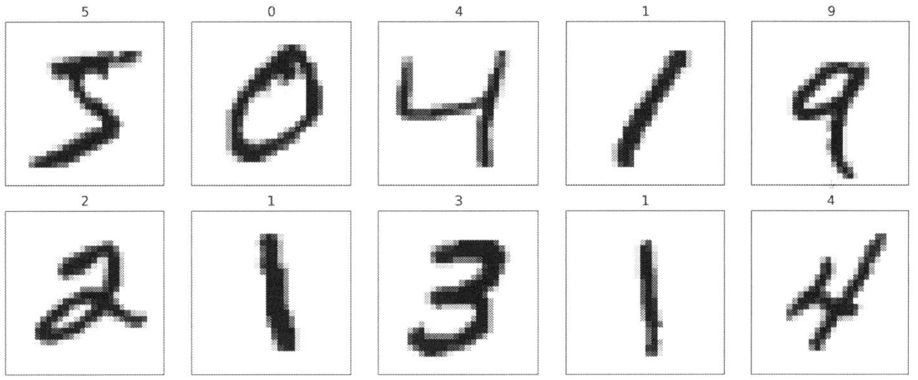

Figure 12.6: Correctly identifying handwritten digits

This concludes our coverage of building and manipulating datasets and fetching datasets from the `torchvision.datasets` library. Next, we will see how to build NN models in PyTorch.

Building an NN model in PyTorch

So far in this chapter, you have learned about the basic utility components of PyTorch for manipulating tensors and organizing data into formats that we can iterate over during training. In this section, we will finally implement our first predictive model in PyTorch. As PyTorch is a bit more flexible but also more complex than machine learning libraries such as scikit-learn, we will start with a simple linear regression model.

The PyTorch neural network module (torch.nn)

`torch.nn` is an elegantly designed module developed to help create and train NNs. It allows easy prototyping and the building of complex models in just a few lines of code.

To fully utilize the power of the module and customize it for your problem, you need to understand what it's doing. To develop this understanding, we will first train a basic linear regression model on a toy dataset without using any features from the `torch.nn` module; we will use nothing but the basic PyTorch tensor operations.

Then, we will incrementally add features from `torch.nn` and `torch.optim`. As you will see in the following subsections, these modules make building an NN model extremely easy. We will also take advantage of the dataset pipeline functionalities supported in PyTorch, such as `Dataset` and `DataLoader`, which you learned about in the previous section. In this book, we will use the `torch.nn` module to build NN models.

The most commonly used approach for building an NN in PyTorch is through `nn.Module`, which allows layers to be stacked to form a network. This gives us more control over the forward pass. We will see examples of building an NN model using the `nn.Module` class.

Finally, as you will see in the following subsections, a trained model can be saved and reloaded for future use.

Building a linear regression model

In this subsection, we will build a simple model to solve a linear regression problem. First, let's create a toy dataset in NumPy and visualize it:

```
>>> X_train = np.arange(10, dtype='float32').reshape((10, 1))
>>> y_train = np.array([1.0, 1.3, 3.1, 2.0, 5.0,
...                     6.3, 6.6,7.4, 8.0,
...                     9.0], dtype='float32')
>>> plt.plot(X_train, y_train, 'o', markersize=10)
>>> plt.xlabel('x')
>>> plt.ylabel('y')
>>> plt.show()
```

As a result, the training examples will be shown in a scatterplot as follows:

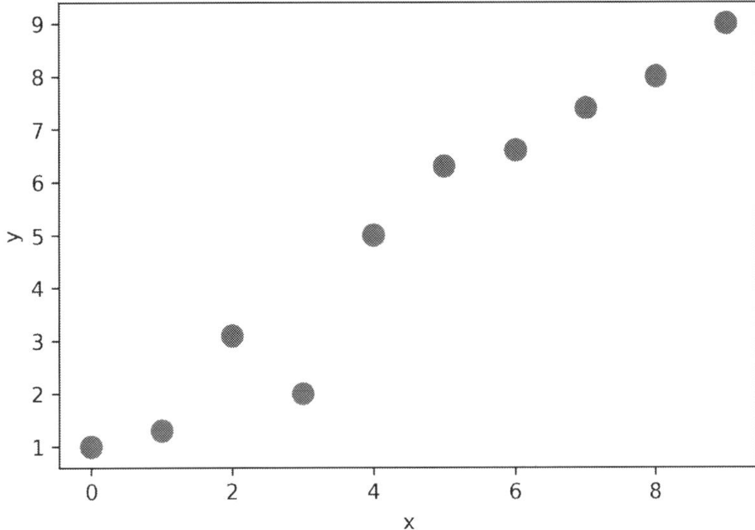

Figure 12.7: A scatterplot of the training examples

Next, we will standardize the features (mean centering and dividing by the standard deviation) and create a PyTorch `Dataset` for the training set and a corresponding `DataLoader`:

```
>>> from torch.utils.data import TensorDataset
>>> X_train_norm = (X_train - np.mean(X_train)) / np.std(X_train)
>>> X_train_norm = torch.from_numpy(X_train_norm)
>>> y_train = torch.from_numpy(y_train).float()
>>> train_ds = TensorDataset(X_train_norm, y_train)
>>> batch_size = 1
>>> train_dl = DataLoader(train_ds, batch_size, shuffle=True)
```

Here, we set a batch size of `1` for the `DataLoader`.

Now, we can define our model for linear regression as $z = wx + b$. Here, we are going to use the `torch.nn` module. It provides predefined layers for building complex NN models, but to start, you will learn how to define a model from scratch. Later in this chapter, you will see how to use those predefined layers.

For this regression problem, we will define a linear regression model from scratch. We will define the parameters of our model, `weight` and `bias`, which correspond to the weight and the bias parameters, respectively. Finally, we will define the `model()` function to determine how this model uses the input data to generate its output:

```
>>> torch.manual_seed(1)
>>> weight = torch.randn(1)
>>> weight.requires_grad_()
>>> bias = torch.zeros(1, requires_grad=True)
>>> def model(xb):
...     return xb @ weight + bias
```

After defining the model, we can define the loss function that we want to minimize to find the optimal model weights. Here, we will choose the **mean squared error (MSE)** as our loss function:

```
>>> def loss_fn(input, target):
...     return (input-target).pow(2).mean()
```

Furthermore, to learn the weight parameters of the model, we will use stochastic gradient descent. In this subsection, we will implement this training via the stochastic gradient descent procedure by ourselves, but in the next subsection, we will use the `SGD` method from the optimization package, `torch.optim`, to do the same thing.

To implement the stochastic gradient descent algorithm, we need to compute the gradients. Rather than manually computing the gradients, we will use PyTorch's `torch.autograd.backward` function. We will cover `torch.autograd` and its different classes and functions for implementing automatic differentiation in *Chapter 13, Going Deeper – The Mechanics of PyTorch*.

Now, we can set the learning rate and train the model for 200 epochs. The code for training the model against the batched version of the dataset is as follows:

```
>>> learning_rate = 0.001
>>> num_epochs = 200
>>> log_epochs = 10
>>> for epoch in range(num_epochs):
...     for x_batch, y_batch in train_dl:
...         pred = model(x_batch)
...         loss = loss_fn(pred, y_batch.long())
...         loss.backward()
...     with torch.no_grad():
...         weight -= weight.grad * learning_rate
...         bias -= bias.grad * learning_rate
...         weight.grad.zero_()
...         bias.grad.zero_()
...     if epoch % log_epochs==0:
```

```
...         print(f'Epoch {epoch}  Loss {loss.item():.4f}')
Epoch 0  Loss 5.1701
Epoch 10  Loss 30.3370
Epoch 20  Loss 26.9436
Epoch 30  Loss 0.9315
Epoch 40  Loss 3.5942
Epoch 50  Loss 5.8960
Epoch 60  Loss 3.7567
Epoch 70  Loss 1.5877
Epoch 80  Loss 0.6213
Epoch 90  Loss 1.5596
Epoch 100  Loss 0.2583
Epoch 110  Loss 0.6957
Epoch 120  Loss 0.2659
Epoch 130  Loss 0.1615
Epoch 140  Loss 0.6025
Epoch 150  Loss 0.0639
Epoch 160  Loss 0.1177
Epoch 170  Loss 0.3501
Epoch 180  Loss 0.3281
Epoch 190  Loss 0.0970
```

Let's look at the trained model and plot it. For the test data, we will create a NumPy array of values evenly spaced between 0 and 9. Since we trained our model with standardized features, we will also apply the same standardization to the test data:

```
>>> print('Final Parameters:', weight.item(), bias.item())
Final Parameters:  2.669806480407715 4.879569053649902
>>> X_test = np.linspace(0, 9, num=100, dtype='float32').reshape(-1, 1)
>>> X_test_norm = (X_test - np.mean(X_train)) / np.std(X_train)
>>> X_test_norm = torch.from_numpy(X_test_norm)
>>> y_pred = model(X_test_norm).detach().numpy()
>>> fig = plt.figure(figsize=(13, 5))
>>> ax = fig.add_subplot(1, 2, 1)
>>> plt.plot(X_train_norm, y_train, 'o', markersize=10)
>>> plt.plot(X_test_norm, y_pred, '--', lw=3)
>>> plt.legend(['Training examples', 'Linear reg.'], fontsize=15)
>>> ax.set_xlabel('x', size=15)
>>> ax.set_ylabel('y', size=15)
>>> ax.tick_params(axis='both', which='major', labelsize=15)
>>> plt.show()
```

Figure 12.8 shows a scatterplot of the training examples and the trained linear regression model:

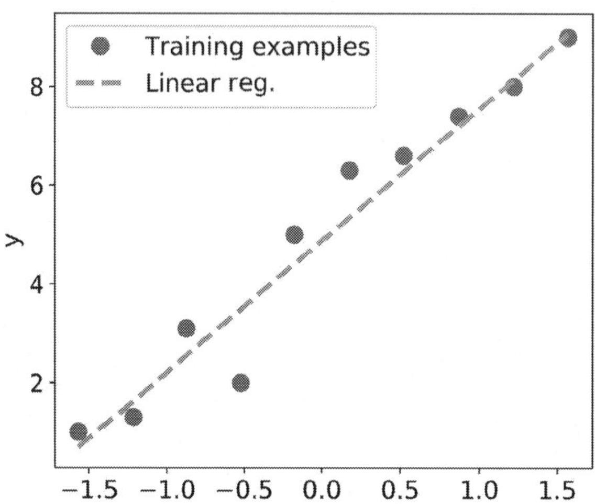

Figure 12.8: The linear regression model fits the data well

Model training via the torch.nn and torch.optim modules

In the previous example, we saw how to train a model by writing a custom loss function `loss_fn()` and applied stochastic gradient descent optimization. However, writing the loss function and gradient updates can be a repeatable task across different projects. The `torch.nn` module provides a set of loss functions, and `torch.optim` supports most commonly used optimization algorithms that can be called to update the parameters based on the computed gradients. To see how they work, let's create a new MSE loss function and a stochastic gradient descent optimizer:

```
>>> import torch.nn as nn
>>> loss_fn = nn.MSELoss(reduction='mean')
>>> input_size = 1
>>> output_size = 1
>>> model = nn.Linear(input_size, output_size)
>>> optimizer = torch.optim.SGD(model.parameters(), lr=learning_rate)
```

Note that here we use the `torch.nn.Linear` class for the linear layer instead of manually defining it.

Now, we can simply call the `step()` method of the `optimizer` to train the model. We can pass a batched dataset (such as `train_dl`, which was created in the previous example):

```
>>> for epoch in range(num_epochs):
...     for x_batch, y_batch in train_dl:
...         # 1. Generate predictions
...         pred = model(x_batch)[:, 0]
...         # 2. Calculate loss
...         loss = loss_fn(pred, y_batch)
...         # 3. Compute gradients
...         loss.backward()
...         # 4. Update parameters using gradients
...         optimizer.step()
...         # 5. Reset the gradients to zero
...         optimizer.zero_grad()
...     if epoch % log_epochs==0:
...         print(f'Epoch {epoch}  Loss {loss.item():.4f}')
```

After the model is trained, visualize the results and make sure that they are similar to the results of the previous method. To obtain the weight and bias parameters, we can do the following:

```
>>> print('Final Parameters:', model.weight.item(), model.bias.item())
Final Parameters: 2.646660089492798 4.883835315704346
```

Building a multilayer perceptron for classifying flowers in the Iris dataset

In the previous example, you saw how to build a model from scratch. We trained this model using stochastic gradient descent optimization. While we started our journey based on the simplest possible example, you can see that defining the model from scratch, even for such a simple case, is neither appealing nor good practice. PyTorch instead provides already defined layers through `torch.nn` that can be readily used as the building blocks of an NN model. In this section, you will learn how to use these layers to solve a classification task using the Iris flower dataset (identifying between three species of irises) and build a two-layer perceptron using the `torch.nn` module. First, let's get the data from `sklearn.datasets`:

```
>>> from sklearn.datasets import load_iris
>>> from sklearn.model_selection import train_test_split
>>> iris = load_iris()
```

```
>>> X = iris['data']
>>> y = iris['target']
>>> X_train, X_test, y_train, y_test = train_test_split(
...     X, y, test_size=1./3, random_state=1)
```

Here, we randomly select 100 samples (2/3) for training and 50 samples (1/3) for testing.

Next, we standardize the features (mean centering and dividing by the standard deviation) and create a PyTorch `Dataset` for the training set and a corresponding `DataLoader`:

```
>>> X_train_norm = (X_train - np.mean(X_train)) / np.std(X_train)
>>> X_train_norm = torch.from_numpy(X_train_norm).float()
>>> y_train = torch.from_numpy(y_train)
>>> train_ds = TensorDataset(X_train_norm, y_train)
>>> torch.manual_seed(1)
>>> batch_size = 2
>>> train_dl = DataLoader(train_ds, batch_size, shuffle=True)
```

Here, we set the batch size to 2 for the `DataLoader`.

Now, we are ready to use the `torch.nn` module to build a model efficiently. In particular, using the `nn.Module` class, we can stack a few layers and build an NN. You can see the list of all the layers that are already available at `https://pytorch.org/docs/stable/nn.html`. For this problem, we are going to use the `Linear` layer, which is also known as a fully connected layer or dense layer, and can be best represented by $f(w \times x + b)$, where x represents a tensor containing the input features, w and b are the weight matrix and the bias vector, and f is the activation function.

Each layer in an NN receives its inputs from the preceding layer; therefore, its dimensionality (rank and shape) is fixed. Typically, we need to concern ourselves with the dimensionality of output only when we design an NN architecture. Here, we want to define a model with two hidden layers. The first one receives an input of four features and projects them to 16 neurons. The second layer receives the output of the previous layer (which has a size of *16*) and projects them to three output neurons, since we have three class labels. This can be done as follows:

```
>>> class Model(nn.Module):
...     def __init__(self, input_size, hidden_size, output_size):
...         super().__init__()
...         self.layer1 = nn.Linear(input_size, hidden_size)
...         self.layer2 = nn.Linear(hidden_size, output_size)
...     def forward(self, x):
...         x = self.layer1(x)
...         x = nn.Sigmoid()(x)
...         x = self.layer2(x)
...         return x
>>> input_size = X_train_norm.shape[1]
```

```
>>> hidden_size = 16
>>> output_size = 3
>>> model = Model(input_size, hidden_size, output_size)
```

Here, we used the sigmoid activation function for the first layer and softmax activation for the last (output) layer. Softmax activation in the last layer is used to support multiclass classification since we have three class labels here (which is why we have three neurons in the output layer). We will discuss the different activation functions and their applications later in this chapter.

Next, we specify the loss function as cross-entropy loss and the optimizer as Adam:

The Adam optimizer is a robust, gradient-based optimization method, which we will talk about in detail in *Chapter 14, Classifying Images with Deep Convolutional Neural Networks*.

```
>>> learning_rate = 0.001
>>> loss_fn = nn.CrossEntropyLoss()
>>> optimizer = torch.optim.Adam(model.parameters(), lr=learning_rate)
```

Now, we can train the model. We will specify the number of epochs to be `100`. The code of training the flower classification model is as follows:

```
>>> num_epochs = 100
>>> loss_hist = [0] * num_epochs
>>> accuracy_hist = [0] * num_epochs
>>> for epoch in range(num_epochs):
...     for x_batch, y_batch in train_dl:
...         pred = model(x_batch)
...         loss = loss_fn(pred, y_batch)
...         loss.backward()
...         optimizer.step()
...         optimizer.zero_grad()
...         loss_hist[epoch] += loss.item()*y_batch.size(0)
...         is_correct = (torch.argmax(pred, dim=1) == y_batch).float()
...         accuracy_hist[epoch] += is_correct.sum()
...     loss_hist[epoch] /= len(train_dl.dataset)
...     accuracy_hist[epoch] /= len(train_dl.dataset)
```

The `loss_hist` and `accuracy_hist` lists keep the training loss and the training accuracy after each epoch. We can use this to visualize the learning curves as follows:

```
>>> fig = plt.figure(figsize=(12, 5))
>>> ax = fig.add_subplot(1, 2, 1)
>>> ax.plot(loss_hist, lw=3)
```

```
>>> ax.set_title('Training loss', size=15)
>>> ax.set_xlabel('Epoch', size=15)
>>> ax.tick_params(axis='both', which='major', labelsize=15)
>>> ax = fig.add_subplot(1, 2, 2)
>>> ax.plot(accuracy_hist, lw=3)
>>> ax.set_title('Training accuracy', size=15)
>>> ax.set_xlabel('Epoch', size=15)
>>> ax.tick_params(axis='both', which='major', labelsize=15)
>>> plt.show()
```

The learning curves (training loss and training accuracy) are as follows:

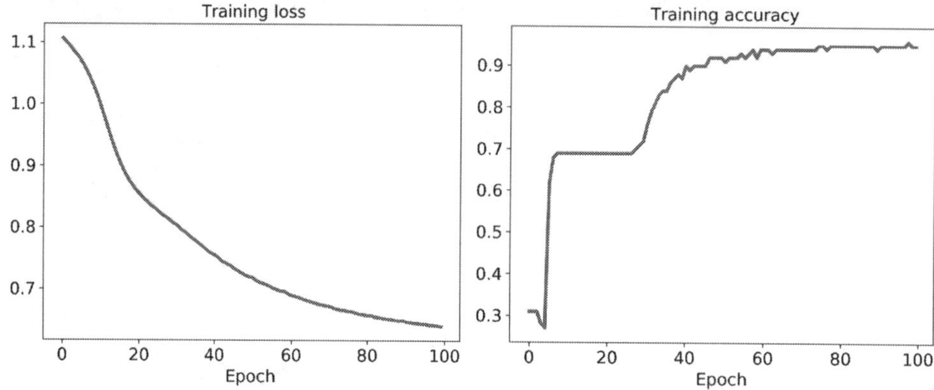

Figure 12.9: Training loss and accuracy curves

Evaluating the trained model on the test dataset

We can now evaluate the classification accuracy of the trained model on the test dataset:

```
>>> X_test_norm = (X_test - np.mean(X_train)) / np.std(X_train)
>>> X_test_norm = torch.from_numpy(X_test_norm).float()
>>> y_test = torch.from_numpy(y_test)
>>> pred_test = model(X_test_norm)
>>> correct = (torch.argmax(pred_test, dim=1) == y_test).float()
>>> accuracy = correct.mean()
>>> print(f'Test Acc.: {accuracy:.4f}')
Test Acc.: 0.9800
```

Since we trained our model with standardized features, we also applied the same standardization to the test data. The classification accuracy is 0.98 (that is, 98 percent).

Saving and reloading the trained model

Trained models can be saved on disk for future use. This can be done as follows:

```
>>> path = 'iris_classifier.pt'
>>> torch.save(model, path)
```

Calling `save(model)` will save both the model architecture and all the learned parameters. As a common convention, we can save models using a `'pt'` or `'pth'` file extension.

Now, let's reload the saved model. Since we have saved both the model architecture and the weights, we can easily rebuild and reload the parameters in just one line:

```
>>> model_new = torch.load(path)
```

Try to verify the model architecture by calling `model_new.eval()`:

```
>>> model_new.eval()
Model(
  (layer1): Linear(in_features=4, out_features=16, bias=True)
  (layer2): Linear(in_features=16, out_features=3, bias=True)
)
```

Finally, let's evaluate this new model that is reloaded on the test dataset to verify that the results are the same as before:

```
>>> pred_test = model_new(X_test_norm)
>>> correct = (torch.argmax(pred_test, dim=1) == y_test).float()
>>> accuracy = correct.mean()
>>> print(f'Test Acc.: {accuracy:.4f}')
Test Acc.: 0.9800
```

If you want to save only the learned parameters, you can use `save(model.state_dict())` as follows:

```
>>> path = 'iris_classifier_state.pt'
>>> torch.save(model.state_dict(), path)
```

To reload the saved parameters, we first need to construct the model as we did before, then feed the loaded parameters to the model:

```
>>> model_new = Model(input_size, hidden_size, output_size)
>>> model_new.load_state_dict(torch.load(path))
```

Choosing activation functions for multilayer neural networks

For simplicity, we have only discussed the sigmoid activation function in the context of multilayer feedforward NNs so far; we have used it in the hidden layer as well as the output layer in the MLP implementation in *Chapter 11*.

Note that in this book, the sigmoidal logistic function, $\sigma(z) = \frac{1}{1+e^{-z}}$, is referred to as the *sigmoid* function for brevity, which is common in machine learning literature. In the following subsections, you will learn more about alternative nonlinear functions that are useful for implementing multilayer NNs.

Technically, we can use any function as an activation function in multilayer NNs as long as it is differentiable. We can even use linear activation functions, such as in Adaline (*Chapter 2, Training Simple Machine Learning Algorithms for Classification*). However, in practice, it would not be very useful to use linear activation functions for both hidden and output layers, since we want to introduce nonlinearity in a typical artificial NN to be able to tackle complex problems. The sum of linear functions yields a linear function after all.

The logistic (sigmoid) activation function that we used in *Chapter 11* probably mimics the concept of a neuron in a brain most closely—we can think of it as the probability of whether a neuron fires. However, the logistic (sigmoid) activation function can be problematic if we have highly negative input, since the output of the sigmoid function will be close to zero in this case. If the sigmoid function returns output that is close to zero, the NN will learn very slowly, and it will be more likely to get trapped in the local minima of the loss landscape during training. This is why people often prefer a hyperbolic tangent as an activation function in hidden layers.

Before we discuss what a hyperbolic tangent looks like, let's briefly recapitulate some of the basics of the logistic function and look at a generalization that makes it more useful for multiclass classification problems.

Logistic function recap

As was mentioned in the introduction to this section, the logistic function is, in fact, a special case of a sigmoid function. You will recall from the section on logistic regression in *Chapter 3, A Tour of Machine Learning Classifiers Using Scikit-Learn*, that we can use a logistic function to model the probability that sample x belongs to the positive class (class 1) in a binary classification task.

The given net input, z, is shown in the following equation:

$$z = w_0 x_0 + w_1 x_1 + \cdots + w_m x_m = \sum_{i=0}^{m} w_i x_i = \boldsymbol{w}^T \boldsymbol{x}$$

The logistic (sigmoid) function will compute the following:

$$\sigma_{\text{logistic}}(z) = \frac{1}{1 + e^{-z}}$$

Note that w_0 is the bias unit (y-axis intercept, which means $x_0 = 1$). To provide a more concrete example, let's take a model for a two-dimensional data point, x, and a model with the following weight coefficients assigned to the w vector:

```
>>> import numpy as np
>>> X = np.array([1, 1.4, 2.5]) ## first value must be 1
>>> w = np.array([0.4, 0.3, 0.5])
>>> def net_input(X, w):
...     return np.dot(X, w)
>>> def logistic(z):
...     return 1.0 / (1.0 + np.exp(-z))
>>> def logistic_activation(X, w):
...     z = net_input(X, w)
...     return logistic(z)
>>> print(f'P(y=1|x) = {logistic_activation(X, w):.3f}')
P(y=1|x) = 0.888
```

If we calculate the net input (z) and use it to activate a logistic neuron with those particular feature values and weight coefficients, we get a value of `0.888`, which we can interpret as an 88.8 percent probability that this particular sample, x, belongs to the positive class.

In *Chapter 11*, we used the one-hot encoding technique to represent multiclass ground truth labels and designed the output layer consisting of multiple logistic activation units. However, as will be demonstrated by the following code example, an output layer consisting of multiple logistic activation units does not produce meaningful, interpretable probability values:

```
>>> # W : array with shape = (n_output_units, n_hidden_units+1)
>>> #     note that the first column are the bias units
>>> W = np.array([[1.1, 1.2, 0.8, 0.4],
...               [0.2, 0.4, 1.0, 0.2],
...               [0.6, 1.5, 1.2, 0.7]])
>>> # A : data array with shape = (n_hidden_units + 1, n_samples)
>>> #     note that the first column of this array must be 1
>>> A = np.array([[1, 0.1, 0.4, 0.6]])
>>> Z = np.dot(W, A[0])
>>> y_probas = logistic(Z)
>>> print('Net Input: \n', Z)
Net Input:
[1.78  0.76  1.65]
>>> print('Output Units:\n', y_probas)
Output Units:
[ 0.85569687  0.68135373  0.83889105]
```

As you can see in the output, the resulting values cannot be interpreted as probabilities for a three-class problem. The reason for this is that they do not sum to 1. However, this is, in fact, not a big concern if we use our model to predict only the class labels and not the class membership probabilities. One way to predict the class label from the output units obtained earlier is to use the maximum value:

```
>>> y_class = np.argmax(Z, axis=0)
>>> print('Predicted class label:', y_class)
Predicted class label: 0
```

In certain contexts, it can be useful to compute meaningful class probabilities for multiclass predictions. In the next section, we will take a look at a generalization of the logistic function, the `softmax` function, which can help us with this task.

Estimating class probabilities in multiclass classification via the softmax function

In the previous section, you saw how we can obtain a class label using the `argmax` function. Previously, in the *Building a multilayer perceptron for classifying flowers in the Iris dataset* section, we determined `activation='softmax'` in the last layer of the MLP model. The `softmax` function is a soft form of the `argmax` function; instead of giving a single class index, it provides the probability of each class. Therefore, it allows us to compute meaningful class probabilities in multiclass settings (multinomial logistic regression).

In `softmax`, the probability of a particular sample with net input z belonging to the ith class can be computed with a normalization term in the denominator, that is, the sum of the exponentially weighted linear functions:

$$p(z) = \sigma(z) = \frac{e^{z_i}}{\sum_{j=1}^{M} e^{z_j}}$$

To see `softmax` in action, let's code it up in Python:

```
>>> def softmax(z):
...     return np.exp(z) / np.sum(np.exp(z))
>>> y_probas = softmax(Z)
>>> print('Probabilities:\n', y_probas)
Probabilities:
[ 0.44668973  0.16107406  0.39223621]
>>> np.sum(y_probas)
1.0
```

As you can see, the predicted class probabilities now sum to 1, as we would expect. It is also notable that the predicted class label is the same as when we applied the `argmax` function to the logistic output.

It may help to think of the result of the `softmax` function as a *normalized* output that is useful for obtaining meaningful class-membership predictions in multiclass settings. Therefore, when we build a multiclass classification model in PyTorch, we can use the `torch.softmax()` function to estimate the probabilities of each class membership for an input batch of examples. To see how we can use the `torch.softmax()` activation function in PyTorch, we will convert `Z` to a tensor in the following code, with an additional dimension reserved for the batch size:

```
>>> torch.softmax(torch.from_numpy(Z), dim=0)
tensor([0.4467, 0.1611, 0.3922], dtype=torch.float64)
```

Broadening the output spectrum using a hyperbolic tangent

Another sigmoidal function that is often used in the hidden layers of artificial NNs is the **hyperbolic tangent** (commonly known as **tanh**), which can be interpreted as a rescaled version of the logistic function:

$$\begin{aligned} \sigma_{\text{logistic}}(z) &= \frac{1}{1+e^{-z}} \\ \sigma_{\tanh}(z) &= 2 \times \sigma_{\text{logistic}}(2z) - 1 = \frac{e^{z}-e^{-z}}{e^{z}+e^{-z}} \end{aligned}$$

The advantage of the hyperbolic tangent over the logistic function is that it has a broader output spectrum ranging in the open interval (–1, 1), which can improve the convergence of the backpropagation algorithm (*Neural Networks for Pattern Recognition, C. M. Bishop, Oxford University Press,* pages: 500-501, *1995*).

In contrast, the logistic function returns an output signal ranging in the open interval (0, 1). For a simple comparison of the logistic function and the hyperbolic tangent, let's plot the two sigmoidal functions:

```
>>> import matplotlib.pyplot as plt
>>> def tanh(z):
...     e_p = np.exp(z)
...     e_m = np.exp(-z)
...     return (e_p - e_m) / (e_p + e_m)
>>> z = np.arange(-5, 5, 0.005)
>>> log_act = logistic(z)
>>> tanh_act = tanh(z)
>>> plt.ylim([-1.5, 1.5])
>>> plt.xlabel('net input $z$')
>>> plt.ylabel('activation $\phi(z)$')
>>> plt.axhline(1, color='black', linestyle=':')
>>> plt.axhline(0.5, color='black', linestyle=':')
>>> plt.axhline(0, color='black', linestyle=':')
```

```
>>> plt.axhline(-0.5, color='black', linestyle=':')
>>> plt.axhline(-1, color='black', linestyle=':')
>>> plt.plot(z, tanh_act,
...          linewidth=3, linestyle='--',
...          label='tanh')
>>> plt.plot(z, log_act,
...          linewidth=3,
...          label='logistic')
>>> plt.legend(loc='lower right')
>>> plt.tight_layout()
>>> plt.show()
```

As you can see, the shapes of the two sigmoidal curves look very similar; however, the `tanh` function has double the output space of the `logistic` function:

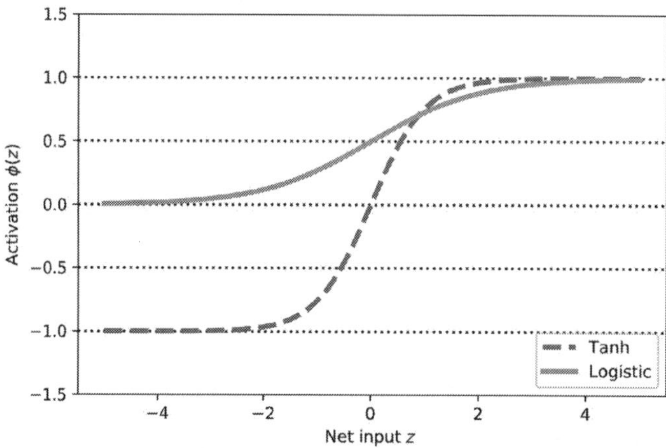

Figure 12.10: A comparison of the tanh and logistic functions

Note that we previously implemented the `logistic` and `tanh` functions verbosely for the purpose of illustration. In practice, we can use NumPy's `tanh` function.

Alternatively, when building an NN model, we can use `torch.tanh(x)` in PyTorch to achieve the same results:

```
>>> np.tanh(z)
array([-0.9999092 , -0.99990829, -0.99990737, ...,  0.99990644,
        0.99990737,  0.99990829])
>>> torch.tanh(torch.from_numpy(z))
tensor([-0.9999, -0.9999, -0.9999,  ...,  0.9999,  0.9999,  0.9999],
       dtype=torch.float64)
```

In addition, the logistic function is available in SciPy's `special` module:

```
>>> from scipy.special import expit
>>> expit(z)
array([0.00669285, 0.00672617, 0.00675966, ..., 0.99320669, 0.99324034,
       0.99327383])
```

Similarly, we can use the `torch.sigmoid()` function in PyTorch to do the same computation, as follows:

```
>>> torch.sigmoid(torch.from_numpy(z))
tensor([0.0067, 0.0067, 0.0068,  ..., 0.9932, 0.9932, 0.9933],
       dtype=torch.float64)
```

Note that using `torch.sigmoid(x)` produces results that are equivalent to `torch.nn.Sigmoid()(x)`, which we used earlier. `torch.nn.Sigmoid` is a class to which you can pass in parameters to construct an object in order to control the behavior. In contrast, `torch.sigmoid` is a function.

Rectified linear unit activation

The **rectified linear unit** (**ReLU**) is another activation function that is often used in deep NNs. Before we delve into ReLU, we should step back and understand the vanishing gradient problem of tanh and logistic activations.

To understand this problem, let's assume that we initially have the net input $z_1 = 20$, which changes to $z_2 = 25$. Computing the tanh activation, we get $\sigma(z_1) = 1.0$ and $\sigma(z_2) = 1.0$, which shows no change in the output (due to the asymptotic behavior of the tanh function and numerical errors).

This means that the derivative of activations with respect to the net input diminishes as z becomes large. As a result, learning the weights during the training phase becomes very slow because the gradient terms may be very close to zero. ReLU activation addresses this issue. Mathematically, ReLU is defined as follows:

$$\sigma(z) = \max(0, z)$$

ReLU is still a nonlinear function that is good for learning complex functions with NNs. Besides this, the derivative of ReLU, with respect to its input, is always 1 for positive input values. Therefore, it solves the problem of vanishing gradients, making it suitable for deep NNs. In PyTorch, we can apply the ReLU activation `torch.relu()` as follows:

```
>>> torch.relu(torch.from_numpy(z))
tensor([0.0000, 0.0000, 0.0000,  ..., 4.9850, 4.9900, 4.9950],
       dtype=torch.float64)
```

We will use the ReLU activation function in the next chapter as an activation function for multilayer convolutional NNs.

Now that we know more about the different activation functions that are commonly used in artificial NNs, let's conclude this section with an overview of the different activation functions that we have encountered so far in this book:

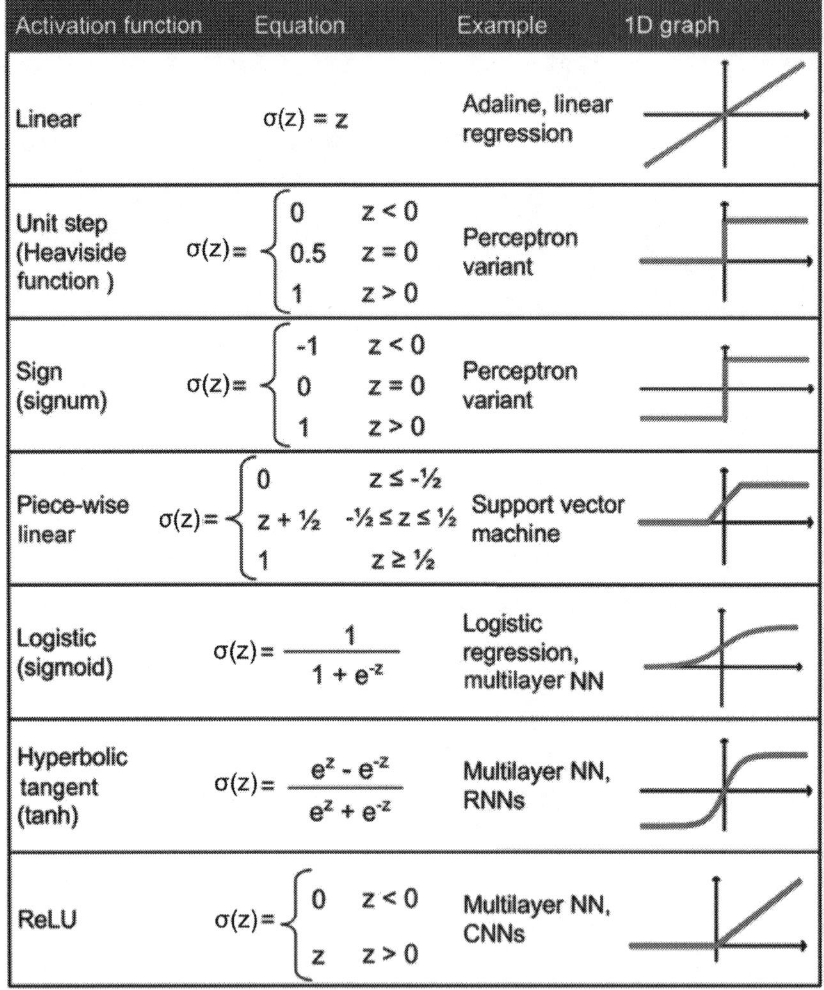

Activation function	Equation	Example	1D graph
Linear	$\sigma(z) = z$	Adaline, linear regression	
Unit step (Heaviside function)	$\sigma(z) = \begin{cases} 0 & z < 0 \\ 0.5 & z = 0 \\ 1 & z > 0 \end{cases}$	Perceptron variant	
Sign (signum)	$\sigma(z) = \begin{cases} -1 & z < 0 \\ 0 & z = 0 \\ 1 & z > 0 \end{cases}$	Perceptron variant	
Piece-wise linear	$\sigma(z) = \begin{cases} 0 & z \leq -\frac{1}{2} \\ z + \frac{1}{2} & -\frac{1}{2} \leq z \leq \frac{1}{2} \\ 1 & z \geq \frac{1}{2} \end{cases}$	Support vector machine	
Logistic (sigmoid)	$\sigma(z) = \frac{1}{1 + e^{-z}}$	Logistic regression, multilayer NN	
Hyperbolic tangent (tanh)	$\sigma(z) = \frac{e^{z} - e^{-z}}{e^{z} + e^{-z}}$	Multilayer NN, RNNs	
ReLU	$\sigma(z) = \begin{cases} 0 & z < 0 \\ z & z > 0 \end{cases}$	Multilayer NN, CNNs	

Figure 12.11: The activation functions covered in this book

You can find the list of all activation functions available in the `torch.nn` module at `https://pytorch.org/docs/stable/nn.functional.html#non-linear-activation-functions`.

Summary

In this chapter, you learned how to use PyTorch, an open source library for numerical computations, with a special focus on deep learning. While PyTorch is more inconvenient to use than NumPy, due to its additional complexity to support GPUs, it allows us to define and train large, multilayer NNs very efficiently.

Also, you learned about using the `torch.nn` module to build complex machine learning and NN models and run them efficiently. We explored model building in PyTorch by defining a model from scratch via the basic PyTorch tensor functionality. Implementing models can be tedious when we have to program at the level of matrix-vector multiplications and define every detail of each operation. However, the advantage is that this allows us, as developers, to combine such basic operations and build more complex models. We then explored `torch.nn`, which makes building NN models a lot easier than implementing them from scratch.

Finally, you learned about different activation functions and understood their behaviors and applications. Specifically, in this chapter, we covered tanh, softmax, and ReLU.

In the next chapter, we'll continue our journey and dive deeper into PyTorch, where we'll find ourselves working with PyTorch computation graphs and the automatic differentiation package. Along the way, you'll learn many new concepts, such as gradient computations.

Join our book's Discord space

Join our Discord community to meet like-minded people and learn alongside more than 2000 members at:

`https://packt.link/MLwPyTorch`

13

Going Deeper – The Mechanics of PyTorch

In *Chapter 12, Parallelizing Neural Network Training with PyTorch*, we covered how to define and manipulate tensors and worked with the `torch.utils.data` module to build input pipelines. We further built and trained a multilayer perceptron to classify the Iris dataset using the PyTorch neural network module (`torch.nn`).

Now that we have some hands-on experience with PyTorch neural network training and machine learning, it's time to take a deeper dive into the PyTorch library and explore its rich set of features, which will allow us to implement more advanced deep learning models in upcoming chapters.

In this chapter, we will use different aspects of PyTorch's API to implement NNs. In particular, we will again use the `torch.nn` module, which provides multiple layers of abstraction to make the implementation of standard architectures very convenient. It also allows us to implement custom NN layers, which is very useful in research-oriented projects that require more customization. Later in this chapter, we will implement such a custom layer.

To illustrate the different ways of model building using the `torch.nn` module, we will also consider the classic **exclusive or** (**XOR**) problem. Firstly, we will build multilayer perceptrons using the `Sequential` class. Then, we will consider other methods, such as subclassing `nn.Module` for defining custom layers. Finally, we will work on two real-world projects that cover the machine learning steps from raw input to prediction.

The topics that we will cover are as follows:

- Understanding and working with PyTorch computation graphs
- Working with PyTorch tensor objects
- Solving the classic XOR problem and understanding model capacity
- Building complex NN models using PyTorch's `Sequential` class and the `nn.Module` class
- Computing gradients using automatic differentiation and `torch.autograd`

The key features of PyTorch

In the previous chapter, we saw that PyTorch provides us with a scalable, multiplatform programming interface for implementing and running machine learning algorithms. After its initial release in 2016 and its 1.0 release in 2018, PyTorch has evolved into one of the two most popular frameworks for deep learning. It uses dynamic computational graphs, which have the advantage of being more flexible compared to its static counterparts. Dynamic computational graphs are debugging friendly: PyTorch allows for interleaving the graph declaration and graph evaluation steps. You can execute the code line by line while having full access to all variables. This is a very important feature that makes the development and training of NNs very convenient.

While PyTorch is an open-source library and can be used for free by everyone, its development is funded and supported by Facebook. This involves a large team of software engineers who expand and improve the library continuously. Since PyTorch is an open-source library, it also has strong support from other developers outside of Facebook, who avidly contribute and provide user feedback. This has made the PyTorch library more useful to both academic researchers and developers. A further consequence of these factors is that PyTorch has extensive documentation and tutorials to help new users.

Another key feature of PyTorch, which was also noted in the previous chapter, is its ability to work with single or multiple **graphical processing units** (**GPUs**). This allows users to train deep learning models very efficiently on large datasets and large-scale systems.

Last but not least, PyTorch supports mobile deployment, which also makes it a very suitable tool for production.

In the next section, we will look at how a tensor and function in PyTorch are interconnected via a computation graph.

PyTorch's computation graphs

PyTorch performs its computations based on a **directed acyclic graph** (**DAG**). In this section, we will see how these graphs can be defined for a simple arithmetic computation. Then, we will see the dynamic graph paradigm, as well as how the graph is created on the fly in PyTorch.

Understanding computation graphs

PyTorch relies on building a computation graph at its core, and it uses this computation graph to derive relationships between tensors from the input all the way to the output. Let's say that we have rank 0 (scalar) tensors a, b, and c and we want to evaluate $z = 2 \times (a - b) + c$.

This evaluation can be represented as a computation graph, as shown in *Figure 13.1*:

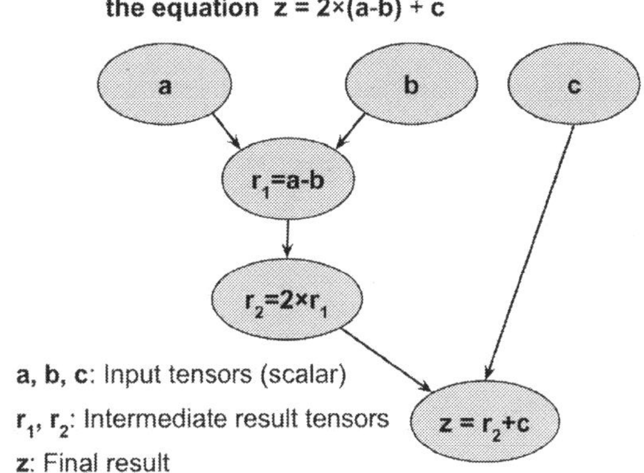

Figure 13.1: How a computation graph works

As you can see, the computation graph is simply a network of nodes. Each node resembles an operation, which applies a function to its input tensor or tensors and returns zero or more tensors as the output. PyTorch builds this computation graph and uses it to compute the gradients accordingly. In the next subsection, we will see some examples of creating a graph for this computation using PyTorch.

Creating a graph in PyTorch

Let's look at a simple example that illustrates how to create a graph in PyTorch for evaluating $z = 2 \times (a - b) + c$, as shown in the previous figure. The variables a, b, and c are scalars (single numbers), and we define these as PyTorch tensors. To create the graph, we can simply define a regular Python function with `a`, `b`, and `c` as its input arguments, for example:

```
>>> import torch
>>> def compute_z(a, b, c):
...     r1 = torch.sub(a, b)
...     r2 = torch.mul(r1, 2)
...     z = torch.add(r2, c)
...     return z
```

Now, to carry out the computation, we can simply call this function with tensor objects as function arguments. Note that PyTorch functions such as `add`, `sub` (or `subtract`), and `mul` (or `multiply`) also allow us to provide inputs of higher ranks in the form of a PyTorch tensor object. In the following code example, we provide scalar inputs (rank 0), as well as rank 1 and rank 2 inputs, as lists:

```
>>> print('Scalar Inputs:', compute_z(torch.tensor(1),
...       torch.tensor(2), torch.tensor(3)))
Scalar Inputs: tensor(1)
>>> print('Rank 1 Inputs:', compute_z(torch.tensor([1]),
...       torch.tensor([2]), torch.tensor([3])))
Rank 1 Inputs: tensor([1])
>>> print('Rank 2 Inputs:', compute_z(torch.tensor([[1]]),
...       torch.tensor([[2]]), torch.tensor([[3]])))
Rank 2 Inputs: tensor([[1]])
```

In this section, you saw how simple it is to create a computation graph in PyTorch. Next, we will look at PyTorch tensors that can be used for storing and updating model parameters.

PyTorch tensor objects for storing and updating model parameters

We covered tensor objects in *Chapter 12, Parallelizing Neural Network Training with PyTorch*. In PyTorch, a special tensor object for which gradients need to be computed allows us to store and update the parameters of our models during training. Such a tensor can be created by just assigning `requires_grad` to `True` on user-specified initial values. Note that as of now (mid-2021), only tensors of floating point and complex `dtype` can require gradients. In the following code, we will generate tensor objects of type `float32`:

```
>>> a = torch.tensor(3.14, requires_grad=True)
>>> print(a)
tensor(3.1400, requires_grad=True)
>>> b = torch.tensor([1.0, 2.0, 3.0], requires_grad=True)
>>> print(b)
tensor([1., 2., 3.], requires_grad=True)
```

Notice that requires_grad is set to False by default. This value can be efficiently set to True by running requires_grad_().

method_() is an in-place method in PyTorch that is used for operations without making a copy of the input.

Let's take a look at the following example:

```
>>> w = torch.tensor([1.0, 2.0, 3.0])
>>> print(w.requires_grad)
False
>>> w.requires_grad_()
>>> print(w.requires_grad)
True
```

You will recall that for NN models, initializing model parameters with random weights is necessary to break the symmetry during backpropagation—otherwise, a multilayer NN would be no more useful than a single-layer NN like logistic regression. When creating a PyTorch tensor, we can also use a random initialization scheme. PyTorch can generate random numbers based on a variety of probability distributions (see https://pytorch.org/docs/stable/torch.html#random-sampling). In the following example, we will take a look at some standard initialization methods that are also available in the torch.nn.init module (see https://pytorch.org/docs/stable/nn.init.html).

So, let's look at how we can create a tensor with Glorot initialization, which is a classic random initialization scheme that was proposed by Xavier Glorot and Yoshua Bengio. For this, we first create an empty tensor and an operator called init as an object of class GlorotNormal. Then, we fill this tensor with values according to the Glorot initialization by calling the xavier_normal_() method. In the following example, we initialize a tensor of shape 2×3:

```
>>> import torch.nn as nn
>>> torch.manual_seed(1)
>>> w = torch.empty(2, 3)
>>> nn.init.xavier_normal_(w)
>>> print(w)
tensor([[ 0.4183,  0.1688,  0.0390],
        [ 0.3930, -0.2858, -0.1051]])
```

Xavier (or Glorot) initialization

In the early development of deep learning, it was observed that random uniform or random normal weight initialization could often result in poor model performance during training.

In 2010, Glorot and Bengio investigated the effect of initialization and proposed a novel, more robust initialization scheme to facilitate the training of deep networks. The general idea behind Xavier initialization is to roughly balance the variance of the gradients across different layers. Otherwise, some layers may get too much attention during training while the other layers lag behind.

According to the research paper by Glorot and Bengio, if we want to initialize the weights in a uniform distribution, we should choose the interval of this uniform distribution as follows:

$$W \sim Uniform\left(-\frac{\sqrt{6}}{\sqrt{n_{in}+n_{out}}}, \frac{\sqrt{6}}{\sqrt{n_{in}+n_{out}}}\right)$$

Here, n_{in} is the number of input neurons that are multiplied by the weights, and n_{out} is the number of output neurons that feed into the next layer. For initializing the weights from Gaussian (normal) distribution, we recommend that you choose the standard deviation of this Gaussian to be:

$$\sigma = \frac{\sqrt{2}}{\sqrt{n_{in}+n_{out}}}$$

PyTorch supports Xavier initialization in both uniform and normal distributions of weights.

For more information about Glorot and Bengio's initialization scheme, including the rationale and mathematical motivation, we recommend the original paper (*Understanding the difficulty of deep feedforward neural networks*, *Xavier Glorot* and *Yoshua Bengio*, 2010), which is freely available at `http://proceedings.mlr.press/v9/glorot10a/glorot10a.pdf`.

Now, to put this into the context of a more practical use case, let's see how we can define two `Tensor` objects inside the base `nn.Module` class:

```
>>> class MyModule(nn.Module):
...     def __init__(self):
...         super().__init__()
...         self.w1 = torch.empty(2, 3, requires_grad=True)
...         nn.init.xavier_normal_(self.w1)
...         self.w2 = torch.empty(1, 2, requires_grad=True)
...         nn.init.xavier_normal_(self.w2)
```

These two tensors can be then used as weights whose gradients will be computed via automatic differentiation.

Computing gradients via automatic differentiation

As you already know, optimizing NNs requires computing the gradients of the loss with respect to the NN weights. This is required for optimization algorithms such as **stochastic gradient descent** (**SGD**). In addition, gradients have other applications, such as diagnosing the network to find out why an NN model is making a particular prediction for a test example. Therefore, in this section, we will cover how to compute gradients of a computation with respect to its input variables.

Computing the gradients of the loss with respect to trainable variables

PyTorch supports *automatic differentiation*, which can be thought of as an implementation of the *chain rule* for computing gradients of nested functions. Note that for the sake of simplicity, we will use the term *gradient* to refer to both partial derivatives and gradients.

Partial derivatives and gradients

A partial derivative $\frac{\partial f}{\partial x_1}$ can be understood as the rate of change of a multivariate function—a function with multiple inputs, $f(x_1, x_2, ...)$, with respect to one of its inputs (here: x_1). The gradient, ∇f, of a function is a vector composed of all the inputs' partial derivatives, $\nabla f = \left(\frac{\partial f}{\partial x_1}, \frac{\partial f}{\partial x_2}, \ldots\right)$.

When we define a series of operations that results in some output or even intermediate tensors, PyTorch provides a context for calculating gradients of these computed tensors with respect to its dependent nodes in the computation graph. To compute these gradients, we can call the `backward` method from the `torch.autograd` module. It computes the sum of gradients of the given tensor with regard to leaf nodes (terminal nodes) in the graph.

Let's work with a simple example where we will compute $z = wx + b$ and define the loss as the squared loss between the target y and prediction z, $Loss = (y - z)^2$. In the more general case, where we may have multiple predictions and targets, we compute the loss as the sum of the squared error, $Loss = \sum_i (y_i - z_i)^2$. In order to implement this computation in PyTorch, we will define the model parameters, w and b, as variables (tensors with the `requires_gradient` attribute set to `True`), and the input, x and y, as default tensors. We will compute the loss tensor and use it to compute the gradients of the model parameters, w and b, as follows:

```
>>> w = torch.tensor(1.0, requires_grad=True)
>>> b = torch.tensor(0.5, requires_grad=True)
>>> x = torch.tensor([1.4])
>>> y = torch.tensor([2.1])
>>> z = torch.add(torch.mul(w, x), b)
>>> loss = (y-z).pow(2).sum()
```

```
>>> loss.backward()
>>> print('dL/dw : ', w.grad)
>>> print('dL/db : ', b.grad)
dL/dw :  tensor(-0.5600)
dL/db :  tensor(-0.4000)
```

Computing the value z is a forward pass in an NN. We used the `backward` method on the `loss` tensor to compute $\frac{\partial Loss}{\partial w}$ and $\frac{\partial Loss}{\partial b}$. Since this is a very simple example, we can obtain $\frac{\partial Loss}{\partial w} = 2x(wx + b - y)$ symbolically to verify that the computed gradients match the results we obtained in the previous code example:

```
>>> # verifying the computed gradient
>>> print(2 * x * ((w * x + b) - y))
tensor([-0.5600], grad_fn=<MulBackward0>)
```

We leave the verification of b as an exercise for the reader.

Understanding automatic differentiation

Automatic differentiation represents a set of computational techniques for computing gradients of arbitrary arithmetic operations. During this process, gradients of a computation (expressed as a series of operations) are obtained by accumulating the gradients through repeated applications of the chain rule. To better understand the concept behind automatic differentiation, let's consider a series of nested computations, $y = f(g(h(x)))$, with input x and output y. This can be broken into a series of steps:

- $u_0 = x$
- $u_1 = h(x)$
- $u_2 = g(u_1)$
- $u_3 = f(u_2) = y$

The derivative $\frac{dy}{dx}$ can be computed in two different ways: forward accumulation, which starts with $\frac{du_3}{dx} = \frac{du_3}{du_2}\frac{du_2}{du_0}$, and reverse accumulation, which starts with $\frac{dy}{du_0} = \frac{dy}{du_1}\frac{du_1}{du_0}$. Note that PyTorch uses the latter, reverse accumulation, which is more efficient for implementing backpropagation.

Adversarial examples

Computing gradients of the loss with respect to the input example is used for generating *adversarial examples* (or *adversarial attacks*). In computer vision, adversarial examples are examples that are generated by adding some small, imperceptible noise (or perturbations) to the input example, which results in a deep NN misclassifying them. Covering adversarial examples is beyond the scope of this book, but if you are interested, you can find the original paper by *Christian Szegedy et al.*, *Intriguing properties of neural networks* at `https://arxiv.org/pdf/1312.6199.pdf`.

Simplifying implementations of common architectures via the torch.nn module

You have already seen some examples of building a feedforward NN model (for instance, a multilayer perceptron) and defining a sequence of layers using the `nn.Module` class. Before we take a deeper dive into `nn.Module`, let's briefly look at another approach for conjuring those layers via `nn.Sequential`.

Implementing models based on nn.Sequential

With `nn.Sequential` (`https://pytorch.org/docs/master/generated/torch.nn.Sequential.html#sequential`), the layers stored inside the model are connected in a cascaded way. In the following example, we will build a model with two densely (fully) connected layers:

```
>>> model = nn.Sequential(
...     nn.Linear(4, 16),
...     nn.ReLU(),
...     nn.Linear(16, 32),
...     nn.ReLU()
... )
>>> model
Sequential(
  (0): Linear(in_features=4, out_features=16, bias=True)
  (1): ReLU()
  (2): Linear(in_features=16, out_features=32, bias=True)
  (3): ReLU()
)
```

We specified the layers and instantiated the `model` after passing the layers to the `nn.Sequential` class. The output of the first fully connected layer is used as the input to the first ReLU layer. The output of the first ReLU layer becomes the input for the second fully connected layer. Finally, the output of the second fully connected layer is used as the input to the second ReLU layer.

We can further configure these layers, for example, by applying different activation functions, initializers, or regularization methods to the parameters. A comprehensive and complete list of available options for most of these categories can be found in the official documentation:

- Choosing activation functions: `https://pytorch.org/docs/stable/nn.html#non-linear-activations-weighted-sum-nonlinearity`
- Initializing the layer parameters via `nn.init`: `https://pytorch.org/docs/stable/nn.init.html`
- Applying L2 regularization to the layer parameters (to prevent overfitting) via the parameter `weight_decay` of some optimizers in `torch.optim`: `https://pytorch.org/docs/stable/optim.html`

- Applying L1 regularization to the layer parameters (to prevent overfitting) by adding the L1 penalty term to the loss tensor, which we will implement next

In the following code example, we will configure the first fully connected layer by specifying the initial value distribution for the weight. Then, we will configure the second fully connected layer by computing the L1 penalty term for the weight matrix:

```
>>> nn.init.xavier_uniform_(model[0].weight)
>>> l1_weight = 0.01
>>> l1_penalty = l1_weight * model[2].weight.abs().sum()
```

Here, we initialized the weight of the first linear layer with Xavier initialization. And we computed the L1 norm of the weight of the second linear layer.

Furthermore, we can also specify the type of optimizer and the loss function for training. Again, a comprehensive list of all available options can be found in the official documentation:

- Optimizers via `torch.optim`: `https://pytorch.org/docs/stable/optim.html#algorithms`
- Loss functions: `https://pytorch.org/docs/stable/nn.html#loss-functions`

Choosing a loss function

Regarding the choices for optimization algorithms, SGD and Adam are the most widely used methods. The choice of loss function depends on the task; for example, you might use mean square error loss for a regression problem.

The family of cross-entropy loss functions supplies the possible choices for classification tasks, which are extensively discussed in *Chapter 14, Classifying Images with Deep Convolutional Neural Networks*.

Furthermore, you can use the techniques you have learned from previous chapters (such as techniques for model evaluation from *Chapter 6, Learning Best Practices for Model Evaluation and Hyperparameter Tuning*) combined with the appropriate metrics for the problem. For example, precision and recall, accuracy, **area under the curve** (AUC), and false negative and false positive scores are appropriate metrics for evaluating classification models.

In this example, we will use the SGD optimizer, and cross-entropy loss for binary classification:

```
>>> loss_fn = nn.BCELoss()
>>> optimizer = torch.optim.SGD(model.parameters(), lr=0.001)
```

Next, we will look at a more practical example: solving the classic XOR classification problem. First, we will use the `nn.Sequential()` class to build the model. Along the way, you will also learn about the capacity of a model for handling nonlinear decision boundaries. Then, we will cover building a model via `nn.Module` that will give us more flexibility and control over the layers of the network.

Solving an XOR classification problem

The XOR classification problem is a classic problem for analyzing the capacity of a model with regard to capturing the nonlinear decision boundary between two classes. We generate a toy dataset of 200 training examples with two features (x_0, x_1) drawn from a uniform distribution between [-1, 1). Then, we assign the ground truth label for training example i according to the following rule:

$$y^{(i)} = \begin{cases} 0 & \text{if } x_0^{(i)} \times x_1^{(i)} < 0 \\ 1 & \text{otherwise} \end{cases}$$

We will use half of the data (100 training examples) for training and the remaining half for validation. The code for generating the data and splitting it into the training and validation datasets is as follows:

```
>>> import matplotlib.pyplot as plt
>>> import numpy as np
>>> torch.manual_seed(1)
>>> np.random.seed(1)
>>> x = np.random.uniform(low=-1, high=1, size=(200, 2))
>>> y = np.ones(len(x))
>>> y[x[:, 0] * x[:, 1]<0] = 0
>>> n_train = 100
>>> x_train = torch.tensor(x[:n_train, :], dtype=torch.float32)
>>> y_train = torch.tensor(y[:n_train], dtype=torch.float32)
>>> x_valid = torch.tensor(x[n_train:, :], dtype=torch.float32)
>>> y_valid = torch.tensor(y[n_train:], dtype=torch.float32)
>>> fig = plt.figure(figsize=(6, 6))
>>> plt.plot(x[y==0, 0], x[y==0, 1], 'o', alpha=0.75, markersize=10)
>>> plt.plot(x[y==1, 0], x[y==1, 1], '<', alpha=0.75, markersize=10)
>>> plt.xlabel(r'$x_1$', size=15)
>>> plt.ylabel(r'$x_2$', size=15)
>>> plt.show()
```

The code results in the following scatterplot of the training and validation examples, shown with different markers based on their class label:

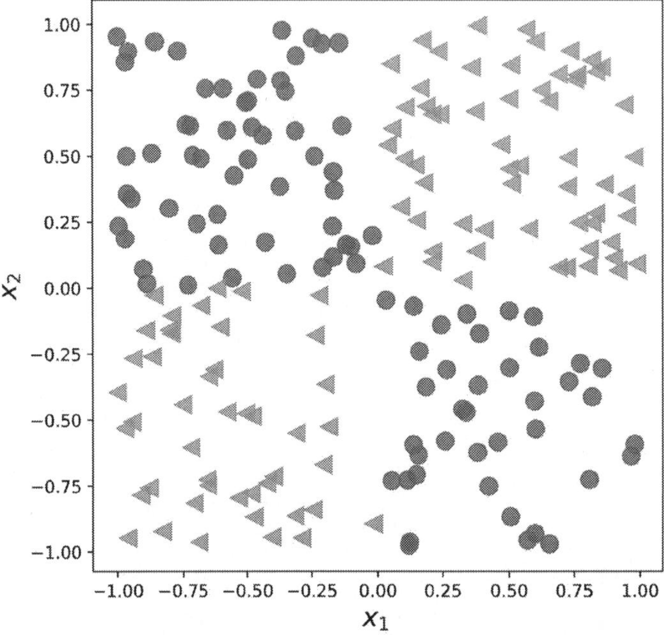

Figure 13.2: Scatterplot of training and validation examples

In the previous subsection, we covered the essential tools that we need to implement a classifier in PyTorch. We now need to decide what architecture we should choose for this task and dataset. As a general rule of thumb, the more layers we have, and the more neurons we have in each layer, the larger the capacity of the model will be. Here, the model capacity can be thought of as a measure of how readily the model can approximate complex functions. While having more parameters means the network can fit more complex functions, larger models are usually harder to train (and prone to overfitting). In practice, it is always a good idea to start with a simple model as a baseline, for example, a single-layer NN like logistic regression:

```
>>> model = nn.Sequential(
...     nn.Linear(2, 1),
...     nn.Sigmoid()
... )
>>> model
Sequential(
  (0): Linear(in_features=2, out_features=1, bias=True)
  (1): Sigmoid()
)
```

After defining the model, we will initialize the cross-entropy loss function for binary classification and the SGD optimizer:

```
>>> loss_fn = nn.BCELoss()
>>> optimizer = torch.optim.SGD(model.parameters(), lr=0.001)
```

Next, we will create a data loader that uses a batch size of 2 for the train data:

```
>>> from torch.utils.data import DataLoader, TensorDataset
>>> train_ds = TensorDataset(x_train, y_train)
>>> batch_size = 2
>>> torch.manual_seed(1)
>>> train_dl = DataLoader(train_ds, batch_size, shuffle=True)
```

Now we will train the model for 200 epochs and record a history of training epochs:

```
>>> torch.manual_seed(1)
>>> num_epochs = 200
>>> def train(model, num_epochs, train_dl, x_valid, y_valid):
...     loss_hist_train = [0] * num_epochs
...     accuracy_hist_train = [0] * num_epochs
...     loss_hist_valid = [0] * num_epochs
...     accuracy_hist_valid = [0] * num_epochs
...     for epoch in range(num_epochs):
...         for x_batch, y_batch in train_dl:
...             pred = model(x_batch)[:, 0]
...             loss = loss_fn(pred, y_batch)
...             loss.backward()
...             optimizer.step()
...             optimizer.zero_grad()
...             loss_hist_train[epoch] += loss.item()
...             is_correct = ((pred>=0.5).float() == y_batch).float()
...             accuracy_hist_train[epoch] += is_correct.mean()
...         loss_hist_train[epoch] /= n_train/batch_size
...         accuracy_hist_train[epoch] /= n_train/batch_size
...         pred = model(x_valid)[:, 0]
...         loss = loss_fn(pred, y_valid)
...         loss_hist_valid[epoch] = loss.item()
...         is_correct = ((pred>=0.5).float() == y_valid).float()
...         accuracy_hist_valid[epoch] += is_correct.mean()
...     return loss_hist_train, loss_hist_valid, \
...            accuracy_hist_train, accuracy_hist_valid
>>> history = train(model, num_epochs, train_dl, x_valid, y_valid)
```

Notice that the history of training epochs includes the train loss and validation loss and the train accuracy and validation accuracy, which is useful for visual inspection after training. In the following code, we will plot the learning curves, including the training and validation loss, as well as their accuracies.

The following code will plot the training performance:

```
>>> fig = plt.figure(figsize=(16, 4))
>>> ax = fig.add_subplot(1, 2, 1)
>>> plt.plot(history[0], lw=4)
>>> plt.plot(history[1], lw=4)
>>> plt.legend(['Train loss', 'Validation loss'], fontsize=15)
>>> ax.set_xlabel('Epochs', size=15)
>>> ax = fig.add_subplot(1, 2, 2)
>>> plt.plot(history[2], lw=4)
>>> plt.plot(history[3], lw=4)
>>> plt.legend(['Train acc.', 'Validation acc.'], fontsize=15)
>>> ax.set_xlabel('Epochs', size=15)
```

This results in the following figure, with two separate panels for the losses and accuracies:

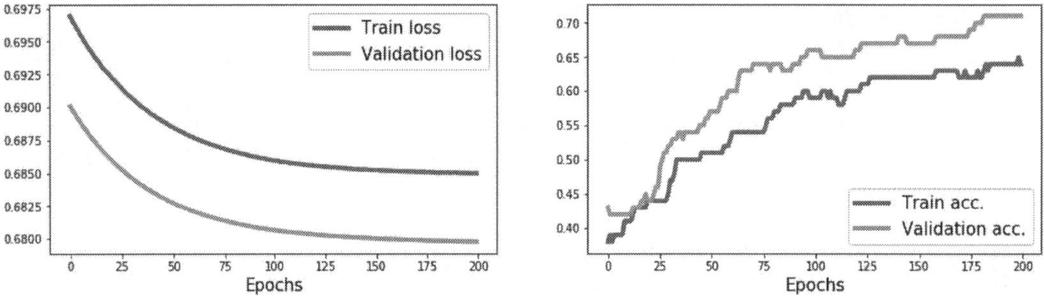

Figure 13.3: Loss and accuracy results

As you can see, a simple model with no hidden layer can only derive a linear decision boundary, which is unable to solve the XOR problem. As a consequence, we can observe that the loss terms for both the training and the validation datasets are very high, and the classification accuracy is very low.

To derive a nonlinear decision boundary, we can add one or more hidden layers connected via nonlinear activation functions. The universal approximation theorem states that a feedforward NN with a single hidden layer and a relatively large number of hidden units can approximate arbitrary continuous functions relatively well. Thus, one approach for tackling the XOR problem more satisfactorily is to add a hidden layer and compare different numbers of hidden units until we observe satisfactory results on the validation dataset. Adding more hidden units would correspond to increasing the width of a layer.

Alternatively, we can also add more hidden layers, which will make the model deeper. The advantage of making a network deeper rather than wider is that fewer parameters are required to achieve a comparable model capacity.

However, a downside of deep (versus wide) models is that deep models are prone to vanishing and exploding gradients, which make them harder to train.

As an exercise, try adding one, two, three, and four hidden layers, each with four hidden units. In the following example, we will take a look at the results of a feedforward NN with two hidden layers:

```
>>> model = nn.Sequential(
...     nn.Linear(2, 4),
...     nn.ReLU(),
...     nn.Linear(4, 4),
...     nn.ReLU(),
...     nn.Linear(4, 1),
...     nn.Sigmoid()
... )
>>> loss_fn = nn.BCELoss()
>>> optimizer = torch.optim.SGD(model.parameters(), lr=0.015)
>>> model
Sequential(
  (0): Linear(in_features=2, out_features=4, bias=True)
  (1): ReLU()
  (2): Linear(in_features=4, out_features=4, bias=True)
  (3): ReLU()
  (4): Linear(in_features=4, out_features=1, bias=True)
  (5): Sigmoid()
)
>>> history = train(model, num_epochs, train_dl, x_valid, y_valid)
```

We can repeat the previous code for visualization, which produces the following:

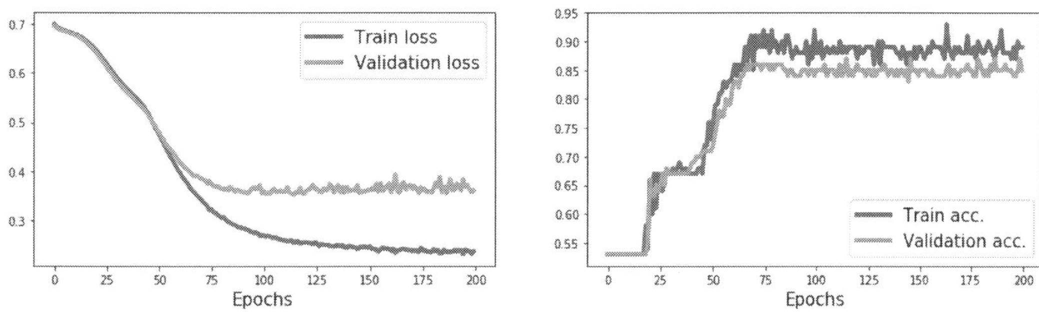

Figure 13.4: Loss and accuracy results after adding two hidden layers

Now, we can see that the model is able to derive a nonlinear decision boundary for this data, and the model reaches 100 percent accuracy on the training dataset. The validation dataset's accuracy is 95 percent, which indicates that the model is slightly overfitting.

Making model building more flexible with nn.Module

In the previous example, we used the PyTorch `Sequential` class to create a fully connected NN with multiple layers. This is a very common and convenient way of building models. However, it unfortunately doesn't allow us to create more complex models that have multiple input, output, or intermediate branches. That's where `nn.Module` comes in handy.

The alternative way to build complex models is by subclassing `nn.Module`. In this approach, we create a new class derived from `nn.Module` and define the method, `__init__()`, as a constructor. The `forward()` method is used to specify the forward pass. In the constructor function, `__init__()`, we define the layers as attributes of the class so that they can be accessed via the `self` reference attribute. Then, in the `forward()` method, we specify how these layers are to be used in the forward pass of the NN. The code for defining a new class that implements the previous model is as follows:

```
>>> class MyModule(nn.Module):
...     def __init__(self):
...         super().__init__()
...         l1 = nn.Linear(2, 4)
...         a1 = nn.ReLU()
...         l2 = nn.Linear(4, 4)
...         a2 = nn.ReLU()
...         l3 = nn.Linear(4, 1)
...         a3 = nn.Sigmoid()
...         l = [l1, a1, l2, a2, l3, a3]
...         self.module_list = nn.ModuleList(l)
...
...     def forward(self, x):
...         for f in self.module_list:
...             x = f(x)
...         return x
```

Notice that we put all layers in the `nn.ModuleList` object, which is just a `list` object composed of `nn.Module` items. This makes the code more readable and easier to follow.

Once we define an instance of this new class, we can train it as we did previously:

```
>>> model = MyModule()
>>> model
MyModule(
  (module_list): ModuleList(
    (0): Linear(in_features=2, out_features=4, bias=True)
    (1): ReLU()
    (2): Linear(in_features=4, out_features=4, bias=True)
    (3): ReLU()
```

```
    (4): Linear(in_features=4, out_features=1, bias=True)
    (5): Sigmoid()
  )
)
>>> loss_fn = nn.BCELoss()
>>> optimizer = torch.optim.SGD(model.parameters(), lr=0.015)
>>> history = train(model, num_epochs, train_dl, x_valid, y_valid)
```

Next, besides the train history, we will use the mlxtend library to visualize the validation data and the decision boundary.

Mlxtend can be installed via `conda` or `pip` as follows:

```
conda install mlxtend -c conda-forge
pip install mlxtend
```

To compute the decision boundary of our model, we need to add a `predict()` method in the `MyModule` class:

```
>>>     def predict(self, x):
...         x = torch.tensor(x, dtype=torch.float32)
...         pred = self.forward(x)[:, 0]
...         return (pred>=0.5).float()
```

It will return the predicted class (0 or 1) for a sample.

The following code will plot the training performance along with the decision region bias:

```
>>> from mlxtend.plotting import plot_decision_regions
>>> fig = plt.figure(figsize=(16, 4))
>>> ax = fig.add_subplot(1, 3, 1)
>>> plt.plot(history[0], lw=4)
>>> plt.plot(history[1], lw=4)
>>> plt.legend(['Train loss', 'Validation loss'], fontsize=15)
>>> ax.set_xlabel('Epochs', size=15)
>>> ax = fig.add_subplot(1, 3, 2)
>>> plt.plot(history[2], lw=4)
>>> plt.plot(history[3], lw=4)
>>> plt.legend(['Train acc.', 'Validation acc.'], fontsize=15)
>>> ax.set_xlabel('Epochs', size=15)
>>> ax = fig.add_subplot(1, 3, 3)
>>> plot_decision_regions(X=x_valid.numpy(),
...                       y=y_valid.numpy().astype(np.integer),
...                       clf=model)
>>> ax.set_xlabel(r'$x_1$', size=15)
```

```
>>> ax.xaxis.set_label_coords(1, -0.025)
>>> ax.set_ylabel(r'$x_2$', size=15)
>>> ax.yaxis.set_label_coords(-0.025, 1)
>>> plt.show()
```

This results in *Figure 13.5*, with three separate panels for the losses, accuracies, and the scatterplot of the validation examples, along with the decision boundary:

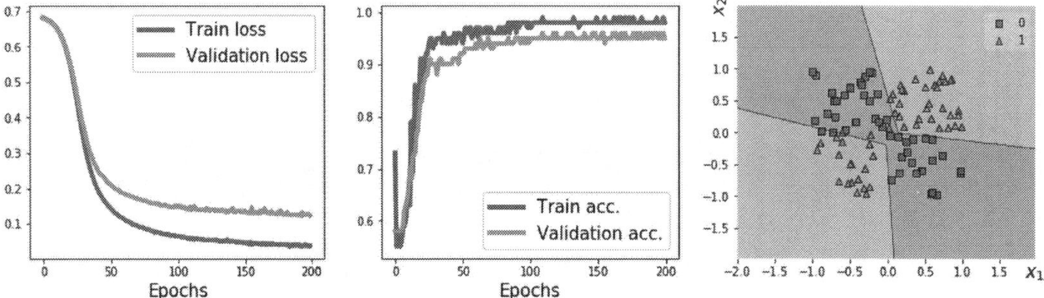

Figure 13.5: Results, including a scatterplot

Writing custom layers in PyTorch

In cases where we want to define a new layer that is not already supported by PyTorch, we can define a new class derived from the `nn.Module` class. This is especially useful when designing a new layer or customizing an existing layer.

To illustrate the concept of implementing custom layers, let's consider a simple example. Imagine we want to define a new linear layer that computes $w(x + \epsilon) + b$, where ϵ refers to a random variable as a noise variable. To implement this computation, we define a new class as a subclass of `nn.Module`. For this new class, we have to define both the constructor `__init__()` method and the `forward()` method. In the constructor, we define the variables and other required tensors for our customized layer. We can create variables and initialize them in the constructor if the `input_size` is given to the constructor. Alternatively, we can delay the variable initialization (for instance, if we do not know the exact input shape upfront) and delegate it to another method for late variable creation.

To look at a concrete example, we are going to define a new layer called `NoisyLinear`, which implements the computation $w(x + \epsilon) + b$, which was mentioned in the preceding paragraph:

```
>>> class NoisyLinear(nn.Module):
...     def __init__(self, input_size, output_size,
...                  noise_stddev=0.1):
...         super().__init__()
...         w = torch.Tensor(input_size, output_size)
...         self.w = nn.Parameter(w)  # nn.Parameter is a Tensor
...                                   # that's a module parameter.
```

```
...             nn.init.xavier_uniform_(self.w)
...             b = torch.Tensor(output_size).fill_(0)
...             self.b = nn.Parameter(b)
...             self.noise_stddev = noise_stddev
...
...         def forward(self, x, training=False):
...             if training:
...                 noise = torch.normal(0.0, self.noise_stddev, x.shape)
...                 x_new = torch.add(x, noise)
...             else:
...                 x_new = x
...             return torch.add(torch.mm(x_new, self.w), self.b)
```

In the constructor, we have added an argument, `noise_stddev`, to specify the standard deviation for the distribution of ϵ, which is sampled from a Gaussian distribution. Furthermore, notice that in the `forward()` method, we have used an additional argument, `training=False`. We use it to distinguish whether the layer is used during training or only for prediction (this is sometimes also called *inference*) or evaluation. Also, there are certain methods that behave differently in training and prediction modes. You will encounter an example of such a method, `Dropout`, in the upcoming chapters. In the previous code snippet, we also specified that the random vector, ϵ, was to be generated and added to the input during training only and not used for inference or evaluation.

Before we go a step further and use our custom `NoisyLinear` layer in a model, let's test it in the context of a simple example.

1. In the following code, we will define a new instance of this layer, and execute it on an input tensor. Then, we will call the layer three times on the same input tensor:

```
>>> torch.manual_seed(1)
>>> noisy_layer = NoisyLinear(4, 2)
>>> x = torch.zeros((1, 4))
>>> print(noisy_layer(x, training=True))
tensor([[ 0.1154, -0.0598]], grad_fn=<AddBackward0>)
>>> print(noisy_layer(x, training=True))
tensor([[ 0.0432, -0.0375]], grad_fn=<AddBackward0>)
>>> print(noisy_layer(x, training=False))
tensor([[0., 0.]], grad_fn=<AddBackward0>)
```

Note that the outputs for the first two calls differ because the `NoisyLinear` layer added random noise to the input tensor. The third call outputs [0, 0] as we didn't add noise by specifying `training=False`.

2. Now, let's create a new model similar to the previous one for solving the XOR classification task. As before, we will use the `nn.Module` class for model building, but this time, we will use our `NoisyLinear` layer as the first hidden layer of the multilayer perceptron. The code is as follows:

```
>>> class MyNoisyModule(nn.Module):
...     def __init__(self):
...         super().__init__()
...         self.l1 = NoisyLinear(2, 4, 0.07)
...         self.a1 = nn.ReLU()
...         self.l2 = nn.Linear(4, 4)
...         self.a2 = nn.ReLU()
...         self.l3 = nn.Linear(4, 1)
...         self.a3 = nn.Sigmoid()
...
...     def forward(self, x, training=False):
...         x = self.l1(x, training)
...         x = self.a1(x)
...         x = self.l2(x)
...         x = self.a2(x)
...         x = self.l3(x)
...         x = self.a3(x)
...         return x
...
...     def predict(self, x):
...         x = torch.tensor(x, dtype=torch.float32)
...         pred = self.forward(x)[:, 0]
...         return (pred>=0.5).float()
...
>>> torch.manual_seed(1)
>>> model = MyNoisyModule()
>>> model
MyNoisyModule(
  (l1): NoisyLinear()
  (a1): ReLU()
  (l2): Linear(in_features=4, out_features=4, bias=True)
```

```
    (a2): ReLU()
    (l3): Linear(in_features=4, out_features=1, bias=True)
    (a3): Sigmoid()
  )
```

3. Similarly, we will train the model as we did previously. At this time, to compute the prediction on the training batch, we use `pred = model(x_batch, True)[:, 0]` instead of `pred = model(x_batch)[:, 0]`:

```
>>> loss_fn = nn.BCELoss()
>>> optimizer = torch.optim.SGD(model.parameters(), lr=0.015)
>>> torch.manual_seed(1)
>>> loss_hist_train = [0] * num_epochs
>>> accuracy_hist_train = [0] * num_epochs
>>> loss_hist_valid = [0] * num_epochs
>>> accuracy_hist_valid = [0] * num_epochs
>>> for epoch in range(num_epochs):
...     for x_batch, y_batch in train_dl:
...         pred = model(x_batch, True)[:, 0]
...         loss = loss_fn(pred, y_batch)
...         loss.backward()
...         optimizer.step()
...         optimizer.zero_grad()
...         loss_hist_train[epoch] += loss.item()
...         is_correct = (
...             (pred>=0.5).float() == y_batch
...         ).float()
...         accuracy_hist_train[epoch] += is_correct.mean()
...     loss_hist_train[epoch] /= n_train/batch_size
...     accuracy_hist_train[epoch] /= n_train/batch_size
...     pred = model(x_valid)[:, 0]
...     loss = loss_fn(pred, y_valid)
...     loss_hist_valid[epoch] = loss.item()
...     is_correct = ((pred>=0.5).float() == y_valid).float()
...     accuracy_hist_valid[epoch] += is_correct.mean()
```

4. After the model is trained, we can plot the losses, accuracies, and the decision boundary:

```
>>> fig = plt.figure(figsize=(16, 4))
>>> ax = fig.add_subplot(1, 3, 1)
>>> plt.plot(loss_hist_train, lw=4)
>>> plt.plot(loss_hist_valid, lw=4)
```

```
>>> plt.legend(['Train loss', 'Validation loss'], fontsize=15)
>>> ax.set_xlabel('Epochs', size=15)
>>> ax = fig.add_subplot(1, 3, 2)
>>> plt.plot(accuracy_hist_train, lw=4)
>>> plt.plot(accuracy_hist_valid, lw=4)
>>> plt.legend(['Train acc.', 'Validation acc.'], fontsize=15)
>>> ax.set_xlabel('Epochs', size=15)
>>> ax = fig.add_subplot(1, 3, 3)
>>> plot_decision_regions(
...     X=x_valid.numpy(),
...     y=y_valid.numpy().astype(np.integer),
...     clf=model
... )
>>> ax.set_xlabel(r'$x_1$', size=15)
>>> ax.xaxis.set_label_coords(1, -0.025)
>>> ax.set_ylabel(r'$x_2$', size=15)
>>> ax.yaxis.set_label_coords(-0.025, 1)
>>> plt.show()
```

5. The resulting figure will be as follows:

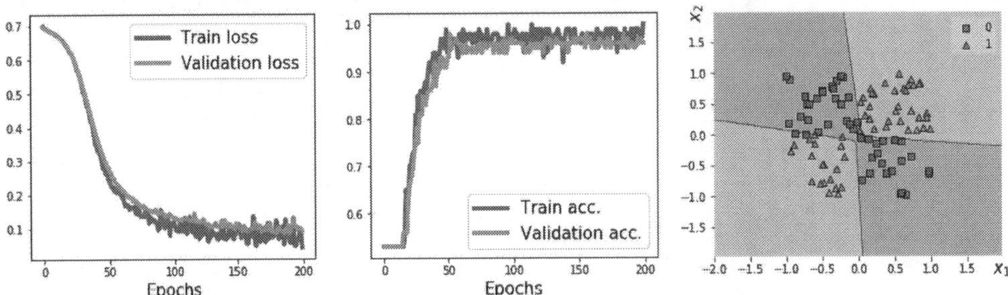

Figure 13.6: Results using NoisyLinear as the first hidden layer

Here, our goal was to learn how to define a new custom layer subclassed from `nn.Module` and to use it as we would use any other standard `torch.nn` layer. Although, with this particular example, `NoisyLinear` did not help to improve the performance, please keep in mind that our objective was to mainly learn how to write a customized layer from scratch. In general, writing a new customized layer can be useful in other applications, for example, if you develop a new algorithm that depends on a new layer beyond the existing ones.

Project one – predicting the fuel efficiency of a car

So far, in this chapter, we have mostly focused on the `torch.nn` module. We used `nn.Sequential` to construct the models for simplicity. Then, we made model building more flexible with `nn.Module` and implemented feedforward NNs, to which we added customized layers. In this section, we will work on a real-world project of predicting the fuel efficiency of a car in miles per gallon (MPG). We will cover the underlying steps in machine learning tasks, such as data preprocessing, feature engineering, training, prediction (inference), and evaluation.

Working with feature columns

In machine learning and deep learning applications, we can encounter various different types of features: continuous, unordered categorical (nominal), and ordered categorical (ordinal). You will recall that in *Chapter 4, Building Good Training Datasets – Data Preprocessing*, we covered different types of features and learned how to handle each type. Note that while numeric data can be either continuous or discrete, in the context of machine learning with PyTorch, "numeric" data specifically refers to continuous data of floating point type.

Sometimes, feature sets are comprised of a mixture of different feature types. For example, consider a scenario with a set of seven different features, as shown in *Figure 13.7*:

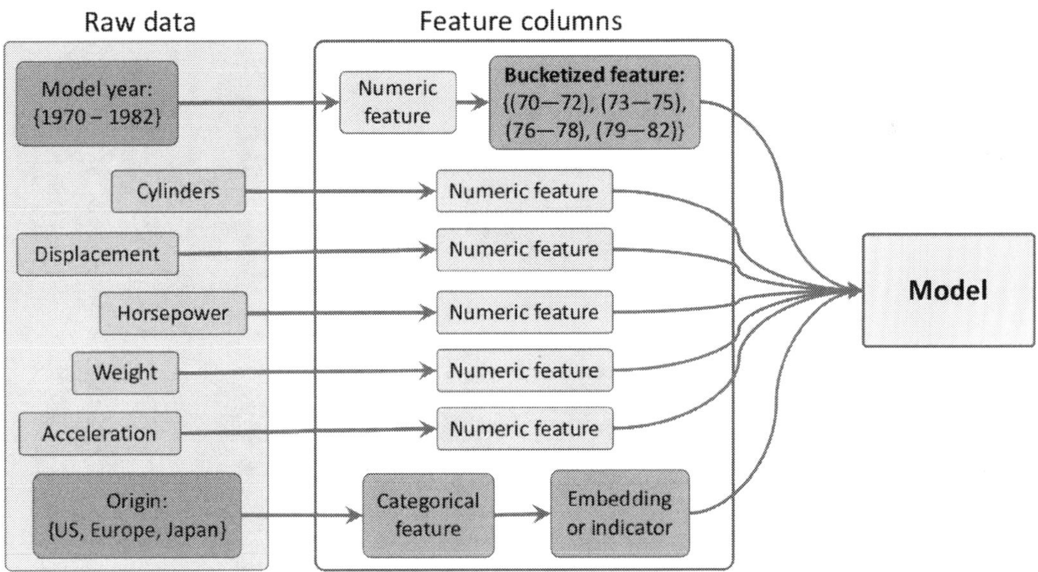

Figure 13.7: Auto MPG data structure

The features shown in the figure (model year, cylinders, displacement, horsepower, weight, acceleration, and origin) were obtained from the Auto MPG dataset, which is a common machine learning benchmark dataset for predicting the fuel efficiency of a car in MPG. The full dataset and its description are available from UCI's machine learning repository at `https://archive.ics.uci.edu/ml/datasets/auto+mpg`.

We are going to treat five features from the Auto MPG dataset (number of cylinders, displacement, horsepower, weight, and acceleration) as "numeric" (here, continuous) features. The model year can be regarded as an ordered categorical (ordinal) feature. Lastly, the manufacturing origin can be regarded as an unordered categorical (nominal) feature with three possible discrete values, 1, 2, and 3, which correspond to the US, Europe, and Japan, respectively.

Let's first load the data and apply the necessary preprocessing steps, including dropping the incomplete rows, partitioning the dataset into training and test datasets, as well as standardizing the continuous features:

```
>>> import pandas as pd
>>> url = 'http://archive.ics.uci.edu/ml/' \
...       'machine-learning-databases/auto-mpg/auto-mpg.data'
>>> column_names = ['MPG', 'Cylinders', 'Displacement', 'Horsepower',
...                 'Weight', 'Acceleration', 'Model Year', 'Origin']
>>> df = pd.read_csv(url, names=column_names,
...                  na_values = "?", comment='\t',
...                  sep=" ", skipinitialspace=True)
>>>
>>> ## drop the NA rows
>>> df = df.dropna()
>>> df = df.reset_index(drop=True)
>>>
>>> ## train/test splits:
>>> import sklearn
>>> import sklearn.model_selection
>>> df_train, df_test = sklearn.model_selection.train_test_split(
...     df, train_size=0.8, random_state=1
... )
>>> train_stats = df_train.describe().transpose()
>>>
>>> numeric_column_names = [
...     'Cylinders', 'Displacement',
...     'Horsepower', 'Weight',
...     'Acceleration'
... ]
```

```
>>> df_train_norm, df_test_norm = df_train.copy(), df_test.copy()
>>> for col_name in numeric_column_names:
...     mean = train_stats.loc[col_name, 'mean']
...     std  = train_stats.loc[col_name, 'std']
...     df_train_norm.loc[:, col_name] = \
...         (df_train_norm.loc[:, col_name] - mean)/std
...     df_test_norm.loc[:, col_name] = \
...         (df_test_norm.loc[:, col_name] - mean)/std
>>> df_train_norm.tail()
```

This results in the following:

	MPG	Cylinders	Displacement	Horsepower	Weight	Acceleration	ModelYear	Origin
203	28.0	-0.824303	-0.901020	-0.736562	-0.950031	0.255202	76	3
255	19.4	0.351127	0.413800	-0.340982	0.293190	0.548737	78	1
72	13.0	1.526556	1.144256	0.713897	1.339617	-0.625403	72	1
235	30.5	-0.824303	-0.891280	-1.053025	-1.072585	0.475353	77	1
37	14.0	1.526556	1.563051	1.636916	1.470420	-1.359240	71	1

Figure 13.8: Preprocessed Auto MG data

The pandas `DataFrame` that we created via the previous code snippet contains five columns with values of the type `float`. These columns will constitute the continuous features.

Next, let's group the rather fine-grained model year (`ModelYear`) information into buckets to simplify the learning task for the model that we are going to train later. Concretely, we are going to assign each car into one of four *year* buckets, as follows:

$$\text{bucket} = \begin{cases} 0 & \text{if year} < 73 \\ 1 & \text{if } 73 \leq \text{year} < 76 \\ 2 & \text{if } 76 \leq \text{year} < 79 \\ 3 & \text{if year} \geq 79 \end{cases}$$

Note that the chosen intervals were selected arbitrarily to illustrate the concepts of "bucketing." In order to group the cars into these buckets, we will first define three cut-off values: [73, 76, 79] for the model year feature. These cut-off values are used to specify half-closed intervals, for instance, $(-\infty, 73)$, $[73, 76)$, $[76, 79)$, and $[76, \infty)$. Then, the original numeric features will be passed to the `torch.bucketize` function (`https://pytorch.org/docs/stable/generated/torch.bucketize.html`) to generate the indices of the buckets. The code is as follows:

```
>>> boundaries = torch.tensor([73, 76, 79])
>>> v = torch.tensor(df_train_norm['Model Year'].values)
>>> df_train_norm['Model Year Bucketed'] = torch.bucketize(
```

```
...     v, boundaries, right=True
... )
>>> v = torch.tensor(df_test_norm['Model Year'].values)
>>> df_test_norm['Model Year Bucketed'] = torch.bucketize(
...     v, boundaries, right=True
... )
>>> numeric_column_names.append('Model Year Bucketed')
```

We added this bucketized feature column to the Python list `numeric_column_names`.

Next, we will proceed with defining a list for the unordered categorical feature, `Origin`. In PyTorch, There are two ways to work with a categorical feature: using an embedding layer via `nn.Embedding` (`https://pytorch.org/docs/stable/generated/torch.nn.Embedding.html`), or using one-hot-encoded vectors (also called *indicator*). In the encoding approach, for example, index 0 will be encoded as [1, 0, 0], index 1 will be encoded as [0, 1, 0], and so on. On the other hand, the embedding layer maps each index to a vector of random numbers of the type `float`, which can be trained. (You can think of the embedding layer as a more efficient implementation of a one-hot encoding multiplied with a trainable weight matrix.)

When the number of categories is large, using the embedding layer with fewer dimensions than the number of categories can improve the performance.

In the following code snippet, we will use the one-hot-encoding approach on the categorical feature in order to convert it into the dense format:

```
>>> from torch.nn.functional import one_hot
>>> total_origin = len(set(df_train_norm['Origin']))
>>> origin_encoded = one_hot(torch.from_numpy(
...     df_train_norm['Origin'].values) % total_origin)
>>> x_train_numeric = torch.tensor(
...     df_train_norm[numeric_column_names].values)
>>> x_train = torch.cat([x_train_numeric, origin_encoded], 1).float()
>>> origin_encoded = one_hot(torch.from_numpy(
...     df_test_norm['Origin'].values) % total_origin)
>>> x_test_numeric = torch.tensor(
...     df_test_norm[numeric_column_names].values)
>>> x_test = torch.cat([x_test_numeric, origin_encoded], 1).float()
```

After encoding the categorical feature into a three-dimensional dense feature, we concatenated it with the numeric features we processed in the previous step. Finally, we will create the label tensors from the ground truth MPG values as follows:

```
>>> y_train = torch.tensor(df_train_norm['MPG'].values).float()
>>> y_test = torch.tensor(df_test_norm['MPG'].values).float()
```

In this section, we have covered the most common approaches for preprocessing and creating features in PyTorch.

Training a DNN regression model

Now, after constructing the mandatory features and labels, we will create a data loader that uses a batch size of 8 for the train data:

```
>>> train_ds = TensorDataset(x_train, y_train)
>>> batch_size = 8
>>> torch.manual_seed(1)
>>> train_dl = DataLoader(train_ds, batch_size, shuffle=True)
```

Next, we will build a model with two fully connected layers where one has 8 hidden units and another has 4:

```
>>> hidden_units = [8, 4]
>>> input_size = x_train.shape[1]
>>> all_layers = []
>>> for hidden_unit in hidden_units:
...     layer = nn.Linear(input_size, hidden_unit)
...     all_layers.append(layer)
...     all_layers.append(nn.ReLU())
...     input_size = hidden_unit
>>> all_layers.append(nn.Linear(hidden_units[-1], 1))
>>> model = nn.Sequential(*all_layers)
>>> model
Sequential(
  (0): Linear(in_features=9, out_features=8, bias=True)
  (1): ReLU()
  (2): Linear(in_features=8, out_features=4, bias=True)
  (3): ReLU()
  (4): Linear(in_features=4, out_features=1, bias=True)
)
```

After defining the model, we will define the MSE loss function for regression and use stochastic gradient descent for optimization:

```
>>> loss_fn = nn.MSELoss()
>>> optimizer = torch.optim.SGD(model.parameters(), lr=0.001)
```

Now we will train the model for 200 epochs and display the train loss for every 20 epochs:

```
>>> torch.manual_seed(1)
>>> num_epochs = 200
>>> log_epochs = 20
```

```
>>> for epoch in range(num_epochs):
...     loss_hist_train = 0
...     for x_batch, y_batch in train_dl:
...         pred = model(x_batch)[:, 0]
...         loss = loss_fn(pred, y_batch)
...         loss.backward()
...         optimizer.step()
...         optimizer.zero_grad()
...         loss_hist_train += loss.item()
...     if epoch % log_epochs==0:
...         print(f'Epoch {epoch}  Loss '
...               f'{loss_hist_train/len(train_dl):.4f}')

Epoch 0  Loss 536.1047
Epoch 20  Loss 8.4361
Epoch 40  Loss 7.8695
Epoch 60  Loss 7.1891
Epoch 80  Loss 6.7062
Epoch 100  Loss 6.7599
Epoch 120  Loss 6.3124
Epoch 140  Loss 6.6864
Epoch 160  Loss 6.7648
Epoch 180  Loss 6.2156
```

After 200 epochs, the train loss was around 5. We can now evaluate the regression performance of the trained model on the test dataset. To predict the target values on new data points, we can feed their features to the model:

```
>>> with torch.no_grad():
...     pred = model(x_test.float())[:, 0]
...     loss = loss_fn(pred, y_test)
...     print(f'Test MSE: {loss.item():.4f}')
...     print(f'Test MAE: {nn.L1Loss()(pred, y_test).item():.4f}')
Test MSE: 9.6130
Test MAE: 2.1211
```

The MSE on the test set is 9.6, and the **mean absolute error** (MAE) is 2.1. After this regression project, we will work on a classification project in the next section.

Project two – classifying MNIST handwritten digits

For this classification project, we are going to categorize MNIST handwritten digits. In the previous section, we covered the four essential steps for machine learning in PyTorch in detail, which we will need to repeat in this section.

You will recall that in *Chapter 12* you learned the way of loading available datasets from the `torchvision` module. First, we are going to load the MNIST dataset using the `torchvision` module.

1. The setup step includes loading the dataset and specifying hyperparameters (the size of the train set and test set, and the size of mini-batches):

```
>>> import torchvision
>>> from torchvision import transforms
>>> image_path = './'
>>> transform = transforms.Compose([
...     transforms.ToTensor()
... ])
>>> mnist_train_dataset = torchvision.datasets.MNIST(
...     root=image_path, train=True,
...     transform=transform, download=False
... )
>>> mnist_test_dataset = torchvision.datasets.MNIST(
...     root=image_path, train=False,
...     transform=transform, download=False
... )
>>> batch_size = 64
>>> torch.manual_seed(1)
>>> train_dl = DataLoader(mnist_train_dataset,
...                       batch_size, shuffle=True)
```

   Here, we constructed a data loader with batches of 64 samples. Next, we will preprocess the loaded datasets.

2. We preprocess the input features and the labels. The features in this project are the pixels of the images we read from **Step 1**. We defined a custom transformation using `torchvision.transforms.Compose`. In this simple case, our transformation consisted only of one method, `ToTensor()`. The `ToTensor()` method converts the pixel features into a floating type tensor and also normalizes the pixels from the [0, 255] to [0, 1] range. In *Chapter 14, Classifying Images with Deep Convolutional Neural Networks*, we will see some additional data transformation methods when we work with more complex image datasets. The labels are integers from 0 to 9 representing ten digits. Hence, we don't need to do any scaling or further conversion. Note that we can access the raw pixels using the `data` attribute, and don't forget to scale them to the range [0, 1].

   We will construct the model in the next step once the data is preprocessed.

3. Construct the NN model:

```
>>> hidden_units = [32, 16]
>>> image_size = mnist_train_dataset[0][0].shape
>>> input_size = image_size[0] * image_size[1] * image_size[2]
>>> all_layers = [nn.Flatten()]
>>> for hidden_unit in hidden_units:
...     layer = nn.Linear(input_size, hidden_unit)
...     all_layers.append(layer)
...     all_layers.append(nn.ReLU())
...     input_size = hidden_unit
>>> all_layers.append(nn.Linear(hidden_units[-1], 10))
>>> model = nn.Sequential(*all_layers)
>>> model
Sequential(
  (0): Flatten(start_dim=1, end_dim=-1)
  (1): Linear(in_features=784, out_features=32, bias=True)
  (2): ReLU()
  (3): Linear(in_features=32, out_features=16, bias=True)
  (4): ReLU()
  (5): Linear(in_features=16, out_features=10, bias=True)
)
```

Note that the model starts with a flatten layer that flattens an input image into a one-dimensional tensor. This is because the input images are in the shape of [1, 28, 28]. The model has two hidden layers, with 32 and 16 units respectively. And it ends with an output layer of ten units representing ten classes, activated by a softmax function. In the next step, we will train the model on the train set and evaluate it on the test set.

4. Use the model for training, evaluation, and prediction:

```
>>> loss_fn = nn.CrossEntropyLoss()
>>> optimizer = torch.optim.Adam(model.parameters(), lr=0.001)
>>> torch.manual_seed(1)
>>> num_epochs = 20
>>> for epoch in range(num_epochs):
...     accuracy_hist_train = 0
...     for x_batch, y_batch in train_dl:
```

```
...             pred = model(x_batch)
...             loss = loss_fn(pred, y_batch)
...             loss.backward()
...             optimizer.step()
...             optimizer.zero_grad()
...             is_correct = (
...                 torch.argmax(pred, dim=1) == y_batch
...             ).float()
...             accuracy_hist_train += is_correct.sum()
...         accuracy_hist_train /= len(train_dl.dataset)
...         print(f'Epoch {epoch}  Accuracy '
...               f'{accuracy_hist_train:.4f}')
Epoch 0  Accuracy 0.8531
...
Epoch 9  Accuracy 0.9691
...
Epoch 19  Accuracy 0.9813
```

We used the cross-entropy loss function for multiclass classification and the Adam optimizer for gradient descent. We will talk about the Adam optimizer in *Chapter 14*. We trained the model for 20 epochs and displayed the train accuracy for every epoch. The trained model reached an accuracy of 96.3 percent on the training set and we will evaluate it on the testing set:

```
>>> pred = model(mnist_test_dataset.data / 255.)
>>> is_correct = (
...     torch.argmax(pred, dim=1) ==
...     mnist_test_dataset.targets
... ).float()
>>> print(f'Test accuracy: {is_correct.mean():.4f}')
Test accuracy: 0.9645
```

The test accuracy is 95.6 percent. You have learned how to solve a classification problem using PyTorch.

Higher-level PyTorch APIs: a short introduction to PyTorch-Lightning

In recent years, the PyTorch community developed several different libraries and APIs on top of PyTorch. Notable examples include fastai (`https://docs.fast.ai/`), Catalyst (`https://github.com/catalyst-team/catalyst`), PyTorch Lightning (`https://www.pytorchlightning.ai`), (`https://lightning-flash.readthedocs.io/en/latest/quickstart.html`), and PyTorch-Ignite (`https://github.com/pytorch/ignite`).

In this section, we will explore PyTorch Lightning (Lightning for short), which is a widely used PyTorch library that makes training deep neural networks simpler by removing much of the boilerplate code. However, while Lightning's focus lies in simplicity and flexibility, it also allows us to use many advanced features such as multi-GPU support and fast low-precision training, which you can learn about in the official documentation at `https://pytorch-lightning.rtfd.io/en/latest/`.

There is also a bonus introduction to PyTorch-Ignite at `https://github.com/rasbt/machine-learning-book/blob/main/ch13/ch13_part4_ignite.ipynb`.

In an earlier section, *Project two – classifying MNIST handwritten digits*, we implemented a multilayer perceptron for classifying handwritten digits in the MNIST dataset. In the next subsections, we will reimplement this classifier using Lightning.

Installing PyTorch Lightning

Lightning can be installed via pip or conda, depending on your preference. For instance, the command for installing Lightning via pip is as follows:

```
pip install pytorch-lightning
```

The following is the command for installing Lightning via conda:

```
conda install pytorch-lightning -c conda-forge
```

The code in the following subsections is based on PyTorch Lightning version 1.5, which you can install by replacing `pytorch-lightning` with `pytorch-lightning==1.5` in these commands.

Setting up the PyTorch Lightning model

We start by implementing the model, which we will train in the next subsections. Defining a model for Lightning is relatively straightforward as it is based on regular Python and PyTorch code. All that is required to implement a Lightning model is to use `LightningModule` instead of the regular PyTorch module. To take advantage of PyTorch's convenience functions, such as the trainer API and automatic logging, we just define a few specifically named methods, which we will see in the following code:

```
import pytorch_lightning as pl
import torch
import torch.nn as nn

from torchmetrics import Accuracy

class MultiLayerPerceptron(pl.LightningModule):
    def __init__(self, image_shape=(1, 28, 28), hidden_units=(32, 16)):
        super().__init__()
```

```
        # new PL attributes:
        self.train_acc = Accuracy()
        self.valid_acc = Accuracy()
        self.test_acc = Accuracy()

        # Model similar to previous section:
        input_size = image_shape[0] * image_shape[1] * image_shape[2]
        all_layers = [nn.Flatten()]
        for hidden_unit in hidden_units:
            layer = nn.Linear(input_size, hidden_unit)
            all_layers.append(layer)
            all_layers.append(nn.ReLU())
            input_size = hidden_unit

        all_layers.append(nn.Linear(hidden_units[-1], 10))
        self.model = nn.Sequential(*all_layers)

    def forward(self, x):
        x = self.model(x)
        return x

    def training_step(self, batch, batch_idx):
        x, y = batch
        logits = self(x)
        loss = nn.functional.cross_entropy(self(x), y)
        preds = torch.argmax(logits, dim=1)
        self.train_acc.update(preds, y)
        self.log("train_loss", loss, prog_bar=True)
        return loss

    def training_epoch_end(self, outs):
        self.log("train_acc", self.train_acc.compute())

    def validation_step(self, batch, batch_idx):
        x, y = batch
        logits = self(x)
        loss = nn.functional.cross_entropy(self(x), y)
        preds = torch.argmax(logits, dim=1)
        self.valid_acc.update(preds, y)
        self.log("valid_loss", loss, prog_bar=True)
        self.log("valid_acc", self.valid_acc.compute(), prog_bar=True)
```

```
        return loss

    def test_step(self, batch, batch_idx):
        x, y = batch
        logits = self(x)
        loss = nn.functional.cross_entropy(self(x), y)
        preds = torch.argmax(logits, dim=1)
        self.test_acc.update(preds, y)
        self.log("test_loss", loss, prog_bar=True)
        self.log("test_acc", self.test_acc.compute(), prog_bar=True)
        return loss

    def configure_optimizers(self):
        optimizer = torch.optim.Adam(self.parameters(), lr=0.001)
        return optimizer
```

Let's now discuss the different methods one by one. As you can see, the `__init__` constructor contains the same model code that we used in a previous subsection. What's new is that we added the accuracy attributes such as `self.train_acc = Accuracy()`. These will allow us to track the accuracy during training. `Accuracy` was imported from the `torchmetrics` module, which should be automatically installed with Lightning. If you cannot import `torchmetrics`, you can try to install it via `pip install torchmetrics`. More information can be found at `https://torchmetrics.readthedocs.io/en/latest/pages/quickstart.html`.

The `forward` method implements a simple forward pass that returns the logits (outputs of the last fully connected layer of our network before the softmax layer) when we call our model on the input data. The logits, computed via the `forward` method by calling `self(x)`, are used for the training, validation, and test steps, which we'll describe next.

The `training_step`, `training_epoch_end`, `validation_step`, `test_step`, and `configure_optimizers` methods are methods that are specifically recognized by Lightning. For instance, `training_step` defines a single forward pass during training, where we also keep track of the accuracy and loss so that we can analyze these later. Note that we compute the accuracy via `self.train_acc.update(preds, y)` but don't log it yet. The `training_step` method is executed on each individual batch during training, and via the `training_epoch_end` method, which is executed at the end of each training epoch, we compute the training set accuracy from the accuracy values we accumulated via training.

The `validation_step` and `test_step` methods define, analogous to the `training_step` method, how the validation and test evaluation process should be computed. Similar to `training_step`, each `validation_step` and `test_step` receives a single batch, which is why we log the accuracy via respective accuracy attributes derived from `Accuracy` of `torchmetric`. However, note that `validation_step` is only called in certain intervals, for example, after each training epoch. This is why we log the validation accuracy inside the validation step, whereas with the training accuracy, we log it after each training epoch, otherwise, the accuracy plot that we inspect later will look too noisy.

Finally, via the `configure_optimizers` method, we specify the optimizer used for training. The following two subsections will discuss how we can set up the dataset and how we can train the model.

Setting up the data loaders for Lightning

There are three main ways in which we can prepare the dataset for Lightning. We can:

- Make the dataset part of the model
- Set up the data loaders as usual and feed them to the `fit` method of a Lightning Trainer—the Trainer is introduced in the next subsection
- Create a `LightningDataModule`

Here, we are going to use a `LightningDataModule`, which is the most organized approach. The `LightningDataModule` consists of five main methods, as we can see in the following:

```
from torch.utils.data import DataLoader
from torch.utils.data import random_split
from torchvision.datasets import MNIST
from torchvision import transforms

class MnistDataModule(pl.LightningDataModule):
    def __init__(self, data_path='./'):
        super().__init__()
        self.data_path = data_path
        self.transform = transforms.Compose([transforms.ToTensor()])

    def prepare_data(self):
        MNIST(root=self.data_path, download=True)

    def setup(self, stage=None):
        # stage is either 'fit', 'validate', 'test', or 'predict'
        # here note relevant
        mnist_all = MNIST(
            root=self.data_path,
            train=True,
            transform=self.transform,
            download=False
        )

        self.train, self.val = random_split(
            mnist_all, [55000, 5000], generator=torch.Generator().manual_
seed(1)
        )
```

```
        self.test = MNIST(
            root=self.data_path,
            train=False,
            transform=self.transform,
            download=False
        )

    def train_dataloader(self):
        return DataLoader(self.train, batch_size=64, num_workers=4)

    def val_dataloader(self):
        return DataLoader(self.val, batch_size=64, num_workers=4)

    def test_dataloader(self):
        return DataLoader(self.test, batch_size=64, num_workers=4)
```

In the `prepare_data` method, we define general steps, such as downloading the dataset. In the `setup` method, we define the datasets used for training, validation, and testing. Note that MNIST does not have a dedicated validation split, which is why we use the `random_split` function to divide the 60,000-example training set into 55,000 examples for training and 5,000 examples for validation.

The data loader methods are self-explanatory and define how the respective datasets are loaded. Now, we can initialize the data module and use it for training, validation, and testing in the next subsections:

```
torch.manual_seed(1)
mnist_dm = MnistDataModule()
```

Training the model using the PyTorch Lightning Trainer class

Now we can reap the rewards from setting up the model with the specifically named methods, as well as the Lightning data module. Lightning implements a `Trainer` class that makes the training model super convenient by taking care of all the intermediate steps, such as calling `zero_grad()`, `backward()`, and `optimizer.step()` for us. Also, as a bonus, it lets us easily specify one or more GPUs to use (if available):

```
mnistclassifier = MultiLayerPerceptron()

if torch.cuda.is_available(): # if you have GPUs
    trainer = pl.Trainer(max_epochs=10, gpus=1)
else:
    trainer = pl.Trainer(max_epochs=10)

trainer.fit(model=mnistclassifier, datamodule=mnist_dm)
```

Via the preceding code, we train our multilayer perceptron for 10 epochs. During training, we see a handy progress bar that keeps track of the epoch and core metrics such as the training and validation losses:

```
Epoch 9: 100% 939/939 [00:07<00:00, 130.42it/s, loss=0.1, v_num=0, train_
loss=0.260, valid_loss=0.166, valid_acc=0.949]
```

After the training has finished, we can also inspect the metrics we logged in more detail, as we will see in the next subsection.

Evaluating the model using TensorBoard

In the previous section, we experienced the convenience of the `Trainer` class. Another nice feature of Lightning is its logging capabilities. Recall that we specified several `self.log` steps in our Lightning model earlier. After, and even during training, we can visualize them in TensorBoard. (Note that Lightning supports other loggers as well; for more information, please see the official documentation at `https://pytorch-lightning.readthedocs.io/en/latest/common/loggers.html`.)

Installing TensorBoard

TensorBoard can be installed via pip or conda, depending on your preference. For instance, the command for installing TensorBoard via pip is as follows:

```
pip install tensorboard
```

The following is the command for installing Lightning via conda:

```
conda install tensorboard -c conda-forge
```

The code in the following subsection is based on TensorBoard version 2.4, which you can install by replacing `tensorboard` with `tensorboard==2.4` in these commands.

By default, Lightning tracks the training in a subfolder named `lightning_logs`. To visualize the training runs, you can execute the following code in the command-line terminal, which will open TensorBoard in your browser:

```
tensorboard --logdir lightning_logs/
```

Alternatively, if you are running the code in a Jupyter notebook, you can add the following code to a Jupyter notebook cell to show the TensorBoard dashboard in the notebook directly:

```
%load_ext tensorboard
%tensorboard --logdir lightning_logs/
```

Figure 13.9 shows the TensorBoard dashboard with the logged training and validation accuracy. Note that there is a `version_0` toggle shown in the lower-left corner. If you run the training code multiple times, Lightning will track them as separate subfolders: `version_0`, `version_1`, `version_2`, and so forth:

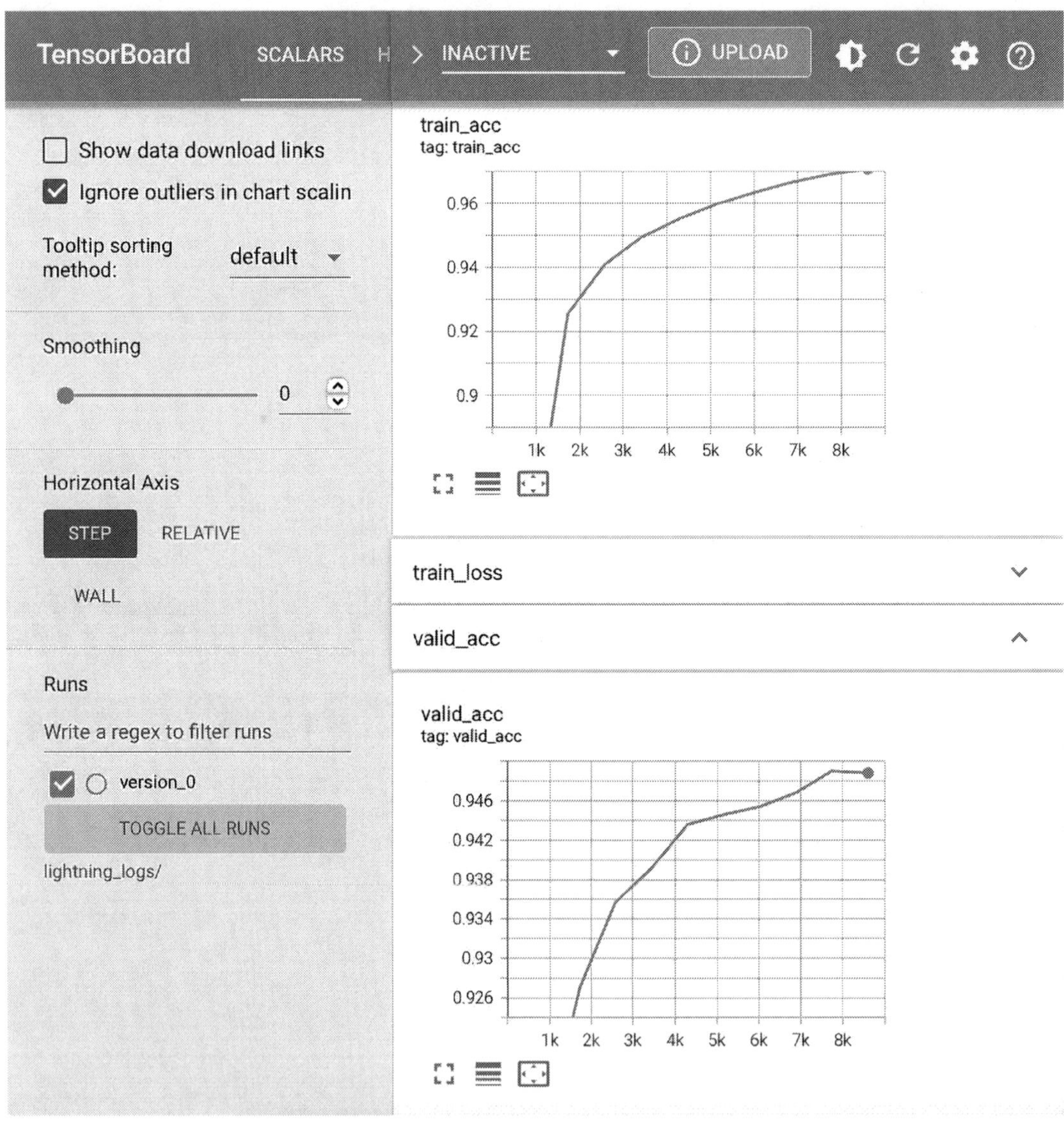

Figure 13.9: TensorBoard dashboard

By looking at the training and validation accuracies in *Figure 13.9*, we can hypothesize that training the model for a few additional epochs can improve performance.

Lightning allows us to load a trained model and train it for additional epochs conveniently. As mentioned previously, Lightning tracks the individual training runs via subfolders. In *Figure 13.10*, we see the contents of the `version_0` subfolder, which contains log files and a model checkpoint for reloading the model:

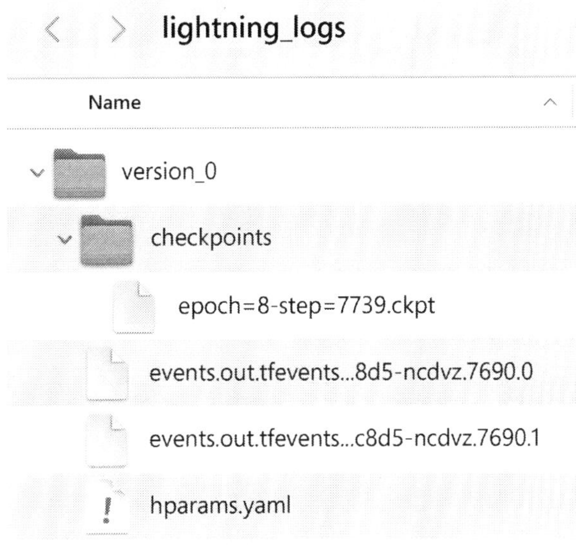

Figure 13.10: PyTorch Lightning log files

For instance, we can use the following code to load the latest model checkpoint from this folder and train the model via `fit`:

```
if torch.cuda.is_available(): # if you have GPUs
    trainer = pl.Trainer(max_epochs=15, resume_from_checkpoint='./lightning_
logs/version_0/checkpoints/epoch=8-step=7739.ckpt', gpus=1)
else:
    trainer = pl.Trainer(max_epochs=15, resume_from_checkpoint='./lightning_
logs/version_0/checkpoints/epoch=8-step=7739.ckpt')

trainer.fit(model=mnistclassifier, datamodule=mnist_dm)
```

Here, we set `max_epochs` to `15`, which trained the model for 5 additional epochs (previously, we trained it for 10 epochs).

Now, let's take a look at the TensorBoard dashboard in *Figure 13.11* and see whether training the model for a few additional epochs was worthwhile:

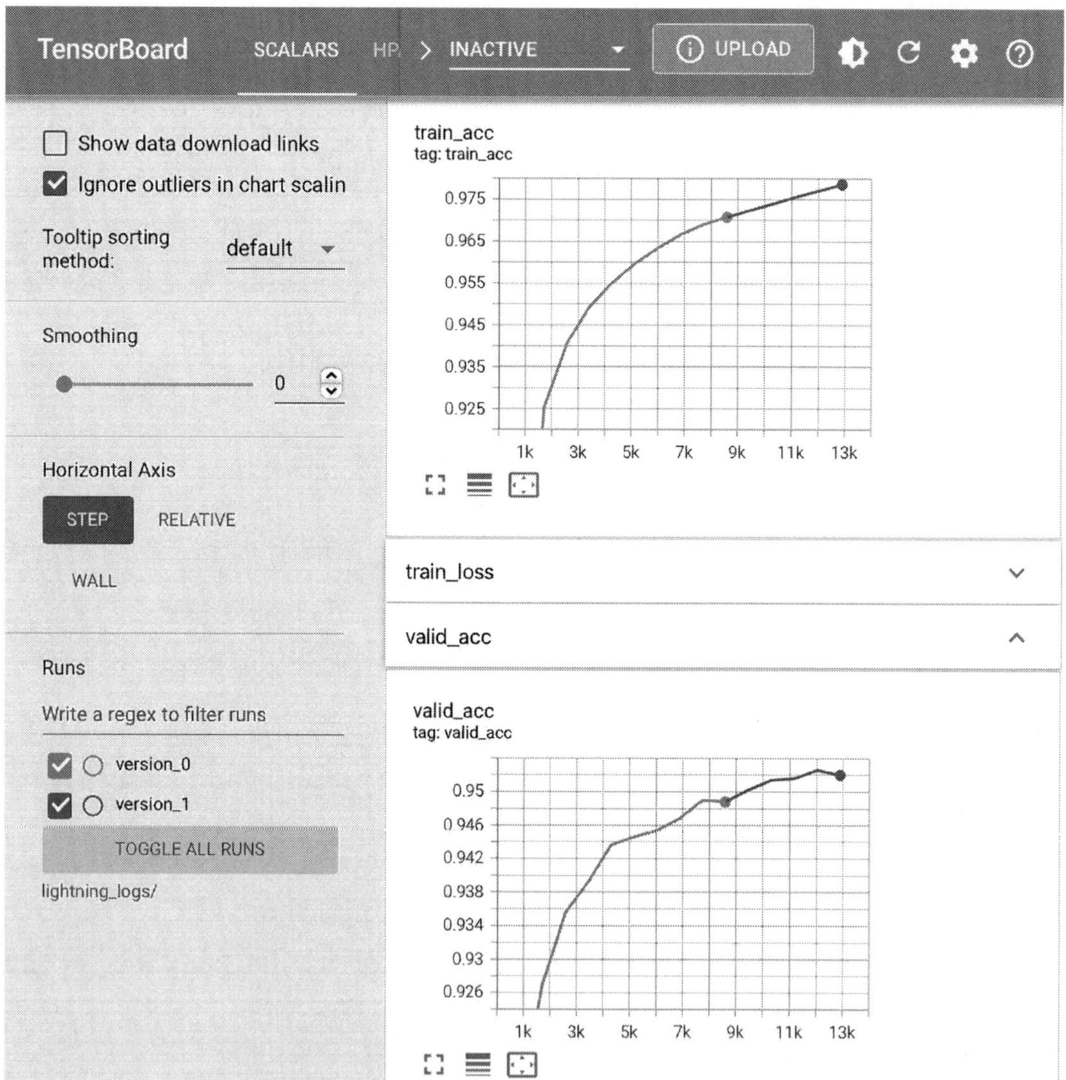

Figure 13.11: TensorBoard dashboard after training for five more epochs

As we can see in *Figure 13.11*, TensorBoard allows us to show the results from the additional training epochs (`version_1`) next to the previous ones (`version_0`), which is very convenient. Indeed, we can see that training for five more epochs improved the validation accuracy. At this point, we may decide to train the model for more epochs, which we leave as an exercise to you.

Once we are finished with training, we can evaluate the model on the test set using the following code:

```
trainer.test(model=mnistclassifier, datamodule=mnist_dm)
```

The resulting test set performance, after training for 15 epochs in total, is approximately 95 percent:

```
[{'test_loss': 0.14912301301956177, 'test_acc': 0.9499600529670715}]
```

Note that PyTorch Lightning also saves the model automatically for us. If you want to reuse the model later, you can conveniently load it via the following code:

```
model = MultiLayerPerceptron.load_from_checkpoint("path/to/checkpoint.ckpt")
```

Learn more about PyTorch Lightning

To learn more about Lightning, please visit the official website, which contains tutorials and examples, at `https://pytorch-lightning.readthedocs.io`.

Lightning also has an active community on Slack that welcomes new users and contributors. To find out more, please visit the official Lightning website at `https://www.pytorchlightning.ai`.

Summary

In this chapter, we covered PyTorch's most essential and useful features. We started by discussing PyTorch's dynamic computation graph, which makes implementing computations very convenient. We also covered the semantics of defining PyTorch tensor objects as model parameters.

After we considered the concept of computing partial derivatives and gradients of arbitrary functions, we covered the `torch.nn` module in more detail. It provides us with a user-friendly interface for building more complex deep NN models. Finally, we concluded this chapter by solving a regression and classification problem using what we have discussed so far.

Now that we have covered the core mechanics of PyTorch, the next chapter will introduce the concept behind **convolutional neural network** (**CNN**) architectures for deep learning. CNNs are powerful models and have shown great performance in the field of computer vision.

Join our book's Discord space

Join our Discord community to meet like-minded people and learn alongside more than 2000 members at:

`https://packt.link/MLwPyTorch`

14

Classifying Images with Deep Convolutional Neural Networks

In the previous chapter, we looked in depth at different aspects of the PyTorch neural network and automatic differentiation modules, you became familiar with tensors and decorating functions, and you learned how to work with `torch.nn`. In this chapter, you will now learn about **convolutional neural networks** (**CNNs**) for image classification. We will start by discussing the basic building blocks of CNNs, using a bottom-up approach. Then, we will take a deeper dive into the CNN architecture and explore how to implement CNNs in PyTorch. In this chapter, we will cover the following topics:

- Convolution operations in one and two dimensions
- The building blocks of CNN architectures
- Implementing deep CNNs in PyTorch
- Data augmentation techniques for improving the generalization performance
- Implementing a facial CNN classifier for recognizing if someone is smiling or not

The building blocks of CNNs

CNNs are a family of models that were originally inspired by how the visual cortex of the human brain works when recognizing objects. The development of CNNs goes back to the 1990s, when Yann LeCun and his colleagues proposed a novel NN architecture for classifying handwritten digits from images (*Handwritten Digit Recognition with a Back-Propagation Network* by *Y. LeCun*, and colleagues, 1989, published at the *Neural Information Processing Systems (NeurIPS)* conference).

The human visual cortex

The original discovery of how the visual cortex of our brain functions was made by David H. Hubel and Torsten Wiesel in 1959, when they inserted a microelectrode into the primary visual cortex of an anesthetized cat. They observed that neurons respond differently after projecting different patterns of light in front of the cat. This eventually led to the discovery of the different layers of the visual cortex. While the primary layer mainly detects edges and straight lines, higher-order layers focus more on extracting complex shapes and patterns.

Due to the outstanding performance of CNNs for image classification tasks, this particular type of feedforward NN gained a lot of attention and led to tremendous improvements in machine learning for computer vision. Several years later, in 2019, Yann LeCun received the Turing award (the most prestigious award in computer science) for his contributions to the field of **artificial intelligence** (**AI**), along with two other researchers, Yoshua Bengio and Geoffrey Hinton, whose names you encountered in previous chapters.

In the following sections, we will discuss the broader concepts of CNNs and why convolutional architectures are often described as "feature extraction layers." Then, we will delve into the theoretical definition of the type of convolution operation that is commonly used in CNNs and walk through examples of computing convolutions in one and two dimensions.

Understanding CNNs and feature hierarchies

Successfully extracting **salient** (**relevant**) **features** is key to the performance of any machine learning algorithm, and traditional machine learning models rely on input features that may come from a domain expert or are based on computational feature extraction techniques.

Certain types of NNs, such as CNNs, can automatically learn the features from raw data that are most useful for a particular task. For this reason, it's common to consider CNN layers as feature extractors: the early layers (those right after the input layer) extract **low-level features** from raw data, and the later layers (often **fully connected layers**, as in a **multilayer perceptron** (**MLP**)) use these features to predict a continuous target value or class label.

Certain types of multilayer NNs, and in particular, deep CNNs, construct a so-called **feature hierarchy** by combining the low-level features in a layer-wise fashion to form high-level features. For example, if we're dealing with images, then low-level features, such as edges and blobs, are extracted from the earlier layers, which are combined to form high-level features. These high-level features can form more complex shapes, such as the general contours of objects like buildings, cats, or dogs.

As you can see in *Figure 14.1*, a CNN computes **feature maps** from an input image, where each element comes from a local patch of pixels in the input image:

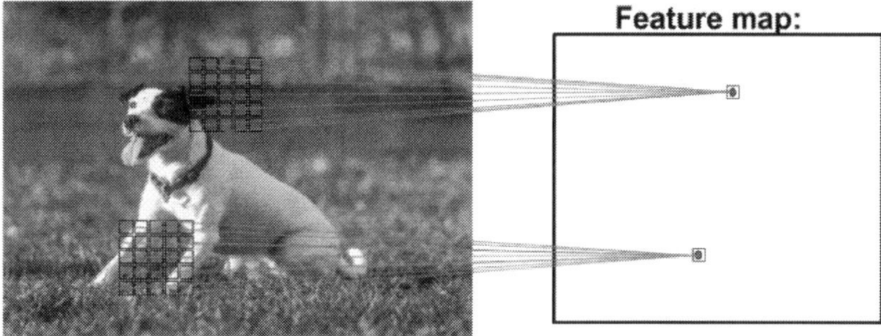

Figure 14.1: Creating feature maps from an image (photo by Alexander Dummer on Unsplash)

This local patch of pixels is referred to as the **local receptive field.** CNNs will usually perform very well on image-related tasks, and that's largely due to two important ideas:

- **Sparse connectivity:** A single element in the feature map is connected to only a small patch of pixels. (This is very different from connecting to the whole input image, as in the case of MLPs. You may find it useful to look back and compare how we implemented a fully connected network that connected to the whole image in *Chapter 11, Implementing a Multilayer Artificial Neural Network from Scratch*.)
- **Parameter sharing:** The same weights are used for different patches of the input image.

As a direct consequence of these two ideas, replacing a conventional, fully connected MLP with a convolution layer substantially decreases the number of weights (parameters) in the network, and we will see an improvement in the ability to capture *salient* features. In the context of image data, it makes sense to assume that nearby pixels are typically more relevant to each other than pixels that are far away from each other.

Typically, CNNs are composed of several **convolutional** and subsampling layers that are followed by one or more fully connected layers at the end. The fully connected layers are essentially an MLP, where every input unit, i, is connected to every output unit, j, with weight w_{ij} (which we covered in more detail in *Chapter 11*).

Please note that subsampling layers, commonly known as **pooling layers**, do not have any learnable parameters; for instance, there are no weights or bias units in pooling layers. However, both the convolutional and fully connected layers have weights and biases that are optimized during training.

In the following sections, we will study convolutional and pooling layers in more detail and see how they work. To understand how convolution operations work, let's start with a convolution in one dimension, which is sometimes used for working with certain types of sequence data, such as text. After discussing one-dimensional convolutions, we will work through the typical two-dimensional ones that are commonly applied to two-dimensional images.

Performing discrete convolutions

A **discrete convolution** (or simply **convolution**) is a fundamental operation in a CNN. Therefore, it's important to understand how this operation works. In this section, we will cover the mathematical definition and discuss some of the **naive** algorithms to compute convolutions of one-dimensional tensors (vectors) and two-dimensional tensors (matrices).

Please note that the formulas and descriptions in this section are solely for understanding how convolution operations in CNNs work. Indeed, much more efficient implementations of convolutional operations already exist in packages such as PyTorch, as you will see later in this chapter.

Mathematical notation

In this chapter, we will use subscript to denote the size of a multidimensional array (tensor); for example, $A_{n_1 \times n_2}$ is a two-dimensional array of size $n_1 \times n_2$. We use brackets, [ ], to denote the indexing of a multidimensional array. For example, $A[i, j]$ refers to the element at index i, j of matrix A. Furthermore, note that we use a special symbol, $*$, to denote the convolution operation between two vectors or matrices, which is not to be confused with the multiplication operator, *, in Python.

Discrete convolutions in one dimension

Let's start with some basic definitions and notations that we are going to use. A discrete convolution for two vectors, x and w, is denoted by $\boldsymbol{y} = \boldsymbol{x} * \boldsymbol{w}$, in which vector x is our input (sometimes called **signal**) and w is called the **filter** or **kernel**. A discrete convolution is mathematically defined as follows:

$$\boldsymbol{y} = \boldsymbol{x} * \boldsymbol{w} \rightarrow y[i] = \sum_{k=-\infty}^{+\infty} x[i-k]\, w[k]$$

As mentioned earlier, the brackets, [ ], are used to denote the indexing for vector elements. The index, i, runs through each element of the output vector, $\boldsymbol{y}$. There are two odd things in the preceding formula that we need to clarify: $-\infty$ to $+\infty$ indices and negative indexing for x.

The fact that the sum runs through indices from $-\infty$ to $+\infty$ seems odd, mainly because in machine learning applications, we always deal with finite feature vectors. For example, if x has 10 features with indices 0, 1, 2, ..., 8, 9, then indices $-\infty$: -1 and 10: $+\infty$ are out of bounds for x. Therefore, to correctly compute the summation shown in the preceding formula, it is assumed that x and w are filled with zeros. This will result in an output vector, y, that also has infinite size, with lots of zeros as well. Since this is not useful in practical situations, x is padded only with a finite number of zeros.

This process is called **zero-padding** or simply **padding**. Here, the number of zeros padded on each side is denoted by p. An example padding of a one-dimensional vector, x, is shown in *Figure 14.2*:

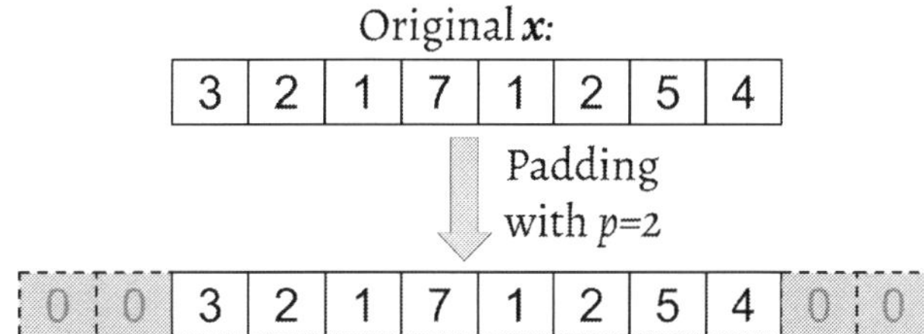

Figure 14.2: An example of padding

Let's assume that the original input, x, and filter, w, have n and m elements, respectively, where $m \leq n$. Therefore, the padded vector, x^p, has size $n + 2p$. The practical formula for computing a discrete convolution will change to the following:

$$\boldsymbol{y} = \boldsymbol{x} * \boldsymbol{w} \rightarrow y[i] = \sum_{k=0}^{k=m-1} x^p[i + m - k]\, w[k]$$

Now that we have solved the infinite index issue, the second issue is indexing x with $i + m - k$. The important point to notice here is that x and w are indexed in different directions in this summation. Computing the sum with one index going in the reverse direction is equivalent to computing the sum with both indices in the forward direction after flipping one of those vectors, x or w, after they are padded. Then, we can simply compute their dot product. Let's assume we flip (rotate) the filter, w, to get the rotated filter, w^r. Then, the dot product, $x[i: i + m].w^r$, is computed to get one element, $y[i]$, where $x[i: i + m]$ is a patch of x with size m. This operation is repeated like in a sliding window approach to get all the output elements.

The following figure provides an example with $\boldsymbol{x} = [3\ 2\ 1\ 7\ 1\ 2\ 5\ 4]$ and $\boldsymbol{w} = \left[\frac{1}{2}\ \frac{3}{4}\ 1\ \frac{1}{4}\right]$ so that the first three output elements are computed:

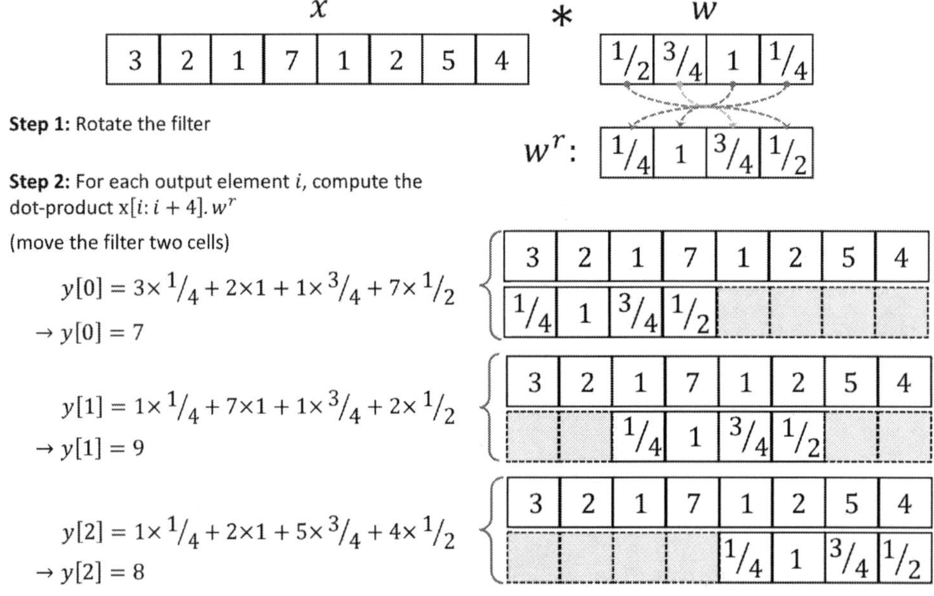

Figure 14.3: The steps for computing a discrete convolution

You can see in the preceding example that the padding size is zero ($p = 0$). Notice that the rotated filter, $\boldsymbol{w}^r$, is shifted by two cells each time we **shift**. This shift is another hyperparameter of a convolution, the **stride**, s. In this example, the stride is two, $s = 2$. Note that the stride has to be a positive number smaller than the size of the input vector. We will talk more about padding and strides in the next section.

Cross-correlation

Cross-correlation (or simply correlation) between an input vector and a filter is denoted by $\boldsymbol{y} = \boldsymbol{x} \star \boldsymbol{w}$ and is very much like a sibling of a convolution, with a small difference: in cross-correlation, the multiplication is performed in the same direction. Therefore, it is not a requirement to rotate the filter matrix, w, in each dimension. Mathematically, cross-correlation is defined as follows:

$$\boldsymbol{y} = \boldsymbol{x} \star \boldsymbol{w} \rightarrow y[i] = \sum_{k=-\infty}^{+\infty} x[i+k]\, w[k]$$

The same rules for padding and stride may be applied to cross-correlation as well. Note that most deep learning frameworks (including PyTorch) implement cross-correlation but refer to it as convolution, which is a common convention in the deep learning field.

Padding inputs to control the size of the output feature maps

So far, we've only used zero-padding in convolutions to compute finite-sized output vectors. Technically, padding can be applied with any $p \geq 0$. Depending on the choice of p, boundary cells may be treated differently than the cells located in the middle of x.

Now, consider an example where $n = 5$ and $m = 3$. Then, with $p = 0$, $x[0]$ is only used in computing one output element (for instance, $y[0]$), while $x[1]$ is used in the computation of two output elements (for instance, $y[0]$ and $y[1]$). So, you can see that this different treatment of elements of x can artificially put more emphasis on the middle element, $x[2]$, since it has appeared in most computations. We can avoid this issue if we choose $p = 2$, in which case, each element of x will be involved in computing three elements of y.

Furthermore, the size of the output, y, also depends on the choice of the padding strategy we use.

There are three modes of padding that are commonly used in practice: *full*, *same*, and *valid*.

In full mode, the padding parameter, p, is set to $p = m - 1$. Full padding increases the dimensions of the output; thus, it is rarely used in CNN architectures.

The same padding mode is usually used to ensure that the output vector has the same size as the input vector, x. In this case, the padding parameter, p, is computed according to the filter size, along with the requirement that the input size and output size are the same.

Finally, computing a convolution in valid mode refers to the case where $p = 0$ (no padding).

Figure 14.4 illustrates the three different padding modes for a simple 5×5 pixel input with a kernel size of 3×3 and a stride of 1:

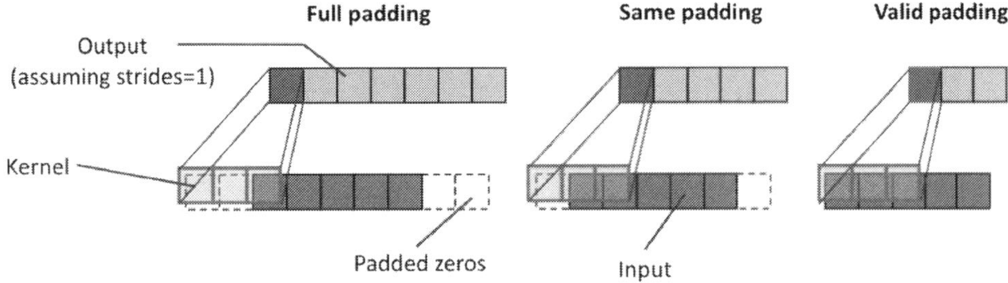

Figure 14.4: The three modes of padding

The most commonly used padding mode in CNNs is same padding. One of its advantages over the other padding modes is that same padding preserves the size of the vector—or the height and width of the input images when we are working on image-related tasks in computer vision—which makes designing a network architecture more convenient.

One big disadvantage of valid padding versus full and same padding is that the volume of the tensors will decrease substantially in NNs with many layers, which can be detrimental to the network's performance. In practice, you should preserve the spatial size using same padding for the convolutional layers and decrease the spatial size via pooling layers or convolutional layers with stride 2 instead, as described in *Striving for Simplicity: The All Convolutional Net* ICLR (workshop track), by *Jost Tobias Springenberg, Alexey Dosovitskiy*, and others, 2015 (`https://arxiv.org/abs/1412.6806`).

As for full padding, its size results in an output larger than the input size. Full padding is usually used in signal processing applications where it is important to minimize boundary effects. However, in a deep learning context, boundary effects are usually not an issue, so we rarely see full padding being used in practice.

Determining the size of the convolution output

The output size of a convolution is determined by the total number of times that we shift the filter, $\boldsymbol{w}$, along the input vector. Let's assume that the input vector is of size n and the filter is of size m. Then, the size of the output resulting from $\boldsymbol{y} = \boldsymbol{x} * \boldsymbol{w}$, with padding p and stride s, would be determined as follows:

$$o = \left\lfloor \frac{n + 2p - m}{s} \right\rfloor + 1$$

Here, $\lfloor \cdot \rfloor$ denotes the *floor* operation.

The floor operation

The floor operation returns the largest integer that is equal to or smaller than the input, for example:

$$\text{floor}(1.77) = \lfloor 1.77 \rfloor = 1$$

Consider the following two cases:

- Compute the output size for an input vector of size 10 with a convolution kernel of size 5, padding 2, and stride 1:

  $$n = 10, m = 5, \quad p = 2, \quad s = 1 \rightarrow o = \left\lfloor \frac{10 + 2 \times 2 - 5}{1} \right\rfloor + 1 = 10$$

  (Note that in this case, the output size turns out to be the same as the input; therefore, we can conclude this to be same padding mode.)

- How does the output size change for the same input vector when we have a kernel of size 3 and stride 2?

  $$n = 10, m = 3, \quad p = 2, \quad s = 2 \rightarrow o = \left\lfloor \frac{10 + 2 \times 2 - 3}{2} \right\rfloor + 1 = 6$$

If you are interested in learning more about the size of the convolution output, we recommend the manuscript *A guide to convolution arithmetic for deep learning* by *Vincent Dumoulin* and *Francesco Visin*, which is freely available at `https://arxiv.org/abs/1603.07285`.

Finally, in order to learn how to compute convolutions in one dimension, a naive implementation is shown in the following code block, and the results are compared with the `numpy.convolve` function. The code is as follows:

```
>>> import numpy as np
>>> def conv1d(x, w, p=0, s=1):
...     w_rot = np.array(w[::-1])
...     x_padded = np.array(x)
...     if p > 0:
...         zero_pad = np.zeros(shape=p)
...         x_padded = np.concatenate([
...             zero_pad, x_padded, zero_pad
...         ])
...     res = []
...     for i in range(0, int((len(x_padded) - len(w_rot))) + 1, s):
...         res.append(np.sum(x_padded[i:i+w_rot.shape[0]] * w_rot))
...     return np.array(res)
>>> ## Testing:
>>> x = [1, 3, 2, 4, 5, 6, 1, 3]
>>> w = [1, 0, 3, 1, 2]
>>> print('Conv1d Implementation:',
...       conv1d(x, w, p=2, s=1))
Conv1d Implementation: [ 5. 14. 16. 26. 24. 34. 19. 22.]
>>> print('NumPy Results:',
...       np.convolve(x, w, mode='same'))
NumPy Results: [ 5 14 16 26 24 34 19 22]
```

So far, we have mostly focused on convolutions for vectors (1D convolutions). We started with the 1D case to make the concepts easier to understand. In the next section, we will cover 2D convolutions in more detail, which are the building blocks of CNNs for image-related tasks.

Performing a discrete convolution in 2D

The concepts you learned in the previous sections are easily extendible to 2D. When we deal with 2D inputs, such as a matrix, $\boldsymbol{X}_{n_1 \times n_2}$, and the filter matrix, $\boldsymbol{W}_{m_1 \times m_2}$, where $m_1 \leq n_1$ and $m_2 \leq n_2$, then the matrix $\boldsymbol{Y} = \boldsymbol{X} * \boldsymbol{W}$ is the result of a 2D convolution between $\boldsymbol{X}$ and $\boldsymbol{W}$. This is defined mathematically as follows:

$$\boldsymbol{Y} = \boldsymbol{X} * \boldsymbol{W} \rightarrow Y[i,j] = \sum_{k_1=-\infty}^{+\infty} \sum_{k_2=-\infty}^{+\infty} X[i-k_1, j-k_2]\, W[k_1, k_2]$$

Notice that if you omit one of the dimensions, the remaining formula is exactly the same as the one we used previously to compute the convolution in 1D. In fact, all the previously mentioned techniques, such as zero padding, rotating the filter matrix, and the use of strides, are also applicable to 2D convolutions, provided that they are extended to both dimensions independently. *Figure 14.5* demonstrates the 2D convolution of an input matrix of size 8×8, using a kernel of size 3×3. The input matrix is padded with zeros with $p = 1$. As a result, the output of the 2D convolution will have a size of 8×8:

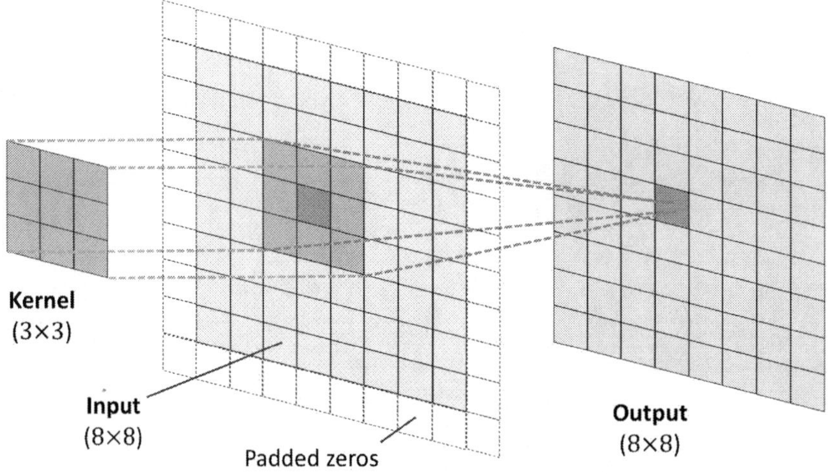

Figure 14.5: The output of a 2D convolution

The following example illustrates the computation of a 2D convolution between an input matrix, $X_{3\times3}$, and a kernel matrix, $W_{3\times3}$, using padding $p = (1, 1)$ and stride $s = (2, 2)$. According to the specified padding, one layer of zeros is added on each side of the input matrix, which results in the padded matrix $\boldsymbol{X}_{5\times5}^{\text{padded}}$, as follows:

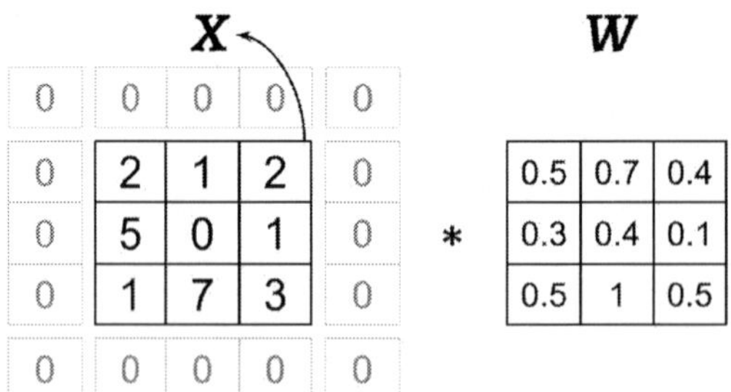

Figure 14.6: Computing a 2D convolution between an input and kernel matrix

With the preceding filter, the rotated filter will be:

$$\boldsymbol{W}^r = \begin{bmatrix} 0.5 & 1 & 0.5 \\ 0.1 & 0.4 & 0.3 \\ 0.4 & 0.7 & 0.5 \end{bmatrix}$$

Note that this rotation is not the same as the transpose matrix. To get the rotated filter in NumPy, we can write `W_rot=W[::-1,::-1]`. Next, we can shift the rotated filter matrix along the padded input matrix, X^{padded}, like a sliding window, and compute the sum of the element-wise product, which is denoted by the ⊙ operator in *Figure 14.7*:

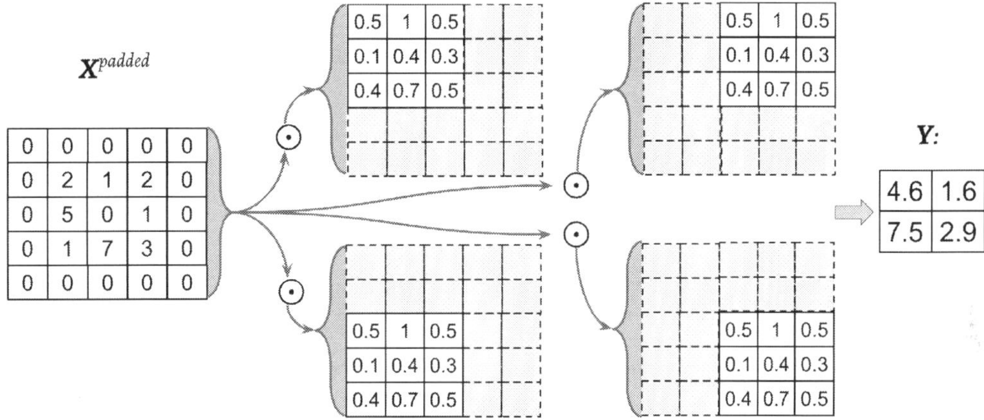

Figure 14.7: Computing the sum of the element-wise product

The result will be the 2×2 matrix, **Y**.

Let's also implement the 2D convolution according to the *naive* algorithm described. The `scipy.signal` package provides a way to compute 2D convolution via the `scipy.signal.convolve2d` function:

```
>>> import numpy as np
>>> import scipy.signal
>>> def conv2d(X, W, p=(0, 0), s=(1, 1)):
...     W_rot = np.array(W)[::-1,::-1]
...     X_orig = np.array(X)
...     n1 = X_orig.shape[0] + 2*p[0]
...     n2 = X_orig.shape[1] + 2*p[1]
...     X_padded = np.zeros(shape=(n1, n2))
...     X_padded[p[0]:p[0]+X_orig.shape[0],
...              p[1]:p[1]+X_orig.shape[1]] = X_orig
...
...     res = []
...     for i in range(0,
...               int((X_padded.shape[0] - \
...               W_rot.shape[0])/s[0])+1, s[0]):
...         res.append([])
```

```
...         for j in range(0,
...                 int((X_padded.shape[1] - \
...                 W_rot.shape[1])/s[1])+1, s[1]):
...             X_sub = X_padded[i:i+W_rot.shape[0],
...                              j:j+W_rot.shape[1]]
...             res[-1].append(np.sum(X_sub * W_rot))
...     return(np.array(res))
>>> X = [[1, 3, 2, 4], [5, 6, 1, 3], [1, 2, 0, 2], [3, 4, 3, 2]]
>>> W = [[1, 0, 3], [1, 2, 1], [0, 1, 1]]
>>> print('Conv2d Implementation:\n',
...       conv2d(X, W, p=(1, 1), s=(1, 1)))
Conv2d Implementation:
[[ 11.  25.  32.  13.]
 [ 19.  25.  24.  13.]
 [ 13.  28.  25.  17.]
 [ 11.  17.  14.   9.]]
>>> print('SciPy Results:\n',
...       scipy.signal.convolve2d(X, W, mode='same'))
SciPy Results:
[[11 25 32 13]
 [19 25 24 13]
 [13 28 25 17]
 [11 17 14  9]]
```

Efficient algorithms for computing convolution

We provided a naive implementation to compute a 2D convolution for the purpose of understanding the concepts. However, this implementation is very inefficient in terms of memory requirements and computational complexity. Therefore, it should not be used in real-world NN applications.

One aspect is that the filter matrix is actually not rotated in most tools like PyTorch. Moreover, in recent years, much more efficient algorithms have been developed that use the Fourier transform to compute convolutions. It is also important to note that in the context of NNs, the size of a convolution kernel is usually much smaller than the size of the input image.

For example, modern CNNs usually use kernel sizes such as 1×1, 3×3, or 5×5, for which efficient algorithms have been designed that can carry out the convolutional operations much more efficiently, such as Winograd's minimal filtering algorithm. These algorithms are beyond the scope of this book, but if you are interested in learning more, you can read the manuscript *Fast Algorithms for Convolutional Neural Networks* by *Andrew Lavin* and *Scott Gray*, 2015, which is freely available at `https://arxiv.org/abs/1509.09308`.

In the next section, we will discuss subsampling or pooling, which is another important operation often used in CNNs.

Subsampling layers

Subsampling is typically applied in two forms of pooling operations in CNNs: **max-pooling** and **mean-pooling** (also known as **average-pooling**). The pooling layer is usually denoted by $P_{n_1 \times n_2}$. Here, the subscript determines the size of the neighborhood (the number of adjacent pixels in each dimension) where the max or mean operation is performed. We refer to such a neighborhood as the **pooling size.**

The operation is described in *Figure 14.8*. Here, max-pooling takes the maximum value from a neighborhood of pixels, and mean-pooling computes their average:

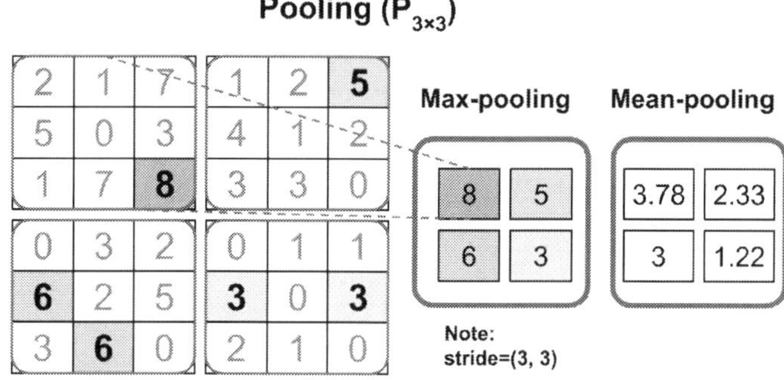

Figure 14.8: An example of max-pooling and mean-pooling

The advantage of pooling is twofold:

- Pooling (max-pooling) introduces a local invariance. This means that small changes in a local neighborhood do not change the result of max-pooling. Therefore, it helps with generating features that are more robust to noise in the input data. Refer to the following example, which shows that the max-pooling of two different input matrices, X_1 and X_2, results in the same output:

$$\left.\begin{array}{l} \boldsymbol{X}_1 = \begin{bmatrix} 10 & 255 & 125 & 0 & 170 & 100 \\ 70 & 255 & 105 & 25 & 25 & 70 \\ 255 & 0 & 150 & 0 & 10 & 10 \\ 0 & 255 & 10 & 10 & 150 & 20 \\ 70 & 15 & 200 & 100 & 95 & 0 \\ 35 & 25 & 100 & 20 & 0 & 60 \end{bmatrix} \\ \\ \boldsymbol{X}_2 = \begin{bmatrix} 100 & 100 & 100 & 50 & 100 & 50 \\ 95 & 255 & 100 & 125 & 125 & 170 \\ 80 & 40 & 10 & 10 & 125 & 150 \\ 255 & 30 & 150 & 20 & 120 & 125 \\ 30 & 30 & 150 & 100 & 70 & 70 \\ 70 & 30 & 100 & 200 & 70 & 95 \end{bmatrix} \end{array}\right\} \xrightarrow{\text{max pooling } P_{2\times 2}} \begin{bmatrix} 255 & 125 & 170 \\ 255 & 150 & 150 \\ 70 & 200 & 95 \end{bmatrix}$$

- Pooling decreases the size of features, which results in higher computational efficiency. Furthermore, reducing the number of features may reduce the degree of overfitting as well.

Overlapping versus non-overlapping pooling

Traditionally, pooling is assumed to be non-overlapping. Pooling is typically performed on non-overlapping neighborhoods, which can be done by setting the stride parameter equal to the pooling size. For example, a non-overlapping pooling layer, $P_{n_1 \times n_2}$, requires a stride parameter $s = (n_1, n_2)$. On the other hand, overlapping pooling occurs if the stride is smaller than the pooling size. An example where overlapping pooling is used in a convolutional network is described in *ImageNet Classification with Deep Convolutional Neural Networks* by *A. Krizhevsky, I. Sutskever*, and *G. Hinton*, 2012, which is freely available as a manuscript at `https://papers.nips.cc/paper/4824-imagenet-classification-with-deep-convolutional-neural-networks`.

While pooling is still an essential part of many CNN architectures, several CNN architectures have also been developed without using pooling layers. Instead of using pooling layers to reduce the feature size, researchers use convolutional layers with a stride of 2.

In a sense, you can think of a convolutional layer with stride 2 as a pooling layer with learnable weights. If you are interested in an empirical comparison of different CNN architectures developed with and without pooling layers, we recommend reading the research article *Striving for Simplicity: The All Convolutional Net* by *Jost Tobias Springenberg, Alexey Dosovitskiy, Thomas Brox*, and *Martin Riedmiller*. This article is freely available at `https://arxiv.org/abs/1412.6806`.

Putting everything together – implementing a CNN

So far, you have learned about the basic building blocks of CNNs. The concepts illustrated in this chapter are not really more difficult than traditional multilayer NNs. We can say that the most important operation in a traditional NN is matrix multiplication. For instance, we use matrix multiplications to compute the pre-activations (or net inputs), as in $\boldsymbol{z} = \boldsymbol{W}\boldsymbol{x} + b$. Here, $\boldsymbol{x}$ is a column vector ($\mathbb{R}^{n \times 1}$ matrix) representing pixels, and $\boldsymbol{W}$ is the weight matrix connecting the pixel inputs to each hidden unit.

In a CNN, this operation is replaced by a convolution operation, as in $\boldsymbol{Z} = \boldsymbol{W} * \boldsymbol{X} + \boldsymbol{b}$, where X is a matrix representing the pixels in a *height×width* arrangement. In both cases, the pre-activations are passed to an activation function to obtain the activation of a hidden unit, $\boldsymbol{A} = \sigma(\boldsymbol{Z})$, where σ is the activation function. Furthermore, you will recall that subsampling is another building block of a CNN, which may appear in the form of pooling, as was described in the previous section.

Working with multiple input or color channels

An input to a convolutional layer may contain one or more 2D arrays or matrices with dimensions $N_1 \times N_2$ (for example, the image height and width in pixels). These $N_1 \times N_2$ matrices are called *channels*. Conventional implementations of convolutional layers expect a rank-3 tensor representation as an input, for example, a three-dimensional array, $\boldsymbol{X}_{N_1 \times N_2 \times C_{in}}$, where C_{in} is the number of input channels. For example, let's consider images as input to the first layer of a CNN. If the image is colored and uses the RGB color mode, then $C_{in} = 3$ (for the red, green, and blue color channels in RGB). However, if the image is in grayscale, then we have $C_{in} = 1$, because there is only one channel with the grayscale pixel intensity values.

Reading an image file

When we work with images, we can read images into NumPy arrays using the `uint8` (unsigned 8-bit integer) data type to reduce memory usage compared to 16-bit, 32-bit, or 64-bit integer types, for example.

Unsigned 8-bit integers take values in the range [0, 255], which are sufficient to store the pixel information in RGB images, which also take values in the same range.

In *Chapter 12, Parallelizing Neural Network Training with PyTorch*, you saw that PyTorch provides a module for loading/storing and manipulating images via `torchvision`. Let's recap how to read an image (this example RGB image is located in the code bundle folder that is provided with this chapter):

```
>>> import torch
>>> from torchvision.io import read_image
>>> img = read_image('example-image.png')
>>> print('Image shape:', img.shape)
Image shape: torch.Size([3, 252, 221])
>>> print('Number of channels:', img.shape[0])
Number of channels: 3
>>> print('Image data type:', img.dtype)
Image data type: torch.uint8
>>> print(img[:, 100:102, 100:102])
tensor([[[179, 182],
         [180, 182]],

        [[134, 136],
         [135, 137]],

        [[110, 112],
         [111, 113]]], dtype=torch.uint8)
```

Note that with `torchvision`, the input and output image tensors are in the format of `Tensor[channels, image_height, image_width]`.

Now that you are familiar with the structure of input data, the next question is, how can we incorporate multiple input channels in the convolution operation that we discussed in the previous sections? The answer is very simple: we perform the convolution operation for each channel separately and then add the results together using the matrix summation. The convolution associated with each channel (c) has its own kernel matrix as $W[:, :, c]$.

The total pre-activation result is computed in the following formula:

$$\text{Given an example } \boldsymbol{X}_{n_1 \times n_2 \times C_{in}}, \text{ a kernel matrix } \boldsymbol{W}_{m_1 \times m_2 \times C_{in}}, \text{ and a bias value } b \quad \Rightarrow \quad \begin{cases} \boldsymbol{Z}^{Conv} = \sum_{c=1}^{C_{in}} \boldsymbol{W}[:,:,c] * \boldsymbol{X}[:,:,c] \\ \text{Pre-activation:} \quad \boldsymbol{Z} = \boldsymbol{Z}^{Conv} + b_c \\ \text{Feature map:} \quad \boldsymbol{A} = \sigma(\boldsymbol{Z}) \end{cases}$$

The final result, A, is a feature map. Usually, a convolutional layer of a CNN has more than one feature map. If we use multiple feature maps, the kernel tensor becomes four-dimensional: $width \times height \times C_{in} \times C_{out}$. Here, $width \times height$ is the kernel size, C_{in} is the number of input channels, and C_{out} is the number of output feature maps. So, now let's include the number of output feature maps in the preceding formula and update it, as follows:

$$\text{Given an example } \boldsymbol{X}_{n_1 \times n_2 \times C_{in}}, \text{ a kernel matrix } \boldsymbol{W}_{m_1 \times m_2 \times C_{in} \times C_{out}}, \text{ and a bias vector } \boldsymbol{b}_{C_{out}} \quad \Rightarrow \quad \begin{cases} \boldsymbol{Z}^{Conv}[:,:,k] = \sum_{c=1}^{C_{in}} \boldsymbol{W}[:,:,c,k] * \boldsymbol{X}[:,:,c] \\ \boldsymbol{Z}[:,:,k] = \boldsymbol{Z}^{Conv}[:,:,k] + b[k] \\ \boldsymbol{A}[:,:,k] = \sigma(\boldsymbol{Z}[:,:,k]) \end{cases}$$

To conclude our discussion of computing convolutions in the context of NNs, let's look at the example in *Figure 14.9*, which shows a convolutional layer, followed by a pooling layer. In this example, there are three input channels. The kernel tensor is four-dimensional. Each kernel matrix is denoted as $m_1 \times m_2$, and there are three of them, one for each input channel. Furthermore, there are five such kernels, accounting for five output feature maps. Finally, there is a pooling layer for subsampling the feature maps:

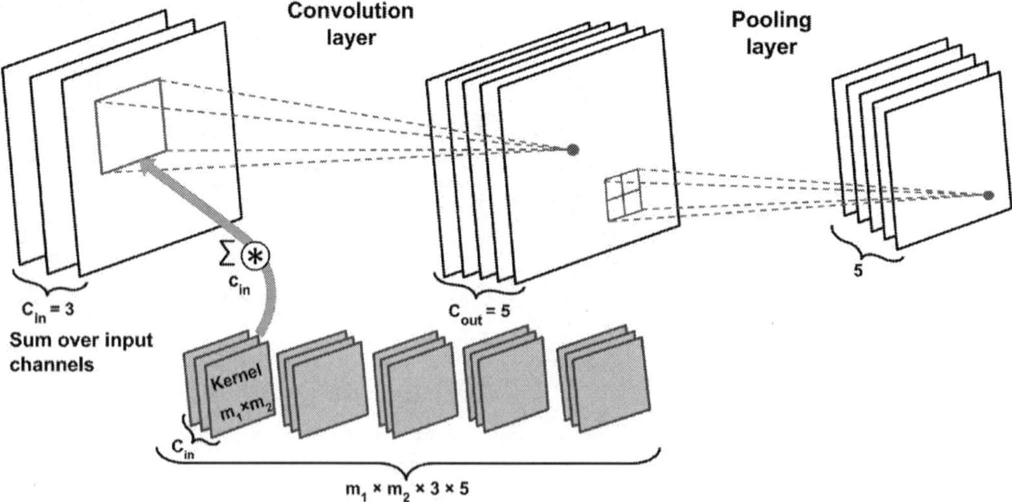

Figure 14.9: Implementing a CNN

How many trainable parameters exist in the preceding example?

To illustrate the advantages of convolution, parameter sharing, and sparse connectivity, let's work through an example. The convolutional layer in the network shown in *Figure 14.9* is a four-dimensional tensor. So, there are $m_1 \times m_2 \times 3 \times 5$ parameters associated with the kernel. Furthermore, there is a bias vector for each output feature map of the convolutional layer. Thus, the size of the bias vector is 5. Pooling layers do not have any (trainable) parameters; therefore, we can write the following:

$$m_1 \times m_2 \times 3 \times 5 + 5$$

If the input tensor is of size $n_1 \times n_2 \times 3$, assuming that the convolution is performed with the same-padding mode, then the size of the output feature maps would be $n_1 \times n_2 \times 5$.

Note that if we use a fully connected layer instead of a convolutional layer, this number will be much larger. In the case of a fully connected layer, the number of parameters for the weight matrix to reach the same number of output units would have been as follows:

$$(n_1 \times n_2 \times 3) \times (n_1 \times n_2 \times 5) = (n_1 \times n_2)^2 \times 3 \times 5$$

In addition, the size of the bias vector is $n_1 \times n_2 \times 5$ (one bias element for each output unit). Given that $m_1 < n_1$ and $m_2 < n_2$, we can see that the difference in the number of trainable parameters is significant.

Lastly, as was already mentioned, the convolution operations typically are carried out by treating an input image with multiple color channels as a stack of matrices; that is, we perform the convolution on each matrix separately and then add the results, as was illustrated in the previous figure. However, convolutions can also be extended to 3D volumes if you are working with 3D datasets, for example, as shown in the paper *VoxNet: A 3D Convolutional Neural Network for Real-Time Object Recognition* by *Daniel Maturana* and *Sebastian Scherer*, 2015, which can be accessed at `https://www.ri.cmu.edu/pub_files/2015/9/voxnet_maturana_scherer_iros15.pdf`.

In the next section, we will talk about how to regularize an NN.

Regularizing an NN with L2 regularization and dropout

Choosing the size of a network, whether we are dealing with a traditional (fully connected) NN or a CNN, has always been a challenging problem. For instance, the size of a weight matrix and the number of layers need to be tuned to achieve a reasonably good performance.

You will recall from *Chapter 13, Going Deeper – The Mechanics of PyTorch,* that a simple network without a hidden layer could only capture a linear decision boundary, which is not sufficient for dealing with an exclusive or (or XOR) or similar problem. The *capacity* of a network refers to the level of complexity of the function that it can learn to approximate. Small networks, or networks with a relatively small number of parameters, have a low capacity and are therefore likely to *underfit*, resulting in poor performance, since they cannot learn the underlying structure of complex datasets. However, very large networks may result in *overfitting*, where the network will memorize the training data and do extremely well on the training dataset while achieving a poor performance on the held-out test dataset. When we deal with real-world machine learning problems, we do not know how large the network should be *a priori*.

One way to address this problem is to build a network with a relatively large capacity (in practice, we want to choose a capacity that is slightly larger than necessary) to do well on the training dataset. Then, to prevent overfitting, we can apply one or multiple regularization schemes to achieve good generalization performance on new data, such as the held-out test dataset.

In *Chapters 3* and *4*, we covered L1 and L2 regularization. Both techniques can prevent or reduce the effect of overfitting by adding a penalty to the loss that results in shrinking the weight parameters during training. While both L1 and L2 regularization can be used for NNs as well, with L2 being the more common choice of the two, there are other methods for regularizing NNs, such as dropout, which we discuss in this section. But before we move on to discussing dropout, to use L2 regularization within a convolutional or fully connected network (recall, fully connected layers are implemented via `torch.nn.Linear` in PyTorch), you can simply add the L2 penalty of a particular layer to the loss function in PyTorch, as follows:

```
>>> import torch.nn as nn
>>> loss_func = nn.BCELoss()
>>> loss = loss_func(torch.tensor([0.9]), torch.tensor([1.0]))
>>> l2_lambda = 0.001
>>> conv_layer = nn.Conv2d(in_channels=3,
...                        out_channels=5,
...                        kernel_size=5)
>>> l2_penalty = l2_lambda * sum(
...     [(p**2).sum() for p in conv_layer.parameters()]
... )
>>> loss_with_penalty = loss + l2_penalty
>>> linear_layer = nn.Linear(10, 16)
```

```
>>> l2_penalty = l2_lambda * sum(
...     [(p**2).sum() for p in linear_layer.parameters()]
... )
>>> loss_with_penalty = loss + l2_penalty
```

Weight decay versus L2 regularization

An alternative way to use L2 regularization is by setting the `weight_decay` parameter in a PyTorch optimizer to a positive value, for example:

```
optimizer = torch.optim.SGD(
    model.parameters(),
    weight_decay=l2_lambda,
    ...
)
```

While L2 regularization and `weight_decay` are not strictly identical, it can be shown that they are equivalent when using **stochastic gradient descent** (**SGD**) optimizers. Interested readers can find more information in the article *Decoupled Weight Decay Regularization* by *Ilya Loshchilov* and *Frank Hutter*, 2019, which is freely available at `https://arxiv.org/abs/1711.05101`.

In recent years, **dropout** has emerged as a popular technique for regularizing (deep) NNs to avoid overfitting, thus improving the generalization performance (*Dropout: A Simple Way to Prevent Neural Networks from Overfitting* by *N. Srivastava*, *G. Hinton*, *A. Krizhevsky*, *I. Sutskever*, and *R. Salakhutdinov*, *Journal of Machine Learning Research 15.1*, pages 1929-1958, 2014, `http://www.jmlr.org/papers/volume15/srivastava14a/srivastava14a.pdf`). Dropout is usually applied to the hidden units of higher layers and works as follows: during the training phase of an NN, a fraction of the hidden units is randomly dropped at every iteration with probability p_{drop} (or keep probability $p_{keep} = 1 - p_{drop}$). This dropout probability is determined by the user and the common choice is $p = 0.5$, as discussed in the previously mentioned article by *Nitish Srivastava* and others, 2014. When dropping a certain fraction of input neurons, the weights associated with the remaining neurons are rescaled to account for the missing (dropped) neurons.

The effect of this random dropout is that the network is forced to learn a redundant representation of the data. Therefore, the network cannot rely on the activation of any set of hidden units, since they may be turned off at any time during training, and is forced to learn more general and robust patterns from the data.

This random dropout can effectively prevent overfitting. *Figure 14.10* shows an example of applying dropout with probability $p = 0.5$ during the training phase, whereby half of the neurons will become inactive randomly (dropped units are selected randomly in each forward pass of training). However, during prediction, all neurons will contribute to computing the pre-activations of the next layer:

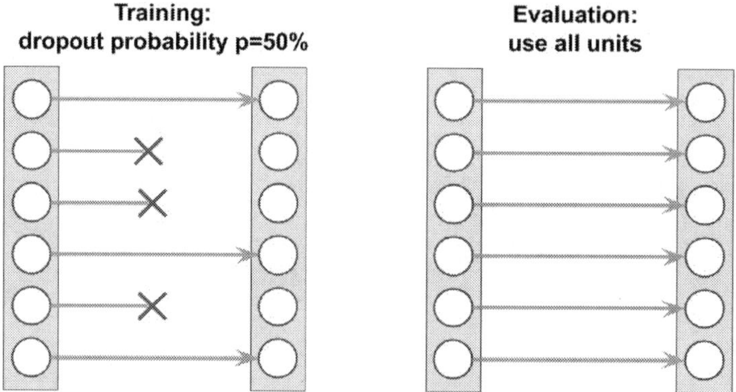

Figure 14.10: Applying dropout during the training phase

As shown here, one important point to remember is that units may drop randomly during training only, whereas for the evaluation (inference) phase, all the hidden units must be active (for instance, $p_{drop} = 0$ or $p_{keep} = 1$). To ensure that the overall activations are on the same scale during training and prediction, the activations of the active neurons have to be scaled appropriately (for example, by halving the activation if the dropout probability was set to $p = 0.5$).

However, since it is inconvenient to always scale activations when making predictions, PyTorch and other tools scale the activations during training (for example, by doubling the activations if the dropout probability was set to $p = 0.5$). This approach is commonly referred to as *inverse dropout*.

While the relationship is not immediately obvious, dropout can be interpreted as the consensus (averaging) of an ensemble of models. As discussed in *Chapter 7, Combining Different Models for Ensemble Learning*, in ensemble learning, we train several models independently. During prediction, we then use the consensus of all the trained models. We already know that model ensembles are known to perform better than single models. In deep learning, however, both training several models and collecting and averaging the output of multiple models is computationally expensive. Here, dropout offers a workaround, with an efficient way to train many models at once and compute their average predictions at test or prediction time.

As mentioned previously, the relationship between model ensembles and dropout is not immediately obvious. However, consider that in dropout, we have a different model for each mini-batch (due to setting the weights to zero randomly during each forward pass).

Then, via iterating over the mini-batches, we essentially sample over $M = 2^h$ models, where h is the number of hidden units.

The restriction and aspect that distinguishes dropout from regular ensembling, however, is that we share the weights over these "different models," which can be seen as a form of regularization. Then, during "inference" (for instance, predicting the labels in the test dataset), we can average over all these different models that we sampled over during training. This is very expensive, though.

Then, averaging the models, that is, computing the geometric mean of the class-membership probability that is returned by a model, i, can be computed as follows:

$$p_{Ensemble} = \left[\prod_{j=1}^{M} p^{\{i\}}\right]^{\frac{1}{M}}$$

Now, the trick behind dropout is that this geometric mean of the model ensembles (here, M models) can be approximated by scaling the predictions of the last (or final) model sampled during training by a factor of $1/(1 - p)$, which is much cheaper than computing the geometric mean explicitly using the previous equation. (In fact, the approximation is exactly equivalent to the true geometric mean if we consider linear models.)

Loss functions for classification

In *Chapter 12, Parallelizing Neural Network Training with PyTorch*, we saw different activation functions, such as ReLU, sigmoid, and tanh. Some of these activation functions, like ReLU, are mainly used in the intermediate (hidden) layers of an NN to add non-linearities to our model. But others, like sigmoid (for binary) and softmax (for multiclass), are added at the last (output) layer, which results in class-membership probabilities as the output of the model. If the sigmoid or softmax activations are not included at the output layer, then the model will compute the logits instead of the class-membership probabilities.

Focusing on classification problems here, depending on the type of problem (binary versus multiclass) and the type of output (logits versus probabilities), we should choose the appropriate loss function to train our model. **Binary cross-entropy** is the loss function for a binary classification (with a single output unit), and **categorical cross-entropy** is the loss function for multiclass classification. In the `torch.nn` module, the categorical cross-entropy loss takes in ground truth labels as integers (for example, y=2, out of three classes, 0, 1, and 2).

Figure 14.11 describes two loss functions available in `torch.nn` for dealing with both cases: binary classification and multiclass with integer labels. Each one of these two loss functions also has the option to receive the predictions in the form of logits or class-membership probabilities:

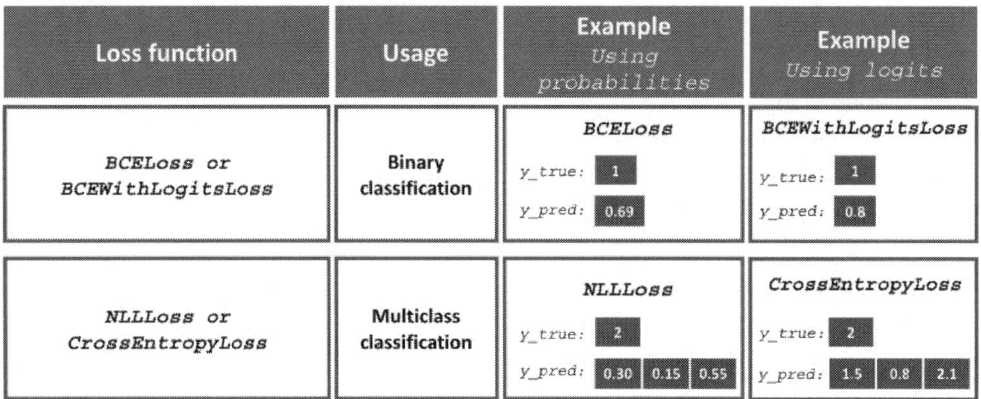

Figure 14.11: Two examples of loss functions in PyTorch

Please note that computing the cross-entropy loss by providing the logits, and not the class-membership probabilities, is usually preferred due to numerical stability reasons. For binary classification, we can either provide logits as inputs to the loss function `nn.BCEWithLogitsLoss()`, or compute the probabilities based on the logits and feed them to the loss function `nn.BCELoss()`. For multiclass classification, we can either provide logits as inputs to the loss function `nn.CrossEntropyLoss()`, or compute the log probabilities based on the logits and feed them to the negative log-likelihood loss function `nn.NLLLoss()`.

The following code will show you how to use these loss functions with two different formats, where either the logits or class-membership probabilities are given as inputs to the loss functions:

```
>>> ####### Binary Cross-entropy
>>> logits = torch.tensor([0.8])
>>> probas = torch.sigmoid(logits)
>>> target = torch.tensor([1.0])
>>> bce_loss_fn = nn.BCELoss()
>>> bce_logits_loss_fn = nn.BCEWithLogitsLoss()
>>> print(f'BCE (w Probas): {bce_loss_fn(probas, target):.4f}')
BCE (w Probas): 0.3711
>>> print(f'BCE (w Logits): '
...       f'{bce_logits_loss_fn(logits, target):.4f}')
BCE (w Logits): 0.3711
```

```
>>> ####### Categorical Cross-entropy
>>> logits = torch.tensor([[1.5, 0.8, 2.1]])
>>> probas = torch.softmax(logits, dim=1)
>>> target = torch.tensor([2])
>>> cce_loss_fn = nn.NLLLoss()
>>> cce_logits_loss_fn = nn.CrossEntropyLoss()
>>> print(f'CCE (w Logits): '
...       f'{cce_logits_loss_fn(logits, target):.4f}')
CCE (w Probas): 0.5996
>>> print(f'CCE (w Probas): '
...       f'{cce_loss_fn(torch.log(probas), target):.4f}')
CCE (w Logits): 0.5996
```

Note that sometimes, you may come across an implementation where a categorical cross-entropy loss is used for binary classification. Typically, when we have a binary classification task, the model returns a single output value for each example. We interpret this single model output as the probability of the positive class (for example, class 1), $P(\text{class} = 1|\boldsymbol{x})$. In a binary classification problem, it is implied that $P(\text{class} = 0|\boldsymbol{x}) = 1 - P(\text{class} = 1|\boldsymbol{x})$; hence, we do not need a second output unit in order to obtain the probability of the negative class. However, sometimes practitioners choose to return two outputs for each training example and interpret them as probabilities of each class: $P(\text{class} = 0|\boldsymbol{x})$ versus $P(\text{class} = 1|\boldsymbol{x})$. Then, in such a case, using a softmax function (instead of the logistic sigmoid) to normalize the outputs (so that they sum to 1) is recommended, and categorical cross-entropy is the appropriate loss function.

Implementing a deep CNN using PyTorch

In *Chapter 13*, as you may recall, we solved the handwritten digit recognition problem using the `torch.nn` module. You may also recall that we achieved about 95.6 percent accuracy using an NN with two linear hidden layers.

Now, let's implement a CNN and see whether it can achieve a better predictive performance compared to the previous model for classifying handwritten digits. Note that the fully connected layers that we saw in *Chapter 13* were able to perform well on this problem. However, in some applications, such as reading bank account numbers from handwritten digits, even tiny mistakes can be very costly. Therefore, it is crucial to reduce this error as much as possible.

The multilayer CNN architecture

The architecture of the network that we are going to implement is shown in *Figure 14.12*. The inputs are 28×28 grayscale images. Considering the number of channels (which is 1 for grayscale images) and a batch of input images, the input tensor's dimensions will be *batchsize*×28×28×1.

The input data goes through two convolutional layers that have a kernel size of 5×5. The first convolution has 32 output feature maps, and the second one has 64 output feature maps. Each convolution layer is followed by a subsampling layer in the form of a max-pooling operation, $P_{2\times2}$. Then a fully connected layer passes the output to a second fully connected layer, which acts as the final *softmax* output layer. The architecture of the network that we are going to implement is shown in *Figure 14.12*:

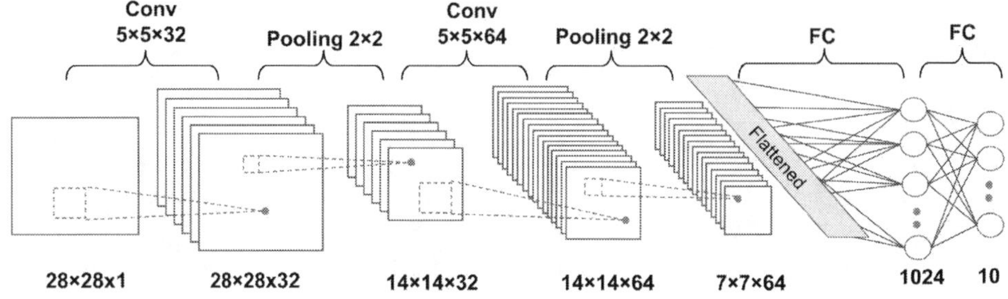

Figure 14.12: A deep CNN

The dimensions of the tensors in each layer are as follows:

- Input: [*batchsize*×28×28×1]
- Conv_1: [*batchsize*×28×28×32]
- Pooling_1: [*batchsize*×14×14×32]
- Conv_2: [*batchsize*×14×14×64]
- Pooling_2: [*batchsize*×7×7×64]
- FC_1: [*batchsize*×1024]
- FC_2 and softmax layer: [*batchsize*×10]

For the convolutional kernels, we are using `stride=1` such that the input dimensions are preserved in the resulting feature maps. For the pooling layers, we are using `kernel_size=2` to subsample the image and shrink the size of the output feature maps. We will implement this network using the PyTorch NN module.

Loading and preprocessing the data

First, we will load the MNIST dataset using the `torchvision` module and construct the training and test sets, as we did in *Chapter 13*:

```
>>> import torchvision
>>> from torchvision import transforms
>>> image_path = './'
>>> transform = transforms.Compose([
...     transforms.ToTensor()
... ])
```

```
>>> mnist_dataset = torchvision.datasets.MNIST(
...     root=image_path, train=True,
...     transform=transform, download=True
... )
>>> from torch.utils.data import Subset
>>> mnist_valid_dataset = Subset(mnist_dataset,
...                              torch.arange(10000))
>>> mnist_train_dataset = Subset(mnist_dataset,
...                              torch.arange(
...                                  10000, len(mnist_dataset)
...                              ))
>>> mnist_test_dataset = torchvision.datasets.MNIST(
...     root=image_path, train=False,
...     transform=transform, download=False
... )
```

The MNIST dataset comes with a pre-specified training and test dataset partitioning scheme, but we also want to create a validation split from the train partition. Hence, we used the first 10,000 training examples for validation. Note that the images are not sorted by class label, so we do not have to worry about whether those validation set images are from the same classes.

Next, we will construct the data loader with batches of 64 images for the training set and validation set, respectively:

```
>>> from torch.utils.data import DataLoader
>>> batch_size = 64
>>> torch.manual_seed(1)
>>> train_dl = DataLoader(mnist_train_dataset,
...                       batch_size,
...                       shuffle=True)
>>> valid_dl = DataLoader(mnist_valid_dataset,
...                       batch_size,
...                       shuffle=False)
```

The features we read are of values in the range [0, 1]. Also, we already converted the images to tensors. The labels are integers from 0 to 9, representing ten digits. Hence, we don't need to do any scaling or further conversion.

Now, after preparing the dataset, we are ready to implement the CNN we just described.

Implementing a CNN using the torch.nn module

For implementing a CNN in PyTorch, we use the `torch.nn` `Sequential` class to stack different layers, such as convolution, pooling, and dropout, as well as the fully connected layers. The `torch.nn` module provides classes for each one: `nn.Conv2d` for a two-dimensional convolution layer; `nn.MaxPool2d` and `nn.AvgPool2d` for subsampling (max-pooling and average-pooling); and `nn.Dropout` for regularization using dropout. We will go over each of these classes in more detail.

Configuring CNN layers in PyTorch

Constructing a layer with the `Conv2d` class requires us to specify the number of output channels (which is equivalent to the number of output feature maps, or the number of output filters) and kernel sizes.

In addition, there are optional parameters that we can use to configure a convolutional layer. The most commonly used ones are the strides (with a default value of 1 in both x, y dimensions) and padding, which controls the amount of implicit padding on both dimensions. Additional configuration parameters are listed in the official documentation: `https://pytorch.org/docs/stable/generated/torch.nn.Conv2d.html`.

It is worth mentioning that usually, when we read an image, the default dimension for the channels is the first dimension of the tensor array (or the second dimension considering the batch dimension). This is called the NCHW format, where *N* stands for the number of images within the batch, *C* stands for channels, and *H* and *W* stand for height and width, respectively.

Note that the `Conv2D` class assumes that inputs are in NCHW format by default. (Other tools, such as TensorFlow, use NHWC format.) However, if you come across some data whose channels are placed at the last dimension, you would need to swap the axes in your data to move the channels to the first dimension (or the second dimension considering the batch dimension). After the layer is constructed, it can be called by providing a four-dimensional tensor, with the first dimension reserved for a batch of examples; the second dimension corresponds to the channel; and the other two dimensions are the spatial dimensions.

As shown in the architecture of the CNN model that we want to build, each convolution layer is followed by a pooling layer for subsampling (reducing the size of feature maps). The `MaxPool2d` and `AvgPool2d` classes construct the max-pooling and average-pooling layers, respectively. The `kernel_size` argument determines the size of the window (or neighborhood) that will be used to compute the max or mean operations. Furthermore, the `stride` parameter can be used to configure the pooling layer, as we discussed earlier.

Finally, the `Dropout` class will construct the dropout layer for regularization, with the argument `p` that denotes the drop probability p_{drop}, which is used to determine the probability of dropping the input units during training, as we discussed earlier. When calling this layer, its behavior can be controlled via `model.train()` and `model.eval()`, to specify whether this call will be made during training or during the inference. When using dropout, alternating between these two modes is crucial to ensure that it behaves correctly; for instance, nodes are only randomly dropped during training, not evaluation or inference.

Constructing a CNN in PyTorch

Now that you have learned about these classes, we can construct the CNN model that was shown in the previous figure. In the following code, we will use the `Sequential` class and add the convolution and pooling layers:

```
>>> model = nn.Sequential()
>>> model.add_module(
...     'conv1',
...     nn.Conv2d(
...         in_channels=1, out_channels=32,
...         kernel_size=5, padding=2
...     )
... )
>>> model.add_module('relu1', nn.ReLU())
>>> model.add_module('pool1', nn.MaxPool2d(kernel_size=2))
>>> model.add_module(
...     'conv2',
...     nn.Conv2d(
...         in_channels=32, out_channels=64,
...         kernel_size=5, padding=2
...     )
... )
>>> model.add_module('relu2', nn.ReLU())
>>> model.add_module('pool2', nn.MaxPool2d(kernel_size=2))
```

So far, we have added two convolution layers to the model. For each convolutional layer, we used a kernel of size 5×5 and `padding=2`. As discussed earlier, using same padding mode preserves the spatial dimensions (vertical and horizontal dimensions) of the feature maps such that the inputs and outputs have the same height and width (and the number of channels may only differ in terms of the number of filters used). As mentioned before, the spatial dimension of the output feature map is calculated by:

$$o = \left\lfloor \frac{n + 2p - m}{s} \right\rfloor + 1$$

where n is the spatial dimension of the input feature map, and p, m, and s denote the padding, kernel size, and stride, respectively. We obtain $p = 2$ in order to achieve $o = i$.

The max-pooling layers with pooling size 2×2 and stride of 2 will reduce the spatial dimensions by half. (Note that if the `stride` parameter is not specified in `MaxPool2D`, by default, it is set equal to the pooling kernel size.)

While we can calculate the size of the feature maps at this stage manually, PyTorch provides a convenient method to compute this for us:

```
>>> x = torch.ones((4, 1, 28, 28))
>>> model(x).shape
torch.Size([4, 64, 7, 7])
```

By providing the input shape as a tuple `(4, 1, 28, 28)` (4 images within the batch, 1 channel, and image size 28×28), specified in this example, we calculated the output to have a shape `(4, 64, 7, 7)`, indicating feature maps with 64 channels and a spatial size of 7×7. The first dimension corresponds to the batch dimension, for which we used 4 arbitrarily.

The next layer that we want to add is a fully connected layer for implementing a classifier on top of our convolutional and pooling layers. The input to this layer must have rank 2, that is, shape [*batchsize* × *input_units*]. Thus, we need to flatten the output of the previous layers to meet this requirement for the fully connected layer:

```
>>> model.add_module('flatten', nn.Flatten())
>>> x = torch.ones((4, 1, 28, 28))
>>> model(x).shape
torch.Size([4, 3136])
```

As the output shape indicates, the input dimensions for the fully connected layer are correctly set up. Next, we will add two fully connected layers with a dropout layer in between:

```
>>> model.add_module('fc1', nn.Linear(3136, 1024))
>>> model.add_module('relu3', nn.ReLU())
>>> model.add_module('dropout', nn.Dropout(p=0.5))
>>> model.add_module('fc2', nn.Linear(1024, 10))
```

The last fully connected layer, named `'fc2'`, has 10 output units for the 10 class labels in the MNIST dataset. In practice, we usually use the sofmax activation to obtain the class-membership probabilities of each input example, assuming that the classes are mutually exclusive, so the probabilities for each example sum to 1. However, the softmax function is already used internally inside PyTorch's `CrossEntropyLoss` implementation, which is why don't have to explicitly add it as a layer after the output layer above. The following code will create the loss function and optimizer for the model:

```
>>> loss_fn = nn.CrossEntropyLoss()
>>> optimizer = torch.optim.Adam(model.parameters(), lr=0.001)
```

The Adam optimizer

Note that in this implementation, we used the `torch.optim.Adam` class for training the CNN model. The Adam optimizer is a robust, gradient-based optimization method suited to nonconvex optimization and machine learning problems. Two popular optimization methods inspired Adam: `RMSProp` and `AdaGrad`.

The key advantage of Adam is in the choice of update step size derived from the running average of gradient moments. Please feel free to read more about the Adam optimizer in the manuscript, *Adam: A Method for Stochastic Optimization* by *Diederik P. Kingma* and *Jimmy Lei Ba*, 2014. The article is freely available at `https://arxiv.org/abs/1412.6980`.

Now we can train the model by defining the following function:

```
>>> def train(model, num_epochs, train_dl, valid_dl):
...     loss_hist_train = [0] * num_epochs
...     accuracy_hist_train = [0] * num_epochs
...     loss_hist_valid = [0] * num_epochs
...     accuracy_hist_valid = [0] * num_epochs
...     for epoch in range(num_epochs):
...         model.train()
...         for x_batch, y_batch in train_dl:
...             pred = model(x_batch)
...             loss = loss_fn(pred, y_batch)
...             loss.backward()
...             optimizer.step()
...             optimizer.zero_grad()
...             loss_hist_train[epoch] += loss.item()*y_batch.size(0)
...             is_correct = (
...                 torch.argmax(pred, dim=1) == y_batch
...             ).float()
...             accuracy_hist_train[epoch] += is_correct.sum()
...         loss_hist_train[epoch] /= len(train_dl.dataset)
...         accuracy_hist_train[epoch] /= len(train_dl.dataset)
...
...         model.eval()
```

```
...         with torch.no_grad():
...             for x_batch, y_batch in valid_dl:
...                 pred = model(x_batch)
...                 loss = loss_fn(pred, y_batch)
...                 loss_hist_valid[epoch] += \
...                     loss.item()*y_batch.size(0)
...                 is_correct = (
...                     torch.argmax(pred, dim=1) == y_batch
...                 ).float()
...                 accuracy_hist_valid[epoch] += is_correct.sum()
...         loss_hist_valid[epoch] /= len(valid_dl.dataset)
...         accuracy_hist_valid[epoch] /= len(valid_dl.dataset)
...
...         print(f'Epoch {epoch+1} accuracy: '
...               f'{accuracy_hist_train[epoch]:.4f} val_accuracy: '
...               f'{accuracy_hist_valid[epoch]:.4f}')
...     return loss_hist_train, loss_hist_valid, \
...            accuracy_hist_train, accuracy_hist_valid
```

Note that using the designated settings for training `model.train()` and evaluation `model.eval()` will automatically set the mode for the dropout layer and rescale the hidden units appropriately so that we do not have to worry about that at all. Next, we will train this CNN model and use the validation dataset that we created for monitoring the learning progress:

```
>>> torch.manual_seed(1)
>>> num_epochs = 20
>>> hist = train(model, num_epochs, train_dl, valid_dl)
Epoch 1 accuracy: 0.9503 val_accuracy: 0.9802
...
Epoch 9 accuracy: 0.9968 val_accuracy: 0.9892
...
Epoch 20 accuracy: 0.9979 val_accuracy: 0.9907
```

Once the 20 epochs of training are finished, we can visualize the learning curves:

```
>>> import matplotlib.pyplot as plt
>>> x_arr = np.arange(len(hist[0])) + 1
>>> fig = plt.figure(figsize=(12, 4))
>>> ax = fig.add_subplot(1, 2, 1)
>>> ax.plot(x_arr, hist[0], '-o', label='Train loss')
>>> ax.plot(x_arr, hist[1], '--<', label='Validation loss')
```

```
>>> ax.legend(fontsize=15)
>>> ax = fig.add_subplot(1, 2, 2)
>>> ax.plot(x_arr, hist[2], '-o', label='Train acc.')
>>> ax.plot(x_arr, hist[3], '--<',
...         label='Validation acc.')
>>> ax.legend(fontsize=15)
>>> ax.set_xlabel('Epoch', size=15)
>>> ax.set_ylabel('Accuracy', size=15)
>>> plt.show()
```

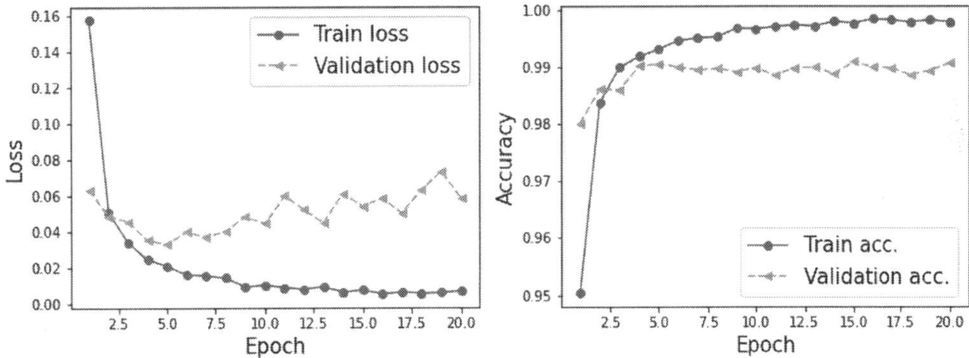

Figure 14.13: Loss and accuracy graphs for the training and validation data

Now, we evaluate the trained model on the test dataset:

```
>>> pred = model(mnist_test_dataset.data.unsqueeze(1) / 255.)
>>> is_correct = (
...     torch.argmax(pred, dim=1) == mnist_test_dataset.targets
... ).float()
>>> print(f'Test accuracy: {is_correct.mean():.4f}')
Test accuracy: 0.9914
```

The CNN model achieves an accuracy of 99.07 percent. Remember that in *Chapter 13*, we got approximately 95 percent accuracy using only fully connected (instead of convolutional) layers.

Finally, we can get the prediction results in the form of class-membership probabilities and convert them to predicted labels by using the `torch.argmax` function to find the element with the maximum probability. We will do this for a batch of 12 examples and visualize the input and predicted labels:

```
>>> fig = plt.figure(figsize=(12, 4))
>>> for i in range(12):
...     ax = fig.add_subplot(2, 6, i+1)
...     ax.set_xticks([]); ax.set_yticks([])
```

```
...     img = mnist_test_dataset[i][0][0, :, :]
...     pred = model(img.unsqueeze(0).unsqueeze(1))
...     y_pred = torch.argmax(pred)
...     ax.imshow(img, cmap='gray_r')
...     ax.text(0.9, 0.1, y_pred.item(),
...             size=15, color='blue',
...             horizontalalignment='center',
...             verticalalignment='center',
...             transform=ax.transAxes)
>>> plt.show()
```

Figure 14.14 shows the handwritten inputs and their predicted labels:

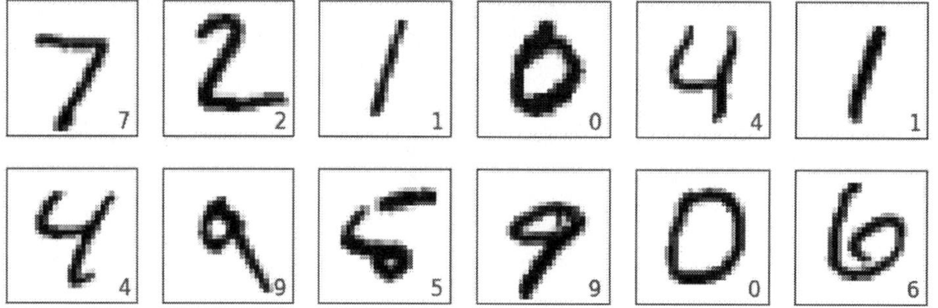

Figure 14.14: Predicted labels for handwritten digits

In this set of plotted examples, all the predicted labels are correct.

We leave the task of showing some of the misclassified digits, as we did in *Chapter 11, Implementing a Multilayer Artificial Neural Network from Scratch,* as an exercise for the reader.

Smile classification from face images using a CNN

In this section, we are going to implement a CNN for smile classification from face images using the CelebA dataset. As you saw in *Chapter 12,* the CelebA dataset contains 202,599 images of celebrities' faces. In addition, 40 binary facial attributes are available for each image, including whether a celebrity is smiling (or not) and their age (young or old).

Based on what you have learned so far, the goal of this section is to build and train a CNN model for predicting the smile attribute from these face images. Here, for simplicity, we will only be using a small portion of the training data (16,000 training examples) to speed up the training process. However, to improve the generalization performance and reduce overfitting on such a small dataset, we will use a technique called **data augmentation**.

Loading the CelebA dataset

First, let's load the data similarly to how we did in the previous section for the MNIST dataset. CelebA data comes in three partitions: a training dataset, a validation dataset, and a test dataset. Next, we will count the number of examples in each partition:

```
>>> image_path = './'
>>> celeba_train_dataset = torchvision.datasets.CelebA(
...     image_path, split='train',
...     target_type='attr', download=True
... )
>>> celeba_valid_dataset = torchvision.datasets.CelebA(
...     image_path, split='valid',
...     target_type='attr', download=True
... )
>>> celeba_test_dataset = torchvision.datasets.CelebA(
...     image_path, split='test',
...     target_type='attr', download=True
... )
>>>
>>> print('Train set:', len(celeba_train_dataset))
Train set:  162770
>>> print('Validation set:', len(celeba_valid_dataset))
Validation: 19867
>>> print('Test set:', len(celeba_test_dataset))
Test set:   19962
```

Alternative ways to download the CelebA dataset

The CelebA dataset is relatively large (approximately 1.5 GB) and the `torchvision` download link is notoriously unstable. If you encounter problems executing the previous code, you can download the files from the official CelebA website manually (`https://mmlab.ie.cuhk.edu.hk/projects/CelebA.html`) or use our download link: `https://drive.google.com/file/d/1m8-EBPgi5MRubrm6iQjafK2QMHDBMSfJ/view?usp=sharing`. If you use our download link, it will download a `celeba.zip` file, which you need to unpack in the current directory where you are running the code. Also, after downloading and unzipping the `celeba` folder, you need to rerun the code above with the setting `download=False` instead of `download=True`. In case you are encountering problems with this approach, please do not hesitate to open a new issue or start a discussion at `https://github.com/rasbt/machine-learning-book` so that we can provide you with additional information.

Next, we will discuss data augmentation as a technique for boosting the performance of deep NNs.

Image transformation and data augmentation

Data augmentation summarizes a broad set of techniques for dealing with cases where the training data is limited. For instance, certain data augmentation techniques allow us to modify or even artificially synthesize more data and thereby boost the performance of a machine or deep learning model by reducing overfitting. While data augmentation is not only for image data, there is a set of transformations uniquely applicable to image data, such as cropping parts of an image, flipping, and changing the contrast, brightness, and saturation. Let's see some of these transformations that are available via the `torchvision.transforms` module. In the following code block, we will first get five examples from the `celeba_train_dataset` dataset and apply five different types of transformation: 1) cropping an image to a bounding box, 2) flipping an image horizontally, 3) adjusting the contrast, 4) adjusting the brightness, and 5) center-cropping an image and resizing the resulting image back to its original size, (218, 178). In the following code, we will visualize the results of these transformations, showing each one in a separate column for comparison:

```
>>> fig = plt.figure(figsize=(16, 8.5))
>>> ## Column 1: cropping to a bounding-box
>>> ax = fig.add_subplot(2, 5, 1)
>>> img, attr = celeba_train_dataset[0]
>>> ax.set_title('Crop to a \nbounding-box', size=15)
>>> ax.imshow(img)
>>> ax = fig.add_subplot(2, 5, 6)
>>> img_cropped = transforms.functional.crop(img, 50, 20, 128, 128)
>>> ax.imshow(img_cropped)
>>>
>>> ## Column 2: flipping (horizontally)
>>> ax = fig.add_subplot(2, 5, 2)
>>> img, attr = celeba_train_dataset[1]
>>> ax.set_title('Flip (horizontal)', size=15)
>>> ax.imshow(img)
>>> ax = fig.add_subplot(2, 5, 7)
>>> img_flipped = transforms.functional.hflip(img)
>>> ax.imshow(img_flipped)
>>>
>>> ## Column 3: adjust contrast
>>> ax = fig.add_subplot(2, 5, 3)
>>> img, attr = celeba_train_dataset[2]
>>> ax.set_title('Adjust constrast', size=15)
>>> ax.imshow(img)
>>> ax = fig.add_subplot(2, 5, 8)
>>> img_adj_contrast = transforms.functional.adjust_contrast(
...     img, contrast_factor=2
... )
>>> ax.imshow(img_adj_contrast)
>>>
>>> ## Column 4: adjust brightness
>>> ax = fig.add_subplot(2, 5, 4)
```

```
>>> img, attr = celeba_train_dataset[3]
>>> ax.set_title('Adjust brightness', size=15)
>>> ax.imshow(img)
>>> ax = fig.add_subplot(2, 5, 9)
>>> img_adj_brightness = transforms.functional.adjust_brightness(
...     img, brightness_factor=1.3
... )
>>> ax.imshow(img_adj_brightness)
>>>
>>> ## Column 5: cropping from image center
>>> ax = fig.add_subplot(2, 5, 5)
>>> img, attr = celeba_train_dataset[4]
>>> ax.set_title('Center crop\nand resize', size=15)
>>> ax.imshow(img)
>>> ax = fig.add_subplot(2, 5, 10)
>>> img_center_crop = transforms.functional.center_crop(
...     img, [0.7*218, 0.7*178]
... )
>>> img_resized = transforms.functional.resize(
...     img_center_crop, size=(218, 178)
... )
>>> ax.imshow(img_resized)
>>> plt.show()
```

Figure 14.15 shows the results:

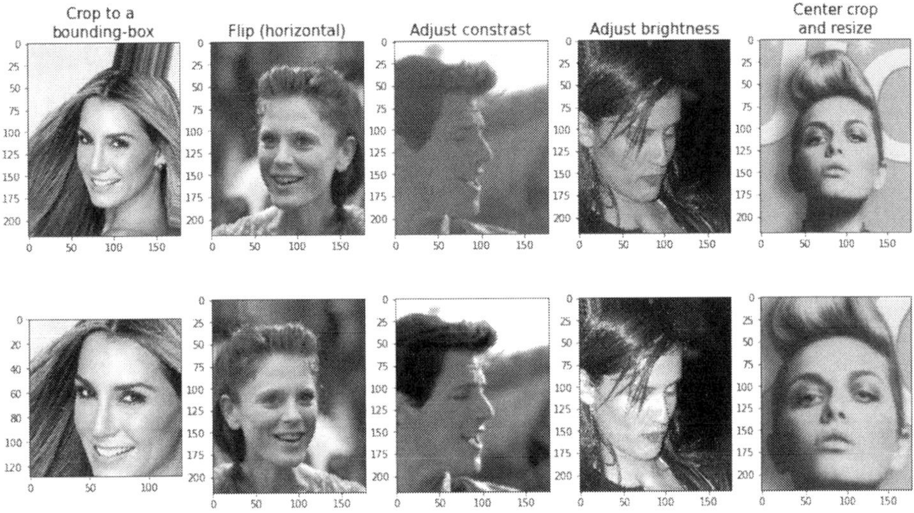

Figure 14.15: Different image transformations

In *Figure 14.15*, the original images are shown in the first row and their transformed versions in the second row. Note that for the first transformation (leftmost column), the bounding box is specified by four numbers: the coordinate of the upper-left corner of the bounding box (here x=20, y=50), and the width and height of the box (width=128, height=128). Also note that the origin (the coordinates at the location denoted as (0, 0)) for images loaded by PyTorch (as well as other packages such as `imageio`) is the upper-left corner of the image.

The transformations in the previous code block are deterministic. However, all such transformations can also be randomized, which is recommended for data augmentation during model training. For example, a random bounding box (where the coordinates of the upper-left corner are selected randomly) can be cropped from an image, an image can be randomly flipped along either the horizontal or vertical axes with a probability of 0.5, or the contrast of an image can be changed randomly, where the `contrast_factor` is selected at random, but with uniform distribution, from a range of values. In addition, we can create a pipeline of these transformations.

For example, we can first randomly crop an image, then flip it randomly, and finally, resize it to the desired size. The code is as follows (since we have random elements, we set the random seed for reproducibility):

```
>>> torch.manual_seed(1)
>>> fig = plt.figure(figsize=(14, 12))
>>> for i, (img, attr) in enumerate(celeba_train_dataset):
...     ax = fig.add_subplot(3, 4, i*4+1)
...     ax.imshow(img)
...     if i == 0:
...         ax.set_title('Orig.', size=15)
...
...     ax = fig.add_subplot(3, 4, i*4+2)
...     img_transform = transforms.Compose([
...         transforms.RandomCrop([178, 178])
...     ])
...     img_cropped = img_transform(img)
...     ax.imshow(img_cropped)
...     if i == 0:
...         ax.set_title('Step 1: Random crop', size=15)
...
...     ax = fig.add_subplot(3, 4, i*4+3)
...     img_transform = transforms.Compose([
...         transforms.RandomHorizontalFlip()
...     ])
...     img_flip = img_transform(img_cropped)
...     ax.imshow(img_flip)
...     if i == 0:
...         ax.set_title('Step 2: Random flip', size=15)
```

```
...
...     ax = fig.add_subplot(3, 4, i*4+4)
...     img_resized = transforms.functional.resize(
...         img_flip, size=(128, 128)
...     )
...     ax.imshow(img_resized)
...     if i == 0:
...         ax.set_title('Step 3: Resize', size=15)
...     if i == 2:
...         break
>>> plt.show()
```

Figure 14.16 shows random transformations on three example images:

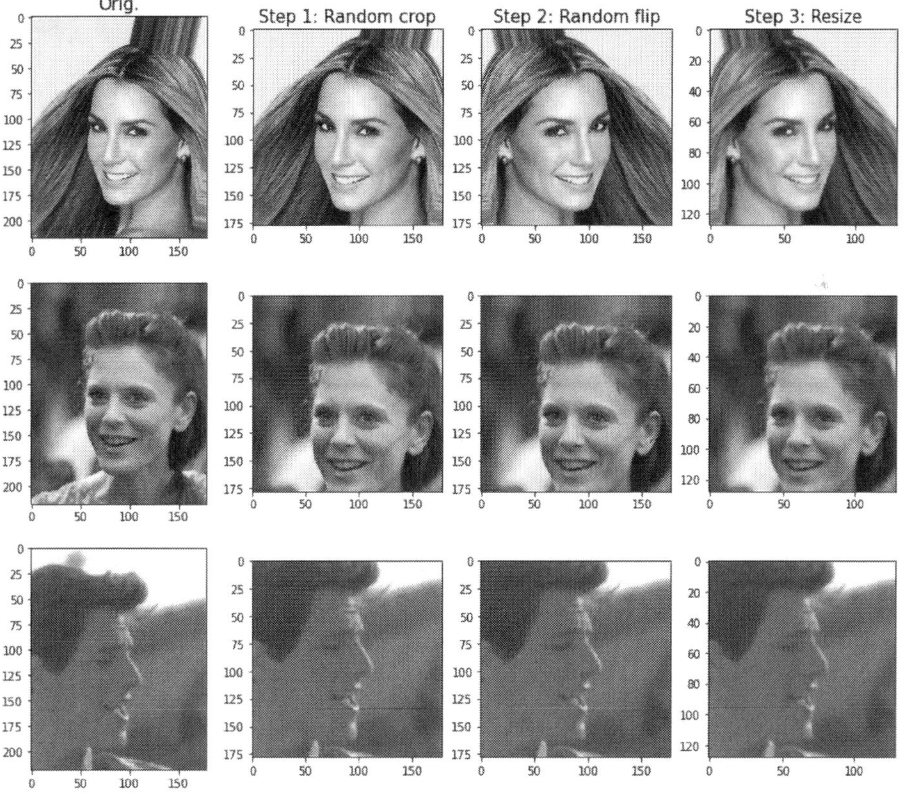

Figure 14.16: Random image transformations

Note that each time we iterate through these three examples, we get slightly different images due to random transformations.

For convenience, we can define transform functions to use this pipeline for data augmentation during dataset loading. In the following code, we will define the function `get_smile`, which will extract the smile label from the `'attributes'` list:

```
>>> get_smile = lambda attr: attr[31]
```

We will define the `transform_train` function that will produce the transformed image (where we will first randomly crop the image, then flip it randomly, and finally, resize it to the desired size 64×64):

```
>>> transform_train = transforms.Compose([
...     transforms.RandomCrop([178, 178]),
...     transforms.RandomHorizontalFlip(),
...     transforms.Resize([64, 64]),
...     transforms.ToTensor(),
... ])
```

We will only apply data augmentation to the training examples, however, and not to the validation or test images. The code for the validation or test set is as follows (where we will first simply crop the image and then resize it to the desired size 64×64):

```
>>> transform = transforms.Compose([
...     transforms.CenterCrop([178, 178]),
...     transforms.Resize([64, 64]),
...     transforms.ToTensor(),
... ])
```

Now, to see data augmentation in action, let's apply the `transform_train` function to our training dataset and iterate over the dataset five times:

```
>>> from torch.utils.data import DataLoader
>>> celeba_train_dataset = torchvision.datasets.CelebA(
...     image_path, split='train',
...     target_type='attr', download=False,
...     transform=transform_train, target_transform=get_smile
... )
>>> torch.manual_seed(1)
>>> data_loader = DataLoader(celeba_train_dataset, batch_size=2)
>>> fig = plt.figure(figsize=(15, 6))
>>> num_epochs = 5
>>> for j in range(num_epochs):
...     img_batch, label_batch = next(iter(data_loader))
...     img = img_batch[0]
```

```
...     ax = fig.add_subplot(2, 5, j + 1)
...     ax.set_xticks([])
...     ax.set_yticks([])
...     ax.set_title(f'Epoch {j}:', size=15)
...     ax.imshow(img.permute(1, 2, 0))
...
...     img = img_batch[1]
...     ax = fig.add_subplot(2, 5, j + 6)
...     ax.set_xticks([])
...     ax.set_yticks([])
...     ax.imshow(img.permute(1, 2, 0))
>>> plt.show()
```

Figure 14.17 shows the five resulting transformations for data augmentation on two example images:

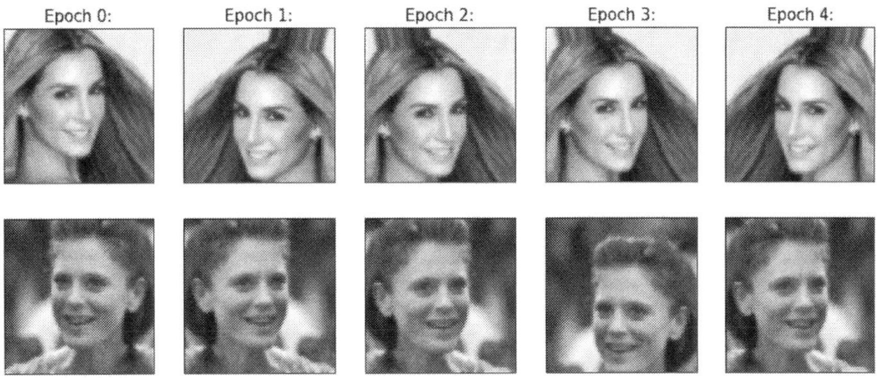

Figure 14.17: The result of five image transformations

Next, we will apply the `transform` function to our validation and test datasets:

```
>>> celeba_valid_dataset = torchvision.datasets.CelebA(
...     image_path, split='valid',
...     target_type='attr', download=False,
...     transform=transform, target_transform=get_smile
... )
>>> celeba_test_dataset = torchvision.datasets.CelebA(
...     image_path, split='test',
...     target_type='attr', download=False,
...     transform=transform, target_transform=get_smile
... )
```

Furthermore, instead of using all the available training and validation data, we will take a subset of 16,000 training examples and 1,000 examples for validation, as our goal here is to intentionally train our model with a small dataset:

```
>>> from torch.utils.data import Subset
>>> celeba_train_dataset = Subset(celeba_train_dataset,
...                               torch.arange(16000))
>>> celeba_valid_dataset = Subset(celeba_valid_dataset,
...                               torch.arange(1000))
>>> print('Train set:', len(celeba_train_dataset))
Train set: 16000
>>> print('Validation set:', len(celeba_valid_dataset))
Validation set: 1000
```

Now, we can create data loaders for three datasets:

```
>>> batch_size = 32
>>> torch.manual_seed(1)
>>> train_dl = DataLoader(celeba_train_dataset,
...                       batch_size, shuffle=True)
>>> valid_dl = DataLoader(celeba_valid_dataset,
...                       batch_size, shuffle=False)
>>> test_dl = DataLoader(celeba_test_dataset,
...                      batch_size, shuffle=False)
```

Now that the data loaders are ready, we will develop a CNN model, and train and evaluate it in the next section.

Training a CNN smile classifier

By now, building a model with `torch.nn` module and training it should be straightforward. The design of our CNN is as follows: the CNN model receives input images of size 3×64×64 (the images have three color channels).

The input data goes through four convolutional layers to make 32, 64, 128, and 256 feature maps using filters with a kernel size of 3×3 and padding of 1 for same padding. The first three convolution layers are followed by max-pooling, $P_{2\times2}$. Two dropout layers are also included for regularization:

```
>>> model = nn.Sequential()
>>> model.add_module(
...     'conv1',
...     nn.Conv2d(
...         in_channels=3, out_channels=32,
...         kernel_size=3, padding=1
...     )
```

```
... )
>>> model.add_module('relu1', nn.ReLU())
>>> model.add_module('pool1', nn.MaxPool2d(kernel_size=2))
>>> model.add_module('dropout1', nn.Dropout(p=0.5))
>>>
>>> model.add_module(
...     'conv2',
...     nn.Conv2d(
...         in_channels=32, out_channels=64,
...         kernel_size=3, padding=1
...     )
... )
>>> model.add_module('relu2', nn.ReLU())
>>> model.add_module('pool2', nn.MaxPool2d(kernel_size=2))
>>> model.add_module('dropout2', nn.Dropout(p=0.5))
>>>
>>> model.add_module(
...     'conv3',
...     nn.Conv2d(
...         in_channels=64, out_channels=128,
...         kernel_size=3, padding=1
...     )
... )
>>> model.add_module('relu3', nn.ReLU())
>>> model.add_module('pool3', nn.MaxPool2d(kernel_size=2))
>>>
>>> model.add_module(
...     'conv4',
...     nn.Conv2d(
...         in_channels=128, out_channels=256,
...         kernel_size=3, padding=1
...     )
... )
>>> model.add_module('relu4', nn.ReLU())
```

Let's see the shape of the output feature maps after applying these layers using a toy batch input (four images arbitrarily):

```
>>> x = torch.ones((4, 3, 64, 64))
>>> model(x).shape
torch.Size([4, 256, 8, 8])
```

There are 256 feature maps (or channels) of size 8×8. Now, we can add a fully connected layer to get to the output layer with a single unit. If we reshape (flatten) the feature maps, the number of input units to this fully connected layer will be 8 × 8 × 256 = 16,384. Alternatively, let's consider a new layer, called *global average-pooling*, which computes the average of each feature map separately, thereby reducing the hidden units to 256. We can then add a fully connected layer. Although we have not discussed global average-pooling explicitly, it is conceptually very similar to other pooling layers. Global average-pooling can be viewed, in fact, as a special case of average-pooling when the pooling size is equal to the size of the input feature maps.

To understand this, consider *Figure 14.18*, showing an example of input feature maps of shape *batchsize*×8×64×64. The channels are numbered *k*=0, 1, ..., 7. The global average-pooling operation calculates the average of each channel so that the output will have the shape [*batchsize*×8]. After this, we will squeeze the output of the global average-pooling layer.

Without squeezing the output, the shape would be [*batchsize*×8×1×1], as the global average-pooling would reduce the spatial dimension of 64×64 to 1×1:

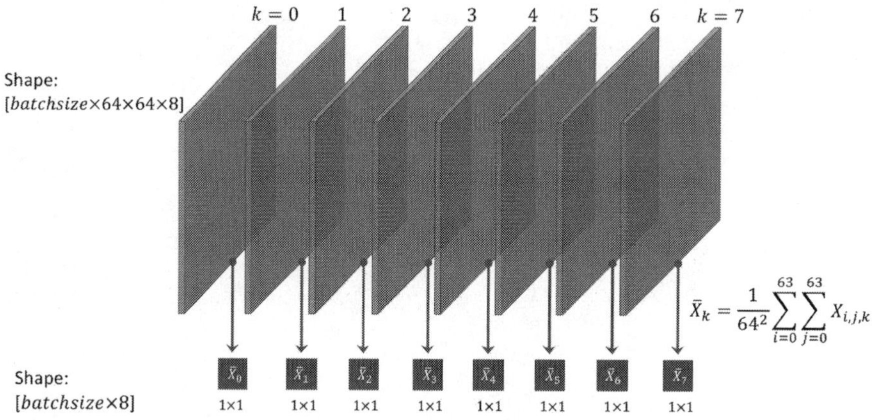

Figure 14.18: Input feature maps

Therefore, given that, in our case, the shape of the feature maps prior to this layer is [*batchsize*×256×8×8], we expect to get 256 units as output, that is, the shape of the output will be [*batchsize*×256]. Let's add this layer and recompute the output shape to verify that this is true:

```
>>> model.add_module('pool4', nn.AvgPool2d(kernel_size=8))
>>> model.add_module('flatten', nn.Flatten())
>>> x = torch.ones((4, 3, 64, 64))
>>> model(x).shape
```

```
torch.Size([4, 256])
```

Finally, we can add a fully connected layer to get a single output unit. In this case, we can specify the activation function to be `'sigmoid'`:

```
>>> model.add_module('fc', nn.Linear(256, 1))
>>> model.add_module('sigmoid', nn.Sigmoid())
>>> x = torch.ones((4, 3, 64, 64))
>>> model(x).shape
torch.Size([4, 1])
>>> model
Sequential(
  (conv1): Conv2d(3, 32, kernel_size=(3, 3), stride=(1, 1), padding=(1, 1))
  (relu1): ReLU()
  (pool1): MaxPool2d(kernel_size=2, stride=2, padding=0, dilation=1, ceil_
mode=False)
  (dropout1): Dropout(p=0.5, inplace=False)
  (conv2): Conv2d(32, 64, kernel_size=(3, 3), stride=(1, 1), padding=(1, 1))
  (relu2): ReLU()
  (pool2): MaxPool2d(kernel_size=2, stride=2, padding=0, dilation=1, ceil_
mode=False)
  (dropout2): Dropout(p=0.5, inplace=False)
  (conv3): Conv2d(64, 128, kernel_size=(3, 3), stride=(1, 1), padding=(1, 1))
  (relu3): ReLU()
  (pool3): MaxPool2d(kernel_size=2, stride=2, padding=0, dilation=1, ceil_
mode=False)
  (conv4): Conv2d(128, 256, kernel_size=(3, 3), stride=(1, 1), padding=(1, 1))
  (relu4): ReLU()
  (pool4): AvgPool2d(kernel_size=8, stride=8, padding=0)
  (flatten): Flatten(start_dim=1, end_dim=-1)
  (fc): Linear(in_features=256, out_features=1, bias=True)
  (sigmoid): Sigmoid()
)
```

The next step is to create a loss function and optimizer (Adam optimizer again). For a binary classification with a single probabilistic output, we use `BCELoss` for the loss function:

```
>>> loss_fn = nn.BCELoss()
>>> optimizer = torch.optim.Adam(model.parameters(), lr=0.001)
```

Now we can train the model by defining the following function:

```
>>> def train(model, num_epochs, train_dl, valid_dl):
...     loss_hist_train = [0] * num_epochs
...     accuracy_hist_train = [0] * num_epochs
...     loss_hist_valid = [0] * num_epochs
...     accuracy_hist_valid = [0] * num_epochs
...     for epoch in range(num_epochs):
...         model.train()
...         for x_batch, y_batch in train_dl:
...             pred = model(x_batch)[:, 0]
...             loss = loss_fn(pred, y_batch.float())
...             loss.backward()
...             optimizer.step()
...             optimizer.zero_grad()
...             loss_hist_train[epoch] += loss.item()*y_batch.size(0)
...             is_correct = ((pred>=0.5).float() == y_batch).float()
...             accuracy_hist_train[epoch] += is_correct.sum()
...         loss_hist_train[epoch] /= len(train_dl.dataset)
...         accuracy_hist_train[epoch] /= len(train_dl.dataset)
...
...         model.eval()
...         with torch.no_grad():
...             for x_batch, y_batch in valid_dl:
...                 pred = model(x_batch)[:, 0]
...                 loss = loss_fn(pred, y_batch.float())
...                 loss_hist_valid[epoch] += \
...                     loss.item() * y_batch.size(0)
...                 is_correct = \
...                     ((pred>=0.5).float() == y_batch).float()
...                 accuracy_hist_valid[epoch] += is_correct.sum()
...         loss_hist_valid[epoch] /= len(valid_dl.dataset)
...         accuracy_hist_valid[epoch] /= len(valid_dl.dataset)
...
...         print(f'Epoch {epoch+1} accuracy: '
...               f'{accuracy_hist_train[epoch]:.4f} val_accuracy: '
...               f'{accuracy_hist_valid[epoch]:.4f}')
...     return loss_hist_train, loss_hist_valid, \
...         accuracy_hist_train, accuracy_hist_valid
```

Next, we will train this CNN model for 30 epochs and use the validation dataset that we created for monitoring the learning progress:

```
>>> torch.manual_seed(1)
>>> num_epochs = 30
>>> hist = train(model, num_epochs, train_dl, valid_dl)
Epoch 1 accuracy: 0.6286 val_accuracy: 0.6540
...
Epoch 15 accuracy: 0.8544 val_accuracy: 0.8700
...
Epoch 30 accuracy: 0.8739 val_accuracy: 0.8710
```

Let's now visualize the learning curve and compare the training and validation loss and accuracies after each epoch:

```
>>> x_arr = np.arange(len(hist[0])) + 1
>>> fig = plt.figure(figsize=(12, 4))
>>> ax = fig.add_subplot(1, 2, 1)
>>> ax.plot(x_arr, hist[0], '-o', label='Train loss')
>>> ax.plot(x_arr, hist[1], '--<', label='Validation loss')
>>> ax.legend(fontsize=15)
>>> ax = fig.add_subplot(1, 2, 2)
>>> ax.plot(x_arr, hist[2], '-o', label='Train acc.')
>>> ax.plot(x_arr, hist[3], '--<',
...         label='Validation acc.')
>>> ax.legend(fontsize=15)
>>> ax.set_xlabel('Epoch', size=15)
>>> ax.set_ylabel('Accuracy', size=15)
>>> plt.show()
```

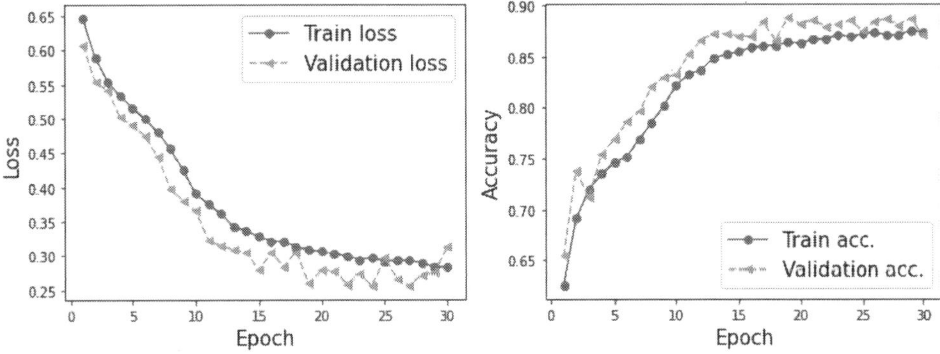

Figure 14.19: A comparison of the training and validation results

Once we are happy with the learning curves, we can evaluate the model on the hold-out test dataset:

```
>>> accuracy_test = 0
>>> model.eval()
>>> with torch.no_grad():
...     for x_batch, y_batch in test_dl:
...         pred = model(x_batch)[:, 0]
...         is_correct = ((pred>=0.5).float() == y_batch).float()
...         accuracy_test += is_correct.sum()
>>> accuracy_test /= len(test_dl.dataset)
>>> print(f'Test accuracy: {accuracy_test:.4f}')
Test accuracy: 0.8446
```

Finally, we already know how to get the prediction results on some test examples. In the following code, we will take a small subset of 10 examples from the last batch of our pre-processed test dataset (`test_dl`). Then, we will compute the probabilities of each example being from class 1 (which corresponds to *smile* based on the labels provided in CelebA) and visualize the examples along with their ground truth label and the predicted probabilities:

```
>>> pred = model(x_batch)[:, 0] * 100
>>> fig = plt.figure(figsize=(15, 7))
>>> for j in range(10, 20):
...     ax = fig.add_subplot(2, 5, j-10+1)
...     ax.set_xticks([]); ax.set_yticks([])
...     ax.imshow(x_batch[j].permute(1, 2, 0))
...     if y_batch[j] == 1:
...         label='Smile'
...     else:
...         label = 'Not Smile'
...     ax.text(
...         0.5, -0.15,
...         f'GT: {label:s}\nPr(Smile)={pred[j]:.0f}%',
...         size=16,
...         horizontalalignment='center',
...         verticalalignment='center',
...         transform=ax.transAxes
...     )
>>> plt.show()
```

In *Figure 14.20*, you can see 10 example images along with their ground truth labels and the probabilities that they belong to class 1, smile:

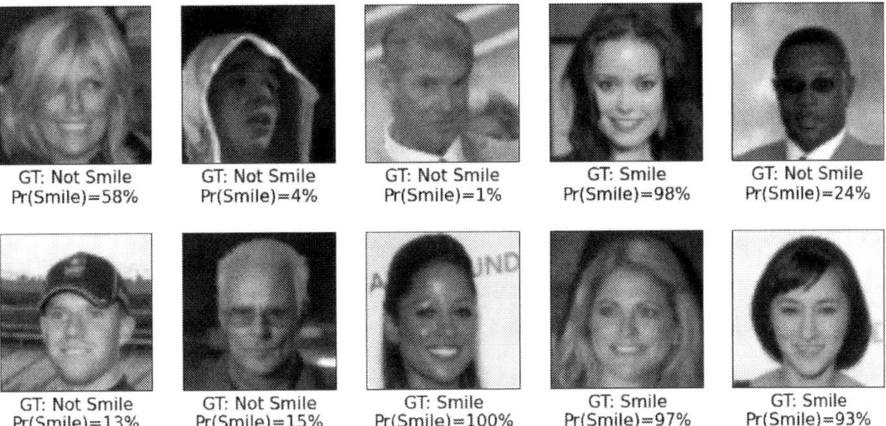

Figure 14.20: Image labels and their probabilities that they belong to class 1

The probabilities of class 1 (that is, *smile* according to CelebA) are provided below each image. As you can see, our trained model is completely accurate on this set of 10 test examples.

As an optional exercise, you are encouraged to try using the entire training dataset instead of the small subset we created. Furthermore, you can change or modify the CNN architecture. For example, you can change the dropout probabilities and the number of filters in the different convolutional layers. Also, you could replace the global average-pooling with a fully connected layer. If you are using the entire training dataset with the CNN architecture we trained in this chapter, you should be able to achieve above 90 percent accuracy.

Summary

In this chapter, we learned about CNNs and their main components. We started with the convolution operation and looked at 1D and 2D implementations. Then, we covered another type of layer that is found in several common CNN architectures: the subsampling or so-called pooling layers. We primarily focused on the two most common forms of pooling: max-pooling and average-pooling.

Next, putting all these individual concepts together, we implemented deep CNNs using the `torch.nn` module. The first network we implemented was applied to the already familiar MNIST handwritten digit recognition problem.

Then, we implemented a second CNN on a more complex dataset consisting of face images and trained the CNN for smile classification. Along the way, you also learned about data augmentation and different transformations that we can apply to face images using the `torchvision.transforms` module.

In the next chapter, we will move on to **recurrent neural networks** (**RNNs**). RNNs are used for learning the structure of sequence data, and they have some fascinating applications, including language translation and image captioning.

Join our book's Discord space

Join our Discord community to meet like-minded people and learn alongside more than 2000 members at:

`https://packt.link/MLwPyTorch`

15

Modeling Sequential Data Using Recurrent Neural Networks

In the previous chapter, we focused on **convolutional neural networks** (CNNs). We covered the building blocks of CNN architectures and how to implement deep CNNs in PyTorch. Finally, you learned how to use CNNs for image classification. In this chapter, we will explore **recurrent neural networks** (**RNNs**) and see their application in modeling sequential data.

We will cover the following topics:

- Introducing sequential data
- RNNs for modeling sequences
- Long short-term memory
- Truncated backpropagation through time
- Implementing a multilayer RNN for sequence modeling in PyTorch
- Project one: RNN sentiment analysis of the IMDb movie review dataset
- Project two: RNN character-level language modeling with LSTM cells, using text data from Jules Verne's *The Mysterious Island*
- Using gradient clipping to avoid exploding gradients

Introducing sequential data

Let's begin our discussion of RNNs by looking at the nature of sequential data, which is more commonly known as sequence data or **sequences**. We will look at the unique properties of sequences that make them different from other kinds of data. We will then see how to represent sequential data and explore the various categories of models for sequential data, which are based on the input and output of a model. This will help us to explore the relationship between RNNs and sequences in this chapter.

Modeling sequential data – order matters

What makes sequences unique, compared to other types of data, is that elements in a sequence appear in a certain order and are not independent of each other. Typical machine learning algorithms for supervised learning assume that the input is **independent and identically distributed** (**IID**) data, which means that the training examples are *mutually independent* and have the same underlying distribution. In this regard, based on the mutual independence assumption, the order in which the training examples are given to the model is irrelevant. For example, if we have a sample consisting of n training examples, $x^{(1)}$, $x^{(2)}$, ..., $x^{(n)}$, the order in which we use the data for training our machine learning algorithm does not matter. An example of this scenario would be the Iris dataset that we worked with previously. In the Iris dataset, each flower has been measured independently, and the measurements of one flower do not influence the measurements of another flower.

However, this assumption is not valid when we deal with sequences—by definition, order matters. Predicting the market value of a particular stock would be an example of this scenario. For instance, assume we have a sample of n training examples, where each training example represents the market value of a certain stock on a particular day. If our task is to predict the stock market value for the next three days, it would make sense to consider the previous stock prices in a date-sorted order to derive trends rather than utilize these training examples in a randomized order.

Sequential data versus time series data

Time series data is a special type of sequential data where each example is associated with a dimension for time. In time series data, samples are taken at successive timestamps, and therefore, the time dimension determines the order among the data points. For example, stock prices and voice or speech records are time series data.

On the other hand, not all sequential data has the time dimension. For example, in text data or DNA sequences, the examples are ordered, but text or DNA does not qualify as time series data. As you will see, in this chapter, we will focus on examples of natural language processing (NLP) and text modeling that are not time series data. However, note that RNNs can also be used for time series data, which is beyond the scope of this book.

Representing sequences

We've established that order among data points is important in sequential data, so we next need to find a way to leverage this ordering information in a machine learning model. Throughout this chapter, we will represent sequences as $\langle \boldsymbol{x}^{(1)}, \boldsymbol{x}^{(2)}, \ldots, \boldsymbol{x}^{(T)} \rangle$. The superscript indices indicate the order of the instances, and the length of the sequence is T. For a sensible example of sequences, consider time series data, where each example point, $x^{(t)}$, belongs to a particular time, t. *Figure 15.1* shows an example of time series data where both the input features (x's) and the target labels (y's) naturally follow the order according to their time axis; therefore, both the x's and y's are sequences.

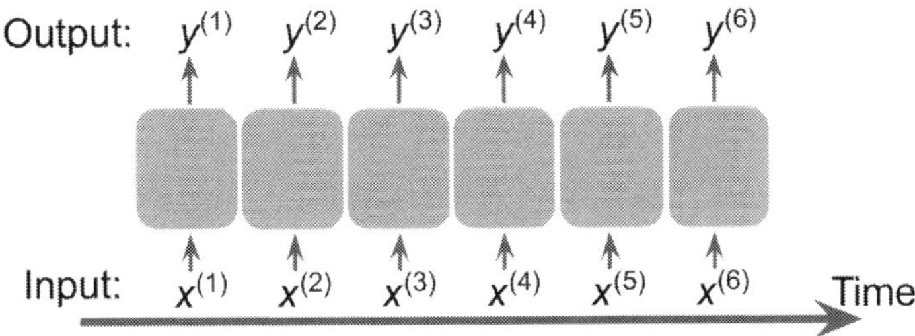

Figure 15.1: An example of time series data

As we have already mentioned, the standard NN models that we have covered so far, such as **multilayer perceptrons** (**MLPs**) and CNNs for image data, assume that the training examples are independent of each other and thus do not incorporate *ordering information*. We can say that such models do not have a *memory* of previously seen training examples. For instance, the samples are passed through the feedforward and backpropagation steps, and the weights are updated independently of the order in which the training examples are processed.

RNNs, by contrast, are designed for modeling sequences and are capable of remembering past information and processing new events accordingly, which is a clear advantage when working with sequence data.

The different categories of sequence modeling

Sequence modeling has many fascinating applications, such as language translation (for example, translating text from English to German), image captioning, and text generation. However, in order to choose an appropriate architecture and approach, we have to understand and be able to distinguish between these different sequence modeling tasks. *Figure 15.2*, based on the explanations in the excellent article *The Unreasonable Effectiveness of Recurrent Neural Networks*, by *Andrej Karpathy*, 2015 (`http://karpathy.github.io/2015/05/21/rnn-effectiveness/`), summarizes the most common sequence modeling tasks, which depend on the relationship categories of input and output data.

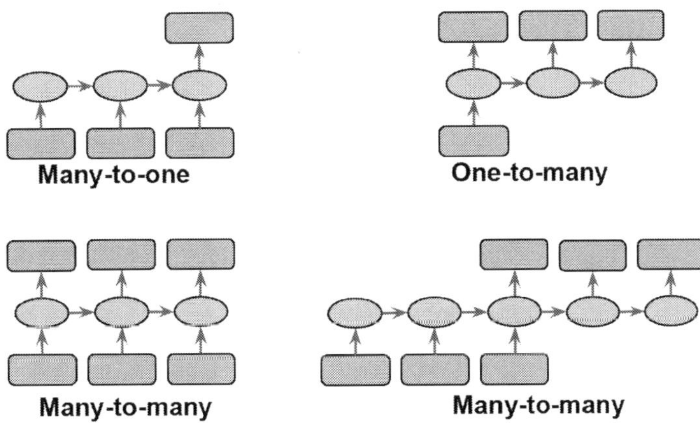

Figure 15.2: The most common sequencing tasks

Let's discuss the different relationship categories between input and output data, which were depicted in the previous figure, in more detail. If neither the input nor output data represent sequences, then we are dealing with standard data, and we could simply use a multilayer perceptron (or another classification model previously covered in this book) to model such data. However, if either the input or output is a sequence, the modeling task likely falls into one of these categories:

- **Many-to-one:** The input data is a sequence, but the output is a fixed-size vector or scalar, not a sequence. For example, in sentiment analysis, the input is text-based (for example, a movie review) and the output is a class label (for example, a label denoting whether a reviewer liked the movie).
- **One-to-many:** The input data is in standard format and not a sequence, but the output is a sequence. An example of this category is image captioning—the input is an image and the output is an English phrase summarizing the content of that image.
- **Many-to-many:** Both the input and output arrays are sequences. This category can be further divided based on whether the input and output are synchronized. An example of a synchronized many-to-many modeling task is video classification, where each frame in a video is labeled. An example of a *delayed* many-to-many modeling task would be translating one language into another. For instance, an entire English sentence must be read and processed by a machine before its translation into German is produced.

Now, after summarizing the three broad categories of sequence modeling, we can move forward to discussing the structure of an RNN.

RNNs for modeling sequences

In this section, before we start implementing RNNs in PyTorch, we will discuss the main concepts of RNNs. We will begin by looking at the typical structure of an RNN, which includes a recursive component to model sequence data. Then, we will examine how the neuron activations are computed in a typical RNN. This will create a context for us to discuss the common challenges in training RNNs, and we will then discuss solutions to these challenges, such as LSTM and **gated recurrent units** (**GRUs**).

Understanding the dataflow in RNNs

Let's start with the architecture of an RNN. *Figure 15.3* shows the dataflow in a standard feedforward NN and in an RNN side by side for comparison:

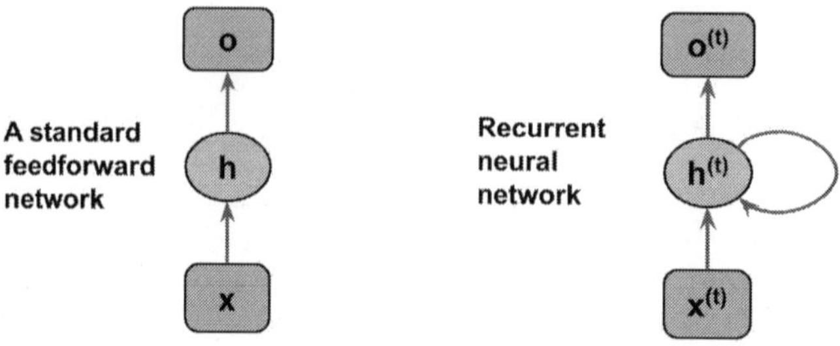

Figure 15.3: The dataflow of a standard feedforward NN and an RNN

Both of these networks have only one hidden layer. In this representation, the units are not displayed, but we assume that the input layer (x), hidden layer (h), and output layer (o) are vectors that contain many units.

Determining the type of output from an RNN

This generic RNN architecture could correspond to the two sequence modeling categories where the input is a sequence. Typically, a recurrent layer can return a sequence as output, $\langle \boldsymbol{o}^{(0)}, \boldsymbol{o}^{(1)}, \ldots, \boldsymbol{o}^{(T)} \rangle$, or simply return the last output (at $t = T$, that is, $o^{(T)}$). Thus, it could be either many-to-many, or it could be many-to-one if, for example, we only use the last element, $o^{(T)}$, as the final output.

We will see later how this is handled in the PyTorch `torch.nn` module, when we take a detailed look at the behavior of a recurrent layer with respect to returning a sequence as output.

In a standard feedforward network, information flows from the input to the hidden layer, and then from the hidden layer to the output layer. On the other hand, in an RNN, the hidden layer receives its input from both the input layer of the current time step and the hidden layer from the previous time step.

The flow of information in adjacent time steps in the hidden layer allows the network to have a memory of past events. This flow of information is usually displayed as a loop, also known as a **recurrent edge** in graph notation, which is how this general RNN architecture got its name.

Similar to multilayer perceptrons, RNNs can consist of multiple hidden layers. Note that it's a common convention to refer to RNNs with one hidden layer as a *single-layer RNN*, which is not to be confused with single-layer NNs without a hidden layer, such as Adaline or logistic regression. *Figure 15.4* illustrates an RNN with one hidden layer (top) and an RNN with two hidden layers (bottom):

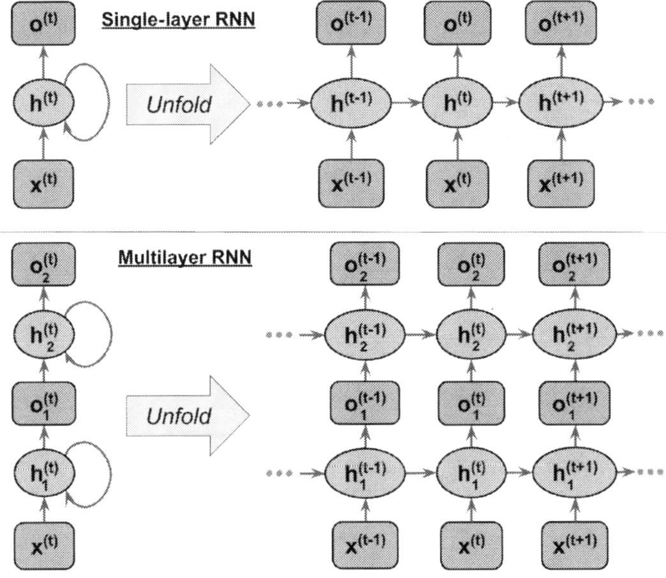

Figure 15.4: Examples of an RNN with one and two hidden layers

To examine the architecture of RNNs and the flow of information, a compact representation with a recurrent edge can be unfolded, which you can see in *Figure 15.4*.

As we know, each hidden unit in a standard NN receives only one input—the net preactivation associated with the input layer. In contrast, each hidden unit in an RNN receives two *distinct* sets of input—the preactivation from the input layer and the activation of the same hidden layer from the previous time step, $t - 1$.

At the first time step, $t = 0$, the hidden units are initialized to zeros or small random values. Then, at a time step where $t > 0$, the hidden units receive their input from the data point at the current time, $\boldsymbol{x}^{(t)}$, and the previous values of hidden units at $t - 1$, indicated as $\boldsymbol{h}^{(t-1)}$.

Similarly, in the case of a multilayer RNN, we can summarize the information flow as follows:

- *layer* = 1: Here, the hidden layer is represented as $\boldsymbol{h}_1^{(t)}$ and it receives its input from the data point, $\boldsymbol{x}^{(t)}$, and the hidden values in the same layer, but at the previous time step, $\boldsymbol{h}_1^{(t-1)}$.
- *layer* = 2: The second hidden layer, $\boldsymbol{h}_2^{(t)}$, receives its inputs from the outputs of the layer below at the current time step ($\boldsymbol{o}_1^{(t)}$) and its own hidden values from the previous time step, $\boldsymbol{h}_2^{(t-1)}$.

Since, in this case, each recurrent layer must receive a sequence as input, all the recurrent layers except the last one must *return a sequence as output* (that is, we will later have to set `return_sequences=True`). The behavior of the last recurrent layer depends on the type of problem.

Computing activations in an RNN

Now that you understand the structure and general flow of information in an RNN, let's get more specific and compute the actual activations of the hidden layers, as well as the output layer. For simplicity, we will consider just a single hidden layer; however, the same concept applies to multilayer RNNs.

Each directed edge (the connections between boxes) in the representation of an RNN that we just looked at is associated with a weight matrix. Those weights do not depend on time, *t*; therefore, they are shared across the time axis. The different weight matrices in a single-layer RNN are as follows:

- $\boldsymbol{W}_{xh}$: The weight matrix between the input, $\boldsymbol{x}^{(t)}$, and the hidden layer, $\boldsymbol{h}$
- $\boldsymbol{W}_{hh}$: The weight matrix associated with the recurrent edge
- $\boldsymbol{W}_{ho}$: The weight matrix between the hidden layer and output layer

These weight matrices are depicted in *Figure 15.5*:

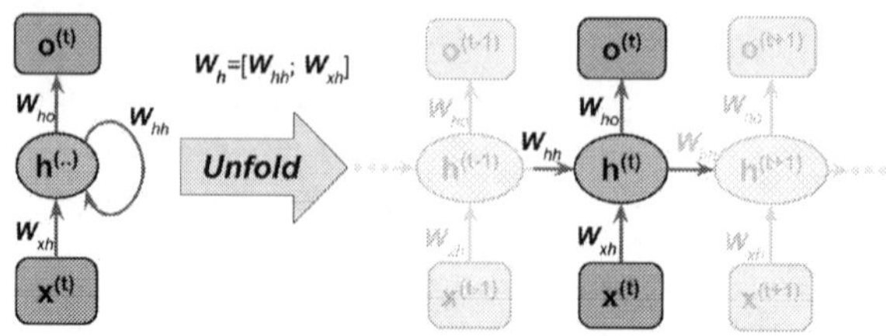

Figure 15.5: Applying weights to a single-layer RNN

In certain implementations, you may observe that the weight matrices, W_{xh} and W_{hh}, are concatenated to a combined matrix, $W_h = [W_{xh}; W_{hh}]$. Later in this section, we will make use of this notation as well.

Computing the activations is very similar to standard multilayer perceptrons and other types of feed-forward NNs. For the hidden layer, the net input, z_h (preactivation), is computed through a linear combination; that is, we compute the sum of the multiplications of the weight matrices with the corresponding vectors and add the bias unit:

$$\boldsymbol{z}_h^{(t)} = \boldsymbol{W}_{xh}\boldsymbol{x}^{(t)} + \boldsymbol{W}_{hh}\boldsymbol{h}^{(t-1)} + \boldsymbol{b}_h$$

Then, the activations of the hidden units at the time step, t, are calculated as follows:

$$\boldsymbol{h}^{(t)} = \sigma_h\left(\boldsymbol{z}_h^{(t)}\right) = \sigma_h\left(\boldsymbol{W}_{xh}\boldsymbol{x}^{(t)} + \boldsymbol{W}_{hh}\boldsymbol{h}^{(t-1)} + \boldsymbol{b}_h\right)$$

Here, b_h is the bias vector for the hidden units and $\sigma(\cdot)$ is the activation function of the hidden layer.

In case you want to use the concatenated weight matrix, $W_h = [W_{xh}; W_{hh}]$, the formula for computing hidden units will change, as follows:

$$\boldsymbol{h}^{(t)} = \sigma_h\left([\boldsymbol{W}_{xh}; \boldsymbol{W}_{hh}]\begin{bmatrix}\boldsymbol{x}^{(t)} \\ \boldsymbol{h}^{(t-1)}\end{bmatrix} + \boldsymbol{b}_h\right)$$

Once the activations of the hidden units at the current time step are computed, then the activations of the output units will be computed, as follows:

$$\boldsymbol{o}^{(t)} = \sigma_o\left(\boldsymbol{W}_{ho}\boldsymbol{h}^{(t)} + \boldsymbol{b}_o\right)$$

To help clarify this further, *Figure 15.6* shows the process of computing these activations with both formulations:

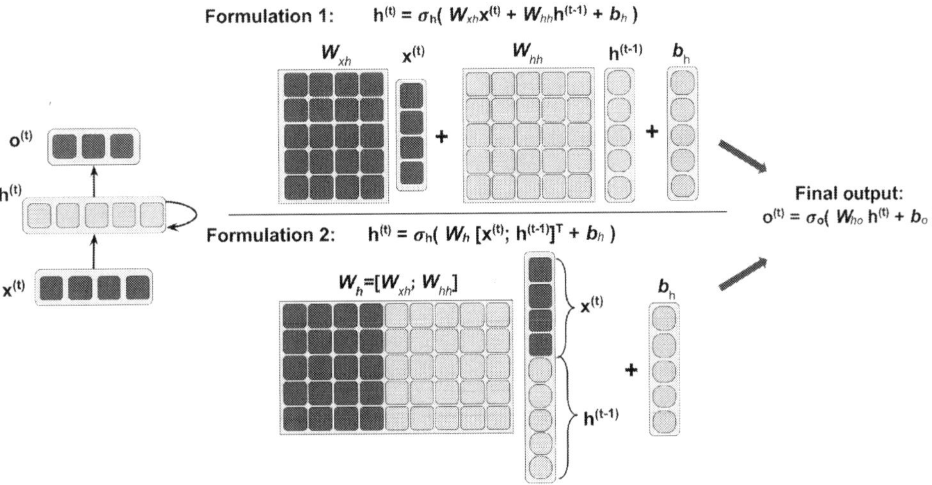

Figure 15.6: Computing the activations

Training RNNs using backpropagation through time (BPTT)

The learning algorithm for RNNs was introduced in 1990: *Backpropagation Through Time: What It Does and How to Do It* (*Paul Werbos, Proceedings of IEEE*, 78(10): 1550-1560, 1990).

The derivation of the gradients might be a bit complicated, but the basic idea is that the overall loss, L, is the sum of all the loss functions at times $t = 1$ to $t = T$:

$$L = \sum_{t=1}^{T} L^{(t)}$$

Since the loss at time t is dependent on the hidden units at all previous time steps $1 : t$, the gradient will be computed as follows:

$$\frac{\partial L^{(t)}}{\partial \boldsymbol{W}_{hh}} = \frac{\partial L^{(t)}}{\partial \boldsymbol{o}^{(t)}} \times \frac{\partial \boldsymbol{o}^{(t)}}{\partial \boldsymbol{h}^{(t)}} \times \left(\sum_{k=1}^{t} \frac{\partial \boldsymbol{h}^{(t)}}{\partial \boldsymbol{h}^{(k)}} \times \frac{\partial \boldsymbol{h}^{(k)}}{\partial \boldsymbol{W}_{hh}} \right)$$

Here, $\frac{\partial \boldsymbol{h}^{(t)}}{\partial \boldsymbol{h}^{(k)}}$ is computed as a multiplication of adjacent time steps:

$$\frac{\partial \boldsymbol{h}^{(t)}}{\partial \boldsymbol{h}^{(k)}} = \prod_{i=k+1}^{t} \frac{\partial \boldsymbol{h}^{(i)}}{\partial \boldsymbol{h}^{(i-1)}}$$

Hidden recurrence versus output recurrence

So far, you have seen recurrent networks in which the hidden layer has the recurrent property. However, note that there is an alternative model in which the recurrent connection comes from the output layer. In this case, the net activations from the output layer at the previous time step, $\boldsymbol{o}^{t-1}$, can be added in one of two ways:

- To the hidden layer at the current time step, $\boldsymbol{h}^t$ (shown in *Figure 15.7* as output-to-hidden recurrence)
- To the output layer at the current time step, $\boldsymbol{o}^t$ (shown in *Figure 15.7* as output-to-output recurrence)

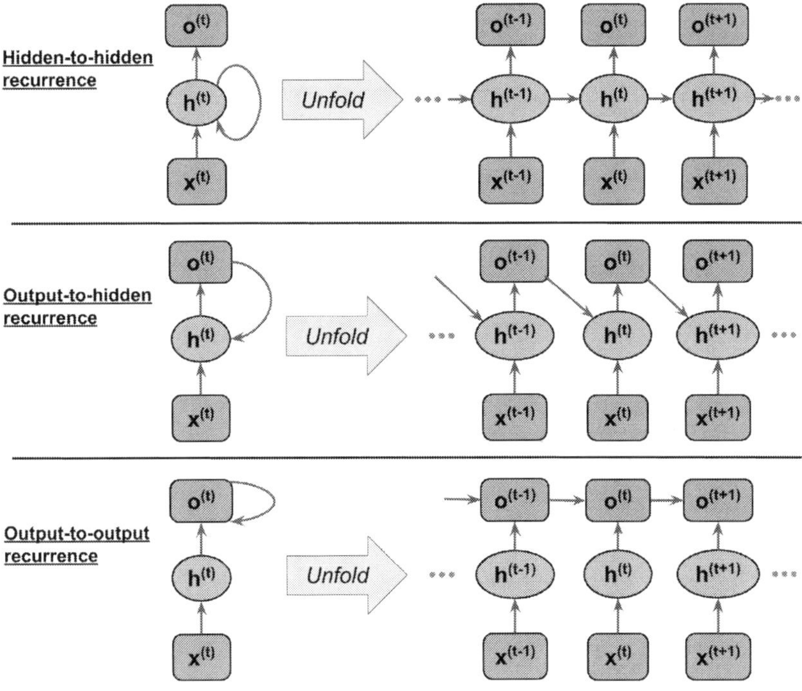

Figure 15.7: Different recurrent connection models

As shown in *Figure 15.7*, the differences between these architectures can be clearly seen in the recurring connections. Following our notation, the weights associated with the recurrent connection will be denoted for the hidden-to-hidden recurrence by W_{hh}, for the output-to-hidden recurrence by W_{oh}, and for the output-to-output recurrence by W_{oo}. In some articles in literature, the weights associated with the recurrent connections are also denoted by W_{rec}.

To see how this works in practice, let's manually compute the forward pass for one of these recurrent types. Using the `torch.nn` module, a recurrent layer can be defined via `RNN`, which is similar to the hidden-to-hidden recurrence. In the following code, we will create a recurrent layer from `RNN` and perform a forward pass on an input sequence of length 3 to compute the output. We will also manually compute the forward pass and compare the results with those of `RNN`.

First, let's create the layer and assign the weights and biases for our manual computations:

```
>>> import torch
>>> import torch.nn as nn
>>> torch.manual_seed(1)
>>> rnn_layer = nn.RNN(input_size=5, hidden_size=2,
...                    num_layers=1, batch_first=True)
>>> w_xh = rnn_layer.weight_ih_l0
>>> w_hh = rnn_layer.weight_hh_l0
>>> b_xh = rnn_layer.bias_ih_l0
>>> b_hh = rnn_layer.bias_hh_l0
>>> print('W_xh shape:', w_xh.shape)
>>> print('W_hh shape:', w_hh.shape)
>>> print('b_xh shape:', b_xh.shape)
>>> print('b_hh shape:', b_hh.shape)
W_xh shape: torch.Size([2, 5])
W_hh shape: torch.Size([2, 2])
b_xh shape: torch.Size([2])
b_hh shape: torch.Size([2])
```

The input shape for this layer is `(batch_size, sequence_length, 5)`, where the first dimension is the batch dimension (as we set `batch_first=True`), the second dimension corresponds to the sequence, and the last dimension corresponds to the features. Notice that we will output a sequence, which, for an input sequence of length 3, will result in the output sequence $\langle \boldsymbol{o}^{(0)}, \boldsymbol{o}^{(1)}, \boldsymbol{o}^{(2)} \rangle$. Also, `RNN` uses one layer by default, and you can set `num_layers` to stack multiple RNN layers together to form a stacked RNN.

Now, we will call the forward pass on the `rnn_layer` and manually compute the outputs at each time step and compare them:

```
>>> x_seq = torch.tensor([[1.0]*5, [2.0]*5, [3.0]*5]).float()
>>> ## output of the simple RNN:
>>> output, hn = rnn_layer(torch.reshape(x_seq, (1, 3, 5)))
>>> ## manually computing the output:
>>> out_man = []
>>> for t in range(3):
...     xt = torch.reshape(x_seq[t], (1, 5))
...     print(f'Time step {t} =>')
...     print('   Input           :', xt.numpy())
...
...     ht = torch.matmul(xt, torch.transpose(w_xh, 0, 1)) + b_xh
...     print('   Hidden          :', ht.detach().numpy())
...
```

```
...     if t > 0:
...         prev_h = out_man[t-1]
...     else:
...         prev_h = torch.zeros((ht.shape))
...     ot = ht + torch.matmul(prev_h, torch.transpose(w_hh, 0, 1)) \
...             + b_hh
...     ot = torch.tanh(ot)
...     out_man.append(ot)
...     print('   Output (manual) :', ot.detach().numpy())
...     print('   RNN output      :', output[:, t].detach().numpy())
...     print()
Time step 0 =>
   Input           : [[1. 1. 1. 1. 1.]]
   Hidden          : [[-0.4701929  0.5863904]]
   Output (manual) : [[-0.3519801   0.52525216]]
   RNN output      : [[-0.3519801   0.52525216]]

Time step 1 =>
   Input           : [[2. 2. 2. 2. 2.]]
   Hidden          : [[-0.88883156  1.2364397 ]]
   Output (manual) : [[-0.68424344  0.76074266]]
   RNN output      : [[-0.68424344  0.76074266]]

Time step 2 =>
   Input           : [[3. 3. 3. 3. 3.]]
   Hidden          : [[-1.3074701  1.886489 ]]
   Output (manual) : [[-0.8649416   0.90466356]]
   RNN output      : [[-0.8649416   0.90466356]]
```

In our manual forward computation, we used the hyperbolic tangent (tanh) activation function since it is also used in `RNN` (the default activation). As you can see from the printed results, the outputs from the manual forward computations exactly match the output of the `RNN` layer at each time step. Hopefully, this hands-on task has enlightened you on the mysteries of recurrent networks.

The challenges of learning long-range interactions

BPTT, which was briefly mentioned earlier, introduces some new challenges. Because of the multiplicative factor, $\frac{\partial h^{(t)}}{\partial h^{(k)}}$, in computing the gradients of a loss function, the so-called **vanishing** and **exploding** gradient problems arise.

These problems are explained by the examples in *Figure 15.8*, which shows an RNN with only one hidden unit for simplicity:

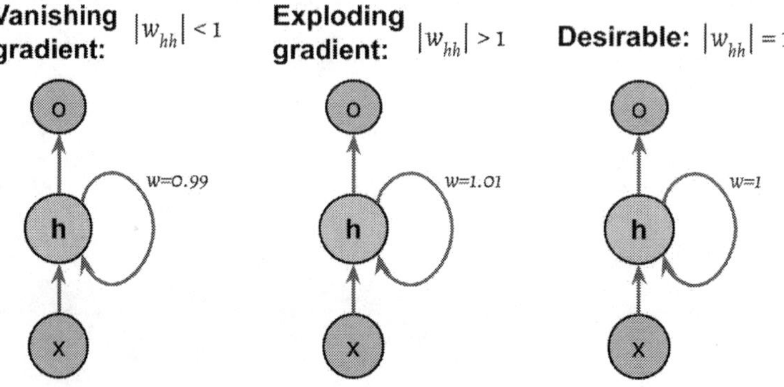

Figure 15.8: Problems in computing the gradients of the loss function

Basically, $\frac{\partial \boldsymbol{h}^{(t)}}{\partial \boldsymbol{h}^{(k)}}$ has $t - k$ multiplications; therefore, multiplying the weight, w, by itself $t - k$ times results in a factor, w^{t-k}. As a result, if $|w| < 1$, this factor becomes very small when $t - k$ is large. On the other hand, if the weight of the recurrent edge is $|w| > 1$, then w^{t-k} becomes very large when $t - k$ is large. Note that a large $t - k$ refers to long-range dependencies. We can see that a naive solution to avoid vanishing or exploding gradients can be reached by ensuring $|w| = 1$. If you are interested and would like to investigate this in more detail, read *On the difficulty of training recurrent neural networks* by *R. Pascanu, T. Mikolov,* and *Y. Bengio*, 2012 (`https://arxiv.org/pdf/1211.5063.pdf`).

In practice, there are at least three solutions to this problem:

- Gradient clipping
- **Truncated backpropagation through time (TBPTT)**
- LSTM

Using gradient clipping, we specify a cut-off or threshold value for the gradients, and we assign this cut-off value to gradient values that exceed this value. In contrast, TBPTT simply limits the number of time steps that the signal can backpropagate after each forward pass. For example, even if the sequence has 100 elements or steps, we may only backpropagate the most recent 20 time steps.

While both gradient clipping and TBPTT can solve the exploding gradient problem, the truncation limits the number of steps that the gradient can effectively flow back and properly update the weights. On the other hand, LSTM, designed in 1997 by Sepp Hochreiter and Jürgen Schmidhuber, has been more successful in vanishing and exploding gradient problems while modeling long-range dependencies through the use of memory cells. Let's discuss LSTM in more detail.

Long short-term memory cells

As stated previously, LSTMs were first introduced to overcome the vanishing gradient problem (*Long Short-Term Memory* by *S. Hochreiter* and *J. Schmidhuber*, *Neural Computation*, 9(8): 1735-1780, 1997). The building block of an LSTM is a **memory cell**, which essentially represents or replaces the hidden layer of standard RNNs.

In each memory cell, there is a recurrent edge that has the desirable weight, $w = 1$, as we discussed, to overcome the vanishing and exploding gradient problems. The values associated with this recurrent edge are collectively called the **cell state**. The unfolded structure of a modern LSTM cell is shown in *Figure 15.9*:

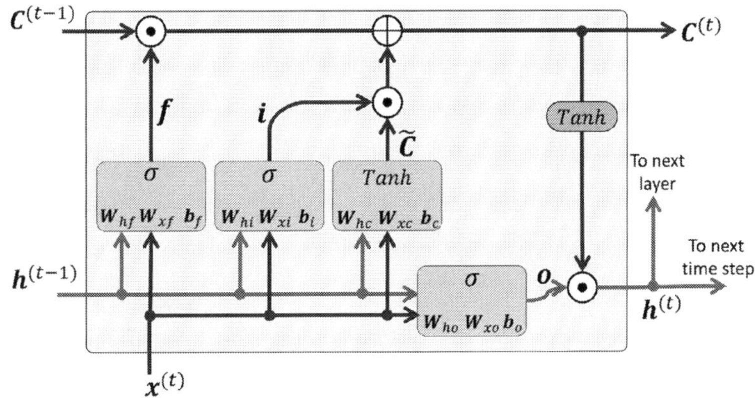

Figure 15.9: The structure of an LSTM cell

Notice that the cell state from the previous time step, $C^{(t-1)}$, is modified to get the cell state at the current time step, $C^{(t)}$, without being multiplied directly by any weight factor. The flow of information in this memory cell is controlled by several computation units (often called *gates*) that will be described here. In the figure, $\odot$ refers to the **element-wise product** (element-wise multiplication) and $\oplus$ means **element-wise summation** (element-wise addition). Furthermore, $x^{(t)}$ refers to the input data at time t, and $h^{(t-1)}$ indicates the hidden units at time $t - 1$. Four boxes are indicated with an activation function, either the sigmoid function (σ) or tanh, and a set of weights; these boxes apply a linear combination by performing matrix-vector multiplications on their inputs (which are $h^{(t-1)}$ and $x^{(t)}$). These units of computation with sigmoid activation functions, whose output units are passed through $\odot$, are called gates.

In an LSTM cell, there are three different types of gates, which are known as the forget gate, the input gate, and the output gate:

The **forget gate** (f_t) allows the memory cell to reset the cell state without growing indefinitely. In fact, the forget gate decides which information is allowed to go through and which information to suppress. Now, f_t is computed as follows:

$$f_t = \sigma\left(\boldsymbol{W}_{xf}\boldsymbol{x}^{(t)} + \boldsymbol{W}_{hf}\boldsymbol{h}^{(t-1)} + \boldsymbol{b}_f\right)$$

Note that the forget gate was not part of the original LSTM cell; it was added a few years later to improve the original model (*Learning to Forget: Continual Prediction with LSTM* by *F. Gers*, *J. Schmidhuber*, and *F. Cummins*, *Neural Computation 12*, 2451-2471, 2000).

The **input gate** (i_t) and **candidate value** ($\widetilde{C}_t$) are responsible for updating the cell state. They are computed as follows:

$$\begin{aligned} \boldsymbol{i}_t &= \sigma\left(\boldsymbol{W}_{xi}\boldsymbol{x}^{(t)} + \boldsymbol{W}_{hi}\boldsymbol{h}^{(t-1)} + \boldsymbol{b}_i\right) \\ \widetilde{\boldsymbol{C}}_t &= \tanh\left(\boldsymbol{W}_{xc}\boldsymbol{x}^{(t)} + \boldsymbol{W}_{hc}\boldsymbol{h}^{(t-1)} + \boldsymbol{b}_c\right) \end{aligned}$$

The cell state at time *t* is computed as follows:

$$\boldsymbol{C}^{(t)} = \left(\boldsymbol{C}^{(t-1)} \odot \boldsymbol{f}_t\right) \oplus \left(\boldsymbol{i}_t \odot \tilde{\boldsymbol{C}}_t\right)$$

The **output gate** (o_t) decides how to update the values of hidden units:

$$\boldsymbol{o}_t = \sigma\left(\boldsymbol{W}_{xo}\boldsymbol{x}^{(t)} + \boldsymbol{W}_{ho}\boldsymbol{h}^{(t-1)} + \boldsymbol{b}_o\right)$$

Given this, the hidden units at the current time step are computed as follows:

$$\boldsymbol{h}^{(t)} = \boldsymbol{o}_t \odot \tanh\left(\boldsymbol{C}^{(t)}\right)$$

The structure of an LSTM cell and its underlying computations might seem very complex and hard to implement. However, the good news is that PyTorch has already implemented everything in optimized wrapper functions, which allows us to define our LSTM cells easily and efficiently. We will apply RNNs and LSTMs to real-world datasets later in this chapter.

Other advanced RNN models

LSTMs provide a basic approach for modeling long-range dependencies in sequences. Yet, it is important to note that there are many variations of LSTMs described in literature (*An Empirical Exploration of Recurrent Network Architectures* by *Rafal Jozefowicz*, *Wojciech Zaremba*, and *Ilya Sutskever*, *Proceedings of ICML*, 2342-2350, 2015). Also worth noting is a more recent approach, **gated recurrent unit** (**GRU**), which was proposed in 2014. GRUs have a simpler architecture than LSTMs; therefore, they are computationally more efficient, while their performance in some tasks, such as polyphonic music modeling, is comparable to LSTMs. If you are interested in learning more about these modern RNN architectures, refer to the paper, *Empirical Evaluation of Gated Recurrent Neural Networks on Sequence Modeling* by *Junyoung Chung* and others, 2014 (`https://arxiv.org/pdf/1412.3555v1.pdf`).

Implementing RNNs for sequence modeling in PyTorch

Now that we have covered the underlying theory behind RNNs, we are ready to move on to the more practical portion of this chapter: implementing RNNs in PyTorch. During the rest of this chapter, we will apply RNNs to two common problem tasks:

1. Sentiment analysis
2. Language modeling

These two projects, which we will walk through together in the following pages, are both fascinating but also quite involved. Thus, instead of providing the code all at once, we will break the implementation up into several steps and discuss the code in detail. If you like to have a big picture overview and want to see all the code at once before diving into the discussion, take a look at the code implementation first.

Project one – predicting the sentiment of IMDb movie reviews

You may recall from *Chapter 8, Applying Machine Learning to Sentiment Analysis*, that sentiment analysis is concerned with analyzing the expressed opinion of a sentence or a text document. In this section and the following subsections, we will implement a multilayer RNN for sentiment analysis using a many-to-one architecture.

In the next section, we will implement a many-to-many RNN for an application of language modeling. While the chosen examples are purposefully simple to introduce the main concepts of RNNs, language modeling has a wide range of interesting applications, such as building chatbots—giving computers the ability to directly talk and interact with humans.

Preparing the movie review data

In *Chapter 8*, we preprocessed and cleaned the review dataset. And we will do the same now. First, we will import the necessary modules and read the data from `torchtext` (which we will install via `pip install torchtext`; version 0.10.0 was used as of late 2021) as follows:

```
>>> from torchtext.datasets import IMDB
>>> train_dataset = IMDB(split='train')
>>> test_dataset = IMDB(split='test')
```

Each set has 25,000 samples. And each sample of the datasets consists of two elements, the sentiment label representing the target label we want to predict (neg refers to negative sentiment and pos refers to positive sentiment), and the movie review text (the input features). The text component of these movie reviews is sequences of words, and the RNN model classifies each sequence as a positive (`1`) or negative (`0`) review.

However, before we can feed the data into an RNN model, we need to apply several preprocessing steps:

1. Split the training dataset into separate training and validation partitions.
2. Identify the unique words in the training dataset
3. Map each unique word to a unique integer and encode the review text into encoded integers (an index of each unique word)
4. Divide the dataset into mini-batches as input to the model

Let's proceed with the first step: creating a training and validation partition from the `train_dataset` we read earlier:

```
>>> ## Step 1: create the datasets
>>> from torch.utils.data.dataset import random_split
>>> torch.manual_seed(1)
>>> train_dataset, valid_dataset = random_split(
...     list(train_dataset), [20000, 5000])
```

The original training dataset contains 25,000 examples. 20,000 examples are randomly chosen for training, and 5,000 for validation.

To prepare the data for input to an NN, we need to encode it into numeric values, as was mentioned in *steps 2* and *3*. To do this, we will first find the unique words (tokens) in the training dataset. While finding unique tokens is a process for which we can use Python datasets, it can be more efficient to use the `Counter` class from the `collections` package, which is part of Python's standard library.

In the following code, we will instantiate a new `Counter` object (`token_counts`) that will collect the unique word frequencies. Note that in this particular application (and in contrast to the bag-of-words model), we are only interested in the set of unique words and won't require the word counts, which are created as a side product. To split the text into words (or tokens), we will reuse the `tokenizer` function we developed in *Chapter 8*, which also removes HTML markups as well as punctuation and other non-letter characters:

The code for collecting unique tokens is as follows:

```
>>> ## Step 2: find unique tokens (words)
>>> import re
>>> from collections import Counter, OrderedDict
>>>
>>> def tokenizer(text):
...     text = re.sub('<[^>]*>', '', text)
...     emoticons = re.findall(
...         '(?::|;|=)(?:-)?(?:\)|\(|D|P)', text.lower()
...     )
...     text = re.sub('[\W]+', ' ', text.lower()) +\
...         ' '.join(emoticons).replace('-', '')
...     tokenized = text.split()
```

```
...     return tokenized
>>>
>>> token_counts = Counter()
>>> for label, line in train_dataset:
...     tokens = tokenizer(line)
...     token_counts.update(tokens)
>>> print('Vocab-size:', len(token_counts))
Vocab-size: 69023
```

If you want to learn more about `Counter`, refer to its documentation at `https://docs.python.org/3/library/collections.html#collections.Counter`.

Next, we are going to map each unique word to a unique integer. This can be done manually using a Python dictionary, where the keys are the unique tokens (words) and the value associated with each key is a unique integer. However, the `torchtext` package already provides a class, `Vocab`, which we can use to create such a mapping and encode the entire dataset. First, we will create a `vocab` object by passing the ordered dictionary mapping tokens to their corresponding occurrence frequencies (the ordered dictionary is the sorted `token_counts`). Second, we will prepend two special tokens to the vocabulary – the padding and the unknown token:

```
>>> ## Step 3: encoding each unique token into integers
>>> from torchtext.vocab import vocab
>>> sorted_by_freq_tuples = sorted(
...     token_counts.items(), key=lambda x: x[1], reverse=True
... )
>>> ordered_dict = OrderedDict(sorted_by_freq_tuples)
>>> vocab = vocab(ordered_dict)
>>> vocab.insert_token("<pad>", 0)
>>> vocab.insert_token("<unk>", 1)
>>> vocab.set_default_index(1)
```

To demonstrate how to use the `vocab` object, we will convert an example input text into a list of integer values:

```
>>> print([vocab[token] for token in ['this', 'is',
...     'an', 'example']])
[11, 7, 35, 457]
```

Note that there might be some tokens in the validation or testing data that are not present in the training data and are thus not included in the mapping. If we have q tokens (that is, the size of `token_counts` passed to `Vocab`, which in this case is 69,023), then all tokens that haven't been seen before, and are thus not included in `token_counts`, will be assigned the integer 1 (a placeholder for the unknown token). In other words, the index 1 is reserved for unknown words. Another reserved value is the integer 0, which serves as a placeholder, a so-called *padding token*, for adjusting the sequence length. Later, when we are building an RNN model in PyTorch, we will consider this placeholder, 0, in more detail.

We can define the `text_pipeline` function to transform each text in the dataset accordingly and the `label_pipeline` function to convert each label to 1 or 0:

```
>>> ## Step 3-A: define the functions for transformation
>>> text_pipeline =\
...      lambda x: [vocab[token] for token in tokenizer(x)]
>>> label_pipeline = lambda x: 1. if x == 'pos' else 0.
```

We will generate batches of samples using `DataLoader` and pass the data processing pipelines declared previously to the argument `collate_fn`. We will wrap the text encoding and label transformation function into the `collate_batch` function:

```
>>> ## Step 3-B: wrap the encode and transformation function
... def collate_batch(batch):
...     label_list, text_list, lengths = [], [], []
...     for _label, _text in batch:
...         label_list.append(label_pipeline(_label))
...         processed_text = torch.tensor(text_pipeline(_text),
...                                       dtype=torch.int64)
...         text_list.append(processed_text)
...         lengths.append(processed_text.size(0))
...     label_list = torch.tensor(label_list)
...     lengths = torch.tensor(lengths)
...     padded_text_list = nn.utils.rnn.pad_sequence(
...         text_list, batch_first=True)
...     return padded_text_list, label_list, lengths
>>>
>>> ## Take a small batch
>>> from torch.utils.data import DataLoader
>>> dataloader = DataLoader(train_dataset, batch_size=4,
...                         shuffle=False, collate_fn=collate_batch)
```

So far, we've converted sequences of words into sequences of integers, and labels of pos or neg into 1 or 0. However, there is one issue that we need to resolve—the sequences currently have different lengths (as shown in the result of executing the following code for four examples). Although, in general, RNNs can handle sequences with different lengths, we still need to make sure that all the sequences in a mini-batch have the same length to store them efficiently in a tensor.

PyTorch provides an efficient method, `pad_sequence()`, which will automatically pad the consecutive elements that are to be combined into a batch with placeholder values (0s) so that all sequences within a batch will have the same shape. In the previous code, we already created a data loader of a small batch size from the training dataset and applied the `collate_batch` function, which itself included a `pad_sequence()` call.

However, to illustrate how padding works, we will take the first batch and print the sizes of the individual elements before combining these into mini-batches, as well as the dimensions of the resulting mini-batches:

```
>>> text_batch, label_batch, length_batch = next(iter(dataloader))
>>> print(text_batch)
tensor([[   35,  1742,     7,   449,   723,     6,   302,     4,
...
0,     0,     0,     0,     0,     0,     0,     0]],
>>> print(label_batch)
tensor([1., 1., 1., 0.])
>>> print(length_batch)
tensor([165,  86, 218, 145])
>>> print(text_batch.shape)
torch.Size([4, 218])
```

As you can observe from the printed tensor shapes, the number of columns in the first batch is 218, which resulted from combining the first four examples into a single batch and using the maximum size of these examples. This means that the other three examples (whose lengths are 165, 86, and 145, respectively) in this batch are padded as much as necessary to match this size.

Finally, let's divide all three datasets into data loaders with a batch size of 32:

```
>>> batch_size = 32
>>> train_dl = DataLoader(train_dataset, batch_size=batch_size,
...                       shuffle=True, collate_fn=collate_batch)
>>> valid_dl = DataLoader(valid_dataset, batch_size=batch_size,
...                       shuffle=False, collate_fn=collate_batch)
>>> test_dl = DataLoader(test_dataset, batch_size=batch_size,
...                      shuffle=False, collate_fn=collate_batch)
```

Now, the data is in a suitable format for an RNN model, which we are going to implement in the following subsections. In the next subsection, however, we will first discuss feature **embedding**, which is an optional but highly recommended preprocessing step that is used to reduce the dimensionality of the word vectors.

Embedding layers for sentence encoding

During the data preparation in the previous step, we generated sequences of the same length. The elements of these sequences were integer numbers that corresponded to the *indices* of unique words. These word indices can be converted into input features in several different ways. One naive way is to apply one-hot encoding to convert the indices into vectors of zeros and ones. Then, each word will be mapped to a vector whose size is the number of unique words in the entire dataset. Given that the number of unique words (the size of the vocabulary) can be in the order of 10^4 – 10^5, which will also be the number of our input features, a model trained on such features may suffer from the **curse of dimensionality**. Furthermore, these features are very sparse since all are zero except one.

A more elegant approach is to map each word to a vector of a fixed size with real-valued elements (not necessarily integers). In contrast to the one-hot encoded vectors, we can use finite-sized vectors to represent an infinite number of real numbers. (In theory, we can extract infinite real numbers from a given interval, for example [-1, 1].)

This is the idea behind embedding, which is a feature-learning technique that we can utilize here to automatically learn the salient features to represent the words in our dataset. Given the number of unique words, n_{words}, we can select the size of the embedding vectors (a.k.a., embedding dimension) to be much smaller than the number of unique words (*embedding_dim* << n_{words}) to represent the entire vocabulary as input features.

The advantages of embedding over one-hot encoding are as follows:

- A reduction in the dimensionality of the feature space to decrease the effect of the curse of dimensionality
- The extraction of salient features since the embedding layer in an NN can be optimized (or learned)

The following schematic representation shows how embedding works by mapping token indices to a trainable embedding matrix:

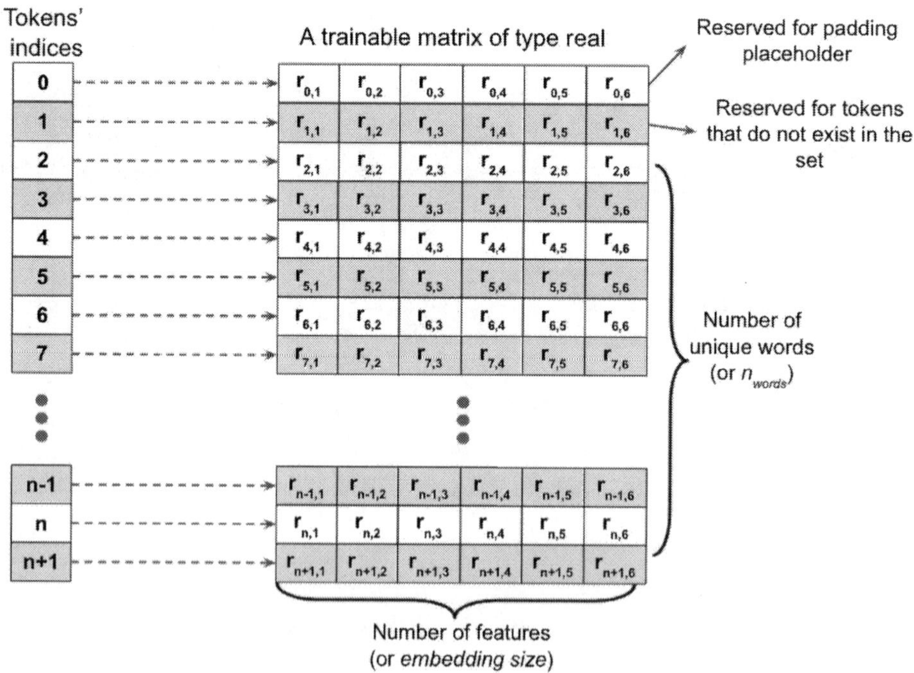

Figure 15.10: A breakdown of how embedding works

Given a set of tokens of size $n + 2$ (n is the size of the token set, plus index 0 is reserved for the padding placeholder, and 1 is for the words not present in the token set), an embedding matrix of size $(n + 2) \times$ *embedding_dim* will be created where each row of this matrix represents numeric features associated with a token. Therefore, when an integer index, i, is given as input to the embedding, it will look up the corresponding row of the matrix at index i and return the numeric features. The embedding matrix serves as the input layer to our NN models. In practice, creating an embedding layer can simply be done using `nn.Embedding`. Let's see an example where we will create an embedding layer and apply it to a batch of two samples, as follows:

```
>>> embedding = nn.Embedding(
...     num_embeddings=10,
...     embedding_dim=3,
...     padding_idx=0)
>>> # a batch of 2 samples of 4 indices each
>>> text_encoded_input = torch.LongTensor([[1,2,4,5],[4,3,2,0]])
>>> print(embedding(text_encoded_input))
tensor([[[-0.7027,  0.3684, -0.5512],
         [-0.4147,  1.7891, -1.0674],
         [ 1.1400,  0.1595, -1.0167],
         [ 0.0573, -1.7568,  1.9067]],

        [[ 1.1400,  0.1595, -1.0167],
         [-0.8165, -0.0946, -0.1881],
         [-0.4147,  1.7891, -1.0674],
         [ 0.0000,  0.0000,  0.0000]]], grad_fn=<EmbeddingBackward>)
```

The input to this model (embedding layer) must have rank 2 with the dimensionality *batchsize* × *input_length*, where *input_length* is the length of sequences (here, 4). For example, an input sequence in the mini-batch could be <1, 5, 9, 2>, where each element of this sequence is the index of the unique words. The output will have the dimensionality *batchsize* × *input_length* × *embedding_dim*, where *embedding_dim* is the size of the embedding features (here, set to 3). The other argument provided to the embedding layer, `num_embeddings`, corresponds to the unique integer values that the model will receive as input (for instance, $n + 2$, set here to 10). Therefore, the embedding matrix in this case has the size 10×3.

`padding_idx` indicates the token index for padding (here, 0), which, if specified, will not contribute to the gradient updates during training. In our example, the length of the original sequence of the second sample is 3, and we padded it with 1 more element 0. The embedding output of the padded element is [0, 0, 0].

Building an RNN model

Now we're ready to build an RNN model. Using the `nn.Module` class, we can combine the embedding layer, the recurrent layers of the RNN, and the fully connected non-recurrent layers. For the recurrent layers, we can use any of the following implementations:

- `RNN`: a regular RNN layer, that is, a fully connected recurrent layer
- `LSTM`: a long short-term memory RNN, which is useful for capturing the long-term dependencies
- `GRU`: a recurrent layer with a gated recurrent unit, as proposed in *Learning Phrase Representations Using RNN Encoder–Decoder for Statistical Machine Translation* by *K. Cho* et al., 2014 (`https://arxiv.org/abs/1406.1078v3`), as an alternative to LSTMs

To see how a multilayer RNN model can be built using one of these recurrent layers, in the following example, we will create an RNN model with two recurrent layers of type `RNN`. Finally, we will add a non-recurrent fully connected layer as the output layer, which will return a single output value as the prediction:

```
>>> class RNN(nn.Module):
...     def __init__(self, input_size, hidden_size):
...         super().__init__()
...         self.rnn = nn.RNN(input_size, hidden_size, num_layers=2,
...                           batch_first=True)
...         # self.rnn = nn.GRU(input_size, hidden_size, num_layers,
...         #                   batch_first=True)
...         # self.rnn = nn.LSTM(input_size, hidden_size, num_layers,
...         #                    batch_first=True)
...         self.fc = nn.Linear(hidden_size, 1)
...
...     def forward(self, x):
...         _, hidden = self.rnn(x)
...         out = hidden[-1, :, :] # we use the final hidden state
...                                # from the last hidden layer as
...                                # the input to the fully connected
...                                # layer
...         out = self.fc(out)
...         return out
>>>
>>> model = RNN(64, 32)
>>> print(model)
>>> model(torch.randn(5, 3, 64))
RNN(
  (rnn): RNN(64, 32, num_layers=2, batch_first=True)
  (fc): Linear(in_features=32, out_features=1, bias=True)
)
```

```
tensor([[ 0.0010],
        [ 0.2478],
        [ 0.0573],
        [ 0.1637],
        [-0.0073]], grad_fn=<AddmmBackward>)
```

As you can see, building an RNN model using these recurrent layers is pretty straightforward. In the next subsection, we will go back to our sentiment analysis task and build an RNN model to solve that.

Building an RNN model for the sentiment analysis task

Since we have very long sequences, we are going to use an LSTM layer to account for long-range effects. We will create an RNN model for sentiment analysis, starting with an embedding layer producing word embeddings of feature size 20 (`embed_dim=20`). Then, a recurrent layer of type LSTM will be added. Finally, we will add a fully connected layer as a hidden layer and another fully connected layer as the output layer, which will return a single class-membership probability value via the logistic sigmoid activation as the prediction:

```
>>> class RNN(nn.Module):
...     def __init__(self, vocab_size, embed_dim, rnn_hidden_size,
...                  fc_hidden_size):
...         super().__init__()
...         self.embedding = nn.Embedding(vocab_size,
...                                       embed_dim,
...                                       padding_idx=0)
...         self.rnn = nn.LSTM(embed_dim, rnn_hidden_size,
...                            batch_first=True)
...         self.fc1 = nn.Linear(rnn_hidden_size, fc_hidden_size)
...         self.relu = nn.ReLU()
...         self.fc2 = nn.Linear(fc_hidden_size, 1)
...         self.sigmoid = nn.Sigmoid()
...
...     def forward(self, text, lengths):
...         out = self.embedding(text)
...         out = nn.utils.rnn.pack_padded_sequence(
...             out, lengths.cpu().numpy(), enforce_sorted=False, batch_first=True
...         )
...         out, (hidden, cell) = self.rnn(out)
...         out = hidden[-1, :, :]
...         out = self.fc1(out)
...         out = self.relu(out)
...         out = self.fc2(out)
...         out = self.sigmoid(out)
...         return out
```

```
>>>
>>> vocab_size = len(vocab)
>>> embed_dim = 20
>>> rnn_hidden_size = 64
>>> fc_hidden_size = 64
>>> torch.manual_seed(1)
>>> model = RNN(vocab_size, embed_dim,
                rnn_hidden_size, fc_hidden_size)
>>> model
RNN(
  (embedding): Embedding(69025, 20, padding_idx=0)
  (rnn): LSTM(20, 64, batch_first=True)
  (fc1): Linear(in_features=64, out_features=64, bias=True)
  (relu): ReLU()
  (fc2): Linear(in_features=64, out_features=1, bias=True)
  (sigmoid): Sigmoid()
)
```

Now we will develop the `train` function to train the model on the given dataset for one epoch and return the classification accuracy and loss:

```
>>> def train(dataloader):
...     model.train()
...     total_acc, total_loss = 0, 0
...     for text_batch, label_batch, lengths in dataloader:
...         optimizer.zero_grad()
...         pred = model(text_batch, lengths)[:, 0]
...         loss = loss_fn(pred, label_batch)
...         loss.backward()
...         optimizer.step()
...         total_acc += (
...             (pred >= 0.5).float() == label_batch
...         ).float().sum().item()
...         total_loss += loss.item()*label_batch.size(0)
...     return total_acc/len(dataloader.dataset), \
...            total_loss/len(dataloader.dataset)
```

Similarly, we will develop the `evaluate` function to measure the model's performance on a given dataset:

```
>>> def evaluate(dataloader):
...     model.eval()
...     total_acc, total_loss = 0, 0
```

```
...     with torch.no_grad():
...         for text_batch, label_batch, lengths in dataloader:
...             pred = model(text_batch, lengths)[:, 0]
...             loss = loss_fn(pred, label_batch)
...             total_acc += (
...                 (pred>=0.5).float() == label_batch
...             ).float().sum().item()
...             total_loss += loss.item()*label_batch.size(0)
...     return total_acc/len(dataloader.dataset), \
...            total_loss/len(dataloader.dataset)
```

The next step is to create a loss function and optimizer (Adam optimizer). For a binary classification with a single class-membership probability output, we use the binary cross-entropy loss (`BCELoss`) as the loss function:

```
>>> loss_fn = nn.BCELoss()
>>> optimizer = torch.optim.Adam(model.parameters(), lr=0.001)
```

Now we will train the model for 10 epochs and display the training and validation performances:

```
>>> num_epochs = 10
>>> torch.manual_seed(1)
>>> for epoch in range(num_epochs):
...     acc_train, loss_train = train(train_dl)
...     acc_valid, loss_valid = evaluate(valid_dl)
...     print(f'Epoch {epoch} accuracy: {acc_train:.4f}'
...           f' val_accuracy: {acc_valid:.4f}')
Epoch 0 accuracy: 0.5843 val_accuracy: 0.6240
Epoch 1 accuracy: 0.6364 val_accuracy: 0.6870
Epoch 2 accuracy: 0.8020 val_accuracy: 0.8194
Epoch 3 accuracy: 0.8730 val_accuracy: 0.8454
Epoch 4 accuracy: 0.9092 val_accuracy: 0.8598
Epoch 5 accuracy: 0.9347 val_accuracy: 0.8630
Epoch 6 accuracy: 0.9507 val_accuracy: 0.8636
Epoch 7 accuracy: 0.9655 val_accuracy: 0.8654
Epoch 8 accuracy: 0.9765 val_accuracy: 0.8528
Epoch 9 accuracy: 0.9839 val_accuracy: 0.8596
```

After training this model for 10 epochs, we will evaluate it on the test data:

```
>>> acc_test, _ = evaluate(test_dl)
>>> print(f'test_accuracy: {acc_test:.4f}')
test_accuracy: 0.8512
```

It showed 85 percent accuracy. (Note that this result is not the best when compared to the state-of-the-art methods used on the IMDb dataset. The goal was simply to show how an RNN works in PyTorch.)

More on the bidirectional RNN

In addition, we will set the `bidirectional` configuration of the `LSTM` to `True`, which will make the recurrent layer pass through the input sequences from both directions, start to end, as well as in the reverse direction:

```
>>> class RNN(nn.Module):
...     def __init__(self, vocab_size, embed_dim,
...                  rnn_hidden_size, fc_hidden_size):
...         super().__init__()
...         self.embedding = nn.Embedding(
...             vocab_size, embed_dim, padding_idx=0
...         )
...         self.rnn = nn.LSTM(embed_dim, rnn_hidden_size,
...                            batch_first=True, bidirectional=True)
...         self.fc1 = nn.Linear(rnn_hidden_size*2, fc_hidden_size)
...         self.relu = nn.ReLU()
...         self.fc2 = nn.Linear(fc_hidden_size, 1)
...         self.sigmoid = nn.Sigmoid()
...
...     def forward(self, text, lengths):
...         out = self.embedding(text)
...         out = nn.utils.rnn.pack_padded_sequence(
...             out, lengths.cpu().numpy(), enforce_sorted=False, batch_first=True
...         )
...         _, (hidden, cell) = self.rnn(out)
...         out = torch.cat((hidden[-2, :, :],
...                          hidden[-1, :, :]), dim=1)
...         out = self.fc1(out)
...         out = self.relu(out)
...         out = self.fc2(out)
...         out = self.sigmoid(out)
...         return out
>>>
>>> torch.manual_seed(1)
>>> model = RNN(vocab_size, embed_dim,
...             rnn_hidden_size, fc_hidden_size)
>>> model
```

```
RNN(
  (embedding): Embedding(69025, 20, padding_idx=0)
  (rnn): LSTM(20, 64, batch_first=True, bidirectional=True)
  (fc1): Linear(in_features=128, out_features=64, bias=True)
  (relu): ReLU()
  (fc2): Linear(in_features=64, out_features=1, bias=True)
  (sigmoid): Sigmoid()
)
```

The bidirectional RNN layer makes two passes over each input sequence: a forward pass and a reverse or backward pass (note that this is not to be confused with the forward and backward passes in the context of backpropagation). The resulting hidden states of these forward and backward passes are usually concatenated into a single hidden state. Other merge modes include summation, multiplication (multiplying the results of the two passes), and averaging (taking the average of the two).

We can also try other types of recurrent layers, such as the regular `RNN`. However, as it turns out, a model built with regular recurrent layers won't be able to reach a good predictive performance (even on the training data). For example, if you try replacing the bidirectional LSTM layer in the previous code with a unidirectional `nn.RNN` (instead of `nn.LSTM`) layer and train the model on full-length sequences, you may observe that the loss will not even decrease during training. The reason is that the sequences in this dataset are too long, so a model with an `RNN` layer cannot learn the long-term dependencies and may suffer from vanishing or exploding gradient problems.

Project two – character-level language modeling in PyTorch

Language modeling is a fascinating application that enables machines to perform human language-related tasks, such as generating English sentences. One of the interesting studies in this area is *Generating Text with Recurrent Neural Networks* by *Ilya Sutskever*, *James Martens*, and *Geoffrey E. Hinton*, *Proceedings of the 28th International Conference on Machine Learning (ICML-11)*, 2011 (`https://pdfs.semanticscholar.org/93c2/0e38c85b69fc2d2eb314b3c1217913f7db11.pdf`).

In the model that we will build now, the input is a text document, and our goal is to develop a model that can generate new text that is similar in style to the input document. Examples of such input are a book or a computer program in a specific programming language.

In character-level language modeling, the input is broken down into a sequence of characters that are fed into our network one character at a time. The network will process each new character in conjunction with the memory of the previously seen characters to predict the next one.

Figure 15.11 shows an example of character-level language modeling (note that EOS stands for "end of sequence"):

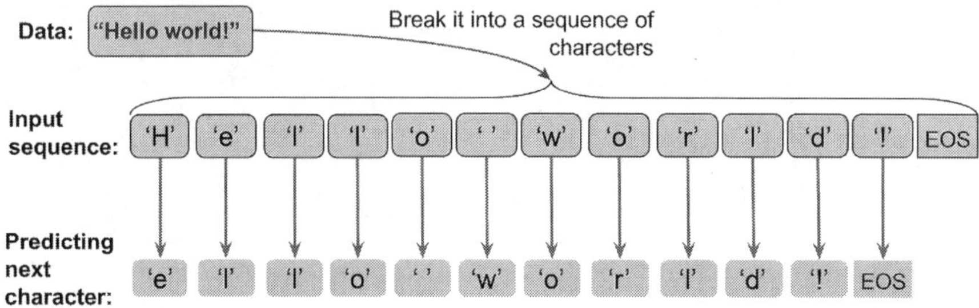

Figure 15.11: Character-level language modeling

We can break this implementation down into three separate steps: preparing the data, building the RNN model, and performing next-character prediction and sampling to generate new text.

Preprocessing the dataset

In this section, we will prepare the data for character-level language modeling.

To obtain the input data, visit the Project Gutenberg website at `https://www.gutenberg.org/`, which provides thousands of free e-books. For our example, you can download the book *The Mysterious Island*, by Jules Verne (published in 1874) in plain text format from `https://www.gutenberg.org/files/1268/1268-0.txt`.

Note that this link will take you directly to the download page. If you are using macOS or a Linux operating system, you can download the file with the following command in the terminal:

```
curl -O https://www.gutenberg.org/files/1268/1268-0.txt
```

If this resource becomes unavailable in the future, a copy of this text is also included in this chapter's code directory in the book's code repository at `https://github.com/rasbt/machine-learning-book`.

Once we have downloaded the dataset, we can read it into a Python session as plain text. Using the following code, we will read the text directly from the downloaded file and remove portions from the beginning and the end (these contain certain descriptions of the Gutenberg project). Then, we will create a Python variable, `char_set`, that represents the set of *unique* characters observed in this text:

```
>>> import numpy as np
>>> ## Reading and processing text
>>> with open('1268-0.txt', 'r', encoding="utf8") as fp:
...     text=fp.read()
>>> start_indx = text.find('THE MYSTERIOUS ISLAND')
>>> end_indx = text.find('End of the Project Gutenberg')
>>> text = text[start_indx:end_indx]
>>> char_set = set(text)
```

```
>>> print('Total Length:', len(text))
Total Length: 1112350
>>> print('Unique Characters:', len(char_set))
Unique Characters: 80
```

After downloading and preprocessing the text, we have a sequence consisting of 1,112,350 characters in total and 80 unique characters. However, most NN libraries and RNN implementations cannot deal with input data in string format, which is why we have to convert the text into a numeric format. To do this, we will create a simple Python dictionary that maps each character to an integer, `char2int`. We will also need a reverse mapping to convert the results of our model back to text. Although the reverse can be done using a dictionary that associates integer keys with character values, using a NumPy array and indexing the array to map indices to those unique characters is more efficient. *Figure 15.12* shows an example of converting characters into integers and the reverse for the words `"Hello"` and `"world"`:

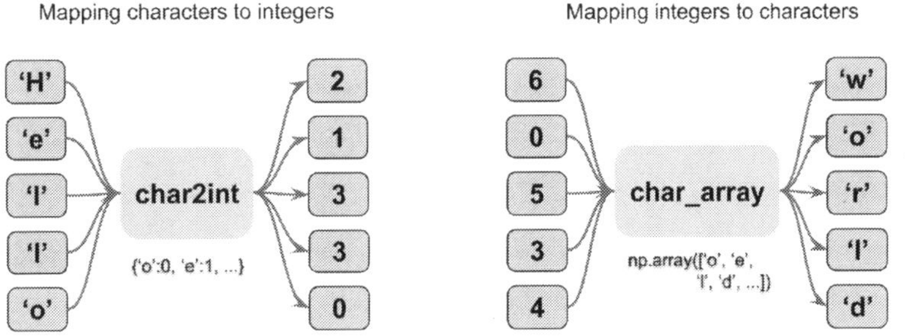

Figure 15.12: Character and integer mappings

Building the dictionary to map characters to integers, and reverse mapping via indexing a NumPy array, as was shown in the previous figure, is as follows:

```
>>> chars_sorted = sorted(char_set)
>>> char2int = {ch:i for i,ch in enumerate(chars_sorted)}
>>> char_array = np.array(chars_sorted)
>>> text_encoded = np.array(
...     [char2int[ch] for ch in text],
...     dtype=np.int32
... )
>>> print('Text encoded shape:', text_encoded.shape)
Text encoded shape: (1112350,)
>>> print(text[:15], '== Encoding ==>', text_encoded[:15])
>>> print(text_encoded[15:21], '== Reverse ==>',
...       ''.join(char_array[text_encoded[15:21]]))
THE MYSTERIOUS == Encoding ==> [44 32 29  1 37 48 43 44 29 42 33 39 45 43  1]
[33 43 36 25 38 28] == Reverse ==> ISLAND
```

The `text_encoded` NumPy array contains the encoded values for all the characters in the text. Now, we will print out the mappings of the first five characters from this array:

```
>>> for ex in text_encoded[:5]:
...     print('{} -> {}'.format(ex, char_array[ex]))
44 -> T
32 -> H
29 -> E
1 -> 
37 -> M
```

Now, let's step back and look at the big picture of what we are trying to do. For the text generation task, we can formulate the problem as a classification task.

Suppose we have a set of sequences of text characters that are incomplete, as shown in *Figure 15.13*:

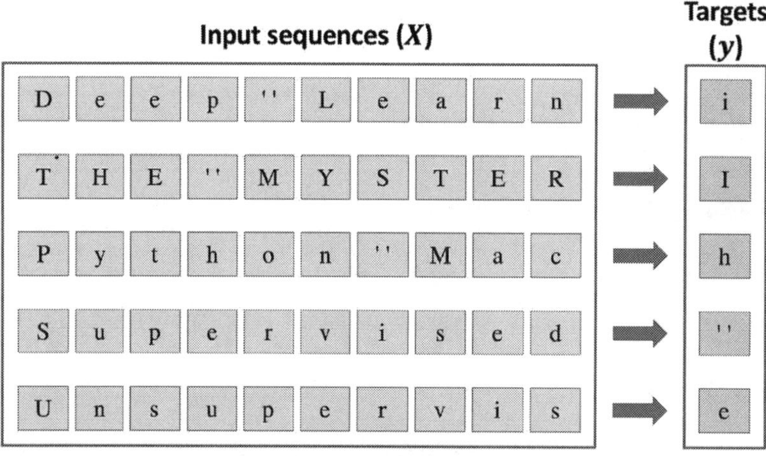

Figure 15.13: Predicting the next character for a text sequence

In *Figure 15.13*, we can consider the sequences shown in the left-hand box to be the input. In order to generate new text, our goal is to design a model that can predict the next character of a given input sequence, where the input sequence represents an incomplete text. For example, after seeing "Deep Learn," the model should predict "i" as the next character. Given that we have 80 unique characters, this problem becomes a multiclass classification task.

Starting with a sequence of length 1 (that is, one single letter), we can iteratively generate new text based on this multiclass classification approach, as illustrated in *Figure 15.14*:

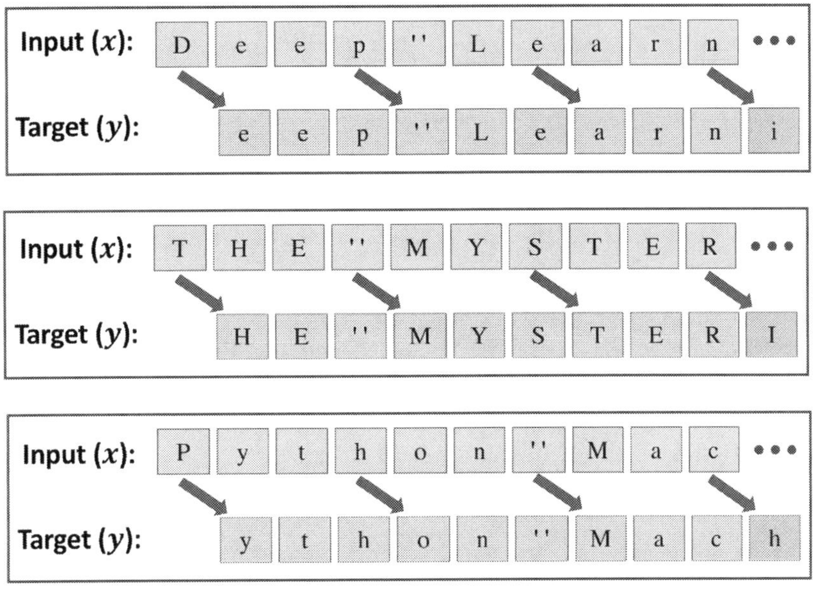

Figure 15.14: Generating next text based on this multiclass classification approach

To implement the text generation task in PyTorch, let's first clip the sequence length to 40. This means that the input tensor, x, consists of 40 tokens. In practice, the sequence length impacts the quality of the generated text. Longer sequences can result in more meaningful sentences. For shorter sequences, however, the model might focus on capturing individual words correctly, while ignoring the context for the most part. Although longer sequences usually result in more meaningful sentences, as mentioned, for long sequences, the RNN model will have problems capturing long-range dependencies. Thus, in practice, finding a sweet spot and good value for the sequence length is a hyperparameter optimization problem, which we have to evaluate empirically. Here, we are going to choose 40, as it offers a good trade-off.

As you can see in the previous figure, the inputs, x, and targets, y, are offset by one character. Hence, we will split the text into chunks of size 41: the first 40 characters will form the input sequence, x, and the last 40 elements will form the target sequence, y.

We have already stored the entire encoded text in its original order in `text_encoded`. We will first create text chunks consisting of 41 characters each. We will further get rid of the last chunk if it is shorter than 41 characters. As a result, the new chunked dataset, named `text_chunks`, will always contain sequences of size 41. The 41-character chunks will then be used to construct the sequence *x* (that is, the input), as well as the sequence *y* (that is, the target), both of which will have 40 elements. For instance, sequence *x* will consist of the elements with indices [0, 1, ..., 39]. Furthermore, since sequence *y* will be shifted by one position with respect to *x*, its corresponding indices will be [1, 2, ..., 40]. Then, we will transform the result into a `Dataset` object by applying a self-defined `Dataset` class:

```
>>> import torch
>>> from torch.utils.data import Dataset
>>> seq_length = 40
>>> chunk_size = seq_length + 1
>>> text_chunks = [text_encoded[i:i+chunk_size]
...                for i in range(len(text_encoded)-chunk_size+1)]
>>> from torch.utils.data import Dataset
>>> class TextDataset(Dataset):
...     def __init__(self, text_chunks):
...         self.text_chunks = text_chunks
...
...     def __len__(self):
...         return len(self.text_chunks)
...
...     def __getitem__(self, idx):
...         text_chunk = self.text_chunks[idx]
...         return text_chunk[:-1].long(), text_chunk[1:].long()
>>>
>>> seq_dataset = TextDataset(torch.tensor(text_chunks))
```

Let's take a look at some example sequences from this transformed dataset:

```
>>> for i, (seq, target) in enumerate(seq_dataset):
...     print(' Input (x): ',
...           repr(''.join(char_array[seq])))
...     print('Target (y): ',
...           repr(''.join(char_array[target])))
...     print()
...     if i == 1:
...         break
 Input (x): 'THE MYSTERIOUS ISLAND ***\n\n\n\n\nProduced b'
Target (y): 'HE MYSTERIOUS ISLAND ***\n\n\n\n\nProduced by'

 Input (x): 'HE MYSTERIOUS ISLAND ***\n\n\n\n\nProduced by'
Target (y): 'E MYSTERIOUS ISLAND ***\n\n\n\n\nProduced by '
```

Finally, the last step in preparing the dataset is to transform this dataset into mini-batches:

```
>>> from torch.utils.data import DataLoader
>>> batch_size = 64
>>> torch.manual_seed(1)
>>> seq_dl = DataLoader(seq_dataset, batch_size=batch_size,
...                     shuffle=True, drop_last=True)
```

Building a character-level RNN model

Now that the dataset is ready, building the model will be relatively straightforward:

```
>>> import torch.nn as nn
>>> class RNN(nn.Module):
...     def __init__(self, vocab_size, embed_dim, rnn_hidden_size):
...         super().__init__()
...         self.embedding = nn.Embedding(vocab_size, embed_dim)
...         self.rnn_hidden_size = rnn_hidden_size
...         self.rnn = nn.LSTM(embed_dim, rnn_hidden_size,
...                            batch_first=True)
...         self.fc = nn.Linear(rnn_hidden_size, vocab_size)
...
...     def forward(self, x, hidden, cell):
...         out = self.embedding(x).unsqueeze(1)
...         out, (hidden, cell) = self.rnn(out, (hidden, cell))
...         out = self.fc(out).reshape(out.size(0), -1)
...         return out, hidden, cell
...
...     def init_hidden(self, batch_size):
...         hidden = torch.zeros(1, batch_size, self.rnn_hidden_size)
...         cell = torch.zeros(1, batch_size, self.rnn_hidden_size)
...         return hidden, cell
```

Notice that we will need to have the logits as outputs of the model so that we can sample from the model predictions in order to generate new text. We will get to this sampling part later.

Then, we can specify the model parameters and create an RNN model:

```
>>> vocab_size = len(char_array)
>>> embed_dim = 256
>>> rnn_hidden_size = 512
>>> torch.manual_seed(1)
>>> model = RNN(vocab_size, embed_dim, rnn_hidden_size)
>>> model
RNN(
  (embedding): Embedding(80, 256)
```

```
  (rnn): LSTM(256, 512, batch_first=True)
  (fc): Linear(in_features=512, out_features=80, bias=True)
)
```

The next step is to create a loss function and optimizer (Adam optimizer). For a multiclass classification (we have `vocab_size=80` classes) with a single logits output for each target character, we use `CrossEntropyLoss` as the loss function:

```
>>> loss_fn = nn.CrossEntropyLoss()
>>> optimizer = torch.optim.Adam(model.parameters(), lr=0.005)
```

Now we will train the model for 10,000 epochs. In each epoch, we will use only one batch randomly chosen from the data loader, `seq_dl`. We will also display the training loss for every 500 epochs:

```
>>> num_epochs = 10000
>>> torch.manual_seed(1)
>>> for epoch in range(num_epochs):
...     hidden, cell = model.init_hidden(batch_size)
...     seq_batch, target_batch = next(iter(seq_dl))
...     optimizer.zero_grad()
...     loss = 0
...     for c in range(seq_length):
...         pred, hidden, cell = model(seq_batch[:, c], hidden, cell)
...         loss += loss_fn(pred, target_batch[:, c])
...     loss.backward()
...     optimizer.step()
...     loss = loss.item()/seq_length
...     if epoch % 500 == 0:
...         print(f'Epoch {epoch} loss: {loss:.4f}')
Epoch 0 loss: 1.9689
Epoch 500 loss: 1.4064
Epoch 1000 loss: 1.3155
Epoch 1500 loss: 1.2414
Epoch 2000 loss: 1.1697
Epoch 2500 loss: 1.1840
Epoch 3000 loss: 1.1469
Epoch 3500 loss: 1.1633
Epoch 4000 loss: 1.1788
Epoch 4500 loss: 1.0828
Epoch 5000 loss: 1.1164
Epoch 5500 loss: 1.0821
Epoch 6000 loss: 1.0764
```

```
Epoch 6500 loss: 1.0561
Epoch 7000 loss: 1.0631
Epoch 7500 loss: 0.9904
Epoch 8000 loss: 1.0053
Epoch 8500 loss: 1.0290
Epoch 9000 loss: 1.0133
Epoch 9500 loss: 1.0047
```

Next, we can evaluate the model to generate new text, starting with a given short string. In the next section, we will define a function to evaluate the trained model.

Evaluation phase – generating new text passages

The RNN model we trained in the previous section returns the logits of size 80 for each unique character. These logits can be readily converted to probabilities, via the softmax function, that a particular character will be encountered as the next character. To predict the next character in the sequence, we can simply select the element with the maximum logit value, which is equivalent to selecting the character with the highest probability. However, instead of always selecting the character with the highest likelihood, we want to (randomly) *sample* from the outputs; otherwise, the model will always produce the same text. PyTorch already provides a class, `torch.distributions.categorical.Categorical`, which we can use to draw random samples from a categorical distribution. To see how this works, let's generate some random samples from three categories [0, 1, 2], with input logits [1, 1, 1]:

```
>>> from torch.distributions.categorical import Categorical
>>> torch.manual_seed(1)
>>> logits = torch.tensor([[1.0, 1.0, 1.0]])
>>> print('Probabilities:',
...       nn.functional.softmax(logits, dim=1).numpy()[0])
Probabilities: [0.33333334 0.33333334 0.33333334]
>>> m = Categorical(logits=logits)
>>> samples = m.sample((10,))
>>> print(samples.numpy())
[[0]
 [0]
 [0]
 [0]
 [1]
 [0]
 [1]
 [2]
 [1]
 [1]]
```

As you can see, with the given logits, the categories have the same probabilities (that is, equiprobable categories). Therefore, if we use a large sample size ($num\_samples \rightarrow \infty$), we would expect the number of occurrences of each category to reach $\approx 1/3$ of the sample size. If we change the logits to [1, 1, 3], then we would expect to observe more occurrences for category 2 (when a very large number of examples are drawn from this distribution):

```
>>> torch.manual_seed(1)
>>> logits = torch.tensor([[1.0, 1.0, 3.0]])
>>> print('Probabilities:', nn.functional.softmax(logits, dim=1).numpy()[0])
Probabilities: [0.10650698 0.10650698 0.78698605]
>>> m = Categorical(logits=logits)
>>> samples = m.sample((10,))
>>> print(samples.numpy())
[[0]
 [2]
 [2]
 [1]
 [2]
 [1]
 [2]
 [2]
 [2]
 [2]]
```

Using `Categorical`, we can generate examples based on the logits computed by our model.

We will define a function, `sample()`, that receives a short starting string, `starting_str`, and generate a new string, `generated_str`, which is initially set to the input string. `starting_str` is encoded to a sequence of integers, `encoded_input`. `encoded_input` is passed to the RNN model one character at a time to update the hidden states. The last character of `encoded_input` is passed to the model to generate a new character. Note that the output of the RNN model represents the logits (here, a vector of size 80, which is the total number of possible characters) for the next character after observing the input sequence by the model.

Here, we only use the `logits` output (that is, $\boldsymbol{o}^{(T)}$), which is passed to the `Categorical` class to generate a new sample. This new sample is converted to a character, which is then appended to the end of the generated string, `generated_text`, increasing its length by 1. Then, this process is repeated until the length of the generated string reaches the desired value. The process of consuming the generated sequence as input for generating new elements is called **autoregression**.

The code for the `sample()` function is as follows:

```
>>> def sample(model, starting_str,
...            len_generated_text=500,
...            scale_factor=1.0):
```

```
...     encoded_input = torch.tensor(
...         [char2int[s] for s in starting_str]
...     )
...     encoded_input = torch.reshape(
...         encoded_input, (1, -1)
...     )
...     generated_str = starting_str
...
...     model.eval()
...     hidden, cell = model.init_hidden(1)
...     for c in range(len(starting_str)-1):
...         _, hidden, cell = model(
...             encoded_input[:, c].view(1), hidden, cell
...         )
...
...     last_char = encoded_input[:, -1]
...     for i in range(len_generated_text):
...         logits, hidden, cell = model(
...             last_char.view(1), hidden, cell
...         )
...         logits = torch.squeeze(logits, 0)
...         scaled_logits = logits * scale_factor
...         m = Categorical(logits=scaled_logits)
...         last_char = m.sample()
...         generated_str += str(char_array[last_char])
...
...     return generated_str
```

Let's now generate some new text:

```
>>> torch.manual_seed(1)
>>> print(sample(model, starting_str='The island'))
The island had been made
and ovylore with think, captain?" asked Neb; "we do."

It was found, they full to time to remove. About this neur prowers, perhaps
ended? It is might be
rather rose?"

"Forward!" exclaimed Pencroft, "they were it? It seems to me?"

"The dog Top--"
```

```
"What can have been struggling sventy."

Pencroft calling, themselves in time to try them what proves that the sailor
and Neb bounded this tenarvan's feelings, and then
still hid head a grand furiously watched to the dorner nor his only
```

As you can see, the model generates mostly correct words, and, in some cases, the sentences are partially meaningful. You can further tune the training parameters, such as the length of input sequences for training, and the model architecture.

Furthermore, to control the predictability of the generated samples (that is, generating text following the learned patterns from the training text versus adding more randomness), the logits computed by the RNN model can be scaled before being passed to `Categorical` for sampling. The scaling factor, α, can be interpreted as an analog to the temperature in physics. Higher temperatures result in more entropy or randomness versus more predictable behavior at lower temperatures. By scaling the logits with $\alpha < 1$, the probabilities computed by the softmax function become more uniform, as shown in the following code:

```
>>> logits = torch.tensor([[1.0, 1.0, 3.0]])
>>> print('Probabilities before scaling:        ',
...       nn.functional.softmax(logits, dim=1).numpy()[0])
>>> print('Probabilities after scaling with 0.5:',
...       nn.functional.softmax(0.5*logits, dim=1).numpy()[0])
>>> print('Probabilities after scaling with 0.1:',
...       nn.functional.softmax(0.1*logits, dim=1).numpy()[0])
Probabilities before scaling:         [0.10650698 0.10650698 0.78698604]
Probabilities after scaling with 0.5: [0.21194156 0.21194156 0.57611688]
Probabilities after scaling with 0.1: [0.31042377 0.31042377 0.37915245]
```

As you can see, scaling the logits by $\alpha = 1$ results in near-uniform probabilities [0.31, 0.31, 0.38]. Now, we can compare the generated text with $\alpha = 2.0$ and $\alpha = 0.5$, as shown in the following points:

- $\alpha = 2.0 \rightarrow$ more predictable:

```
>>> torch.manual_seed(1)
>>> print(sample(model, starting_str='The island',
...              scale_factor=2.0))
The island is one of the colony?" asked the sailor, "there is not to be
able to come to the shores of the Pacific."
"Yes," replied the engineer, "and if it is not the position of the
forest, and the marshy way have been said, the dog was not first on the
shore, and
found themselves to the corral.
```

```
The settlers had the sailor was still from the surface of the sea, they
were not received for the sea. The shore was to be able to inspect the
windows of Granite House.
The sailor turned the sailor was the hor
```

- $\alpha = 0.5 \rightarrow$ more randomness:

```
>>> torch.manual_seed(1)
>>> print(sample(model, starting_str='The island',
...                  scale_factor=0.5))
The island
deep incomele.
Manyl's', House, won's calcon-sglenderlessly," everful ineriorouins.,
pyra" into
truth. Sometinivabes, iskumar gave-zen."

Bleshed but what cotch quadrap which little cedass
fell oprely
by-andonem. Peditivall--"i dove Gurgeon. What resolt-eartnated to him
ran trail.

Withinhe)tiny turns returned, after owner plan bushelsion lairs; they
were
know? Whalerin branch I
pites, Dougg!-iteun," returnwe aid masses atong thoughts! Dak,
Hem-arches yone, Veay wantzer? Woblding,
Herbert, omep
```

The results show that scaling the logits with $\alpha = 0.5$ (increasing the temperature) generates more random text. There is a trade-off between the novelty of the generated text and its correctness.

In this section, we worked with character-level text generation, which is a sequence-to-sequence (seq2seq) modeling task. While this example may not be very useful by itself, it is easy to think of several useful applications for these types of models; for example, a similar RNN model can be trained as a chatbot to assist users with simple queries.

Summary

In this chapter, you first learned about the properties of sequences that make them different from other types of data, such as structured data or images. We then covered the foundations of RNNs for sequence modeling. You learned how a basic RNN model works and discussed its limitations with regard to capturing long-term dependencies in sequence data. Next, we covered LSTM cells, which consist of a gating mechanism to reduce the effect of exploding and vanishing gradient problems, which are common in basic RNN models.

After discussing the main concepts behind RNNs, we implemented several RNN models with different recurrent layers using PyTorch. In particular, we implemented an RNN model for sentiment analysis, as well as an RNN model for generating text.

In the next chapter, we will see how we can augment an RNN with an attention mechanism, which helps it with modeling long-range dependencies in translation tasks. Then, we will introduce a new deep learning architecture called *transformer*, which has recently been used to further push the state of the art in the natural language processing domain.

Join our book's Discord space

Join our Discord community to meet like-minded people and learn alongside more than 2000 members at:

`https://packt.link/MLwPyTorch`

16

Transformers – Improving Natural Language Processing with Attention Mechanisms

In the previous chapter, we learned about **recurrent neural networks** (**RNNs**) and their applications in **natural language processing** (**NLP**) through a sentiment analysis project. However, a new architecture has recently emerged that has been shown to outperform the RNN-based **sequence-to-sequence** (**seq2seq**) models in several NLP tasks. This is the so-called **transformer** architecture.

Transformers have revolutionized natural language processing and have been at the forefront of many impressive applications ranging from automated language translation (`https://ai.googleblog.com/2020/06/recent-advances-in-google-translate.html`) and modeling fundamental properties of protein sequences (`https://www.pnas.org/content/118/15/e2016239118.short`) to creating an AI that helps people write code (`https://github.blog/2021-06-29-introducing-github-copilot-ai-pair-programmer`).

In this chapter, you will learn about the basic mechanisms of *attention* and *self-attention* and see how they are used in the original transformer architecture. Then, equipped with an understanding of how transformers work, we will explore some of the most influential NLP models that emerged from this architecture and learn how to use a large-scale language model, the so-called BERT model, in PyTorch.

We will cover the following topics:

- Improving RNNs with an attention mechanism
- Introducing the stand-alone self-attention mechanism
- Understanding the original transformer architecture
- Comparing transformer-based large-scale language models
- Fine-tuning BERT for sentiment classification

Adding an attention mechanism to RNNs

In this section, we discuss the motivation behind developing an **attention mechanism**, which helps predictive models to focus on certain parts of the input sequence more than others, and how it was originally used in the context of RNNs. Note that this section provides a historical perspective explaining why the attention mechanism was developed. If individual mathematical details appear complicated, you can feel free to skip over them as they are not needed for the next section, explaining the self-attention mechanism for transformers, which is the focus of this chapter.

Attention helps RNNs with accessing information

To understand the development of an attention mechanism, consider the traditional RNN model for a **seq2seq task** like language translation, which parses the entire input sequence (for instance, one or more sentences) before producing the translation, as shown in *Figure 16.1*:

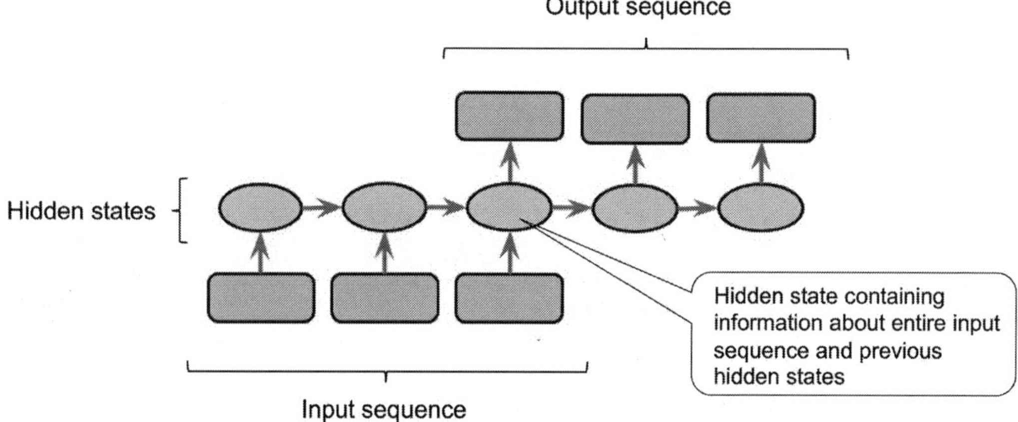

Figure 16.1: A traditional RNN encoder-decoder architecture for a seq2seq modeling task

Why is the RNN parsing the whole input sentence before producing the first output? This is motivated by the fact that translating a sentence word by word would likely result in grammatical errors, as illustrated in *Figure 16.2*:

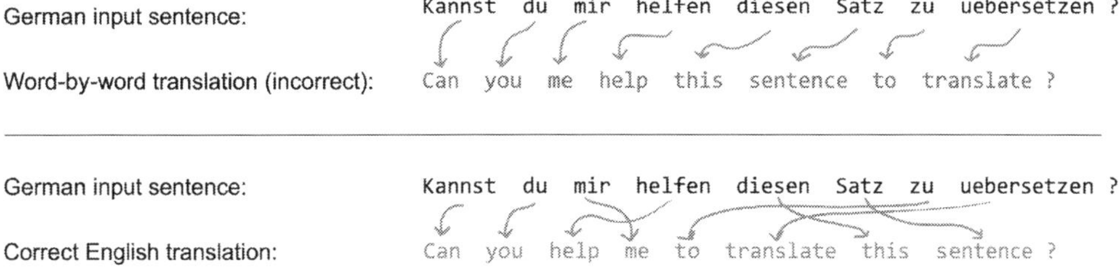

Figure 16.2: Translating a sentence word by word can lead to grammatical errors

However, as illustrated in *Figure 16.2*, one limitation of this seq2seq approach is that the RNN is trying to remember the entire input sequence via one single hidden unit before translating it. Compressing all the information into one hidden unit may cause loss of information, especially for long sequences. Thus, similar to how humans translate sentences, it may be beneficial to have access to the whole input sequence at each time step.

In contrast to a regular RNN, an attention mechanism lets the RNN access all input elements at each given time step. However, having access to all input sequence elements at each time step can be overwhelming. So, to help the RNN focus on the most relevant elements of the input sequence, the attention mechanism assigns different attention weights to each input element. These attention weights designate how important or relevant a given input sequence element is at a given time step. For example, revisiting *Figure 16.2*, the words "mir, helfen, zu" may be more relevant for producing the output word "help" than the words "kannst, du, Satz."

The next subsection introduces an RNN architecture that was outfitted with an attention mechanism to help process long sequences for language translation.

The original attention mechanism for RNNs

In this subsection, we will summarize the mechanics of the attention mechanism that was originally developed for language translation and first appeared in the following paper: *Neural Machine Translation by Jointly Learning to Align and Translate* by *Bahdanau, D., Cho, K., and Bengio, Y.,* 2014, `https://arxiv.org/abs/1409.0473`.

Given an input sequence $x = \left(x^{(1)}, x^{(2)}, \ldots, x^{(T)}\right)$, the attention mechanism assigns a weight to each element $x^{(i)}$ (or, to be more specific, its hidden representation) and helps the model identify which part of the input it should focus on. For example, suppose our input is a sentence, and a word with a larger weight contributes more to our understanding of the whole sentence. The RNN with the attention mechanism shown in *Figure 16.3* (modeled after the previously mentioned paper) illustrates the overall concept of generating the second output word:

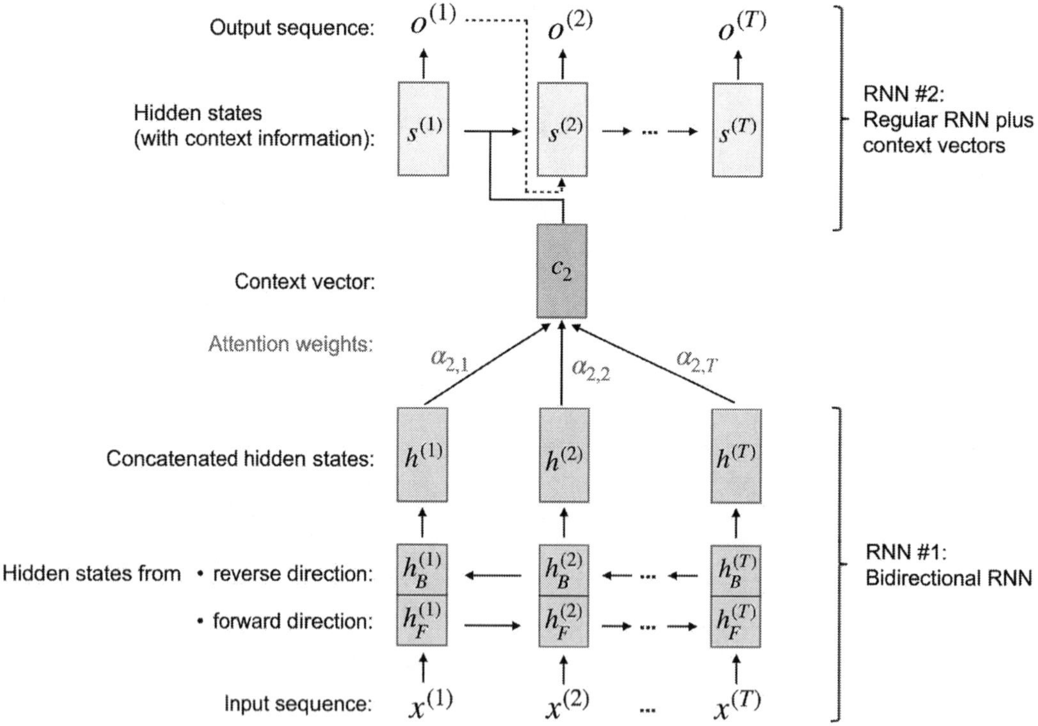

Figure 16.3: RNN with attention mechanism

The attention-based architecture depicted in the figure consists of two RNN models, which we will explain in the next subsections.

Processing the inputs using a bidirectional RNN

The first RNN (RNN #1) of the attention-based RNN in *Figure 16.3* is a bidirectional RNN that generates context vectors, c_i. You can think of a context vector as an augmented version of the input vector, $x^{(i)}$. In other words, the c_i input vector also incorporates information from all other input elements via an attention mechanism. As we can see in *Figure 16.3*, RNN #2 then uses this context vector, prepared by RNN #1, to generate the outputs. In the remainder of this subsection, we will discuss how RNN #1 works, and we will revisit RNN #2 in the next subsection.

The bidirectional RNN #1 processes the input sequence x in the regular forward direction $(1...T)$ as well as backward $(T...1)$. Parsing a sequence in the backward direction has the same effect as reversing the original input sequence—think of reading a sentence in reverse order. The rationale behind this is to capture additional information since current inputs may have a dependence on sequence elements that came either before or after it in a sentence, or both.

Consequently, from reading the input sequence twice (that is, forward and backward), we have two hidden states for each input sequence element. For instance, for the second input sequence element $x^{(2)}$, we obtain the hidden state $h_F^{(2)}$from the forward pass and the hidden state $h_B^{(2)}$ from the backward pass. These two hidden states are then concatenated to form the hidden state $h^{(2)}$. For example, if both $h_F^{(2)}$ and $h_B^{(2)}$ are 128-dimensional vectors, the concatenated hidden state $h^{(2)}$ will consist of 256 elements. We can consider this concatenated hidden state as the "annotation" of the source word since it contains the information of the *j*th word in both directions.

In the next section, we will see how these concatenated hidden states are further processed and used by the second RNN to generate the outputs.

Generating outputs from context vectors

In *Figure 16.3*, we can consider RNN #2 as the main RNN that is generating the outputs. In addition to the hidden states, it receives so-called context vectors as input. A context vector c_i is a weighted version of the concatenated hidden states, $h^{(1)} ... h^{(T)}$, which we obtained from RNN #1 in the previous subsection. We can compute the context vector of the *i*th input as a weighted sum:

$$c_i = \sum_{j=1}^{T} \alpha_{ij} h^{(j)}$$

Here, α_{ij} represents the attention weights over the input sequence $j = 1...T$ in the context of the *i*th input sequence element. Note that each *i*th input sequence element has a unique set of attention weights. We will discuss the computation of the attention weights α_{ij} in the next subsection.

For the remainder of this subsection, let us discuss how the context vectors are used via the second RNN in the preceding figure (RNN #2). Just like a vanilla (regular) RNN, RNN #2 also uses hidden states. Considering the hidden layer between the aforementioned "annotation" and final output, let us denote the hidden state at time i as $s^{(i)}$. Now, RNN #2 receives the aforementioned context vector c_i at each time step i as input.

In *Figure 16.3*, we saw that the hidden state $s^{(i)}$ depends on the previous hidden state $s^{(i-1)}$, the previous target word $y^{(i-1)}$, and the context vector $c^{(i)}$, which are used to generate the predicted output $o^{(i)}$ for target word $y^{(i)}$ at time i. Note that the sequence vector $\boldsymbol{y}$ refers to the sequence vector representing the correct translation of input sequence $\boldsymbol{x}$ that is available during training. During training, the true label (word) $y^{(i)}$ is fed into the next state $s^{(i+1)}$; since this true label information is not available for prediction (inference), we feed the predicted output $o^{(i)}$ instead, as depicted in the previous figure.

To summarize what we have just discussed above, the attention-based RNN consists of two RNNs. RNN #1 prepares context vectors from the input sequence elements, and RNN #2 receives the context vectors as input. The context vectors are computed via a weighted sum over the inputs, where the weights are the attention weights α_{ij}.The next subsection discusses how we compute these attention weights.

Computing the attention weights

Finally, let us visit the last missing piece in our puzzle—attention weights. Because these weights pairwise connect the inputs (annotations) and the outputs (contexts), each attention weight α_{ij} has two subscripts: j refers to the index position of the input and i corresponds to the output index position. The attention weight α_{ij} is a normalized version of the alignment score e_{ij}, where the alignment score evaluates how well the input around position j matches with the output at position i. To be more specific, the attention weight is computed by normalizing the alignment scores as follows:

$$\alpha_{ij} = \frac{\exp(e_{ij})}{\sum_{k=1}^{T} \exp(e_{ik})}$$

Note that this equation is similar to the softmax function, which we discussed in *Chapter 12, Parallelizing Neural Network Training with PyTorch*, in the section *Estimating class probabilities in multiclass classification via the softmax function*. Consequently, the attention weights $\alpha_{i1}...\alpha_{iT}$ sum up to 1.

Now, to summarize, we can structure the attention-based RNN model into three parts. The first part computes bidirectional annotations of the input. The second part consists of the recurrent block, which is very much like the original RNN, except that it uses context vectors instead of the original input. The last part concerns the computation of the attention weights and context vectors, which describe the relationship between each pair of input and output elements.

The transformer architecture also utilizes an attention mechanism, but unlike the attention-based RNN, it solely relies on the **self-attention** mechanism and does not include the recurrent process found in the RNN. In other words, a transformer model processes the whole input sequence all at once instead of reading and processing the sequence one element at a time. In the next section, we will introduce a basic form of the self-attention mechanism before we discuss the transformer architecture in more detail in the following section.

Introducing the self-attention mechanism

In the previous section, we saw that attention mechanisms can help RNNs with remembering context when working with long sequences. As we will see in the next section, we can have an architecture entirely based on attention, without the recurrent parts of an RNN. This attention-based architecture is known as **transformer**, and we will discuss it in more detail later.

In fact, transformers can appear a bit complicated at first glance. So, before we discuss transformers in the next section, let us dive into the **self-attention** mechanism used in transformers. In fact, as we will see, this self-attention mechanism is just a different flavor of the attention mechanism that we discussed in the previous section. We can think of the previously discussed attention mechanism as an operation that connects two different modules, that is, the encoder and decoder of the RNN. As we will see, self-attention focuses only on the input and captures only dependencies between the input elements. without connecting two modules.

In the first subsection, we will introduce a basic form of self-attention without any learning parameters, which is very much like a pre-processing step to the input. Then in the second subsection, we will introduce the common version of self-attention that is used in the transformer architecture and involves learnable parameters.

Starting with a basic form of self-attention

To introduce self-attention, let's assume we have an input sequence of length T, $\boldsymbol{x}^{(1)}, \dots, \boldsymbol{x}^{(T)}$, as well as an output sequence, $\boldsymbol{z}^{(1)}, \boldsymbol{z}^{(2)}, \dots, \boldsymbol{z}^{(T)}$. To avoid confusion, we will use $\boldsymbol{o}$ as the final output of the whole transformer model and $\boldsymbol{z}$ as the output of the self-attention layer because it is an intermediate step in the model.

Each ith element in these sequences, $\boldsymbol{x}^{(i)}$ and $\boldsymbol{z}^{(i)}$, are vectors of size d (that is, $\boldsymbol{x}^{(i)} \in R^d$) representing the feature information for the input at position i, which is similar to RNNs. Then, for a seq2seq task, the goal of self-attention is to model the dependencies of the current input element to all other input elements. To achieve this, self-attention mechanisms are composed of three stages. First, we derive importance weights based on the similarity between the current element and all other elements in the sequence. Second, we normalize the weights, which usually involves the use of the already familiar softmax function. Third, we use these weights in combination with the corresponding sequence elements to compute the attention value.

More formally, the output of self-attention, $\boldsymbol{z}^{(i)}$, is the weighted sum of all T input sequences, $\boldsymbol{x}^{(j)}$ (where $j = 1 \dots T$). For instance, for the ith input element, the corresponding output value is computed as follows:

$$\boldsymbol{z}^{(i)} = \sum_{j=1}^{T} \alpha_{ij} \boldsymbol{x}^{(j)}$$

Hence, we can think of $\boldsymbol{z}^{(i)}$ as a context-aware embedding vector in input vector $\boldsymbol{x}^{(i)}$ that involves all other input sequence elements weighted by their respective attention weights. Here, the attention weights, α_{ij}, are computed based on the similarity between the current input element, $\boldsymbol{x}^{(i)}$, and all other elements in the input sequence, $\boldsymbol{x}^{(1)} \dots \boldsymbol{x}^{(T)}$. More concretely, this similarity is computed in two steps explained in the next paragraphs.

First, we compute the dot product between the current input element, $\boldsymbol{x}^{(i)}$, and another element in the input sequence, $\boldsymbol{x}^{(j)}$:

$$\omega_{ij} = \boldsymbol{x}^{(i)^\top} \boldsymbol{x}^{(j)}$$

Before we normalize the ω_{ij} values to obtain the attention weights, a_{ij}, let's illustrate how we compute the ω_{ij} values with a code example. Here, let's assume we have an input sentence "can you help me to translate this sentence" that has already been mapped to an integer representation via a dictionary as explained in *Chapter 15, Modeling Sequential Data Using Recurrent Neural Networks*:

```
>>> import torch
>>> sentence = torch.tensor(
>>>     [0, # can
>>>      7, # you
>>>      1, # help
>>>      2, # me
>>>      5, # to
>>>      6, # translate
>>>      4, # this
>>>      3] # sentence
>>> )

>>> sentence
tensor([0, 7, 1, 2, 5, 6, 4, 3])
```

Let's also assume that we already encoded this sentence into a real-number vector representation via an embedding layer. Here, our embedding size is 16, and we assume that the dictionary size is 10. The following code will produce the word embeddings of our eight words:

```
>>> torch.manual_seed(123)
>>> embed = torch.nn.Embedding(10, 16)
>>> embedded_sentence = embed(sentence).detach()
>>> embedded_sentence.shape
torch.Size([8, 16])
```

Now, we can compute ω_{ij} as the dot product between the *i*th and *j*th word embeddings. We can do this for all ω_{ij} values as follows:

```
>>> omega = torch.empty(8, 8)
>>> for i, x_i in enumerate(embedded_sentence):
>>>     for j, x_j in enumerate(embedded_sentence):
>>>         omega[i, j] = torch.dot(x_i, x_j)
```

While the preceding code is easy to read and understand, `for` loops can be very inefficient, so let's compute this using matrix multiplication instead:

```
>>> omega_mat = embedded_sentence.matmul(embedded_sentence.T)
```

We can use the `torch.allclose` function to check that this matrix multiplication produces the expected results. If two tensors contain the same values, `torch.allclose` returns `True`, as we can see here:

```
>>> torch.allclose(omega_mat, omega)
True
```

We have learned how to compute the similarity-based weights for the ith input and all inputs in the sequence ($\boldsymbol{x}^{(1)}$ to $\boldsymbol{x}^{(T)}$), the "raw" weights (ω_{i1} to ω_{iT}). We can obtain the attention weights, α_{ij}, by normalizing the ω_{ij} values via the familiar softmax function, as follows:

$$\alpha_{ij} = \frac{\exp(\omega_{ij})}{\sum_{j=1}^{T} \exp(\omega_{ij})} = \text{softmax}\left(\left[\omega_{ij}\right]_{j=1\ldots T}\right)$$

Notice that the denominator involves a sum over all input elements ($1 \ldots T$). Hence, due to applying this softmax function, the weights will sum to 1 after this normalization, that is,

$$\sum_{j=1}^{T} \alpha_{ij} = 1$$

We can compute the attention weights using PyTorch's softmax function as follows:

```
>>> import torch.nn.functional as F
>>> attention_weights = F.softmax(omega, dim=1)
>>> attention_weights.shape
torch.Size([8, 8])
```

Note that `attention_weights` is an 8×8 matrix, where each element represents an attention weight, α_{ij}. For instance, if we are processing the ith input word, the ith row of this matrix contains the corresponding attention weights for all words in the sentence. These attention weights indicate how relevant each word is to the ith word. Hence, the columns in this attention matrix should sum to 1, which we can confirm via the following code:

```
>>> attention_weights.sum(dim=1)
tensor([1.0000, 1.0000, 1.0000, 1.0000, 1.0000, 1.0000, 1.0000, 1.0000])
```

Now that we have seen how to compute the attention weights, let us recap and summarize the three main steps behind the self-attention operation:

1. For a given input element, $\boldsymbol{x}^{(i)}$, and each jth element in the set $\{1, ..., T\}$, compute the dot product, $\boldsymbol{x}^{(i)^\top} \boldsymbol{x}^{(j)}$
2. Obtain the attention weight, α_{ij}, by normalizing the dot products using the softmax function
3. Compute the output, $\boldsymbol{z}^{(i)}$, as the weighted sum over the entire input sequence: $\boldsymbol{z}^{(i)} = \sum_{j=1}^{T} \alpha_{ij} \boldsymbol{x}^{(j)}$

These steps are further illustrated in *Figure 16.4*:

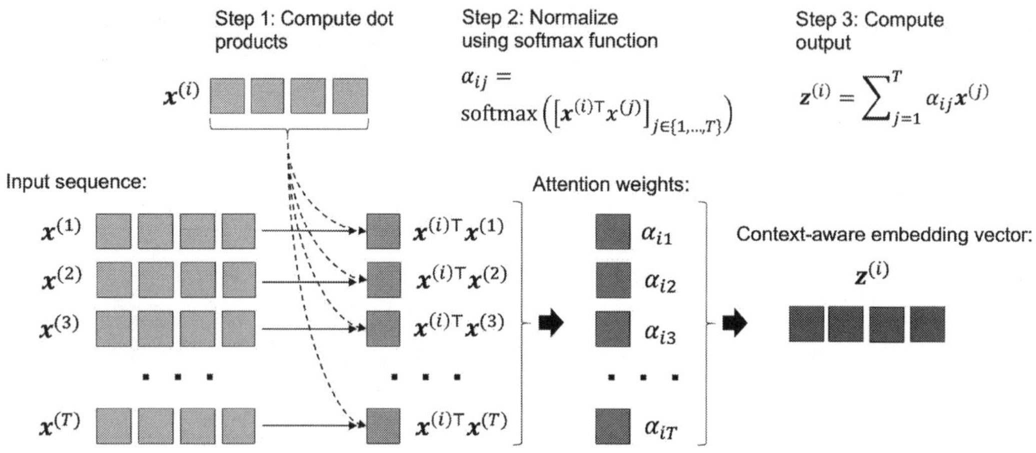

Figure 16.4: A basic self-attention process for illustration purposes

Lastly, let us see a code example for computing the context vectors, $\boldsymbol{z}^{(i)}$, as the attention-weighted sum of the inputs (step 3 in *Figure 16.4*). In particular, let's assume we are computing the context vector for the second input word, that is, $\boldsymbol{z}^{(2)}$:

```
>>> x_2 = embedded_sentence[1, :]
>>> context_vec_2 = torch.zeros(x_2.shape)
>>> for j in range(8):
...     x_j = embedded_sentence[j, :]
...     context_vec_2 += attention_weights[1, j] * x_j
>>> context_vec_2
tensor([-9.3975e-01, -4.6856e-01,  1.0311e+00, -2.8192e-01,  4.9373e-01,
-1.2896e-02, -2.7327e-01, -7.6358e-01,  1.3958e+00, -9.9543e-01,
-7.1288e-04,  1.2449e+00, -7.8077e-02,  1.2765e+00, -1.4589e+00,
-2.1601e+00])
```

Again, we can achieve this more efficiently by using matrix multiplication. Using the following code, we are computing the context vectors for all eight input words:

```
>>> context_vectors = torch.matmul(
...     attention_weights, embedded_sentence)
```

Similar to the input word embeddings stored in `embedded_sentence`, the `context_vectors` matrix has dimensionality 8 × 16. The second row in this matrix contains the context vector for the second input word, and we can check the implementation using `torch.allclose()` again:

```
>>> torch.allclose(context_vec_2, context_vectors[1])
True
```

As we can see, the manual `for` loop and matrix computations of the second context vector yielded the same results.

This section implemented a basic form of self-attention, and in the next section, we will modify this implementation using learnable parameter matrices that can be optimized during neural network training.

Parameterizing the self-attention mechanism: scaled dot-product attention

Now that you have been introduced to the basic concept behind self-attention, this subsection summarizes the more advanced self-attention mechanism called **scaled dot-product attention** that is used in the transformer architecture. Note that in the previous subsection, we did not involve any learnable parameters when computing the outputs. In other words, using the previously introduced basic self-attention mechanism, the transformer model is rather limited regarding how it can update or change the attention values during model optimization for a given sequence. To make the self-attention mechanism more flexible and amenable to model optimization, we will introduce three additional weight matrices that can be fit as model parameters during model training. We denote these three weight matrices as $\boldsymbol{U}_q$, $\boldsymbol{U}_k$, and $\boldsymbol{U}_v$. They are used to project the inputs into query, key, and value sequence elements, as follows:

- Query sequence: $\boldsymbol{q}^{(i)} = \boldsymbol{U}_q\boldsymbol{x}^{(i)}$ for $i \in [1, T]$
- Key sequence: $\boldsymbol{k}^{(i)} = \boldsymbol{U}_k\boldsymbol{x}^{(i)}$ for $i \in [1, T]$
- Value sequence: $\boldsymbol{v}^{(i)} = \boldsymbol{U}_v\boldsymbol{x}^{(i)}$ for $i \in [1, T]$

Figure 16.5 illustrates how these individual components are used to compute the context-aware embedding vector corresponding to the second input element:

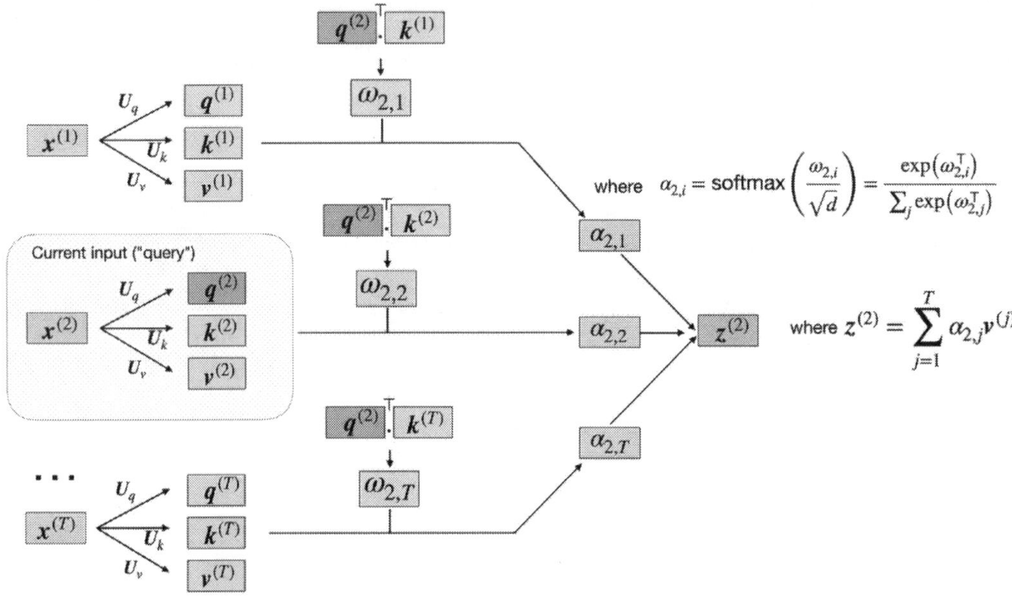

Figure 16.5: Computing the context-aware embedding vector of the second sequence element

Query, key, and value terminology

The terms query, key, and value that were used in the original transformer paper are inspired by information retrieval systems and databases. For example, if we enter a query, it is matched against the key values for which certain values are retrieved.

Here, both $\boldsymbol{q}^{(i)}$ and $\boldsymbol{k}^{(i)}$ are vectors of size d_k. Therefore, the projection matrices $\boldsymbol{U}_q$ and $\boldsymbol{U}_k$ have the shape $d_k \times d$, while $\boldsymbol{U}_v$ has the shape $d_v \times d$. (Note that d is the dimensionality of each word vector, $\boldsymbol{x}^{(i)}$.) For simplicity, we can design these vectors to have the same shape, for example, using $d_k = d_v = d$. To provide additional intuition via code, we can initialize these projection matrices as follows:

```
>>> torch.manual_seed(123)
>>> d = embedded_sentence.shape[1]
>>> U_query = torch.rand(d, d)
>>> U_key = torch.rand(d, d)
>>> U_value = torch.rand(d, d)
```

Using the query projection matrix, we can then compute the query sequence. For this example, consider the second input element, $\boldsymbol{x}^{(i)}$, as our query, as illustrated in *Figure 16.5*:

```
>>> x_2 = embedded_sentence[1]
>>> query_2 = U_query.matmul(x_2)
```

In a similar fashion, we can compute the key and value sequences, $\boldsymbol{k}^{(i)}$and $\boldsymbol{v}^{(i)}$:

```
>>> key_2 = U_key.matmul(x_2)
>>> value_2 = U_value.matmul(x_2)
```

However, as we can see from *Figure 16.5*, we also need the key and value sequences for all other input elements, which we can compute as follows:

```
>>> keys = U_key.matmul(embedded_sentence.T).T
>>> values = U_value.matmul(embedded_sentence.T).T
```

In the key matrix, the *i*th row corresponds to the key sequence of the *i*th input element, and the same applies to the value matrix. We can confirm this by using `torch.allclose()` again, which should return `True`:

```
>>> keys = U_key.matmul(embedded_sentence.T).T
>>> torch.allclose(key_2, keys[1])
>>> values = U_value.matmul(embedded_sentence.T).T
>>> torch.allclose(value_2, values[1])
```

In the previous section, we computed the unnormalized weights, ω_{ij}, as the pairwise dot product between the given input sequence element, $\boldsymbol{x}^{(i)}$, and the *j*th sequence element, $\boldsymbol{x}^{(j)}$. Now, in this parameterized version of self-attention, we compute ω_{ij} as the dot product between the query and key:

$$\omega_{ij} = \boldsymbol{q}^{(i)^\top} \boldsymbol{k}^{(j)}$$

For example, the following code computes the unnormalized attention weight, ω_{23}, that is, the dot product between our query and the third input sequence element:

```
>>> omega_23 = query_2.dot(keys[2])
>>> omega_23
tensor(14.3667)
```

Since we will be needing these later, we can scale up this computation to all keys:

```
>>> omega_2 = query_2.matmul(keys.T)
>>> omega_2
tensor([-25.1623,   9.3602,  14.3667,  32.1482,  53.8976,  46.6626,  -1.2131,
-32.9391])
```

The next step in self-attention is to go from the unnormalized attention weights, ω_{ij}, to the normalized attention weights, α_{ij}, using the softmax function. We can then further use $1/\sqrt{m}$ to scale ω_{ij} before normalizing it via the softmax function, as follows:

$$\alpha_{ij} = \text{softmax}\left(\frac{\omega_{ij}}{\sqrt{m}}\right)$$

Note that scaling ω_{ij} by $1/\sqrt{m}$, where typically $m = d_k$, ensures that the Euclidean length of the weight vectors will be approximately in the same range.

The following code is for implementing this normalization to compute the attention weights for the entire input sequence with respect to the second input element as the query:

```
>>> attention_weights_2 = F.softmax(omega_2 / d**0.5, dim=0)
>>> attention_weights_2
tensor([2.2317e-09, 1.2499e-05, 4.3696e-05, 3.7242e-03, 8.5596e-01, 1.4025e-01,
8.8896e-07, 3.1936e-10])
```

Finally, the output is a weighted average of value sequences: $\boldsymbol{z}^{(i)} = \sum_{j=1}^{T} \alpha_{ij}\boldsymbol{v}^{(j)}$, which can be implemented as follows:

```
>>> context_vector_2 = attention_weights_2.matmul(values)
>>> context_vector_2
tensor([-1.2226, -3.4387, -4.3928, -5.2125, -1.1249, -3.3041,
-1.4316, -3.2765, -2.5114, -2.6105, -1.5793, -2.8433, -2.4142,
-0.3998, -1.9917, -3.3499])
```

In this section, we introduced a self-attention mechanism with trainable parameters that lets us compute context-aware embedding vectors by involving all input elements, which are weighted by their respective attention scores. In the next section, we will learn about the transformer architecture, a neural network architecture centered around the self-attention mechanism introduced in this section.

Attention is all we need: introducing the original transformer architecture

Interestingly, the original transformer architecture is based on an attention mechanism that was first used in an RNN. Originally, the intention behind using an attention mechanism was to improve the text generation capabilities of RNNs when working with long sentences. However, only a few years after experimenting with attention mechanisms for RNNs, researchers found that an attention-based language model was even more powerful when the recurrent layers were deleted. This led to the development of the **transformer architecture**, which is the main topic of this chapter and the remaining sections.

The transformer architecture was first proposed in the NeurIPS 2017 paper *Attention Is All You Need* by *A. Vaswani* and colleagues (`https://arxiv.org/abs/1706.03762`). Thanks to the self-attention mechanism, a transformer model can capture long-range dependencies among the elements in an input sequence—in an NLP context; for example, this helps the model better "understand" the meaning of an input sentence.

Although this transformer architecture was originally designed for language translation, it can be generalized to other tasks such as English constituency parsing, text generation, and text classification. Later, we will discuss popular language models, such as BERT and GPT, which were derived from this original transformer architecture. *Figure 16.6*, which we adapted from the original transformer paper, illustrates the main architecture and components we will be discussing in this section:

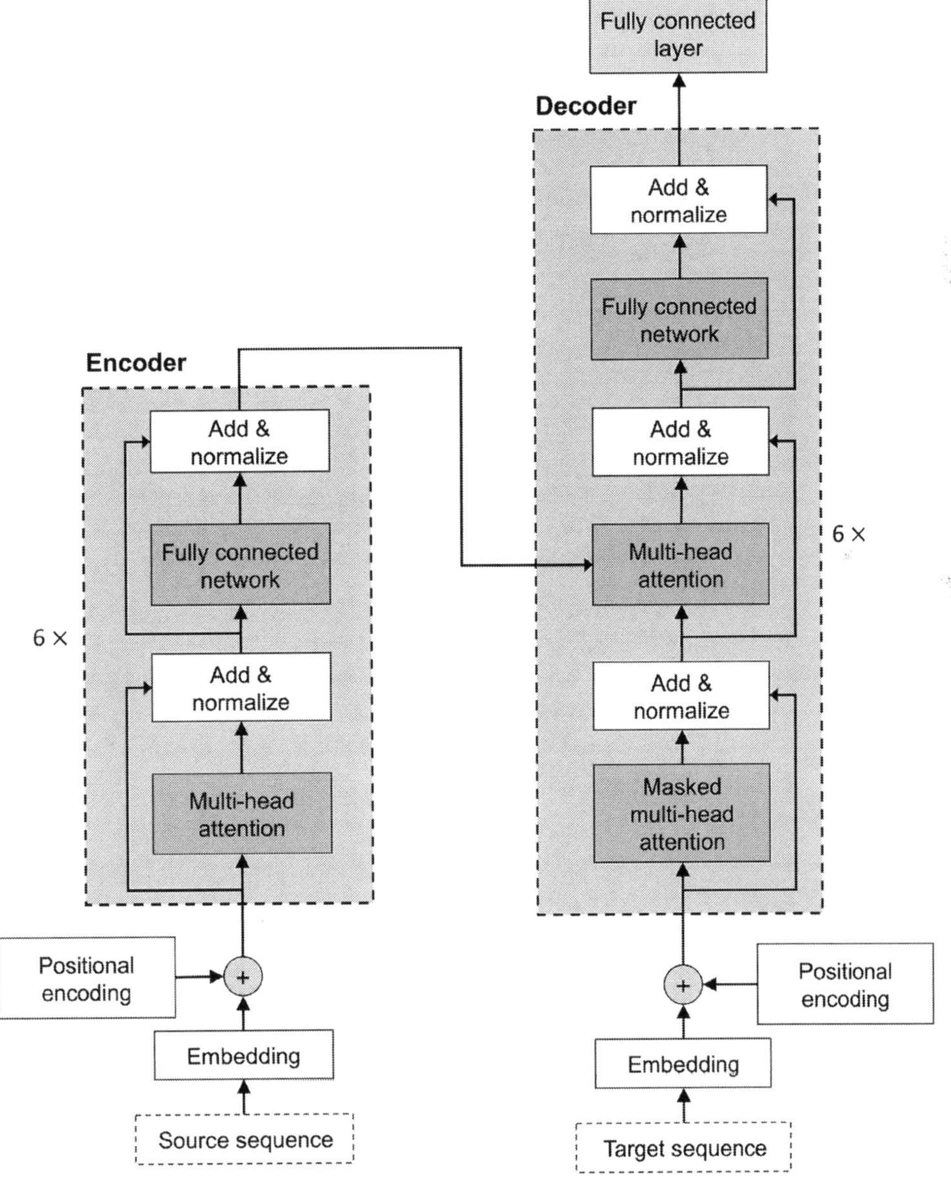

Figure 16.6: The original transformer architecture

In the following subsections, we go over this original transformer model step by step, by decomposing it into two main blocks: an encoder and a decoder. The encoder receives the original sequential input and encodes the embeddings using a multi-head self-attention module. The decoder takes in the processed input and outputs the resulting sequence (for instance, the translated sentence) using a *masked* form of self-attention.

Encoding context embeddings via multi-head attention

The overall goal of the **encoder** block is to take in a sequential input $\boldsymbol{X} = \left(\boldsymbol{x}^{(1)}, \boldsymbol{x}^{(2)}, \ldots, \boldsymbol{x}^{(T)}\right)$ and map it into a continuous representation $\boldsymbol{Z} = \left(\boldsymbol{z}^{(1)}, \boldsymbol{z}^{(2)}, \ldots, \boldsymbol{z}^{(T)}\right)$ that is then passed on to the decoder.

The encoder is a stack of six identical layers. Six is not a magic number here but merely a hyperparameter choice made in the original transformer paper. You can adjust the number of layers according to the model performance. Inside each of these identical layers, there are two sublayers: one computes the multi-head self-attention, which we will discuss below, and the other one is a fully connected layer, which you have already encountered in previous chapters.

Let's first talk about the **multi-head self-attention**, which is a simple modification of scaled dot-product attention covered earlier in this chapter. In the scaled dot-product attention, we used three matrices (corresponding to query, value, and key) to transform the input sequence. In the context of multi-head attention, we can think of this set of three matrices as one attention *head*. As indicated by its name, in multi-head attention, we now have multiple of such heads (sets of query, value, and key matrices) similar to how convolutional neural networks can have multiple kernels.

To explain the concept of multi-head self-attention with h heads in more detail, let's break it down into the following steps.

First, we read in the sequential input $\boldsymbol{X} = \left(\boldsymbol{x}^{(1)}, \boldsymbol{x}^{(2)}, \ldots, \boldsymbol{x}^{(T)}\right)$. Suppose each element is embedded by a vector of length d. Here, the input can be embedded into a $T \times d$ matrix. Then, we create h sets of the query, key, and value learning parameter matrices:

- $\boldsymbol{U}_{q_1}, \boldsymbol{U}_{k_1}, \boldsymbol{U}_{v_1}$
- $\boldsymbol{U}_{q_2}, \boldsymbol{U}_{k_2}, \boldsymbol{U}_{v_2}$
- ...
- $\boldsymbol{U}_{q_h}, \boldsymbol{U}_{k_h}, \boldsymbol{U}_{v_h}$

Because we are using these weight matrices to project each element $\boldsymbol{x}^{(i)}$ for the required dimension-matching in the matrix multiplications, both $\boldsymbol{U}_{q_j}$ and $\boldsymbol{U}_{k_j}$ have the shape $d_k \times d$, and $\boldsymbol{U}_{v_j}$ has the shape $d_v \times d$. As a result, both resulting sequences, query and key, have length d_k, and the resulting value sequence has length d_v. In practice, people often choose $d_k = d_v = m$ for simplicity.

To illustrate the multi-head self-attention stack in code, first consider how we created the single query projection matrix in the previous subsection, *Parameterizing the self-attention mechanism: scaled dot-product attention*:

```
>>> torch.manual_seed(123)
>>> d = embedded_sentence.shape[1]
>>> one_U_query = torch.rand(d, d)
```

Now, assume we have eight attention heads similar to the original transformer, that is, $h = 8$:

```
>>> h = 8
>>> multihead_U_query = torch.rand(h, d, d)
>>> multihead_U_key = torch.rand(h, d, d)
>>> multihead_U_value = torch.rand(h, d, d)
```

As we can see in the code, multiple attention heads can be added by simply adding an additional dimension.

Splitting data across multiple attention heads

In practice, rather than having a separate matrix for each attention head, transformer implementations use a single matrix for all attention heads. The attention heads are then organized into logically separate regions in this matrix, which can be accessed via Boolean masks. This makes it possible to implement multi-head attention more efficiently because multiple matrix multiplications can be implemented as a single matrix multiplication instead. However, for simplicity, we are omitting this implementation detail in this section.

After initializing the projection matrices, we can compute the projected sequences similar to how it's done in scaled dot-product attention. Now, instead of computing one set of query, key, and value sequences, we need to compute h sets of them. More formally, for example, the computation involving the query projection for the ith data point in the jth head can be written as follows:

$$\boldsymbol{q}_j^{(i)} = \boldsymbol{U}_{q_j} \boldsymbol{x}^{(i)}$$

We then repeat this computation for all heads $j \in \{1, \dots h\}$.

In code, this looks like the following for the second input word as the query:

```
>>> multihead_query_2 = multihead_U_query.matmul(x_2)
>>> multihead_query_2.shape
torch.Size([8, 16])
```

The `multihead_query_2` matrix has eight rows, where each row corresponds to the jth attention head.

Similarly, we can compute key and value sequences for each head:

```
>>> multihead_key_2 = multihead_U_key.matmul(x_2)
>>> multihead_value_2 = multihead_U_value.matmul(x_2)
>>> multihead_key_2[2]
tensor([-1.9619, -0.7701, -0.7280, -1.6840, -1.0801, -1.6778,  0.6763,  0.6547,
         1.4445, -2.7016, -1.1364, -1.1204, -2.4430, -0.5982, -0.8292, -1.4401])
```

The code output shows the key vector of the second input element via the third attention head.

However, remember that we need to repeat the key and value computations for all input sequence elements, not just x_2—we need this to compute self-attention later. A simple and illustrative way to do this is by expanding the input sequence embeddings to size 8 as the first dimension, which is the number of attention heads. We use the `.repeat()` method for this:

```
>>> stacked_inputs = embedded_sentence.T.repeat(8, 1, 1)
>>> stacked_inputs.shape
torch.Size([8, 16, 8])
```

Then, we can have a batch matrix multiplication, via `torch.bmm()`, with the attention heads to compute all keys:

```
>>> multihead_keys = torch.bmm(multihead_U_key, stacked_inputs)
>>> multihead_keys.shape
torch.Size([8, 16, 8])
```

In this code, we now have a tensor that refers to the eight attention heads in its first dimension. The second and third dimensions refer to the embedding size and the number of words, respectively. Let us swap the second and third dimensions so that the keys have a more intuitive representation, that is, the same dimensionality as the original input sequence `embedded_sentence`:

```
>>> multihead_keys = multihead_keys.permute(0, 2, 1)
>>> multihead_keys.shape
torch.Size([8, 8, 16])
```

After rearranging, we can access the second key value in the second attention head as follows:

```
>>> multihead_keys[2, 1]
tensor([-1.9619, -0.7701, -0.7280, -1.6840, -1.0801, -1.6778,  0.6763,  0.6547,
         1.4445, -2.7016, -1.1364, -1.1204, -2.4430, -0.5982, -0.8292, -1.4401])
```

We can see that this is the same key value that we got via `multihead_key_2[2]` earlier, which indicates that our complex matrix manipulations and computations are correct. So, let's repeat it for the value sequences:

```
>>> multihead_values = torch.matmul(
        multihead_U_value, stacked_inputs)
>>> multihead_values = multihead_values.permute(0, 2, 1)
```

We follow the steps of the single head attention calculation to calculate the context vectors as described in the *Parameterizing the self-attention mechanism: scaled dot-product attention* section. We will skip the intermediate steps for brevity and assume that we have computed the context vectors for the second input element as the query and the eight different attention heads, which we represent as `multihead_z_2` via random data:

```
>>> multihead_z_2 = torch.rand(8, 16)
```

Note that the first dimension indexes over the eight attention heads, and the context vectors, similar to the input sentences, are 16-dimensional vectors. If this appears complicated, think of `multihead_z_2` as eight copies of the $z^{(2)}$ shown in *Figure 16.5*; that is, we have one $z^{(2)}$ for each of the eight attention heads.

Then, we concatenate these vectors into one long vector of length $d_v \times h$ and use a linear projection (via a fully connected layer) to map it back to a vector of length d_v. This process is illustrated in *Figure 16.7*:

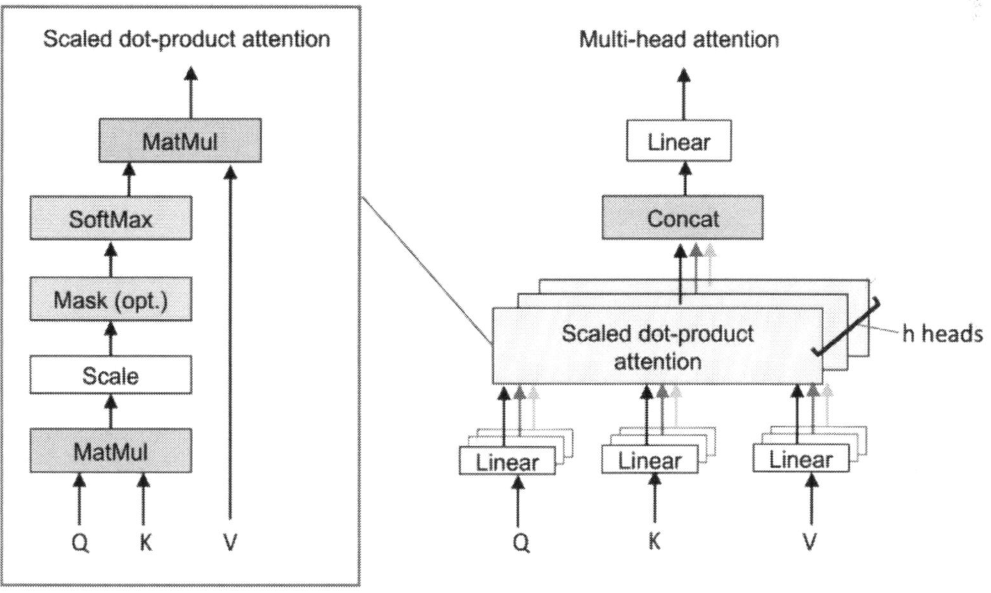

Figure 16.7: Concatenating the scaled dot-product attention vectors into one vector and passing it through a linear projection

In code, we can implement the concatenation and squashing as follows:

```
>>> linear = torch.nn.Linear(8*16, 16)
>>> context_vector_2 = linear(multihead_z_2.flatten())
>>> context_vector_2.shape
torch.Size([16])
```

To summarize, multi-head self-attention is repeating the scaled dot-product attention computation multiple times in parallel and combining the results. It works very well in practice because the multiple heads help the model to capture information from different parts of the input, which is very similar to how the multiple kernels produce multiple channels in a convolutional network, where each channel can capture different feature information. Lastly, while multi-head attention sounds computationally expensive, note that the computation can all be done in parallel because there are no dependencies between the multiple heads.

Learning a language model: decoder and masked multi-head attention

Similar to the encoder, the **decoder** also contains several repeated layers. Besides the two sublayers that we have already introduced in the previous encoder section (the multi-head self-attention layer and fully connected layer), each repeated layer also contains a masked multi-head attention sublayer.

Masked attention is a variation of the original attention mechanism, where masked attention only passes a limited input sequence into the model by "masking" out a certain number of words. For example, if we are building a language translation model with a labeled dataset, at sequence position i during the training procedure, we only feed in the correct output words from positions 1,...,i-1. All other words (for instance, those that come after the current position) are hidden from the model to prevent the model from "cheating." This is also consistent with the nature of text generation: although the true translated words are known during training, we know nothing about the ground truth in practice. Thus, we can only feed the model the solutions to what it has already generated, at position i.

Figure 16.8 illustrates how the layers are arranged in the decoder block:

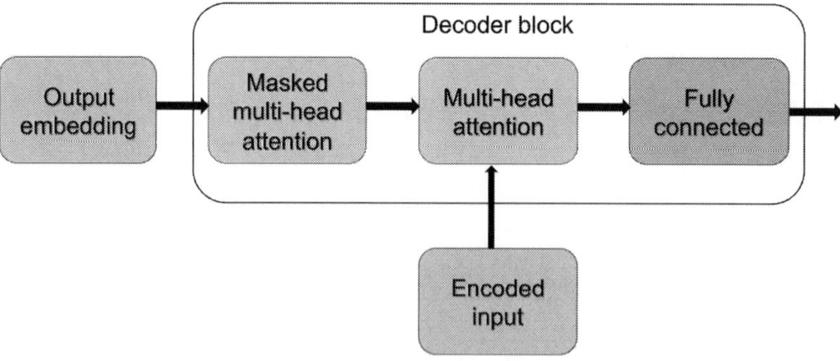

Figure 16.8: Layer arrangement in the decoder part

First, the previous output words (output embeddings) are passed into the masked multi-head attention layer. Then, the second layer receives both the encoded inputs from the encoder block and the output of the masked multi-head attention layer into a multi-head attention layer. Finally, we pass the multi-head attention outputs into a fully connected layer that generates the overall model output: a probability vector corresponding to the output words.

Note that we can use an argmax function to obtain the predicted words from these word probabilities similar to the overall approach we took in the recurrent neural network in *Chapter 15, Modeling Sequential Data Using Recurrent Neural Networks.*

Comparing the decoder with the encoder block, the main difference is the range of sequence elements that the model can attend to. In the encoder, for each given word, the attention is calculated across all the words in a sentence, which can be considered as a form of bidirectional input parsing. The decoder also receives the bidirectionally parsed inputs from the encoder. However, when it comes to the output sequence, the decoder only considers those elements that are preceding the current input position, which can be interpreted as a form of unidirectional input parsing.

Implementation details: positional encodings and layer normalization

In this subsection, we will discuss some of the implementation details of transformers that we have glanced over so far but are worth mentioning.

First, let's consider the **positional encodings** that were part of the original transformer architecture from *Figure 16.6*. Positional encodings help with capturing information about the input sequence ordering and are a crucial part of transformers because both scaled dot-product attention layers and fully connected layers are permutation-invariant. This means, without positional encoding, the order of words is ignored and does not make any difference to the attention-based encodings. However, we know that word order is essential for understanding a sentence. For example, consider the following two sentences:

1. Mary gives John a flower
2. John gives Mary a flower

The words occurring in the two sentences are exactly the same; the meanings, however, are very different.

Transformers enable the same words at different positions to have slightly different encodings by adding a vector of small values to the input embeddings at the beginning of the encoder and decoder blocks. In particular, the original transformer architecture uses a so-called sinusoidal encoding:

$$PE_{(i,2k)} = \sin(pos/10000^{2k/d_{\text{model}}})$$

$$PE_{(i,2k+1)} = \cos(pos/10000^{2k/d_{\text{model}}})$$

Here i is the position of the word and k denotes the length of the encoding vector, where we choose k to have the same dimension as the input word embeddings so that the positional encoding and word embeddings can be added together. Sinusoidal functions are used to prevent positional encodings from becoming too large. For instance, if we used absolute position 1,2,3..., n to be positional encodings, they would dominate the word encoding and make the word embedding values negligible.

In general, there are two types of positional encodings, an *absolute* one (as shown in the previous formula) and a *relative* one. The former will record absolute positions of words and is sensitive to word shifts in a sentence. That is to say, absolute positional encodings are fixed vectors for each given position. On the other hand, relative encodings only maintain the relative position of words and are invariant to sentence shift.

Next, let's look at the **layer normalization** mechanism, which was first introduced by J. Ba, J.R. Kiros, and G.E. Hinton in 2016 in the same-named paper *Layer Normalization* (URL: `https://arxiv.org/abs/1607.06450`). While batch normalization, which we will discuss in more detail in *Chapter 17, Generative Adversarial Networks for Synthesizing New Data*, is a popular choice in computer vision contexts, layer normalization is the preferred choice in NLP contexts, where sentence lengths can vary. *Figure 16.9* illustrates the main differences of layer and batch normalization side by side:

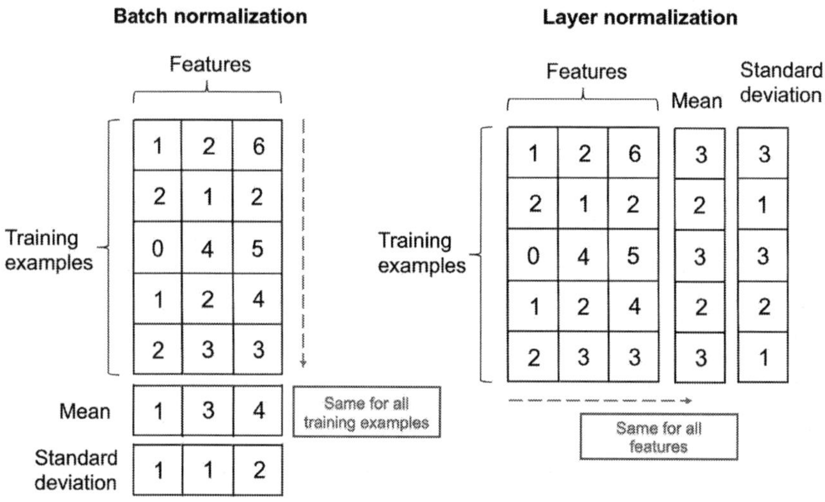

Figure 16.9: A comparison of batch and layer normalization

While layer normalization is traditionally performed across all elements in a given feature for each feature independently, the layer normalization used in transformers extends this concept and computes the normalization statistics across all feature values independently for each training example.

Since layer normalization computes mean and standard deviation for each training example, it relaxes minibatch size constraints or dependencies. In contrast to batch normalization, layer normalization is thus capable of learning from data with small minibatch sizes and varying lengths. However, note that the original transformer architecture does not have varying-length inputs (sentences are padded when needed), and unlike RNNs, there is no recurrence in the model. So, how can we then justify the use of layer normalization over batch normalization? Transformers are usually trained on very large text corpora, which requires parallel computation; this can be challenging to achieve with batch normalization, which has a dependency between training examples. Layer normalization has no such dependency and is thus a more natural choice for transformers.

Building large-scale language models by leveraging unlabeled data

In this section, we will discuss popular large-scale transformer models that emerged from the original transformer. One common theme among these transformers is that they are pre-trained on very large, unlabeled datasets and then fine-tuned for their respective target tasks. First, we will introduce the common training procedure of transformer-based models and explain how it is different from the original transformer. Then, we will focus on popular large-scale language models including **Generative Pre-trained Transformer** (GPT), **Bidirectional Encoder Representations from Transformers** (BERT), and **Bidirectional and Auto-Regressive Transformers** (BART).

Pre-training and fine-tuning transformer models

In an earlier section, *Attention is all we need: introducing the original transformer architecture*, we discussed how the original transformer architecture can be used for language translation. Language translation is a supervised task and requires a labeled dataset, which can be very expensive to obtain. The lack of large, labeled datasets is a long-lasting problem in deep learning, especially for models like the transformer, which are even more data hungry than other deep learning architectures. However, given that large amounts of text (books, websites, and social media posts) are generated every day, an interesting question is how we can use such unlabeled data for improving the model training.

The answer to whether we can leverage unlabeled data in transformers is *yes*, and the trick is a process called **self-supervised learning**: we can generate "labels" from supervised learning from plain text itself. For example, given a large, unlabeled text corpus, we train the model to perform **next-word prediction**, which enables the model to learn the probability distribution of words and can form a strong basis for becoming a powerful language model.

Self-supervised learning is traditionally also referred to as **unsupervised pre-training** and is essential for the success of modern transformer-based models. The "unsupervised" in unsupervised pre-training supposedly refers to the fact that we use unlabeled data; however, since we use the structure of the data to generate labels (for example, the next-word prediction task mentioned previously), it is still a supervised learning process.

To elaborate a bit further on how unsupervised pre-training and next-word prediction works, if we have a sentence containing *n* words, the pre-training procedure can be decomposed into the following three steps:

1. At time *step 1*, feed in the ground-truth words 1, ..., *i*-1.
2. Ask the model to predict the word at position *i* and compare it with the ground-truth word *i*.
3. Update the model and time step, *i*:= *i*+1. Go back to step 1 and repeat until all words are processed.

We should note that in the next iteration, we always feed the model the ground-truth (correct) words instead of what the model has generated in the previous round.

The main idea of pre-training is to make use of plain text and then transfer and fine-tune the model to perform some specific tasks for which a (smaller) labeled dataset is available. Now, there are many different types of pre-training techniques. For example, the previously mentioned next-word prediction task can be considered as a unidirectional pre-training approach. Later, we will introduce additional pre-training techniques that are utilized in different language models to achieve various functionalities.

A complete training procedure of a transformer-based model consists of two parts: (1) pre-training on a large, unlabeled dataset and (2) training (that is, fine-tuning) the model for specific downstream tasks using a labeled dataset. In the first step, the pre-trained model is not designed for any specific task but rather trained as a "general" language model. Afterward, via the second step, it can be generalized to any customized task via regular supervised learning on a labeled dataset.

With the representations that can be obtained from the pre-trained model, there are mainly two strategies for transferring and adopting a model to a specific task: (1) a **feature-based approach** and (2) a **fine-tuning approach**. (Here, we can think of these representations as the hidden layer activations of the last layers of a model.)

The feature-based approach uses the pre-trained representations as additional features to a labeled dataset. This requires us to learn how to extract sentence features from the pre-trained model. An early model that is well-known for this feature extraction approach is **ELMo** (**Embeddings from Language Models**) proposed by Peters and colleagues in 2018 in the paper *Deep Contextualized Word Representations* (URL: `https://arxiv.org/abs/1802.05365`). ELMo is a pre-trained bidirectional language model that masks words at a certain rate. In particular, it randomly masks 15 percent of the input words during pre-training, and the modeling task is to fill in these blanks, that is, predicting the missing (masked) words. This is different from the unidirectional approach we introduced previously, which hides all the future words at time step i. Bidirectional masking enables a model to learn from both ends and can thus capture more holistic information about a sentence. The pre-trained ELMo model can generate high-quality sentence representations that, later on, serve as input features for specific tasks. In other words, we can think of the feature-based approach as a model-based feature extraction technique similar to principal component analysis, which we covered in *Chapter 5, Compressing Data via Dimensionality Reduction*.

The fine-tuning approach, on the other hand, updates the pre-trained model parameters in a regular supervised fashion via backpropagation. Unlike the feature-based method, we usually also add another fully connected layer to the pre-trained model, to accomplish certain tasks such as classification, and then update the whole model based on the prediction performance on the labeled training set. One popular model that follows this approach is BERT, a large-scale transformer model pre-trained as a bidirectional language model. We will discuss BERT in more detail in the following subsections. In addition, in the last section of this chapter, we will see a code example showing how to fine-tune a pre-trained BERT model for sentiment classification using the movie review dataset we worked with in *Chapter 8, Applying Machine Learning to Sentiment Analysis*, and *Chapter 15, Modeling Sequential Data Using Recurrent Neural Networks*.

Before we move on to the next section and start our discussion of popular transformer-based language models, the following figure summarizes the two stages of training transformer models and illustrates the difference between the feature-based and fine-tuning approaches:

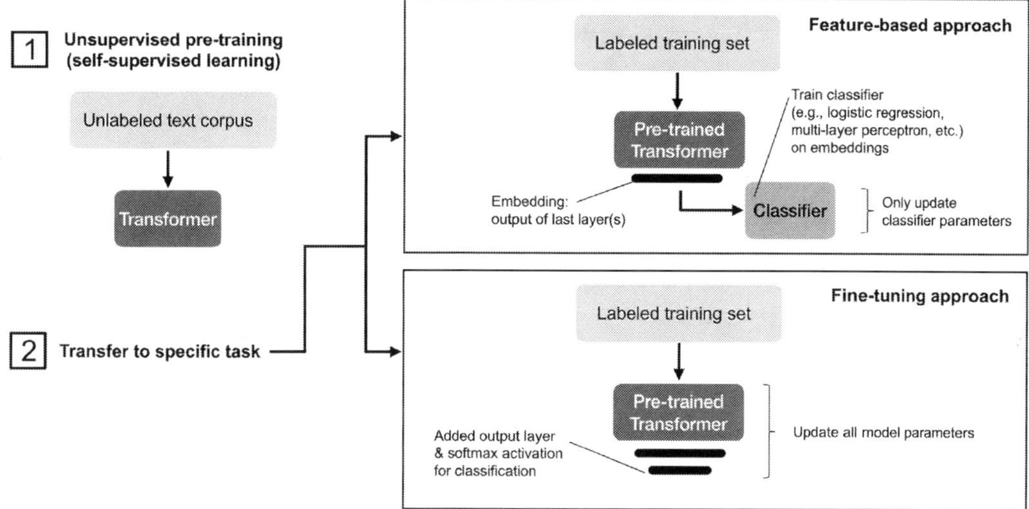

Figure 16.10: The two main ways to adopt a pre-trained transformer for downstream tasks

Leveraging unlabeled data with GPT

The **Generative Pre-trained Transformer** (**GPT**) is a popular series of large-scale language models for generating text developed by OpenAI. The most recent model, GPT-3, which was released in May 2020 (*Language Models are Few-Shot Learners*), is producing astonishing results. The quality of the text generated by GPT-3 is very hard to distinguish from human-generated texts. In this section, we are going to discuss how the GPT model works on a high level, and how it has evolved over the years.

As listed in *Table 16.1*, one obvious evolution within the GPT model series is the number of parameters:

Model	Release year	Number of parameters	Title	Paper link
GPT-1	2018	110 million	Improving Language Understanding by Generative Pre-Training	`https://www.cs.ubc.ca/~amuham01/LING530/papers/radford2018improving.pdf`
GPT-2	2019	1.5 billion	Language Models are Unsupervised Multitask Learners	`https://www.semanticscholar.org/paper/Language-Models-are-Unsupervised-Multitask-Learners-Radford-Wu/9405cc0d6169988371b2755e573cc28650d14dfe`
GPT-3	2020	175 billion	Language Models are Few-Shot Learners	`https://arxiv.org/pdf/2005.14165.pdf`

Table 16.1: Overview of the GPT models

But let's not get ahead of ourselves, and take a closer look at the GPT-1 model first, which was released in 2018. Its training procedure can be decomposed into two stages:

1. Pre-training on a large amount of unlabeled plain text
2. Supervised fine-tuning

As *Figure 16.11* (adapted from the GPT-1 paper) illustrates, we can consider GPT-1 as a transformer consisting of (1) a decoder (and without an encoder block) and (2) an additional layer that is added later for the supervised fine-tuning to accomplish specific tasks:

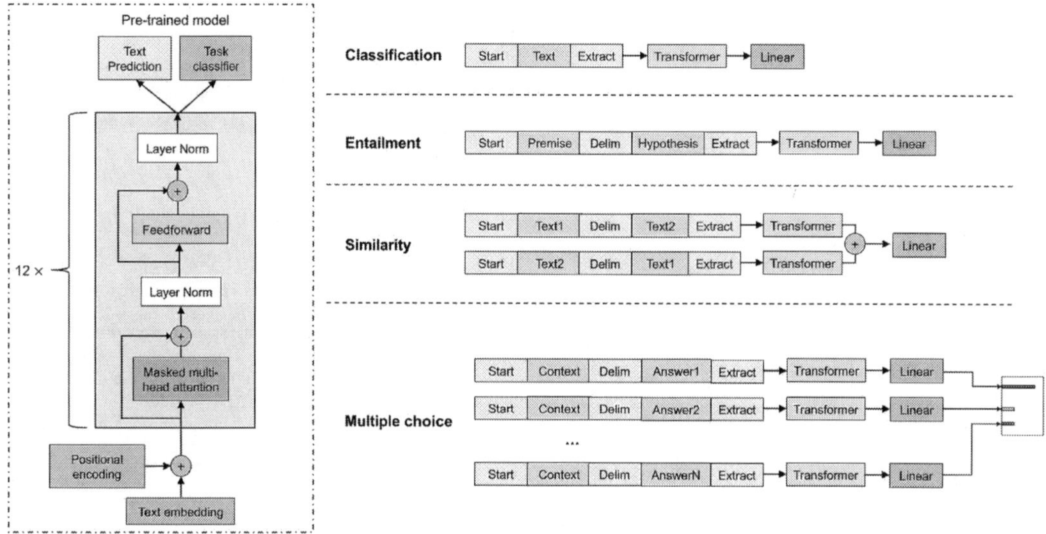

Figure 16.11: The GPT-1 transformer

In the figure, note that if our task is *Text Prediction* (predicting the next word), then the model is ready after the pre-training step. Otherwise, for example, if our task is related to classification or regression, then supervised fine-tuning is required.

During pre-training, GPT-1 utilizes a transformer decoder structure, where, at a given word position, the model only relies on preceding words to predict the next word. GPT-1 utilizes a unidirectional self-attention mechanism, as opposed to a bidirectional one as in BERT (which we will cover later in this chapter), because GPT-1 is focused on text generation rather than classification. During text generation, it produces words one by one with a natural left-to-right direction. There is one other aspect worth highlighting here: during the training procedure, for each position, we always feed the correct words from the previous positions to the model. However, during inference, we just feed the model whatever words it has generated to be able to generate new texts.

After obtaining the pre-trained model (the block in the previous figure labeled as *Transformer*), we then insert it between the input pre-processing block and a linear layer, where the linear layer serves as an output layer (similar to previous deep neural network models we discussed earlier in this book). For classification tasks, fine-tuning is as simple as first tokenizing the input and then feeding it into the pre-trained model and the newly added linear layer, which is followed by a softmax activation function. However, for more complicated tasks such as question answering, inputs are organized in a certain format that is not necessarily matching the pre-trained model, which requires an extra processing step customized for each task. Readers who are interested in specific modifications are encouraged to read the GPT-1 paper for additional details (the link is provided in the previous table).

GPT-1 also performs surprisingly well on **zero-shot tasks**, which proves its ability to be a general language model that can be customized for different types of tasks with minimal task-specific fine-tuning. Zero-shot learning generally describes a special circumstance in machine learning where during testing and inference, the model is required to classify samples from classes that were not observed during training. In the context of GPT, the zero-shot setting refers to unseen tasks.

GPT's adaptability inspired researchers to get rid of the task-specific input and model setup, which led to the development of GPT-2. Unlike its predecessor, GPT-2 does not require any additional modification during the input or fine-tuning stages anymore. Instead of rearranging sequences to match the required format, GPT-2 can distinguish between different types of inputs and perform the corresponding downstream tasks with minor hints, the so-called "contexts." This is achieved by modeling output probabilities conditioned on both input and task type, $p(output|input, task)$, instead of only conditioning on the input. For example, the model is expected to recognize a translation task if the context includes `translate to French, English text, French text.`

This sounds much more "artificially intelligent" than GPT and is indeed the most noticeable improvement besides the model size. Just as the title of its corresponding paper indicates (*Language Models are Unsupervised Multitask Learners*), an unsupervised language model may be key to zero-shot learning, and GPT-2 makes full use of zero-shot task transfer to build this multi-task learner.

Compared with GPT-2, GPT-3 is less "ambitious" in the sense that it shifts the focus from zero- to one-shot and **few-shot learning** via in-context learning. While providing no task-specific training examples seems to be too strict, few-shot learning is not only more realistic but also more human-like: humans usually need to see a few examples to be able to learn a new task. Just as its name suggests, few-shot learning means that the model sees a *few* examples of the task while one-shot learning is restricted to exactly one example.

Figure 16.12 illustrates the difference between zero-shot, one-shot, few-shot, and fine-tuning procedures:

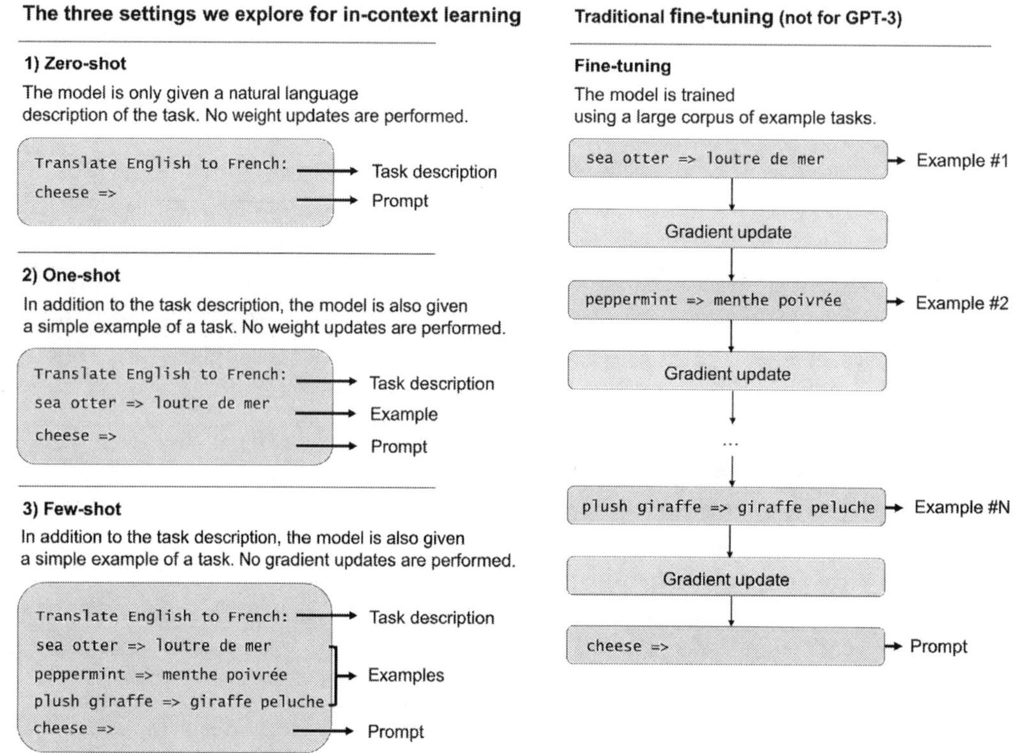

Figure 16.12: A comparison of zero-shot, one-shot, and few-shot learning

The model architecture of GPT-3 is pretty much the same as GPT-2 except for the 100-fold parameter size increase and the use of a sparse transformer. In the original (dense) attention mechanism we discussed earlier, each element attends to all other elements in the input, which scales with $O(n^2)$ complexity. **Sparse attention** improves the efficiency by only attending to a subset of elements with limited size, normally proportional to $n^{1/p}$. Interested readers can learn more about the specific subset selection by visiting the sparse transformer paper: *Generating Long Sequences with Sparse Transformers by Rewon Child et al.* 2019 (URL: `https://arxiv.org/abs/1904.10509`).

Using GPT-2 to generate new text

Before we move on to the next transformer architecture, let us take a look at how we can use the latest GPT models to generate new text. Note that GPT-3 is still relatively new and is currently only available as a beta version via the OpenAI API at `https://openai.com/blog/openai-api/`. However, an implementation of GPT-2 has been made available by Hugging Face (a popular NLP and machine learning company; `http://huggingface.co`), which we will use.

We will be accessing GPT-2 via `transformers`, which is a very comprehensive Python library created by Hugging Face that provides various transformer-based models for pre-training and fine-tuning. Users can also discuss and share their customized models on the forum. Feel free to check out and engage with the community if you are interested: `https://discuss.huggingface.co`.

Installing transformers version 4.9.1

Because this package is evolving rapidly, you may not be able to replicate the results in the following subsections. For reference, this tutorial uses version 4.9.1 released in June 2021. To install the version we used in this book, you can execute the following command in your terminal to install it from PyPI:

```
pip install transformers==4.9.1
```

We also recommend checking the latest instructions on the official installation page:

`https://huggingface.co/transformers/installation.html`

Once we have installed the `transformers` library, we can run the following code to import a pre-trained GPT model that can generate new text:

```
>>> from transformers import pipeline, set_seed
>>> generator = pipeline('text-generation', model='gpt2')
```

Then, we can prompt the model with a text snippet and ask it to generate new text based on that input snippet:

```
>>> set_seed(123)
>>> generator("Hey readers, today is",
...           max_length=20,
...           num_return_sequences=3)

[{'generated_text': "Hey readers, today is not the last time we'll be seeing
one of our favorite indie rock bands"},
 {'generated_text': 'Hey readers, today is Christmas. This is not Christmas,
because Christmas is so long and I hope'},
 {'generated_text': "Hey readers, today is CTA Day!\n\nWe're proud to be
hosting a special event"}]
```

As we can see from the output, the model generated three reasonable sentences based on our text snippet. If you want to explore more examples, please feel free to change the random seed and the maximum sequence length.

Also, as previously illustrated in *Figure 16.10*, we can use a transformer model to generate features for training other models. The following code illustrates how we can use GPT-2 to generate features based on an input text:

```
>>> from transformers import GPT2Tokenizer
>>> tokenizer = GPT2Tokenizer.from_pretrained('gpt2')
>>> text = "Let us encode this sentence"
>>> encoded_input = tokenizer(text, return_tensors='pt')
>>> encoded_input
{'input_ids': tensor([[ 5756,   514, 37773,   428,  6827]]), 'attention_mask':
tensor([[1, 1, 1, 1, 1]])}
```

This code encoded the input sentence text into a tokenized format for the GPT-2 model. As we can see, it mapped the strings to an integer representation, and it set the attention mask to all 1s, which means that all words will be processed when we pass the encoded input to the model, as shown here:

```
>>> from transformers import GPT2Model
>>> model = GPT2Model.from_pretrained('gpt2')
>>> output = model(**encoded_input)
```

The `output` variable stores the last hidden state, that is, our GPT-2-based feature encoding of the input sentence:

```
>>> output['last_hidden_state'].shape
torch.Size([1, 5, 768])
```

To suppress the verbose output, we only showed the shape of the tensor. Its first dimension is the batch size (we only have one input text), which is followed by the sentence length and size of the feature encoding. Here, each of the five words is encoded as a 768-dimensional vector.

Now, we could apply this feature encoding to a given dataset and train a downstream classifier based on the GPT-2-based feature representation instead of using a bag-of-words model as discussed in *Chapter 8, Applying Machine Learning to Sentiment Analysis*.

Moreover, an alternative approach to using large pre-trained language models is fine-tuning, as we discussed earlier. We will be seeing a fine-tuning example later in this chapter.

If you are interested in additional details on using GPT-2, we recommend the following documentation pages:

- `https://huggingface.co/gpt2`
- `https://huggingface.co/docs/transformers/model_doc/gpt2`

Bidirectional pre-training with BERT

BERT, its full name being **Bidirectional Encoder Representations from Transformers**, was created by a Google research team in 2018 (*BERT: Pre-training of Deep Bidirectional Transformers for Language Understanding* by *J. Devlin, M. Chang, K. Lee,* and *K. Toutanova*, `https://arxiv.org/abs/1810.04805`). For reference, even though we cannot compare GPT and BERT directly as they are different architectures, BERT has 345 million parameters (which makes it only slightly larger than GPT-1, and its size is only 1/5 of GPT-2).

As its name suggests, BERT has a transformer-encoder-based model structure that utilizes a bidirectional training procedure. (Or, more accurately, we can think of BERT as using "nondirectional" training because it reads in all input elements all at once.) Under this setting, the encoding of a certain word depends on both the preceding and the succeeding words. Recall that in GPT, input elements are read in with a natural left-to-right order, which helps to form a powerful generative language model. Bidirectional training disables BERT's ability to generate a sentence word by word but provides input encodings of higher quality for other tasks, such as classification, since the model can now process information in both directions.

Recall that in a transformer's encoder, token encoding is a summation of positional encodings and token embeddings. In the BERT encoder, there is an additional segment embedding indicating which segment this token belongs to. This means that each token representation contains three ingredients, as *Figure 16.13* illustrates:

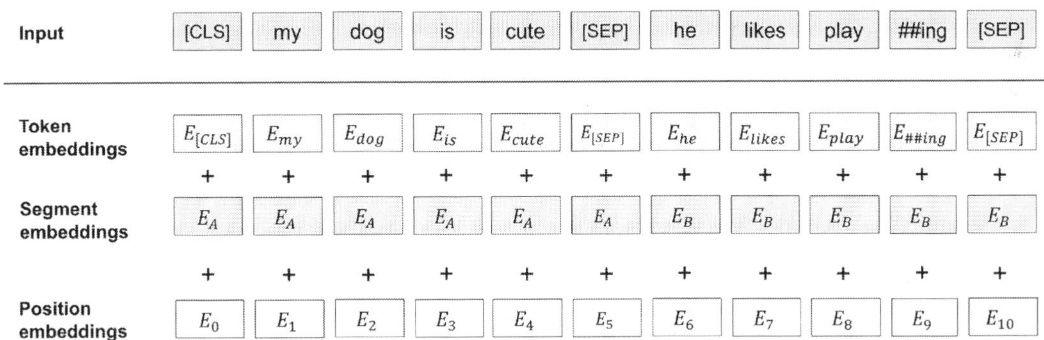

Figure 16.13: Preparing the inputs for the BERT encoder

Why do we need this additional segment information in BERT? The need for this segment information originated from the special pre-training task of BERT called *next-sentence prediction*. In this pre-training task, each training example includes two sentences and thus requires special segment notation to denote whether it belongs to the first or second sentence.

Now, let us look at BERT's pre-training tasks in more detail. Similar to all other transformer-based language models, BERT has two training stages: pre-training and fine-tuning. And pre-training includes two unsupervised tasks: *masked language modeling* and *next-sentence prediction*.

In the **masked language model** (**MLM**), tokens are randomly replaced by so-called *mask tokens*, `[MASK]`, and the model is required to predict these hidden words. Compared with the next-word prediction in GPT, MLM in BERT is more akin to "filling in the blanks" because the model can attend to all tokens in the sentence (except the masked ones). However, simply masking words out can result in inconsistencies between pre-training and fine-tuning since `[MASK]` tokens do not appear in regular texts. To alleviate this, there are further modifications to the words that are selected for masking. For instance, 15 percent of the words in BERT are marked for masking. These 15 percent of randomly selected words are then further treated as follows:

1. Keep the word unchanged 10 percent of the time
2. Replace the original word token with a random word 10 percent of the time
3. Replace the original word token with a mask token, `[MASK]`, 80 percent of the time

Besides avoiding the aforementioned inconsistency between pre-training and fine-tuning when introducing `[MASK]` tokens into the training procedure, these modifications also have other benefits. Firstly, unchanged words include the possibility of maintaining the information of the original token; otherwise, the model can only learn from the context and nothing from the masked words. Secondly, the 10 percent random words prevent the model from becoming lazy, for instance, learning nothing but returning what it is being given. The probabilities for masking, randomizing, and leaving words unchanged were chosen by an ablation study (see the GPT-2 paper); for instance, authors tested different settings and found that this combination worked best.

Figure 16.14 illustrates an example where the word *fox* is masked and, with a certain probability, remains unchanged or is replaced by `[MASK]` or *coffee*. The model is then required to predict what the masked (highlighted) word is as illustrated in *Figure 16.14*:

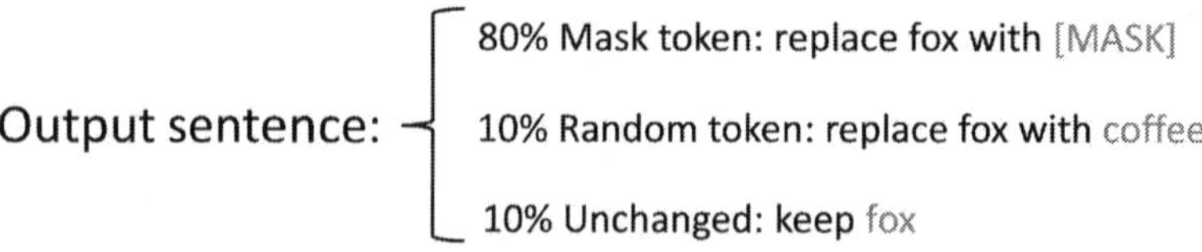

Figure 16.14: An example of MLM

Next-sentence prediction is a natural modification of the next-word prediction task considering the bidirectional encoding of BERT. In fact, many important NLP tasks, such as question answering, depend on the relationship of two sentences in the document. This kind of relationship is hard to capture via regular language models because next-word prediction training usually occurs on a single-sentence level due to input length constraints.

In the next-sentence prediction task, the model is given two sentences, A and B, in the following format:

[CLS] A [SEP] B [SEP]

[CLS] is a classification token, which serves as a placeholder for the predicted label in the decoder output, as well as a token denoting the beginning of the sentences. The [SEP] token, on the other hand, is attached to denote the end of each sentence. The model is then required to classify whether B is the next sentence ("IsNext") of A or not. To provide the model with a balanced dataset, 50 percent of the samples are labeled as "IsNext" while the remaining samples are labeled as "NotNext."

BERT is pre-trained on these two tasks, masked sentences and next-sentence prediction, at the same time. Here, the training objective of BERT is to minimize the combined loss function of both tasks.

Starting from the pre-trained model, specific modifications are required for different downstream tasks in the fine-tuning stage. Each input example needs to match a certain format; for example, it should begin with a [CLS] token and be separated using [SEP] tokens if it consists of more than one sentence.

Roughly speaking, BERT can be fine-tuned on four categories of tasks: (a) sentence pair classification; (b) single-sentence classification; (c) question answering; (d) single-sentence tagging.

Among them, (a) and (b) are sequence-level classification tasks, which only require an additional softmax layer to be added to the output representation of the [CLS] token. (c) and (d), on the other hand, are token-level classification tasks. This means that the model passes output representations of all related tokens to the softmax layer to predict a class label for each individual token.

Question answering

Task (c), question answering, appears to be less often discussed compared to other popular classification tasks such as sentiment classification or speech tagging. In question answering, each input example can be split into two parts, the question and the paragraph that helps to answer the question. The model is required to point out both the start and end token in the paragraph that forms a proper answer to the question. This means that the model needs to generate a tag for every single token in the paragraph, indicating whether this token is a start or end token, or neither. As a side note, it is worth mentioning that the output may contain an end token that appears before the start token, which will lead to a conflict when generating the answer. This kind of output will be recognized as "No Answer" to the question.

As *Figure 16.15* indicates, the model fine-tuning setup has a very simple structure: an input encoder is attached to a pre-trained BERT, and a softmax layer is added for classification. Once the model structure is set up, all the parameters will be adjusted along the learning process.

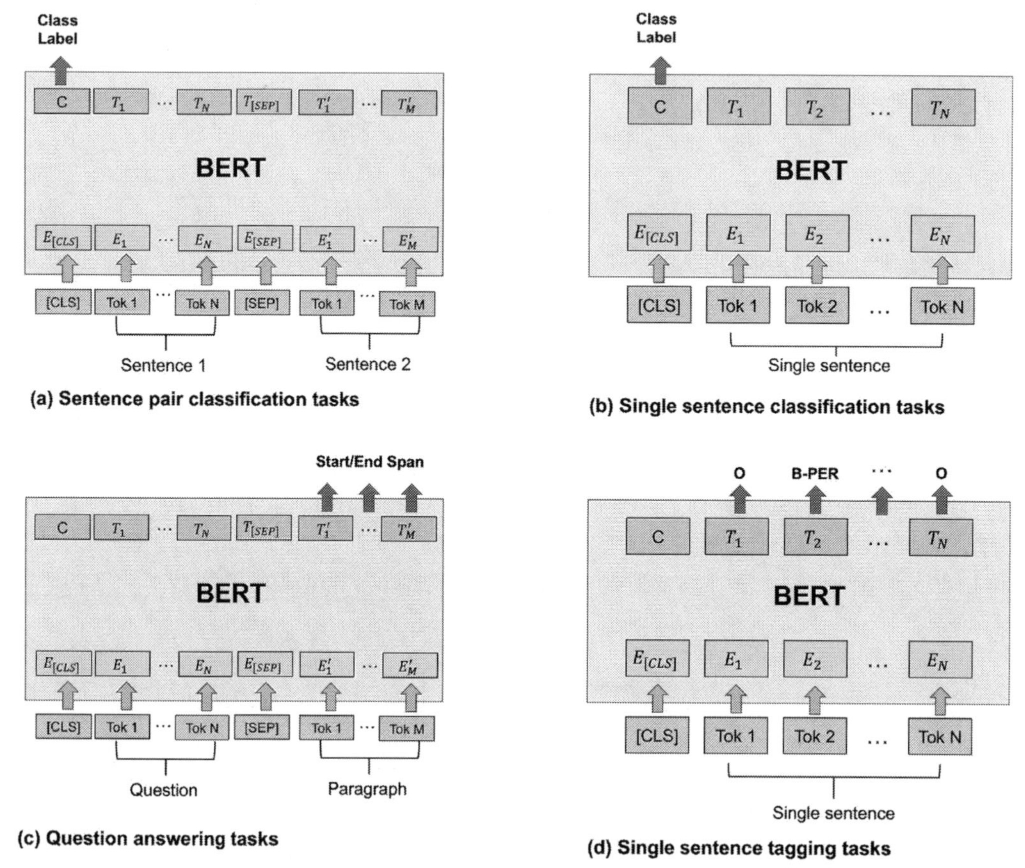

Figure 16.15: Using BERT to fine-tune different language tasks

The best of both worlds: BART

The **Bidirectional and Auto-Regressive Transformer**, abbreviated as **BART**, was developed by researchers at Facebook AI Research in 2019: *BART: Denoising Sequence-to-Sequence Pre-training for Natural Language Generation, Translation, and Comprehension, Lewis* and colleagues, `https://arxiv.org/abs/1910.13461`. Recall that in previous sections we argued that GPT utilizes a transformer's decoder structure, whereas BERT utilizes a transformer's encoder structure. Those two models are thus capable of performing different tasks well: GPT's specialty is generating text, whereas BERT performs better on classification tasks. BART can be viewed as a generalization of both GPT and BERT. As the title of this section suggests, BART is able to accomplish both tasks, generating and classifying text. The reason why it can handle both tasks well is that the model comes with a bidirectional encoder as well as a left-to-right autoregressive decoder.

You may wonder how this is different from the original transformer. There are a few changes to the model size along with some minor changes such as activation function choices. However, one of the more interesting changes is that BART works with different model inputs. The original transformer model was designed for language translation so there are two inputs: the text to be translated (source sequence) for the encoder and the translation (target sequence) for the decoder. Additionally, the decoder also receives the encoded source sequence, as illustrated earlier in *Figure 16.6*. However, in BART, the input format was generalized such that it only uses the source sequence as input. BART can perform a wider range of tasks including language translation, where a target sequence is still required to compute the loss and fine-tune the model, but it is not necessary to feed it directly into the decoder.

Now let us take a closer look at the BART's model structure. As previously mentioned, BART is composed of a bidirectional encoder and an autoregressive decoder. Upon receiving a training example as plain text, the input will first be "corrupted" and then encoded by the encoder. These input encodings will then be passed to the decoder, along with the generated tokens. The cross-entropy loss between encoder output and the original text will be calculated and then optimized through the learning process. Think of a transformer where we have two texts in different languages as input to the decoder: the initial text to be translated (source text) and the generated text in the target language. BART can be understood as replacing the former with corrupted text and the latter with the input text itself.

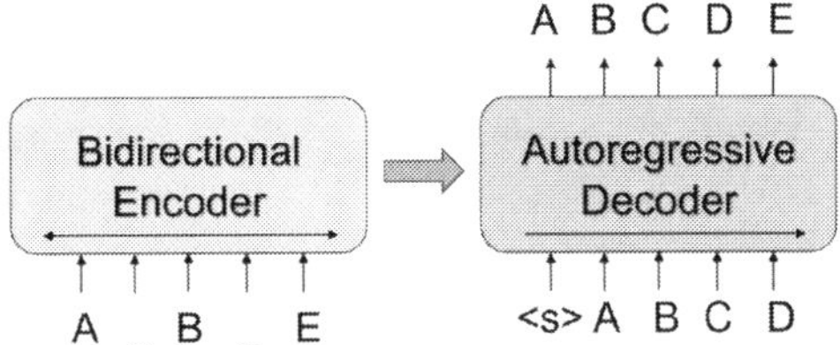

Figure 16.16: BART's model structure

To explain the corruption step in a bit more detail, recall that BERT and GPT are pre-trained by reconstructing masked words: BERT is "filling in the blanks" and GPT is "predicting the next word." These pre-training tasks can also be recognized as reconstructing corrupted sentences because masking words is one way of corrupting a sentence. BART provides the following corruption methods that can be applied to the clean text:

- Token masking
- Token deletion
- Text infilling
- Sentence permutation
- Document rotation

One or more of the techniques listed above can be applied to the same sentence; in the worst scenario, where all the information is contaminated and corrupted, the text becomes useless. Hence, the encoder has limited utility, and with only the decoder module working properly, the model will essentially become more similar to a unidirectional language.

BART can be fine-tuned on a wide range of downstream tasks including (a) sequence classification, (b) token classification, (c) sequence generation, and (d) machine translation. As with BERT, small changes to the inputs need to be made in order to perform different tasks.

In the sequence classification task, an additional token needs to be attached to the input to serve as the generated label token, which is similar to the [CLS] token in BERT. Also, instead of disturbing the input, uncorrupted input is fed into both the encoder and decoder so that the model can make full use of the input.

For token classification, additional tokens become unnecessary, and the model can directly use the generated representation for each token for classification.

Sequence generation in BART differs a bit from GPT because of the existence of the encoder. Instead of generating text from the ground up, sequence generation tasks via BART are more comparable to summarization, where the model is given a corpus of contexts and asked to generate a summary or an abstractive answer to certain questions. To this end, whole input sequences are fed into the encoder while the decoder generates output autoregressively.

Finally, it's natural for BART to perform machine translation considering the similarity between BART and the original transformer. However, instead of following the exact same procedure as for training the original transformer, researchers considered the possibility of incorporating the entire BART model as a pre-trained decoder. To complete the translation model, a new set of randomly initialized parameters is added as a new, additional encoder. Then, the fine-tuning stage can be accomplished in two steps:

1. First, freeze all the parameters except the encoder
2. Then, update all parameters in the model

BART was evaluated on several benchmark datasets for various tasks, and it obtained very competitive results compared to other famous language models such as BERT. In particular, for generation tasks including abstractive question answering, dialogue response, and summarization tasks, BART achieved state-of-the-art results.

Fine-tuning a BERT model in PyTorch

Now that we have introduced and discussed all the necessary concepts and the theory behind the original transformer and popular transformer-based models, it's time to take a look at the more practical part! In this section, you will learn how to fine-tune a BERT model for **sentiment classification** in PyTorch.

Note that although there are many other transformer-based models to choose from, BERT provides a nice balance between model popularity and having a manageable model size so that it can be fine-tuned on a single GPU. Note also that pre-training a BERT from scratch is painful and quite unnecessary considering the availability of the `transformers` Python package provided by Hugging Face, which includes a bunch of pre-trained models that are ready for fine-tuning.

In the following sections, you'll see how to prepare and tokenize the IMDb movie review dataset and fine-tune the distilled BERT model to perform sentiment classification. We deliberately chose sentiment classification as a simple but classic example, though there are many other fascinating applications of language models. Also, by using the familiar IMDb movie review dataset, we can get a good idea of the predictive performance of the BERT model by comparing it to the logistic regression model in *Chapter 8, Applying Machine Learning to Sentiment Analysis,* and the RNN in *Chapter 15, Modeling Sequential Data Using Recurrent Neural Networks.*

Loading the IMDb movie review dataset

In this subsection, we will begin by loading the required packages and the dataset, split into train, validation, and test sets.

For the BERT-related parts of this tutorial, we will mainly use the open-source `transformers` library (`https://huggingface.co/transformers/`) created by Hugging Face, which we installed in the previous section, *Using GPT-2 to generate new text.*

The **DistilBERT** model we are using in this chapter is a lightweight transformer model created by distilling a pre-trained BERT base model. The original uncased BERT base model contains over 110 million parameters while DistilBERT has 40 percent fewer parameters. Also, DistilBERT runs 60 percent faster and still preserves 95 percent of BERT's performance on the GLUE language understanding benchmark.

The following code imports all the packages we will be using in this chapter to prepare the data and fine-tune the DistilBERT model:

```
>>> import gzip
>>> import shutil
>>> import time

>>> import pandas as pd
>>> import requests
>>> import torch
>>> import torch.nn.functional as F
>>> import torchtext

>>> import transformers
>>> from transformers import DistilBertTokenizerFast
>>> from transformers import DistilBertForSequenceClassification
```

Next, we specify some general settings, including the number of epochs we train the network on, the device specification, and the random seed. To reproduce the results, make sure to set a specific random seed such as 123:

```
>>> torch.backends.cudnn.deterministic = True
>>> RANDOM_SEED = 123
>>> torch.manual_seed(RANDOM_SEED)
```

```
>>> DEVICE = torch.device('cuda' if torch.cuda.is_available() else 'cpu')

>>> NUM_EPOCHS = 3
```

We will be working on the IMDb movie review dataset, which you have already seen in *Chapters 8* and *15*. The following code fetches the compressed dataset and unzips it:

```
>>> url = ("https://github.com/rasbt/"
...        "machine-learning-book/raw/"
...        "main/ch08/movie_data.csv.gz")
>>> filename = url.split("/")[-1]

>>> with open(filename, "wb") as f:
...     r = requests.get(url)
...     f.write(r.content)

>>> with gzip.open('movie_data.csv.gz', 'rb') as f_in:
...     with open('movie_data.csv', 'wb') as f_out:
...         shutil.copyfileobj(f_in, f_out)
```

If you have the `movie_data.csv` file from *Chapter 8* still on your hard drive, you can skip this download and unzip procedure.

Next, we load the data into a pandas `DataFrame` and make sure it looks all right:

```
>>> df = pd.read_csv('movie_data.csv')
>>> df.head(3)
```

	review	sentiment
0	In 1974, the teenager Martha Moxley (Maggie Gr...	1
1	OK... so... I really like Kris Kristofferson a...	0
2	***SPOILER*** Do not read this, if you think a...	0

Figure 16.17: The first three rows of the IMDb movie review dataset

The next step is to split the dataset into separate training, validation, and test sets. Here, we use 70 percent of the reviews for the training set, 10 percent for the validation set, and the remaining 20 percent for testing:

```
>>> train_texts = df.iloc[:35000]['review'].values
>>> train_labels = df.iloc[:35000]['sentiment'].values

>>> valid_texts = df.iloc[35000:40000]['review'].values
```

```
>>> valid_labels = df.iloc[35000:40000]['sentiment'].values

>>> test_texts = df.iloc[40000:]['review'].values
>>> test_labels = df.iloc[40000:]['sentiment'].values
```

Tokenizing the dataset

So far, we have obtained the texts and labels for the training, validation, and test sets. Now, we are going to tokenize the texts into individual word tokens using the tokenizer implementation inherited from the pre-trained model class:

```
>>> tokenizer = DistilBertTokenizerFast.from_pretrained(
...     'distilbert-base-uncased'
... )

>>> train_encodings = tokenizer(list(train_texts), truncation=True, padding=True)
>>> valid_encodings = tokenizer(list(valid_texts), truncation=True, padding=True)
>>> test_encodings = tokenizer(list(test_texts), truncation=True, padding=True)
```

Choosing different tokenizers

If you are interested in applying different types of tokenizers, feel free to explore the `tokenizers` package (`https://huggingface.co/docs/tokenizers/python/latest/`), which is also built and maintained by Hugging Face. However, inherited tokenizers maintain the consistency between the pre-trained model and the dataset, which saves us the extra effort of finding the specific tokenizer corresponding to the model. In other words, using an inherited tokenizer is the recommended approach if you want to fine-tune a pre-trained model.

Finally, let's pack everything into a class called `IMDbDataset` and create the corresponding data loaders. Such a self-defined dataset class lets us customize all the related features and functions for our custom movie review dataset in `DataFrame` format:

```
>>> class IMDbDataset(torch.utils.data.Dataset):
...     def __init__(self, encodings, labels):
...         self.encodings = encodings
...         self.labels = labels

>>>     def __getitem__(self, idx):
...         item = {key: torch.tensor(val[idx])
...                 for key, val in self.encodings.items()}
...         item['labels'] = torch.tensor(self.labels[idx])
```

```
...             return item

>>>     def __len__(self):
...         return len(self.labels)


>>> train_dataset = IMDbDataset(train_encodings, train_labels)
>>> valid_dataset = IMDbDataset(valid_encodings, valid_labels)
>>> test_dataset = IMDbDataset(test_encodings, test_labels)

>>> train_loader = torch.utils.data.DataLoader(
...     train_dataset, batch_size=16, shuffle=True)
>>> valid_loader = torch.utils.data.DataLoader(
...     valid_dataset, batch_size=16, shuffle=False)
>>> test_loader = torch.utils.data.DataLoader(
...     test_dataset, batch_size=16, shuffle=False)
```

While the overall data loader setup should be familiar from previous chapters, one noteworthy detail is the `item` variable in the `__getitem__` method. The encodings we produced previously store a lot of information about the tokenized texts. Via the dictionary comprehension that we use to assign the dictionary to the `item` variable, we are only extracting the most relevant information. For instance, the resulting dictionary entries include `input_ids` (unique integers from the vocabulary corresponding to the tokens), `labels` (the class labels), and `attention_mask`. Here, `attention_mask` is a tensor with binary values (0s and 1s) that denotes which tokens the model should attend to. In particular, 0s correspond to tokens used for padding the sequence to equal lengths and are ignored by the model; the 1s correspond to the actual text tokens.

Loading and fine-tuning a pre-trained BERT model

Having taken care of the data preparation, in this subsection, you will see how to load the pre-trained DistilBERT model and fine-tune it using the dataset we just created. The code for loading the pre-trained model is as follows:

```
>>> model = DistilBertForSequenceClassification.from_pretrained(
...     'distilbert-base-uncased')
>>> model.to(DEVICE)
>>> model.train()

>>> optim = torch.optim.Adam(model.parameters(), lr=5e-5)
```

`DistilBertForSequenceClassification` specifies the downstream task we want to fine-tune the model on, which is sequence classification in this case. As mentioned before, `'distilbert-base-uncased'` is a lightweight version of a BERT uncased base model with manageable size and good performance. Note that "uncased" means that the model does not distinguish between upper- and lower-case letters.

Using other pre-trained transformers

The *transformers* package also provides many other pre-trained models and various downstream tasks for fine-tuning. Check them out at `https://huggingface.co/transformers/`.

Now, it's time to train the model. We can break this up into two parts. First, we need to define an accuracy function to evaluate the model performance. Note that this accuracy function computes the conventional classification accuracy. Why is it so verbose? Here, we are loading the dataset batch by batch to work around RAM or GPU memory (VRAM) limitations when working with a large deep learning model:

```
>>> def compute_accuracy(model, data_loader, device):
...         with torch.no_grad():
...             correct_pred, num_examples = 0, 0
...             for batch_idx, batch in enumerate(data_loader):
...                 ### Prepare data
...                 input_ids = batch['input_ids'].to(device)
...                 attention_mask = \
...                     batch['attention_mask'].to(device)
...                 labels = batch['labels'].to(device)

...                 outputs = model(input_ids,
...                    attention_mask=attention_mask)
...                 logits = outputs['logits']
...                 predicted_labels = torch.argmax(logits, 1)
...                 num_examples += labels.size(0)
...                 correct_pred += \
...                     (predicted_labels == labels).sum()
...         return correct_pred.float()/num_examples * 100
```

In the `compute_accuracy` function, we load a given batch and then obtain the predicted labels from the outputs. While doing this, we keep track of the total number of examples via `num_examples`. Similarly, we keep track of the number of correct predictions via the `correct_pred` variable. Finally, after we iterate over the complete dataset, we compute the accuracy as the proportion of correctly predicted labels.

Overall, via the `compute_accuracy` function, you can already get a glimpse at how we can use the transformer model to obtain the class labels. That is, we feed the model the `input_ids` along with the `attention_mask` information that, here, denotes whether a token is an actual text token or a token for padding the sequences to equal length. The `model` call then returns the outputs, which is a transformer library-specific `SequenceClassifierOutput` object. From this object, we then obtain the logits that we convert into class labels via the `argmax` function as we have done in previous chapters.

Finally, let us get to the main part: the training (or rather, fine-tuning) loop. As you will notice, fine-tuning a model from the *transformers* library is very similar to training a model in pure PyTorch from scratch:

```
>>> start_time = time.time()

>>> for epoch in range(NUM_EPOCHS):

...     model.train()

...     for batch_idx, batch in enumerate(train_loader):

...         ### Prepare data
...         input_ids = batch['input_ids'].to(DEVICE)
...         attention_mask = batch['attention_mask'].to(DEVICE)
...         labels = batch['labels'].to(DEVICE)

...         ### Forward pass
...         outputs = model(input_ids,
...                         attention_mask=attention_mask,
...                         labels=labels)
...         loss, logits = outputs['loss'], outputs['logits']

...         ### Backward pass
...         optim.zero_grad()
...         loss.backward()
...         optim.step()

...         ### Logging
...         if not batch_idx % 250:
...             print(f'Epoch: {epoch+1:04d}/{NUM_EPOCHS:04d}'
...                   f' | Batch'
...                   f'{batch_idx:04d}/'
...                   f'{len(train_loader):04d} | '
...                   f'Loss: {loss:.4f}')

...     model.eval()

...     with torch.set_grad_enabled(False):
...         print(f'Training accuracy: '
...             f'{compute_accuracy(model, train_loader, DEVICE):.2f}%'
```

```
...                 f'\nValid accuracy: '
...                 f'{compute_accuracy(model, valid_loader, DEVICE):.2f}%')

...       print(f'Time elapsed: {(time.time() - start_time)/60:.2f} min')

... print(f'Total Training Time: {(time.time() - start_time)/60:.2f} min')
... print(f'Test accuracy: {compute_accuracy(model, test_loader, DEVICE):.2f}%')
```

The output produced by the preceding code is as follows (note that the code is not fully deterministic, which is why the results you are getting may be slightly different):

```
Epoch: 0001/0003 | Batch 0000/2188 | Loss: 0.6771
Epoch: 0001/0003 | Batch 0250/2188 | Loss: 0.3006
Epoch: 0001/0003 | Batch 0500/2188 | Loss: 0.3678
Epoch: 0001/0003 | Batch 0750/2188 | Loss: 0.1487
Epoch: 0001/0003 | Batch 1000/2188 | Loss: 0.6674
Epoch: 0001/0003 | Batch 1250/2188 | Loss: 0.3264
Epoch: 0001/0003 | Batch 1500/2188 | Loss: 0.4358
Epoch: 0001/0003 | Batch 1750/2188 | Loss: 0.2579
Epoch: 0001/0003 | Batch 2000/2188 | Loss: 0.2474
Training accuracy: 96.32%
Valid accuracy: 92.34%
Time elapsed: 20.67 min
Epoch: 0002/0003 | Batch 0000/2188 | Loss: 0.0850
Epoch: 0002/0003 | Batch 0250/2188 | Loss: 0.3433
Epoch: 0002/0003 | Batch 0500/2188 | Loss: 0.0793
Epoch: 0002/0003 | Batch 0750/2188 | Loss: 0.0061
Epoch: 0002/0003 | Batch 1000/2188 | Loss: 0.1536
Epoch: 0002/0003 | Batch 1250/2188 | Loss: 0.0816
Epoch: 0002/0003 | Batch 1500/2188 | Loss: 0.0786
Epoch: 0002/0003 | Batch 1750/2188 | Loss: 0.1395
Epoch: 0002/0003 | Batch 2000/2188 | Loss: 0.0344
Training accuracy: 98.35%
Valid accuracy: 92.46%
Time elapsed: 41.41 min
Epoch: 0003/0003 | Batch 0000/2188 | Loss: 0.0403
Epoch: 0003/0003 | Batch 0250/2188 | Loss: 0.0036
Epoch: 0003/0003 | Batch 0500/2188 | Loss: 0.0156
Epoch: 0003/0003 | Batch 0750/2188 | Loss: 0.0114
Epoch: 0003/0003 | Batch 1000/2188 | Loss: 0.1227
Epoch: 0003/0003 | Batch 1250/2188 | Loss: 0.0125
```

```
Epoch: 0003/0003 | Batch 1500/2188 | Loss: 0.0074
Epoch: 0003/0003 | Batch 1750/2188 | Loss: 0.0202
Epoch: 0003/0003 | Batch 2000/2188 | Loss: 0.0746
Training accuracy: 99.08%
Valid accuracy: 91.84%
Time elapsed: 62.15 min
Total Training Time: 62.15 min
Test accuracy: 92.50%
```

In this code, we iterate over multiple epochs. In each epoch we perform the following steps:

1. Load the input into the device we are working on (GPU or CPU)
2. Compute the model output and loss
3. Adjust the weight parameters by backpropagating the loss
4. Evaluate the model performance on both the training and validation set

Note that the training time may vary on different devices. After three epochs, accuracy on the test dataset reaches around 93 percent, which is a substantial improvement compared to the 85 percent test accuracy that the RNN achieved in *Chapter 15*.

Fine-tuning a transformer more conveniently using the Trainer API

In the previous subsection, we implemented the training loop in PyTorch manually to illustrate that fine-tuning a transformer model is really not that much different from training an RNN or CNN model from scratch. However, note that the `transformers` library contains several nice extra features for additional convenience, like the Trainer API, which we will introduce in this subsection.

The Trainer API provided by Hugging Face is optimized for transformer models with a wide range of training options and various built-in features. When using the Trainer API, we can skip the effort of writing training loops on our own, and training or fine-tuning a transformer model is as simple as a function (or method) call. Let's see how this works in practice.

After loading the pre-trained model via

```
>>> model = DistilBertForSequenceClassification.from_pretrained(
...     'distilbert-base-uncased')
>>> model.to(DEVICE)
>>> model.train();
```

The training loop from the previous section can then be replaced by the following code:

```
>>> optim = torch.optim.Adam(model.parameters(), lr=5e-5)

>>> from transformers import Trainer, TrainingArguments
```

```
>>> training_args = TrainingArguments(
...     output_dir='./results',
...     num_train_epochs=3,
...     per_device_train_batch_size=16,
...     per_device_eval_batch_size=16,
...     logging_dir='./logs',
...     logging_steps=10,
... )

>>> trainer = Trainer(
...    model=model,
...    args=training_args,
...    train_dataset=train_dataset,
...    optimizers=(optim, None) # optim and learning rate scheduler
... )
```

In the preceding code snippets, we first defined the training arguments, which are relatively self-explanatory settings regarding the input and output locations, number of epochs, and batch sizes. We tried to keep the settings as simple as possible; however, there are many additional settings available, and we recommend consulting the `TrainingArguments` documentation page for additional details: `https://huggingface.co/transformers/main_classes/trainer.html#trainingarguments`.

We then passed these `TrainingArguments` settings to the `Trainer` class to instantiate a new `trainer` object. After initiating the `trainer` with the settings, the model to be fine-tuned, and the training and evaluation sets, we can train the model by calling the `trainer.train()` method (we will use this method further shortly). That's it, using the Trainer API is as simple as shown in the preceding code, and no further boilerplate code is required.

However, you may have noticed that the test dataset was not involved in these code snippets, and we haven't specified any evaluation metrics in this subsection. This is because the Trainer API only shows the training loss and does not provide model evaluation along the training process by default. There are two ways to display the final model performance, which we will illustrate next.

The first method for evaluating the final model is to define an evaluation function as the `compute_metrics` argument for another `Trainer` instance. The `compute_metrics` function operates on the models' test predictions as logits (which is the default output of the model) and the test labels. To instantiate this function, we recommend installing Hugging Face's `datasets` library via `pip install datasets` and use it as follows:

```
>>> from datasets import load_metric
>>> import numpy as np

>>> metric = load_metric("accuracy")

>>> def compute_metrics(eval_pred):
```

```
...         logits, labels = eval_pred
...         # note: logits are a numpy array, not a pytorch tensor
...         predictions = np.argmax(logits, axis=-1)
...         return metric.compute(
...             predictions=predictions, references=labels)
```

The updated `Trainer` instantiation (now including `compute_metrics`) is then as follows:

```
>>> trainer=Trainer(
...     model=model,
...     args=training_args,
...     train_dataset=train_dataset,
...     eval_dataset=test_dataset,
...     compute_metrics=compute_metrics,
...     optimizers=(optim, None) # optim and learning rate scheduler
... )
```

Now, let's train the model (again, note that the code is not fully deterministic, which is why you might be getting slightly different results):

```
>>> start_time = time.time()
>>> trainer.train()

***** Running training *****
  Num examples = 35000
  Num Epochs = 3
  Instantaneous batch size per device = 16
  Total train batch size (w. parallel, distributed & accumulation) = 16
  Gradient Accumulation steps = 1
  Total optimization steps = 6564

Step  Training Loss
10    0.705800
20    0.684100
30    0.681500
40    0.591600
50    0.328600
60    0.478300
...


>>> print(f'Total Training Time: '
...       f'{(time.time() - start_time)/60:.2f} min')
Total Training Time: 45.36 min
```

After the training has completed, which can take up to an hour depending on your GPU, we can call `trainer.evaluate()` to obtain the model performance on the test set:

```
>>> print(trainer.evaluate())

***** Running Evaluation *****
Num examples = 10000
Batch size = 16
100%|                                        | 625/625 [10:59<00:00,  1.06s/
it]
{'eval_loss': 0.30534815788269043,
 'eval_accuracy': 0.9327,
 'eval_runtime': 87.1161,
 'eval_samples_per_second': 114.789,
 'eval_steps_per_second': 7.174,
 'epoch': 3.0}
```

As we can see, the evaluation accuracy is around 94 percent, similar to our own previously used PyTorch training loop. (Note that we have skipped the training step, because the `model` is already fine-tuned after the previous `trainer.train()` call.) There is a small discrepancy between our manual training approach and using the `Trainer` class, because the `Trainer` class uses some different and some additional settings.

The second method we could employ to compute the final test set accuracy is re-using our `compute_accuracy` function that we defined in the previous section. We can directly evaluate the performance of the fine-tuned model on the test dataset by running the following code:

```
>>> model.eval()
>>> model.to(DEVICE)

>>> print(f'Test accuracy: {compute_accuracy(model, test_loader,
DEVICE):.2f}%')

Test accuracy: 93.27%
```

In fact, if you want to check the model's performance regularly during training, you can require the trainer to print the model evaluation after each epoch by defining the training arguments as follows:

```
>>> from transformers import TrainingArguments

>>> training_args = TrainingArguments("test_trainer",
...     evaluation_strategy="epoch", ...)
```

However, if you are planning to change or optimize hyperparameters and repeat the fine-tuning procedure several times, we recommend using the validation set for this purpose, in order to keep the test set independent. We can achieve this by instantiating the `Trainer` using `valid_dataset`:

```
>>> trainer=Trainer(
...     model=model,
...     args=training_args,
...     train_dataset=train_dataset,
...     eval_dataset=valid_dataset,
...     compute_metrics=compute_metrics,
... )
```

In this section, we saw how we can fine-tune a BERT model for classification. This is different from using other deep learning architectures like RNNs, which we usually train from scratch. However, unless we are doing research and are trying to develop new transformer architectures—a very expensive endeavor—pre-training transformer models is not necessary. Since transformer models are trained on general, unlabeled dataset resources, pre-training them ourselves may not be a good use of our time and resources; fine-tuning is the way to go.

Summary

In this chapter, we introduced a whole new model architecture for natural language processing, the transformer architecture. The transformer architecture is built on a concept called self-attention, and we started introducing this concept step by step. First, we looked at an RNN outfitted with attention in order to improve its translation capabilities for long sentences. Then, we gently introduced the concept of self-attention and explained how it is used in the multi-head attention module within the transformer.

Many different derivatives of the transformer architecture have emerged and evolved since the original transformer was published in 2017. In this chapter, we focused on a selection of some of the most popular ones: the GPT model family, BERT, and BART. GPT is a unidirectional model that is particularly good at generating new text. BERT takes a bidirectional approach, which is better suited for other types of tasks, for example, classification. Lastly, BART combines both the bidirectional encoder from BERT and the unidirectional decoder from GPT. Interested readers can find out about additional transformer-based architectures via the following two survey articles:

1. *Pre-trained Models for Natural Language Processing: A Survey* by *Qiu* and colleagues, 2020. Available at `https://arxiv.org/abs/2003.08271`
2. *AMMUS : A Survey of Transformer-based Pretrained Models in Natural Language Processing* by *Kayan* and colleagues, 2021. Available at `https://arxiv.org/abs/2108.05542`

Transformer models are generally more data hungry than RNNs and require large amounts of data for pre-training. The pre-training leverages large amounts of unlabeled data to build a general language model that can then be specialized to specific tasks by fine-tuning it on smaller labeled datasets.

To see how this works in practice, we downloaded a pre-trained BERT model from the Hugging Face `transformers` library and fine-tuned it for sentiment classification on the IMDb movie review dataset.

In the next chapter, we will discuss generative adversarial networks. As the name suggests, generative adversarial networks are models that can be used for generating new data, similar to the GPT models we discussed in this chapter. However, we are now leaving the natural language modeling topic behind us and will look at generative adversarial networks in the context of computer vision and generating new images, the task that these networks were originally designed for.

Join our book's Discord space

Join our Discord community to meet like-minded people and learn alongside more than 2000 members at:
`https://packt.link/MLwPyTorch`

17

Generative Adversarial Networks for Synthesizing New Data

In the previous chapter, we focused on **recurrent neural networks** for modeling sequences. In this chapter, we will explore **generative adversarial networks** (**GANs**) and see their application in synthesizing new data samples. GANs are considered to be one of the most important breakthroughs in deep learning, allowing computers to generate new data (such as new images).

In this chapter, we will cover the following topics:

- Introducing generative models for synthesizing new data
- Autoencoders, variational autoencoders, and their relationship to GANs
- Understanding the building blocks of GANs
- Implementing a simple GAN model to generate handwritten digits
- Understanding transposed convolution and batch normalization
- Improving GANs: deep convolutional GANs and GANs using the Wasserstein distance

Introducing generative adversarial networks

Let's first look at the foundations of GAN models. The overall objective of a GAN is to synthesize new data that has the same distribution as its training dataset. Therefore, GANs, in their original form, are considered to be in the unsupervised learning category of machine learning tasks, since no labeled data is required. It is worth noting, however, that extensions made to the original GAN can lie in both the semi-supervised and supervised domains.

The general GAN concept was first proposed in 2014 by Ian Goodfellow and his colleagues as a method for synthesizing new images using deep **neural networks** (**NNs**) (*Generative Adversarial Nets*, in *Advances in Neural Information Processing Systems* by *I. Goodfellow, J. Pouget-Abadie, M. Mirza, B. Xu, D. Warde-Farley, S. Ozair, A. Courville*, and *Y. Bengio*, pp. 2672-2680, 2014). While the initial GAN architecture proposed in this paper was based on fully connected layers, similar to multilayer perceptron architectures, and trained to generate low-resolution MNIST-like handwritten digits, it served more as a proof of concept to demonstrate the feasibility of this new approach.

However, since its introduction, the original authors, as well as many other researchers, have proposed numerous improvements and various applications in different fields of engineering and science; for example, in computer vision, GANs are used for image-to-image translation (learning how to map an input image to an output image), image super-resolution (making a high-resolution image from a low-resolution version), image inpainting (learning how to reconstruct the missing parts of an image), and many more applications. For instance, recent advances in GAN research have led to models that are able to generate new, high-resolution face images. Examples of such high-resolution images can be found on `https://www.thispersondoesnotexist.com/`, which showcases synthetic face images generated by a GAN.

Starting with autoencoders

Before we discuss how GANs work, we will first start with autoencoders, which can compress and decompress training data. While standard autoencoders cannot generate new data, understanding their function will help you to navigate GANs in the next section.

Autoencoders are composed of two networks concatenated together: an **encoder** network and a **decoder** network. The encoder network receives a *d*-dimensional input feature vector associated with example x (that is, $\boldsymbol{x} \in R^d$) and encodes it into a *p*-dimensional vector, z (that is, $\boldsymbol{z} \in R^p$). In other words, the role of the encoder is to learn how to model the function $z = f(x)$. The encoded vector, z, is also called the **latent vector**, or the latent feature representation. Typically, the dimensionality of the latent vector is less than that of the input examples; in other words, $p < d$. Hence, we can say that the encoder acts as a data compression function. Then, the decoder decompresses $\hat{x}$ from the lower-dimensional latent vector, z, where we can think of the decoder as a function, $\hat{x} = g(\boldsymbol{z})$. A simple autoencoder architecture is shown in *Figure 17.1*, where the encoder and decoder parts consist of only one fully connected layer each:

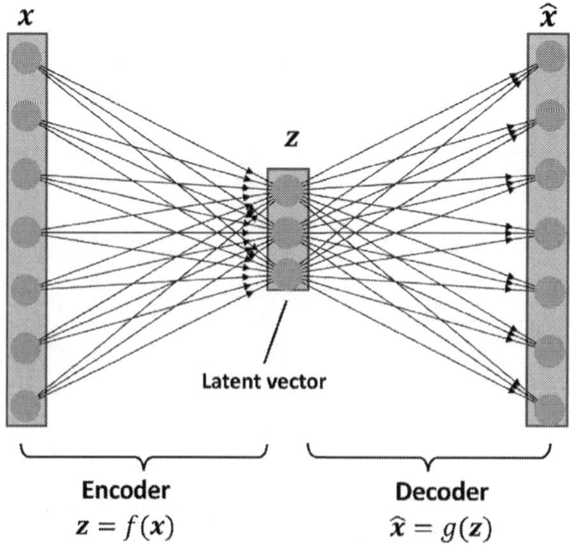

Figure 17.1: The architecture of an autoencoder

The connection between autoencoders and dimensionality reduction

In *Chapter 5, Compressing Data via Dimensionality Reduction*, you learned about dimensionality reduction techniques, such as **principal component analysis** (PCA) and **linear discriminant analysis** (LDA). Autoencoders can be used as a dimensionality reduction technique as well. In fact, when there is no nonlinearity in either of the two subnetworks (encoder and decoder), then the autoencoder approach is *almost identical* to PCA.

In this case, if we assume the weights of a single-layer encoder (no hidden layer and no nonlinear activation function) are denoted by the matrix *U*, then the encoder models $\boldsymbol{z} = \boldsymbol{U}^T\boldsymbol{x}$. Similarly, a single-layer linear decoder models $\hat{\boldsymbol{x}} = \boldsymbol{U}\boldsymbol{z}$. Putting these two components together, we have $\hat{\boldsymbol{x}} = \boldsymbol{U}\boldsymbol{U}^T\boldsymbol{x}$. This is exactly what PCA does, with the exception that PCA has an additional orthonormal constraint: $\boldsymbol{U}\boldsymbol{U}^T = \boldsymbol{I}_{n \times n}$.

While *Figure 17.1* depicts an autoencoder without hidden layers within the encoder and decoder, we can, of course, add multiple hidden layers with nonlinearities (as in a multilayer NN) to construct a deep autoencoder that can learn more effective data compression and reconstruction functions. Also, note that the autoencoder mentioned in this section uses fully connected layers. When we work with images, however, we can replace the fully connected layers with convolutional layers, as you learned in *Chapter 14, Classifying Images with Deep Convolutional Neural Networks*.

Other types of autoencoders based on the size of latent space

As previously mentioned, the dimensionality of an autoencoder's latent space is typically lower than the dimensionality of the inputs ($p < d$), which makes autoencoders suitable for dimensionality reduction. For this reason, the latent vector is also often referred to as the "bottleneck," and this particular configuration of an autoencoder is also called **undercomplete**. However, there is a different category of autoencoders, called **overcomplete**, where the dimensionality of the latent vector, *z*, is, in fact, greater than the dimensionality of the input examples ($p > d$).

When training an overcomplete autoencoder, there is a trivial solution where the encoder and the decoder can simply learn to copy (memorize) the input features to their output layer. Obviously, this solution is not very useful. However, with some modifications to the training procedure, overcomplete autoencoders can be used for *noise reduction*.

In this case, during training, random noise, $\boldsymbol{\epsilon}$, is added to the input examples and the network learns to reconstruct the clean example, *x*, from the noisy signal, $\boldsymbol{x} + \boldsymbol{\epsilon}$. Then, at evaluation time, we provide the new examples that are naturally noisy (that is, noise is already present such that no additional artificial noise, $\boldsymbol{\epsilon}$, is added) in order to remove the existing noise from these examples. This particular autoencoder architecture and training method is referred to as a *denoising autoencoder*.

If you are interested, you can learn more about it in the research article *Stacked denoising autoencoders: Learning useful representations in a deep network with a local denoising criterion* by *Pascal Vincent* and colleagues, 2010 (`http://www.jmlr.org/papers/v11/vincent10a.html`).

Generative models for synthesizing new data

Autoencoders are deterministic models, which means that after an autoencoder is trained, given an input, x, it will be able to reconstruct the input from its compressed version in a lower-dimensional space. Therefore, it cannot generate new data beyond reconstructing its input through the transformation of the compressed representation.

A generative model, on the other hand, can generate a new example, $\tilde{x}$, from a random vector, z (corresponding to the latent representation). A schematic representation of a generative model is shown in the following figure. The random vector, z, comes from a distribution with fully known characteristics, so we can easily sample from such a distribution. For example, each element of z may come from the uniform distribution in the range [-1, 1] (for which we write $z_i \sim Uniform(-1, 1)$) or from a standard normal distribution (in which case, we write $z_i \sim Normal(\mu = 0, \sigma^2 = 1)$):

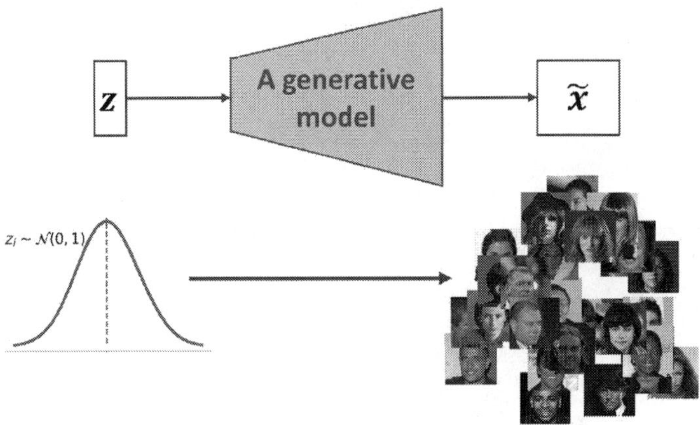

Figure 17.2: A generative model

As we have shifted our attention from autoencoders to generative models, you may have noticed that the decoder component of an autoencoder has some similarities with a generative model. In particular, they both receive a latent vector, z, as input and return an output in the same space as x. (For the autoencoder, $\hat{x}$ is the reconstruction of an input, x, and for the generative model, $\tilde{x}$ is a synthesized sample.)

However, the major difference between the two is that we do not know the distribution of z in the autoencoder, while in a generative model, the distribution of z is fully characterizable. It is possible to generalize an autoencoder into a generative model, though. One approach is the **variational autoencoder** (VAE).

In a VAE receiving an input example, x, the encoder network is modified in such a way that it computes two moments of the distribution of the latent vector: the mean, $\boldsymbol{\mu}$, and variance, $\boldsymbol{\sigma}^2$. During the training of a VAE, the network is forced to match these moments with those of a standard normal distribution (that is, zero mean and unit variance). Then, after the VAE model is trained, the encoder is discarded, and we can use the decoder network to generate new examples, $\tilde{x}$, by feeding random z vectors from the "learned" Gaussian distribution.

Besides VAEs, there are other types of generative models, for example, *autoregressive models* and *normalizing flow models*. However, in this chapter, we are only going to focus on GAN models, which are among the most recent and most popular types of generative models in deep learning.

What is a generative model?

Note that generative models are traditionally defined as algorithms that model data input distributions, $p(x)$, or the joint distributions of the input data and associated targets, $p(x, y)$. By definition, these models are also capable of sampling from some feature, x_i, conditioned on another feature, x_j, which is known as **conditional inference**. In the context of deep learning, however, the term **generative model** is typically used to refer to models that generate realistic-looking data. This means that we can sample from input distributions, $p(x)$, but we are not necessarily able to perform conditional inference.

Generating new samples with GANs

To understand what GANs do in a nutshell, let's first assume we have a network that receives a random vector, $\boldsymbol{z}$, sampled from a known distribution, and generates an output image, $\boldsymbol{x}$. We will call this network **generator** (G) and use the notation $\tilde{\boldsymbol{x}} = G(\boldsymbol{z})$ to refer to the generated output. Assume our goal is to generate some images, for example, face images, images of buildings, images of animals, or even handwritten digits such as MNIST.

As always, we will initialize this network with random weights. Therefore, the first output images, before these weights are adjusted, will look like white noise. Now, imagine there is a function that can assess the quality of images (let's call it an *assessor function*).

If such a function exists, we can use the feedback from that function to tell our generator network how to adjust its weights to improve the quality of the generated images. This way, we can train the generator based on the feedback from that assessor function, such that the generator learns to improve its output toward producing realistic-looking images.

While an assessor function, as described in the previous paragraph, would make the image generation task very easy, the question is whether such a universal function to assess the quality of images exists and, if so, how it is defined. Obviously, as humans, we can easily assess the quality of output images when we observe the outputs of the network; although, we cannot (yet) backpropagate the result from our brain to the network. Now, if our brain can assess the quality of synthesized images, can we design an NN model to do the same thing? In fact, that's the general idea of a GAN.

As shown in *Figure 17.3*, a GAN model consists of an additional NN called **discriminator** (*D*), which is a classifier that learns to detect a synthesized image, $\tilde{x}$, from a real image, x:

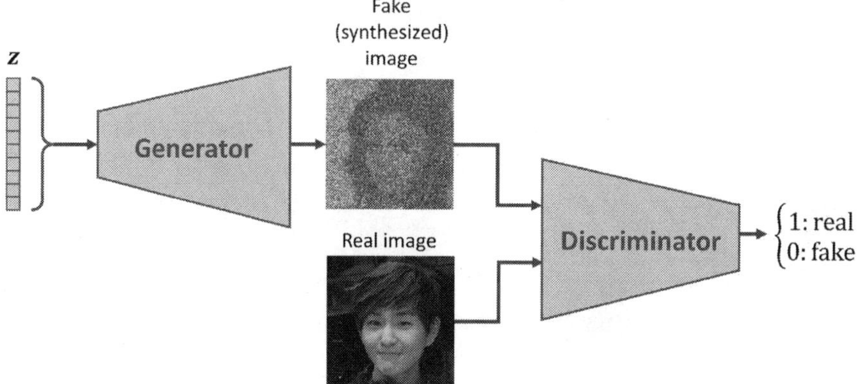

Figure 17.3: The discriminator distinguishes between the real image and the one created by the generator

In a GAN model, the two networks, generator and discriminator, are trained together. At first, after initializing the model weights, the generator creates images that do not look realistic. Similarly, the discriminator does a poor job of distinguishing between real images and images synthesized by the generator. But over time (that is, through training), both networks become better as they interact with each other. In fact, the two networks play an adversarial game, where the generator learns to improve its output to be able to fool the discriminator. At the same time, the discriminator becomes better at detecting the synthesized images.

Understanding the loss functions of the generator and discriminator networks in a GAN model

The objective function of GANs, as described in the original paper *Generative Adversarial Nets* by *I. Goodfellow* and colleagues (`https://papers.nips.cc/paper/5423-generative-adversarial-nets.pdf`), is as follows:

$$V\left(\theta^{(D)}, \theta^{(G)}\right) = E_{x \sim p_{data}(x)}[\log D(\boldsymbol{x})] + E_{z \sim p_z(z)}\left[\log\left(1 - D\left(G(\boldsymbol{z})\right)\right)\right]$$

Here, $V\left(\theta^{(D)}, \theta^{(G)}\right)$ is called the **value function**, which can be interpreted as a payoff: we want to maximize its value with respect to the discriminator (*D*), while minimizing its value with respect to the generator (*G*), that is, $\min_G \max_D V\left(\theta^{(D)}, \theta^{(G)}\right)$. *D*(*x*) is the probability that indicates whether the input example, x, is real or fake (that is, generated). The expression $E_{x \sim p_{data}(x)}[\log D(\boldsymbol{x})]$ refers to the expected value of the quantity in brackets with respect to the examples from the data distribution (distribution of the real examples); $E_{z \sim p_z(z)}\left[\log\left(1 - D\left(G(\boldsymbol{z})\right)\right)\right]$ refers to the expected value of the quantity with respect to the distribution of the input, z, vectors.

One training step of a GAN model with such a value function requires two optimization steps: (1) maximizing the payoff for the discriminator and (2) minimizing the payoff for the generator. A practical way of training GANs is to alternate between these two optimization steps: (1) fix (freeze) the parameters of one network and optimize the weights of the other one, and (2) fix the second network and optimize the first one. This process should be repeated at each training iteration. Let's assume that the generator network is fixed, and we want to optimize the discriminator. Both terms in the value function $V\left(\theta^{(D)}, \theta^{(G)}\right)$ contribute to optimizing the discriminator, where the first term corresponds to the loss associated with the real examples, and the second term is the loss for the fake examples. Therefore, when G is fixed, our objective is to *maximize* $V\left(\theta^{(D)}, \theta^{(G)}\right)$, which means making the discriminator better at distinguishing between real and generated images.

After optimizing the discriminator using the loss terms for real and fake samples, we then fix the discriminator and optimize the generator. In this case, only the second term in $V\left(\theta^{(D)}, \theta^{(G)}\right)$ contributes to the gradients of the generator. As a result, when *D* is fixed, our objective is to *minimize* $V\left(\theta^{(D)}, \theta^{(G)}\right)$, which can be written as $\min_G E_{\boldsymbol{z}\sim p_z(\boldsymbol{z})}\left[\log\left(1 - D\left(G(\boldsymbol{z})\right)\right)\right]$. As was mentioned in the original GAN paper by Goodfellow and colleagues, this function, $\log\left(1 - D\left(G(\boldsymbol{z})\right)\right)$, suffers from vanishing gradients in the early training stages. The reason for this is that the outputs, *G*(*z*), early in the learning process, look nothing like real examples, and therefore *D*(*G*(*z*)) will be close to zero with high confidence. This phenomenon is called **saturation.** To resolve this issue, we can reformulate the minimization objective, $\min_G E_{\boldsymbol{z}\sim p_z(\boldsymbol{z})}\left[\log\left(1 - D\left(G(\boldsymbol{z})\right)\right)\right]$, by rewriting it as $\max_G E_{\boldsymbol{z}\sim p_z(\boldsymbol{z})}\left[\log\left(D\left(G(\boldsymbol{z})\right)\right)\right]$.

This replacement means that for training the generator, we can swap the labels of real and fake examples and carry out a regular function minimization. In other words, even though the examples synthesized by the generator are fake and are therefore labeled 0, we can flip the labels by assigning label 1 to these examples and *minimize* the binary cross-entropy loss with these new labels instead of maximizing $\max_G E_{\boldsymbol{z}\sim p_z(\boldsymbol{z})}\left[\log\left(D\left(G(\boldsymbol{z})\right)\right)\right]$.

Now that we have covered the general optimization procedure for training GAN models, let's explore the various data labels that we can use when training GANs. Given that the discriminator is a binary classifier (the class labels are 0 and 1 for fake and real images, respectively), we can use the binary cross-entropy loss function. Therefore, we can determine the ground truth labels for the discriminator loss as follows:

$$\begin{matrix}\text{Ground truth labels} \\ \text{for the discriminator}\end{matrix} = \begin{cases} 1: & \text{for real images, i.e., } \boldsymbol{x} \\ 0: & \text{for outputs of } G\text{, i.e., } G(\boldsymbol{z}) \end{cases}$$

What about the labels to train the generator? As we want the generator to synthesize realistic images, we want to penalize the generator when its outputs are not classified as real by the discriminator. This means that we will assume the ground truth labels for the outputs of the generator to be 1 when computing the loss function for the generator.

Putting all of this together, the following figure displays the individual steps in a simple GAN model:

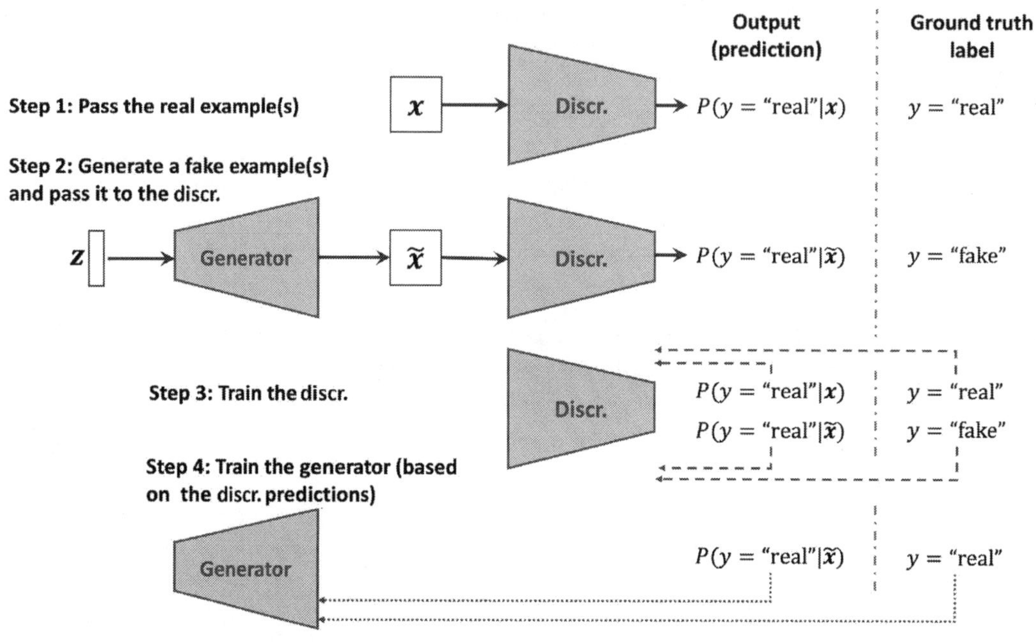

Figure 17.4: The steps in building a GAN model

In the following section, we will implement a GAN from scratch to generate new handwritten digits.

Implementing a GAN from scratch

In this section, we will cover how to implement and train a GAN model to generate new images such as MNIST digits. Since the training on a normal **central processing unit** (CPU) may take a long time, in the following subsection, we will cover how to set up the Google Colab environment, which will allow us to run the computations on **graphics processing units** (GPUs).

Training GAN models on Google Colab

Some of the code examples in this chapter may require extensive computational resources that go beyond a conventional laptop or a workstation without a GPU. If you already have an NVIDIA GPU-enabled computing machine available, with CUDA and cuDNN libraries installed, you can use that to speed up the computations.

However, since many of us do not have access to high-performance computing resources, we will use the Google Colaboratory environment (often referred to as Google Colab), which is a free cloud computing service (available in most countries).

Google Colab provides Jupyter Notebook instances that run on the cloud; the notebooks can be saved on Google Drive or GitHub. While the platform provides various different computing resources, such as CPUs, GPUs, and even **tensor processing units** (**TPUs**), it is important to highlight that the execution time is currently limited to 12 hours. Therefore, any notebook running longer than 12 hours will be interrupted.

The code blocks in this chapter will need a maximum computing time of two to three hours, so this will not be an issue. However, if you decide to use Google Colab for other projects that take longer than 12 hours, be sure to use checkpointing and save intermediate checkpoints.

Jupyter Notebook

Jupyter Notebook is a graphical user interface (GUI) for running code interactively and interleaving it with text documentation and figures. Due to its versatility and ease of use, it has become one of the most popular tools in data science.

For more information about the general Jupyter Notebook GUI, please view the official documentation at `https://jupyter-notebook.readthedocs.io/en/stable/`. All the code in this book is also available in the form of Jupyter notebooks, and a short introduction can be found in the code directory of the first chapter.

Lastly, we highly recommend *Adam Rule* et al.'s article *Ten simple rules for writing and sharing computational analyses in Jupyter Notebooks* on using Jupyter Notebook effectively in scientific research projects, which is freely available at `https://journals.plos.org/ploscompbiol/article?id=10.1371/journal.pcbi.1007007`.

Accessing Google Colab is very straightforward. You can visit `https://colab.research.google.com`, which automatically takes you to a prompt window where you can see your existing Jupyter notebooks. From this prompt window, click the **Google Drive** tab, as shown in *Figure 17.5*. This is where you will save the notebook on your Google Drive.

Then, to create a new notebook, click on the **New notebook** link at the bottom of the prompt window:

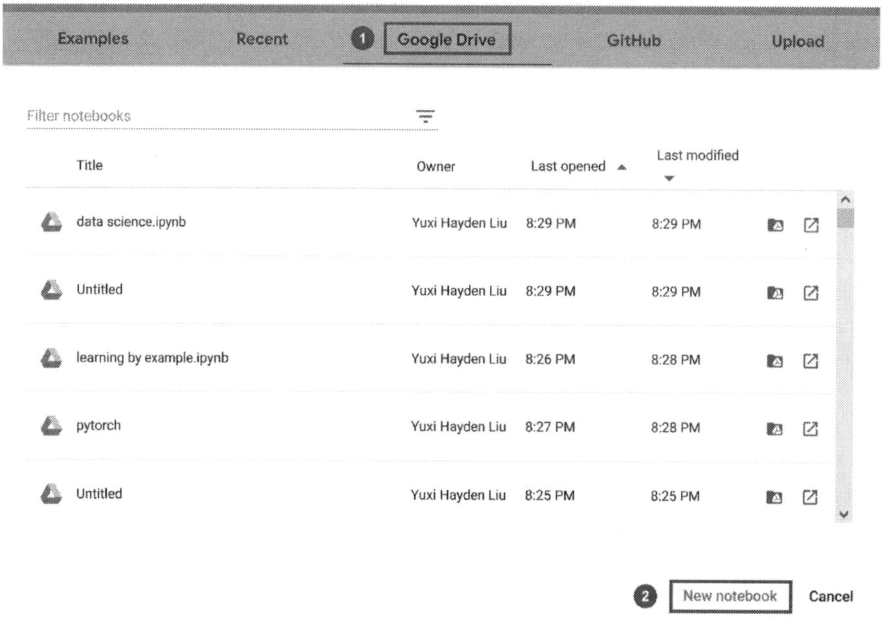

Figure 17.5: Creating a new Python notebook in Google Colab

This will create and open a new notebook for you. All the code examples you write in this notebook will be automatically saved, and you can later access the notebook from your Google Drive in a directory called **Colab Notebooks.**

In the next step, we want to utilize GPUs to run the code examples in this notebook. To do this, from the **Runtime** option in the menu bar of this notebook, click on **Change runtime type** and select **GPU**, as shown in *Figure 17.6*:

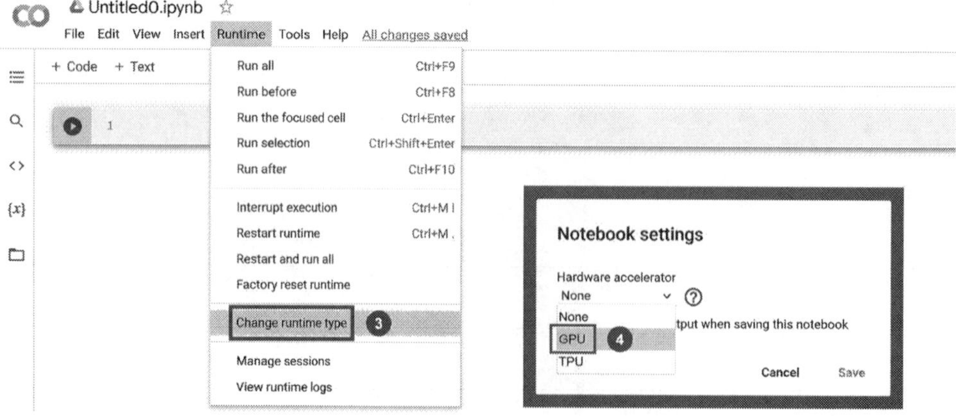

Figure 17.6: Utilizing GPUs in Google Colab

In the last step, we just need to install the Python packages that we will need for this chapter. The Colab Notebooks environment already comes with certain packages, such as NumPy, SciPy, and the latest stable version of PyTorch. At the time of writing, the latest stable version on Google Colab is PyTorch 1.9.

Now, we can test the installation and verify that the GPU is available using the following code:

```
>>> import torch
>>> print(torch.__version__)
1.9.0+cu111
>>> print("GPU Available:", torch.cuda.is_available())
GPU Available: True
>>> if torch.cuda.is_available():
...     device = torch.device("cuda:0")
... else:
...     device = "cpu"
>>> print(device)
cuda:0
```

Furthermore, if you want to save the model to your personal Google Drive, or transfer or upload other files, you need to mount Google Drive. To do this, execute the following in a new cell of the notebook:

```
>>> from google.colab import drive
>>> drive.mount('/content/drive/')
```

This will provide a link to authenticate the Colab Notebook accessing your Google Drive. After following the instructions for authentication, it will provide an authentication code that you need to copy and paste into the designated input field below the cell you have just executed. Then, your Google Drive will be mounted and available at `/content/drive/My Drive`. Alternatively, you can mount it via the GUI interface as highlighted in *Figure 17.7*:

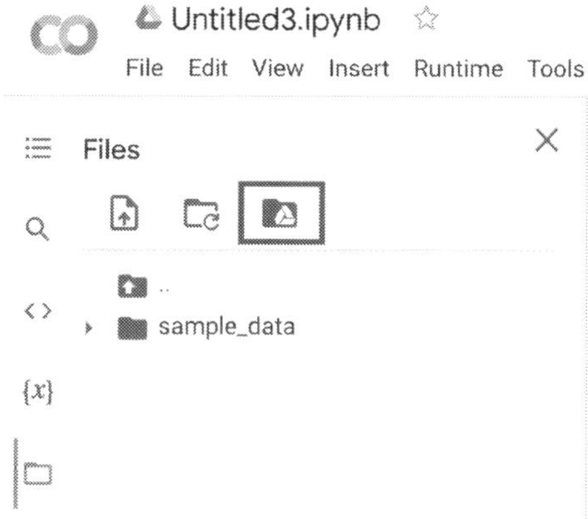

Figure 17.7: Mounting your Google Drive

Implementing the generator and the discriminator networks

We will start the implementation of our first GAN model with a generator and a discriminator as two fully connected networks with one or more hidden layers, as shown in *Figure 17.8*:

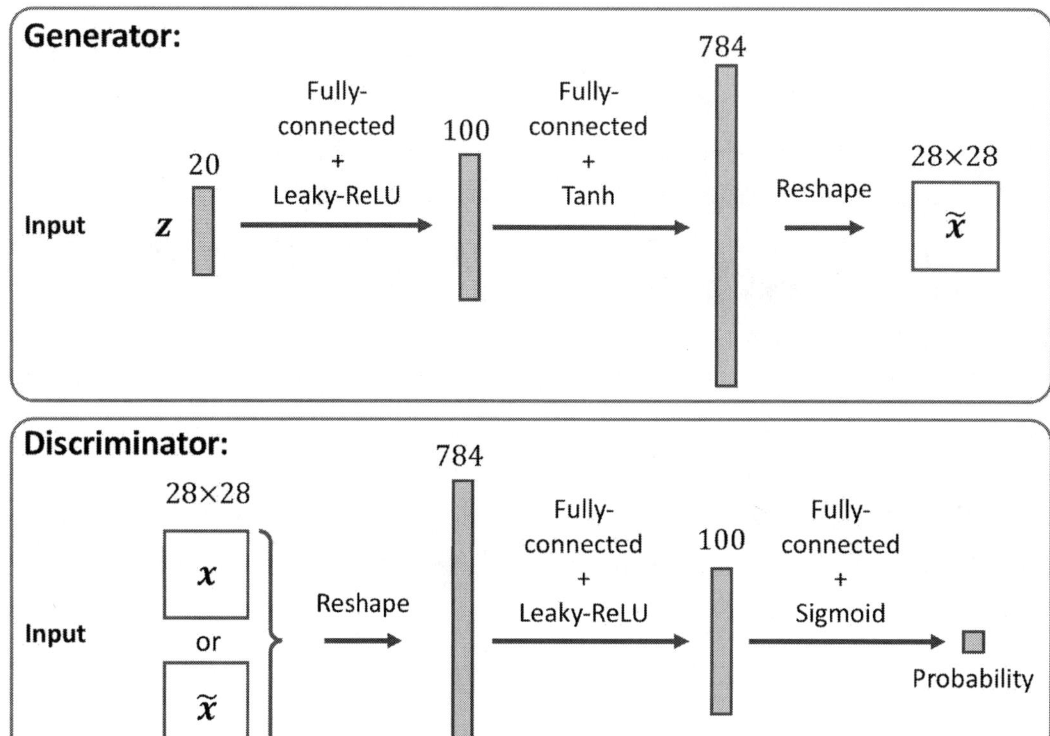

Figure 17.8: A GAN model with a generator and discriminator as two fully connected networks

Figure 17.8 depicts the original GAN based on fully connected layers, which we will refer to as a *vanilla GAN*.

In this model, for each hidden layer, we will apply the leaky ReLU activation function. The use of ReLU results in sparse gradients, which may not be suitable when we want to have the gradients for the full range of input values. In the discriminator network, each hidden layer is also followed by a dropout layer. Furthermore, the output layer in the generator uses the hyperbolic tangent (tanh) activation function. (Using tanh activation is recommended for the generator network since it helps with the learning.)

The output layer in the discriminator has no activation function (that is, linear activation) to get the logits. Alternatively, we can use the sigmoid activation function to get probabilities as output.

Leaky rectified linear unit (ReLU) activation function

In *Chapter 12, Parallelizing Neural Network Training with PyTorch,* we covered different nonlinear activation functions that can be used in an NN model. If you recall, the ReLU activation function was defined as $\sigma(z) = \max(0, z)$, which suppresses the negative (preactivation) inputs; that is, negative inputs are set to zero. Consequently, using the ReLU activation function may result in sparse gradients during backpropagation. Sparse gradients are not always detrimental and can even benefit models for classification. However, in certain applications, such as GANs, it can be beneficial to obtain the gradients for the full range of input values, which we can achieve by making a slight modification to the ReLU function such that it outputs small values for negative inputs. This modified version of the ReLU function is also known as **leaky ReLU**. In short, the leaky ReLU activation function permits non-zero gradients for negative inputs as well, and as a result, it makes the networks more expressive overall.

The leaky ReLU activation function is defined as follows:

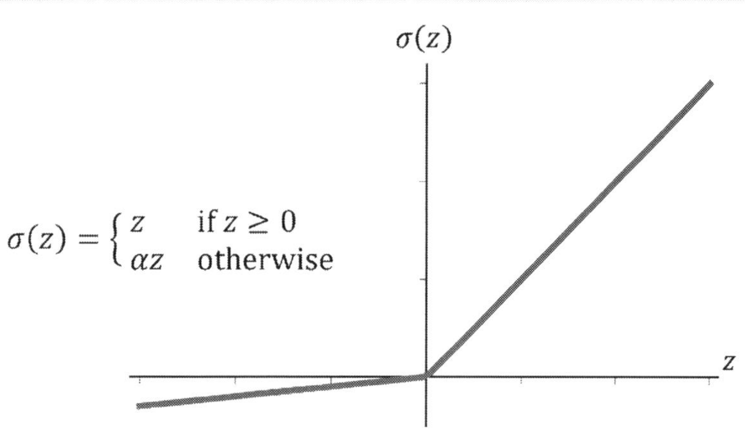

Figure 17.9: The leaky ReLU activation function

Here, α determines the slope for the negative (preactivation) inputs.

We will define two helper functions for each of the two networks, instantiate a model from the PyTorch `nn.Sequential` class, and add the layers as described. The code is as follows:

```
>>> import torch.nn as nn
>>> import numpy as np
>>> import matplotlib.pyplot as plt
>>> ## define a function for the generator:
>>> def make_generator_network(
...         input_size=20,
...         num_hidden_layers=1,
...         num_hidden_units=100,
...         num_output_units=784):
...     model = nn.Sequential()
...     for i in range(num_hidden_layers):
...         model.add_module(f'fc_g{i}',
...                          nn.Linear(input_size, num_hidden_units))
...         model.add_module(f'relu_g{i}', nn.LeakyReLU())
...         input_size = num_hidden_units
...     model.add_module(f'fc_g{num_hidden_layers}',
...                      nn.Linear(input_size, num_output_units))
...     model.add_module('tanh_g', nn.Tanh())
...     return model
>>>
>>> ## define a function for the discriminator:
>>> def make_discriminator_network(
...         input_size,
...         num_hidden_layers=1,
...         num_hidden_units=100,
...         num_output_units=1):
...     model = nn.Sequential()
...     for i in range(num_hidden_layers):
...         model.add_module(
...             f'fc_d{i}',
...             nn.Linear(input_size, num_hidden_units, bias=False)
...         )
...         model.add_module(f'relu_d{i}', nn.LeakyReLU())
...         model.add_module('dropout', nn.Dropout(p=0.5))
...         input_size = num_hidden_units
...     model.add_module(f'fc_d{num_hidden_layers}',
...                      nn.Linear(input_size, num_output_units))
...     model.add_module('sigmoid', nn.Sigmoid())
...     return model
```

Next, we will specify the training settings for the model. As you will remember from previous chapters, the image size in the MNIST dataset is 28×28 pixels. (That is only one color channel because MNIST contains only grayscale images.) We will further specify the size of the input vector, z, to be 20. Since we are implementing a very simple GAN model for illustration purposes only and using fully connected layers, we will only use a single hidden layer with 100 units in each network. In the following code, we will specify and initialize the two networks, and print their summary information:

```
>>> image_size = (28, 28)
>>> z_size = 20
>>> gen_hidden_layers = 1
>>> gen_hidden_size = 100
>>> disc_hidden_layers = 1
>>> disc_hidden_size = 100
>>> torch.manual_seed(1)
>>> gen_model = make_generator_network(
...     input_size=z_size,
...     num_hidden_layers=gen_hidden_layers,
...     num_hidden_units=gen_hidden_size,
...     num_output_units=np.prod(image_size)
... )
>>> print(gen_model)
Sequential(
  (fc_g0): Linear(in_features=20, out_features=100, bias=False)
  (relu_g0): LeakyReLU(negative_slope=0.01)
  (fc_g1): Linear(in_features=100, out_features=784, bias=True)
  (tanh_g): Tanh()
)

>>> disc_model = make_discriminator_network(
...     input_size=np.prod(image_size),
...     num_hidden_layers=disc_hidden_layers,
...     num_hidden_units=disc_hidden_size
... )
>>> print(disc_model)
Sequential(
  (fc_d0): Linear(in_features=784, out_features=100, bias=False)
  (relu_d0): LeakyReLU(negative_slope=0.01)
  (dropout): Dropout(p=0.5, inplace=False)
  (fc_d1): Linear(in_features=100, out_features=1, bias=True)
  (sigmoid): Sigmoid()
)
```

Defining the training dataset

In the next step, we will load the MNIST dataset from PyTorch and apply the necessary preprocessing steps. Since the output layer of the generator is using the tanh activation function, the pixel values of the synthesized images will be in the range (-1, 1). However, the input pixels of the MNIST images are within the range [0, 255] (with a data type `PIL.Image.Image`). Thus, in the preprocessing steps, we will use the `torchvision.transforms.ToTensor` function to convert the input image tensors to a tensor. As a result, besides changing the data type, calling this function will also change the range of input pixel intensities to [0, 1]. Then, we can shift them by –0.5 and scale them by a factor of 0.5 such that the pixel intensities will be rescaled to be in the range [–1, 1], which can improve gradient descent-based learning:

```
>>> import torchvision
>>> from torchvision import transforms
>>> image_path = './'
>>> transform = transforms.Compose([
...     transforms.ToTensor(),
...     transforms.Normalize(mean=(0.5), std=(0.5)),
... ])
>>> mnist_dataset = torchvision.datasets.MNIST(
...     root=image_path, train=True,
...     transform=transform, download=False
... )
>>> example, label = next(iter(mnist_dataset))
>>> print(f'Min: {example.min()} Max: {example.max()}')
>>> print(example.shape)
Min: -1.0 Max: 1.0
torch.Size([1, 28, 28])
```

Furthermore, we will also create a random vector, z, based on the desired random distribution (in this code example, uniform or normal, which are the most common choices):

```
>>> def create_noise(batch_size, z_size, mode_z):
...     if mode_z == 'uniform':
...         input_z = torch.rand(batch_size, z_size)*2 - 1
...     elif mode_z == 'normal':
...         input_z = torch.randn(batch_size, z_size)
...     return input_z
```

Let's inspect the dataset object that we created. In the following code, we will take one batch of examples and print the array shapes of this sample of input vectors and images. Furthermore, in order to understand the overall data flow of our GAN model, in the following code, we will process a forward pass for our generator and discriminator.

First, we will feed the batch of input, z, vectors to the generator and get its output, g_output. This will be a batch of fake examples, which will be fed to the discriminator model to get the probabilities for the batch of fake examples, d_proba_fake. Furthermore, the processed images that we get from the dataset object will be fed to the discriminator model, which will result in the probabilities for the real examples, d_proba_real. The code is as follows:

```
>>> from torch.utils.data import DataLoader
>>> batch_size = 32
>>> dataloader = DataLoader(mnist_dataset, batch_size, shuffle=False)
>>> input_real, label = next(iter(dataloader))
>>> input_real = input_real.view(batch_size, -1)
>>> torch.manual_seed(1)
>>> mode_z = 'uniform'  # 'uniform' vs. 'normal'
>>> input_z = create_noise(batch_size, z_size, mode_z)
>>> print('input-z -- shape:', input_z.shape)
>>> print('input-real -- shape:', input_real.shape)
input-z -- shape: torch.Size([32, 20])
input-real -- shape: torch.Size([32, 784])

>>> g_output = gen_model(input_z)
>>> print('Output of G -- shape:', g_output.shape)
Output of G -- shape: torch.Size([32, 784])

>>> d_proba_real = disc_model(input_real)
>>> d_proba_fake = disc_model(g_output)
>>> print('Disc. (real) -- shape:', d_proba_real.shape)
>>> print('Disc. (fake) -- shape:', d_proba_fake.shape)
Disc. (real) -- shape: torch.Size([32, 1])
Disc. (fake) -- shape: torch.Size([32, 1])
```

The two probabilities, d_proba_fake and d_proba_real, will be used to compute the loss functions for training the model.

Training the GAN model

As the next step, we will create an instance of nn.BCELoss as our loss function and use that to calculate the binary cross-entropy loss for the generator and discriminator associated with the batches that we just processed. To do this, we also need the ground truth labels for each output. For the generator, we will create a vector of 1s with the same shape as the vector containing the predicted probabilities for the generated images, d_proba_fake. For the discriminator loss, we have two terms: the loss for detecting the fake examples involving d_proba_fake and the loss for detecting the real examples based on d_proba_real.

The ground truth labels for the fake term will be a vector of 0s that we can generate via the `torch.zeros()` (or `torch.zeros_like()`) function. Similarly, we can generate the ground truth values for the real images via the `torch.ones()` (or `torch.ones_like()`) function, which creates a vector of 1s:

```
>>> loss_fn = nn.BCELoss()
>>> ## Loss for the Generator
>>> g_labels_real = torch.ones_like(d_proba_fake)
>>> g_loss = loss_fn(d_proba_fake, g_labels_real)
>>> print(f'Generator Loss: {g_loss:.4f}')
Generator Loss: 0.6863

>>> ## Loss for the Discriminator
>>> d_labels_real = torch.ones_like(d_proba_real)
>>> d_labels_fake = torch.zeros_like(d_proba_fake)
>>> d_loss_real = loss_fn(d_proba_real, d_labels_real)
>>> d_loss_fake = loss_fn(d_proba_fake, d_labels_fake)
>>> print(f'Discriminator Losses: Real {d_loss_real:.4f} Fake {d_loss_
fake:.4f}')
Discriminator Losses: Real 0.6226 Fake 0.7007
```

The previous code example shows the step-by-step calculation of the different loss terms for the purpose of understanding the overall concept behind training a GAN model. The following code will set up the GAN model and implement the training loop, where we will include these calculations in a `for` loop.

We will start with setting up the data loader for the real dataset, the generator and discriminator model, as well as a separate Adam optimizer for each of the two models:

```
>>> batch_size = 64
>>> torch.manual_seed(1)
>>> np.random.seed(1)
>>> mnist_dl = DataLoader(mnist_dataset, batch_size=batch_size,
...                       shuffle=True, drop_last=True)

>>> gen_model = make_generator_network(
...     input_size=z_size,
...     num_hidden_layers=gen_hidden_layers,
...     num_hidden_units=gen_hidden_size,
...     num_output_units=np.prod(image_size)
... ).to(device)
>>> disc_model = make_discriminator_network(
...     input_size=np.prod(image_size),
...     num_hidden_layers=disc_hidden_layers,
...     num_hidden_units=disc_hidden_size
... ).to(device)
```

```
>>> loss_fn = nn.BCELoss()
>>> g_optimizer = torch.optim.Adam(gen_model.parameters())
>>> d_optimizer = torch.optim.Adam(disc_model.parameters())
```

In addition, we will compute the loss gradients with respect to the model weights and optimize the parameters of the generator and discriminator using two separate Adam optimizers. We will write two utility functions for training the discriminator and the generator as follows:

```
>>> ## Train the discriminator
>>> def d_train(x):
...     disc_model.zero_grad()
...     # Train discriminator with a real batch
...     batch_size = x.size(0)
...     x = x.view(batch_size, -1).to(device)
...     d_labels_real = torch.ones(batch_size, 1, device=device)
...     d_proba_real = disc_model(x)
...     d_loss_real = loss_fn(d_proba_real, d_labels_real)
...     # Train discriminator on a fake batch
...     input_z = create_noise(batch_size, z_size, mode_z).to(device)
...     g_output = gen_model(input_z)
...     d_proba_fake = disc_model(g_output)
...     d_labels_fake = torch.zeros(batch_size, 1, device=device)
...     d_loss_fake = loss_fn(d_proba_fake, d_labels_fake)
...     # gradient backprop & optimize ONLY D's parameters
...     d_loss = d_loss_real + d_loss_fake
...     d_loss.backward()
...     d_optimizer.step()
...     return d_loss.data.item(), d_proba_real.detach(), \
...            d_proba_fake.detach()
>>>
>>> ## Train the generator
>>> def g_train(x):
...     gen_model.zero_grad()
...     batch_size = x.size(0)
...     input_z = create_noise(batch_size, z_size, mode_z).to(device)
...     g_labels_real = torch.ones(batch_size, 1, device=device)
...
...     g_output = gen_model(input_z)
...     d_proba_fake = disc_model(g_output)
...     g_loss = loss_fn(d_proba_fake, g_labels_real)
```

```
...     # gradient backprop & optimize ONLY G's parameters
...     g_loss.backward()
...     g_optimizer.step()
...     return g_loss.data.item()
```

Next, we will alternate between the training of the generator and the discriminator for 100 epochs. For each epoch, we will record the loss for the generator, the loss for the discriminator, and the loss for the real data and fake data respectively. Furthermore, after each epoch, we will generate some examples from a fixed noise input using the current generator model by calling the `create_samples()` function. We will store the synthesized images in a Python list. The code is as follows:

```
>>> fixed_z = create_noise(batch_size, z_size, mode_z).to(device)
>>> def create_samples(g_model, input_z):
...     g_output = g_model(input_z)
...     images = torch.reshape(g_output, (batch_size, *image_size))
...     return (images+1)/2.0
>>>
>>> epoch_samples = []
>>> all_d_losses = []
>>> all_g_losses = []
>>> all_d_real = []
>>> all_d_fake = []
>>> num_epochs = 100
>>>
>>> for epoch in range(1, num_epochs+1):
...     d_losses, g_losses = [], []
...     d_vals_real, d_vals_fake = [], []
...     for i, (x, _) in enumerate(mnist_dl):
...         d_loss, d_proba_real, d_proba_fake = d_train(x)
...         d_losses.append(d_loss)
...         g_losses.append(g_train(x))
...         d_vals_real.append(d_proba_real.mean().cpu())
...         d_vals_fake.append(d_proba_fake.mean().cpu())
...
...     all_d_losses.append(torch.tensor(d_losses).mean())
...     all_g_losses.append(torch.tensor(g_losses).mean())
...     all_d_real.append(torch.tensor(d_vals_real).mean())
...     all_d_fake.append(torch.tensor(d_vals_fake).mean())
...     print(f'Epoch {epoch:03d} | Avg Losses >>'
...           f' G/D {all_g_losses[-1]:.4f}/{all_d_losses[-1]:.4f}'
...           f' [D-Real: {all_d_real[-1]:.4f}'
...           f' D-Fake: {all_d_fake[-1]:.4f}]')
```

```
...     epoch_samples.append(
...         create_samples(gen_model, fixed_z).detach().cpu().numpy()
...     )

Epoch 001 | Avg Losses >> G/D 0.9546/0.8957 [D-Real: 0.8074 D-Fake: 0.4687]
Epoch 002 | Avg Losses >> G/D 0.9571/1.0841 [D-Real: 0.6346 D-Fake: 0.4155]
Epoch ...
Epoch 100 | Avg Losses >> G/D 0.8622/1.2878 [D-Real: 0.5488 D-Fake: 0.4518]
```

Using a GPU on Google Colab, the training process that we implemented in the previous code block should be completed in less than an hour. (It may even be faster on your personal computer if you have a recent and capable CPU and a GPU.) After the model training has completed, it is often helpful to plot the discriminator and generator losses to analyze the behavior of both subnetworks and assess whether they converged.

It is also helpful to plot the average probabilities of the batches of real and fake examples as computed by the discriminator in each iteration. We expect these probabilities to be around 0.5, which means that the discriminator is not able to confidently distinguish between real and fake images:

```
>>> import itertools
>>> fig = plt.figure(figsize=(16, 6))
>>> ## Plotting the losses
>>> ax = fig.add_subplot(1, 2, 1)
>>> plt.plot(all_g_losses, label='Generator loss')
>>> half_d_losses = [all_d_loss/2 for all_d_loss in all_d_losses]
>>> plt.plot(half_d_losses, label='Discriminator loss')
>>> plt.legend(fontsize=20)
>>> ax.set_xlabel('Iteration', size=15)
>>> ax.set_ylabel('Loss', size=15)
>>>
>>> ## Plotting the outputs of the discriminator
>>> ax = fig.add_subplot(1, 2, 2)
>>> plt.plot(all_d_real, label=r'Real: $D(\mathbf{x})$')
>>> plt.plot(all_d_fake, label=r'Fake: $D(G(\mathbf{z}))$')
>>> plt.legend(fontsize=20)
>>> ax.set_xlabel('Iteration', size=15)
>>> ax.set_ylabel('Discriminator output', size=15)
>>> plt.show()
```

Figure 17.10 shows the results:

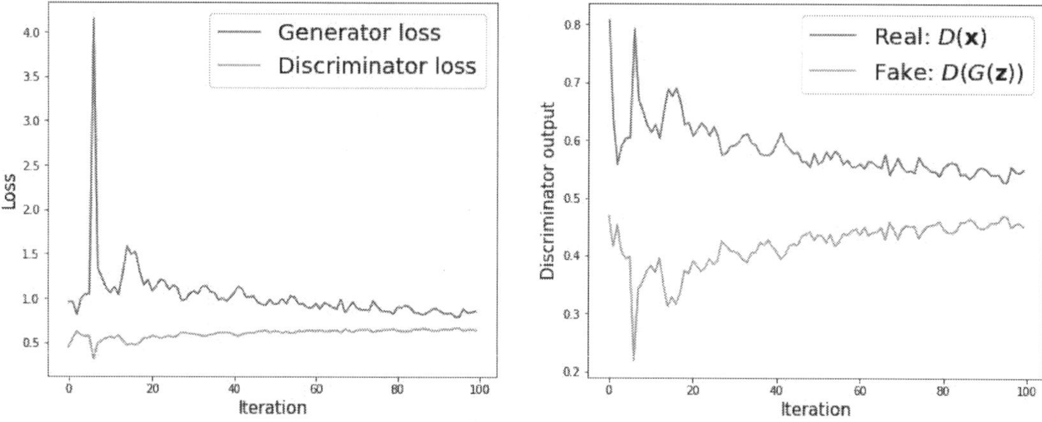

Figure 17.10: The discriminator performance

As you can see from the discriminator outputs in the previous figure, during the early stages of the training, the discriminator was able to quickly learn to distinguish quite accurately between the real and fake examples; that is, the fake examples had probabilities close to 0, and the real examples had probabilities close to 1. The reason for that was that the fake examples were nothing like the real ones; therefore, distinguishing between real and fake was rather easy. As the training proceeds further, the generator will become better at synthesizing realistic images, which will result in probabilities of both real and fake examples that are close to 0.5.

Furthermore, we can also see how the outputs of the generator, that is, the synthesized images, change during training. In the following code, we will visualize some of the images produced by the generator for a selection of epochs:

```
>>> selected_epochs = [1, 2, 4, 10, 50, 100]
>>> fig = plt.figure(figsize=(10, 14))
>>> for i,e in enumerate(selected_epochs):
...     for j in range(5):
...         ax = fig.add_subplot(6, 5, i*5+j+1)
...         ax.set_xticks([])
...         ax.set_yticks([])
...         if j == 0:
...             ax.text(
...                 -0.06, 0.5, f'Epoch {e}',
...                 rotation=90, size=18, color='red',
...                 horizontalalignment='right',
...                 verticalalignment='center',
...                 transform=ax.transAxes
...             )
```

```
...
...         image = epoch_samples[e-1][j]
...         ax.imshow(image, cmap='gray_r')
...
>>> plt.show()
```

Figure 17.11 shows the produced images:

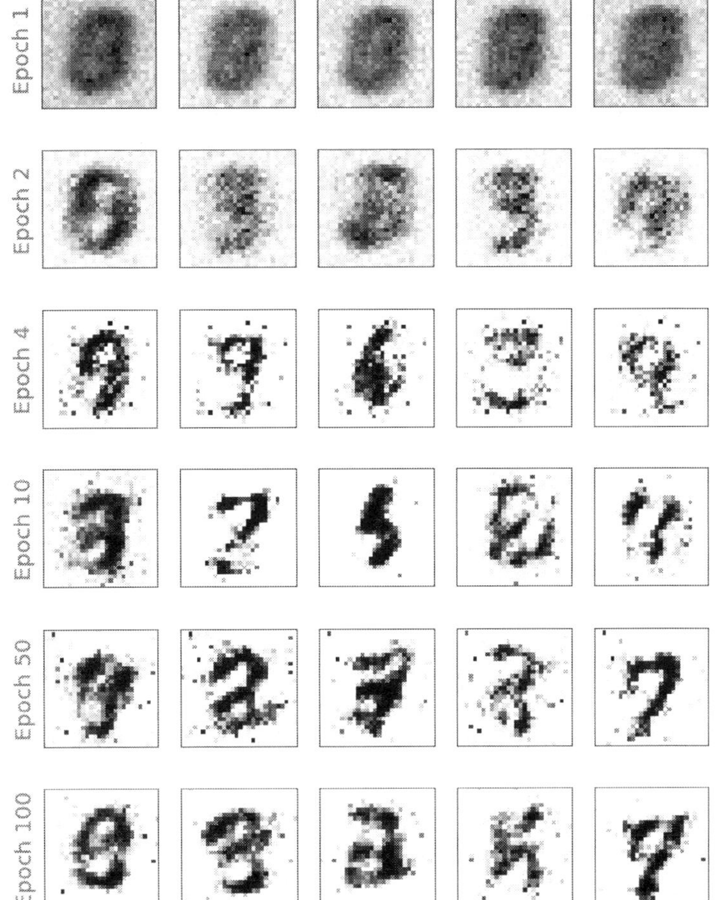

Figure 17.11: Images produced by the generator

As you can see from *Figure 17.11*, the generator network produced more and more realistic images as the training progressed. However, even after 100 epochs, the produced images still look very different from the handwritten digits contained in the MNIST dataset.

In this section, we designed a very simple GAN model with only a single fully connected hidden layer for both the generator and discriminator. After training the GAN model on the MNIST dataset, we were able to achieve promising, although not yet satisfactory, results with the new handwritten digits.

As we learned in *Chapter 14, Classifying Images with Deep Convolutional Neural Networks,* NN architectures with convolutional layers have several advantages over fully connected layers when it comes to image classification. In a similar sense, adding convolutional layers to our GAN model to work with image data might improve the outcome. In the next section, we will implement a **deep convolutional GAN (DCGAN)**, which uses convolutional layers for both the generator and the discriminator networks.

Improving the quality of synthesized images using a convolutional and Wasserstein GAN

In this section, we will implement a DCGAN, which will enable us to improve the performance we saw in the previous GAN example. Additionally, we will briefly talk about an extra key technique, **Wasserstein GAN (WGAN)**.

The techniques that we will cover in this section will include the following:

- Transposed convolution
- Batch normalization (BatchNorm)
- WGAN

The DCGAN was proposed in 2016 by *A. Radford, L. Metz,* and *S. Chintala* in their article *Unsupervised representation learning with deep convolutional generative adversarial networks,* which is freely available at `https://arxiv.org/pdf/1511.06434.pdf`. In this article, the researchers proposed using convolutional layers for both the generator and discriminator networks. Starting from a random vector, z, the DCGAN first uses a fully connected layer to project z into a new vector with a proper size so that it can be reshaped into a spatial convolution representation ($h \times w \times c$), which is smaller than the output image size. Then, a series of convolutional layers, known as **transposed convolution**, are used to upsample the feature maps to the desired output image size.

Transposed convolution

In *Chapter 14,* you learned about the convolution operation in one- and two-dimensional spaces. In particular, we looked at how the choices for the padding and strides change the output feature maps. While a convolution operation is usually used to downsample the feature space (for example, by setting the stride to 2, or by adding a pooling layer after a convolutional layer), a *transposed convolution* operation is usually used for *upsampling* the feature space.

To understand the transposed convolution operation, let's go through a simple thought experiment. Assume that we have an input feature map of size $n \times n$. Then, we apply a 2D convolution operation with certain padding and stride parameters to this $n \times n$ input, resulting in an output feature map of size $m \times m$. Now, the question is, how we can apply another convolution operation to obtain a feature map with the initial dimension $n \times n$ from this $m \times m$ output feature map while maintaining the connectivity patterns between the input and output? Note that only the shape of the $n \times n$ input matrix is recovered and not the actual matrix values.

This is what transposed convolution does, as shown in *Figure 17.12*:

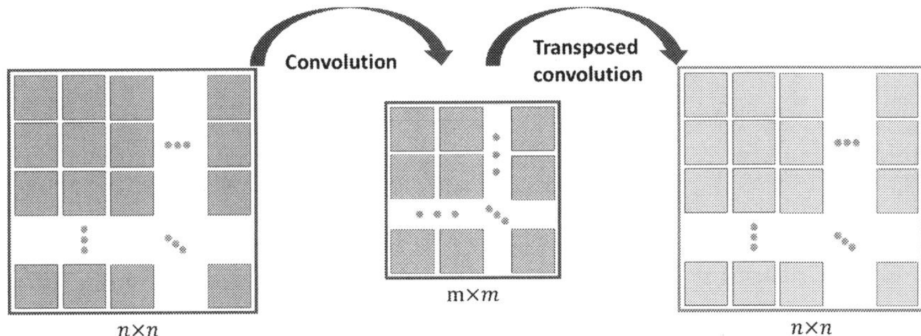

Figure 17.12: Transposed convolution

Transposed convolution versus deconvolution

Transposed convolution is also called **fractionally strided convolution.** In deep learning literature, another common term that is used to refer to transposed convolution is **deconvolution.** However, note that deconvolution was originally defined as the inverse of a convolution operation, f, on a feature map, x, with weight parameters, w, producing feature map x', $f_w(x) = x'$. A deconvolution function, f^{-1}, can then be defined as $f_w^{-1}(f(x)) = x$. However, note that the transposed convolution is merely focused on recovering the dimensionality of the feature space and not the actual values.

Upsampling feature maps using transposed convolution works by inserting 0s between the elements of the input feature maps. *Figure 17.13* shows an example of applying transposed convolution to an input of size 4×4, with a stride of 2×2 and kernel size of 2×2. The matrix of size 9×9 in the center shows the results after inserting such 0s into the input feature map. Then, performing a normal convolution using the 2×2 kernel with a stride of 1 results in an output of size 8×8. We can verify the backward direction by performing a regular convolution on the output with a stride of 2, which results in an output feature map of size 4×4, which is the same as the original input size:

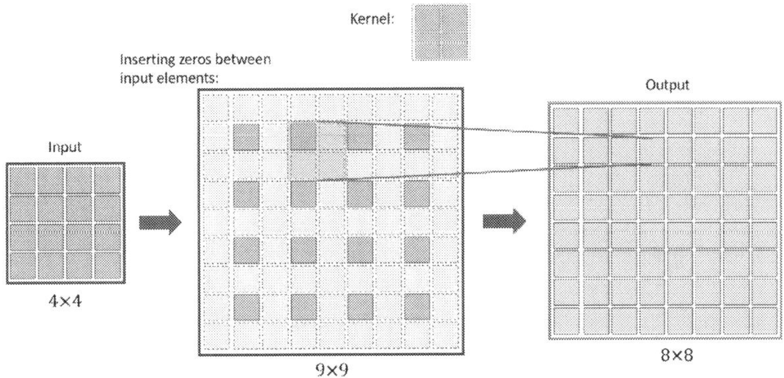

Figure 17.13: Applying transposed convolution to a 4×4 input

Figure 17.13 shows how transposed convolution works in general. There are various cases in which input size, kernel size, strides, and padding variations can change the output. If you want to learn more about all these different cases, refer to the tutorial *A Guide to Convolution Arithmetic for Deep Learning* by *Vincent Dumoulin* and *Francesco Visin*, 2018 (`https://arxiv.org/pdf/1603.07285.pdf`.)

Batch normalization

BatchNorm was introduced in 2015 by Sergey Ioffe and Christian Szegedy in the article *Batch Normalization: Accelerating Deep Network Training by Reducing Internal Covariate Shift*, which you can access via arXiv at `https://arxiv.org/pdf/1502.03167.pdf`. One of the main ideas behind BatchNorm is normalizing the layer inputs and preventing changes in their distribution during training, which enables faster and better convergence.

BatchNorm transforms a mini-batch of features based on its computed statistics. Assume that we have the net preactivation feature maps obtained after a convolutional layer in a four-dimensional tensor, *Z*, with the shape [*m*×*c*×*h*×*w*], where *m* is the number of examples in the batch (i.e., batch size), *h*×*w* is the spatial dimension of the feature maps, and *c* is the number of channels. BatchNorm can be summarized in three steps, as follows:

1. Compute the mean and standard deviation of the net inputs for each mini-batch:

$$\boldsymbol{\mu}_B = \frac{1}{m \times h \times w} \sum_{i,j,k} \boldsymbol{Z}^{[i,j,k]}$$

$$\boldsymbol{\sigma}_B^2 = \frac{1}{m \times h \times w} \sum_{i,j,k} \left(\boldsymbol{Z}^{[i,j,k]} - \boldsymbol{\mu}_B\right)^2$$

   where $\boldsymbol{\mu}_B$ and $\boldsymbol{\sigma}_B^2$ both have size *c*.

2. Standardize the net inputs for all examples in the batch:

$$\boldsymbol{Z}_{\text{std}}^{[i]} = \frac{\boldsymbol{Z}^{[i]} - \boldsymbol{\mu}_B}{\boldsymbol{\sigma}_B + \epsilon}$$

   where ϵ is a small number for numerical stability (that is, to avoid division by zero).

3. Scale and shift the normalized net inputs using two learnable parameter vectors, $\boldsymbol{\gamma}$ and $\boldsymbol{\beta}$, of size *c* (number of channels):

$$\boldsymbol{A}_{\text{pre}}^{[i]} = \boldsymbol{\gamma} \boldsymbol{Z}_{\text{std}}^{[i]} + \boldsymbol{\beta}$$

Figure 17.14 illustrates the process:

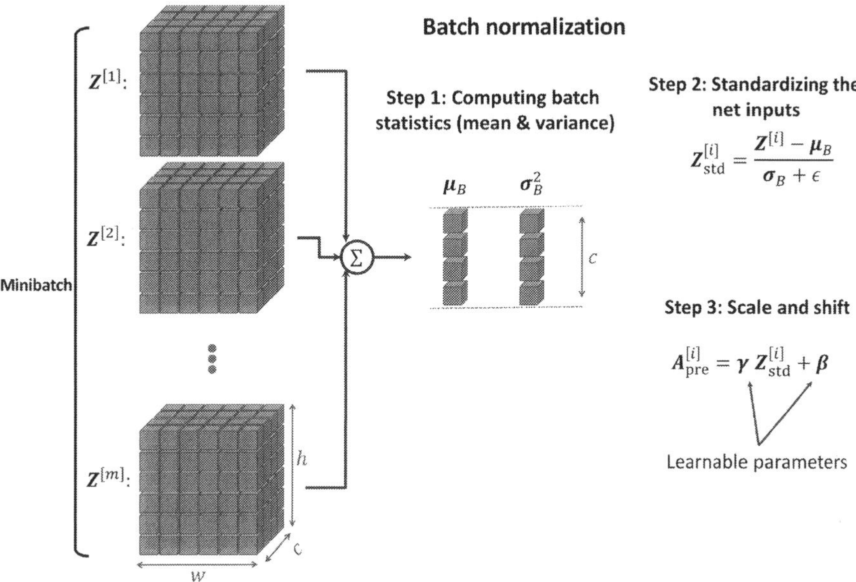

Figure 17.14: The process of batch normalization

In the first step of BatchNorm, the mean, $\boldsymbol{\mu}_B$, and standard deviation, $\boldsymbol{\sigma}_B$, of the mini-batch are computed. Both $\boldsymbol{\mu}_B$ and $\boldsymbol{\sigma}_B$ are vectors of size *c* (where *c* is the number of channels). Then, these statistics are used in *step 2* to scale the examples in each mini-batch via z-score normalization (standardization), resulting in standardized net inputs, $\boldsymbol{Z}_{\text{std}}^{[i]}$. As a consequence, these net inputs are mean-centered and have *unit variance*, which is generally a useful property for gradient descent-based optimization. On the other hand, always normalizing the net inputs such that they have the same properties across the different mini-batches, which can be diverse, can severely impact the representational capacity of NNs. This can be understood by considering a feature, $x \sim N(0,1)$, which, after sigmoid activation to $\sigma(x)$, results in a linear region for values close to 0. Therefore, in step 3, the learnable parameters, $\boldsymbol{\beta}$ and $\boldsymbol{\gamma}$, which are vectors of size *c* (number of channels), allow BatchNorm to control the shift and spread of the normalized features.

During training, the running averages, $\boldsymbol{\mu}_B$, and running variance, $\boldsymbol{\sigma}_B^2$, are computed, which are used along with the tuned parameters, $\boldsymbol{\beta}$ and $\boldsymbol{\gamma}$, to normalize the test example(s) at evaluation.

Why does BatchNorm help optimization?

Initially, BatchNorm was developed to reduce the so-called **internal covariance shift**, which is defined as the changes that occur in the distribution of a layer's activations due to the updated network parameters during training.

To explain this with a simple example, consider a fixed batch that passes through the network at epoch 1. We record the activations of each layer for this batch. After iterating through the whole training dataset and updating the model parameters, we start the second epoch, where the previously fixed batch passes through the network. Then, we compare the layer activations from the first and second epochs. Since the network parameters have changed, we observe that the activations have also changed. This phenomenon is called the **internal covariance shift**, which was believed to decelerate NN training.

However, in 2018, S. Santurkar, D. Tsipras, A. Ilyas, and A. Madry further investigated what makes BatchNorm so effective. In their study, the researchers observed that the effect of BatchNorm on the internal covariance shift is marginal. Based on the outcome of their experiments, they hypothesized that the effectiveness of BatchNorm is, instead, based on a smoother surface of the loss function, which makes the non-convex optimization more robust.

If you are interested in learning more about these results, read through the original paper, *How Does Batch Normalization Help Optimization?*, which is freely available at `http://papers.nips.cc/paper/7515-how-does-batch-normalization-help-optimization.pdf`.

The PyTorch API provides a class, `nn.BatchNorm2d()` (`nn.BatchNorm1d()` for 1D input), that we can use as a layer when defining our models; it will perform all of the steps that we described for BatchNorm. Note that the behavior for updating the learnable parameters, $\boldsymbol{\gamma}$ and $\boldsymbol{\beta}$, depends on whether the model is a training model not. These parameters are learned only during training and are then used for normalization during evaluation.

Implementing the generator and discriminator

At this point, we have covered the main components of a DCGAN model, which we will now implement. The architectures of the generator and discriminator networks are summarized in the following two figures.

The generator takes a vector, $\boldsymbol{z}$, of size 100 as input. Then, a series of transposed convolutions using `nn.ConvTranspose2d()` upsamples the feature maps until the spatial dimension of the resulting feature maps reaches 28×28. The number of channels is reduced by half after each transposed convolutional layer, except the last one, which uses only one output filter to generate a grayscale image. Each transposed convolutional layer is followed by BatchNorm and leaky ReLU activation functions, except the last one, which uses tanh activation (without BatchNorm).

The architecture for the generator (the feature maps after each layer) is shown in *Figure 17.15*:

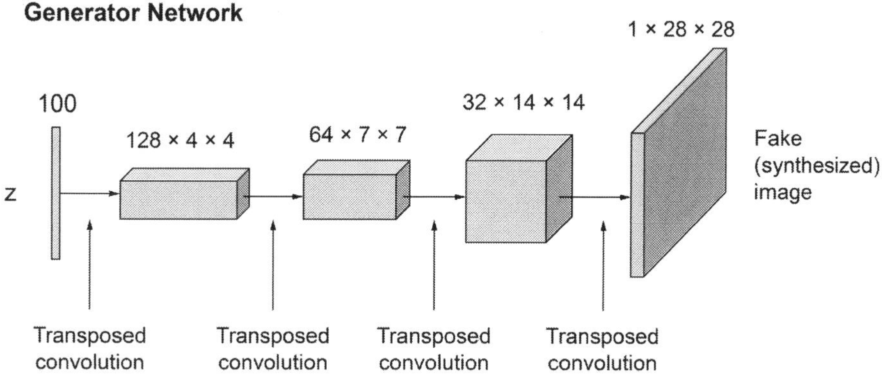

Figure 17.15: The generator network

The discriminator receives images of size 1×28×28, which are passed through four convolutional layers. The first three convolutional layers reduce the spatial dimensionality by 4 while increasing the number of channels of the feature maps. Each convolutional layer is also followed by BatchNorm and leaky ReLU activation. The last convolutional layer uses kernels of size 4×4 and a single filter to reduce the spatial dimensionality of the output to 1×1×1. Finally, the convolutional output is followed by a sigmoid function and squeezed to one dimension:

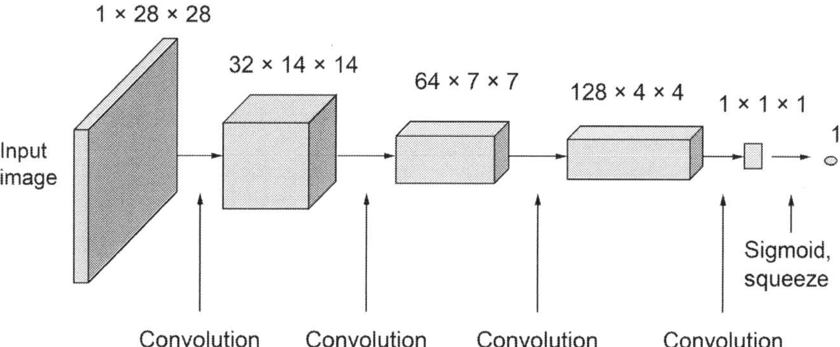

Figure 17.16: The discriminator network

Architecture design considerations for convolutional GANs

Notice that the number of feature maps follows different trends between the generator and the discriminator. In the generator, we start with a large number of feature maps and decrease them as we progress toward the last layer. On the other hand, in the discriminator, we start with a small number of channels and increase it toward the last layer. This is an important point for designing CNNs with the number of feature maps and the spatial size of the feature maps in reverse order. When the spatial size of the feature maps increases, the number of feature maps decreases and vice versa.

In addition, note that it's usually not recommended to use bias units in the layer that follows a BatchNorm layer. Using bias units would be redundant in this case, since BatchNorm already has a shift parameter, $\boldsymbol{\beta}$. You can omit the bias units for a given layer by setting `bias=False` in `nn.ConvTranspose2d` or `nn.Conv2d`.

The code for the helper function to make the generator and the discriminator network class is as follows:

```
>>> def make_generator_network(input_size, n_filters):
...     model = nn.Sequential(
...         nn.ConvTranspose2d(input_size, n_filters*4, 4,
...                            1, 0, bias=False),
...         nn.BatchNorm2d(n_filters*4),
...         nn.LeakyReLU(0.2),
...         nn.ConvTranspose2d(n_filters*4, n_filters*2,
...                            3, 2, 1, bias=False),
...         nn.BatchNorm2d(n_filters*2),
...         nn.LeakyReLU(0.2),
...         nn.ConvTranspose2d(n_filters*2, n_filters,
...                            4, 2, 1, bias=False),
...         nn.BatchNorm2d(n_filters),
...         nn.LeakyReLU(0.2),
...         nn.ConvTranspose2d(n_filters, 1, 4, 2, 1,
...                            bias=False),
...         nn.Tanh()
...     )
...     return model
>>>
>>> class Discriminator(nn.Module):
...     def __init__(self, n_filters):
...         super().__init__()
...         self.network = nn.Sequential(
...             nn.Conv2d(1, n_filters, 4, 2, 1, bias=False),
```

```
...             nn.LeakyReLU(0.2),
...             nn.Conv2d(n_filters, n_filters*2,
...                       4, 2, 1, bias=False),
...             nn.BatchNorm2d(n_filters * 2),
...             nn.LeakyReLU(0.2),
...             nn.Conv2d(n_filters*2, n_filters*4,
...                       3, 2, 1, bias=False),
...             nn.BatchNorm2d(n_filters*4),
...             nn.LeakyReLU(0.2),
...             nn.Conv2d(n_filters*4, 1, 4, 1, 0, bias=False),
...             nn.Sigmoid()
...         )
...
...     def forward(self, input):
...         output = self.network(input)
...         return output.view(-1, 1).squeeze(0)
```

With the helper function and class, you can build a DCGAN model and train it by using the same MNIST dataset object we initialized in the previous section when we implemented the simple, fully connected GAN. We can create the generator networks using the helper function and print its architecture as follows:

```
>>> z_size = 100
>>> image_size = (28, 28)
>>> n_filters = 32
>>> gen_model = make_generator_network(z_size, n_filters).to(device)
>>> print(gen_model)
Sequential(
  (0): ConvTranspose2d(100, 128, kernel_size=(4, 4), stride=(1, 1), bias=False)
  (1): BatchNorm2d(128, eps=1e-05, momentum=0.1, affine=True, track_running_
stats=True)
  (2): LeakyReLU(negative_slope=0.2)
  (3): ConvTranspose2d(128, 64, kernel_size=(3, 3), stride=(2, 2), padding=(1,
1), bias=False)
  (4): BatchNorm2d(64, eps=1e-05, momentum=0.1, affine=True, track_running_
stats=True)
  (5): LeakyReLU(negative_slope=0.2)
  (6): ConvTranspose2d(64, 32, kernel_size=(4, 4), stride=(2, 2), padding=(1,
1), bias=False)
  (7): BatchNorm2d(32, eps=1e-05, momentum=0.1, affine=True, track_running_
stats=True)
```

```
  (8): LeakyReLU(negative_slope=0.2)
  (9): ConvTranspose2d(32, 1, kernel_size=(4, 4), stride=(2, 2), padding=(1, 1), bias=False)
  (10): Tanh()
)
```

Similarly, we can generate the discriminator network and see its architecture:

```
>>> disc_model = Discriminator(n_filters).to(device)
>>> print(disc_model)
Discriminator(
  (network): Sequential(
    (0): Conv2d(1, 32, kernel_size=(4, 4), stride=(2, 2), padding=(1, 1), bias=False)
    (1): LeakyReLU(negative_slope=0.2)
    (2): Conv2d(32, 64, kernel_size=(4, 4), stride=(2, 2), padding=(1, 1), bias=False)
    (3): BatchNorm2d(64, eps=1e-05, momentum=0.1, affine=True, track_running_stats=True)
    (4): LeakyReLU(negative_slope=0.2)
    (5): Conv2d(64, 128, kernel_size=(3, 3), stride=(2, 2), padding=(1, 1), bias=False)
    (6): BatchNorm2d(128, eps=1e-05, momentum=0.1, affine=True, track_running_stats=True)
    (7): LeakyReLU(negative_slope=0.2)
    (8): Conv2d(128, 1, kernel_size=(4, 4), stride=(1, 1), bias=False)
    (9): Sigmoid()
  )
)
```

Also, we can use the same loss functions and optimizers as we did in the *Training the GAN model* subsection:

```
>>> loss_fn = nn.BCELoss()
>>> g_optimizer = torch.optim.Adam(gen_model.parameters(), 0.0003)
>>> d_optimizer = torch.optim.Adam(disc_model.parameters(), 0.0002)
```

We will be making a few small modifications to the training procedure. The `create_noise()` function for generating random input must change to output a tensor of four dimensions instead of a vector:

```
>>> def create_noise(batch_size, z_size, mode_z):
...     if mode_z == 'uniform':
...         input_z = torch.rand(batch_size, z_size, 1, 1)*2 - 1
...     elif mode_z == 'normal':
...         input_z = torch.randn(batch_size, z_size, 1, 1)
...     return input_z
```

The `d_train()` function for training the discriminator doesn't need to reshape the input image:

```
>>> def d_train(x):
...     disc_model.zero_grad()
...     # Train discriminator with a real batch
...     batch_size = x.size(0)
...     x = x.to(device)
...     d_labels_real = torch.ones(batch_size, 1, device=device)
...     d_proba_real = disc_model(x)
...     d_loss_real = loss_fn(d_proba_real, d_labels_real)
...     # Train discriminator on a fake batch
...     input_z = create_noise(batch_size, z_size, mode_z).to(device)
...     g_output = gen_model(input_z)
...     d_proba_fake = disc_model(g_output)
...     d_labels_fake = torch.zeros(batch_size, 1, device=device)
...     d_loss_fake = loss_fn(d_proba_fake, d_labels_fake)
...     # gradient backprop & optimize ONLY D's parameters
...     d_loss = d_loss_real + d_loss_fake
...     d_loss.backward()
...     d_optimizer.step()
...     return d_loss.data.item(), d_proba_real.detach(), \
...            d_proba_fake.detach()
```

Next, we will alternate between the training of the generator and the discriminator for 100 epochs. After each epoch, we will generate some examples from a fixed noise input using the current generator model by calling the `create_samples()` function. The code is as follows:

```
>>> fixed_z = create_noise(batch_size, z_size, mode_z).to(device)
>>> epoch_samples = []
>>> torch.manual_seed(1)
>>> for epoch in range(1, num_epochs+1):
...     gen_model.train()
...     for i, (x, _) in enumerate(mnist_dl):
...         d_loss, d_proba_real, d_proba_fake = d_train(x)
...         d_losses.append(d_loss)
...         g_losses.append(g_train(x))
...     print(f'Epoch {epoch:03d} | Avg Losses >>'
...           f' G/D {torch.FloatTensor(g_losses).mean():.4f}'
...           f'/{torch.FloatTensor(d_losses).mean():.4f}')
...     gen_model.eval()
...     epoch_samples.append(
...         create_samples(
...             gen_model, fixed_z
...         ).detach().cpu().numpy()
...     )
Epoch 001 | Avg Losses >> G/D 4.7016/0.1035
Epoch 002 | Avg Losses >> G/D 5.9341/0.0438
...
Epoch 099 | Avg Losses >> G/D 4.3753/0.1360
Epoch 100 | Avg Losses >> G/D 4.4914/0.1120
```

Finally, let's visualize the saved examples at some epochs to see how the model is learning and how the quality of synthesized examples changes over the course of learning:

```
>>> selected_epochs = [1, 2, 4, 10, 50, 100]
>>> fig = plt.figure(figsize=(10, 14))
>>> for i,e in enumerate(selected_epochs):
...     for j in range(5):
...         ax = fig.add_subplot(6, 5, i*5+j+1)
...         ax.set_xticks([])
...         ax.set_yticks([])
...         if j == 0:
...             ax.text(-0.06, 0.5,  f'Epoch {e}',
...                     rotation=90, size=18, color='red',
...                     horizontalalignment='right',
...                     verticalalignment='center',
```

```
...                     transform=ax.transAxes)
...
...         image = epoch_samples[e-1][j]
...         ax.imshow(image, cmap='gray_r')
>>> plt.show()
```

Figure 17.17 shows the results:

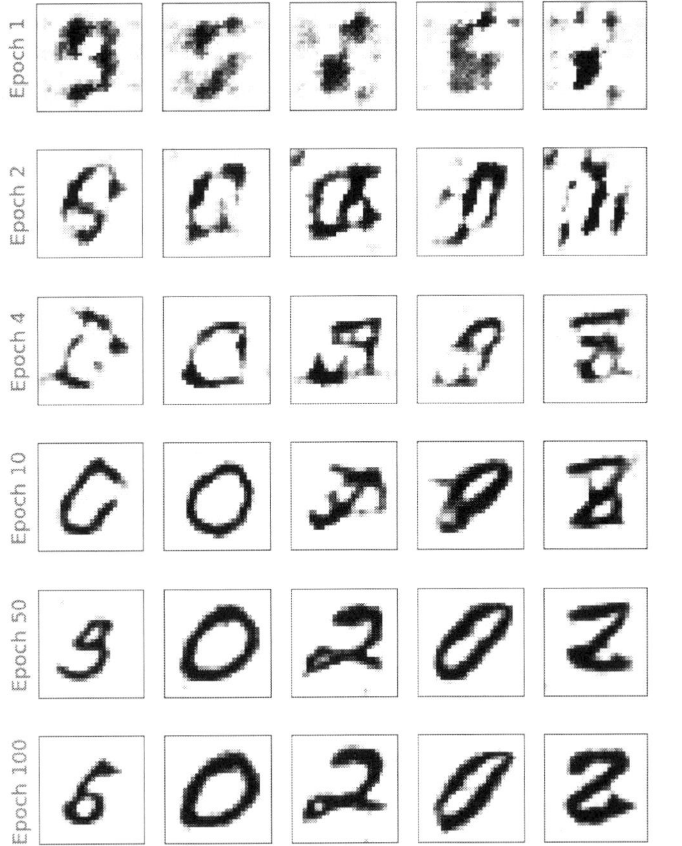

Figure 17.17: Generated images from the DCGAN

We used the same code to visualize the results as in the section on vanilla GAN. Comparing the new examples shows that DCGAN can generate images of a much higher quality.

You may wonder how we can evaluate the results of GAN generators. The simplest approach is visual assessment, which involves evaluating the quality of the synthesized images in the context of the target domain and the project objective. Furthermore, there have been several more sophisticated evaluation methods proposed that are less subjective and less limited by domain knowledge. For a detailed survey, see *Pros and Cons of GAN Evaluation Measures: New Developments* (`https://arxiv.org/abs/2103.09396`). The paper summarizes generator evaluation into qualitative and quantitative measures.

There is a theoretical argument that training the generator should seek to minimize the dissimilarity between the distribution observed in the real data and the distribution observed in synthesized examples. Hence our current architecture would not perform very well when using cross-entropy as a loss function.

In the next subsection, we will cover WGAN, which uses a modified loss function based on the so-called Wasserstein-1 (or earth mover's) distance between the distributions of real and fake images for improving the training performance.

Dissimilarity measures between two distributions

We will first see different measures for computing the divergence between two distributions. Then, we will see which one of these measures is already embedded in the original GAN model. Finally, switching this measure in GANs will lead us to the implementation of a WGAN.

As mentioned at the beginning of this chapter, the goal of a generative model is to learn how to synthesize new samples that have the same distribution as the distribution of the training dataset. Let *P*(*x*) and *Q*(*x*) represent the distribution of a random variable, *x*, as shown in the following figure.

First, let's look at some ways, shown in *Figure 17.18*, that we can use to measure the dissimilarity between two distributions, *P* and *Q*:

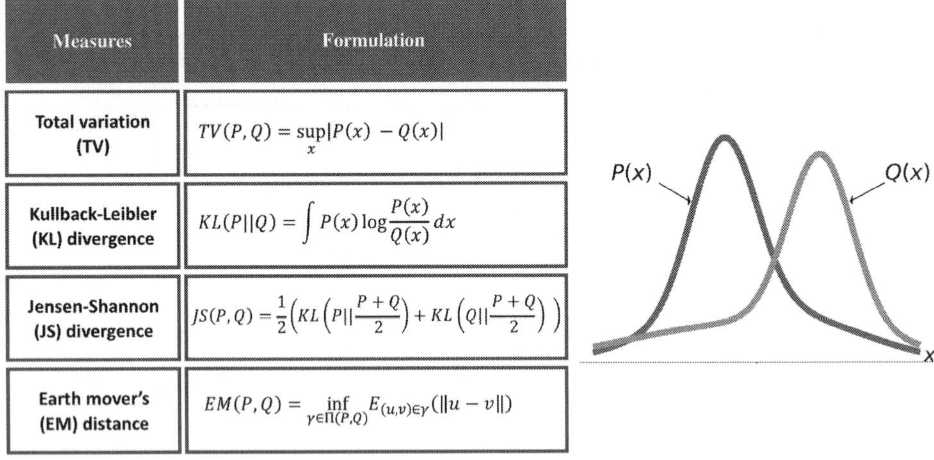

Measures	Formulation
Total variation (TV)	$TV(P,Q) = \sup_x \lvert P(x) - Q(x) \rvert$
Kullback-Leibler (KL) divergence	$KL(P\|\|Q) = \int P(x) \log \frac{P(x)}{Q(x)} dx$
Jensen-Shannon (JS) divergence	$JS(P,Q) = \frac{1}{2}\left(KL\left(P\|\|\frac{P+Q}{2}\right) + KL\left(Q\|\|\frac{P+Q}{2}\right)\right)$
Earth mover's (EM) distance	$EM(P,Q) = \inf_{\gamma \in \Pi(P,Q)} E_{(u,v)\in\gamma}(\|u - v\|)$

Figure 17.18: Methods to measure the dissimilarity between distributions P and Q

The function supremum, *sup*(*S*), used in the **total variation** (**TV**) measure, refers to the smallest value that is greater than all elements of *S*. In other words, *sup*(*S*) is the least upper bound for *S*. Vice versa, the infimum function, *inf*(*S*), which is used in EM distance, refers to the largest value that is smaller than all elements of *S* (the greatest lower bound).

Let's gain an understanding of these measures by briefly stating what they are trying to accomplish in simple words:

- The first one, TV distance, measures the largest difference between the two distributions at each point.
- The EM distance can be interpreted as the minimal amount of work needed to transform one distribution into the other. The infimum function in the EM distance is taken over $\Pi(P, Q)$, which is the collection of all joint distributions whose marginals are P or Q. Then, $\gamma(u, v)$ is a transfer plan, which indicates how we redistribute the earth from location u to v, subject to some constraints for maintaining valid distributions after such transfers. Computing EM distance is an optimization problem by itself, which is to find the optimal transfer plan, $\gamma(u, v)$.
- The **Kullback-Leibler** (KL) and **Jensen-Shannon** (JS) divergence measures come from the field of information theory. Note that KL divergence is not symmetric, that is, $KL(P\|Q) \neq KL(Q\|P)$ in contrast to JS divergence.

The dissimilarity equations provided in *Figure 17.18* correspond to continuous distributions but can be extended for discrete cases. An example of calculating these different dissimilarity measures with two simple discrete distributions is illustrated in *Figure 17.19*:

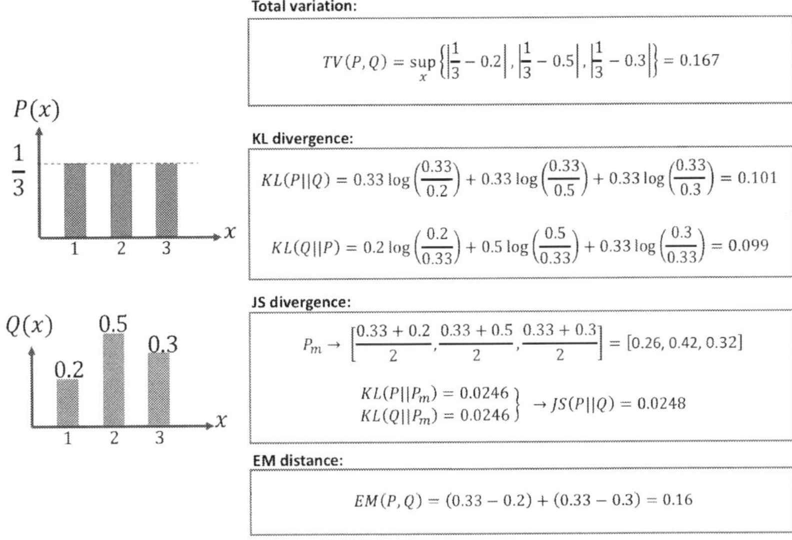

Figure 17.19: An example of calculating the different dissimilarity measures

Note that, in the case of the EM distance, for this simple example, we can see that $Q(x)$ at $x = 2$ has the excess value of $0.5 - \frac{1}{3} = 0.166$, while the value of Q at the other two x's is below 1/3. Therefore, the minimal amount of work is when we transfer the extra value at $x = 2$ to $x = 1$ and $x = 3$, as shown in *Figure 17.19*. For this simple example, it's easy to see that these transfers will result in the minimal amount of work out of all possible transfers. However, this may be infeasible to do for more complex cases.

The relationship between KL divergence and cross-entropy

KL divergence, $KL(P\|Q)$, measures the relative entropy of the distribution, P, with respect to a reference distribution, Q. The formulation for KL divergence can be extended as:

$$KL(P\|Q) = -\int P(x)\log(Q(x))\,dx - \left(-\int P(x)\log(P(x))\right)$$

Moreover, for discrete distributions, KL divergence can be written as:

$$KL(P\|Q) = -\sum_i P(x_i)\log\left(\frac{P(x_i)}{Q(x_i)}\right)$$

which can be similarly extended as:

$$KL(P\|Q) = -\sum_i P(x_i)\log(Q(x_i)) - \left(-\sum_i P(x_i)\log(P(x_i))\right)$$

Based on the extended formulation (either discrete or continuous), KL divergence is viewed as the cross-entropy between P and Q (the first term in the preceding equation) subtracted by the (self-) entropy of P (second term), that is, $KL(P\|Q) = H(P,Q) - H(P)$.

Now, going back to our discussion of GANs, let's see how these different distance measures are related to the loss function for GANs. It can be mathematically shown that the loss function in the original GAN indeed *minimizes the JS divergence between the distribution of real and fake examples*. But, as discussed in an article by *Martin Arjovsky* and colleagues (*Wasserstein Generative Adversarial Networks*, `http://proceedings.mlr.press/v70/arjovsky17a/arjovsky17a.pdf`), JS divergence has problems training a GAN model, and therefore, in order to improve the training, the researchers proposed using the EM distance as a measure of dissimilarity between the distribution of real and fake examples.

What is the advantage of using EM distance?

To answer this question, we can consider an example that was given in the previously mentioned article by Martin Arjovsky and colleagues. To put it in simple words, assume we have two distributions, P and Q, which are two parallel lines. One line is fixed at $x = 0$ and the other line can move across the x-axis but is initially located at $x = \theta$, where $\theta > 0$.

It can be shown that the KL, TV, and JS dissimilarity measures are $KL(P\|Q) = +\infty$, $TV(P,Q) = 1$, and $JS(P,Q) = \frac{1}{2}\log 2$. None of these dissimilarity measures are a function of the parameter θ, and therefore, they cannot be differentiated with respect to θ toward making the distributions, P and Q, become similar to each other. On the other hand, the EM distance is $EM(P,Q) = |\theta|$, whose gradient with respect to θ exists and can push Q toward P.

Now, let's focus our attention on how EM distance can be used to train a GAN model. Let's assume P_r is the distribution of the real examples and P_g denotes the distributions of fake (generated) examples. P_r and P_g replace P and Q in the EM distance equation. As was mentioned earlier, computing the EM distance is an optimization problem by itself; therefore, this becomes computationally intractable, especially if we want to repeat this computation in each iteration of the GAN training loop. Fortunately, though, the computation of the EM distance can be simplified using a theorem called **Kantorovich-Rubinstein duality**, as follows:

$$W(P_r, P_g) = \sup_{\|f\|_L \leq 1} E_{u \in P_r}[f(u)] - E_{v \in P_g}[f(v)]$$

Here, the supremum is taken over all the *1-Lipschitz* continuous functions denoted by $\|f\|_L \leq 1$.

Lipschitz continuity

Based on 1-Lipschitz continuity, the function, *f*, must satisfy the following property:

$$|f(x_1) - f(x_2)| \leq |x_1 - x_2|$$

Furthermore, a real function, *f:R→R*, that satisfies the property

$$|f(x_1) - f(x_2)| \leq K|x_1 - x_2|$$

is called **K-Lipschitz continuous.**

Using EM distance in practice for GANs

Now, the question is, how do we find such a 1-Lipschitz continuous function to compute the Wasserstein distance between the distribution of real (P_r) and fake (P_g) outputs for a GAN? While the theoretical concepts behind the WGAN approach may seem complicated at first, the answer to this question is simpler than it may appear. Recall that we consider deep NNs to be universal function approximators. This means that we can simply train an NN model to approximate the Wasserstein distance function. As you saw in the previous section, the simple GAN uses a discriminator in the form of a classifier. For WGAN, the discriminator can be changed to behave as a *critic*, which returns a scalar score instead of a probability value. We can interpret this score as how realistic the input images are (like an art critic giving scores to artworks in a gallery).

To train a GAN using the Wasserstein distance, the losses for the discriminator, *D*, and generator, *G*, are defined as follows. The critic (that is, the discriminator network) returns its outputs for the batch of real image examples and the batch of synthesized examples. We use the notations $D(x)$ and $D(G(z))$, respectively.

Then, the following loss terms can be defined:

- The real component of the discriminator's loss:

$$L_{\text{real}}^{D} = -\frac{1}{N}\sum_{i} D(\boldsymbol{x}_i)$$

- The fake component of the discriminator's loss:

$$L_{\text{fake}}^{D} = \frac{1}{N}\sum_{i} D\big(G(\boldsymbol{z}_i)\big)$$

- The loss for the generator:

$$L^{G} = -\frac{1}{N}\sum_{i} D\big(G(\boldsymbol{z}_i)\big)$$

That will be all for the WGAN, except that we need to ensure that the 1-Lipschitz property of the critic function is preserved during training. For this purpose, the WGAN paper proposes clamping the weights to a small region, for example, [–0.01, 0.01].

Gradient penalty

In the paper by Arjovsky and colleagues, weight clipping is suggested for the 1-Lipschitz property of the discriminator (or critic). However, in another paper titled *Improved Training of Wasserstein GANs* by *Ishaan Gulrajani* and colleagues, 2017, which is freely available at `https://arxiv.org/pdf/1704.00028.pdf`, Ishaan Gulrajani and colleagues showed that clipping the weights can lead to exploding and vanishing gradients. Furthermore, weight clipping can also lead to capacity underuse, which means that the critic network is limited to learning only some simple functions, as opposed to more complex functions. Therefore, rather than clipping the weights, Ishaan Gulrajani and colleagues proposed **gradient penalty** (**GP**) as an alternative solution. The result is the **WGAN with gradient penalty** (**WGAN-GP**).

The procedure for the GP that is added in each iteration can be summarized by the following sequence of steps:

1. For each pair of real and fake examples $\left(\boldsymbol{x}^{[i]}, \tilde{\boldsymbol{x}}^{[i]}\right)$ in a given batch, choose a random number, $\alpha^{[i]}$, sampled from a uniform distribution, that is, $\alpha^{[i]} \in U(0,1)$.
2. Calculate an interpolation between the real and fake examples: $\breve{\boldsymbol{x}}^{[i]} = \alpha \boldsymbol{x}^{[i]} + (1-\alpha)\tilde{\boldsymbol{x}}^{[i]}$, resulting in a batch of interpolated examples.
3. Compute the discriminator (critic) output for all the interpolated examples, $D\left(\breve{\boldsymbol{x}}^{[i]}\right)$.
4. Calculate the gradients of the critic's output with respect to each interpolated example, that is, $\nabla_{\breve{\boldsymbol{x}}^{[i]}} D\left(\breve{\boldsymbol{x}}^{[i]}\right)$.
5. Compute the GP as:

$$L_{gp}^{D} = \frac{1}{N}\sum_{i}\left(\left\|\nabla_{\breve{\boldsymbol{x}}^{[i]}} D\left(\breve{\boldsymbol{x}}^{[i]}\right)\right\|_2 - 1\right)^2$$

The total loss for the discriminator is then as follows:

$$L_{\text{total}}^{D} = L_{\text{real}}^{D} + L_{\text{fake}}^{D} + \lambda L_{gp}^{D}$$

Here, λ is a tunable hyperparameter.

Implementing WGAN-GP to train the DCGAN model

We have already defined the helper function and class that create the generator and discriminator networks for DCGAN (`make_generator_network()` and `Discriminator()`). It is recommended to use layer normalization in WGAN instead of batch normalization. Layer normalization normalizes the inputs across features instead of across the batch dimension in batch normalization. The code to build the WGAN model is as follows:

```
>>> def make_generator_network_wgan(input_size, n_filters):
...     model = nn.Sequential(
...         nn.ConvTranspose2d(input_size, n_filters*4, 4,
...                            1, 0, bias=False),
...         nn.InstanceNorm2d(n_filters*4),
...         nn.LeakyReLU(0.2),
...
...         nn.ConvTranspose2d(n_filters*4, n_filters*2,
...                            3, 2, 1, bias=False),
...         nn.InstanceNorm2d(n_filters*2),
...         nn.LeakyReLU(0.2),
...
...         nn.ConvTranspose2d(n_filters*2, n_filters, 4,
...                            2, 1, bias=False),
...         nn.InstanceNorm2d(n_filters),
...         nn.LeakyReLU(0.2),
...
...         nn.ConvTranspose2d(n_filters, 1, 4, 2, 1, bias=False),
...         nn.Tanh()
...     )
...     return model
>>>
>>> class DiscriminatorWGAN(nn.Module):
...     def __init__(self, n_filters):
...         super().__init__()
...         self.network = nn.Sequential(
...             nn.Conv2d(1, n_filters, 4, 2, 1, bias=False),
...             nn.LeakyReLU(0.2),
...
```

```
...             nn.Conv2d(n_filters, n_filters*2, 4, 2, 1,
...                       bias=False),
...             nn.InstanceNorm2d(n_filters * 2),
...             nn.LeakyReLU(0.2),
...
...             nn.Conv2d(n_filters*2, n_filters*4, 3, 2, 1,
...                       bias=False),
...             nn.InstanceNorm2d(n_filters*4),
...             nn.LeakyReLU(0.2),
...
...             nn.Conv2d(n_filters*4, 1, 4, 1, 0, bias=False),
...             nn.Sigmoid()
...         )
...
...     def forward(self, input):
...         output = self.network(input)
...         return output.view(-1, 1).squeeze(0)
```

Now we can initiate the networks and their optimizers as follows:

```
>>> gen_model = make_generator_network_wgan(
...     z_size, n_filters
... ).to(device)
>>> disc_model = DiscriminatorWGAN(n_filters).to(device)
>>> g_optimizer = torch.optim.Adam(gen_model.parameters(), 0.0002)
>>> d_optimizer = torch.optim.Adam(disc_model.parameters(), 0.0002)
```

Next, we will define the function to compute the GP component as follows:

```
>>> from torch.autograd import grad as torch_grad
>>> def gradient_penalty(real_data, generated_data):
...     batch_size = real_data.size(0)
...
...     # Calculate interpolation
...     alpha = torch.rand(real_data.shape[0], 1, 1, 1,
...                        requires_grad=True, device=device)
...     interpolated = alpha * real_data + \
...                    (1 - alpha) * generated_data
...
...     # Calculate probability of interpolated examples
...     proba_interpolated = disc_model(interpolated)
...
```

```
...     # Calculate gradients of probabilities
...     gradients = torch_grad(
...         outputs=proba_interpolated, inputs=interpolated,
...         grad_outputs=torch.ones(proba_interpolated.size(),
...                                 device=device),
...         create_graph=True, retain_graph=True
...     )[0]
...
...     gradients = gradients.view(batch_size, -1)
...     gradients_norm = gradients.norm(2, dim=1)
...     return lambda_gp * ((gradients_norm - 1)**2).mean()
```

The WGAN version of discriminator and generator training functions are as follows:

```
>>> def d_train_wgan(x):
...     disc_model.zero_grad()
...
...     batch_size = x.size(0)
...     x = x.to(device)
...
...     # Calculate probabilities on real and generated data
...     d_real = disc_model(x)
...     input_z = create_noise(batch_size, z_size, mode_z).to(device)
...     g_output = gen_model(input_z)
...     d_generated = disc_model(g_output)
...     d_loss = d_generated.mean() - d_real.mean() + \
...              gradient_penalty(x.data, g_output.data)
...     d_loss.backward()
...     d_optimizer.step()
...     return d_loss.data.item()
>>>
>>> def g_train_wgan(x):
...     gen_model.zero_grad()
...
...     batch_size = x.size(0)
...     input_z = create_noise(batch_size, z_size, mode_z).to(device)
...     g_output = gen_model(input_z)
...
...     d_generated = disc_model(g_output)
...     g_loss = -d_generated.mean()
...
```

```
...     # gradient backprop & optimize ONLY G's parameters
...     g_loss.backward()
...     g_optimizer.step()
...     return g_loss.data.item()
```

Then we will train the model for 100 epochs and record the generator output of a fixed noise input:

```
>>> epoch_samples_wgan = []
>>> lambda_gp = 10.0
>>> num_epochs = 100
>>> torch.manual_seed(1)
>>> critic_iterations = 5
>>> for epoch in range(1, num_epochs+1):
...     gen_model.train()
...     d_losses, g_losses = [], []
...     for i, (x, _) in enumerate(mnist_dl):
...         for _ in range(critic_iterations):
...             d_loss = d_train_wgan(x)
...         d_losses.append(d_loss)
...         g_losses.append(g_train_wgan(x))
...
...     print(f'Epoch {epoch:03d} | D Loss >>'
...           f' {torch.FloatTensor(d_losses).mean():.4f}')
...     gen_model.eval()
...     epoch_samples_wgan.append(
...         create_samples(
...             gen_model, fixed_z
...         ).detach().cpu().numpy()
...     )
```

Finally, let's visualize the saved examples at some epochs to see how the WGAN model is learning and how the quality of synthesized examples changes over the course of learning. The following figure shows the results, which demonstrate slightly better image quality than what the DCGAN model generated:

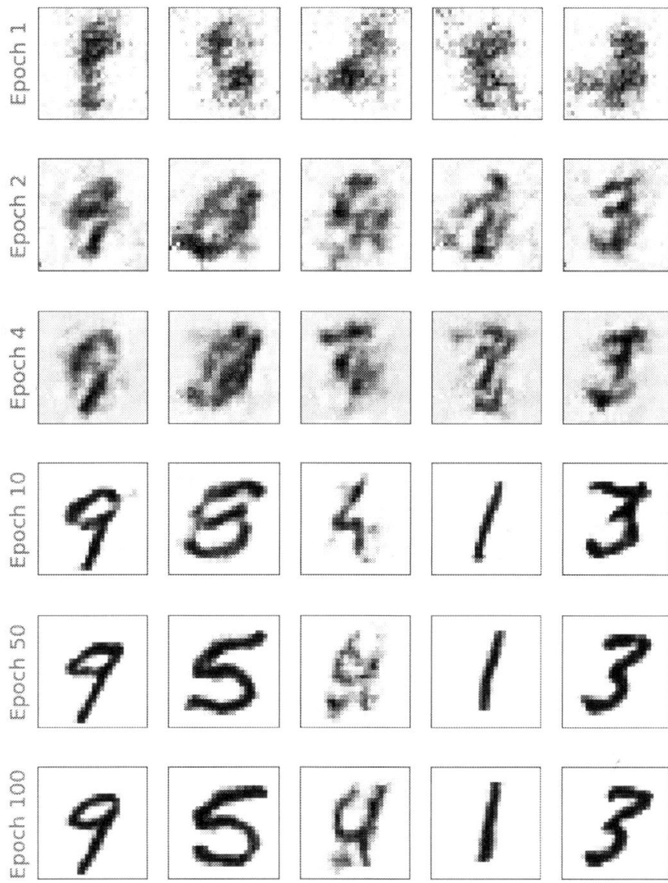

Figure 17.20: Generated images using WGAN

Mode collapse

Due to the adversarial nature of GAN models, it is notoriously hard to train them. One common cause of failure in training GANs is when the generator gets stuck in a small subspace and learns to generate similar samples. This is called **mode collapse**, and an example is shown in *Figure 17.21*.

The synthesized examples in this figure are not cherry-picked. This shows that the generator has failed to learn the entire data distribution, and instead, has taken a lazy approach focusing on a subspace:

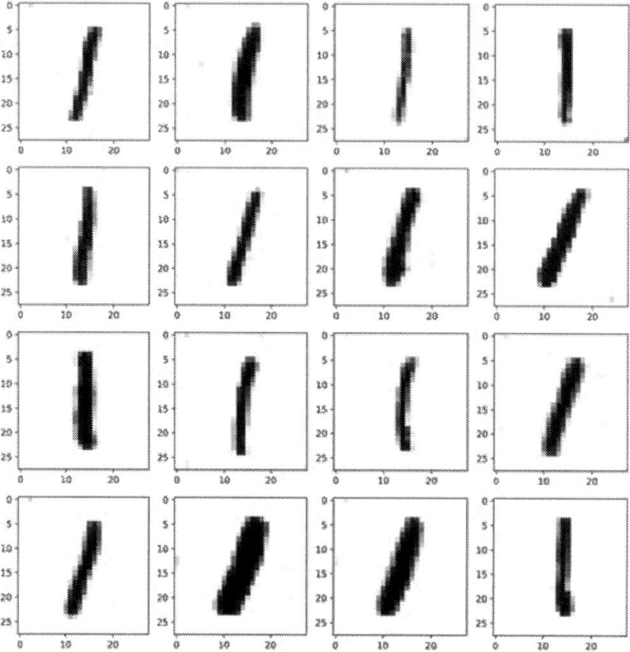

Figure 17.21: An example of mode collapse

Besides the vanishing and exploding gradient problems that we saw previously, there are some further aspects that can also make training GAN models difficult (indeed, it is an art). Here are a few suggested tricks from GAN artists.

One approach is called **mini-batch discrimination**, which is based on the fact that batches consisting of only real or fake examples are fed separately to the discriminator. In mini-batch discrimination, we let the discriminator compare examples across these batches to see whether a batch is real or fake. The diversity of a batch consisting of only real examples is most likely higher than the diversity of a fake batch if a model suffers from mode collapse.

Another technique that is commonly used for stabilizing GAN training is *feature matching*. In feature matching, we make a slight modification to the objective function of the generator by adding an extra term that minimizes the difference between the original and synthesized images based on intermediate representations (feature maps) of the discriminator. We encourage you to read more about this technique in the original article by *Ting-Chun Wang* and colleagues, titled *High Resolution Image Synthesis and Semantic Manipulation with Conditional GANs,* which is freely available at `https://arxiv.org/pdf/1711.11585.pdf`.

During the training, a GAN model can also get stuck in several modes and just hop between them. To avoid this behavior, you can store some old examples and feed them to the discriminator to prevent the generator from revisiting previous modes. This technique is referred to as *experience replay*. Furthermore, you can train multiple GANs with different random seeds so that the combination of all of them covers a larger part of the data distribution than any single one of them.

Other GAN applications

In this chapter, we mainly focused on generating examples using GANs and looked at a few tricks and techniques to improve the quality of synthesized outputs. The applications of GANs are expanding rapidly, including in computer vision, machine learning, and even other domains of science and engineering. A nice list of different GAN models and application areas can be found at `https://github.com/hindupuravinash/the-gan-zoo`.

It is worth mentioning that we covered GANs in an unsupervised fashion; that is, no class label information was used in the models that were covered in this chapter. However, the GAN approach can be generalized to semi-supervised and supervised tasks, as well. For example, the **conditional GAN (cGAN)** proposed by *Mehdi Mirza* and *Simon Osindero* in the paper *Conditional Generative Adversarial Nets*, 2014 (`https://arxiv.org/pdf/1411.1784.pdf`) uses the class label information and learns to synthesize new images conditioned on the provided label, that is, $\tilde{\boldsymbol{x}} = G(\mathbf{z}|y)$—applied to MNIST. This allows us to generate different digits in the range 0-9 selectively. Furthermore, conditional GANs allow us to do image-to-image translation, which is to learn how to convert a given image from a specific domain to another. In this context, one interesting work is the Pix2Pix algorithm, published in the paper *Image-to-Image Translation with Conditional Adversarial Networks* by *Philip Isola* and colleagues, 2018 (`https://arxiv.org/pdf/1611.07004.pdf`). It is worth mentioning that in the Pix2Pix algorithm, the discriminator provides the real/fake predictions for multiple patches across the image as opposed to a single prediction for an entire image.

CycleGAN is another interesting GAN model built on top of the cGAN, also for image-to-image translation. However, note that in CycleGAN, the training examples from the two domains are unpaired, meaning that there is no one-to-one correspondence between inputs and outputs. For example, using a CycleGAN, we could change the season of a picture taken in summer to winter. In the paper *Unpaired Image-to-Image Translation Using Cycle-Consistent Adversarial Networks* by *Jun-Yan Zhu* and colleagues, 2020 (`https://arxiv.org/pdf/1703.10593.pdf`), an impressive example shows horses converted into zebras.

Summary

In this chapter, you first learned about generative models in deep learning and their overall objective: synthesizing new data. We then covered how GAN models use a generator network and a discriminator network, which compete with each other in an adversarial training setting to improve each other. Next, we implemented a simple GAN model using only fully connected layers for both the generator and the discriminator.

We also covered how GAN models can be improved. First, you saw a DCGAN, which uses deep convolutional networks for both the generator and the discriminator. Along the way, you also learned about two new concepts: transposed convolution (for upsampling the spatial dimensionality of feature maps) and BatchNorm (for improving convergence during training).

We then looked at a WGAN, which uses the EM distance to measure the distance between the distributions of real and fake samples. Finally, we talked about the WGAN with GP to maintain the 1-Lipschitz property instead of clipping the weights.

In the next chapter, we will look at graph neural networks. Previously, we have been focused on tabular and image datasets. In contrast, graph neural networks are designed for graph-structured data, which allows us to work with datasets that are ubiquitous in social sciences, engineering, and biology. Popular examples of graph-structure data include social network graphs and molecules consisting of atoms connected by covalent bonds.

Join our book's Discord space

Join our Discord community to meet like-minded people and learn alongside more than 2000 members at:

`https://packt.link/MLwPyTorch`

18

Graph Neural Networks for Capturing Dependencies in Graph Structured Data

In this chapter, we will introduce a class of deep learning models that operates on graph data, namely, **graph neural networks** (**GNNs**). GNNs have been an area of rapid development in recent years. According to the *State of AI* report from 2021 (`https://www.stateof.ai/2021-report-launch.html`), GNNs have evolved "from niche to one of the hottest fields of AI research."

GNNs have been applied in a variety of areas, including the following:

- Text classification (`https://arxiv.org/abs/1710.10903`)
- Recommender systems (`https://arxiv.org/abs/1704.06803`)
- Traffic forecasting (`https://arxiv.org/abs/1707.01926`)
- Drug discovery (`https://arxiv.org/abs/1806.02473`)

While we can't cover every new idea in this rapidly developing space, we'll provide a basis to understand how GNNs function and how they can be implemented. In addition, we'll introduce the **PyTorch Geometric** library, which provides resources for managing graph data for deep learning as well as implementations of many different kinds of graph layers that you can use in your deep learning models.

The topics that will be covered in this chapter are as follows:

- An introduction to graph data and how it can be represented for use in deep neural networks
- An explanation of graph convolutions, a major building block of common GNNs
- A tutorial showing how to implement GNNs for molecular property prediction using PyTorch Geometric
- An overview of methods at the cutting edge of the GNN field

Introduction to graph data

Broadly speaking, graphs represent a certain way we describe and capture relationships in data. Graphs are a particular kind of data structure that is nonlinear and abstract. And since graphs are abstract objects, a concrete representation needs to be defined so the graphs can be operated on. Furthermore, graphs can be defined to have certain properties that may require different representations. *Figure 18.1* summarizes the common types of graphs, which we will discuss in more detail in the following subsections:

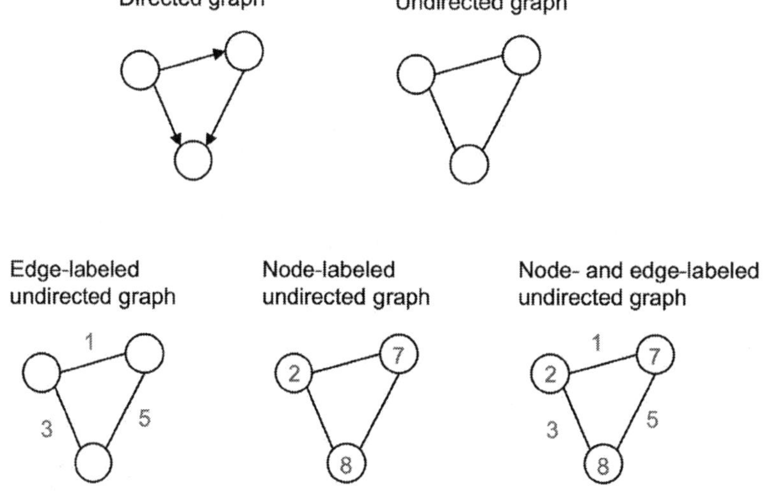

Figure 18.1: Common types of graphs

Undirected graphs

An **undirected graph** consists of **nodes** (in graph theory also often called **vertices**) that are connected via edges where the order of the nodes and their connection does not matter. *Figure 18.2* sketches two typical examples of undirected graphs, a friend graph, and a graph of a chemical molecule consisting of atoms connected through chemical bonds (we will be discussing such molecular graphs in much more detail in later sections):

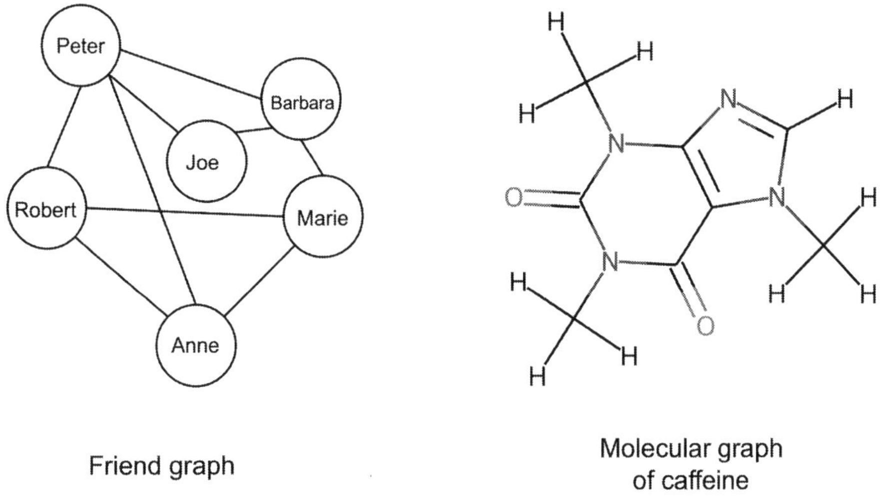

Figure 18.2: Two examples of undirected graphs

Other common examples of data that can be represented as undirected graphs include images, protein-protein interaction networks, and point clouds.

Mathematically, an undirected graph G is a pair (V, E), where V is a set of the graph's nodes, and E is the set of edges making up the paired nodes. The graph can then be encoded as a $|V|\times|V|$ **adjacency matrix** A. Each element x_{ij} in matrix A is either a 1 or a 0, with 1 denoting an edge between nodes i and j (vice versa, 0 denotes the absence of an edge). Since the graph is undirected, an additional property of A is that $x_{ij} = x_{ji}$.

Directed graphs

Directed graphs, in contrast to undirected graphs discussed in the previous section, connect nodes via *directed* edges. Mathematically they are defined in the same way as an undirected graph, except that E, the set of edges, is a set of *ordered* pairs. Therefore, element x_{ij} of A does need not equal x_{ji}.

An example of a directed graph is a citation network, where nodes are publications and edges from a node are directed toward the nodes of papers that a given paper cited.

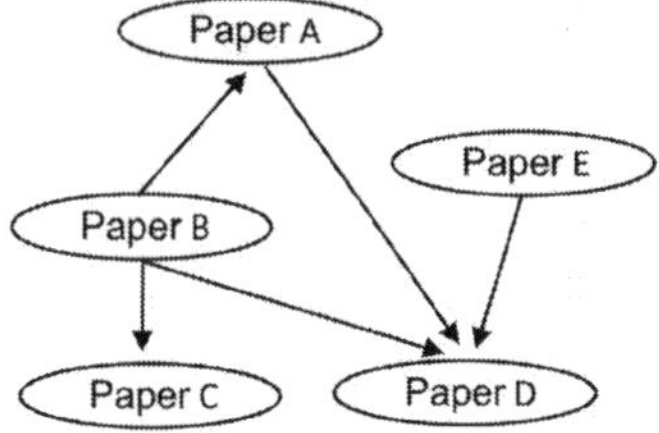

Figure 18.3: An example of a directed graph

Labeled graphs

Many graphs we are interested in working with have additional information associated with each of their nodes and edges. For example, if you consider the caffeine molecule shown earlier, molecules can be represented as graphs where each node is a chemical element (for example, O, C, N, or H atoms) and each edge is the type of bond (for example, single or double bond) between its two nodes. These node and edge features need to be encoded in some capacity. Given graph G, defined by the node set and edge set tuple (V, E), we define a $|V|\times f_V$ node feature matrix $\boldsymbol{X}$, where f_V is the length of the label vector of each node. For edge labels, we define an $|E|\times f_E$ edge feature matrix $\boldsymbol{X}_E$, where f_E is the length of the label vector of each edge.

Molecules are an excellent example of data that can be represented as a **labeled graph**, and we will be working with molecular data throughout the chapter. As such, we will take this opportunity to cover their representation in detail in the next section.

Representing molecules as graphs

As a chemical overview, molecules can be thought of as groups of atoms held together by chemical bonds. There are different atoms corresponding to different chemical elements, for example, common elements include carbon (C), oxygen (O), nitrogen (N), and hydrogen (H). Also, there are different kinds of bonds that form the connection between atoms, for example, single or double bonds.

We can represent a molecule as an undirected graph with a node label matrix, where each row is a one-hot encoding of the associated node's atom type. Additionally, there is an edge label matrix where each row is a one-hot encoding of the associated edge's bond type. To simplify this representation, hydrogen atoms are sometimes made implicit since their location can be inferred with basic chemical rules. Considering the caffeine molecule we saw earlier, an example of a graph representation with implicit hydrogen atoms is shown in *Figure 18.4*:

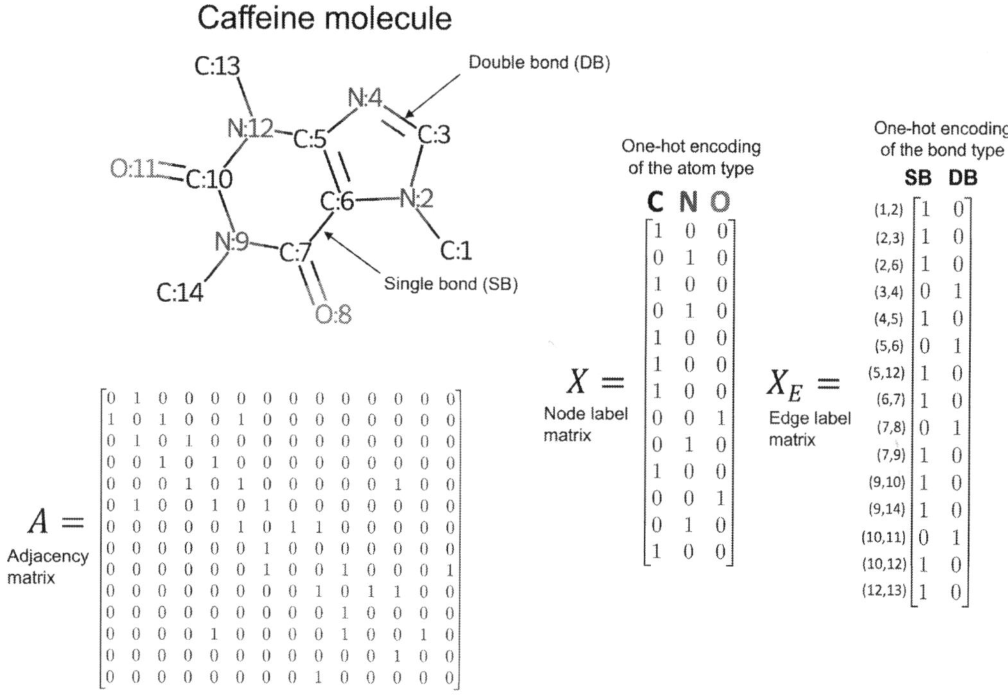

Figure 18.4: Graph representation of a caffeine molecule

Understanding graph convolutions

The previous section showed how graph data can be represented. The next logical step is to discuss what tools we have that can effectively utilize those representations.

In the following subsections, we will introduce graph convolutions, which are the key component for building GNNs. In this section, we'll see why we want to use convolutions on graphs and discuss what attributes we want those convolutions to have. We'll then introduce graph convolutions through an implementation example.

The motivation behind using graph convolutions

To help explain graph convolutions, let's briefly recap how convolutions are utilized in convolutional neural networks (CNNs), which we discussed in *Chapter 14, Classifying Images with Deep Convolutional Neural Networks*. In the context of images, we can think of a convolution as the process of sliding a convolutional filter over an image, where, at each step, a weighted sum is computed between the filter and the receptive field (the part of the image it is currently on top of).

As discussed in the CNN chapter, the filter can be viewed as a detector for a specific feature. This approach to feature detection is well-suited for images for several reasons, for instance, the following priors we can place on image data:

1. **Shift-invariance:** We can still recognize a feature in an image regardless of where it is located (for example, after translation). A cat can be recognized as a cat whether it is in the top left, bottom right, or another part of an image.
2. **Locality:** Nearby pixels are closely related.
3. **Hierarchy:** Larger parts of an image can often be broken down into combinations of associated smaller parts. A cat has a head and legs; the head has eyes and a nose; the eyes have pupils and irises.

Interested readers can find a more formal description of these priors, and priors assumed by GNNs, in the 2019 article *Understanding the Representation Power of Graph Neural Networks in Learning Graph Topology*, by *N. Dehmamy, A.-L. Barabasi*, and *R. Yu* (`https://arxiv.org/abs/1907.05008`).

Another reason convolutions are well-suited for processing images is that the number of trainable parameters does not depend on the dimensionality of the input. You could train a series of 3×3 convolutional filters on, for example, a 256×256 or a 9×9 image. (However, if the same image is presented in different resolutions, the receptive fields and, therefore, the extracted features will differ. And for higher-resolution images, we may want to choose larger kernels or add additional layers to extract useful features effectively.)

Like images, graphs also have natural priors that justify a convolutional approach. Both kinds of data, images and graphs, share the locality prior. However, how we define locality differs. In images, the prior is on locality in 2D space, while with graphs, it is structural locality. Intuitively, this means that a node that is one edge away is more likely to be related than a node five edges away. For example, in a citation graph, a directly cited publication, which would be one edge away, is more likely to have similar subject matter than a publication with multiple degrees of separation.

A strict prior for graph data is **permutation invariance**, which means that the ordering of the nodes does not affect the output. This is illustrated in *Figure 18.5*, where changing the ordering of a graph's nodes does not change the graph's structure:

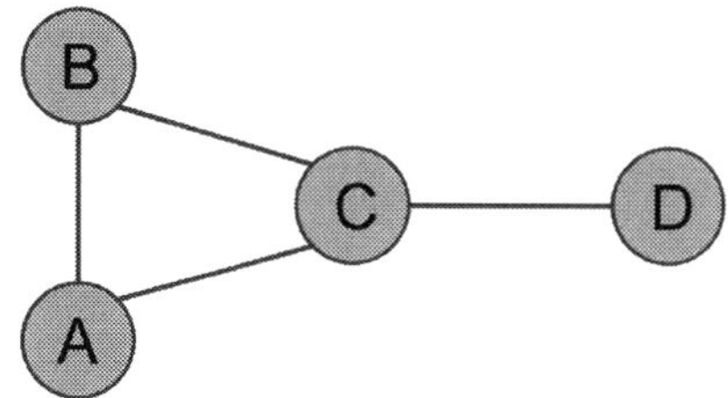

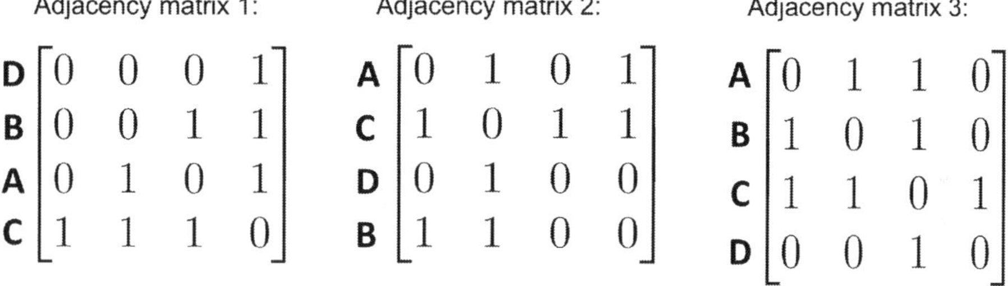

Figure 18.5: Different adjacency matrices representing the same graph

Since the same graph can be represented by multiple adjacency matrices, as illustrated in *Figure 18.5*, consequently, any graph convolution needs to be permutation invariant.

A convolutional approach is also desirable for graphs because it can function with a fixed parameter set for graphs of different sizes. This property is arguably even more important for graphs than images. For instance, there are many image datasets with a fixed resolution where a fully connected approach (for example, using a multilayer perceptron) could be possible, as we have seen in *Chapter 11, Implementing a Multilayer Artificial Neural Network from Scratch*. In contrast, most graph datasets contain graphs of varying sizes.

While image convolutional operators are standardized, there are many different kinds of graph convolutions, and the development of new graph convolutions is a very active area of research. Our focus is on providing general ideas so that readers can rationalize about the GNNs they wish to utilize. To this end, the following subsection will show how to implement a basic graph convolution in PyTorch. Then, in the next section, we will construct a simple GNN in PyTorch from the ground up.

Implementing a basic graph convolution

In this subsection, we will introduce a basic graph convolution function and see what happens when it is applied to a graph. Consider the following graph and its representation:

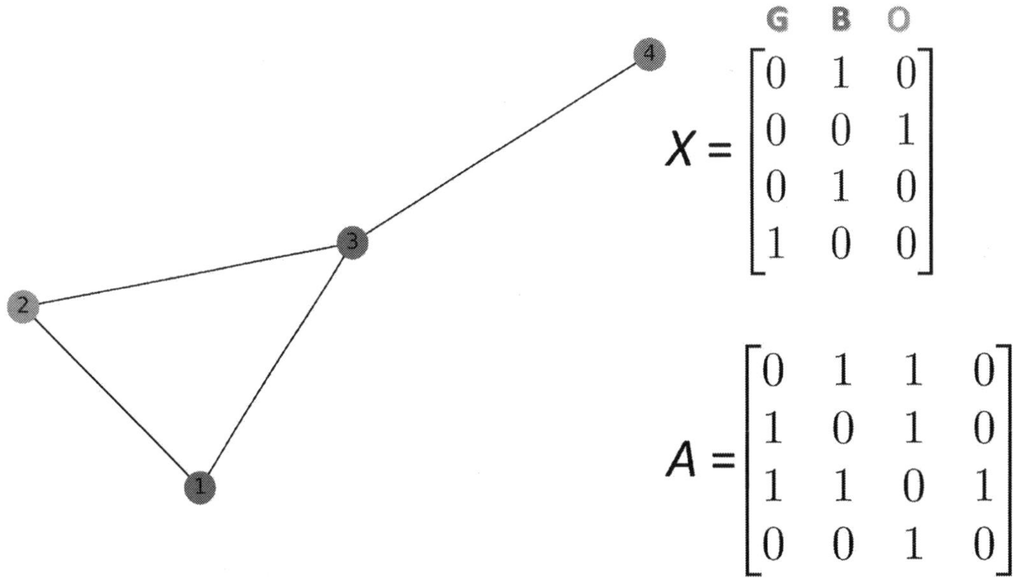

Figure 18.6: A representation of a graph

Figure 18.6 depicts an undirected graph with node labels specified by an $n \times n$ adjacency matrix A and $n \times f_{in}$ node feature matrix X, where the only feature is a one-hot representation of each node's color—green (G), blue (B), or orange (O).

One of the most versatile libraries for graph manipulation and visualization is NetworkX, which we will be using to illustrate how to construct graphs from a label matrix X and a node matrix A.

Installing NetworkX

NetworkX is a handy Python library for manipulating and visualizing graphs. It can be installed via `pip`:

```
pip install networkx
```

We used version 2.6.2 to create the graph visualizations in this chapter. For more information, please visit the official website at `https://networkx.org`.

Using NetworkX, we can construct the graph shown in *Figure 18.6* as follows:

```
>>> import numpy as np
>>> import networkx as nx
```

```
>>> G = nx.Graph()
... # Hex codes for colors if we draw graph
>>> blue, orange, green = "#1f77b4", "#ff7f0e", "#2ca02c"
>>> G.add_nodes_from([
...     (1, {"color": blue}),
...     (2, {"color": orange}),
...     (3, {"color": blue}),
...     (4, {"color": green})
... ])
>>> G.add_edges_from([(1,2), (2,3), (1,3), (3,4)])
>>> A = np.asarray(nx.adjacency_matrix(G).todense())
>>> print(A)
[[0 1 1 0]
[1 0 1 0]
[1 1 0 1]
[0 0 1 0]]

>>> def build_graph_color_label_representation(G, mapping_dict):
...     one_hot_idxs = np.array([mapping_dict[v] for v in
...         nx.get_node_attributes(G, 'color').values()])
>>>     one_hot_encoding = np.zeros(
...         (one_hot_idxs.size, len(mapping_dict)))
>>>     one_hot_encoding[
...         np.arange(one_hot_idxs.size), one_hot_idxs] = 1
>>>     return one_hot_encoding
>>> X = build_graph_color_label_representation(
...     G, {green: 0, blue: 1, orange: 2})
>>> print(X)
[[0., 1., 0.],
[0., 0., 1.],
[0., 1., 0.],
[1., 0., 0.]]
```

To draw the graph constructed in the preceding code, we can then use the following code:

```
>>> color_map = nx.get_node_attributes(G, 'color').values()
>>> nx.draw(G,with_labels=True, node_color=color_map)
```

In the preceding code example, we first initiated a new `Graph` object from NetworkX. We then added nodes 1 to 4 together with color specifications for visualization. After adding the nodes, we specified their connections (edges). Using the `adjacency_matrix` constructor from NetworkX, we create the adjacency matrix A, and our custom `build_graph_color_label_representation` function creates the node label matrix X from the information we added to the `Graph` object earlier.

With graph convolutions, we can interpret each row of X as being an embedding of the information that is stored at the node corresponding to that row. Graph convolutions update the embeddings at each node based on the embeddings of their neighbors and themselves. For our example implementation, the graph convolution will take the following form:

$$\boldsymbol{x}_i' = \boldsymbol{x}_i \boldsymbol{W}_1 + \sum_{j \in N(i)} \boldsymbol{x}_j \boldsymbol{W}_2 + b$$

Here, $\boldsymbol{x}_i'$ is the updated embedding for node i; $\boldsymbol{W}_1$ and $\boldsymbol{W}_2$ are $f_{in} \times f_{out}$ matrices of learnable filter weights; and b is a learnable bias vector of length f_{out}.

The two weight matrices $\boldsymbol{W}_1$ and $\boldsymbol{W}_2$ can be considered filter banks, where each column is an individual filter. Note that this filter design is most effective when the locality prior on graph data holds. If a value at a node is highly correlated with the value at another node many edges away, a single convolution will not capture that relationship. Stacking convolutions will capture more distant relationships, as illustrated in *Figure 18.7* (we set the bias to zero for simplicity):

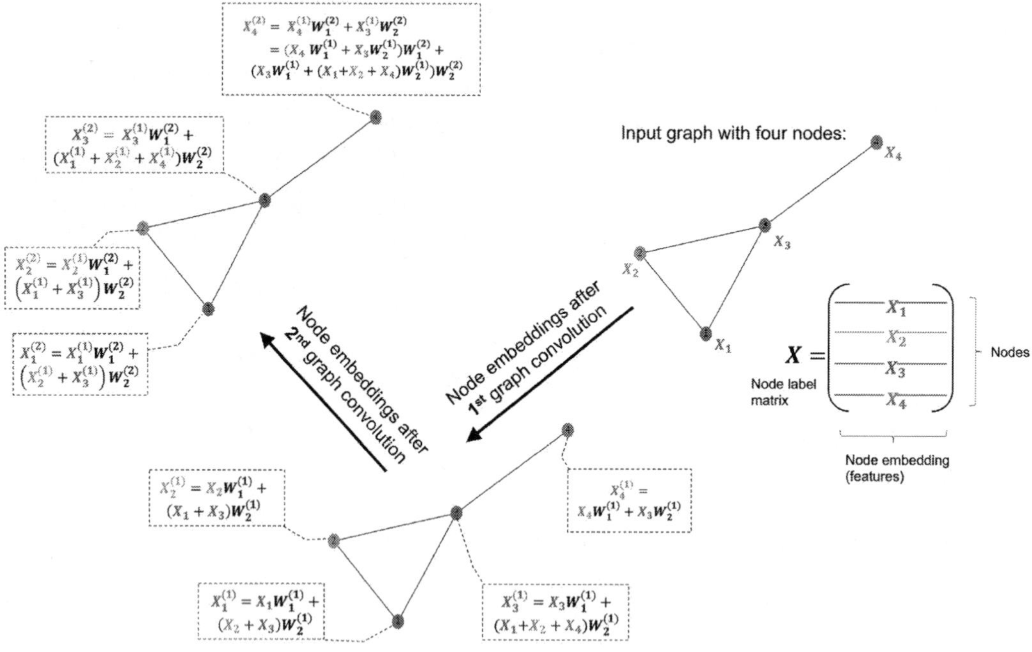

Figure 18.7: Capturing relationships from a graph

The design of the graph convolution illustrated in *Figure 18.7* fits our priors on graph data, but it may not be clear how to implement the sum over neighbors in matrix form. This is where we utilize the adjacency matrix A. The matrix form of this convolution is $XW_1 + AXW_2$. Here, the adjacency matrix, consisting of 1s and 0s, acts as a mask to select nodes and compute the desired sums. In NumPy, initializing this layer and computing a forward pass on the previous graph could be written as follows:

```
>>> f_in, f_out = X.shape[1], 6
>>> W_1 = np.random.rand(f_in, f_out)
>>> W_2 = np.random.rand(f_in, f_out)
>>> h = np.dot(X, W_1)+ np.dot(np.dot(A,X), W_2)
```

Computing a forward pass of a graph convolution is that easy.

Ultimately, we want a graph convolutional layer to update the representation of the node information encoded in X by utilizing the structural (connectivity) information provided by A. There are many potential ways to do this, and this plays out in the numerous kinds of graph convolutions that have been developed.

To talk about different graph convolutions, generally, it would be nice for them to have a unifying framework. Thankfully, such a framework was presented in *Neural Message Passing for Quantum Chemistry* by *Justin Gilmer* and colleagues, 2017, `https://arxiv.org/abs/1704.01212`.

In this **message-passing** framework, each node in the graph has an associated hidden state $h_i^{(t)}$, where i is the node's index at time step t. The initial value $h_i^{(0)}$ is defined as X_i, which is the row of X associated with node i.

Each graph convolution can be split into a message-passing phase and a node update phase. Let $N(i)$ be the neighbors of node i. For undirected graphs, $N(i)$ is the set of nodes that share an edge with node i. For directed graphs, $N(i)$ is the set of nodes that have an edge whose endpoint is node i. The message-passing phase can be formulated as follows:

$$m_i = \sum_{j \in N(i)} M_t\left(h_i^{(t)}, h_j^{(t)}, e_{ij}\right)$$

Here, M_t is a message function. In our example layer, we define this message function as $M_t = h_j^{(t)} W_2$. The node update phase with the update function U_t is $h_i^{(t+1)} = U_t\left(h_i^{(t)}, m_i\right)$. In our example layer, this update is $h_i^{(t+1)} = h_i^{(t)} W_1 + m_i + b$.

Figure 18.8 visualizes the message-passing idea and summarizes the convolution we have implemented:

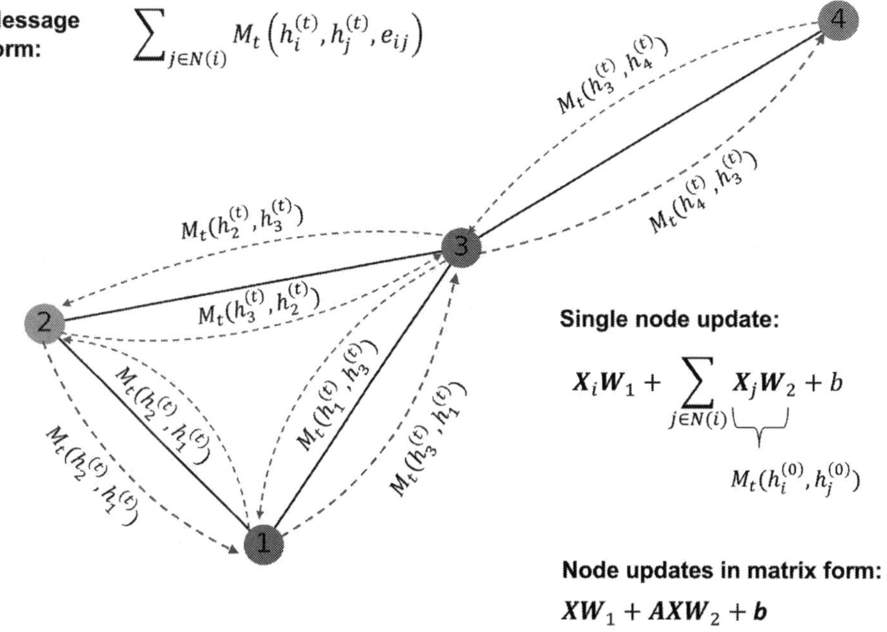

Figure 18.8: The convolutions implemented on the graph and the message form

In the next section, we'll incorporate this graph convolution layer into a GNN model implemented in PyTorch.

Implementing a GNN in PyTorch from scratch

The previous section focused on understanding and implementing a graph convolution operation. In this section, we'll walk you through a basic implementation of a graph neural network to illustrate how to apply these methods to graphs if you start from scratch. If this approach appears complicated, don't worry; GNNs are relatively complex models to implement. Thus, we'll introduce PyTorch Geometric in a later section, which provides tools to ease the implementation of, and the data management for, graph neural networks.

Defining the NodeNetwork model

We will start this section by showing a PyTorch from-scratch implementation of a GNN. We will take a top-down approach, starting with the main neural network model, which we call `NodeNetwork`, and then we will fill in the individual details:

```
import networkx as nx
import torch
from torch.nn.parameter import Parameter
import numpy as np
import math
import torch.nn.functional as F

class NodeNetwork(torch.nn.Module):
    def __init__(self, input_features):
        super().__init__()
        self.conv_1 = BasicGraphConvolutionLayer (
            input_features, 32)
        self.conv_2 = BasicGraphConvolutionLayer(32, 32)
        self.fc_1 = torch.nn.Linear(32, 16)
        self.out_layer = torch.nn.Linear(16, 2)

    def forward(self, X, A, batch_mat):
        x = F.relu(self.conv_1(X, A))
        x = F.relu(self.conv_2(x, A))
        output = global_sum_pool(x, batch_mat)
        output = self.fc_1(output)
        output = self.out_layer(output)
        return F.softmax(output, dim=1)
```

The `NodeNetwork` model we just defined can be summarized as follows:

1. Perform two graph convolutions (`self.conv_1` and `self.conv_2`)
2. Pool all the node embeddings via `global_sum_pool`, which we will define later
3. Run the pooled embeddings through two fully connected layers (`self.fc_1` and `self.out_layer`)
4. Output a class-membership probability via softmax

The structure of the network along with a visualization of what each layer is doing is summarized in *Figure 18.9*:

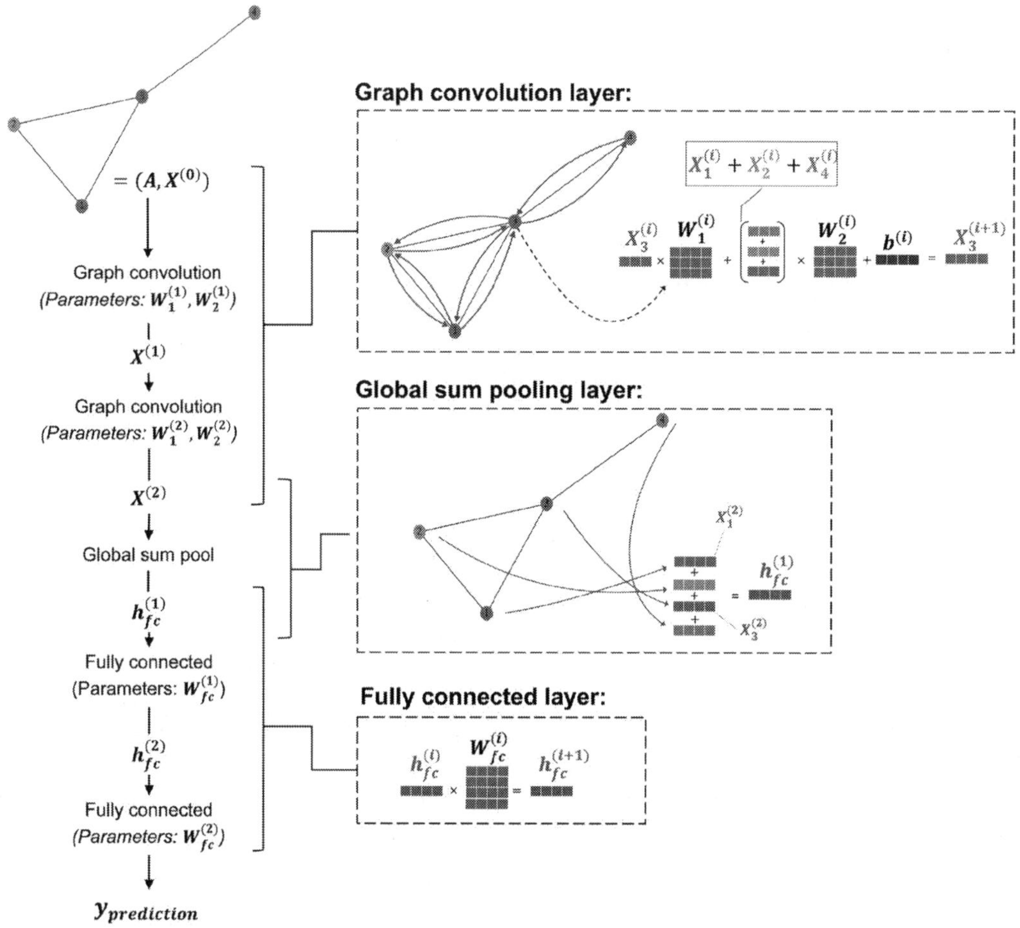

Figure 18.9: A visualization of each neural network layer

The individual aspects, such as the graph convolution layers and global pooling, will be discussed in the next subsections.

Coding the NodeNetwork's graph convolution layer

Now, let's define the graph convolution operation (`BasicGraphConvolutionLayer`) that was used inside the previous `NodeNetwork` class:

```
class BasicGraphConvolutionLayer(torch.nn.Module):
    def __init__(self, in_channels, out_channels):
        super().__init__()
        self.in_channels = in_channels
```

```
        self.out_channels = out_channels
        self.W2 = Parameter(torch.rand(
            (in_channels, out_channels), dtype=torch.float32))
        self.W1 = Parameter(torch.rand(
            (in_channels, out_channels), dtype=torch.float32))

        self.bias = Parameter(torch.zeros(
                out_channels, dtype=torch.float32))
    def forward(self, X, A):
        potential_msgs = torch.mm(X, self.W2)
        propagated_msgs = torch.mm(A, potential_msgs)
        root_update = torch.mm(X, self.W1)
        output = propagated_msgs + root_update + self.bias
        return output
```

As with fully connected layers and image convolutional layers, we add a bias term so that the intercept of the linear combination of the layer outputs (prior to the application of a nonlinearity like ReLU) can vary. The `forward()` method implements the matrix form of the forward pass, which we discussed in the previous subsection, with the addition of a bias term.

To try out the `BasicGraphConvolutionLayer`, let's apply it to the graph and adjacency matrix that we defined in the section *Implementing a basic graph convolution* previously:

```
>>> print('X.shape:', X.shape)
X.shape: (4, 3)

>>> print('A.shape:', A.shape)
A.shape: (4, 4)

>>> basiclayer = BasicGraphConvolutionLayer(3, 8)
>>> out = basiclayer(
...     X=torch.tensor(X, dtype=torch.float32),
...     A=torch.tensor(A, dtype=torch.float32)
... )

>>> print('Output shape:', out.shape)
Output shape: torch.Size([4, 8])
```

Based on the code example above, we can see that our `BasicGraphConvolutionLayer` converted the four-node graph consisting of three features into a representation with eight features.

Adding a global pooling layer to deal with varying graph sizes

Next, we define the `global_sum_pool()` function that was used in the `NodeNetwork` class, where `global_sum_pool()` implements a global pooling layer. Global pooling layers aggregate all of a graph's node embeddings into a fixed-sized output. As shown in *Figure 18.9*, `global_sum_pool()` sums all the node embeddings of a graph. We note that this global pooling is relatively similar to the global average pooling used in CNNs, which is used before the data is run through fully connected layers, as we have seen in *Chapter 14, Classifying Images with Deep Convolutional Neural Networks.*

Summing all the node embeddings results in a loss of information, so reshaping the data would be preferable, but since graphs can have different sizes, this is not feasible. Global pooling can be done with any permutation invariant function, for example, `sum`, `max`, and `mean`. Here is the implementation of `global_sum_pool()`:

```
def global_sum_pool(X, batch_mat):
    if batch_mat is None or batch_mat.dim() == 1:
        return torch.sum(X, dim=0).unsqueeze(0)
    else:
        return torch.mm(batch_mat, X)
```

If data is not batched or the batch size is one, this function just sums over the current node embeddings. Otherwise, the embeddings are multiplied with `batch_mat`, which has a structure based on how graph data is batched.

When all data in a dataset has the same dimensionality, batching the data is as straightforward as adding a dimension by stacking the data. (Side note: the function called in the default batching function in PyTorch is literally called `stack`.) Since graph sizes vary, this approach is not feasible with graph data unless padding is used. However, padding can be inefficient in cases where graph sizes can vary substantially. Usually, the better way to deal with varying graph sizes is to treat each batch as a single graph where each graph in the batch is a subgraph that is disconnected from the rest. This is illustrated in *Figure 18.10*:

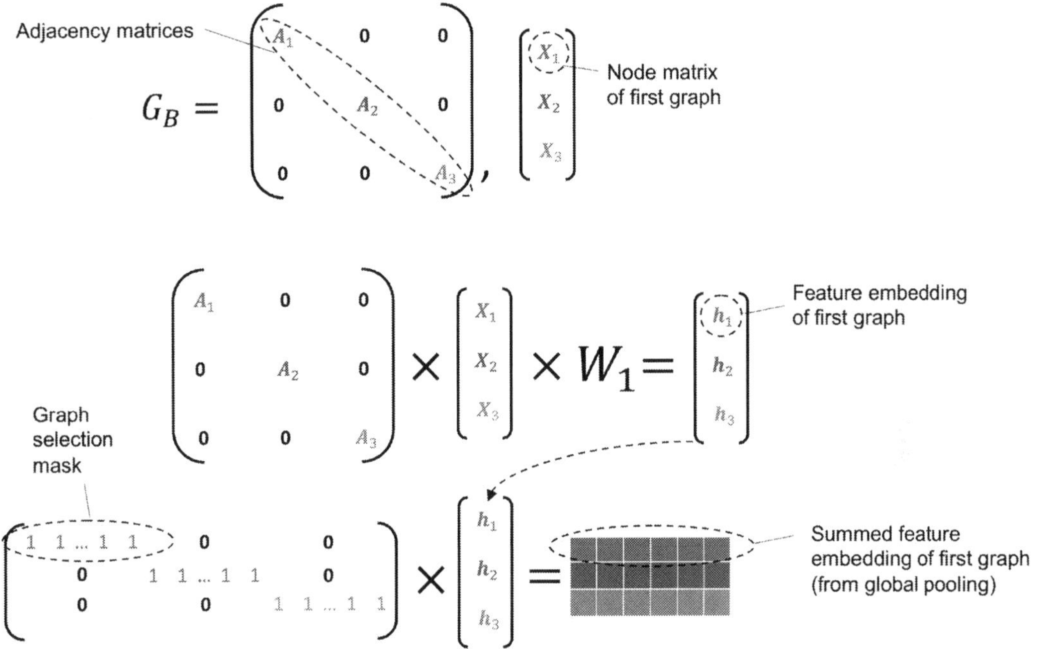

Figure 18.10: How to deal with varying graph sizes

To describe *Figure 18.10* more formally, suppose we are given graphs $G_1, \ldots, G_k$ of sizes $n_1, \ldots, n_k$ with f features per node. In addition, we are given the corresponding adjacency matrices $A_1, \ldots, A_k$ and feature matrices $X_1, \ldots, X_k$. Let N be the total number of nodes, $N = \sum_{i=1}^{k} n_i$, $s_1 = 0$, and $s_i = s_{i-1} + n_{i-1}$ for $1 < i \leq k$. As shown in the figure, we define a graph G_B with $N{\times}N$ adjacency matrix A_B and $N{\times}f$ feature matrix X_B. Using Python index notation, $A_B[s_i{:}s_i + n_i, s_i + n_i] = A_i$, and all other elements of A_B outside these index sets are 0. Additionally, $X_B[s_i{:}s_i + n_i, :] = X_i$.

By design, disconnected nodes will never be in the same receptive field of a graph convolution. As a result, when backpropagating gradients of G_B through graph convolutions, the gradients attached to each graph in the batch will be independent. This means that if we treat a set of graph convolutions as a function f, if $h_B = f(X_B, A_B)$ and $h_i = f(X_i, A_i)$, then $h_B[s_i{:}s_i + n, :] = h_i$. If the sum global pooling extracts the sums of each h_i from h_B as separate vectors, passing that stack of vectors through fully connected layers would keep the gradients of each item in the batch separate throughout the entire backpropagation.

This is the purpose of `batch_mat` in `global_sum_pool()`—to serve as a graph selection mask that keeps the graphs in the batch separate. We can generate this mask for graphs of sizes n_1, ..., n_k with the following code:

```
def get_batch_tensor(graph_sizes):
    starts = [sum(graph_sizes[:idx])
              for idx in range(len(graph_sizes))]
    stops = [starts[idx] + graph_sizes[idx]
             for idx in range(len(graph_sizes))]
    tot_len = sum(graph_sizes)
    batch_size = len(graph_sizes)
    batch_mat = torch.zeros([batch_size, tot_len]).float()
    for idx, starts_and_stops in enumerate(zip(starts, stops)):
        start = starts_and_stops[0]
        stop = starts_and_stops[1]
        batch_mat[idx,start:stop] = 1
    return batch_mat
```

Thus, given a batch size, b, `batch_mat` is a $b \times N$ matrix where batch_mat[i–1, s_i:$s_i + n_i$] = 1 for $1 \leq i \leq k$ and where elements outside these index sets are 0. The following is a collate function for constructing a representation of some G_B and a corresponding batch matrix:

```
# batch is a list of dictionaries each containing
# the representation and label of a graph
def collate_graphs(batch):
    adj_mats = [graph['A'] for graph in batch]
    sizes = [A.size(0) for A in adj_mats]
    tot_size = sum(sizes)
    # create batch matrix
    batch_mat = get_batch_tensor(sizes)
    # combine feature matrices
    feat_mats = torch.cat([graph['X'] for graph in batch], dim=0)
    # combine labels
    labels = torch.cat([graph['y'] for graph in batch], dim=0)
    # combine adjacency matrices
    batch_adj = torch.zeros([tot_size, tot_size], dtype=torch.float32)
    accum = 0
    for adj in adj_mats:
        g_size = adj.shape[0]
        batch_adj[accum:accum+g_size,accum:accum+g_size] = adj
        accum = accum + g_size
    repr_and_label = {'A': batch_adj,
```

```
            'X': feat_mats, 'y': labels,
            'batch': batch_mat}
    return repr_and_label
```

Preparing the DataLoader

In this section, we will see how the code from the previous subsections all comes together. First, we will generate some graphs and put them into a PyTorch `Dataset`. Then, we will use our `collate` function in a `DataLoader` for our GNN.

But before we define the graphs, let's implement a function that builds a dictionary representation that we will use later:

```
def get_graph_dict(G, mapping_dict):
    # Function builds dictionary representation of graph G
    A = torch.from_numpy(
        np.asarray(nx.adjacency_matrix(G).todense())).float()
    # build_graph_color_label_representation()
    # was introduced with the first example graph
    X = torch.from_numpy(
      build_graph_color_label_representation(
              G, mapping_dict)).float()
    # kludge since there is not specific task for this example
    y = torch.tensor([[1,0]]).float()
    return {'A': A, 'X': X, 'y': y, 'batch': None}
```

This function takes a NetworkX graph and returns a dictionary containing its adjacency matrix `A`, its node feature matrix `X`, and a binary label `y`. Since we won't actually be training this model on a real-world task, we just set the labels arbitrarily. Then, `nx.adjacency_matrix()` takes a NetworkX graph and returns a sparse representation that we convert to a dense `np.array` form using `todense()`.

We'll now construct graphs and use the `get_graph_dict` function to convert NetworkX graphs to a format our network can handle:

```
>>> # building 4 graphs to treat as a dataset
>>> blue, orange, green = "#1f77b4", "#ff7f0e","#2ca02c"
>>> mapping_dict= {green:0, blue:1, orange:2}
>>> G1 = nx.Graph()
>>> G1.add_nodes_from([
...     (1,{"color": blue}),
...     (2,{"color": orange}),
...     (3,{"color": blue}),
...     (4,{"color": green})
... ])
```

```
>>> G1.add_edges_from([(1, 2), (2, 3), (1, 3), (3, 4)])
>>> G2 = nx.Graph()
>>> G2.add_nodes_from([
...     (1,{"color": green}),
...     (2,{"color": green}),
...     (3,{"color": orange}),
...     (4,{"color": orange}),
...     (5,{"color": blue})
... ])
>>> G2.add_edges_from([(2, 3),(3, 4),(3, 1),(5, 1)])
>>> G3 = nx.Graph()
>>> G3.add_nodes_from([
...     (1,{"color": orange}),
...     (2,{"color": orange}),
...     (3,{"color": green}),
...     (4,{"color": green}),
...     (5,{"color": blue}),
...     (6,{"color":orange})
... ])
>>> G3.add_edges_from([(2,3), (3,4), (3,1), (5,1), (2,5), (6,1)])
>>> G4 = nx.Graph()
>>> G4.add_nodes_from([
...     (1,{"color": blue}),
...     (2,{"color": blue}),
...     (3,{"color": green})
... ])
>>> G4.add_edges_from([(1, 2), (2, 3)])
>>> graph_list = [get_graph_dict(graph, mapping_dict) for graph in
...     [G1, G2, G3, G4]]
```

The graphs this code generates are visualized in *Figure 18.11*:

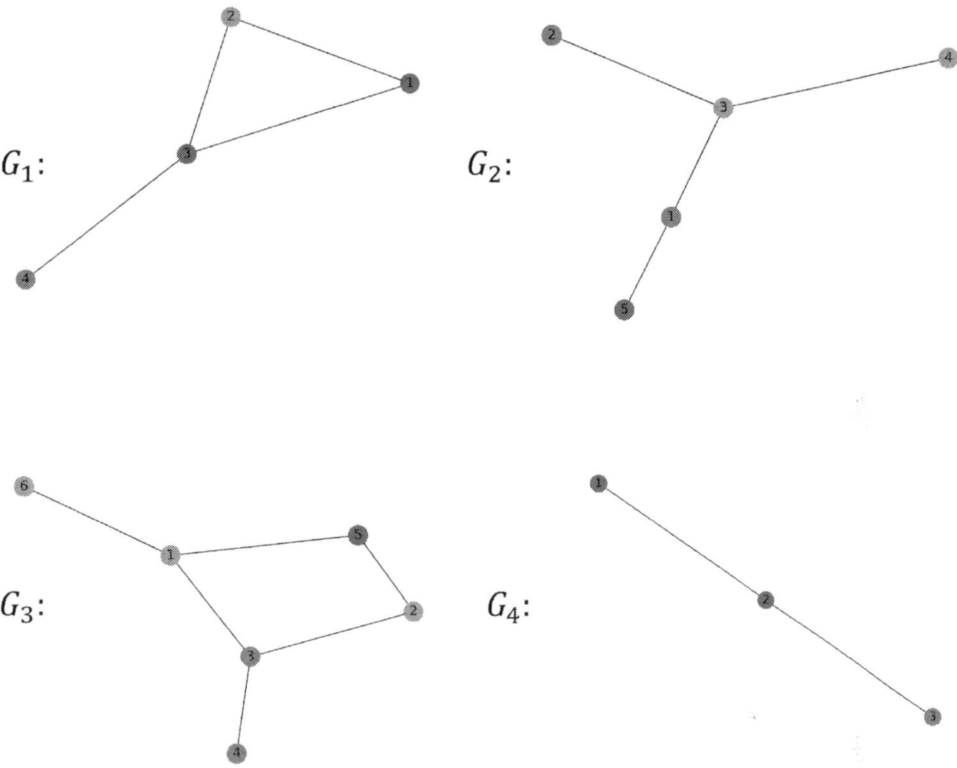

Figure 18.11: Four generated graphs

This code block constructs four NetworkX graphs and stores them in a list. Here, the constructor of `nx.Graph()` initializes an empty graph, and `add_nodes_from()` adds nodes to the empty graph from a list of tuples. The first item in each tuple is the node's name, and the second item is a dictionary of that node's attributes.

The add_edges_from() method of a graph takes a list of tuples where each tuple defines an edge between its elements (nodes). Now, we can construct a PyTorch Dataset for these graphs:

```
from torch.utils.data import Dataset
class ExampleDataset(Dataset):
    # Simple PyTorch dataset that will use our list of graphs
    def __init__(self, graph_list):
        self.graphs = graph_list
    def __len__(self):
        return len(self.graphs)

    def __getitem__(self,idx):
        mol_rep = self.graphs[idx]
        return mol_rep
```

While using a custom Dataset may seem like unnecessary effort, it allows us to exhibit how collate_graphs() can be used in a DataLoader:

```
>>> from torch.utils.data import DataLoader
>>> dset = ExampleDataset(graph_list)
>>> # Note how we use our custom collate function
>>> loader = DataLoader(
...     dset, batch_size=2, shuffle=False,
...     collate_fn=collate_graphs)
```

Using the NodeNetwork to make predictions

After we have defined all the necessary functions and set up the DataLoader, we now initialize a new NodeNetwork and apply it to our graph data:

```
>>> node_features = 3
>>> net = NodeNetwork(node_features)

>>> batch_results = []
>>> for b in loader:
...     batch_results.append(
...         net(b['X'], b['A'], b['batch']).detach())
```

Note that for brevity, we didn't include a training loop; however, the GNN model could be trained in a regular fashion by computing the loss between predicted and true class labels, backpropagating the loss via .backward(), and updating the model weights via a gradient descent-based optimizer. We leave this as an optional exercise for the reader. In the next section, we will show how to do that with a GNN implementation from PyTorch Geometric, which implements more sophisticated GNN code.

To continue with our previous code, let's now provide a single input graph to the model directly without the `DataLoader`:

```
>>> G1_rep = dset[1]
>>> G1_single = net(
...     G1_rep['X'], G1_rep['A'], G1_rep['batch']).detach()
```

We can now compare the results from applying the GNN to a single graph (`G1_single`) and to the first graph from the `DataLoader` (also the first graph, `G1`, which we guaranteed, since we set `shuffle=False`) to double-check that the batch loader works correctly. As we can see by using `torch.isclose()` (to account for rounding errors), the results are equivalent, as we would have hoped:

```
>>> G1_batch = batch_results[0][1]
>>> torch.all(torch.isclose(G1_single, G1_batch))
tensor(True)
```

Congrats! You now understand how to construct, set up, and run a basic GNN. However, from this introduction, you probably realize that managing and manipulating graph data can be somewhat laborious. Also, we didn't even build a graph convolution that uses edge labels, which would complicate matters further. Thankfully, there is PyTorch Geometric, a package that makes this much easier by providing implementations of many GNN layers. We'll introduce this library with an end-to-end example of implementing and training a more complex GNN on molecule data in the next subsection.

Implementing a GNN using the PyTorch Geometric library

In this section, we will implement a GNN using the PyTorch Geometric library, which simplifies the process of training GNNs. We apply the GNN to QM9, a dataset consisting of small molecules, to predict isotropic polarizability, which is a measure of a molecule's tendency to have its charge distorted by an electric field.

Installing PyTorch Geometric

PyTorch Geometric can be installed via conda or pip. We recommend you visit the official documentation website at `https://pytorch-geometric.readthedocs.io/en/latest/notes/installation.html` to select the installation command recommended for your operating system. For this chapter, we used pip to install version 2.0.2 along with its `torch-scatter` and `torch-sparse` dependencies:

```
pip install torch-scatter==2.0.9
pip install torch-sparse==0.6.12
pip install torch-geometric==2.0.2
```

Let's start by loading a dataset of small molecules and look at how PyTorch Geometric stores the data:

```
>>> # For all examples in this section we use the following imports.
>>> # Note that we are using torch_geometric's DataLoader.
>>> import torch
>>> from torch_geometric.datasets import QM9
>>> from torch_geometric.loader import DataLoader
>>> from torch_geometric.nn import NNConv, global_add_pool
>>> import torch.nn.functional as F
>>> import torch.nn as nn
>>> import numpy as np
>>> # let's load the QM9 small molecule dataset
>>> dset = QM9('.')
>>> len(dset)
130831
>>> # Here's how torch geometric wraps data
>>> data = dset[0]
>>> data
Data(edge_attr=[8, 4], edge_index=[2, 8], idx=[1], name="gdb_1", pos=[5, 3],
x=[5, 11], y=[1, 19], z=[5])
>>> # can access attributes directly
>>> data.z
tensor([6, 1, 1, 1, 1])
>>> # the atomic number of each atom can add attributes
>>> data.new_attribute = torch.tensor([1, 2, 3])
>>> data
Data(edge_attr=[8, 4], edge_index=[2, 8], idx=[1], name="gdb_1", new_
attribute=[3], pos=[5, 3], x=[5, 11], y=[1, 19], z=[5])
>>> # can move all attributes between devices
>>> device = torch.device(
...     "cuda:0" if torch.cuda.is_available() else "cpu"
... )
>>> data.to(device)
>>> data.new_attribute.is_cuda
True
```

The `Data` object is a convenient, flexible wrapper for graph data. Note that many PyTorch Geometric objects require certain keywords in data objects to process them correctly. Specifically, `x` should contain node features, `edge_attr` should contain edge features, `edge_index` should include an edge list, and `y` should contain labels. The QM9 data contains some additional attributes of note: `pos`, the position of each of the molecules' atoms in a 3D grid, and `z`, the atomic number of each atom in the molecule. The labels in the QM9 are a bunch of physical properties of the molecules, such as dipole moment, free energy, enthalpy, or isotropic polarization. We are going to implement a GNN and train it on QM9 to predict isotropic polarization.

The QM9 dataset

The QM9 dataset contains 133,885 small organic molecules labeled with several geometric, energetic, electronic, and thermodynamic properties. QM9 is a common benchmark dataset for developing methods for predicting chemical structure-property relationships and hybrid quantum mechanic/machine learning methods. More information about the dataset can be found at `http://quantum-machine.org/datasets/`.

The bond types of molecules are important; that is, which atoms are connected via a certain bond type, for example, single or double bonds, matters. Hence, we'll want to use a graph convolution that can utilize edge features. For this, we'll use the `torch_geometric.nn.NNConv` layer. (If you are interested in the implementation details, its source code be found at `https://pytorch-geometric.readthedocs.io/en/latest/_modules/torch_geometric/nn/conv/nn_conv.html#NNConv`.)

This convolution in the `NNConv` layer takes the following form:

$$\boldsymbol{X}_i^{(t)} = \boldsymbol{W}\boldsymbol{X}_i^{(t-1)} + \sum_{j \in N(i)} \boldsymbol{X}_j^{(t-1)} . h_{\Theta}(e_{i,j})$$

Here, h is a neural network parameterized by a set of weights Θ, and W is a weight matrix for the node labels. This graph convolution is very similar to the one we implemented previously from scratch:

$$\boldsymbol{X}_i^{(t)} = \boldsymbol{W}_1\boldsymbol{X}_i^{(t-1)} + \sum_{j \in N(i)} \boldsymbol{X}_j^{(t-1)}\boldsymbol{W}_2$$

The only real difference is that the W_2 equivalent, the neural network h, is parametrized based on the edge labels, which allows the weights to vary for different edge labels. Via the following code, we implement a GNN utilizing two such graph convolutional layers (`NNConv`):

```
class ExampleNet(torch.nn.Module):
    def __init__(self, num_node_features, num_edge_features):
        super().__init__()
        conv1_net = nn.Sequential(
            nn.Linear(num_edge_features, 32),
            nn.ReLU(),
            nn.Linear(32, num_node_features*32))

        conv2_net = nn.Sequential(
            nn.Linear(num_edge_features, 32),
            nn.ReLU(),
            nn.Linear(32, 32*16))

        self.conv1 = NNConv(num_node_features, 32, conv1_net)
        self.conv2 = NNConv(32,16, conv2_net)
```

```
        self.fc_1 = nn.Linear(16, 32)
        self.out = nn.Linear(32, 1)

    def forward(self, data):
        batch, x, edge_index, edge_attr = (
            data.batch, data.x, data.edge_index, data.edge_attr)
        # First graph conv layer
        x = F.relu(self.conv1(x, edge_index, edge_attr))
        # Second graph conv layer
        x = F.relu(self.conv2(x, edge_index, edge_attr))
        x = global_add_pool(x,batch)
        x = F.relu(self.fc_1(x))
        output = self.out(x)
        return output
```

We'll train this GNN to predict a molecule's isotropic polarizability, a measure of the relative tendency of a molecule's charge distribution to be distorted by an external electric field. We'll split the QM9 dataset into training, validation, and test sets, and use PyTorch Geometric `DataLoader`. Note that these do not require a special collate function, but require a `Data` object with appropriately named attributes.

Next, let's split the dataset:

```
>>> from torch.utils.data import random_split
>>> train_set, valid_set, test_set = random_split(
...     dset,[110000, 10831, 10000])
>>> trainloader = DataLoader(train_set, batch_size=32, shuffle=True)
>>> validloader = DataLoader(valid_set, batch_size=32, shuffle=True)
>>> testloader = DataLoader(test_set, batch_size=32, shuffle=True)
```

The following code will initialize and train a network on a GPU (if available):

```
>>> # initialize a network
>>> qm9_node_feats, qm9_edge_feats = 11, 4
>>> net = ExampleNet(qm9_node_feats, qm9_edge_feats)

>>> # initialize an optimizer with some reasonable parameters
>>> optimizer = torch.optim.Adam(
...     net.parameters(), lr=0.01)
>>> epochs = 4
>>> target_idx = 1 # index position of the polarizability label
>>> device = torch.device("cuda:0" if
...                       torch.cuda.is_available() else "cpu")
>>> net.to(device)
```

The training loop, shown in the following code, follows the familiar pattern we have encountered in previous PyTorch chapters, so we can skip the explanation details. However, one detail that is worth highlighting is that here we are computing the mean squared error (MSE) loss instead of the cross-entropy, since polarizability is a continuous target and not a class label:

```
>>> for total_epochs in range(epochs):
...     epoch_loss = 0
...     total_graphs = 0
...     net.train()
...     for batch in trainloader:
...         batch.to(device)
...         optimizer.zero_grad()
...         output = net(batch)
...         loss = F.mse_loss(
...             output,batch.y[:, target_idx].unsqueeze(1))
...         loss.backward()
...         epoch_loss += loss.item()
...         total_graphs += batch.num_graphs
...         optimizer.step()
...     train_avg_loss = epoch_loss / total_graphs
...     val_loss = 0
...     total_graphs = 0
...     net.eval()
...     for batch in validloader:
...         batch.to(device)
...         output = net(batch)
...         loss = F.mse_loss(
...             output,batch.y[:, target_idx].unsqueeze(1))
...         val_loss += loss.item()
...         total_graphs += batch.num_graphs
...     val_avg_loss = val_loss / total_graphs
...     print(f"Epochs: {total_epochs} | "
...           f"epoch avg. loss: {train_avg_loss:.2f} | "
...           f"validation avg. loss: {val_avg_loss:.2f}")
Epochs: 0 | epoch avg. loss: 0.30 | validation avg. loss: 0.10
Epochs: 1 | epoch avg. loss: 0.12 | validation avg. loss: 0.07
Epochs: 2 | epoch avg. loss: 0.10 | validation avg. loss: 0.05
Epochs: 3 | epoch avg. loss: 0.09 | validation avg. loss: 0.07
```

Over the first four training epochs, both training and validation loss are decreasing. The dataset is large and may take a little while to train on a CPU, so we stop training after four epochs. However, if we train the model further, the loss will continue to improve. You can train the model for additional epochs to see how that changes the performance.

The following code predicts the values on the test data and collects the true labels:

```
>>> net.eval()
>>> predictions = []
>>> real = []
>>> for batch in testloader:
...     output = net(batch.to(device))
...     predictions.append(output.detach().cpu().numpy())
...     real.append(
...             batch.y[:,target_idx] .detach().cpu().numpy())
>>> real = np.concatenate(real)
>>> predictions = np.concatenate(predictions)
```

Now we can make a scatterplot with a subset of the test data. Since the test dataset is relatively large (10,000 molecules), the results can be a bit cluttered, and for simplicity, we only plot the first 500 predictions and targets:

```
>>> import matplotlib.pyplot as plt
>>> plt.scatter(real[:500], predictions[:500])
>>> plt.xlabel('Isotropic polarizability')
>>> plt.ylabel('Predicted isotropic polarizability')
```

The resulting figure is shown here:

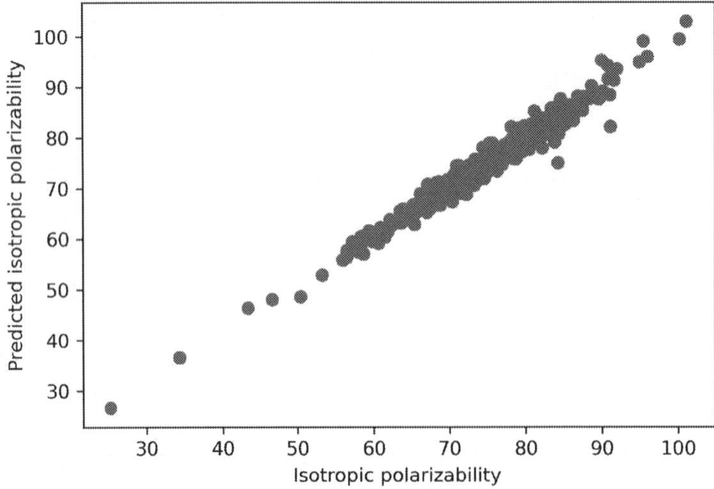

Figure 18.12: Predicted isotropic polarizability plotted against the actual isotropic polarizability

Based on the plot, given that the points lie relatively near the diagonal, our simple GNN appears to have done a decent job with predicting isotropic polarization values, even without hyperparameter tuning.

TorchDrug – A PyTorch-based library for drug discovery

PyTorch Geometric is a comprehensive general-purpose library for working with graphs, including molecules, as you have seen in this section. If you are interested in more in-depth molecule work and drug discovery, we also recommend considering the recently developed TorchDrug library, which offers many convenient utilities for working with molecules. You can find out more about TorchDrug here: `https://torchdrug.ai/`.

Other GNN layers and recent developments

This section will introduce a selection of additional layers that you can utilize in your GNNs, in addition to providing a high-level overview of some recent developments in the field. While we will provide background on the intuition behind these layers and their implementations, these concepts can become a little complicated mathematically speaking, but don't get discouraged. These are optional topics, and it is not necessary to grasp the minutiae of all these implementations. Understanding the general ideas behind the layers will be sufficient to experiment with the PyTorch Geometric implementations that we reference.

The following subsections will introduce spectral graph convolution layers, graph pooling layers, and normalization layers for graphs. Lastly, the final subsection will provide a bird's eye view of some more advanced kinds of graph neural networks.

Spectral graph convolutions

The graph convolutions we have utilized up to this point have all been spatial in nature. This means that they aggregate information based on the topological space associated with the graph, which is just a fancy way of saying that spatial convolutions operate on local neighborhoods of nodes. As a consequence of this, if a GNN that utilizes spatial convolutions needs to capture complex global patterns in graph data, then the network will need to stack multiple spatial convolutions. In situations where these global patterns are important, but network depth needs to be limited, spectral graph convolutions are an alternative kind of convolution to consider.

Spectral graph convolutions operate differently than spatial graph convolutions. Spectral graph convolutions operate by utilizing the graph's spectrum—its set of eigenvalues—by computing the eigendecomposition of a normalized version of the graph's adjacency matrix called the *graph Laplacian*. That last sentence may seem like a doozy, so let's break it down and go over it step by step.

For an undirected graph, the Laplacian matrix of a graph is defined as $L = D - A$, where A is the adjacency matrix of the graph and D is the degree matrix. A degree matrix is a diagonal matrix where the element on the diagonal in the row with index i is the number of edges in and out of the node associated with the ith row of the adjacency matrix.

L is a real-valued symmetric matrix, and it has been proven that real-valued symmetric matrices can be decomposed as $\boldsymbol{L} = \boldsymbol{Q \Lambda Q^T}$, where Q is an orthogonal matrix whose columns are the eigenvectors of L, and $\boldsymbol{\Lambda}$ is a diagonal matrix whose elements are the eigenvalues of L. You can think of Q as providing an underlying representation of the graph's structure. Unlike spatial convolutions, which use local neighborhoods of the graph that are defined by A, spectral convolutions utilize the alternative representation of the structure from Q to update the node embeddings.

The following example of a spectral convolution utilizes the eigendecomposition of the *symmetric normalized graph Laplacian*, which is defined for a graph as follows:

$$\boldsymbol{L}_{sym} = \boldsymbol{I} - \boldsymbol{D}^{-\frac{1}{2}}\boldsymbol{A}\boldsymbol{D}^{-\frac{1}{2}}$$

Here, $\boldsymbol{I}$ is the identity matrix. This is used because the normalization of the graph Laplacian can help stabilize the gradient-based training procedure similar to feature standardization.

Given that $\boldsymbol{Q\Lambda Q^T}$ is the eigendecomposition of L_{sym}, the graph convolution is defined as follows:

$$\boldsymbol{X}' = \boldsymbol{Q}(\boldsymbol{Q}^T\boldsymbol{X} \odot \boldsymbol{Q}^T\boldsymbol{W})$$

Here, $\boldsymbol{W}$ is a trainable weight matrix. The inside of the parentheses essentially multiplies X and W by a matrix that encodes structural relationships in the graph. The $\odot$ operator here denotes element-wise multiplication of the inner terms, while the outside Q maps the result back into the original basis. This convolution has a few undesirable properties, since computing a graph's eigendecomposition has a computational complexity of $O(n^3)$. This means that it is slow, and as it is structured, $\boldsymbol{W}$ is dependent on the size of the graph. Consequently, the spectral convolution can only be applied to graphs of the same size. Furthermore, the receptive field of this convolution is the whole graph, and this cannot be tuned in the current formulation. However, various techniques and convolutions have been developed to address these issues.

For example, Bruna and colleagues (`https://arxiv.org/abs/1312.6203`) introduced a smoothing method that addresses the size dependence of W by approximating it with a set of functions, each multiplied by their own scalar parameter, α. That is, given the set of functions $f_1, ..., f_n$, $\boldsymbol{W} \approx \sum \alpha_i f_i$. The set of functions is such that the dimensionality can be varied. However, since α remains scalar, the convolutions parameter space can be independent of the graph size.

Other spectral convolutions worth mentioning include the Chebyshev graph convolution (`https://arxiv.org/abs/1606.09375`), which can approximate the original spectral convolution at a lower time complexity and can have receptive fields with varying sizes. Kipf and Welling (`https://arxiv.org/abs/1609.02907`) introduce a convolution with properties similar to the Chebyshev convolutions, but with a reduced parameter burden. Implementations of both of these are available in PyTorch Geometric as `torch_geometric.nn.ChebConv` and `torch_geometric.nn.GCNConv` and are reasonable places to start if you want to play around with spectral convolutions.

Pooling

We will briefly discuss some examples of pooling layers that have been developed for graphs. While the downsampling provided by pooling layers has been beneficial in CNN architectures, the benefit of downsampling in GNNs has not been realized as clearly.

Pooling layers for image data (ab)use spatial locality, which graphs do not have. If a clustering of the nodes in a graph is provided, we can define how a graph pooling layer should pool nodes. However, it is unclear how to define optimal clustering, and different clustering approaches may be favored for different contexts. Even after clustering is determined, if nodes are downsampled, it is unclear how the remaining nodes should be connected. While these are still open research questions, we'll look at a few graph pooling layers and point out their approaches to the aforementioned issues.

As with CNNs, there are mean and max pooling layers that can be applied to GNNs. As shown in *Figure 18.13*, given a clustering of nodes, each cluster becomes a node in a new graph:

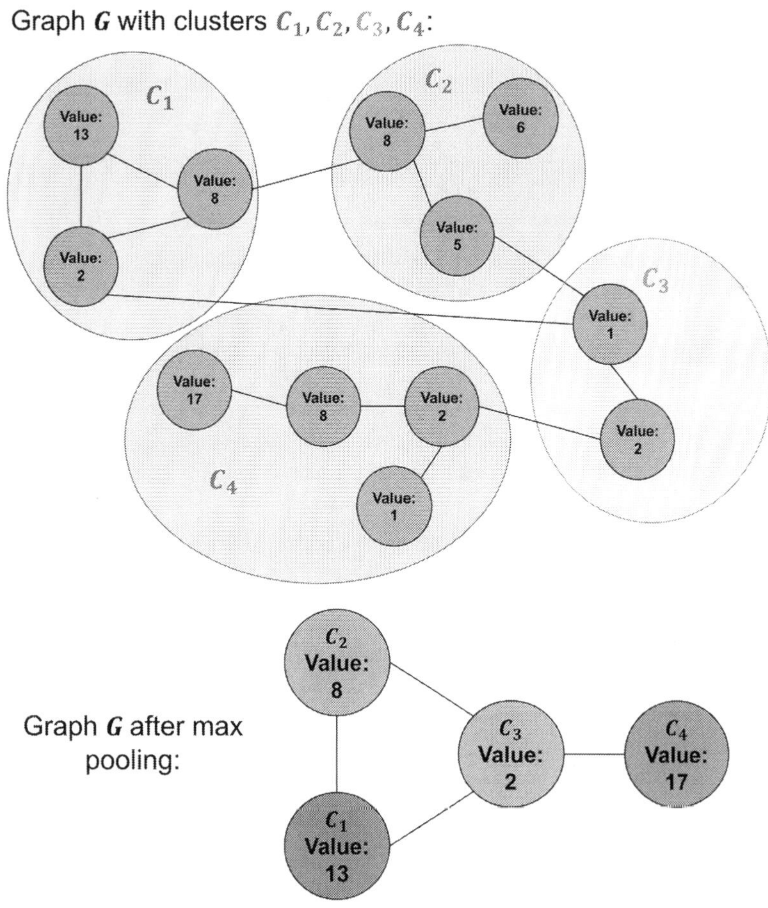

Figure 18.13: Applying max pooling to a graph

Each cluster's embedding is equal to the mean or max of the embeddings of the nodes in the cluster. To address connectivity, the cluster is assigned the union of all edge indices in the cluster. For example, if nodes *i*, *j*, *k* are assigned to cluster c_1, any node, or cluster containing a node, that shared an edge with *i*, *j*, or *k* will share an edge with c_1.

A more complex pooling layer, *DiffPool* (`https://arxiv.org/abs/1806.08804`), tries to address both clustering and downsampling simultaneously. This layer learns a soft cluster assignment matrix $\boldsymbol{S} \in \mathbb{R}^{n\times c}$, which distributes *n* node embeddings into *c* clusters. (For a refresher on soft versus hard clustering, refer to the section *Hard versus soft clustering* in *Chapter 10, Working with Unlabeled Data – Clustering Analysis*.) With this, *X* is updated as $X' = S^T X$ and *A* as $A' = S^T A^T S$. Notably, A' no longer contains discrete values and can instead be viewed as a matrix of edge weightings. Over time, *DiffPool* converges to an almost hard clustering assignment with interpretable structure.

Another pooling method, top-*k* pooling, drops nodes from the graph instead of aggregating them, which circumvents clustering and connectivity issues. While this seemingly comes with a loss of the information in the dropped nodes, in the context of a network, as long as a convolution occurs before pooling, the network can learn to avoid this. The dropped nodes are selected using a projection score against a learnable vector *p*. The actual formulation to compute (*X'*, *A'*), as stated in *Towards Sparse Hierarchical Graph Classifiers* (`https://arxiv.org/abs/1811.01287`), is:

$$y = \frac{X_p}{||p||}, \quad i = \text{top-k}(\boldsymbol{y}, k), \quad \boldsymbol{X}' = (\boldsymbol{X} \odot \tanh(\boldsymbol{y}))_i, \quad \boldsymbol{A}' = A_{ii}$$

Here, top-*k* selects the indexes of **y**, with the top *k* values and the index vector *i* being used to drop rows of ***X*** and ***A***. Top-*k* pooling is implemented in PyTorch Geometric as `torch_geometric.nn.TopKPooling`. Additionally, max and mean pooling are implemented as `torch_geometric.nn.max_pool_x` and `torch_geometric.nn.avg_pool_x`, respectively.

Normalization

Normalization techniques are utilized in many kinds of neural networks to help stabilize and/or speed up the training process. Many approaches, such as batch normalization (discussed in *Chapter 17, Generative Adversarial Networks for Synthesizing New Data*), can be readily applied in GNNs with appropriate bookkeeping. In this section, we will briefly describe some of the normalization layers that have been designed specifically for graph data.

As a quick review of normalization, we mean that given a set of feature values $x_1, ..., x_n$, we update the values with $\frac{x_i-\mu}{\sigma}$, where μ is the mean and σ the standard deviation of the set of values. Typically, most neural network normalization methods take the general form $\gamma\frac{x_i-\mu}{\sigma} + \beta$, where γ and β are learnable parameters, and the difference between methods has to do with the set of features the normalization is applied over.

GraphNorm: A Principled Approach to Accelerating Graph Neural Network Training by *Tianle Cai* and colleagues, 2020 (`https://arxiv.org/abs/2009.03294`), showed that the mean statistic after aggregation in a graph convolution can contain meaningful information, so discarding it completely may not be desirable. To address this, they introduced *GraphNorm*.

Borrowing notation from the original manuscript, let h be the matrix of node embeddings. Let $h_{i,j}$ be the jth feature value of node v_i, where $i = 1, \ldots, n$, and $j = 1, \ldots, d$. *GraphNorm* takes the following form:

$$\gamma_j \frac{h_{i,j} - \alpha_j \cdot \mu_j}{\hat{\sigma}_j} + \beta_j$$

Here, $\mu_j = \frac{\sum_{i=1}^{n} h_{i,j}}{n}$ and $\hat{\sigma}_j = \frac{\sum_{i=1}^{n}\left(h_{i,j} - \alpha_j \mu_j\right)^2}{n}$. The key addition is the learnable parameter, α, which can control how much of the mean statistic, μ_j, to discard.

Another graph normalization technique is *MsgNorm,* which was described by *Guohao Li* and colleagues in the manuscript *DeeperGCN: All You Need to Train Deeper GCNs* in 2020 (`https://arxiv.org/abs/2006.07739`). *MsgNorm* corresponds to the message-passing formulation of graph convolutions mentioned earlier in the chapter. Using message-passing network nomenclature (defined at the end of the subsection *Implementing a basic graph convolution*), after a graph convolution has summed over M_t and produced m_i but before updating the nodes embedding with U_t, *MsgNorm* normalizes m_i with the following formula:

$$m_i' = s \cdot \|h_i\|_2 \cdot \frac{m_i}{\|m_i\|_2}$$

Here, s is a learnable scaling factor and the intuition behind this approach is to normalize the features of the aggregated messages in a graph convolution. While there is no theory to support this normalization approach, it has worked well in practice.

The normalization layers we've discussed are all implemented and available via PyTorch Geometric as `BatchNorm`, `GroupNorm`, and `MessageNorm`. For more information, please visit the PyTorch Geometric documentation at `https://pytorch-geometric.readthedocs.io/en/latest/modules/nn.html#normalization-layers`.

Unlike graph pooling layers, which may require an additional clustering setup, graph normalization layers can be more readily plugged into an existing GNN model. Testing a variety of normalization methods during model development and optimization is a reasonable and recommended approach.

Pointers to advanced graph neural network literature

The field of deep learning focused on graphs is developing rapidly, and there are many methods that we can't cover in reasonable detail in this introductory chapter. So, before we conclude this chapter, we want to provide interested readers with a selection of pointers to noteworthy literature for more in-depth studies of this topic.

As you might remember from *Chapter 16, Transformers – Improving Natural Language Processing with Attention Mechanisms,* attention mechanisms can improve the capabilities of models by providing additional contexts. In this regard, a variety of attention methods for GNNs have been developed. Examples of GNNs augmented with attention include *Graph Attention Networks,* by *Petar Veličković* and colleagues, 2017 (`https://arxiv.org/abs/1710.10903`) and *Relational Graph Attention Networks* by *Dan Busbridge* and colleagues, 2019 (`https://arxiv.org/abs/1904.05811`).

Recently, these attention mechanisms have also been utilized in graph transformers proposed by *Seongjun Yun* and colleagues, 2020 (`https://arxiv.org/abs/1911.06455`) and *Heterogeneous Graph Transformer* by *Ziniu Hu* and colleagues, 2020 (`https://arxiv.org/abs/2003.01332`).

Next to the aforementioned graph transformers, other deep generative models have been developed specifically for graphs. There are graph variational autoencoders such as those introduced in *Variational Graph Auto-Encoders* by *Kipf* and *Welling*, 2016 (`https://arxiv.org/abs/1611.07308`), *Constrained Graph Variational Autoencoders for Molecule Design* by Qi Liu and colleagues, 2018 (`https://arxiv.org/abs/1805.09076`), and *GraphVAE: Towards Generation of Small Graphs Using Variational Autoencoders* by *Simonovsky* and *Komodakis*, 2018 (`https://arxiv.org/abs/1802.03480`). Another notable graph variational autoencoder that has been applied to molecule generation is the *Junction Tree Variational Autoencoder for Molecular Graph Generation* by *Wengong Jin* and colleagues, 2019 (`https://arxiv.org/abs/1802.04364`).

Some GANs have been designed to generate graph data, though, as of this writing, the performance of GANs on graphs is much less convincing than in the image domain. Examples include *GraphGAN: Graph Representation Learning with Generative Adversarial Nets* by *Hongwei Wang* and colleagues, 2017 (`https://arxiv.org/abs/1711.08267`) and *MolGAN: An Implicit Generative Model for Small Molecular Graphs* by *Cao* and *Kipf*, 2018 (`https://arxiv.org/abs/1805.11973`).

GNNs have also been incorporated into deep reinforcement learning models—you will learn more about reinforcement learning in the next chapter. Examples include *Graph Convolutional Policy Network for Goal-Directed Molecular Graph Generation* by *Jiaxuan You* and colleagues, 2018 (`https://arxiv.org/abs/1806.02473`) and a deep Q-network proposed in *Optimization of Molecules via Deep Reinforcement Learning* by *Zhenpeng Zhou* and colleagues, 2018 (`https://arxiv.org/abs/1810.08678`), which utilizes a GNN that was applied to molecule generation tasks.

Lastly, while not technically graph data, 3D point clouds are sometimes represented as such using distance cutoffs to create edges. Applications of graph networks in this space include *Point-GNN: Graph Neural Network for 3D Object Detection in a Point Cloud* by *Weijing Shi* and colleagues, 2020 (`https://arxiv.org/abs/2003.01251`), which detects 3D objects in LiDAR point clouds. In addition, *GAPNet: Graph Attention based Point Neural Network for Exploiting Local Feature of Point Cloud* by *Can Chen* and colleagues, 2019 (`https://arxiv.org/abs/1905.08705`) was designed to detect local features in point cloud data, which had been challenging for other deep architectures.

Summary

As the amount of data we have access to continues to increase, so too will our need to understand interrelations within the data. While this will be done in numerous ways, graphs function as a distilled representation of these relationships, so the amount of graph data available will only increase.

In this chapter, we explained graph neural networks from the ground up by implementing a graph convolution layer and a GNN from scratch. We saw that implementing GNNs, due to the nature of graph data, is actually quite complex. Thus, to apply GNNs to a real-world example, such as predicting molecular polarization, we learned how to utilize the PyTorch Geometric library, which provides implementations of many of the building blocks we need. Lastly, we went over some of the notable literature for diving into the GNN literature more deeply.

Hopefully, this chapter provided an introduction to how deep learning can be leveraged to learn on graphs. Methods in this space are currently a hot area of research, and many of the ones we have mentioned were published in the last couple of years. With this text as a starting point, maybe the next advancement in the space can be made by you.

In the next chapter, we will look at reinforcement learning, which is a completely different category of machine learning compared to what we have covered so far in this book.

Join our book's Discord space

Join our Discord community to meet like-minded people and learn alongside more than 2000 members at:

`https://packt.link/MLwPyTorch`

19

Reinforcement Learning for Decision Making in Complex Environments

In the previous chapters, we focused on supervised and unsupervised machine learning. We also learned how to leverage artificial neural networks and deep learning to tackle problems encountered with these types of machine learning. As you'll recall, supervised learning focuses on predicting a category label or continuous value from a given input feature vector. Unsupervised learning focuses on extracting patterns from data, making it useful for data compression (*Chapter 5, Compressing Data via Dimensionality Reduction*), clustering (*Chapter 10, Working with Unlabeled Data – Clustering Analysis*), or approximating the training set distribution for generating new data (*Chapter 17, Generative Adversarial Networks for Synthesizing New Data*).

In this chapter, we turn our attention to a separate category of machine learning, **reinforcement learning** (**RL**), which is different from the previous categories as it is focused on learning *a series of actions* for optimizing an overall reward—for example, winning at a game of chess. In summary, this chapter will cover the following topics:

- Learning the basics of RL, getting familiar with agent/environment interactions, and understanding how the reward process works, in order to help make decisions in complex environments
- Introducing different categories of RL problems, model-based and model-free learning tasks, Monte Carlo, and temporal difference learning algorithms
- Implementing a Q-learning algorithm in a tabular format
- Understanding function approximation for solving RL problems, and combining RL with deep learning by implementing a *deep* Q-learning algorithm

RL is a complex and vast area of research, and this chapter focuses on the fundamentals. As this chapter serves as an introduction, and to keep our attention on the important methods and algorithms, we will work mainly with basic examples that illustrate the main concepts. However, toward the end of this chapter, we will go over a more challenging example and utilize deep learning architectures for a particular RL approach known as deep Q-learning.

Introduction – learning from experience

In this section, we will first introduce the concept of RL as a branch of machine learning and see its major differences compared with other tasks of machine learning. After that, we will cover the fundamental components of an RL system. Then, we will see the RL mathematical formulation based on the Markov decision process.

Understanding reinforcement learning

Until this point, this book has primarily focused on *supervised* and *unsupervised* learning. Recall that in *supervised* learning, we rely on labeled training examples, which are provided by a supervisor or a human expert, and the goal is to train a model that can generalize well to unseen, unlabeled test examples. This means that the supervised learning model should learn to assign the same labels or values to a given input example as the supervisor human expert. On the other hand, in *unsupervised* learning, the goal is to learn or capture the underlying structure of a dataset, such as in clustering and dimensionality reduction methods; or learning how to generate new, synthetic training examples with a similar underlying distribution. RL is substantially different from supervised and unsupervised learning, and so RL is often regarded as the "third category of machine learning."

The key element that distinguishes RL from other subtasks of machine learning, such as supervised and unsupervised learning, is that RL is centered around the concept of *learning by interaction*. This means that in RL, the model learns from interactions with an environment to maximize a *reward function*.

While maximizing a reward function is related to the concept of minimizing the loss function in supervised learning, the *correct* labels for learning a series of actions are not known or defined upfront in RL—instead, they need to be learned through interactions with the environment to achieve a certain desired outcome—such as winning at a game. With RL, the model (also called an **agent**) interacts with its environment, and by doing so generates a sequence of interactions that are together called an **episode**. Through these interactions, the agent collects a series of rewards determined by the environment. These rewards can be positive or negative, and sometimes they are not disclosed to the agent until the end of an episode.

For example, imagine that we want to teach a computer to play the game of chess and win against human players. The labels (rewards) for each individual chess move made by the computer are not known until the end of the game, because during the game itself, we don't know whether a particular move will result in winning or losing that game. Only right at the end of the game is the feedback determined. That feedback would likely be a positive reward given if the computer won the game because the agent had achieved the overall desired outcome; and vice versa, a negative reward would likely be given if the computer had lost the game.

Furthermore, considering the example of playing chess, the input is the current configuration, for instance, the arrangement of the individual chess pieces on the board. Given the large number of possible inputs (the states of the system), it is impossible to label each configuration or state as positive or negative. Therefore, to define a learning process, we provide rewards (or penalties) at the end of each game, when we know whether we reached the desired outcome—whether we won the game or not.

This is the essence of RL. In RL, we cannot or do not teach an agent, computer, or robot *how* to do things; we can only specify *what* we want the agent to achieve. Then, based on the outcome of a particular trial, we can determine rewards depending on the agent's success or failure. This makes RL very attractive for decision making in complex environments, especially when the problem-solving task requires a series of steps, which are unknown, or hard to explain, or hard to define.

Besides applications in games and robotics, examples of RL can also be found in nature. For example, training a dog involves RL—we hand out rewards (treats) to the dog when it performs certain desirable actions. Or consider a medical dog that is trained to warn its partner of an oncoming seizure. In this case, we do not know the exact mechanism by which the dog is able to detect an oncoming seizure, and we certainly wouldn't be able to define a series of steps to learn seizure detection, even if we had precise knowledge of this mechanism. However, we can reward the dog with a treat if it successfully detects a seizure to *reinforce* this behavior!

While RL provides a powerful framework for learning an arbitrary series of actions to achieve a certain goal, please do keep in mind that RL is still a relatively young and active area of research with many unresolved challenges. One aspect that makes training RL models particularly challenging is that the consequent model inputs depend on actions taken previously. This can lead to all sorts of problems, and usually results in unstable learning behavior. Also, this sequence-dependence in RL creates a so-called *delayed effect*, which means that the action taken at a time step t may result in a future reward appearing some arbitrary number of steps later.

Defining the agent-environment interface of a reinforcement learning system

In all examples of RL, we can find two distinct entities: an agent and an environment. Formally, an **agent** is defined as an entity that learns how to make decisions and interacts with its surrounding environment by taking an action. In return, as a consequence of taking an action, the agent receives observations and a reward signal as governed by the environment. The **environment** is anything that falls outside the agent. The environment communicates with the agent and determines the reward signal for the agent's action as well as its observations.

The **reward signal** is the feedback that the agent receives from interacting with the environment, which is usually provided in the form of a scalar value and can be either positive or negative. The purpose of the reward is to tell the agent how well it has performed. The frequency at which the agent receives the reward depends on the given task or problem. For example, in the game of chess, the reward would be determined after a full game based on the outcome of all the moves: a win or a loss. On the other hand, we could define a maze such that the reward is determined after each time step. In such a maze, the agent then tries to maximize its accumulated rewards over its lifetime—where lifetime describes the duration of an episode.

Figure 19.1 illustrates the interactions and communication between the agent and the environment:

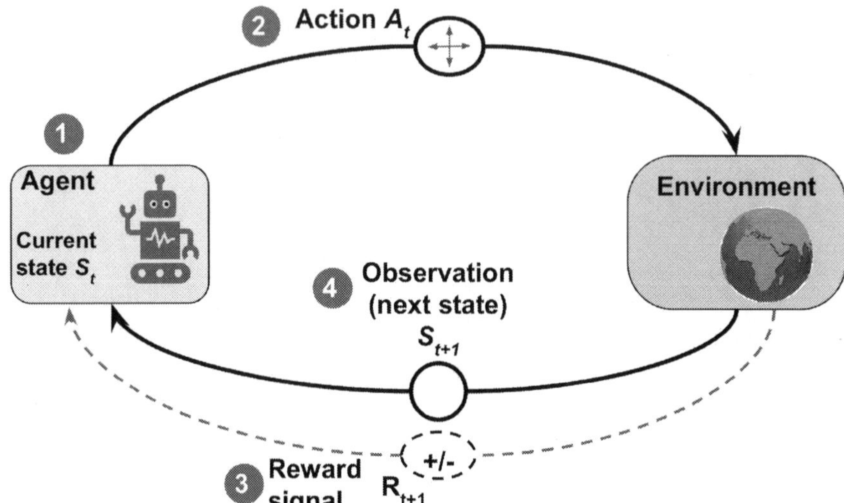

Figure 19.1: The interaction between the agent and its environment

The state of the agent, as illustrated in *Figure 19.1*, is the set of all of its variables (1). For example, in the case of a robot drone, these variables could include the drone's current position (longitude, latitude, and altitude), the drone's remaining battery life, the speed of each fan, and so forth. At each time step, the agent interacts with the environment through a set of available actions A_t (2). Based on the action taken by the agent denoted by A_t, while it is at state S_t, the agent will receive a reward signal R_{t+1} (3), and its state will become S_{t+1} (4).

During the learning process, the agent must try different actions (**exploration**) so that it can progressively learn which actions to prefer and perform more often (**exploitation**) in order to maximize the total, cumulative reward. To understand this concept, let's consider a very simple example where a new computer science graduate with a focus on software engineering is wondering whether to start working at a company (exploitation) or to pursue a master's or Ph.D. degree to learn more about data science and machine learning (exploration). In general, exploitation will result in choosing actions with a greater short-term reward, whereas exploration can potentially result in greater total rewards in the long run. The tradeoff between exploration and exploitation has been studied extensively, and yet, there is no universal answer to this decision-making dilemma.

The theoretical foundations of RL

Before we jump into some practical examples and start training an RL model, which we will be doing later in this chapter, let's first understand some of the theoretical foundations of RL. The following sections will begin by first examining the mathematical formulation of **Markov decision processes**, episodic versus continuing tasks, some key RL terminology, and dynamic programming using the **Bellman equation**. Let's start with Markov decision processes.

Markov decision processes

In general, the type of problems that RL deals with are typically formulated as **Markov decision processes (MDPs)**. The standard approach for solving MDP problems is by using dynamic programming, but RL offers some key advantages over dynamic programming.

Dynamic programming

Dynamic programming refers to a set of computer algorithms and programming methods that was developed by Richard Bellman in the 1950s. In a sense, dynamic programming is about recursive problem solving—solving relatively complicated problems by breaking them down into smaller subproblems.

The key difference between recursion and dynamic programming is that dynamic programming stores the results of subproblems (usually as a dictionary or other form of lookup table) so that they can be accessed in constant time (instead of recalculating them) if they are encountered again in future.

Examples of some famous problems in computer science that are solved by dynamic programming include sequence alignment and computing the shortest path from point A to point B.

Dynamic programming is not a feasible approach, however, when the size of states (that is, the number of possible configurations) is relatively large. In such cases, RL is considered a much more efficient and practical alternative approach for solving MDPs.

The mathematical formulation of Markov decision processes

The types of problems that require learning an interactive and sequential decision-making process, where the decision at time step t affects the subsequent situations, are mathematically formalized as MDPs.

In the case of the agent/environment interactions in RL, if we denote the agent's starting state as S_0, the interactions between the agent and the environment result in a sequence as follows:

$$\{S_0, A_0, R_1\},\quad \{S_1, A_1, R_2\},\quad \{S_2, A_2, R_3\},\quad \ldots$$

Note that the braces serve only as a visual aid. Here, S_t and A_t stand for the state and the action taken at time step t. R_{t+1} denotes the reward received from the environment after performing action A_t. Note that S_t, R_{t+1}, and A_t are time-dependent random variables that take values from predefined finite sets denoted by $s \in \hat{S}$, $r \in \hat{R}$, and $a \in \hat{A}$, respectively. In an MDP, these time-dependent random variables, S_t and R_{t+1}, have probability distributions that only depend on their values at the preceding time step, $t - 1$. The probability distribution for $S_{t+1} = s'$ and $R_{t+1} = r$ can be written as a conditional probability over the preceding state (S_t) and taken action (A_t) as follows:

$$p(s', r|s, a) \stackrel{\text{def}}{=} P(S_{t+1} = s', R_{t+1} = r|S_t = s, A_t = a)$$

This probability distribution completely defines the **dynamics of the environment** (or model of the environment) because, based on this distribution, all transition probabilities of the environment can be computed. Therefore, the environment dynamics are a central criterion for categorizing different RL methods. The types of RL methods that require a model of the environment or try to learn a model of the environment (that is, the environment dynamics) are called *model-based* methods, as opposed to *model-free* methods.

Model-free and model-based RL

When the probability $p(s', r|s, a)$ is known, then the learning task can be solved with dynamic programming. But when the dynamics of the environment are not known, as is the case in many real-world problems, then we would need to acquire a large number of samples by interacting with the environment to compensate for the unknown environment dynamics.

Two main approaches for dealing with this problem are the model-free **Monte Carlo (MC)** and **temporal difference (TD)** methods. The following chart displays the two main categories and the branches of each method:

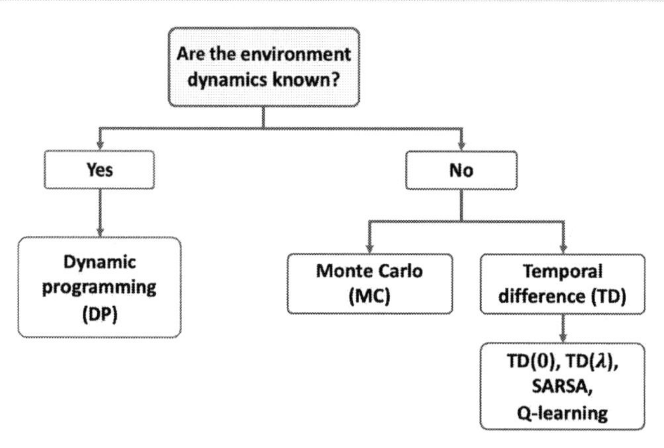

Figure 19.2: The different models to use based on the environment dynamics

We will cover these different approaches and their branches from theory to practical algorithms in this chapter.

The environment dynamics can be considered deterministic if particular actions for given states are always or never taken, that is, $p(s', r|s, a) \in \{0,1\}$. Otherwise, in the more general case, the environment would have stochastic behavior.

To make sense of this stochastic behavior, let's consider the probability of observing the future state $S_{t+1} = s'$ conditioned on the current state $S_t = s$ and the performed action $A_t = a$. This is denoted by:

$$p(s'|s, a) \stackrel{\text{def}}{=} P(S_{t+1} = s'|S_t = s, A_t = a)$$

It can be computed as a marginal probability by taking the sum over all possible rewards:

$$p(s'|s,a) \stackrel{\text{def}}{=} \sum_{r \in \hat{R}} p(s',r|s,a)$$

This probability is called **state-transition probability.** Based on the state-transition probability, if the environment dynamics are deterministic, then it means that when the agent takes action $A_t = a$ at state $S_t = s$, the transition to the next state, $S_{t+1} = s'$, will be 100 percent certain, that is, $p(s'|s,a) = 1$.

Visualization of a Markov process

A Markov process can be represented as a directed cyclic graph in which the nodes in the graph represent the different states of the environment. The edges of the graph (that is, the connections between the nodes) represent the transition probabilities between the states.

For example, let's consider a student deciding between three different situations: (A) studying for an exam at home, (B) playing video games at home, or (C) studying at the library. Furthermore, there is a terminal state (T) for going to sleep. The decisions are made every hour, and after making a decision, the student will remain in a chosen situation for that particular hour. Then, assume that when staying at home (state A), there is a 50 percent likelihood that the student switches the activity to playing video games. On the other hand, when the student is at state B (playing video games), there is a relatively high chance (80 percent) that the student will continue playing video games in the subsequent hours.

The dynamics of the student's behavior is shown as a Markov process in *Figure 19.3*, which includes a cyclic graph and a transition table:

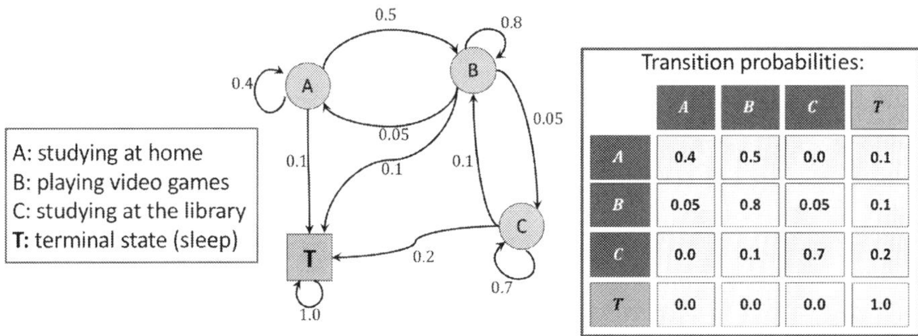

	A	B	C	T
A	0.4	0.5	0.0	0.1
B	0.05	0.8	0.05	0.1
C	0.0	0.1	0.7	0.2
T	0.0	0.0	0.0	1.0

Figure 19.3: The Markov process of the student

The values on the edges of the graph represent the transition probabilities of the student's behavior, and their values are also shown in the table to the right. When considering the rows in the table, please note that the transition probabilities coming out of each state (node) always sum to 1.

Episodic versus continuing tasks

As the agent interacts with the environment, the sequence of observations or states forms a trajectory. There are two types of trajectories. If an agent's trajectory can be divided into subparts such that each starts at time $t = 0$ and ends in a terminal state S_T (at $t = T$), the task is called an *episodic task*.

On the other hand, if the trajectory is infinitely continuous without a terminal state, the task is called a *continuing task*.

The task related to a learning agent for the game of chess is an episodic task, whereas a cleaning robot that is keeping a house tidy is typically performing a continuing task. In this chapter, we only consider episodic tasks.

In episodic tasks, an **episode** is a sequence or trajectory that an agent takes from a starting state, S_0, to a terminal state, S_T:

$$S_0, A_0, R_1, S_1, A_1, R_2, ..., S_t, A_t, R_{t+1}, ..., S_{t-1}, A_{t-1}, R_t, S_t$$

For the Markov process shown in *Figure 19.3*, which depicts the task of a student studying for an exam, we may encounter episodes like the following three examples:

Episode 1: $BBCCCCBAT$ $\rightarrow$ pass (final reward = +1)

Episode 2: $ABBBBBBBBBT$ $\rightarrow$ fail (final reward = −1)

Episode 3: $BCCCCCT$ $\rightarrow$ pass (final reward = +1)

RL terminology: return, policy, and value function

Next, let's define some additional RL-specific terminology that we will need for the remainder of this chapter.

The return

The so-called *return* at time *t* is the cumulated reward obtained from the entire duration of an episode. Recall that $R_{t+1} = r$ is the *immediate reward* obtained after performing an action, A_t, at time t; the *subsequent* rewards are R_{t+2}, R_{t+3}, and so forth.

The return at time t can then be calculated from the immediate reward as well as the subsequent ones, as follows:

$$G_t \stackrel{\text{def}}{=} R_{t+1} + \gamma R_{t+2} + \gamma^2 R_{t+3} + \cdots = \sum_{k=0} \gamma^k R_{t+k+1}$$

Here, γ is the *discount factor* in range [0, 1]. The parameter γ indicates how much the future rewards are "worth" at the current moment (time t). Note that by setting $\gamma = 0$, we would imply that we do not care about future rewards. In this case, the return will be equal to the immediate reward, ignoring the subsequent rewards after $t + 1$, and the agent will be short-sighted. On the other hand, if $\gamma = 1$, the return will be the unweighted sum of all subsequent rewards.

Moreover, note that the equation for the return can be expressed in a simpler way by using *recursion* as follows:

$$G_t = R_{t+1} + \gamma G_{t+1} = r + \gamma G_{t+1}$$

This means that the return at time t is equal to the immediate reward r plus the discounted future return at time $t+1$. This is a very important property, which facilitates the computations of the return.

Intuition behind the discount factor

To get an understanding of the discount factor, consider *Figure 19.4*, showing the value of earning a $100 bill today compared to earning it in a year from now. Under certain economic situations, like inflation, earning this $100 bill right now could be worth more than earning it in the future:

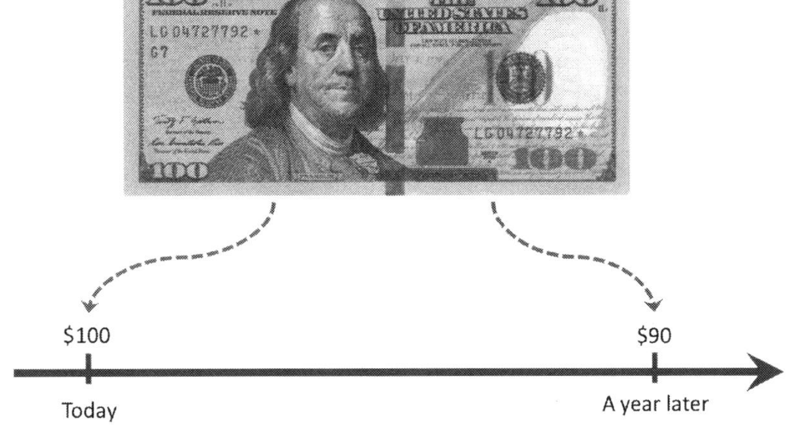

Figure 19.4: An example of a discount factor based on the value of a $100 bill over time

Therefore, we say that if this bill is worth $100 right now, then it would be worth $90 in a year with a discount factor $\gamma = 0.9$.

Let's compute the return at different time steps for the episodes in our previous student example. Assume $\gamma = 0.9$ and that the only reward given is based on the result of the exam (+1 for passing the exam, and –1 for failing it). The rewards for intermediate time steps are 0.

Episode 1: $BBCCCCBAT \rightarrow \text{pass (final reward} = +1)$:

- $t = 0 \quad : \quad G_0 = R_1 + \gamma R_2 + \gamma^2 R_3 + \cdots + \gamma^6 R_7$

  $\rightarrow \quad G_0 = 0 + 0 \times \gamma + \cdots + 1 \times \gamma^6 = 0.9^6 \approx 0.531$

- $t = 1 \quad : \quad G_1 = 1 \times \gamma^5 = 0.590$
- $t = 2 \quad : \quad G_2 = 1 \times \gamma^4 = 0.656$
- ...
- $t = 6 \quad : \quad G_6 = 1 \times \gamma = 0.9$
- $t = 7 \quad : \quad G_7 = 1 = 1$

Episode 2: $ABBBBBBBBBBT$ → fail (final reward = −1):

- $t = 0 \quad : \quad G_0 = -1 \times \gamma^8 = -0.430$
- $t = 1 \quad : \quad G_0 = -1 \times \gamma^7 = -0.478$
- ...
- $t = 8 \quad : \quad G_0 = -1 \times \gamma = -0.9$
- $t = 9 \quad : \quad G_{10} = -1$

We leave the computation of the returns for the third episode as an exercise for the reader.

Policy

A *policy* typically denoted by $\pi(a|s)$ is a function that determines the next action to take, which can be either deterministic or stochastic (that is, the probability for taking the next action). A stochastic policy then has a probability distribution over actions that an agent can take at a given state:

$$\pi(a|s) \stackrel{\text{def}}{=} P[A_t = a|S_t = s]$$

During the learning process, the policy may change as the agent gains more experience. For example, the agent may start from a random policy, where the probability of all actions is uniform; meanwhile, the agent will hopefully learn to optimize its policy toward reaching the optimal policy. The *optimal policy* $\pi_*(a|s)$ is the policy that yields the highest return.

Value function

The *value function*, also referred to as the *state-value function*, measures the *goodness* of each state—in other words, how good or bad it is to be in a particular state. Note that the criterion for goodness is based on the return.

Now, based on the return G_t, we define the value function of state s as the expected return (the average return over all possible episodes) after *following policy* π:

$$v_\pi(s) \stackrel{\text{def}}{=} E_\pi[G_t|S_t = s] = E_\pi\left[\sum_{k=0} \gamma^{k+1} R_{t+k+1} \middle| S_t = s\right]$$

In an actual implementation, we usually estimate the value function using lookup tables, so we do not have to recompute it multiple times. (This is the dynamic programming aspect.) For example, in practice, when we estimate the value function using such tabular methods, we store all the state values in a table denoted by $V(s)$. In a Python implementation, this could be a list or a NumPy array whose indices refer to different states; or, it could be a Python dictionary, where the dictionary keys map the states to the respective values.

Moreover, we can also define a value for each state-action pair, which is called the *action-value function* and is denoted by $q_\pi(s, a)$. The action-value function refers to the expected return G_t when the agent is at state $S_t = s$ and takes action $A_t = a$.

Extending the definition of the state-value function to state-action pairs, we get the following:

$$q_{\pi}(s,a) \stackrel{\text{def}}{=} E_{\pi}[G_t|S_t = s, A_t = a] = E_{\pi}\left[\sum_{k=0} \gamma^{k+1}R_{t+k+1}\middle| S_t = s, A_t = a\right]$$

This is similar to referring to the optimal policy as $\pi_*(a|s)$, $v_*(s)$, and $q_*(s,a)$ also denote the optimal state-value and action-value functions.

Estimating the value function is an essential component of RL methods. We will cover different ways of calculating and estimating the state-value function and action-value function later in this chapter.

The difference between the reward, return, and value function

The *reward* is a consequence of the agent taking an action given the current state of the environment. In other words, the reward is a signal that the agent receives when performing an action to transition from one state to the next. However, remember that not every action yields a positive or negative reward—think back to our chess example, where a positive reward is only received upon winning the game, and the reward for all intermediate actions is zero.

A state itself has a certain value, which we assign to it, to measure how good or bad this state is—this is where the *value function* comes into play. Typically, the states with a "high" or "good" value are those states that have a high expected *return* and will likely yield a high reward given a particular policy.

For example, let's consider a chess-playing computer once more. A positive reward may only be given at the end of the game if the computer wins the game. There is no (positive) reward if the computer loses the game. Now, imagine the computer performs a particular chess move that captures the opponent's queen without any negative consequences for the computer. Since the computer only receives a reward for winning the game, it does not get an immediate reward by making this move that captures the opponent's queen. However, the new state (the state of the board after capturing the queen) may have a high value, which may yield a reward (if the game is won afterward). Intuitively, we can say that the high value associated with capturing the opponent's queen is associated with the fact that capturing the queen often results in winning the game—and thus the high expected return, or value. However, note that capturing the opponent's queen does not always lead to winning the game; hence, the agent is likely to receive a positive reward, but it is not guaranteed.

In short, the return is the weighted sum of rewards for an entire episode, which would be equal to the discounted final reward in our chess example (since there is only one reward). The value function is the expectation over all possible episodes, which basically computes how "valuable" it is, on average, to make a certain move.

Before we move directly ahead into some RL algorithms, let's briefly go over the derivation for the Bellman equation, which we can use to implement the policy evaluation.

Dynamic programming using the Bellman equation

The Bellman equation is one of the central elements of many RL algorithms. The Bellman equation simplifies the computation of the value function, such that rather than summing over multiple time steps, it uses a recursion that is similar to the recursion for computing the return.

Based on the recursive equation for the total return $G_t = r + \gamma G_{t+1}$, we can rewrite the value function as follows:

$$\begin{aligned} v_\pi(s) &\stackrel{\text{def}}{=} E_\pi[G_t|S_t = s] \\ &= E_\pi[r + \gamma G_{t+1}|S_t = s] \\ &= r + \gamma\, E_\pi[G_{t+1}|S_t = s] \end{aligned}$$

Notice that the immediate reward r is taken out of the expectation since it is a constant and known quantity at time t.

Similarly, for the action-value function, we could write:

$$\begin{aligned} q_\pi(s,a) &\stackrel{\text{def}}{=} E_\pi[G_t|S_t = s, A_t = a] \\ &= E_\pi[r + \gamma G_{t+1}|S_t = s, A_t = a] \\ &= r + \gamma\, E_\pi[G_{t+1}|S_t = s, A_t = a] \end{aligned}$$

We can use the environment dynamics to compute the expectation by summing all the probabilities of the next state s' and the corresponding rewards r:

$$v_\pi(s) = \sum_{a\in\hat{A}} \pi(a|s) \sum_{s'\in\hat{S},r\in\hat{R}} p(s',r|s,a)[r + \gamma\, E_\pi[G_{t+1}|S_{t+1} = s']]$$

Now, we can see that expectation of the return, $E_\pi[G_{t+1}|S_t = s']$, is essentially the state-value function $v_\pi(s')$. So, we can write $v_\pi(s)$ as a function of $v_\pi(s')$:

$$v_\pi(s) = \sum_{a\in\hat{A}} \pi(a|s) \sum_{s'\in\hat{S},r\in\hat{R}} p(s',r|s,a)[r + \gamma\, v_\pi(s')]$$

This is called the **Bellman equation**, which relates the value function for a state, s, to the value function of its subsequent state, s'. This greatly simplifies the computation of the value function because it eliminates the iterative loop along the time axis.

Reinforcement learning algorithms

In this section, we will cover a series of learning algorithms. We will start with dynamic programming, which assumes that the transition dynamics—or the environment dynamics, that is, $p(s',r|s,a)$—are known. However, in most RL problems, this is not the case. To work around the unknown environment dynamics, RL techniques were developed that learn through interacting with the environment. These techniques include **Monte Carlo (MC)**, **temporal difference (TD)** learning, and the increasingly popular Q-learning and deep Q-learning approaches.

Figure 19.5 describes the course of advancing RL algorithms, from dynamic programming to Q-learning:

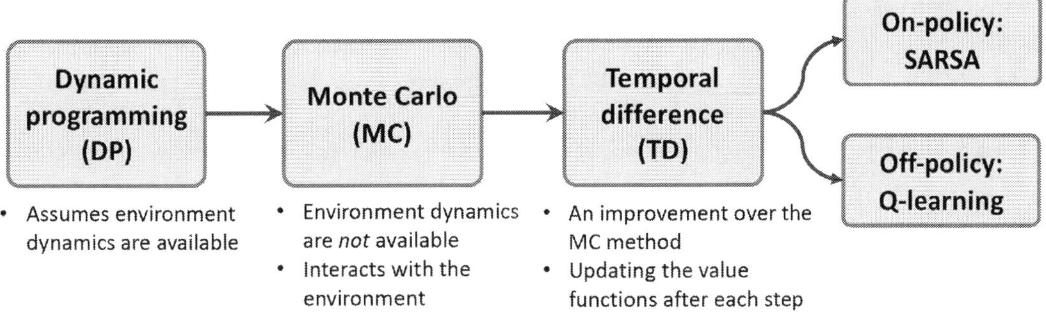

Figure 19.5: Different types of RL algorithms

In the following sections of this chapter, we will step through each of these RL algorithms. We will start with dynamic programming, before moving on to MC, and finally on to TD and its branches of on-policy **SARSA** (**state–action–reward–state–action**) and off-policy Q-learning. We will also move into deep Q-learning while we build some practical models.

Dynamic programming

In this section, we will focus on solving RL problems under the following assumptions:

- We have full knowledge of the environment dynamics; that is, all transition probabilities $p(s', r|s, a)$—are known.
- The agent's state has the Markov property, which means that the next action and reward depend only on the current state and the choice of action we make at this moment or current time step.

The mathematical formulation for RL problems using a **Markov decision process** (**MDP**) was introduced earlier in this chapter. If you need a refresher, please refer to the section entitled *The mathematical formulation of Markov decision processes*, which introduced the formal definition of the value function $v_\pi(s)$ following the policy π, and the Bellman equation, which was derived using the environment dynamics.

We should emphasize that dynamic programming is not a practical approach for solving RL problems. The problem with using dynamic programming is that it assumes full knowledge of the environment dynamics, which is usually unreasonable or impractical for most real-world applications. However, from an educational standpoint, dynamic programming helps with introducing RL in a simple fashion and motivates the use of more advanced and complicated RL algorithms.

There are two main objectives via the tasks described in the following subsections:

1. Obtain the true state-value function, $v_\pi(s)$; this task is also known as the prediction task and is accomplished with *policy evaluation*.
2. Find the optimal value function, $v_*(s)$, which is accomplished via *generalized policy iteration*.

Policy evaluation – predicting the value function with dynamic programming

Based on the Bellman equation, we can compute the value function for an arbitrary policy π with dynamic programming when the environment dynamics are known. For computing this value function, we can adapt an iterative solution, where we start from $v^{\langle 0 \rangle}(s)$, which is initialized to zero values for each state. Then, at each iteration $i + 1$, we update the values for each state based on the Bellman equation, which, in turn, is based on the values of states from a previous iteration, i, as follows:

$$v^{\langle i+1 \rangle}(s) = \sum_{a} \pi(a|s) \sum_{s' \in \hat{S}, r \in \hat{R}} p(s', r|s, a)\left[r + \gamma\, v^{\langle i \rangle}(s')\right]$$

It can be shown that as the iterations increase to infinity, $v^{\langle i \rangle}(s)$ converges to the true state-value function, $v_\pi(s)$.

Also, notice here that we do not need to interact with the environment. The reason for this is that we already know the environment dynamics accurately. As a result, we can leverage this information and estimate the value function easily.

After computing the value function, an obvious question is how that value function can be useful for us if our policy is still a random policy. The answer is that we can actually use this computed $v_\pi(s)$ to improve our policy, as we will see next.

Improving the policy using the estimated value function

Now that we have computed the value function $v_\pi(s)$ by following the existing policy, π, we want to use $v_\pi(s)$ and improve the existing policy, π. This means that we want to find a new policy, π', that, for each state, s, following π', would yield higher or at least equal value than using the current policy, π. In mathematical terms, we can express this objective for the improved policy, π', as:

$$v_{\pi'}(s) \geq v_\pi(s) \quad \forall s \in \hat{S}$$

First, recall that a policy, π, determines the probability of choosing each action, a, while the agent is at state s. Now, in order to find π' that always has a better or equal value for each state, we first compute the action-value function, $q_\pi(s, a)$, for each state, s, and action, a, based on the computed state value using the value function $v_\pi(s)$. We iterate through all the states, and for each state, s, we compare the value of the next state, s', that would occur if action a was selected.

After we have obtained the highest state value by evaluating all state-action pairs via $q_\pi(s, a)$, we can compare the corresponding action with the action selected by the current policy. If the action suggested by the current policy (that is, $\arg\max_a \pi(a|s)$) is different than the action suggested by the action-value function (that is, $\arg\max_a q_\pi(s, a)$), then we can update the policy by reassigning the probabilities of actions to match the action that gives the highest action value, $q_\pi(s, a)$. This is called the *policy improvement* algorithm.

Policy iteration

Using the policy improvement algorithm described in the previous subsection, it can be shown that the policy improvement will strictly yield a better policy, unless the current policy is already optimal (which means $v_\pi(s) = v_{\pi'}(s) = v_*(s)$ for each $s \in \hat{S}$). Therefore, if we iteratively perform policy evaluation followed by policy improvement, we are guaranteed to find the optimal policy.

Note that this technique is referred to as **generalized policy iteration (GPI)**, which is common among many RL methods. We will use the GPI in later sections of this chapter for the MC and TD learning methods.

Value iteration

We saw that by repeating the policy evaluation (compute $v_\pi(s)$ and $q_\pi(s,a)$) and policy improvement (finding π' such that $v_{\pi'}(s) \geq v_\pi(s) \;\; \forall s \in \hat{S}$), we can reach the optimal policy. However, it can be more efficient if we combine the two tasks of policy evaluation and policy improvement into a single step. The following equation updates the value function for iteration $i+1$ (denoted by $v^{\langle i+1 \rangle}$) based on the action that maximizes the weighted sum of the next state value and its immediate reward ($r + \gamma\, v^{\langle i \rangle}(s')$):

$$v^{\langle i+1 \rangle}(s) = \max_a \sum_{s',r} p(s',r|s,a)\left[r + \gamma\, v^{\langle i \rangle}(s')\right]$$

In this case, the updated value for $v^{\langle i+1 \rangle}(s)$ is maximized by choosing the best action out of all possible actions, whereas in policy evaluation, the updated value was using the weighted sum over all actions.

Notation for tabular estimates of the state-value and action-value functions

In most RL literature and textbooks, the lowercase v_π and q_π are used to refer to the true state-value and true action-value functions, respectively, as mathematical functions.

Meanwhile, for practical implementations, these value functions are defined as lookup tables. The tabular estimates of these value functions are denoted by $V(S_t = s) \approx v_\pi(s)$ and $Q_\pi(S_t = s, A_t = a) \approx q_\pi(s,a)$. We will also use this notation in this chapter.

Reinforcement learning with Monte Carlo

As we saw in the previous section, dynamic programming relies on a simplistic assumption that the environment's dynamics are fully known. Moving away from the dynamic programming approach, we now assume that we do not have any knowledge about the environment dynamics.

That is, we do not know the state-transition probabilities of the environment, and instead, we want the agent to learn through *interacting* with the environment. Using MC methods, the learning process is based on the so-called *simulated experience*.

For MC-based RL, we define an agent class that follows a probabilistic policy, π, and based on this policy, our agent takes an action at each step. This results in a simulated episode.

Earlier, we defined the state-value function, such that the value of a state indicates the expected return from that state. In dynamic programming, this computation relied on the knowledge of the environment dynamics, that is, $p(s', r|s, a)$.

However, from now on, we will develop algorithms that do not require the environment dynamics. MC-based methods solve this problem by generating simulated episodes where an agent interacts with the environment. From these simulated episodes, we will be able to compute the average return for each state visited in that simulated episode.

State-value function estimation using MC

After generating a set of episodes, for each state, *s*, the set of episodes that all pass through state *s* is considered for calculating the value of state *s*. Let's assume that a lookup table is used for obtaining the value corresponding to the value function, $V(S_t = s)$. MC updates for estimating the value function are based on the total return obtained in that episode starting from the first time that state *s* is visited. This algorithm is called *first-visit Monte Carlo* value prediction.

Action-value function estimation using MC

When the environment dynamics are known, we can easily infer the action-value function from a state-value function by looking one step ahead to find the action that gives the maximum value, as was shown in the *Dynamic programming* section. However, this is not feasible if the environment dynamics are unknown.

To solve this issue, we can extend the algorithm for estimating the first-visit MC state-value prediction. For instance, we can compute the *estimated* return for each state-action pair using the action-value function. To obtain this estimated return, we consider visits to each state-action pair (*s*, *a*), which refers to visiting state *s* and taking action *a*.

However, a problem arises since some actions may never be selected, resulting in insufficient exploration. There are a few ways to resolve this. The simplest approach is called *exploratory start*, which assumes that every state-action pair has a non-zero probability at the beginning of the episode.

Another approach for dealing with this lack-of-exploration issue is called the ϵ*-greedy policy*, which will be discussed in the next section on policy improvement.

Finding an optimal policy using MC control

MC control refers to the optimization procedure for improving a policy. Similar to the policy iteration approach in the previous section (*Dynamic programming*), we can repeatedly alternate between policy evaluation and policy improvement until we reach the optimal policy. So, starting from a random policy, π_0, the process of alternating between policy evaluation and policy improvement can be illustrated as follows:

$$\pi_0 \xrightarrow{Eval.} q_{\pi_0} \xrightarrow{Improve} \pi_1 \xrightarrow{Eval.} q_{\pi_1} \xrightarrow{Improve} \pi_2 \quad \ldots \quad \xrightarrow{Eval.} q_* \xrightarrow{Improve} \pi_*$$

Policy improvement – computing the greedy policy from the action-value function

Given an action-value function, $q(s, a)$, we can generate a greedy (deterministic) policy as follows:

$$\pi(s) \stackrel{\text{def}}{=} \arg\max_a q(s,a)$$

To avoid the lack-of-exploration problem, and to consider the non-visited state-action pairs as discussed earlier, we can let the non-optimal actions have a small chance (ϵ) to be chosen. This is called the ϵ-greedy policy, according to which, all non-optimal actions at state s have a minimal $\frac{\epsilon}{|A(s)|}$ probability of being selected (instead of 0), and the optimal action has a probability of $1 - \frac{(|A(s)|-1)\times\epsilon}{|A(s)|}$ (instead of 1).

Temporal difference learning

So far, we have seen two fundamental RL techniques—dynamic programming and MC-based learning. Recall that dynamic programming relies on the complete and accurate knowledge of the environment dynamics. The MC-based method, on the other hand, learns by simulated experience. In this section, we will now introduce a third RL method called *TD learning*, which can be considered as an improvement or extension of the MC-based RL approach.

Similar to the MC technique, TD learning is also based on learning by experience and, therefore, does not require any knowledge of environment dynamics and transition probabilities. The main difference between the TD and MC techniques is that in MC, we have to wait until the end of the episode to be able to calculate the total return.

However, in TD learning, we can leverage some of the learned properties to update the estimated values before reaching the end of the episode. This is called *bootstrapping* (in the context of RL, the term *bootstrapping* is not to be confused with the bootstrap estimates we used in *Chapter 7, Combining Different Models for Ensemble Learning*).

Similar to the dynamic programming approach and MC-based learning, we will consider two tasks: estimating the value function (which is also called value prediction) and improving the policy (which is also called the control task).

TD prediction

Let's first revisit the value prediction by MC. At the end of each episode, we are able to estimate the return, G_t, for each time step t. Therefore, we can update our estimates for the visited states as follows:

$$V(S_t) \leftarrow V(S_t) + \alpha(G_t - V(S_t))$$

Here, G_t is used as the *target return* to update the estimated values, and $(G_t - V(S_t))$ is a *correction* term added to our current estimate of the value $V(S_t)$. The value α is a hyperparameter denoting the learning rate, which is kept constant during learning.

Notice that in MC, the correction term uses the *actual* return, G_t, which is not known until the end of the episode. To clarify this, we can rename the actual return, G_t, to $G_{t:T}$, where the subscript $t{:}T$ indicates that this is the return obtained at time step t while considering all the events that occurred from time step t until the final time step, T.

In TD learning, we replace the actual return, $G_{t:T}$, with a new target return, $G_{t:t+1}$, which significantly simplifies the updates for the value function, $V(S_t)$. The update formula based on TD learning is as follows:

$$V(S_t) \leftarrow V(S_t) + \alpha(G_{t:t+1} - V(S_t))$$

Here, the target return, $G_{t:t+1} \stackrel{\text{def}}{=} R_{t+1} + \gamma V(S_{t+1}) = r + \gamma V(S_{t+1})$, is using the observed reward, R_{t+1}, and the estimated value of the next immediate step. Notice the difference between MC and TD. In MC, $G_{t:T}$ is not available until the end of the episode, so we should execute as many steps as needed to get there. On the contrary, in TD, we only need to go one step ahead to get the target return. This is also known as TD(0).

Furthermore, the TD(0) algorithm can be generalized to the so-called *n-step TD* algorithm, which incorporates more future steps—more precisely, the weighted sum of n future steps. If we define $n = 1$, then the n-step TD procedure is identical to TD(0), which was described in the previous paragraph. If $n \to \infty$, however, the n-step TD algorithm will be the same as the MC algorithm. The update rule for n-step TD is as follows:

$$V(S_t) \leftarrow V(S_t) + \alpha(G_{t:t+n} - V(S_t))$$

And $G_{t:t+n}$ is defined as:

$$G_{t:t+n} \stackrel{\text{def}}{=} \begin{cases} R_{t+1} + \gamma R_{t+2} + \cdots + \gamma^{n-1} R_{t+n} + \gamma^n V(S_{t+n}) & \text{if } t + n < T \\ G_{t:T} & \text{otherwise} \end{cases}$$

MC versus TD: which method converges faster?

While the precise answer to this question is still unknown, in practice, it is empirically shown that TD can converge faster than MC. If you are interested, you can find more details on the convergences of MC and TD in the book entitled *Reinforcement Learning: An Introduction*, by *Richard S. Sutton* and *Andrew G. Barto*.

Now that we have covered the prediction task using the TD algorithm, we can move on to the control task. We will cover two algorithms for TD control: an *on-policy* control and an *off-policy* control. In both cases, we use the GPI that was used in both the dynamic programming and MC algorithms. In on-policy TD control, the value function is updated based on the actions from the same policy that the agent is following; while in an off-policy algorithm, the value function is updated based on actions outside the current policy.

On-policy TD control (SARSA)

For simplicity, we only consider the one-step TD algorithm, or TD(0). However, the on-policy TD control algorithm can be readily generalized to n-step TD. We will start by extending the prediction formula for defining the state-value function to describe the action-value function. To do this, we use a lookup table, that is, a tabular 2D array, $Q(S_t, A_t)$, which represents the action-value function for each state-action pair. In this case, we will have the following:

$$Q(S_t, A_t) \leftarrow Q(S_t, A_t) + \alpha[R_{t+1} + \gamma\, Q(S_{t+1}, A_{t+1}) - Q(S_t, A_t)]$$

This algorithm is often called SARSA, referring to the quintuple (S_t, A_t, R_{t+1}, S_{t+1}, A_{t+1}) that is used in the update formula.

As we saw in the previous sections describing the dynamic programming and MC algorithms, we can use the GPI framework, and starting from the random policy, we can repeatedly estimate the action-value function for the current policy and then optimize the policy using the ϵ-greedy policy based on the current action-value function.

Off-policy TD control (Q-learning)

We saw when using the previous on-policy TD control algorithm that how we estimate the action-value function is based on the policy that is used in the simulated episode. After updating the action-value function, a separate step for policy improvement is performed by taking the action that has the higher value.

An alternative (and better) approach is to combine these two steps. In other words, imagine the agent is following policy π, generating an episode with the current transition quintuple (S_t, A_t, R_{t+1}, S_{t+1}, A_{t+1}). Instead of updating the action-value function using the action value of A_{t+1} that is taken by the agent, we can find the best action even if it is not actually chosen by the agent following the current policy. (That's why this is considered an *off-policy* algorithm.)

To do this, we can modify the update rule to consider the maximum Q-value by varying different actions in the next immediate state. The modified equation for updating the Q-values is as follows:

$$Q(S_t, A_t) \leftarrow Q(S_t, A_t) + \alpha\left[R_{t+1} + \gamma \max_a Q(S_{t+1}, a) - Q(S_t, A_t)\right]$$

We encourage you to compare the update rule here with that of the SARSA algorithm. As you can see, we find the best action in the next state, S_{t+1}, and use that in the correction term to update our estimate of $Q(S_t, A_t)$.

To put these materials into perspective, in the next section, we will see how to implement the Q-learning algorithm for solving a *grid world problem*.

Implementing our first RL algorithm

In this section, we will cover the implementation of the Q-learning algorithm to solve a *grid world problem* (a grid world is a two-dimensional, cell-based environment where the agent moves in four directions to collect as much reward as possible). To do this, we use the OpenAI Gym toolkit.

Introducing the OpenAI Gym toolkit

OpenAI Gym is a specialized toolkit for facilitating the development of RL models. OpenAI Gym comes with several predefined environments. Some basic examples are CartPole and MountainCar, where the tasks are to balance a pole and to move a car up a hill, respectively, as the names suggest. There are also many advanced robotics environments for training a robot to fetch, push, and reach for items on a bench or training a robotic hand to orient blocks, balls, or pens. Moreover, OpenAI Gym provides a convenient, unified framework for developing new environments. More information can be found on its official website: `https://gym.openai.com/`.

To follow the OpenAI Gym code examples in the next sections, you need to install the `gym` library (at the time of writing, version 0.20.0 was used), which can be easily done using `pip`:

```
pip install gym==0.20
```

If you need additional help with the installation, please refer to the official installation guide at `https://gym.openai.com/docs/#installation`.

Working with the existing environments in OpenAI Gym

For practice with the Gym environments, let's create an environment from `CartPole-v1`, which already exists in OpenAI Gym. In this example environment, there is a pole attached to a cart that can move horizontally, as shown in *Figure 19.6*:

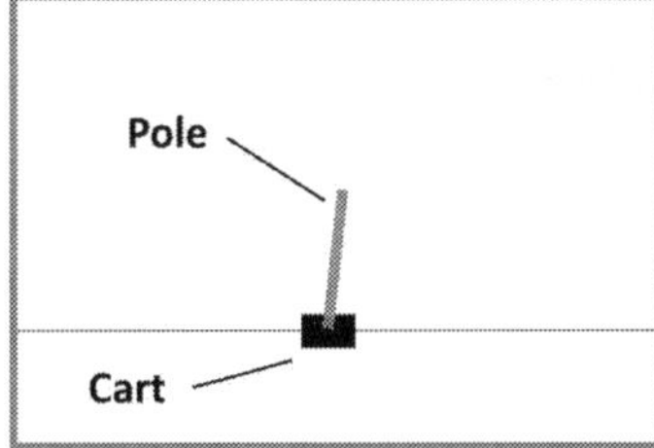

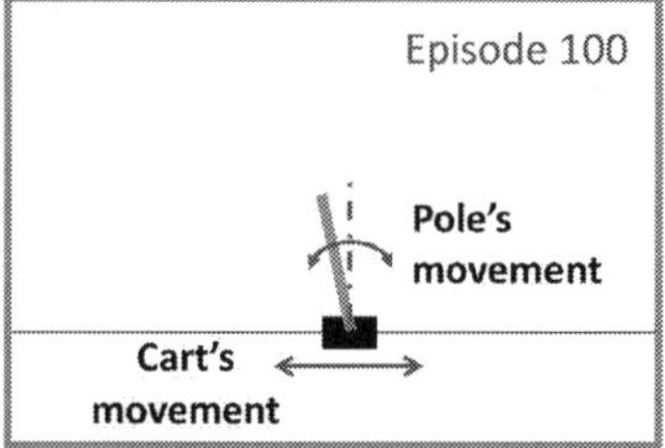

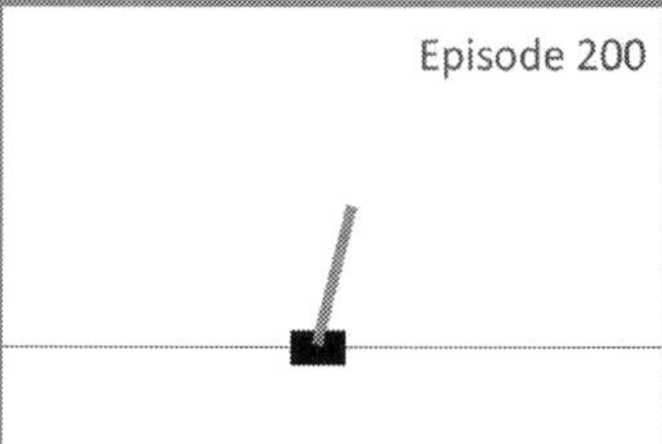

Figure 19.6: The CartPole example in Gym

The movements of the pole are governed by the laws of physics, and the goal for RL agents is to learn how to move the cart to stabilize the pole and prevent it from tipping over to either side.

Now, let's look at some properties of the CartPole environment in the context of RL, such as its state (or observation) space, action space, and how to execute an action:

```
>>> import gym
>>> env = gym.make('CartPole-v1')
>>> env.observation_space
Box(-3.4028234663852886e+38, 3.4028234663852886e+38, (4,), float32)
>>> env.action_space
Discrete(2)
```

In the preceding code, we created an environment for the CartPole problem. The observation space for this environment is `Box(4,)` (with float values from `-inf` to `inf`), which represents a four-dimensional space corresponding to four real-valued numbers: the position of the cart, the cart's velocity, the angle of the pole, and the velocity of the tip of the pole. The action space is a discrete space, `Discrete(2)`, with two choices: pushing the cart either to the left or to the right.

The environment object, `env`, that we previously created by calling `gym.make('CartPole-v1')` has a `reset()` method that we can use to reinitialize an environment prior to each episode. Calling the `reset()` method will basically set the pole's starting state (S_0):

```
>>> env.reset()
array([-0.03908273, -0.00837535,  0.03277162, -0.0207195 ])
```

The values in the array returned by the `env.reset()` method call mean that the initial position of the cart is –0.039, with a velocity –0.008, and the angle of the pole is 0.033 radians, while the angular velocity of its tip is –0.021. Upon calling the `reset()` method, these values are initialized with random values with uniform distribution in the range [–0.05, 0.05].

After resetting the environment, we can interact with the environment by choosing an action and executing it by passing the action to the `step()` method:

```
>>> env.step(action=0)
(array([-0.03925023, -0.20395158,  0.03235723,  0.28212046]), 1.0, False, {})
>>> env.step(action=1)
(array([-0.04332927, -0.00930575,  0.03799964, -0.00018409]), 1.0, False, {})
```

Via the previous two commands, `env.step(action=0)` and `env.step(action=1)`, we pushed the cart to the left (`action=0`) and then to the right (`action=1`), respectively. Based on the selected action, the cart and its pole can move as governed by the laws of physics. Every time we call `env.step()`, it returns a tuple consisting of four elements:

- An array for the new state (or observations)
- A reward (a scalar value of type `float`)
- A termination flag (`True` or `False`)
- A Python dictionary containing auxiliary information

The `env` object also has a `render()` method, which we can execute after each step (or a series of steps) to visualize the environment and the movements of the pole and cart, through time.

The episode terminates when the angle of the pole becomes larger than 12 degrees (from either side) with respect to an imaginary vertical axis, or when the position of the cart is more than 2.4 units from the center position. The reward defined in this example is to maximize the time the cart and pole are stabilized within the valid regions—in other words, the total reward (that is, return) can be maximized by maximizing the length of the episode.

A grid world example

After introducing the CartPole environment as a warm-up exercise for working with the OpenAI Gym toolkit, we will now switch to a different environment. We will work with a grid world example, which is a simplistic environment with m rows and n columns. Considering $m = 5$ and $n = 6$, we can summarize this environment as shown in *Figure 19.7*:

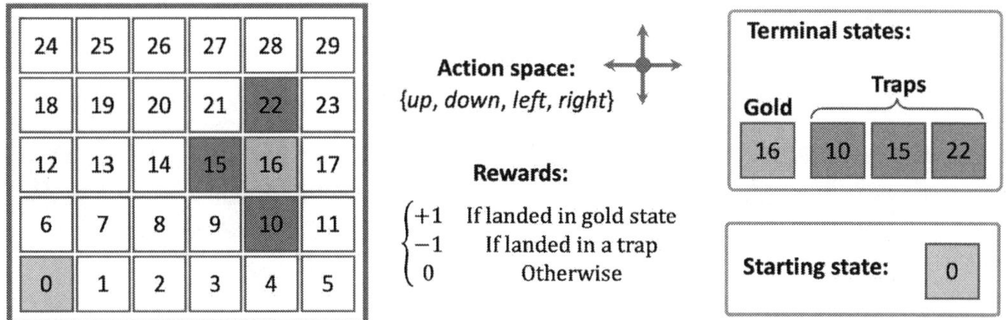

Figure 19.7: An example of a grid world environment

In this environment, there are 30 different possible states. Four of these states are terminal states: a pot of gold at state 16 and three traps at states 10, 15, and 22. Landing in any of these four terminal states will end the episode, but with a difference between the gold and trap states. Landing on the gold state yields a positive reward, +1, whereas moving the agent onto one of the trap states yields a negative reward, -1. All other states have a reward of 0. The agent always starts from state 0. Therefore, every time we reset the environment, the agent will go back to state 0. The action space consists of four directions: move up, down, left, and right.

When the agent is at the outer boundary of the grid, selecting an action that would result in leaving the grid will not change the state.

Next, we will see how to implement this environment in Python using the OpenAI Gym package.

Implementing the grid world environment in OpenAI Gym

For experimenting with the grid world environment via OpenAI Gym, using a script editor or IDE rather than executing the code interactively is highly recommended.

First, we create a new Python script named `gridworld_env.py` and then proceed by importing the necessary packages and two helper functions that we define for building the visualization of the environment.

To render the environments for visualization purposes, the OpenAI Gym library uses the pyglet library and provides wrapper classes and functions for our convenience. We will use these wrapper classes for visualizing the grid world environment in the following code example. More details about these wrapper classes can be found at `https://github.com/openai/gym/blob/58ed658d9b15fd410c50d1fdb25a7cad9acb7fa4/gym/envs/classic_control/rendering.py`.

The following code example uses those wrapper classes:

```
## Script: gridworld_env.py
import numpy as np
from gym.envs.toy_text import discrete
from collections import defaultdict
import time
import pickle
import os
from gym.envs.classic_control import rendering

CELL_SIZE = 100
MARGIN = 10


def get_coords(row, col, loc='center'):
    xc = (col+1.5) * CELL_SIZE
    yc = (row+1.5) * CELL_SIZE
    if loc == 'center':
        return xc, yc
    elif loc == 'interior_corners':
        half_size = CELL_SIZE//2 - MARGIN
        xl, xr = xc - half_size, xc + half_size
        yt, yb = xc - half_size, xc + half_size
        return [(xl, yt), (xr, yt), (xr, yb), (xl, yb)]
    elif loc == 'interior_triangle':
        x1, y1 = xc, yc + CELL_SIZE//3
        x2, y2 = xc + CELL_SIZE//3, yc - CELL_SIZE//3
        x3, y3 = xc - CELL_SIZE//3, yc - CELL_SIZE//3
        return [(x1, y1), (x2, y2), (x3, y3)]

def draw_object(coords_list):
    if len(coords_list) == 1: # -> circle
        obj = rendering.make_circle(int(0.45*CELL_SIZE))
        obj_transform = rendering.Transform()
        obj.add_attr(obj_transform)
        obj_transform.set_translation(*coords_list[0])
        obj.set_color(0.2, 0.2, 0.2) # -> black
    elif len(coords_list) == 3: # -> triangle
        obj = rendering.FilledPolygon(coords_list)
        obj.set_color(0.9, 0.6, 0.2) # -> yellow
    elif len(coords_list) > 3: # -> polygon
        obj = rendering.FilledPolygon(coords_list)
```

```
        obj.set_color(0.4, 0.4, 0.8) # -> blue
    return obj
```

Using Gym 0.22 or newer

Note that `gym` is currently undergoing some internal restructuring. In version 0.22 and newer, you may have to update the previous code example (from `gridworld_env.py`) and replace the following line

```
from gym.envs.classic_control import rendering
```

with the following code:

```
from gym.utils import pyglet_rendering
```

For more details, please refer to the code repository at `https://github.com/rasbt/machine-learning-book/tree/main/ch19`

The first helper function, `get_coords()`, returns the coordinates of the geometric shapes that we will use to annotate the grid world environment, such as a triangle to display the gold or circles to display the traps. The list of coordinates is passed to `draw_object()`, which decides to draw a circle, a triangle, or a polygon based on the length of the input list of coordinates.

Now, we can define the grid world environment. In the same file (`gridworld_env.py`), we define a class named `GridWorldEnv`, which inherits from OpenAI Gym's `DiscreteEnv` class. The most important function of this class is the constructor method, `__init__()`, where we define the action space, specify the role of each action, and determine the terminal states (gold as well as traps) as follows:

```
class GridWorldEnv(discrete.DiscreteEnv):
    def __init__(self, num_rows=4, num_cols=6, delay=0.05):
        self.num_rows = num_rows
        self.num_cols = num_cols
        self.delay = delay
        move_up = lambda row, col: (max(row-1, 0), col)
        move_down = lambda row, col: (min(row+1, num_rows-1), col)
        move_left = lambda row, col: (row, max(col-1, 0))
        move_right = lambda row, col: (
            row, min(col+1, num_cols-1))
        self.action_defs={0: move_up, 1: move_right,
                          2: move_down, 3: move_left}
        ## Number of states/actions
        nS = num_cols*num_rows
        nA = len(self.action_defs)
        self.grid2state_dict={(s//num_cols, s%num_cols):s
                              for s in range(nS)}
        self.state2grid_dict={s:(s//num_cols, s%num_cols)
```

```
                                  for s in range(nS)}
        ## Gold state
        gold_cell = (num_rows//2, num_cols-2)

        ## Trap states
        trap_cells = [((gold_cell[0]+1), gold_cell[1]),
                       (gold_cell[0], gold_cell[1]-1),
                       ((gold_cell[0]-1), gold_cell[1])]
        gold_state = self.grid2state_dict[gold_cell]
        trap_states = [self.grid2state_dict[(r, c)]
                       for (r, c) in trap_cells]
        self.terminal_states = [gold_state] + trap_states
        print(self.terminal_states)
        ## Build the transition probability
        P = defaultdict(dict)
        for s in range(nS):
            row, col = self.state2grid_dict[s]
            P[s] = defaultdict(list)
            for a in range(nA):
                action = self.action_defs[a]
                next_s = self.grid2state_dict[action(row, col)]

                ## Terminal state
                if self.is_terminal(next_s):
                    r = (1.0 if next_s == self.terminal_states[0]
                         else -1.0)
                else:
                    r = 0.0
                if self.is_terminal(s):
                    done = True
                    next_s = s
                else:
                    done = False
                P[s][a] = [(1.0, next_s, r, done)]
        ## Initial state distribution
        isd = np.zeros(nS)
        isd[0] = 1.0
        super().__init__(nS, nA, P, isd)
        self.viewer = None
        self._build_display(gold_cell, trap_cells)
```

```
    def is_terminal(self, state):
        return state in self.terminal_states


    def _build_display(self, gold_cell, trap_cells):
        screen_width = (self.num_cols+2) * CELL_SIZE
        screen_height = (self.num_rows+2) * CELL_SIZE
        self.viewer = rendering.Viewer(screen_width,
                                       screen_height)
        all_objects = []
        ## List of border points' coordinates
        bp_list = [
            (CELL_SIZE-MARGIN, CELL_SIZE-MARGIN),
            (screen_width-CELL_SIZE+MARGIN, CELL_SIZE-MARGIN),
            (screen_width-CELL_SIZE+MARGIN,
             screen_height-CELL_SIZE+MARGIN),
            (CELL_SIZE-MARGIN, screen_height-CELL_SIZE+MARGIN)
        ]
        border = rendering.PolyLine(bp_list, True)
        border.set_linewidth(5)
        all_objects.append(border)
        ## Vertical lines
        for col in range(self.num_cols+1):
            x1, y1 = (col+1)*CELL_SIZE, CELL_SIZE
            x2, y2 = (col+1)*CELL_SIZE,\
                     (self.num_rows+1)*CELL_SIZE
            line = rendering.PolyLine([(x1, y1), (x2, y2)], False)
            all_objects.append(line)

        ## Horizontal lines
        for row in range(self.num_rows+1):
            x1, y1 = CELL_SIZE, (row+1)*CELL_SIZE
            x2, y2 = (self.num_cols+1)*CELL_SIZE,\
                     (row+1)*CELL_SIZE
            line=rendering.PolyLine([(x1, y1), (x2, y2)], False)
            all_objects.append(line)

        ## Traps: --> circles
        for cell in trap_cells:
            trap_coords = get_coords(*cell, loc='center')
            all_objects.append(draw_object([trap_coords]))
```

```
        ## Gold: --> triangle
        gold_coords = get_coords(*gold_cell,
                                 loc='interior_triangle')
        all_objects.append(draw_object(gold_coords))
        ## Agent --> square or robot
        if (os.path.exists('robot-coordinates.pkl') and
                CELL_SIZE==100):
            agent_coords = pickle.load(
                open('robot-coordinates.pkl', 'rb'))
            starting_coords = get_coords(0, 0, loc='center')
            agent_coords += np.array(starting_coords)
        else:
            agent_coords = get_coords(
                0, 0, loc='interior_corners')
        agent = draw_object(agent_coords)
        self.agent_trans = rendering.Transform()
        agent.add_attr(self.agent_trans)
        all_objects.append(agent)
        for obj in all_objects:
            self.viewer.add_geom(obj)


    def render(self, mode='human', done=False):
        if done:
            sleep_time = 1
        else:
            sleep_time = self.delay
        x_coord = self.s % self.num_cols
        y_coord = self.s // self.num_cols
        x_coord = (x_coord+0) * CELL_SIZE
        y_coord = (y_coord+0) * CELL_SIZE
        self.agent_trans.set_translation(x_coord, y_coord)
        rend = self.viewer.render(
             return_rgb_array=(mode=='rgb_array'))
        time.sleep(sleep_time)
        return rend


    def close(self):
        if self.viewer:
            self.viewer.close()
            self.viewer = None
```

This code implements the grid world environment, from which we can create instances of this environment. We can then interact with it in a manner similar to that in the CartPole example. The implemented class, `GridWorldEnv`, inherits methods such as `reset()` for resetting the state and `step()` for executing an action. The details of the implementation are as follows:

- We defined the four different actions using lambda functions: `move_up()`, `move_down()`, `move_left()`, and `move_right()`.
- The NumPy array `isd` holds the probabilities of the starting states so that a random state will be selected based on this distribution when the `reset()` method (from the parent class) is called. Since we always start from state 0 (the lower-left corner of the grid world), we set the probability of state 0 to 1.0 and the probabilities of all other 29 states to 0.0.
- The transition probabilities, defined in the Python dictionary `P` determine the probabilities of moving from one state to another state when an action is selected. This allows us to have a probabilistic environment where taking an action could have different outcomes based on the stochasticity of the environment. For simplicity, we just use a single outcome, which is to change the state in the direction of the selected action. Finally, these transition probabilities will be used by the `env.step()` function to determine the next state.
- Furthermore, the `_build_display()` function will set up the initial visualization of the environment, and the `render()` function will show the movements of the agent.

Note that during the learning process, we do not know about the transition probabilities, and the goal is to learn by interacting with the environment. Therefore, we do not have access to `P` outside the class definition.

Now, we can test this implementation by creating a new environment and visualizing a random episode by taking random actions at each state. Include the following code at the end of the same Python script (`gridworld_env.py`) and then execute the script:

```
if __name__ == '__main__':
    env = GridWorldEnv(5, 6)
    for i in range(1):
        s = env.reset()
        env.render(mode='human', done=False)
        while True:
            action = np.random.choice(env.nA)
            res = env.step(action)
            print('Action  ', env.s, action, ' -> ', res)
            env.render(mode='human', done=res[2])
            if res[2]:
                break
    env.close()
```

After executing the script, you should see a visualization of the grid world environment as depicted in *Figure 19.8*:

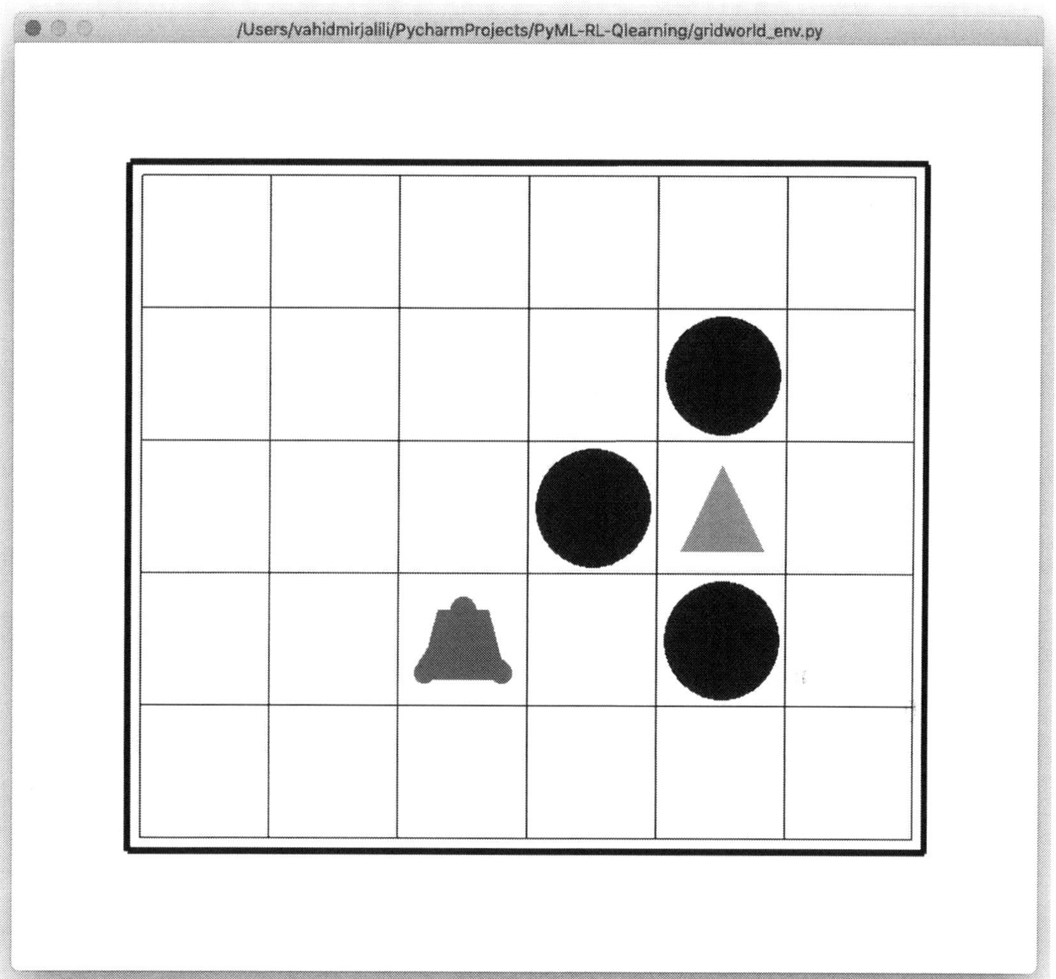

Figure 19.8: A visualization of our grid world environment

Solving the grid world problem with Q-learning

After focusing on the theory and the development process of RL algorithms, as well as setting up the environment via the OpenAI Gym toolkit, we will now implement the currently most popular RL algorithm, Q-learning. For this, we will use the grid world example that we already implemented in the script `gridworld_env.py`.

Now, we create a new script and name it `agent.py`. In this `agent.py` script, we define an agent for interacting with the environment as follows:

```
## Script: agent.py
from collections import defaultdict
import numpy as np

class Agent:
    def __init__(
            self, env,
            learning_rate=0.01,
            discount_factor=0.9,
            epsilon_greedy=0.9,
            epsilon_min=0.1,
            epsilon_decay=0.95):
        self.env = env
        self.lr = learning_rate
        self.gamma = discount_factor
        self.epsilon = epsilon_greedy
        self.epsilon_min = epsilon_min
        self.epsilon_decay = epsilon_decay
        ## Define the q_table
        self.q_table = defaultdict(lambda: np.zeros(self.env.nA))

    def choose_action(self, state):
        if np.random.uniform() < self.epsilon:
            action = np.random.choice(self.env.nA)
        else:
            q_vals = self.q_table[state]
            perm_actions = np.random.permutation(self.env.nA)
            q_vals = [q_vals[a] for a in perm_actions]
            perm_q_argmax = np.argmax(q_vals)
            action = perm_actions[perm_q_argmax]
        return action

    def _learn(self, transition):
        s, a, r, next_s, done = transition
        q_val = self.q_table[s][a]
        if done:
            q_target = r
```

```
        else:
            q_target = r + self.gamma*np.max(self.q_table[next_s])
        ## Update the q_table
        self.q_table[s][a] += self.lr * (q_target - q_val)
        ## Adjust the epsilon
        self._adjust_epsilon()

    def _adjust_epsilon(self):
        if self.epsilon > self.epsilon_min:
            self.epsilon *= self.epsilon_decay
```

The `__init__()` constructor sets up various hyperparameters, such as the learning rate, discount factor (γ), and the parameters for the ϵ-greedy policy. Initially, we start with a high value of ϵ, but the `_adjust_epsilon()` method reduces it until it reaches the minimum value, ϵ_{min}. The `choose_action()` method chooses an action based on the ϵ-greedy policy as follows. A random uniform number is selected to determine whether the action should be selected randomly or otherwise, based on the action-value function. The `_learn()` method implements the update rule for the Q-learning algorithm. It receives a tuple for each transition, which consists of the current state (*s*), selected action (*a*), observed reward (*r*), next state (*s'*), as well as a flag to determine whether the end of the episode has been reached. The target value is equal to the observed reward (*r*) if this is flagged as end-of-episode; otherwise, the target is $r + \gamma \max_{a} Q(s', a)$.

Finally, for our next step, we create a new script, `qlearning.py`, to put everything together and train the agent using the Q-learning algorithm.

In the following code, we define a function, `run_qlearning()`, that implements the Q-learning algorithm, simulating an episode by calling the `_choose_action()` method of the agent and executing the environment. Then, the transition tuple is passed to the `_learn()` method of the agent to update the action-value function. In addition, for monitoring the learning process, we also store the final reward of each episode (which could be -1 or +1), as well as the length of episodes (the number of moves taken by the agent from the start of the episode until the end).

The list of rewards and the number of moves is then plotted using the `plot_learning_history()` function:

```
## Script: qlearning.py
from gridworld_env import GridWorldEnv
from agent import Agent
from collections import namedtuple
import matplotlib.pyplot as plt
import numpy as np
np.random.seed(1)
```

```
Transition = namedtuple(
    'Transition', ('state', 'action', 'reward',
                   'next_state', 'done'))


def run_qlearning(agent, env, num_episodes=50):
    history = []
    for episode in range(num_episodes):
        state = env.reset()
        env.render(mode='human')
        final_reward, n_moves = 0.0, 0
        while True:
            action = agent.choose_action(state)
            next_s, reward, done, _ = env.step(action)
            agent._learn(Transition(state, action, reward,
                                    next_s, done))
            env.render(mode='human', done=done)
            state = next_s
            n_moves += 1
            if done:
                break
            final_reward = reward
        history.append((n_moves, final_reward))
        print(f'Episode {episode}: Reward {final_reward:.2} '
              f'#Moves {n_moves}')
    return history


def plot_learning_history(history):
    fig = plt.figure(1, figsize=(14, 10))
    ax = fig.add_subplot(2, 1, 1)
    episodes = np.arange(len(history))
    moves = np.array([h[0] for h in history])
    plt.plot(episodes, moves, lw=4,
             marker='o', markersize=10)
    ax.tick_params(axis='both', which='major', labelsize=15)
    plt.xlabel('Episodes', size=20)
    plt.ylabel('# moves', size=20)
    ax = fig.add_subplot(2, 1, 2)
    rewards = np.array([h[1] for h in history])
```

```
    plt.step(episodes, rewards, lw=4)
    ax.tick_params(axis='both', which='major', labelsize=15)
    plt.xlabel('Episodes', size=20)
    plt.ylabel('Final rewards', size=20)
    plt.savefig('q-learning-history.png', dpi=300)
    plt.show()

if __name__ == '__main__':
    env = GridWorldEnv(num_rows=5, num_cols=6)
    agent = Agent(env)
    history = run_qlearning(agent, env)
    env.close()
    plot_learning_history(history)
```

Executing this script will run the Q-learning program for 50 episodes. The behavior of the agent will be visualized, and you can see that at the beginning of the learning process, the agent mostly ends up in the trap states. But over time, it learns from its failures and eventually finds the gold state (for instance, the first time in episode 7). *Figure 19.9* shows the agent's number of moves and rewards:

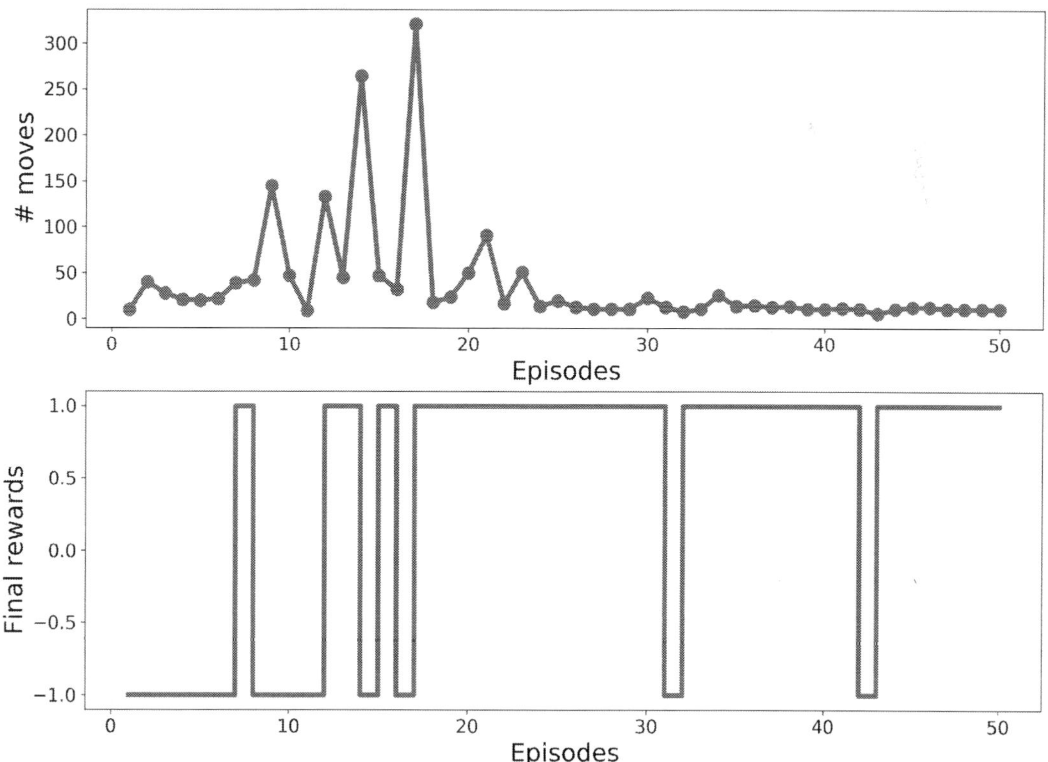

Figure 19.9: The agent's number of moves and rewards

The plotted learning history shown in the previous figure indicates that the agent, after 30 episodes, learns a short path to get to the gold state. As a result, the lengths of the episodes after the 30th episode are more or less the same, with minor deviations due to the ϵ-greedy policy.

A glance at deep Q-learning

In the previous code, we saw an implementation of the popular Q-learning algorithm for the grid world example. This example consisted of a discrete state space of size 30, where it was sufficient to store the Q-values in a Python dictionary.

However, we should note that sometimes the number of states can get very large, possibly almost infinitely large. Also, we may be dealing with a continuous state space instead of working with discrete states. Moreover, some states may not be visited at all during training, which can be problematic when generalizing the agent to deal with such unseen states later.

To address these problems, instead of representing the value function in a tabular format like $V(S_t)$, or $Q(S_t, A_t)$, for the action-value function, we use a *function approximation* approach. Here, we define a parametric function, $v_w(x_s)$, that can learn to approximate the true value function, that is, $v_w(x_s) \approx v_\pi(s)$, where x_s is a set of input features (or "featurized" states).

When the approximator function, $q_w(x_s, a)$, is a **deep neural network** (**DNN**), the resulting model is called a **deep Q-network** (**DQN**). For training a DQN model, the weights are updated according to the Q-learning algorithm. An example of a DQN model is shown in *Figure 19.10*, where the states are represented as features passed to the first layer:

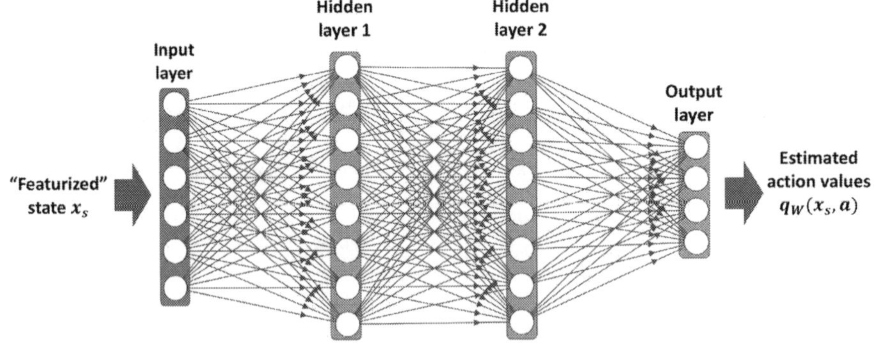

Figure 19.10: An example of a DQN

Now, let's see how we can train a DQN using the *deep Q-learning* algorithm. Overall, the main approach is very similar to the tabular Q-learning method. The main difference is that we now have a multilayer NN that computes the action values.

Training a DQN model according to the Q-learning algorithm

In this section, we describe the procedure for training a DQN model using the Q-learning algorithm. The deep Q-learning approach requires us to make some modifications to our previously implemented standard Q-learning approach.

One such modification is in the agent's `choose_action()` method, which, in the code of the previous section for Q-learning, was simply accessing the action values stored in a dictionary. Now, this function should be changed to perform a forward pass of the NN model for computing the action values.

The other modifications needed for the deep Q-learning algorithm are described in the following two subsections.

Replay memory

Using the previous tabular method for Q-learning, we could update the values for specific state-action pairs without affecting the values of others. However, now that we approximate $q(s, a)$ with an NN model, updating the weights for a state-action pair will likely affect the output of other states as well. When training NNs using stochastic gradient descent for a supervised task (for example, a classification task), we use multiple epochs to iterate through the training data multiple times until it converges.

This is not feasible in Q-learning, since the episodes will change during the training and, as a result, some states that were visited in the early stages of training will become less likely to be visited later.

Furthermore, another problem is that when we train an NN, we assume that the training examples are **IID** (**independent and identically distributed**). However, the samples taken from an episode of the agent are not IID, as they form a sequence of transitions.

To solve these issues, as the agent interacts with the environment and generates a transition quintuple $q_w(x_s, a)$, we store a large (but finite) number of such transitions in a memory buffer, often called *replay memory*. After each new interaction (that is, the agent selects an action and executes it in the environment), the resulting new transition quintuple is appended to the memory.

To keep the size of the memory bounded, the oldest transition will be removed from the memory (for example, if it is a Python list, we can use the `pop(0)` method to remove the first element of the list). Then, a mini-batch of examples is randomly selected from the memory buffer, which will be used for computing the loss and updating the network parameters. *Figure 19.11* illustrates the process:

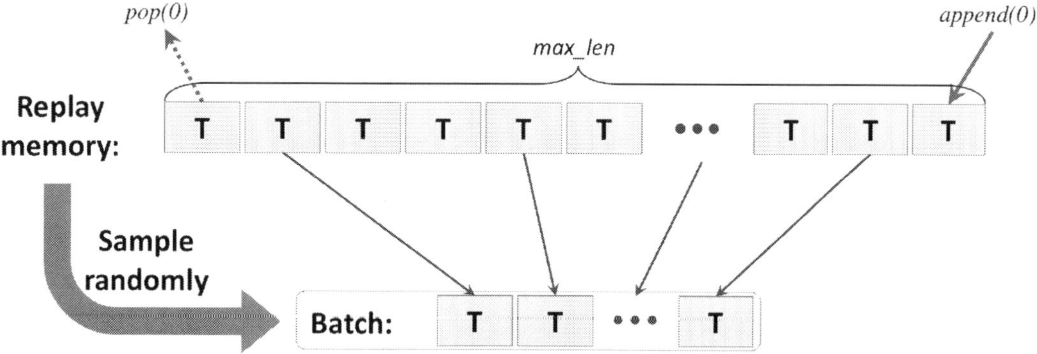

Figure 19.11: The replay memory process

Implementing the replay memory

The replay memory can be implemented using a Python list, where every time we add a new element to the list, we need to check the size of the list and call `pop(0)` if needed.

Alternatively, we can use the `deque` data structure from the Python `collections` library, which allows us to specify an optional argument, `max_len`. By specifying the `max_len` argument, we will have a bounded deque. Therefore, when the object is full, appending a new element results in automatically removing an element from it.

Note that this is more efficient than using a Python list, since removing the first element of a list using `pop(0)` has O(n) complexity, while the deque's runtime complexity is O(1). You can learn more about the deque implementation from the official documentation that is available at `https://docs.python.org/3.9/library/collections.html#collections.deque`.

Determining the target values for computing the loss

Another required change from the tabular Q-learning method is how to adapt the update rule for training the DQN model parameters. Recall that a transition quintuple, *T*, stored in the batch of examples, contains $(x_s, a, r, x_{s'}, \text{done})$.

As shown in *Figure 19.12*, we perform two forward passes of the DQN model. The first forward pass uses the features of the current state (x_s). Then, the second forward pass uses the features of the next state ($x_{s'}$). As a result, we will obtain the estimated action values, $q_w(x_s, :)$ and $q_w(x_{s'}, :)$, from the first and second forward pass, respectively. (Here, this $q_w(x_s, :)$ notation means a vector of Q-values for all actions in $\hat{A}$.) From the transition quintuple, we know that action a is selected by the agent.

Therefore, according to the Q-learning algorithm, we need to update the action value corresponding to the state-action pair (x_s, a) with the scalar target value $r + \gamma \max_{a' \in \hat{A}} q_w(x_{s'}, a')$. Instead of forming a scalar target value, we will create a target action-value vector that retains the action values for other actions, $a' \neq a$, as shown in *Figure 19.12*:

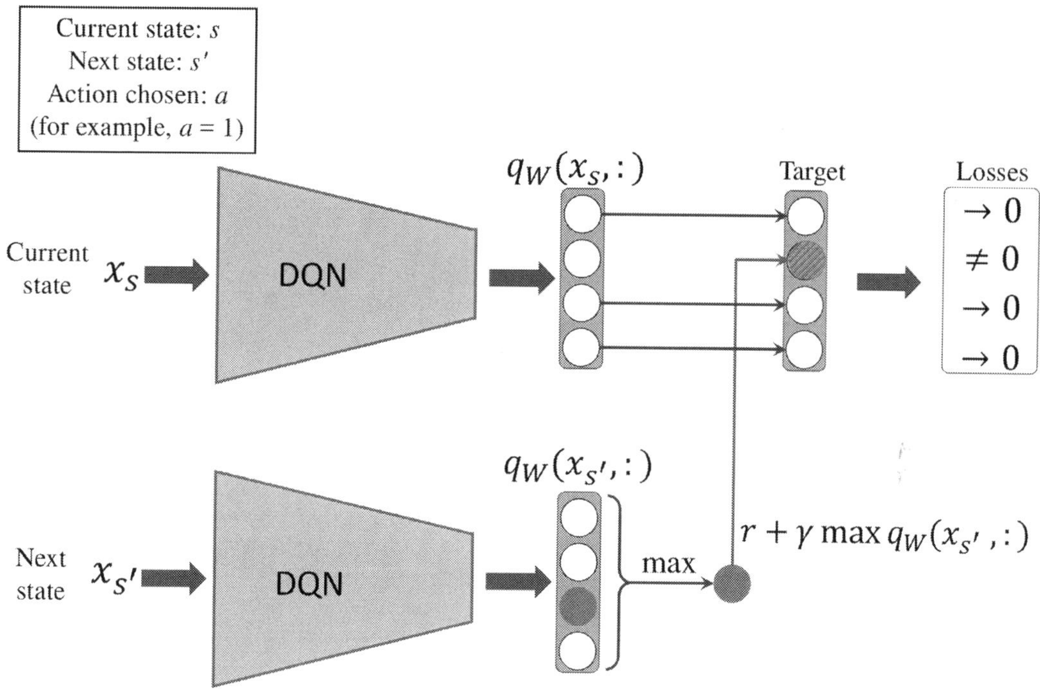

Figure 19.12: Determining the target value using the DQN

We treat this as a regression problem, using the following three quantities:

- The currently predicted values, $q_w(x_s, :)$
- The target value vector as described
- The standard **mean squared error** (**MSE**) loss function

As a result, the losses will be zero for every action except for a. Finally, the computed loss will be backpropagated to update the network parameters.

Implementing a deep Q-learning algorithm

Finally, we will use all these techniques to implement a deep Q-learning algorithm. This time, we use the CartPole environment from the OpenAI Gym environment that we introduced earlier. Recall that the CartPole environment has a continuous state space of size 4. In the following code, we define a class, `DQNAgent`, that builds the model and specifies various hyperparameters.

This class has two additional methods compared to the previous agent that was based on tabular Q-learning. The `remember()` method will append a new transition quintuple to the memory buffer, and the `replay()` method will create a mini-batch of example transitions and pass that to the `_learn()` method for updating the network's weight parameters:

```
import gym
import numpy as np
import torch
import torch.nn as nn
import random
import matplotlib.pyplot as plt
from collections import namedtuple
from collections import deque
np.random.seed(1)
torch.manual_seed(1)

Transition = namedtuple(
            'Transition', ('state', 'action', 'reward',
                           'next_state', 'done'))
class DQNAgent:
    def __init__(
            self, env, discount_factor=0.95,
            epsilon_greedy=1.0, epsilon_min=0.01,
            epsilon_decay=0.995, learning_rate=1e-3,
            max_memory_size=2000):
        self.env = env
        self.state_size = env.observation_space.shape[0]
        self.action_size = env.action_space.n
        self.memory = deque(maxlen=max_memory_size)
        self.gamma = discount_factor
        self.epsilon = epsilon_greedy
        self.epsilon_min = epsilon_min
        self.epsilon_decay = epsilon_decay
        self.lr = learning_rate
```

```
        self._build_nn_model()

    def _build_nn_model(self):
        self.model = nn.Sequential(nn.Linear(self.state_size, 256),
                          nn.ReLU(),
                          nn.Linear(256, 128),
                          nn.ReLU(),
                          nn.Linear(128, 64),
                          nn.ReLU(),
                          nn.Linear(64, self.action_size))
        self.loss_fn = nn.MSELoss()
        self.optimizer = torch.optim.Adam(
                            self.model.parameters(), self.lr)

    def remember(self, transition):
        self.memory.append(transition)

    def choose_action(self, state):
        if np.random.rand() <= self.epsilon:
            return np.random.choice(self.action_size)
        with torch.no_grad():
            q_values = self.model(torch.tensor(state,
                              dtype=torch.float32))[0]
        return torch.argmax(q_values).item()  # returns action

    def _learn(self, batch_samples):
        batch_states, batch_targets = [], []
        for transition in batch_samples:
            s, a, r, next_s, done = transition
            with torch.no_grad():
                if done:
                    target = r
                else:
                    pred = self.model(torch.tensor(next_s,
                                  dtype=torch.float32))[0]
                    target = r + self.gamma * pred.max()
            target_all = self.model(torch.tensor(s,
                                  dtype=torch.float32))[0]
            target_all[a] = target
```

```
                batch_states.append(s.flatten())
                batch_targets.append(target_all)
                self._adjust_epsilon()
                self.optimizer.zero_grad()
                pred = self.model(torch.tensor(batch_states,
                                  dtype=torch.float32))
                loss = self.loss_fn(pred, torch.stack(batch_targets))
                loss.backward()
                self.optimizer.step()
            return loss.item()

    def _adjust_epsilon(self):
        if self.epsilon > self.epsilon_min:
            self.epsilon *= self.epsilon_decay

    def replay(self, batch_size):
        samples = random.sample(self.memory, batch_size)
        return self._learn(samples)
```

Finally, with the following code, we train the model for 200 episodes, and at the end visualize the learning history using the `plot_learning_history()` function:

```
def plot_learning_history(history):
    fig = plt.figure(1, figsize=(14, 5))
    ax = fig.add_subplot(1, 1, 1)
    episodes = np.arange(len(history))+1
    plt.plot(episodes, history, lw=4,
             marker='o', markersize=10)
    ax.tick_params(axis='both', which='major', labelsize=15)
    plt.xlabel('Episodes', size=20)
    plt.ylabel('Total rewards', size=20)
    plt.show()

## General settings
EPISODES = 200
batch_size = 32
init_replay_memory_size = 500

if __name__ == '__main__':
    env = gym.make('CartPole-v1')
    agent = DQNAgent(env)
```

```
state = env.reset()
state = np.reshape(state, [1, agent.state_size])
## Filling up the replay-memory
for i in range(init_replay_memory_size):
    action = agent.choose_action(state)
    next_state, reward, done, _ = env.step(action)
    next_state = np.reshape(next_state, [1, agent.state_size])
    agent.remember(Transition(state, action, reward,
                              next_state, done))
    if done:
        state = env.reset()
        state = np.reshape(state, [1, agent.state_size])
    else:
        state = next_state
total_rewards, losses = [], []
for e in range(EPISODES):
    state = env.reset()
    if e % 10 == 0:
        env.render()
    state = np.reshape(state, [1, agent.state_size])
    for i in range(500):
        action = agent.choose_action(state)
        next_state, reward, done, _ = env.step(action)
        next_state = np.reshape(next_state,
                                [1, agent.state_size])
        agent.remember(Transition(state, action, reward,
                                  next_state, done))
        state = next_state
        if e % 10 == 0:
            env.render()
        if done:
            total_rewards.append(i)
            print(f'Episode: {e}/{EPISODES}, Total reward: {i}')
            break
        loss = agent.replay(batch_size)
        losses.append(loss)
plot_learning_history(total_rewards)
```

After training the agent for 200 episodes, we see that the agent indeed learned to increase the total rewards over time, as shown in *Figure 19.13*:

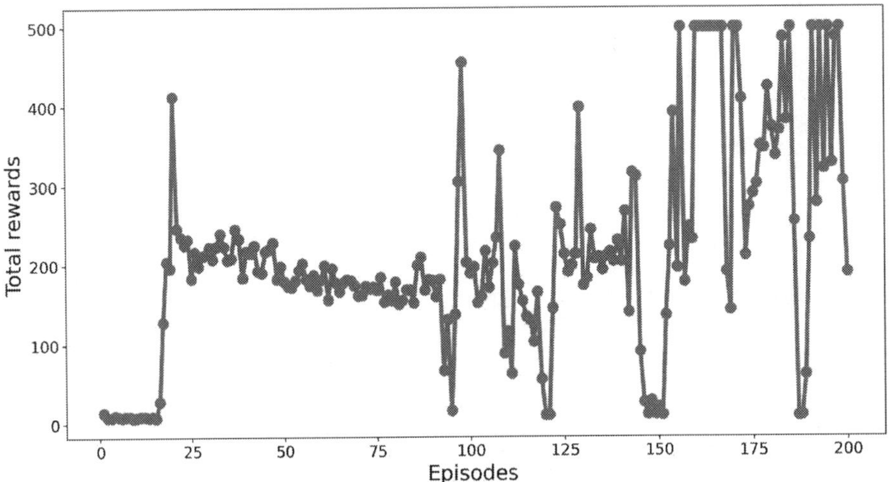

Figure 19.13: The agent's rewards increased over time

Note that the total rewards obtained in an episode are equal to the amount of time that the agent is able to balance the pole. The learning history plotted in this figure shows that after about 30 episodes, the agent learns how to balance the pole and hold it for more than 200 time steps.

Chapter and book summary

In this chapter, we covered the essential concepts in RL, starting from the very foundations, and how RL can support decision making in complex environments.

We learned about agent-environment interactions and **Markov decision processes** (**MDPs**), and we considered three main approaches for solving RL problems: dynamic programming, MC learning, and TD learning. We discussed the fact that the dynamic programming algorithm assumes that the full knowledge of environment dynamics is available, an assumption that is not typically true for most real-world problems.

Then, we saw how the MC- and TD-based algorithms learn by allowing an agent to interact with the environment and generate a simulated experience. After discussing the underlying theory, we implemented the Q-learning algorithm as an off-policy subcategory of the TD algorithm for solving the grid world example. Finally, we covered the concept of function approximation and deep Q-learning in particular, which can be used for problems with large or continuous state spaces.

We hope you enjoyed this last chapter of *Python Machine Learning* and our exciting tour of machine learning and deep learning. Throughout the journey of this book, we've covered the essential topics that this field has to offer, and you should now be well equipped to put those techniques into action to solve real-world problems.

We started our journey in *Chapter 1, Giving Computers the Ability to Learn from Data,* with a brief overview of the different types of learning tasks: supervised learning, reinforcement learning, and unsupervised learning.

We then discussed several different learning algorithms that you can use for classification, starting with simple single-layer NNs in *Chapter 2, Training Simple Machine Learning Algorithms for Classification*.

We continued to discuss advanced classification algorithms in *Chapter 3, A Tour of Machine Learning Classifiers Using Scikit-Learn*, and we learned about the most important aspects of a machine learning pipeline in *Chapter 4, Building Good Training Datasets – Data Preprocessing*, and *Chapter 5, Compressing Data via Dimensionality Reduction*.

Remember that even the most advanced algorithm is limited by the information in the training data that it gets to learn from. So, in *Chapter 6, Learning Best Practices for Model Evaluation and Hyperparameter Tuning*, we learned about the best practices to build and evaluate predictive models, which is another important aspect in machine learning applications.

If one single learning algorithm does not achieve the performance we desire, it can sometimes be helpful to create an ensemble of experts to make a prediction. We explored this in *Chapter 7, Combining Different Models for Ensemble Learning*.

Then, in *Chapter 8, Applying Machine Learning to Sentiment Analysis*, we applied machine learning to analyze one of the most popular and interesting forms of data in the modern age, which is dominated by social media platforms on the internet—text documents.

For the most part, our focus was on algorithms for classification, which is probably the most popular application of machine learning. However, this is not where our journey ended! In *Chapter 9, Predicting Continuous Target Variables with Regression Analysis*, we explored several algorithms for regression analysis to predict continuous target variables.

Another exciting subfield of machine learning is clustering analysis, which can help us find hidden structures in the data, even if our training data does not come with the right answers to learn from. We worked with this in *Chapter 10, Working with Unlabeled Data – Clustering Analysis*.

We then shifted our attention to one of the most exciting algorithms in the whole machine learning field—artificial neural networks. We started by implementing a multilayer perceptron from scratch with NumPy in *Chapter 11, Implementing a Multilayer Artificial Neural Network from Scratch*.

The benefits of PyTorch for deep learning became obvious in *Chapter 12, Parallelizing Neural Network Training with PyTorch*, where we used PyTorch to facilitate the process of building NN models, worked with PyTorch `Dataset` objects, and learned how to apply preprocessing steps to a dataset.

We delved deeper into the mechanics of PyTorch in *Chapter 13, Going Deeper – The Mechanics of PyTorch*, and discussed the different aspects and mechanics of PyTorch, including tensor objects, computing gradients of a computation, as well as the neural network module, `torch.nn`.

In *Chapter 14, Classifying Images with Deep Convolutional Neural Networks*, we dived into convolutional neural networks, which are widely used in computer vision at the moment, due to their great performance in image classification tasks.

In *Chapter 15, Modeling Sequential Data Using Recurrent Neural Networks*, we learned about sequence modeling using RNNs.

In *Chapter 16, Transformers – Improving Natural Language Processing with Attention Mechanisms*, we introduced the attention mechanism to address one of the weaknesses of RNNs, that is, remembering previous input elements when dealing with long sequences. We then explored various kinds of transformer architectures, which are deep learning architectures that are centered around the self-attention mechanism and constitute the state of the art for creating large-scale language models.

In *Chapter 17*, *Generative Adversarial Networks for Synthesizing New Data*, we saw how to generate new images using GANs and, along the way, we also learned about autoencoders, batch normalization, transposed convolution, and Wasserstein GANs.

Previous chapters were centered around tabular datasets as well as text and image data. In *Chapter 18*, *Graph Neural Networks for Capturing Dependencies in Graph Structured Data*, we focused on deep learning for graph-structured data, which is commonly used data representation for social networks and molecules (chemical compounds). Moreover, we learned about so-called graph neural networks, which are deep neural networks that are compatible with such data.

Finally, in this chapter, we covered a separate category of machine learning tasks and saw how to develop algorithms that learn by interacting with their environment through a reward process.

While a comprehensive study of deep learning is well beyond the scope of this book, we hope that we've kindled your interest enough to follow the most recent advancements in this field of deep learning.

If you're considering a career in machine learning, or you just want to keep up to date with the current advancements in this field, we can recommend that you keep an eye on the recent literature published in this field. The following are some resources that we find particularly useful:

- A subreddit and community dedicated to learning machine learning: `https://www.reddit.com/r/learnmachinelearning/`
- A daily updated list of the latest machine learning manuscripts uploaded to the arXiv preprint server: `https://arxiv.org/list/cs.LG/recent`
- A paper recommendation engine built on top of arXiv: `http://www.arxiv-sanity.com`

Lastly, you can find out what we, the authors, are up to at these sites:

- Sebastian Raschka: `https://sebastianraschka.com`
- Hayden Liu: `https://www.mlexample.com/`
- Vahid Mirjalili: `http://vahidmirjalili.com`

You're always welcome to contact us if you have any questions about this book or if you need some general tips on machine learning.

Join our book's Discord space

Join our Discord community to meet like-minded people and learn alongside more than 2000 members at:
`https://packt.link/MLwPyTorch`

packt.com

Subscribe to our online digital library for full access to over 7,000 books and videos, as well as industry leading tools to help you plan your personal development and advance your career. For more information, please visit our website.

Why subscribe?

- Spend less time learning and more time coding with practical eBooks and Videos from over 4,000 industry professionals
- Improve your learning with Skill Plans built especially for you
- Get a free eBook or video every month
- Fully searchable for easy access to vital information
- Copy and paste, print, and bookmark content

At www.packt.com, you can also read a collection of free technical articles, sign up for a range of free newsletters, and receive exclusive discounts and offers on Packt books and eBooks.

Other Books You May Enjoy

If you enjoyed this book, you may be interested in these other books by Packt:

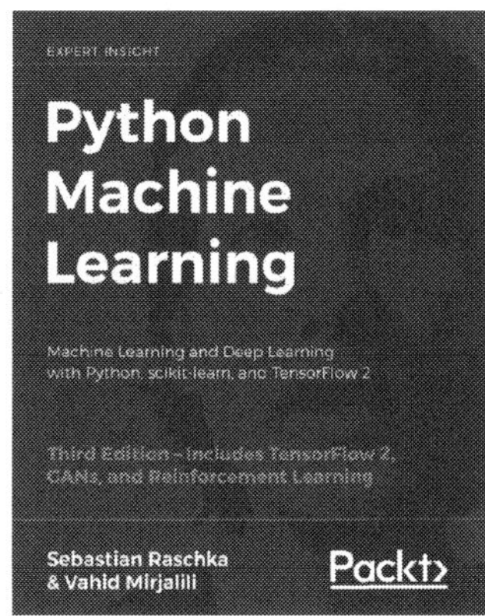

Python Machine Learning, Third Edition

Sebastian Raschka

Vahid Mirjalili

ISBN: 9781789955750

- Master the frameworks, models, and techniques that enable machines to 'learn' from data
- Use scikit-learn for machine learning and TensorFlow for deep learning
- Apply machine learning to image classification, sentiment analysis, intelligent web applications, and more
- Build and train neural networks, GANs, and other models
- Discover best practices for evaluating and tuning models
- Predict continuous target outcomes using regression analysis
- Dig deeper into textual and social media data using sentiment analysis

Transformers for Natural Language Processing

Denis Rothman

ISBN: 9781800565791

- Use the latest pretrained transformer models
- Grasp the workings of the original Transformer, GPT-2, BERT, T5, and other transformer models
- Create language understanding Python programs using concepts that outperform classical deep learning models
- Use a variety of NLP platforms, including Hugging Face, Trax, and AllenNLP
- Apply Python, TensorFlow, and Keras programs to sentiment analysis, text summarization, speech recognition, machine translations, and more
- Measure the productivity of key transformers to define their scope, potential, and limits in production

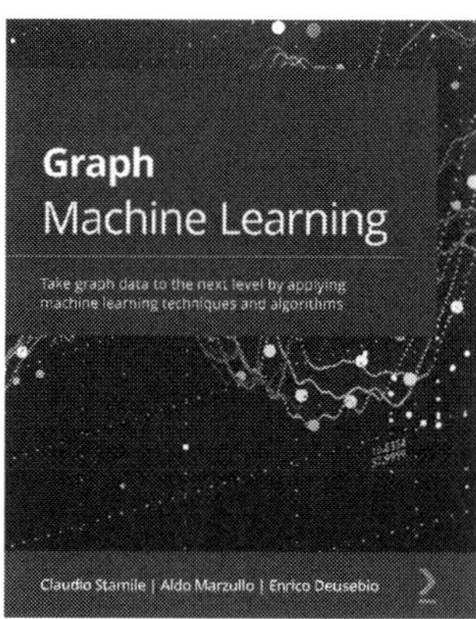

Graph Machine Learning

Claudio Stamile

Aldo Marzullo

Enrico Deusebio

ISBN: 9781800204492

- Write Python scripts to extract features from graphs
- Distinguish between the main graph representation learning techniques
- Become well-versed with extracting data from social networks, financial transaction systems, and more
- Implement the main unsupervised and supervised graph embedding techniques
- Get to grips with shallow embedding methods, graph neural networks, graph regularization methods, and more
- Deploy and scale out your application seamlessly

Packt is searching for authors like you

If you're interested in becoming an author for Packt, please visit `authors.packtpub.com` and apply today. We have worked with thousands of developers and tech professionals, just like you, to help them share their insight with the global tech community. You can make a general application, apply for a specific hot topic that we are recruiting an author for, or submit your own idea.

Share your thoughts

Now you've finished *Machine Learning with PyTorch and Scikit-Learn,* we'd love to hear your thoughts! Scan the QR code below to go straight to the Amazon review page for this book and share your feedback or leave a review on the site that you purchased it from.

https://packt.link/r/1801819319

Your review is important to us and the tech community and will help us make sure we're delivering excellent quality content.

Index

Symbols

A

G

H

I

J

K

N

O

Q

R

S

T

U

V

Download a Free PDF copy of this book

Thanks for purchasing this book!

Do you like to read on the go but are unable to carry your print books everywhere? Is your eBook purchase not compatible with the device of your choice?

Don't worry, now with every Packt book you get a DRM-free PDF version of that book at no cost.

Read anywhere, any place, on any device. Search, copy, and paste code from your favorite technical books directly into your application.

The perks don't stop there, you can get exclusive access to discounts, newsletters, and great free content in your inbox daily

Follow these simple steps to get the benefits:

1. Scan the QR code or visit the link below

`https://packt.link/free-ebook/9781801819312`

2. Submit your proof of purchase
3. That's it! We'll send your free PDF and other benefits to your email directly

Made in United States
Orlando, FL
25 May 2025

61562741R00424